CRITICAL SURVEY
OF
SHORT FICTION
Fourth Edition

CRITICAL SURVEY
OF
SHORT FICTION
Fourth Edition

Volume 2
British, Irish, and Commonwealth Writers

Arthur Machen - William Butler Yeats

Appendixes - Indexes

Editor
Charles E. May
California State University, Long Beach

SALEM PRESS
Ipswich, Massachusetts   Hackensack, New Jersey

Cover Photo: Alice Munro © (David Levenson/Getty Images)

Copyright © 1981, 1987, 1993, 2001, 2012, Salem Press, A Division of EBSCO Publishing, Inc.

Some of the essays in this work, which have been updated, originally appeared in the following Salem Press publications, *Critical Survey of Short Fiction* (1981), *Critical Survey of Short Fiction, Supplement* (1987), *Critical Survey of Short Fiction, Revised Edition*, (1993; preceding volumes edited by Frank N. Magill), *Critical Survey of Short Fiction, Second Revised Edition* (2001; edited by Charles E. May).

The paper used in these volumes conforms to the American National Standard for Permanence of Paper for Printed Library Materials, X39.48-1992 (R1997).

LIBRARY OF CONGRESS CATALOGING-IN-PUBLICATION DATA

Critical survey of short fiction / editor, Charles E. May. -- 4th ed.

     p. cm.

Includes bibliographical references and index.
ISBN 978-1-58765-789-4 (set : alk. paper) -- ISBN 978-1-58765-790-0 (set, american : alk. paper) --
ISBN 978-1-58765-791-7 (vol. 1, american : alk. paper) -- ISBN 978-1-58765-792-4 (vol. 2, american : alk. paper) --
ISBN 978-1-58765-793-1 (vol. 3, american : alk. paper) -- ISBN 978-1-58765-794-8 (vol. 4, american : alk. paper) --
ISBN 978-1-58765-795-5 (set, british : alk. paper) -- ISBN 978-1-58765-796-2 (vol. 1, british : alk. paper) --
ISBN 978-1-58765-797-9 (vol. 2, british : alk. paper) -- ISBN 978-1-58765-798-6 (european : alk. paper) --
ISBN 978-1-58765-799-3 (world : alk. paper) -- ISBN 978-1-58765-800-6 (topical essays : alk. paper) --
ISBN 978-1-58765-803-7 (cumulative index : alk. paper)

1. Short story. 2. Short story--Bio-bibliography. I. May, Charles E. (Charles Edward), 1941-
PN3321.C7 2011
809.3'1--dc23

2011026000

First Printing

PRINTED IN THE UNITED STATES OF AMERICA

CONTENTS

Contents v
Contributors vii
Complete List of Contents xi
Key to Pronunciation xiii
Machen, Arthur 457
MacLaverty, Bernard 461
MacLeod, Alistair 465
Malory, Sir Thomas 469
Malouf, David 473
Mansfield, Katherine 477
Mars-Jones, Adam 486
Marshall, Owen 490
Maugham, W. Somerset 494
McCann, Colum 501
McEwan, Ian 505
McGahern, John 510
Mistry, Rohinton 514
Moore, George 518
Munro, Alice 523
O'Brien, Edna 534
O'Brien, Fitz-James 541
O'Connor, Frank 545
O'Faoláin, Seán 552
O'Flaherty, Liam 558
Plomer, William 565
Pritchett, V. S. 569
Rhys, Jean 578
Richler, Mordecai 583
Rooke, Leon 589
Saki 594
Sansom, William 598
Scott, Sir Walter 605

Seiffert, Rachel 610
Shields, Carol 614
Sillitoe, Alan 619
Spark, Muriel 624
Steele, Sir Richard 630
Stevenson, Robert Louis 635
Swift, Graham 641
Taylor, Elizabeth 645
Thackeray, William Makepeace 649
Thomas, Dylan 655
Tóibín, Colm 661
Tremain, Rose 665
Trevor, William 670
Tuohy, Frank 678
Vanderhaeghe, Guy 683
Wain, John 687
Warner, Sylvia Townsend 691
Welch, Denton 698
Weldon, Fay 704
Wells, H. G. 710
Wilson, Angus 716
Winton, Tim 720
Woolf, Virginia 724
Yeats, William Butler 731
Terms and Techniques 739
Bibliography 753
Guide to Online Resources 780
Timeline 785
Major Awards 789
Chronological List of Writers 853
Categorical Index 857
Subject Index 866

CONTRIBUTORS

Michael Adams
CUNY Graduate Center

Stanley S. Atherton
Original Contributor

Bryan Aubrey
Fairfield, Iowa

L. Michelle Baker
The Catholic University of America

Carol M. Barnum
Southern Polytechnic State University

Mary Baron
Original Contributor

David Barratt
Montreat College

Bert Bender
Original Contributor

Nicholas Birns
Eugene Lang College, The New School

Julia B. Boken
Indiana University, Southeast

Jerry Bradley
New Albany, Indiana

Harold Branam
Savannah State University

Peter Brigg
University of Guelph

J. R. Brink
Henry E. Huntington Library

Edmund J. Campion
University of Tennessee, Knoxville

Mary LeDonne Cassidy
South Carolina State University

Richard Hauer Costa
Texas A&M University

Richard H. Dammers
Normal, Illinois

Mary Virginia Davis
University of California, Davis

Danielle A. DeFoe
Sierra College

Bill Delaney
San Diego, California

John F. Desmond
Original Contributor

Marcia B. Dinneen
Bridgewater State University

Grace Eckley
Drake University

Thomas L. Erskine
Salisbury University

Christine Ferrari
Monash University

John W. Fiero
University of Louisiana at Lafayette

Mary Fitzgerald-Hoyt
Siena College

Kathy Ruth Frazier
Original Contributor

Kenneth Funsten
Original Contributor

Ann Davison Garbett
Averett University

Janet E. Gardner
Falmouth, Massachusetts

James W. Garvey
Original Contributor

Sheldon Goldfarb
University of British Colulmbia

Peter W. Graham
Virginia Polytechnic Institute and State University

James L. Green
Arizona State University

John L. Grigsby
Appalachian Research & Defense Fund of Kentucky, Inc.

Marcus Hammond
Longview Community College

Cheryl Herr
Original Contributor

Joseph W. Hinton
Portland, Oregon

William Hoffman
Fort Meyers, Florida

Mary Hurd
East Tennessee State University

Earl G. Ingersoll
SUNY College at Brockport

Archibald E. Irwin
Indiana University, Southeast

Kimberley L. Jacobs
Miami University-Ohio

Paul Kane
Vassar College

Karen A. Kildahl
South Dakota State University

Sue L. Kimball
Methodist College

Grove Koger
Boise Public Library

Uma Kukathas
Seattle, Washingtom

Rebecca Kuzins
Pasadena, California

Eugene S. Larson
Los Angeles Pierce College

Donald F. Larsson
Mankato State University

Leon Lewis
Appalachian State University

R. C. Lutz
CII Group

Joanne McCarthy
Tacoma, Washington

Gina Macdonald
Loyola University

James MacDonald
Humber College

Karen M. Cleveland Marwick
Hemel Hempstead, Hertfordshire, England

J. Greg Matthews
Washington State University Libraries

Charles E. May
California State University, Long Beach

Kenneth W. Meadwell
University of Winnipeg

Patrick Meanor
SUNY College at Oneonta

Paula M. Miller
Biola University

Robert W. Millett
Original Contributor

Melissa Molloy
Rhode Island College

Sherry Morton-Mollo
California State University, Fullerton

Brian Murray
Youngstown State University

Keith Neilson
California State University, Fullerton

William Nelles

University of Massachusetts-Dartmouth

Evelyn Newlyn

Virginia Polytechnic Institute and State University

Emma Coburn Norris

Troy State University

George O'Brien

Georgetown University

James Norman O'Neill

Bryant College

Katherine Orr

University of Chichester

Robert M. Otten

Marymount University

Cóilín Owens

George Mason University

Leslie A. Pearl

San Diego, California

William Peden

University of Missouri-Columbia

Chapel Louise Petty

Blackwell, Oklahoma

Allene Phy-Olsen

Austin Peay State University

Valerie A. Murrenus Pilmaier

University of Wisconsin-Sheboygan

Karen Priest

Lamar State College, Orange

Norman Prinsky

Augusta State University

Charles Pullen

Queens University

Rosemary M. Canfield Reisman

Sonoma, California

Martha E. Rhynes

Oklahoma East Central University

Dorothy Dodge Robbins

Louisiana Tech University

James Curry Robison

Original Contributor

Mary Rohrberger

New Orleans, Louisiana

Douglas Rollins

Dawson College

Jill Rollins

Trafalgar College

Ruth Rosenberg

Brooklyn, NY

Chaman L. Sahni

Boise State University

David N. Samuelson

California State University, Long Beach

Charles L. P. Silet

Iowa State University

Amy Sisson

Houston Community College

Roger Smith

Portland, Oregon

Will Smith

University of Nottingham

George Soule

Carleton College

Brian Stableford

Reading, United Kingdom

Karen F. Stein

University of Rhode Island

W. J. Stuckey

Purdue University

Alvin Sullivan

Alton, Illinois

Eileen A. Sullivan

Tallahassee, Florida

James Sullivan

California State University, Los Angeles

Catherine Swanson

Austin, Texas

Roy Arthur Swanson

University of Wisconsin-Milwaukee

Christopher J. Thaiss

George Mason University

Terry Theodore

University of North Carolina at Wilmington

Lou Thompson

Texas Woman's University

Dennis Vannatta

University of Arkansas at Little Rock

Mark A. Weinstein

Original Contributor

Barbara Wiedemann

Auburn University at Montgomery

Thomas Willard

University of Arizona

Michael Witkoski

University of South Carolina

Jennifer L. Wyatt

Civic Memorial High School

COMPLETE LIST OF CONTENTS

British Volume 1

Publisher's Note vii
Contributors x
Key to Pronunciation xix
Addison, Joseph 1
Amis, Martin 6
Atwood, Margaret 11
Austen, Jane 20
Ballard, J. G. 25
Barker, Nicola 32
Barnes, Julian 36
Bates, H. E. 41
Beerbohm, Max 47
Bezmozgis, David 52
Bissoondath, Neil 56
Blackwood, Algernon 60
Bowen, Elizabeth 64
Boylan, Clare 70
Boyle, Patrick 74
Byatt, A. S. 78
Callaghan, Barry 83
Callaghan, Morley 87
Carey, Peter 94
Carleton, William 98
Carter, Angela 104
Chaucer, Geoffrey 108
Chesterton, G. K. 122
Christie, Agatha 129
Clarke, Arthur C. 136
Collier, John 143
Congreve, William 149
Conrad, Joseph 152
Coppard, A. E. 162
Dahl, Roald 168
Davies, Rhys 174
de la Mare, Walter 179
Dickens, Charles 184

Donovan, Gerard 190
Doyle, Sir Arthur Conan 194
Lord Dunsany 203
Edgeworth, Maria 209
Eliot, George 218
Enright, Anne 222
Fitzgerald, Penelope 227
Forster, E. M. 231
Fowles, John 237
Friel, Brian 243
Gallant, Mavis 248
Galloway, Janice 254
Galsworthy, John 258
Gilliatt, Penelope 263
Goldsmith, Oliver 269
Greene, Graham 275
Greene, Robert 282
Hardy, Thomas 288
Hawkesworth, John 294
Higgins, Aidan 298
Hogan, Desmond 303
Hospital, Janette Turner 308
Huxley, Aldous 312
Ishiguro, Kazuo 318
Jacobs, W. W. 323
James, M. R. 327
Jhabvala, Ruth Prawer 332
Johnson, Samuel 336
Jordan, Neil 342
Joyce, James 346
Kavan, Anna 355
Keegan, Claire 360
Kelman, James 364
Kennedy, A. L. 368
Kiely, Benedict 373
Kinsella, W. P. 379
Kipling, Rudyard 385

Kureishi, Hanif.............................394
Lasdun, James.............................399
Laurence, Margaret.......................403
Lavin, Mary................................408
Lawrence, D. H.............................415

Lawson, Henry.............................424
Le, Nam....................................429
Le Fanu, Joseph Sheridan 432
Lessing, Doris.............................439
Lewis, Wyndham 447

British Volume 2

Contents v
Contributors vii
Complete List of Contents xi
Key to Pronunciation xiii
Machen, Arthur 457
MacLaverty, Bernard 461
MacLeod, Alistair 465
Malory, Sir Thomas..........................469
Malouf, David 473
Mansfield, Katherine 477
Mars-Jones, Adam 486
Marshall, Owen.............................490
Maugham, W. Somerset 494
McCann, Colum 501
McEwan, Ian 505
McGahern, John 510
Mistry, Rohinton 514
Moore, George 518
Munro, Alice 523
O'Brien, Edna 534
O'Brien, Fitz-James 541
O'Connor, Frank 545
O'Faoláin, Seán.............................552
O'Flaherty, Liam 558
Plomer, William 565
Pritchett, V. S. 569
Rhys, Jean 578
Richler, Mordecai...........................583
Rooke, Leon 589
Saki 594
Sansom, William 598
Scott, Sir Walter 605

Seiffert, Rachel.............................610
Shields, Carol 614
Sillitoe, Alan 619
Spark, Muriel 624
Steele, Sir Richard..........................630
Stevenson, Robert Louis 635
Swift, Graham 641
Taylor, Elizabeth 645
Thackeray, William Makepeace..............649
Thomas, Dylan 655
Tóibín, Colm 661
Tremain, Rose 665
Trevor, William 670
Tuohy, Frank 678
Vanderhaeghe, Guy 683
Wain, John 687
Warner, Sylvia Townsend 691
Welch, Denton..............................698
Weldon, Fay 704
Wells, H. G. 710
Wilson, Angus 716
Winton, Tim 720
Woolf, Virginia..............................724
Yeats, William Butler 731
Terms and Techniques.......................739
Bibliography 753
Guide to Online Resources 780
Timeline 785
Major Awards 789
Chronological List of Writers 853
Categorical Index 857
Subject Index 866

KEY TO PRONUNCIATION

To help users of the *Critical Survey of Short Fiction* pronounce unfamiliar names of profiled writers correctly, phonetic spellings using the character symbols listed below appear in parentheses immediately after the first mention of the writer's name in the narrative text. Stressed syllables are indicated in capital letters, and syllables are separated by hyphens.

VOWEL SOUNDS
Symbol: Spelled (Pronounced)

a: answer (AN-suhr), laugh (laf), sample (SAM-puhl), that (that)
ah: father (FAH-thur), hospital (HAHS-pih-tuhl)
aw: awful (AW-fuhl), caught (kawt)
ay: blaze (blayz), fade (fayd), waiter (WAYT-ur), weigh (way)
eh: bed (behd), head (hehd), said (sehd)
ee: believe (bee-LEEV), cedar (SEE-dur), leader (LEED-ur), liter (LEE-tur)
ew: boot (bewt), lose (lewz)
i: buy (bi), height (hit), lie (li), surprise (sur-PRIZ)
ih: bitter (BIH-tur), pill (pihl)
o: cotton (KO-tuhn), hot (hot)
oh: below (bee-LOH), coat (koht), note (noht), wholesome (HOHL-suhm)
oo: good (good), look (look)
ow: couch (kowch), how (how)
oy: boy (boy), coin (koyn)
uh: about (uh-BOWT), butter (BUH-tuhr), enough (ee-NUHF), other (UH-thur)

CONSONANT SOUNDS
Symbol: Spelled (Pronounced)

ch: beach (beech), chimp (chihmp)
g: beg (behg), disguise (dihs-GIZ), get (geht)
j: digit (DIH-juht), edge (ehj), jet (jeht)
k: cat (kat), kitten (KIH-tuhn), hex (hehks)
s: cellar (SEHL-ur), save (sayv), scent (sehnt)
sh: champagne (sham-PAYN), issue (IH-shew), shop (shop)
ur: birth (burth), disturb (dihs-TURB), earth (urth), letter (LEH-tur)
y: useful (YEWS-fuhl), young (yuhng)
z: business (BIHZ-nehs), zest (zehst)
zh: vision (VIH-zhuhn)

CRITICAL SURVEY
OF
SHORT FICTION

Fourth Edition

M

ARTHUR MACHEN

Born: Caerleon-on-Usk, Wales; March 3, 1863
Died: Beaconsfield, Buckinghamshire, England;
    December 15, 1947
Also Known As: Arthur Llewellyn Jones

PRINCIPAL SHORT FICTION

The Chronicle of Clemendy: Or, The History of the
    IX Joyous Journeys, 1888
The Great God Pan, 1890 (novella)
"The Great God Pan" and "The Inmost Light,"
    1894 (novellas)
The Three Impostors: Or, The Transmutations, 1895
The House of Souls, 1906
The Angels of Mons, the Bowmen, and Other
    Legends of the War, 1915
The Children of the Pool, and Other Stories, 1936
The Cosy Room, and Other Stories, 1936
Holy Terrors, 1946
Tales of Horror and the Supernatural, 1948
Ritual, and Other Stories, 1992

OTHER LITERARY FORMS

Early in his career Arthur Machen (MAHK-ehn) translated several works from French, including *The Memoirs of Jacques Casanova* (1894). His major novel is *The Hill of Dreams* (1907). Autobiographical volumes include *Far Off Things* (1922) and *Things Near and Far* (1923). Machen's highly readable essays are collected in such volumes as *Dog and Duck* (1924).

ACHIEVEMENTS

In recognition of his literary accomplishments, Arthur Machen received a civil-list pension from King George V in 1933. Over the years several societies of enthusiastic readers have been formed to reprint Machen's works and advance his reputation.

BIOGRAPHY

Arthur Llewellyn Jones was born on the border between England and Wales in the Welsh village of Caerleon-on-Usk on March 3, 1863, the son of an Anglican clergyman, John Edward Jones. "Machen," Jones's mother's name, was legally taken by his father a few years later to fulfill the requirements of an inheritance. The childhood he spent in this remote countryside, which still bore the traces of ancient Roman occupation, would remain with him all his life.

Having foiled his parents' plans for a formal education, Machen moved to London at the age of eighteen, earning a bare subsistence as a journalist and translator. His first important literary effort was *The Great God Pan*, a controversial novella of supernatural horror that was to be followed by many more works in the same vein. Machen wrote his most important novel, *The Hill of Dreams*, during the mid-1890's but was not able to find a publisher until about ten years later. Referring to Daniel Defoe's famous novel, Machen described his own effort as "a *Robinson Crusoe* of the soul," and in it he described the agonizing experiences of a sensitive writer much like him in the vast, impersonal metropolis of London.

Machen had made a name for himself as a novelist and short-story writer, but his income was negligible. Although he never quite gave up fiction, he made a living as an actor, journalist, and essayist during the latter part of his life. Machen died in Beaconsfield, Buckinghamshire, on December 15, 1947.

ANALYSIS

Almost all of Arthur Machen's works--fiction and nonfiction alike--are touched by his sense of the marvelous, his belief that another, more meaningful world lies behind the facade of routine, everyday sense experience. Sometimes this other world is one of horror--as in the nightmarish events described in "The White

People"--and sometimes it is a world of wonder and joy. As a character in his story "The Red Hand" puts it, "There are sacraments of evil as well as of good about us, and we live and move to my belief in an unknown world, a place where there are caves and shadows and dwellers in twilights."

In many cases Machen's protagonists use drugs or other medical means to pierce the veil of so-called reality. A theory that Machen dramatized in many of his works--that the folklore of elves and fairies has its origin in the survival of a primitive dwarf race driven underground by the invading Celts--represents an extension of this belief. His interests and subject matter place Machen outside the realistic tradition of British fiction but mark him as an important and highly influential figure in the development of modern fantasy.

Machen's writings defy easy classification. His best fictional writings inhabit a middle ground between the short story and the novel; his works in the former category are often developed with the indirection and leisurely pace readers associate with the latter. One important volume, *The Three Impostors: Or, The Transmutations*, incorporates several stories into a larger and more complex framework. In addition, many of Machen's apparently fictional works have the expository tone of nonfiction, and a number of the shorter pieces he wrote toward the end of his career can be read as either stories or essays.

THE GREAT GOD PAN

Although critics have pointed out its crudity, this early novella is the work most modern readers associate with Machen's name. It introduced many of its author's themes and methods, and despite its wayward approach and its reliance on the most outlandish coincidences, it remains a gripping if disquieting reading experience. The story is told from several points of view but deals essentially with an unorthodox brain operation that will allow a young woman to "see" the Great God Pan. Although Pan is ostensibly the Greek god of pastures and flocks, in this case he represents the hideous reality that lies behind the day-to-day world. The patient--Mary Vaughan--ultimately dies, but not before giving birth to a daughter. It is this daughter who, years later, is the cause of a series of suicides in London society. It turns out that she is the daughter of

Arthur Machen (Getty Images)

Mary Vaughan and Pan and, when confronted, commits suicide herself and regresses through a series of devolutionary steps to a kind of primeval slime.

THE THREE IMPOSTORS

Machen's 1895 collection works several stories into a larger framework that defies logical summary but that clearly conveys his belief in a reality underlying the everyday. The stories involve or are told to one or the other of two friends, Dyson and Phillipps, the former a romantic dreamer and unpublished writer and the latter a pragmatic scientist, the two having met in a London tobacco shop. Aside from the work's obvious horror, it is also surprisingly humorous.

In "Adventure of the Gold Tiberius" Dyson recovers an extraordinarily rare coin after observing a violent pursuit. A young woman tells Phillipps the "Novel of the Black Seal," in which famous scientist Dr. Gregg pursues the "little people," much to his subsequent regret. In "Novel of the Iron Maid," an acquaintance describes to Dyson how a third party is beset by his own instrument of torture. "Novel of the White Powder" is related to Dyson by a young woman (who seems somehow familiar to the reader) and concerns a medical prescription that has unluckily degenerated into a potion that witches once took at their Sabbaths. Through all these strange adventures passes an enigmatic figure, a "young man with spectacles," who is somehow the key to the entire series of events.

The Everyman edition of this intriguing work (Rutland, Vt.: Tuttle, 1995) contains an introduction by critic David Trotter, as well as other valuable supplementary material. Two of the embedded stories, "Novel of the Black Seal" and "Novel of the White Powder," are regarded as classics of fantasy and are often reprinted individually under shortened titles.

"THE WHITE PEOPLE"

Originally published in 1899, "The White People" is regarded not only as a high point in Machen's writing career but also as one of the best supernatural stories ever written. The heart of the story, "The Green Book," is framed by a discussion between two characters about the nature of evil. One of the two, Ambrose, announces a central belief of Machen's, that "Sorcery and sanctity . . . are the only realities. Each is an ecstasy, a withdrawal from the common life."

"The Green Book" itself is the diary of a young girl and recounts in naïve, largely unpunctuated fashion the girl's "ecstasy," her initiation into Satanism by her nurse. Machen incorporated both authentic and imaginary folklore into the girl's account and wrote it in a run-on "stream-of-consciousness" style that would later be identified with novelist James Joyce. Looking far beyond the logical (and thus inadequate) utterances of Ambrose and his friend, this fragment illustrates literature's ability to create a viable world outside the confines of realism.

"THE BOWMEN"

"The Bowmen" became Machen's most famous story during World War I. It originally appeared in the London newspaper the *Evening News* for September 29, 1914, and professed--in an age-old fictional ploy--to be a true account of extraordinary events. During the recent Battle of Mons, Machen said, an inadvertent reference to St. George had resulted in the appearance of phantom bowmen in shining armor who had attacked the Germans. The implication was that the British patron saint of soldiers had summoned the archers from the Battle of Agincourt (1415), where they had saved the day for the British, to fight once again for their descendants. Almost immediately, "witnesses" stepped forward to testify to the reality of these and similar events. Although Machen made it clear after the fact that his brief tale was fiction, he was inspired to write further works on the same theme. These were collected as *The Angel of Mons, The Bowmen, and Other Legends of the War*. The material of these stories subsequently became part of the folklore of Britain's wartime experience.

"N"

"N" is Machen's most important later story, a leisurely and elegiacal variation on one of his favorite themes. It originally appeared in *The Cosy Room, and Other Stories*, a collection of what were otherwise reprints. The story is set in the London suburb of Stoke Newington and concerns a small group of friends who discover through their idle talk that an interpenetration of two worlds has taken place. This phenomenon results in stories of an unusually pleasant if confoundingly elusive garden somewhere in the area. Machen even coined a term, "perichoresis," to describe the phenomenon. "N" has been criticized as somewhat diffuse, but it is hard to imagine that a more tightly developed story could have conveyed the fragile wonder that Machen produces in this work. Another of Machen's works, his novel *The Green Round* (1933), develops some of the same material, although not so memorably.

OTHER MAJOR WORKS

LONG FICTION: *The Hill of Dreams*, 1907; *The Great Return*, 1915; *The Terror*, 1917; *The Secret Glory*, 1922 (complete edition 1998); *The Shining Pyramid*, 1923; *A Fragment of Life*, 1928; *The Green Round*, 1933.

NONFICTION: *The Anatomy of Tobacco*, 1884; *Hieroglyphics: A Note upon Ecstasy in Literature*, 1902; *Far Off Things*, 1922 (autobiography); *Strange Roads*, 1923; *Things Near and Far*, 1923 (autobiography); *Dog and Duck*, 1924; *The London Adventure*, 1924; *The Canning Wonder*, 1925; *Dreads and Drolls*, 1926; *Notes and Queries*, 1926; *Arthur Machen and Montgomery Evans: Letters of a Literary Friendship, 1923-1947*, 1994; *The Secret of Sangraal*, 1995.

TRANSLATIONS: *The Heptameron: Or, Tales and Novels of Marguerite, Queen of Navarre*, 1886; *The Memoirs of Jacques Casanova*, 1894.

BIBLIOGRAPHY

Cavaliero, Glen. "Watchers on the Threshold." In *The Supernatural and English Fiction*. Oxford, England: Oxford University Press, 1995. Cavaliero stresses the importance of landscape and cityscape in Machen's works, as well as the sexual content of his stories. Like most commentators, he praises "The White People" in particular.

Jones, Daryl. "Borderlands: Spiritualism and the Occult in Fin de Siècle and Edwardian Welsh and Irish Horror." *Irish Studies Review* 17, no. 1 (February, 2009): 31-44. Examines the influence of spiritualism, occultism, and Celtic theories and rhetoric on Machen and other writers of horror fiction set in Wales and Ireland. Argues that these writers viewed themselves as straddling between the spiritual and material worlds and depicted this state in their works.

Joshi, S. T. "Arthur Machen: The Mystery of the Universe." In *The Weird Tale*. Austin: University of Texas Press, 1990. Taking a largely negative view of Machen's work, Joshi dismisses the author's philosophy and his narrative skill. He observes that, with few exceptions, Machen's best works were written during the decade 1889-1899.

MacLeod, Kirsten. "Arthur Machen's *Great God Pan* and Decadent Pan(ic)." In *Fictions of British Decadence: High Art, Popular Writing, and the Fin de Siècle*. New York: Palgrave Macmillan, 2006. Places *The Great God Pan* in the context of Decadence, pointing out the themes and techniques in Marchen's novella that reflect the ideas and writing style of this literary movement.

Nash, Berta. "Arthur Machen Among the Arthurians." In *Minor British Novelists*, edited by Charles Alva Hoyt. Carbondale: Southern Illinois University Press, 1967. Examines Machen's use of the Matter of Arthur, particularly the Holy Grail, which Nash believes functioned for Machen as a symbol of humankind. Despite the title of the volume, Machen's short fiction, as well as his novels, are considered.

Reynolds, Aidan, and William Charlton. *Arthur Machen: A Short Account of His Life and Work*. Oxford, England: Caermaen, 1988. As the standard biography of Machen, this volume is not likely to be surpassed. Originally published in 1963, it includes illustrations, notes, brief bibliographies, and an index.

Schoolfield, George C. *A Baedeker of Decadence: Charting a Literary Fashion, 1884-1927*. New Haven, Conn.: Yale University Press, 2003. Devotes a chapter to an examination of Machen's short fiction and novels, focusing on these works as examples of the literary Decadence movement that was popular at the end of the nineteenth and beginning of the twentieth centuries.

Sparks, Tabitha. "New Women, Avenging Doctors: Gothic Medicine in Bram Stoker." In *The Doctor in the Victorian Novel: Family Practices*. Burlington, Vt.: Ashgate, 2009. Discusses Stocker's *Dracula* and Machen's novellas *The Great God Pan* and *The Inmost Light*, all of which were published after the Contagious Diseases Act was repealed in 1886. The repeal was hailed as a victory for the physical autonomy of women, and it engendered hostility between physicians and feminists. Sparks demonstrates how the three works reflect this conflict by depicting physicians who seize control of women's sexuality and reproductive capabilities.

Sweetser, Wesley D. *Arthur Machen*. Boston: Twayne, 1964. Sweetser's study remains the most complete book on Machen, summarizing his life and discussing almost all his vast production. Includes useful (although now dated) primary and secondary bibliographies.

Valentine, Mark. *Arthur Machen*. Bridgend, Mid Glamorgan, Wales: Seren, 1995. A sympathetic introduction to Machen, briefer than Sweetser's but taking advantage of more recent scholarship and taking issue with Joshi on several points. Includes illustrations and a select bibliography but no index.

Wagenknecht, Edward. "Arthur Machen." In *Seven Masters of Supernatural Fiction*. New York: Greenwood Press, 1991. This survey by an objective critic gives fair consideration to Machen's later, lesser-known stories and novels, as well as his more familiar works.

Grove Koger.

BERNARD MACLAVERTY

Born: Belfast, Northern Ireland; September 14, 1942

PRINCIPAL SHORT FICTION
Secrets, and Other Stories, 1977
A Time to Dance, and Other Stories, 1982
The Great Profundo, and Other Stories, 1987
Walking the Dog, and Other Stories, 1994
Matters of Life and Death, and Other Stories, 2006

OTHER LITERARY FORMS

Bernard MacLaverty (muh-KLA-vur-tee) published his first novel, *Lamb,* in 1980. His novel *Cal* was published in 1983, and the novel *Grace Notes* appeared in 1997, followed by *The Anatomy School* in 2001. He also has written a number of screenplays and has adapted works for radio.

ACHIEVEMENTS

MacLaverty won the Scottish Arts Council Award for *Secrets, and Other Stories,* for *A Time to Dance, and Other Stories,* and for *The Great Profundo, and Other Stories.* He was joint winner of Scottish Writer of the Year in 1988 (McVitie's Prize), and the Irish Post Award in 1989. *Walking the Dog* was shortlisted for the Saltire Society Scottish Book of the Year in 1994. His novel *Grace Notes* won the Saltire Scottish Book of the Year Award in 1997 and was shortlisted for the Booker Prize, the Writers Guild Best Fiction Book, the Whitbread Novel of the Year, and the Mind Book of the Year. His novel *The Anatomy School* was shortlisted for the Saltire Scottish Book of the Year award in 2004. For his film *Bye-Child,* he won the British Academy of Film and Television Arts Scotland Best First Director Award in 2004.

BIOGRAPHY

Bernard MacLaverty was born in 1942 in Belfast, Northern Ireland, where he attended the Catholic school St. Malachy's College. When his scores did not qualify him for university, he worked for ten years as a medical laboratory technician at Queen's University. With the encouragement of an anatomy professor and Phillip Hobsbaum, a lecturer in English at Queen's, who ran a writers' course for some of his promising students, MacLaverty, at age twenty-eight, entered Queen's University as a student, where he earned an honors degree in English and qualified to be a teacher. Concerned about his children's safety because of the violence in Northern Ireland, he moved with his family to Scotland in 1975. After living for three years in Edinburgh, he moved to the Isle of Islay, where he taught for eight years. During this time, he published his first collection of stories, *Secrets,* to good reviews and gave up teaching to spend full time writing. For two years he was writer-in-residence at the University of Aberdeen, and he published his first novel, *Lamb,* in 1980. He later moved to Glasgow, with his wife, Madeline, and their four children, to teach fiction at the Research Institute of Irish and Scottish Studies. MacLaverty was a leader of the Glasgow Committee that campaigned for the release of the so-called Birmingham Six, Northern Irish Catholics convicted and later released on appeal for bombing a pub in Birmingham, England. After his novel *Cal* was made into a successful film starring Helen Mirren, MacLaverty began writing film scripts, adapting MacGill's novel *Children of the Dead End* (1915). MacLaverty is a member of Aosdána, an organization of writers sponsored by the Arts Council of Ireland, and is visiting writer and professor at the University of Strathclyde.

ANALYSIS

Although Bernard MacLaverty writes about a wide range of subjects, featuring a variety of characters, the fact that he was born and raised in Belfast, Northern Ireland, surrounded by the sectarian violence of the so-called Troubles, has had an unmistakable influence on his fiction. Although this is obvious in his novel *Cal* (in which an Irish Republican Army terrorist falls in love with the widow of a Protestant policeman the terrorist has helped to assassinate), it is also true in a number of his short stories. MacLaverty once said he used to think that the short story would be overburdened with a death in it, but many of his stories, as indicated by the title of his collection *Matters of Life and Death* are haunted by the threat of violence and death. However, in spite of the hostility that hovers over much of his work, MacLaverty's stories exhibit a tight Chekhovian control, reminiscent of his fellow Irishman, Frank O'Connor, that does not allow them to become merely visceral. In one of his stories, "The Clinic," a man waiting to take a diabetes test in the hospital reads a story by Anton Chekhov, admiring Chekhov's ability to use prose so precisely that it seems as "if the thing is happening in front of your eyes." MacLaverty has some of that same Chekhovian ability with language. Although his stories do not have the subtle complexity of his famous Irish short-story colleague, William Trevor, they are carefully crafted evocations of Irish life, especially as it has been conditioned by sectarian hostility in Northern Ireland.

"Secrets"

The title story of MacLaverty's debut collection is one of his best known. It focuses on a young man who has been called to the home of his Great Aunt Mary, who is dying. As he sits at her deathbed, he recalls an incident when he was a child and became curious about a soldier named Brother Benignus, from whom the aunt received letters when she was young. He sneaks into the aunt's bedroom and begins reading love letters from the young soldier, which are largely about the horrors of death he has witnessed. In the final letter the boy reads, the young soldier, who has been wounded and is in a hospital, writes that he feels he must sacrifice something to make up for the horrors he has seen, concluding that in some strange way Christ has spoken to him through all the carnage. This is obviously in reference to the soldier's decision to become a priest after the war, which would, of course, make it impossible for him and the aunt to be together. When the aunt discovers the boy reading the letters, she is furious and tells him, "You are dirt and always will be dirt. I shall remember this till the day I die." When the aunt dies and the boy's mother burns the letters in the fireplace, he asks if the aunt said anything about him before she died. Learning that she did not, he begins to cry for the first time since her death, for the woman who had been his "teller of tales," that she might forgive him.

"Umberto Verdi, Chimney-Sweep"

This is one of the more subtle stories in *Secrets*. It focuses on Nan, a housewife with four small children, whose life is characterized by the everyday struggles of domesticity. She calls a chimney-sweep to take care of her smoking chimney, choosing him for no other reason than his name reminds her of fantasies of a past visit to Italy before she met her husband. She goes to a wine shop and buys a bottle of Italian wine, recalling its smell and the romantic fragrances of Italy. She also recalls a man named Kamel, who asked her out many times when she was young and impressed her with his gentlemanly manners. When Kamel asks her to marry him and to come live with him in the Middle East, the cultural difference is too much for her, and she turns him down. However, she has fantasies about what her

Bernard MacLaverty (Geray Sweeney/Corbis)

life would have been like had she accepted his proposal. On the day the chimney-sweep is to come to take care of her fireplace, she dresses up in a white frock, puts the baby down for a nap, sends the other children to a neighbor's house, and waits for what she thinks will be a romantic encounter. However, the sweep is a short, fat man of fifty. When the work is done, she opens the wine and takes only two sips before pouring the rest of it down the sink because of its acrid taste. Although the conflict between romantic expectation and reality in this story is simple, Nan's mixed feelings of memory and regret and her inchoate expectations are subtle and complex.

"PHONEFUN LIMITED"

This story from MacLaverty's second collection, *A Time to Dance*, is well known primarily because he adapted it for a radio program that was heard widely in the United Kingdom. It is a relatively light scenario about two ex-prostitutes, Sadie and Agnes, who run a telephone sex business out of their home. Most of the story focuses on the dialogue between the two women while they eat dinner and recall men they have known in the past. They count the money they have received, justify what they do as being better than walking the streets, and read aloud and laugh at some of the letters they receive from men they call. Agnes, who does most of the calling, contacts some of her clients, pretending that she is engaging in sex with them. She recalls those who have disgusted her or amused her with the absurdity of what they request her to do or say. The story ends with the two women going to bed and Agnes rebuffing Sadie's sexual overtures. The two women seem superior to their male clients but evoke sadness at the loneliness of their situation. The story is so dependent on dialogue that it seems a natural for a radio program.

WALKING THE DOG

MacLaverty has said that he patterned the structure of his collection *Walking the Dog*, with its interchapters, after Ernest Hemingway's *In Our Time* (1924, 1925), although MacLaverty decided to make his interchapters comic considerations of the life or technique of the writer. The italicized interstories all begin with the phrase "Your man," which MacLaverty says is an Irish phrase hard to translate but means something like "Our hero walked into a bar," which names someone

but does not actually give him a name. The first italicized introit story is entitled "On the Art of the Short Story" and consists of the descriptive line, "This is a story with a trick beginning," followed by: "Your man put down his pen and considered the possibility that if he left this as the only sentence, then his story would also have a trick ending."

"WALKING THE DOG"

The title story of MacLaverty's collection recounts a simple but chilling encounter that illustrates the tension of the Troubles in Northern Ireland. A man walking his dog one night is accosted by two men with guns, who threaten to blow his head off and force him into their car. The men tell him they are from the Irish Republican Army (IRA), the Catholic group determined to force Northern Ireland to become part of the Republic in the south. They want to know if he is Catholic or Protestant, but since he does not know for sure if they are IRA or Protestants, he says he does not believe in any of that crap and that he is neither. They then force him to say his alphabet, but he knows that Catholics and Protestants, because of their different schooling pronounce the letter "H" differently. Therefore, when he gets to that letter, he pronounces it both ways-- "aitch" and "haitch." When they force him to tell them what he thinks of the IRA, he says he hates everything for which they stand. The two men, who finally agree that he is no more a Catholic than they are, let him out of the car and drive away. The story has a simple plot line and simple character interaction but effectively suggests the delicate nature of religious and political differences in Northern Ireland during the time of the Troubles.

MATTERS OF LIFE AND DEATH

The first story in Bernard MacLaverty's collection *Matters of Life and Death* is an emblematic introit that he says encapsulates many of the horrors of Northern Ireland since Bloody Friday. Metaphorically titled "On the Roundabout," to suggest the never-ending, dizzying circularity of sectarian violence in the North, the story takes place soon after the beginnings of the Troubles in the early 1970's. A man driving into a traffic circle with what he calls his Norman Rockwell family rescues a young man being savagely beaten by two laughing assailants. That is all that happens, but in its restrained elegance, the story epitomizes the deep-seated hatred that has crippled the country for years.

Three additional stories derive either directly or indirectly from the Troubles. In "A Trusted Neighbor," a Protestant policeman seems like a friend to his Catholic neighbor, until, with something of a shock at the end, the reader learns that he is setting him up for a vicious attack. "The Trojan Sofa" is a comic tour de force told from the point of view of an eleven-year-old boy whose Catholic father sews him up in a sofa, which he then sells to a British major. Once the boy is in the house, he is to let his father in to loot it--a robbery his father justifies by saying that the wrong done to Ireland by the British is so great that anything done to them in retaliation is honorable. "Learning to Dance" is a sad and subtle sonata about two young boys placed in the temporary care of a childless doctor and his wife when their father, a prominent man, is killed in what the reader assumes was an act of sectarian violence. As usual in a MacLaverty tale, nothing much happens, but the story is a moving, elegiac evocation of loss, sadness, and perplexity.

Like many other writers, MacLaverty learned to write this kind of subtle atmospheric story from Chekhov--a mentor to whom he pays tribute in "The Clinic," in which a man passes the time in a doctor's office, while anxiously waiting to hear if he has diabetes, by reading a Chekhov story entitled "The Beauties." The man's experience with his fear and his experience with the story merge in the end, when love and beauty are reaffirmed as both the man in Chekhov's story and the man in MacLaverty's story feel the "wind blow across [their] soul."

In "Visiting Takabuti," another Chekhovian story, a maiden aunt takes her two nephews to see a famous female mummy in a Belfast museum. On the bus ride home, she thinks about a traditional Irish tale in which, at the moment of death, the soul tiptoes to the door but then turns back and kisses the body that has sheltered it all these years. Although the story's ending may seem a bit too symbolically pat and predictable, MacLaverty creates the woman so delicately that the reader cannot help but be moved.

The longest story in the collection, "Up the Coast," moves back and forth between the point of view of a young woman who has gone to a remote area to paint and a young man who hunts her down and rapes her. MacLaverty refuses to sensationalize or politicize the act, choosing instead to focus on the understated artistic means by which the woman transcends the violation.

OTHER MAJOR WORKS

LONG FICTION: *Lamb*, 1980; *Cal*, 1983; *Grace Notes*, 1997; *The Anatomy School*, 2001.

SCREENPLAYS: *Cal*, 1984 (adaptation of his novel); *Lamb*, 1986.

RADIO PLAYS: *My Dear Palestrina*, 1980; *Secrets*, 1981; *No Joke*, 1983; *Some Surrender*, 1988; *The Break*, 1988.

CHILDREN'S LITERATURE: *A Man in Search of a Pet*, 1978; *Andrew McAndrew*, 1988.

BIBLIOGRAPHY

Griffith, Benjamin. "Ireland's Ironies, Grim and Droll: The Fiction of Bernard MacLaverty." *Sewanee Review* 106 (Spring, 1998): 334-339. Griffith says that most of MacLaverty's characters are beset by religion and the Irish Troubles and besotted by sex and drink, acting out their lives of noisy desperation with minimal plots. Discusses stories from *Walking the Dog*, including "Silent Retreat," "Just Visiting," and "At the Beach."

Ladrón, Marisol Morales. "Writing Is a State of Mind, Not an Achievement: An Interview with Bernard MacLaverty." *Atlantis* 23 (December, 2001): 201-211. MacLaverty says his devotion to writing began with his admiration of Michael MacLaverty. He insists that, although writing need not be overtly political, all writing, even writing that pretends not to be, is political.

"Mac the Strife." *The Sunday Herald*, October 10, 1999, p. 12. In this profile, MacLaverty is called a Celtic Chekhov, whose émigré position as a man from Northern Ireland living in Scotland often characterizes his fiction.

MacLaverty, Bernard. "Bernard MacLaverty: Writer's Corner." *Europe*, July 1995, p. 45. In this interview after the publication of *Walking the Dog*, MacLaverty talks about the importance of humor in stories of Northern Ireland, the source of the title story in the collection, and why Irish writers are so popular around the world.

Saxton, Arnold. "An Introduction to the Stories of Bernard MacLaverty." *Journal of the Short Story in English* 8 (Spring, 1987): 113-123. Discusses

several stories from *Secrets* and *A Time to Dance*, including "Secrets," "Life Drawing," "Phonefun Limited," "Between Two Shores," "My Dear Palestrina," and "Umberto Verdi, Chimney-Sweep." Argues that MacLaverty's primary themes are loneliness, isolation, and discontent.

Charles E. May

ALISTAIR MACLEOD

Born: North Battleford, Saskatchewan, Canada; July 20, 1936

PRINCIPAL SHORT FICTION

The Lost Salt Gift of Blood, 1978

As Birds Bring Forth the Sun, and Other Stories, 1986

The Lost Salt Gift of Blood: New and Selected Stories, 1988

Island: The Collected Stories of Alistair MacLeod (pb. in U.S. as Island: The Complete Stories, 2001)

OTHER LITERARY FORMS

Alistair MacLeod (AL-ih-stayr muh-KLOWD) adapted his novel *No Great Mischief* (1999) for production as a play in 2004. He had previously written a play entitled *The Lost Salt Gift of Blood*, which was produced in the Maritimes in 1982. Another play, *The Boat*, based on the short story of that name, toured Canada, England, and Scotland in 1983 and 1984. MacLeod's primary nonfiction work is his doctoral dissertation, *A Textual Study of Thomas Hardy's "A Group of Noble Dames"* (1968).

ACHIEVEMENTS

Despite the fact that his output is relatively small, Alistair MacLeod is ranked as one of the finest fiction

writers that Canada has produced. In his short fiction, MacLeod captured the spirit of a people and described a rapidly vanishing way of life. Early in his career, MacLeod was chosen to represent Canada in a writers' exchange program between Canada and Scotland. In 2009, MacLeod's lifetime of achievement as a writer of short stories was recognized when he was awarded the PEN/Malamud Award for Short Fiction. MacLeod's novel *No Great Mischief* had the same setting and reflected the same values as his short fiction. It won the Trillium Prize, the Thomas Head Raddall Atlantic Fiction Award, the Dartmouth Book and Writing Award for Fiction, the Atlantic Provinces Booksellers Choice Award, and the 2001 International IMPAC Dublin Literary Award. In 2008, MacLeod was appointed an Officer of the Order of Canada.

BIOGRAPHY

Alistair MacLeod was born in North Battleford, Saskatchewan, the son of Alexander Duncan MacLeod and Christene MacLellan, whose families had lived on Cape Breton Island, Nova Scotia, for many generations. However, because their area was especially hard hit economically during the Great Depression, the MacLeods had to leave Nova Scotia, and as a result, Alistair MacLeod spent the first ten years of his life outside the area with which he would come to be identified. After five years in Saskatchewan and another five in Alberta, the MacLeods moved back to Cape Breton and the family farm. There Alistair MacLeod was surrounded by members of an extended family, united in their adherence to their Highland Scots traditions and in their loyalty to the small community in which they lived. MacLeod soon learned how to catch fish and do farm chores. Over the years, he also worked as a miner and as a logger.

After graduating from high school, in 1956 MacLeod earned a certificate from the Nova Scotia Teachers' College of Truro. He then taught for one year on Port Hood Island, near Cape Breton. In 1957, he entered St. Francis Xavier University in Antigonish, where he earned B.A. and B.Ed. degrees. He then proceeded to graduate school at the University of New Brunswick, completing an M.A. in 1961 with a thesis on the Canadian short story. That same year, his short story "The Greater Good" appeared in *Intervales*, a New Brunswick magazine. MacLeod spent the next two years as a lecturer in English at Nova Scotia Teachers' College. From 1966 to 1969, he lived in the United States, studying for his doctorate at the University of Notre Dame, while teaching English at Indiana University in Fort Wayne. In 1968, he received his doctorate; again, his research involved the short story. The subject of his dissertation was a volume of short fiction by the Victorian writer Thomas Hardy. MacLeod had already begun turning out poetry and short stories, which by the end of the 1960's began appearing regularly in various literary periodicals. His first book-length publication, *The Lost Salt Gift of Blood*, a collection of seven stories, did not appear until 1978.

In 1969, MacLeod accepted a faculty position at the University of Windsor in Windsor, Ontario. In 1971, MacLeod married Anita MacLellan, who also was a native of Cape Breton. They had six children: Alexander, Lewis, Kenneth, Marion, Daniel, and Andrew. MacLeod spent the rest of his academic career at the University of Windsor, teaching English and creative writing. In 1973, he became the fiction editor of the *University of Windsor Review*.

Analysis

Though all but one of his short stories involve the people of Scottish ancestry who immigrated to Nova Scotia in the late eighteenth and early nineteenth centuries, Alistair MacLeod does not write fiction that has a

limited application. His stories deal with such universal themes as human beings versus nature, tradition versus innovation, the past versus the present, reason versus emotion, duty versus ambition, and age versus youth. Their appeal is based not only on MacLeod's flawless style but also on his evenhanded approach to conflicts. On one hand, he has no qualms about exposing the self-centered, as in "The Return," in which a snobbish, city-bred wife has kept her son away from his grandmother for ten years, or in "The Road to Rankin's Point," where only one of an elderly woman's many descendants regard her as anything more than a problem to be solved. On the other hand, as a man who chose to escape from Cape Breton and live in the larger world that an education opens up to, MacLeod can sympathize with the young man in "The Boat," who is torn between his desire to please his mother by becoming a fisherman and his own certainty that he belongs in the world of books. Although the clarity of his style may give the reader the impression that his stories are simple, in fact MacLeod's fiction is as complicated as life itself.

Alistair MacLeod (Getty Images)

"The Tuning of Perfection"

One example of MacLeod's commitment to total honesty is his short story "The Tuning of Perfection." The protagonist is a lonely, seventy-eight-year-old widower known only as Archibald, a man who has always lived by absolute values: reverence for the past, respect for nature, and insistence on the truth. However, it seems that the world no longer lives by those values. After Archibald has sold a fine young mare, confident that her offspring will carry on her line, the buyer tells him that she will be bred constantly so that her urine can be used in human birth control pills and that her colts will be killed. Another betrayal of his values concerns the bald eagles that wheel above his mountain home, which Archibald has always viewed with delight. When he mentions them to visiting folklorists, he is told that they have already disappeared in other areas and that they will be seen above Cape Breton only until the forestry industry in Nova Scotia decides that it will be profitable to use pesticides and herbicides.

If nature is at risk in the modern world, Archibald at least believes that the Gaelic songs he loves can be preserved intact. He is looking forward to taking a group made up of his extended family to Halifax, where they will perform authentic Gaelic music on a television show. However, just when the arrangements appear to be complete, the producer of the show informs Archibald that each narrative must be cut in half and suggests that he find a way to make the songs sound less melancholy. Though Archibald knows that his singers will be bitterly disappointed, he cannot violate his principles, and he turns down the producer. To his horror, his place is taken by some friends of a rough young man called Carver, who cannot sing, does not know Gaelic, and is interested only in making money.

Up to this point, it appears that the conflict has been between a principled past and an unprincipled present. However, when Carver and some of his friends arrive at Archibald's house, roaring drunk but bearing a gift of whiskey, the old man has to rethink his most cherished beliefs. These young men, he realizes, are not unlike the Scots celebrated in the songs he so values. Thus while their songs may not have been true to the tradition, the men who sang them brought the Highlands to that stage in Halifax.

"In the Fall"

Often MacLeod utilizes a story of initiation to demonstrate the complexity of life. In "In the Fall," the narrator is a thirteen-year-old boy named James. His father and mother are arguing about whether or not to keep an old horse through the winter. The father had befriended the horse when they were both working in the coal mines. When he left, he bought the horse, named him Scott, and brought him home to work on the farm. He has often told his children about the time long ago when, after he got drunk and fell asleep in the bootlegger's house, he emerged the next morning to find Scott standing in the snow, waiting patiently for his master. However, the father has a wife and six children to support, and the horse is old, frail, and, in the mother's opinion, not worth his keep. Although the father is hesitant to have the horse put down, the mother has made up her mind. She announces that she has called the drover MacRae to pick up the horse that morning. However, when MacRae arrives, his task turns out to be more difficult than he had expected. Scott balks at the ramp of the truck and then runs away, to the delight of James's ten-year-old brother David, who has made a pet of the horse. At this point, James realizes that his father has no choice, that they are too poor to keep the horse any longer. He sees his father lead the docile horse into the truck that will take him to his death.

Suddenly James realizes that David has disappeared. He finds him in the chicken-house, swinging an ax, surrounded by the dead bodies of his mother's prized capons. At the end of the story, the mother and the father embrace, evidently having reached an understanding, and James goes to find his brother, hoping to persuade him to forgive their mother, hoping to show him what he has learned: that survival forces people to make hard choices.

"Winter Dog"

In another moving story of an animal sacrificed to human necessity, a father recalls an episode from his childhood on Cape Breton. When he was twelve, his father bought a collie pup. However, though he grew into a beautiful dog, the most rigorous training failed to make him skilled at herding cattle. The narrator does find a use for him, however; he is strong enough to pull a sleigh. One snowy day, the narrator takes his dog and the sleigh out onto the ice, finds a frozen seal, and loads it onto the sleigh. The seal soon falls off, and when it becomes clear that the ice is not solid, the boy releases the dog, who runs off. Then the boy falls through the ice. When he cries out, the dog comes to him, pulls him out, and guides him from one ice pan to another until they are near home. After they get indoors and begin to thaw out, the boy is too embarrassed to tell anyone about his adventure or to admit that the dog saved his life.

Two years later, the narrator and his father take the dog for a walk, and he is shot by a neighbor. It turns out that the father had asked to neighbor to kill the dog. His explanation is that people were afraid of the dog, but the narrator suspects that the community does not want the dog's bloodlines to become dominant. The narrator reflects that had he told his father about the dog's saving his life, the animal might have been allowed to live. In any case, the dog lives on in the narrator's memory and in the golden-gray dogs on Cape Breton that are his descendants. Again, MacLeod is emphasizing the tragic complexities of human existence, while at the same time demonstrating the value of memory and the continuing presence of the past.

OTHER MAJOR WORKS

LONG FICTION: *No Great Mischief*, 1999.

DRAMA: *The Lost Salt Gift of Blood*, pr. 1982 (adaptation of his short story); *The Boat*, pr. 1983 (adaptation of his short story); *No Great Mischief*, pr. 2004, pb. 2006 (with David Young; adaptation of his novel).

NONFICTION: *A Textual Study of Thomas Hardy's "A Group of Noble Dames,"* 1968 (doctoral dissertation).

BIBLIOGRAPHY

Creelman, David. "'Hoping to Strike Some Sort of Solidarity': The Shifting Fictions of Alistair MacLeod." *Studies in Canadian Literature* 24, no. 2 (1999): 79-99. Argues that MacLeod's short stories reflect a change in attitude over the years. While in the early stories, he wrote sympathetically about the desire to escape from the pressures of the past, increasingly he sees tradition as a vital need both for society and for the individual.

Eichler, Leah. "Alistair MacLeod of Scotsmen in Canada." *Publishers Weekly* 247, no. 17 (April 24, 2000): 54-55. In an informal interview conducted after the publication of *No Great Mischief*, the MacLeod compares writing a novel with writing short stories. He also comments on the importance of his native landscape in his works, his writing techniques, and the values he attempts to impart to the students in his writing classes.

Govier, Katherine. "Fathers and Sons: Alistair MacLeod Plumbs the Generational Chasm That Includes Social Class and Geography." *Time International* 155, no. 18 (May 8, 2000): 57. In a review of *Island*, MacLeod is praised for his poignant stories about conflicts between fathers who remain on the land and sons who escape to the city, thus moving into a higher social class but, in the view of those left behind, abandoning their heritage.

Guilford, Irene, ed. *Alistair MacLeod: Essays on His Works*. Buffalo, N.Y.: Guernica, 2002. The first book-length volume devoted to MacLeod and his work. Includes essays by writers Jane Urquhart and Janice Kulyk Keefer and by several prominent scholars. Also contains a revealing interview. The editor's introduction is an excellent starting point for a study of MacLeod.

Kocan, Peter. "The Shelter of Each Other." *Quadrant* 47, no. 12 (December, 2003): 87-89. Shows how the stories in *Island* reflect such themes as the loss of continuity and the weakening of familial loyalties. Includes perceptive comments on the importance of animals as symbols of their loyalty and of human betrayal.

Omhovère, Claire. "Roots and Routes in a Selection of Stories by Alistair MacLeod." *Canadian Literature* 189 (Summer, 2006): 50-67. A detailed analysis of four stories, emphasizing their reflection of the conflicts between confinement and escape, man and nature. Notes and bibliography.

Wood, James. "Clearances." *New Republic* 224, no. 4509 (June 18, 2001): 31-35. Despite occasional lapses into sentimentality and melodrama, MacLeod can produce "remarkable stories," worthy of comparison with the best contemporary works. This point is illustrated with an analysis of "The Tuning of Perfection."

Rosemary M. Canfield Reisman

SIR THOMAS MALORY

Born: Warwickshire, England; Early fifteenth
century
Died: Newgate Prison, London, England; March 14,
1471

PRINCIPAL SHORT FICTION
Le Morte d'Arthur, 1485 (the Winchester manuscript,
1934; discovered by W. F. Oakeshott).

OTHER LITERARY FORMS
Le Morte d'Arthur, published in 1485, is the only
work that has been attributed to Sir Thomas Malory.

ACHIEVEMENTS
Although a vast body of Arthurian legend, fable,
and romance existed before Sir Thomas Malory's *Le
Morte d'Arthur* in works such as the Latin *Historia
Regum Britanniae* by Geoffrey of Monmouth, the
French verse romances of Chrétien de Troyes, and the
English Layamon's *Brut*, Malory was the first writer to
give unity and coherence to this mass of material. Popular for centuries after its publication by William
Caxton in 1485, Malory's collection of Arthurian tales
served as inspiration to many later writers such as Alfred, Lord Tennyson (*Idylls of the King*, 1859-1885)
and T. H. White (*The Once and Future King*, 1958). In
addition, Malory is credited with being the first English
writer to use prose with a sensitivity and expressive-
ness that had hitherto been reserved for poetry.

BIOGRAPHY
Controversy surrounds the precise identity of the
Sir Thomas Malory who wrote *Le Morte d'Arthur*.
Long identified as a knight born in Newbold Revell,
Warwickshire, who wrote his work in prison, and
died in 1471, modern scholars have identified several
other contenders. Opinion seems divided concerning
whether he supported the York or the Lancastrian side
in the Wars of the Roses, which ravaged England in
the fifteenth century.

ANALYSIS
Although in 1570 Roger Ascham attributed the popularity of Sir Thomas Malory's work to an unhealthy
interest in "open manslaughter and bold bawdy," the
continuing popularity of *Le Morte d'Arthur* is itself
evidence of this medieval author's remarkable grasp of
narrative technique. The aesthetic principles governing
Malory's art have been a matter of debate since the discovery of the Winchester manuscript in 1934. Eugène
Vinaver, who edited the modern standard edition, *The
Works of Sir Thomas Malory* (1947), has argued that
Malory unraveled the complicated *entrelacement* of his
French sources, focusing on narrative units which approach the unity readers expect in modern short stories.
Since the appearance of his edition, critics have argued
that whatever Malory's intentions, *Le Morte d'Arthur*
is one work with a cumulative effect. This controversy
seems to have subsided, with most scholars agreeing
that Malory wrote eight separate tales rather than one
unified narrative and that each of the tales exists within
a well-defined cycle. Malory's work thus represents an
important transition from the medieval romance to the
modern narrative or short story.

"THE TALE OF KING ARTHUR"
"The Tale of King Arthur," Malory's first treatment
of Arthur, describes Arthur's battles to consolidate
England as one kingdom. Within this one large unit,
there are a number of tales that, although linked to the
overall theme of Arthur's conquests, illustrate Malory's narrative techniques. "The Tale of Balin," for example, is a self-contained story in which one learns all
that is needed to know about Balin; on the other hand,
Malory includes inscriptions on tombs, puzzling
prophecies by Merlin, and other interpolations that al-
lude to incidents in the stories of Galahad, Lancelot,

and Tristram. These vestiges of the medieval *entrelacement* supply information which is not necessary to an understanding of Balin's adventures; their existence makes it impossible to claim "The Tale of Balin" an absolute unity of effect. Nevertheless, the presence of this unnecessary information does not make the story of Balin any less a self-contained and independent narrative unit. This story affords a particularly interesting example of Malory's characteristic style and use of techniques which were to find their greatest themes in "The Quest of the Holy Grail" and "The Death of King Arthur."

"THE TALE OF BALIN"

"The Tale of Balin" begins when a mysterious damsel appears at Arthur's court, wearing a sword that can only be drawn out of its sheath by a virtuous knight. All of Arthur's knights try and fail to unsheathe the sword. Balin, however, draws out the sword only to be told by the damsel that if he keeps it, he will destroy his best friend and the man whom he most loves. It is then that the Lady of the Lake appears, demanding that Arthur give her the heads of Balin and the sword-damsel. Hearing this, Balin claims that the sword-damsel caused his mother's death and cuts off her head. By this action Balin violates Arthur's safe conduct and loses his favor.

In the incidents which follow, Balin tries to regain Arthur's favor by conquering his enemies; however, in adventure after adventure Balin's success as a knight, the greatest in the world, is juxtaposed with prophecies of disaster and tragedy. He unintentionally causes the suicides of two sets of lovers and strikes a "dolorous stroke" in self-defense which lays waste three kingdoms. Finally, he meets his brother Balan, his best friend and the person he most loves. Disguised with unfamiliar shields, they fail to recognize each other and fight to the death. Just before they die, they recognize each other and ask to be buried in the same tomb.

While readers accept the supernatural prophecies as tragic foreshadowings, Balin refuses to believe them. Reluctant as he is to accept the validity of the prophetic warnings, he accepts the disasters themselves with a simple fortitude. At three different points in the narrative, he says: "I shall take the aventure that God woll ordayne me." This courageous acceptance of a tragic

fate becomes a compelling secondary theme in the tale.

Of the foreshadowings, the most significant occurs just before the final episode in which Balin and his brother engage in fatal battle. Balin hears a horn blow "as it had ben the dethe of a best. . . . 'That blast,' said Balyn, 'is blowen for me, for I am the pryse, and yet am I not dede.'" After causing the death of innocent lovers and the waste of three kingdoms, Balin says with stark but effective simplicity that he is the prize or victim of the hunt, but he is not yet dead. At this point, he realizes that he is being pursued by supernatural forces.

In fact, this image of fate as the hunter and Balin as the prize or victim epitomizes the irony and pathos of Balin's fortunes. Through the use of tragic foreshadowing, Malory contrasts Balin's success as a knight, his demonstration of faith and virtue by winning the sword, with his human vulnerability to fate.

"THE QUEST OF THE HOLY GRAIL"

"The Quest of the Holy Grail" is linked somewhat loosely to "The Tale of Balin" by allusions to the failure of all knights, even Lancelot, to draw out Balin's sword, but it is principally concerned with parallelism between Galahad and his father Lancelot. Malory emphasizes Lancelot's supremacy over all earthly knights, but it is Galahad who serves as model for the followers of Christ and becomes the spiritual ideal.

Traditionally, the Grail is the name of the cup Jesus used at the Last Supper. Later, Joseph of Arimethea was supposed to have caught Christ's blood in it during the Crucifixion. A vision of the Grail was seen by a nun, the sister of one of the Knights of the Round Table, but only three knights achieve the quest--Galahad, Percival, and Bors. At the conclusion of the tale, a multitude of angels appear and bear Galahad's soul to heaven; a hand descends to take the Grail and the sacred spear which pierced Christ's body into heaven.

At the very outset of the quest for the Grail, Arthur laments that however worthy this quest may be, it will destroy the solidarity of the Round Table. Lancelot insists that the quest will bring great honor to the knights. It is a tribute to Malory's success as a storyteller that he does justice both to the spiritual ideal of the quest and the earthly, but splendid, fellowship of the Round Table.

"THE DEATH OF KING ARTHUR"

Malory's "The Death of King Arthur" is both his greatest work and the one in which he demonstrates the most independence from his sources. With profound psychological understanding, he dramatizes the conflict between two loyalties: the chivalric code with its emphasis upon comradeship and devotion to one's lord, epitomized in the Round Table, and the service of the knight-lover for his lady, the romantic theme of courtly chronicles. In rescuing Queen Guinevere whom he loves and serves as knight, Lancelot is forced to kill Sir Gareth, the brother of Gawain and the knight who loves Lancelot more than all other men. This incident is Malory's own invention; his sources describe only vaguely the death of Gawain's brothers.

Faced with the prospect of battle against Lancelot, Arthur realizes that this battle will indeed result in the destruction of the fellowship of the Round Table. His lament emphasizes the tragedy of the loss: "I am soryar for my good knyghtes losse than for the losse of my fayre queen; for quenys I myght have inow, but such felyship of good knyghtes shall never be togydirs in no company." Eugène Vinaver has commented:

> . . . it is not through sin or weakness of heart that the end comes about, but through the devotion of the truest friend and the truest lover, though a tragic greatness which fixes forever the complex and delicate meaning of Arthur's epic.

Confronted with accusations by Agravain and Mordred, his bastard son and nephew, that Lancelot has traitorously loved the queen, Arthur is reluctant to take action. When he agrees to test Lancelot, it is with misgivings because, as he acknowledges, "sir Launcelot had done so much for hym and for the quene so many tymes." After Lancelot is discovered in the queen's chamber, Guinevere is sentenced to burning. Lancelot rescues her, and in the process of saving her from the flames, slays Gareth. The war which follows destroys everything.

Even after Lancelot returns the queen to Arthur, Lancelot is exiled and then attacked in France by Arthur and Gawain. While Arthur is gone, Mordred seizes the kingdom and Guinevere, whom he plans to marry. In the first battle with Mordred, Arthur wins, although

Gawain receives his death wound and writes repentantly to Lancelot, begging him to come to Arthur's assistance. Arthur dies on the plains of Salisbury and with him pass the ideals of the Round Table.

When Lancelot returns to avenge the king and queen, he finds that Guinevere has entered a convent. As she explains to Lancelot, she has renounced the world because she feels that their love has caused the wars and the death of Arthur. Although she urges Lancelot to marry and to find his own happiness, he insists that he will become a hermit for her sake: "And therefore, lady, sithen you have taken you to perfection I must needs take me to perfection of right."

Finally, in an episode that seems to be Malory's invention, Lancelot learns of Guinevere's death in a dream and is told to bury her near Arthur. During her burial he swoons in sorrow. When he dies shortly afterward, consumed by grief for the king and queen, the bishop hermit relates a vision in which he sees angels raising Lancelot to heaven. At his burial his brother Ector delivers a eulogy which represents Malory's definitive statement on the chivalric ideal:

> Thou were never matched of erthely knyghtes hande. . . . And thou were the truest frende to thy lovar that ever bestrade hors, and thou were the trewest lover of a synful man that ever loved woman, and thou were the kyndest man that ever strake wyth swerde. And thou were the godelyest persone that ever cam emonge prees of knyghtes, and thou was the mekest man and the jentyllest that ever ete in halle emonge ladyes, and thou were the sternest knyght to thy mortal foo that ever put spere in reeste.

Malory's handling of the Arthurian materials have made the stories of King Arthur part of the English literary tradition. From the complexity of his French sources he produced narratives which remain vital and appealing to the modern reader. Perhaps, however, the best critical summary of Malory's achievement was offered by William Caxton, Malory's first editor and critic, who tells readers that in *Le Morte d'Arthur* they will find "many joyous and playsaunt hystoryes and noble and renomed actes of humanyte, gentylnesse, and chyvalryes."

BIBLIOGRAPHY

Archibald, Elizabeth, and A. S. G. Edwards, eds. *A Companion to Malory*. Woodbridge, England, 1996. Collection of critical essays examining various aspects of *Le Morte d'Arthur*, including the editing and creation of Malory's text, the depiction of chivalry and of women's place in the work, Malory's sources, his style and use of language, and the work's reception.

Batt, Catherine. *Malory's Morte Darthur*: Remaking Arthurian Tradition. New York: Palgrave, 2002. Traces the sources of Malory's work in French and English Arthurian legends and examines how Malory transformed these sources to create new concepts of masculine heroism. Analyzes individual sections of *Le Morte d'Arthur*, including Merlin's narratives and the tales of Arthur and Lucius, Sir Lancelot, Sir Gareth of Orkney, and Sir Tristram.

Bennet, J. A. W., ed. *Essays on Malory*. Oxford, England: Clarendon Press, 1963. Collection of seven essays by such outstanding Middle English scholars as C. S. Lewis, Derek Stanley Brewer, and W. F. Oakeshott. Included is an essay on art and nature by Eugène Vinaver, one of the most prominent Malory scholars of his day, written in the form of an open letter to C. S. Lewis, which responds to many of the points made by Lewis in his own essay in this collection ("The English Prose *Morte*"). A lengthy examination of chivalry in *Le Morte d'Arthur* is also included.

Benson, Larry D. *Malory's "Morte Darthur."* Cambridge, Mass.: Harvard University Press, 1976. Four aspects of Malory's work are examined in a study concerned chiefly with the context in which Malory wrote: a discussion of the relationship of the genre of *Le Morte d'Arthur* to Arthurian legend and traditional romances; the structure of Malory's work, particularly as it relates to the English romance; a historical perspective on chivalric traditions and chivalry in Malory; and a detailed literary and historical interpretation of the tale of the Sancgreal, the book of Sir Lancelot and Guinevere, and the death of Arthur.

Falcetta, Jennie-Rebecca. "The Enduring Sacred Strain: The Place of the Tale of the Sankgreal Within Sir Thomas Malory's *Le Morte d'Arthur*." *Christianity and Literature* 47 (Autumn, 1997): 21-34. Discusses the Grail's effects on three levels: its association with sensuous trappings, its effect on the main characters of the Arthuriad, and its impact on the conclusion of *Le Morte d'Arthur*.

Field, P. J. C. *The Life and Times of Sir Thomas Malory*. Cambridge, England: D. S. Brewer, 1993. A detailed, scholarly retelling of Malory's life. Recommended for advanced students and scholars.

_____. *Malory: Texts and Sources*. Cambridge, England: D. S. Brewer, 1998. An examination of the sources for Malory and Arthurian tales.

Hanks, Dorrel Thomas, Jr., and Jessica Gentry Brogdon, eds. *The Social and Literary Contexts of Malory's "Morte Darthur."* Woodbridge, England: Boydell and Brewer, 2001. A collection of essays that place Malory's work in the context of English medieval history and society.

Hardyment, Christina. Malory: *The Knight Who Became King Arthur's Chronicler*. New York: HarperCollins Publishers, 2005. Chronicles Malory's life, including his service as a soldier during the War of the Roses and other battles and his subsequent imprisonment. Places his life in the context of English political history. Traces the sources of *Le Morte d'Arthur* in French romances and in early English history and popular ballads.

Kennedy, Beverly. *Knighthood in the Morte Darthur*. Cambridge, England: D. S. Brewer, 1985. A comprehensive, detailed examination of knighthood and chivalry and a meticulous discussion of *Le Morte d'Arthur* in this light. Kennedy considers different facets of knighthood, such as "The High Order of Knighthood," "Worshipful Knighthood," and "True Knighthood."

McCarthy, Terence. *Reading the "Morte d'Arthur."* Wolfeboro, N.H.: Boydell and Brewer, 1988. An excellent introduction to *Le Morte d'Arthur*. McCarthy outlines the structure of the work, book by book, with plenty of background and analysis, then offers more in-depth discussions of the chivalric tradition, historical background, Malory's style, and his method of storytelling. He also suggests a selection of passages for closer study to give the newcomer to Malory a representative and manageable introduction to an occasionally difficult text.

Parry, Joseph D. "Following Malory out of Arthur's World." *Modern Philology* 95 (November, 1997): 147-169. Argues that the final resting place of King Arthur at Avalon is fitting in terms of the narrative's focus on two types of locations that correspond to two concurrent but contradictory narratives of the dissolution of Arthurian society.

Takamiya, Toshiyuki, and Derek Brewer, eds. *Aspects of Malory*. Totowa, N.J.: Rowman & Littlefield, 1981. Contains eleven essays on Malory. The essays examine topics such as Malory's sources, the structure of his tales, and the Malory manuscript. Eugène Vinaver discusses Malory's prose style, and Richard R. Griffiths offers a new theory on the author's identity.

Whetter, K. S., and Raluca L. Radulescu, eds. *Re-Viewing "Le Morte Darthur": Texts and Contexts, Characters and Themes*. Rochester, N.Y.: D. S. Brewer, 2005. Collection of essays on *Le Morte d'Arthur*, including discussions of the text's production and printing; the political geography of fifteenth century England; and violence and knighthood, the depiction of women, and genre and cohesion in the work.

J. R. Brink
Updated by Catherine Swanson

DAVID MALOUF

Born: Brisbane, Queensland, Australia; March 20, 1934

PRINCIPAL SHORT FICTION
Child's Play, 1982
Antipodes, 1985
Dream Stuff, 2000
Every Move You Make, 2006
The Complete Stories, 2007

OTHER LITERARY FORMS

David Malouf (mah-LEWF) began his career as a poet. His collection of poems titled *Neighbours in the Thicket: Poems* (1974) helped him gain a reputation as a rising talent in Australian writing. He continued his career as a poet with *First Things Last* (1981) and *Wild Lemons: Poems* (1980). Several collections of his notable poetry, including *Poems, 1975-1976* (1976), *Selected Poems, 1959-1989* (1994), and *Revolving Days: Selected Poems* (2008), have been published. While Malouf began his career as a poet, he also has produced eight novels, including *Remembering Babylon* (1993), for which he received critical acclaim. Malouf has not limited himself to the genres of poetry and fiction. Throughout his career he has written or cowritten several dramatic and libretto works, including *Blood Relations* (1988) and *Jane Eyre* (2000). He also has produced a collection of autobiographical essays titled *Twelve Edmondstone Street* (1985), which provides insight into different locations that have helped shape him as an author.

ACHIEVEMENTS

David Malouf has won multiple Australian and international literary awards for his poetry, novels, and short stories. In 1974, Malouf began receiving critical acclaim for his writing when he won the Australian Literature Society Gold Medal for his poetry collection *Neighbours in the Thicket: Poems*. He won the award again for his novel *Ransom* (2009). His novel *Remembering Babylon* is his most highly recognized piece of literature. It received the Miles Franklin Award in Australia and the Prix Femina Étranger Award in France, and was shortlisted for the Man Booker Prize in 1994. Along with the awards he has received for his poetry and novels, Malouf has won several awards for his short fiction. In 1985, he was awarded the Victorian Premier Prize for *Antipodes*. In 2000, Malouf received the

Lannan Literary Fiction Award for the short-story collection *Dream Stuff*. That same year, Malouf also was honored as the sixteenth laureate of the Neustadt International Prize for Literature, which recognizes the work of poets, novelists, and playwrights. Malouf's career-spanning collection *The Complete Stories* (2007) was awarded the Australia Asia Literary Award in 2008. The award is Australia's richest literary prize, providing the winning author with $110,000 to continue producing literary work.

BIOGRAPHY

David George Joseph Malouf was born on March 20, 1934, in Brisbane, Queensland, Australia, to Lebanese English parents. Malouf graduated from Brisbane Grammar School in 1950 and then attended the University of Queensland. He received a bachelor's degree, with honors in English, in 1954 and opted to stay at the university in order to teach. As he taught, he wrote and published poetry. After teaching for several years in Australia, Malouf relocated to England, where he taught at schools in London and Birkenhead, Cheshire.

David Malouf (Sophie Bassouls/Sygma/Corbis)

In 1968, Malouf returned to Australia and took a lecturing position in the English department at the University of Sydney. As he taught, Malouf published collections of his poetry through the University of Queensland Press. In the late 1970's, he branched out from poetry into prose. Using his experiences to construct a fictional narrative, Malouf published his first novel, *Johnno* (1975). After the publication of Malouf's second novel, *An Imaginary Life* (1978), the Literature Board of the Australia Council awarded him a three-year fellowship. The fellowship allowed Malouf to become a full-time writer.

Malouf again relocated to Europe, moving to Italy until 1985. While living in Italy, Malouf enjoyed the ambiguity of writing away from his native land, and he began producing not only poetry and longer fiction but also short stories, plays, and libretti. Later, he settled in Australia, where he has continued to add to his catalog of work.

ANALYSIS

David Malouf witnessed great change in Australia as he grew up. The multiple cultures that immigrated into Australia made it hard to define a cohesive Australian identity. As Malouf matured, the concept of an Australian cultural identity began to interest him. The descendant of immigrants himself, he became interested in the social and cultural relationships between immigrants and natives. As immigrants are faced with transitions, so are Malouf's characters, ranging from childhood innocence to hardened maturity, from past memories to future aspirations. By facing transitional challenges, Malouf's characters are led toward a realization of identity.

"EUSTACE"

One of Malouf's early short stories, "Eustace" was written in conjunction with the novella *Child's Play*. The story draws on the transitional experiences of a girl from the communal protection of her childhood to the individual risks of adulthood. The story opens with a teenage boy breaking into a dormitory for girls at an orphanage. A young girl named Jane wakes to discover the boy.

She keeps his visits to the dormitory a secret; the boy's presence breaks the monotonous routines that she is used to at the orphanage. The repetitive daily lessons and the events that the girls experience are designed to protect them from the hardships of life outside the orphanage. As the boy continues to visit Jane, the other girls become aware of him. They do not find the boy's presence to be as unique or as exciting as Jane does.

While collectively the girls are comforted by the monotonous routines of the orphanage, Jane wants to experience more. At the end of the story, Jane runs away from the security of the dormitory in order to be with the boy. To Jane, the boy represents an outside world full of new experiences. Her desire to connect with the outside world symbolizes her process of transition. The other girls childishly push the boy's visits aside, opting to remain ignorant of the outside world the boy represents. Jane, however, internalizes the experience and begins to understand that in order to continue maturing she must leave the safety of her childhood. Through her interpretation of the boy's visits, she has moved out of childhood and into adolescence.

"That Antic Jezebel"

Within "That Antic Jezebel," Malouf presents the experiences and inner thoughts of Clay McHugh, an elderly European migrant living in Sydney, Australia. As a young woman, Clay placed importance on her social standing instead of intimacy. She has lived her entire life economically and free of intimate commitments, while maintaining the appearance of wealth. As a reminder of her choices, Clay wears a chain around her wrist that is adorned by various trinkets left behind by the men to whom she refused to commit. While showing little regret for her lifestyle, the chain, with its collection of memories, constantly acts as a reminder of her past experiences.

The story transitions from the memories of Clay's youth to the events of her senior years. Throughout her life, Clay maintained her attachment to social standing and her detachment to commitment. As the story concludes, Clay discovers, while at a symphony performance in Sydney, that her current lover has died from a heart attack. The man's son, about whom she realizes she knows very little, tells her of his death. The news is

shocking, but she reacts to it in the same detached way she has always treated commitment. In the privacy of her room, however, she begins to feel the weight of all the memories attached to the chain around her wrist.

As Clay remembers her youthful indiscretions, she realizes she has become old. The sudden awakening to her lover's mortality places her own into focus. The chain, with its trinkets, begins to represent not only the men who passed through her life but also the choices she has made. As her own mortality is brought into focus, her loneliness is emphasized. At the end of the story, Clay takes off the clothes she wore to the symphony and the chain. As she lies in bed, completely stripped of material matter and outside society's view, she realizes that the chain of memories is heavy and that her own end may not be far off.

"Sally's Story"

In "Sally's Story," Malouf constructs an environment of sadness and growth surrounding the events of the Vietnam War. As a teenager in Australia, Sally Prentiss decides she is too inexperienced to become the actress she dreams of being. She takes a position as a domestic companion to American soldiers during the Vietnam War. In her position, Sally provides a pretend domestic environment to Americans on combat leave. Her duties as a domestic companion require her to take care of and be intimate with the soldiers. Through the fantasy of domesticity that Sally provides, the soldiers escape the reality of the war. Sally eventually becomes haunted by the realities of war, as she begins to find it difficult to provide the necessary domestic fantasy without succumbing to emotional attachment. She realizes that the apparition of marriage that she is involved in forces her to have an extreme sense of self-control, so that she does not fall for the fantasy.

In need of relief from the emotionally draining experiences with the soldiers, Sally returns to her hometown. While visiting her mother, Sally meets a young man named Brad, a single father. As Sally gets to know Brad and his children, she becomes more relaxed, allowing the experiences of her domestic partnerships to recede into her memory.

Malouf mirrors Sally's experience as a domestic provider to the soldiers through her experience with the local man to portray the transitions between innocence and adulthood. Sally's desires to gain experience as a teenager were the result of a childlike fantasy. She gained the experience she had sought, but the experience caused her to mature more quickly than she expected. As a result, she returned to a place of protection in order to find her own domestic fantasy.

"THE VALLEY OF LAGOONS"

In "The Valley of Lagoons," Angus, the story's narrator, is an outsider who wants to belong to a group. By making a connection, he can form his own identity. As the only male sibling in a family of three children, he looks toward the family of his best friend to provide a group identity. Growing up around the customs of the McGowan family, Angus yearns to take part in their annual hunting trip. As a child, Angus's parents denied him permission to go on the trip. As a teenager on the cusp of adulthood, Angus is allowed to go on the trip that marks his best friend's eighteenth birthday. As Angus anticipates the trip, his view of the McGowan family identity is challenged. As the boys mature, they begin to grow apart as they become interested in different courses of study.

During this time, Braden's older brother Stuart becomes involved with Angus's sister Katie. As the hunting trip approaches, Katie ends the relationship. Isolated in the Australian wilderness with the McGowans, Angus realizes the manipulation he has been subjected to by Stuart, as he pleads with Angus to convince Katie to take him back. Disgusted by Stuart's selfishness, Angus walks into the Australian wilderness. As Angus contemplates his relationships and the beauty of nature, he hears the sound of a rifle. As a final plea for attention, Stuart shoots himself in the leg. Angus, seeing how mixed up and emotional Stuart is, realizes that personal action defines a person's identity more effectively than does a collective identity. Malouf represents the struggles of Australians to form a cohesive cultural identity through Angus's discovery of his identity. As Angus clarifies his identity throughout the story, Malouf expresses the hope that Australians can find cultural unity through the beauty of Australia's landscape.

OTHER MAJOR WORKS

LONG FICTION: *Johnno*, 1975; *An Imaginary Life*, 1978; *The Bread of Time to Come*, 1981 (also known as *Fly Away Peter*, 1982); *Harland's Half Acre*, 1984; *The Great World*, 1990; *Remembering Babylon*, 1993; *The Conversations at Curlow Creek*, 1996; *Ransom*, 2009.

PLAYS: *Voss*, pr. 1986 (opera libretto); *Blood Relations*, pr., pb. 1988; *Mer de Glace*, pr. 1991 (opera libretto, with Richard Meale); *Baa Baa Black Sheep: A Jungle Tale*, pr. 1993 (libretto; music by Michael Berkeley); *Jane Eyre*, pr. 2000 (opera libretto; music by Berkeley).

POETRY: "Interiors," in *Four Poets*, 1962; *Bicycle, and Other Poems*, 1970 (also known as *The Year of the Foxes, and Other Poems*, 1979); *Neighbours in the Thicket*, 1974; *Poems, 1975-1976*, 1976; *Wild Lemons: Poems*, 1980; *First Things Last*, 1981; *Selected Poems*, 1981; *Selected Poems*, 1991; *Selected Poems, 1959-1989*, 1994; *Typewriter Music*, 2007; *Revolving Days: Selected Poems*, 2008.

NONFICTION: *Twelve Edmonstone Street*, 1985 (autobiography); *A Spirit of Play: The Making of Australian Consciousness*, 1998.

EDITED TEXTS: *We Took Their Orders and Are Dead: An Anti-War Anthology*, 1971 (with Shirley Cass, Ros Cheney, and Michael Wilding); *Gesture of a Hand*, 1975; *New Currents in Australian Writing*, 1978 (with Katharine Brisbane and R. F. Brissenden).

MISCELLANEOUS: *David Malouf: "Johnno," Short Stories, Poems, Essays, and Interview*, 1990 (James Tulip, editor).

BIBLIOGRAPHY

Bliss, Carolyn. "Reimagining the Remembered: David Malouf and Moral Implications of Myth." *World Literature Today* 74, no. 4 (Autumn, 2000): 724-732. In his construction of Australian literature, Malouf interprets Australian culture and the myths surrounding it. Bliss investigates the patterns Malouf uses to create a connection between his work and these myths.

Indyk, Ivor, and National Library of Australia. *David Malouf: A Celebration*. Canberra, Australia: National Library of Australia, 2001. This book gathers several essays by contemporaries of Malouf that detail his profound impact on Australian literature and provide descriptions of personal experiences the contributors have had with Malouf.

Levasseur, Jennifer, and Kevin Rabalais. "Public Dreaming." *The Kenyon Review* (2000): 164-169. Levasseur and Rabalais interview Malouf after receiving the Neustadt International Prize for Literature. The interview provides a firsthand look at Malouf's influences and writing style.

Malouf, David. "A Writing Life." *World Literature Today* 74, no. 4 (Autumn, 2000): 701-705. "A Writing Life" is the transcript of Malouf's 2000 Neustadt lecture. In it, he describes several experiences and places that

have influenced him as a writer. Since the award recognized his work for its success as international literature, Malouf discusses the importance of Australian traditions and settings within his work.

Sharrad, Paul. "Delicate Business': David Malouf's Shorter Prose." *World Literature Today* 74, no. 4 (Autumn, 2000): 759-768. In this short article, Sharrad discusses the themes and style found in Malouf's short fiction. Sharrad discusses Malouf's work up to the publication of *Dream Stuff*, Malouf's short-story collection.

Marcus Hammond

KATHERINE MANSFIELD

Born: Wellington, New Zealand; October 14, 1888
Died: Fontainebleau, France; January 9, 1923

PRINCIPAL SHORT FICTION

In a German Pension, 1911
Bliss, and Other Stories, 1920
The Garden Party, and Other Stories, 1922
The Doves' Nest, and Other Stories, 1923
Something Childish, and Other Stories, 1924 (also known as *The Little Girl, and Other Stories,* 1924)
Katherine Mansfield's Short Stories, 2008

OTHER LITERARY FORMS

Although Katherine Mansfield is best known as a writer of short stories, she also wrote poems and book reviews, which were collected and edited posthumously by her second husband, John Middleton Murry. She once began a novel, and several fragments of plays have survived. She left a considerable amount of personal documents; their bulk greatly exceeds that of her published work. Murry edited the *Journal of Katherine Mansfield* (1927; "Definitive Edition," 1954), *The Letters of Katherine Mansfield* (1928), *The Scrapbook of Katherine Mansfield* (1939), and *Katherine Mansfield's Letters to John Middleton Murry, 1913-1922* (1951).

ACHIEVEMENTS

Although extravagant claims have been made for her, many critics insist that Mansfield's achievements were modest. She completed no novel, and, although she wrote about one hundred stories, her fame rests on no more than a dozen. However, in any age, her stories would be remarkable for their precise and evocative descriptions, their convincing dialogue, their economy and wit, and their dazzling insights into the shifting emotions of their characters.

In her own age, she was a pioneer. She and James Joyce are often credited with creating the modern short story. Though this claim may be an exaggeration, her stories did without the old-fashioned overbearing author-narrators, the elaborate settings of scenes, and the obvious explanations of motives and themes of earlier fiction. Instead, she provided images and metaphors, dialogues and monologues with little in between. Like T. S. Eliot's *The Waste Land* (1922), her stories seem to have had their nonpoetic dross deleted.

Her stories have influenced such writers as Elizabeth Bowen, Katherine Anne Porter, and Christopher Isherwood; the standard "*New Yorker* story" owes much to her. Most important, many decades after her death, her stories continue to be read with pleasure.

BIOGRAPHY

Almost everything Katherine Mansfield wrote was autobiographical in some way. It helps a reader to know about Mansfield's life because she often does not identify her stories' locations. For example, readers may be puzzled by her combining English manners and exotic flora in her New Zealand stories.

The author was born Kathleen Mansfield Beauchamp in Wellington, New Zealand, on October 14, 1888. (In her lifetime, she used many names. Her family called her "Kass." She took "Katherine Mansfield" as her name in 1910.) Her father, Harold Beauchamp, was an importer who became chairman of the Bank of New Zealand and was knighted in 1923. In 1903, the Beauchamps sailed for London, where Kass was enrolled at Queen's College, an institution for young women much like a university. She remained at Queen's until 1906, reading advanced authors, such as Oscar Wilde, and publishing stories in the college magazine. Her parents brought her back to Wellington in 1906, where she published her first stories in a newspaper. She left New Zealand for London in 1908, never to return.

Her next decade was one of personal complexities and artistic growth. She was sexually attracted to both women and men. At Queen's College, she met Ida Baker, her friend and companion for much of her life. Back in London, she fell in love with a violinist whom she had known in New Zealand. After she learned that she was pregnant by him, she abruptly married George C. Bowden on March 2, 1909, and as abruptly left him. At her mother's insistence, she traveled to Germany, where she had a miscarriage. The Bowdens were not divorced until April, 1918.

In Germany she met the Polish translator Floryan Sobieniowski, who, in the opinion of biographer Claire Tomalin, infected her with gonorrhea. Most of her medical problems may have come from this infection: the removal of a Fallopian tube, rheumatic symptoms, pleurisy, and eventually tuberculosis. Back in London, Mansfield met the future editor and critic John Middleton Murry. Their on-again, off-again relationship endured until her death. They were married on May 3, 1918; after she died, Murry edited her stories, letters, and journals. Meanwhile, she was strongly affected when her brother was killed in France in 1915. His death and her own worsening health were probably strong influences on her stories.

During these years, she and Murry knew many famous writers and artists, particularly those who frequented Lady Ottoline Morrell's famous salon at Garsington: Lytton Strachey, Dora Carrington, David Garnett, Aldous Huxley, Dorothy Brett, J. M. Keynes, and T. S. Eliot. She and Virginia Woolf had an off-and-on friendship and professional association; she seriously flirted with Bertrand Russell. The Murrys' most notable friendship was with D. H. and Frieda Lawrence; the character Gudrun in D. H. Lawrence's *Women in Love* (1920) is said to be based on Mansfield. Both Woolf and Lawrence were influenced by Mansfield; both made nasty remarks about her in her last years.

Another result of meeting Sobieniowski in Germany may have been reading the works of Anton Chekhov; Mansfield's story "The Child-Who-Was-Tired" is a free adaptation--perhaps a plagiarism--of a Chekhov story. During 1910 and 1911, she published a number of bitter stories with German settings, collected in *In a German Pension*. For the next seven years, Mansfield experimented with many styles and published stories in journals, such as *New Age, Rhythm*, and *Blue Review*, before she discovered a mature voice. Her first great story, "Prelude," was published as a booklet in July, 1918, by Virginia and Leonard Woolf's Hogarth Press.

Her health had not been good for several years; her gonorrhea remained undiagnosed until 1918. From the time she learned that she had tuberculosis in December, 1917, she spent most of each year out of England. Accompanied by Murry or Ida Baker, she traveled to France, Switzerland, and Italy, trying to fight off her disease. In 1922, her search led her to George Ivanovitch Gurdjieff's Institute of the Harmonious Development of Man near Paris, where she seems to have been moderately happy until she died the following year.

During her last five years, she wrote most of the stories for which she is best known. They were often published in journals, such as *Athenaeum, Arts and Letters, London Mercury*, and *Sphere*. Many were then collected in *Bliss, and Other Stories* and *The Garden-Party, and Other Stories*.

Katherine Mansfield (Getty Images)

ANALYSIS

Katherine Mansfield's themes are not hard to discover. In 1918, she set herself the tasks of communicating the exhilarating delicacy and peacefulness of the world's beauty and also of crying out against "corruption." A reader will soon make his or her own list of themes: the yearnings, complexities, and misunderstandings of love; loneliness, particularly of independent women; the superficiality of much of modern life; the erosions of time and forgetfulness; and the beauty and indifferent power of the natural world, especially plant life and the sea. Her exact meanings are not so easily pinned down, for her tone is complex: She mixes witty satire and shattering emotional reversals. Moreover, she uses dialogue and indirect speech extensively, and she does not often seem to speak directly in her own voice; the reader is not sure exactly who is speaking. It is vital for readers to understand that Mansfield (like Chekhov, to whom she is often compared) does not conceal a hidden "message" in her stories. If a story appears to point in many directions, not all of which are logically consistent, that is the way

Mansfield feels the whole truth is most honestly communicated. This essay suggests some of the ways these stories may be read.

The action of her stories (again, like Chekhov's) does not surge powerfully forward. Often her stories are designed, by means of quick changes in time and by surprise turns, to lead the reader to unexpected moments of illumination or epiphanies. Her stories are economical, edited so that there is usually not one unnecessary or insignificant word. She can be witty if she chooses, but more often her stories provide arresting descriptions and startling metaphors, which evoke shifting states of happiness, yearning, or despair.

"IN A CAFÉ"

Mansfield's stories often evoke the complexities of the conversational give-and-take between women and men and the unexpected courses that passion can take. An early story, "In a Café," portrays a youthful "new woman" and her male acquaintance, a musician. They flirt as they discuss life, art, and the future. Before he leaves, he asks the girl for her violets, but once outside he drops them because he must keep his hands warm for performing. The young woman is totally happy until she sees the violets on the sidewalk. The reader knows that her love has been crushed, but, new woman that she is, she kicks the flowers and goes her way laughing.

"EPILOGUE II"

"Epilogue II" (also known as "Violet") is more complex. At a pension in France, where the acidly worldly narrator is recovering from an attack of nerves, she reports a long conversation with an exasperating woman named Violet, who in turns tells of a conversation she has had with a man named Arthur. Violet says that, after a few dances, Arthur asked her if she believed in Pan and kissed her. It was her first adult kiss, and they immediately became engaged. The narrator can hardly believe what Violet tells her and is repelled by how easily the naïve Violet and Arthur have found each other. The story (a conversation within a conversation) ends with the narrator thinking that she herself might be too sophisticated. (In this story, Mansfield has imported a piece of conversation from real life. Sometime before she wrote "Epilogue II," she startled a man by asking him if he believed in Pan.)

"PSYCHOLOGY"

In "Psychology," Mansfield dissects the ebb and flow of attraction between two older artists, culminating in a moment of potential, a moment which, because of their agonizing self-consciousness, they miss. This story shows both minds, but readers are left with the woman and with another characteristically unexpected psychological twist. An older female acquaintance brings her flowers--violets again. This spontaneous gift revitalizes the woman, and with renewed hope she begins an intense letter to the man who has left her. Readers may guess that their next meeting will be no more satisfying than their last.

"JE NE PARLE PAS FRANÇAIS"

Mansfield often portrays more complex and ambiguous sexual and psychological relationships and, as usual, constructs her story to lead her reader in roundabout ways into unexpected territory. Though she often takes readers briefly into male minds, the story "Je Ne Parle Pas Français" has one of her rare male narrators. Raoul Duqette, a grubby Parisian writer, pimp, and gigolo, tells of an Englishman, Dick Harmon, and the woman nicknamed "Mouse," whom he brings to Paris. Not all critics agree on whom the story concerns. Although the reader learns much about the English couple's tortured relationship (Dick leaves Mouse because he cannot betray his mother, and Mouse knows she cannot return to England), many readers think that the story centers on the Frenchman. Incapable of deep emotion, Raoul spies on those with fuller lives than his own; he despises women, is sexually attracted to Dick, and is able to recognize only dimly the suffering that he has witnessed. At the end, he revels in Mouse's sorrow and imagines selling a girl like her to an old lecher.

"BLISS"

The triangle in "Bliss" is different, and again, Mansfield mixes her tones. Bertha seems childishly happy in her marriage, her home, her child, and her arty friends. She gives a marvelous party in which sophisticated guests make inane, decadent conversation. Meanwhile, Bertha finds herself physically attracted to one of her guests, the cool Miss Fulton, and thinks that she detects Miss Fulton giving her a signal. Together in the garden, they contemplate a lovely, flowering pear tree, and Bertha senses that they understand each other

intuitively. Again Mansfield surprises the reader. Bertha transfers her feelings for Miss Fulton to her husband; for the first time, she really desires him. When she overhears him making an assignation with Miss Fulton, however, her life is shattered. In "Bliss," as elsewhere, Mansfield's brilliant and precise descriptions of the nonhuman world are always evocative. Although sometimes nature simply reveals an unsympathetic force, allied to human passions but beyond human control, some natural features demand to be interpreted as symbols, such as the phallic pear tree in this story. Phallic it is, but it may be feminine as well, for Bertha identifies with it. The story is read however, and the pear tree cannot be explained simply. Neither can the reader's final reaction: Is Bertha trapped in an evil world? Is she a free adult at last?

"THE LOST BATTLE"

Mansfield also explores the problems of lonely women, often by showing the reader their inmost trains of thought. In "The Lost Battle," a woman traveling alone is escorted to her room in a French hotel by an overbearing man who makes demeaning and insinuating remarks: A bed in a small room will be enough for her, he implies. She asserts herself and demands a better room, one with a table on which to write. She wins her struggle and is happy with her new room--its size, the view from its windows, and its sturdy table. When she overtips the boy who delivers her bags, however, her joy somehow leaves her. In a convincing but mysterious moment typical of Mansfield's stories, the woman's bravery collapses in self-consciousness, memory, tears, and desire.

"MISS BRILL"

Perhaps Mansfield's best-known version of the lonely woman is the central character of "Miss Brill." The reader follows Miss Brill's thoughts as she arrives at the public gardens. The first faint chill of fall and the noise of the band signal that a new season has begun. Miss Brill's sympathetic interest extends to the various sorts of people in the park; the reader senses an older, precise woman who yearns that happiness and gentleness will come for herself and others. Even some unpleasantries fail to shake Miss Brill's enjoyment, as she rejoices that everyone there is performing in some wonderful, happy play. Her illusions, however, are shattered by two insensitive young lovers who simply wish that the fussy old woman would move. Again the reader is taken into a lonely woman's mind as she undergoes a psychic shock.

"THE DAUGHTERS OF THE LATE COLONEL"

In "The Daughters of the Late Colonel," the shock is muffled, and the reader does not enter the two sisters' minds so deeply so soon. The story at first appears to center on the familiar Mansfield theme of male domination. The sisters seem to react alike to the death of their domineering father. They are still under his spell. Mansfield shows her dry wit as their hesitant and ineffectual efforts to assert themselves with the nurse and their maid are pathetic and hilarious at the same time. Even sisters, however, may be alone. Not only have they lost their father and are without prospects of marriage, but also they differ so much in temperament that they will never understand each other--the older sister is prosaic, the younger one dreamy. It is only at the end of the story that each sister shows small signs of vitality. The prosaic sister hears a cry from within, muses on lost chances, and feels a hint of hope. When Mansfield takes readers into the thoughts of the younger sister, they discover that all along she has been living in a secret and extravagant imaginary world of repressed desire: her real life. For a moment, each sister thinks that some action could be taken, but the moment passes without communication. Their lives will never bear fruit.

Mansfield's wit is sometimes closer to the center of a story. In "Bliss," many early pages show a devastating view of the world of artists that Mansfield knew so well at Garsington and elsewhere. "Marriage à la Mode" is more purely a social satire. A nice, plodding husband, William, supports his wife Isabel's ambitions. They move from a cozy little house to the suburbs and entertain her artistic friends. Mansfield's acute ear for conversation enables her to give the reader the wonderful remarks that pass for wit among the arty set. The reader cheers when William, in a dignified letter, asks for a divorce. Isabel's friends mock the letter. Isabel herself realizes how shallow they are, but she runs to them laughing. The story has a moral, but its chief impact is satirical. This is also true of "The Young Girl." The title character is the disgustingly spoiled and overdressed teenage daughter of a selfish mother who is mainly interested in gambling at a casino. By the end of the story, the girl has revealed her youth and vulnerability, but the reader probably remembers the story's vapid world most vividly.

"THE FLY"

Mansfield's modernist method seldom gives the reader straightforward statements of her themes; the reader needs to interpret them carefully. Her most deliberately ambiguous and hotly debated story is "The Fly." A businessman ("the boss") is reminded of his beloved son's death in World War I and how he has grieved. Now, however, the boss is troubled because he can no longer feel or cry. At this point, he rescues a fly caught in his inkwell; the fly carefully cleans itself. Then the Mansfield surprise: The boss drops another gob of ink on the fly, admires its courage as it cleans itself again, but then drops more ink. The fly is dead. The boss feels wretched and bullies an employee. The story may remind some readers of William Shakespeare's "As flies to wanton boys are we to the gods;/ They kill us for their sport."

Murry said that "The Fly" represents Mansfield's revulsion from the cruelty of war; other critics discover her antipathy to her own father. Whatever its biographical source, the reader must try to decide his or her reaction to the boss. Where are the readers' sympathies? At first they are with the aged employee who jogs the boss's memory and perhaps with the boss himself. When readers hear of the son's death, they do sympathize with the father. What do they make of his torturing--yet admiring--the fly? Do readers despise him as a sadistic bully? Do they sympathize with him? Is the fly simply another victim of society's brutality, the boss's brutality? Are readers to see Mansfield as the fly, unfairly stricken with tuberculosis? Does the boss refuse to admit his own mortality until he sees himself as a victim, like the fly? At the very end, is he repressing such thoughts again? Critics are divided about this story, but what is clear is that its ambiguities raise a host of issues for consideration.

"THE MAN WITHOUT A TEMPERAMENT"

Another story that poses problems is "The Man Without a Temperament." The reader has trouble establishing where the story is taking place and who are its characters. Gradually it can be determined that the story takes place at a continental hotel and that the central characters are not the grotesque guests, like The Two Topknots, but The Man (Robert Salesby) and his invalid wife (Jinnie--Mrs. Salesby). The Mansfield woman here is not only lonely but also sick--sick with something that resembles the author's own tuberculosis. The reader's difficulties are slightly compounded when Mansfield manipulates time; readers soon decide that the dislocations in the story are Robert's memories of happier days in England. This story's greatest problem, however, is what the reader is to think of Robert. At first glance, he seems without temperament; all his care is for his wife, her comfort, her health, and her whims. Soon, the tension that he is under becomes obvious. He is tortured by his memories. When his wife encourages him to take a walk by himself, he quickly agrees and almost forgets to return. The exquisite tact and humor that his wife loves so much ring hollow: Readers know that he suspects that she will not live much longer. Is he an icy, resentful, and disgusting hypocrite? Some readers may think so. Is he admirably patient and forbearing? Murry, who acknowledged that Robert was a portrait of himself, thought it was drawn with admiration.

NEW ZEALAND STORIES

Soon after her return to London, Mansfield wrote some stories based on her experiences among the common people of New Zealand. "The Woman at the Store" is a chilling and dramatic tale in which three travelers stop far from civilization at a dilapidated store run by a slatternly woman and her child. Although the travelers feel sympathy for the woman's hard life, they also laugh at the woman and child--laugh until the child's drawing makes clear that the woman has murdered her husband. The travelers leave quickly. "Ole Underwood," a character sketch based on a real Wellington character, lets readers see into the mind of a deranged former convict as he makes his way around town, driven by memories of his wife's infidelity. In both cases, Mansfield tries to get into the minds of lower-class people, people much different from those she usually depicts. Another story that deals sympathetically with the doomed struggles of a lower-class character is "The Life of Ma Parker."

When Mansfield returned in earnest to telling stories of the New Zealand life that she knew best, she produced her finest work. (The critic Rhoda B. Nathan thinks that the New Zealand stories, taken as a group, can be considered as a bildungsroman, or story of an artist's growth.) The family drama of her childhood provided material for many of these stories. Her mother was attractive but delicate. Her father was forceful and successful. They lived in a substantial house in Wellington just on the edge of a poor district, then in a nearby village, and later at the edge of the sea in Wellington harbor. She was the third of five surviving children living among a number of aunts and cousins, an uncle and a grandmother.

"PRELUDE"

Mansfield's two longest works of fiction, "Prelude" and "At the Bay," are strikingly different from conventional short stories. Both take a slight narrative line and string on it a number of short episodes and intense renderings of the inner lives of members--mainly female--of an extended family. In both, readers are set down among these people without preparation; they must work out their relations for themselves. In both, readers must take time to discover the rich vision that Mansfield is giving them.

In "Prelude," the reader enters the consciousness of several members of the family as they adjust to a new house in the country. (The Beauchamps moved from Wellington to Karori in 1893.) The reader is led into the minds of the child Kezia (the character who resembles the author as a girl), her hearty father (Stanley), her pregnant mother (Linda), and her unfulfilled aunt (Beryl). Their relations are strained, and they reveal their hopes, loves, and anxieties. Gradually, Mansfield's emphasis becomes clear. She gives most weight to Linda and Beryl, whose inner worlds invite a range of analysis. Analysis begins with the aloe tree. Mansfield had earlier prepared readers for this huge, ugly, ominous growth, which flowers only once every one hundred years. Readers sense that the tree is somehow symbolic. Linda is fascinated by it. When she sees the tree by moonlight, its cruel thorns seem to embody the hate that she often feels, or do they embody the masculine force that she hates? Either way, the aloe tree brings out for the reader the secret that Linda keeps from everyone else: Alongside her other emotions (dislike for her children, love and concern for her husband) is pure hatred. She wonders what Stanley would think of that. Beryl also has her secret self. The story ends with her taking an inventory of her attractive qualities and wondering if she can ever get beyond her poses, her false life, to the warm authentic life that she thinks is still within her. Mansfield's apparently haphazard plot has in fact been drawing the reader to two striking female visions.

"AT THE BAY"

"At the Bay" tells about the same household perhaps a year later. Some characters, such as Kezia, appear to have changed. Mansfield's methods, however, are much the same, though the sea that frames this story does not insist on its symbolic force so obviously as did the aloe tree. Stanley forges off to work. The women he leaves are happy that he is gone, especially Linda, his strangely passive wife, who still loves him but dislikes their children, including a new baby boy. The children and their cousins play games. Kezia almost faces death when she pleads with her grandmother not to leave them. Linda's weak brother does face his failure. Beryl has a new friend, a vivid witch-like woman with an attractive younger husband. Though Linda briefly finds love with Stanley, this story, like "Prelude," ends with two dissimilar kinds of unfulfilled love. Linda loves her baby only for a moment. Beryl yearns for sexual contact but is terrified and revolted when she finds the real thing. Perhaps at the end, the sea (as a possible symbol of female fecundity, time, and destruction) sympathizes with human desires, perhaps not. Mansfield's way of presenting her incidents and structuring her story creates intense sympathy for her characters, yet simultaneously lets readers see them, without obviously judging them, from a distance.

"THE DOLL'S HOUSE"

Two shorter New Zealand stories probably show Mansfield at her finest, and they demonstrate most clearly how her narrative surprises and moments of brilliant revelation of character and motive can be concentrated in a single phrase, in what might be called a domestic epiphany: a small moment of great importance not easily summarized. In "The Doll's House,"

Kezia and her sisters are given a vulgar plaything. The house is despised by Aunt Beryl but loved by the girls (Kezia is particularly enthralled by a tiny lamp in the diminutive dining room) and much admired by their schoolmates. The story seems to be about adult cruelty and juvenile snobbery. All along, however, there appear to be two social outcasts, Lil Kelvey and her silent little sister, Else, both daughters of a washerwoman and (perhaps) a criminal. When Kezia impulsively invites them to look at the house, Aunt Beryl orders them away. Lil says nothing, but her silent, wretched little sister had got one glimpse of the beautiful doll's house and remembers, not her humiliation, but that she saw the house's tiny lamp. A small human spirit asserts itself.

"THE GARDEN-PARTY"

"The Garden-Party" is based on what happened at a real party that the Beauchamps gave in Wellington in 1907. Part of its meaning concerns the relations between two social classes. The central character is Laura, clearly a Mansfield-like character, an adolescent Kezia. Laura is thrilled by the promise of festivity, but in the middle of the expensive preparations--canna lilies, dainty sandwiches, a small band to play under the marquee--she learns of the death of a poor man who lived close by in a wretched house. Readers see the clash of generations when Laura demands that the party be canceled, but her worldly mother says no. The party is a grand success. As usual in Mansfield, important matters slip the mind; Laura enjoys herself immensely, especially because her large new hat is widely admired. After the guests have left, her mother sends Laura with a basket of party food to the house of the dead man. Her journey at dusk is phantasmagoric. Her sympathies, forgotten at the party, return. She is shocked by the somber house of death and by the grieving wife, and she is overwhelmed by the stillness, even the beauty, of the corpse. Laura feels that she must say something: "Forgive my hat." What she says is certainly inadequate, but it seems to signal a moment of understanding and growth--or does it? Laura has found a moment of beauty in death. Is that evasive or profound? She accepts the sympathy of her brother at the very end. He understands--or does he?

OTHER MAJOR WORKS

POETRY: *Poems*, 1923 (J. M. Murry, editor).

NONFICTION: *Novels and Novelists*, 1930 (J. M. Murry, editor); *The Collected Letters of Katherine Mansfield*, 1984-2008 (5 volumes; Vincent O'Sullivan and Margaret Scott, editors); *The Katherine Mansfield Notebooks*, 1997 (2 volumes).

BIBLIOGRAPHY

Alpers, Antony. *The Life of Katherine Mansfield*. Rev. ed. New York: Viking Press, 1980. The standard biography, sensible, balanced, and detailed. Alpers draws on years of research and includes interviews with people who knew Mansfield, such as John Middleton Murry and Ida Baker, and their comments on his earlier book, *Katherine Mansfield: A Biography* (1953). He offers some analyses, including passages on "At the Bay," "Prelude," and "Je Ne Parle Pas Français." Includes notes, illustrations, index, a detailed chronology, and a full bibliography.

Bateson, F. W. "The Fly." *Essays in Criticism* 12 (1962): 39-53. Two critics interpret "The Fly," giving it the kind of close reading usually reserved for lyric poetry. Other correspondents support and contest the original reading. Although they discuss the functions of characters and many details, they focus on the mind of the boss and a reader's reaction to him.

Berkman, Sylvia. *Katherine Mansfield: A Critical Study*. New Haven, Conn.: Yale University Press, 1951. Includes a chapter describing how Mansfield used details of her family's life to write "The Aloe" and then to revise it as "Prelude." The final chapter compares Mansfield with Anton Chekhov and James Joyce.

Daly, Saralyn R. *Katherine Mansfield*. Rev. ed. New York: Twayne, 1994. A revision of Daly's earlier Twayne study of Mansfield, based on the availability of Mansfield manuscripts and letters. Interweaves biographical information with discussions of individual stories, focusing on method of composition and typical themes.

Darrohn, Christine. "'Blown to Bits': Katherine Mansfield's 'The Garden-Party' and the Great War." *Modern Fiction Studies* 44 (Fall, 1998): 514-539. Argues that in "The Garden-Party' Mansfield tries to imagine a moment when class and gender do not matter. Maintains the story explores the conflicting demands of the postwar period, specifically, the painful task of mourning and recovery and the ways in which this task complicates the project of critiquing a society that is founded on the structures of exclusion, hierarchy, and dominance that foster wars.

Fulbrook, Kate. *Katherine Mansfield*. Bloomington: Indiana University Press, 1986. The chapters on the stories focus on Mansfield's continual attention to the distortions in social relations created by gender. Argues that Mansfield's stories are overtly feminist and demand to be read as critical accounts of social injustice grounded in the pretense of a natural psychological or biological order.

Hankin, C. A. *Katherine Mansfield and Her Confessional Stories*. New York: St. Martin's Press, 1983. Hankin's thesis is that Mansfield's stories are confessional, with the result that this book connects each story as precisely as possible to its sources in Mansfield's life. The detailed analyses of each of the major stories are more valuable than this thesis suggests. Hankin's readings are subtle and detailed, especially when they discuss the complexities of characters and symbols.

Head, Dominic. "Katherine Mansfield: The Impersonal Short Story." In *The Modernist Short Story: A Study in Theory and Practice*. 1992. Reprint. New York: Cambridge University Press, 2009. Head's examination of modernist innovations in short fiction devotes a chapter to Mansfield, in which he analyzes many of her stories and discusses the use of conflicting voices in her narratives, her symbolism, her theme of female victimization, and other aspects of her writing.

Hunter, Adrian. "Katherine Mansfield." In *The Cambridge Introduction to the Short Story in English*. Cambridge, England: Cambridge University Press, 2007. An overview of Mansfield's short fiction, discussing the influence of Anton Chekhov on her work, her views about writing, and the style and themes of some of the short stories.

Mansfield, Katherine. *The Complete Stories of Katherine Mansfield*, edited by Antony Alpers. Auckland: Golden Press/Whitcombe & Tombs, 1974. Not the complete short stories but a full and comprehensive collection of almost all of them, scrupulously edited and arranged chronologically in natural and instructive groups. Alpers's notes provide basic facts about each story and much essential information about many of them. The notes also list all the stories not included in this collection, thus forming a complete catalog of Mansfield's short fiction.

_____. *Katherine Mansfield's Selected Stories: The Texts of the Stories, Katherine Mansfield--from Her Letters, Criticism.* Selected and edited by Vincent O'Sullivan. New York: W.W. Norton, 2006. In addition to the texts of some of Mansfield's stories, this volume contains excerpts from twenty of her letters and analytical essays about her works. Some of these essays were written by other well-known writers, such as Conrad Aiken, T. S. Eliot, Katherine Anne Porter, V. S. Pritchett, Elizabeth Bowen, and Frank O'Connor.

McDonnell, Jenny. *Katherine Mansfield and the Modernist Marketplace: At the Mercy of the Public.* New York: Palgrave Macmillan, 2010. Charts Mansfield's development as writer in the context of her book and periodical publishing contracts. Demonstrates how she created experimental short stories that not only conformed with the modernist aesthetic but also were commercially viable.

Nathan, Rhoda B. *Critical Essays on Katherine Mansfield.* New York: G. K. Hall, 1993. Organizes previously published and new essays on Mansfield into three categories: "The New Zealand Experience," "The Craft of the Story," and "The Artist in Context." Essays represent a variety of approaches, including feminist, postcolonial, and historicist.

_____. *Katherine Mansfield.* New York: Continuum, 1988. Provides a detailed and useful chapter on the New Zealand stories considered as a group. Includes comments on the "painterly" qualities of "Je Ne Parle Pas Français." The final two chapters discuss Mansfield's achievement with regard to other writers.

Robinson, Roger, ed. *Katherine Mansfield: In from the Margin.* Baton Rouge: Louisiana State University Press, 1994. Reprints papers from two Mansfield centenary conferences. The papers examine Mansfield's feminine discourse, her interest in the cult of childhood, the narrative technique of her stories, and her place in the modernist tradition.

Tomalin, Claire. *Katherine Mansfield: A Secret Life.* New York: Alfred A. Knopf, 1987. A readable biography, though without many critical comments, emphasizing the medical consequences of Mansfield's sexual freedom and treating the question of her plagiarizing "The Child Who-Was-Tired."

George Soule

Adam Mars-Jones

Born: London, England; October 26, 1954

Principal short fiction

Fabrications, 1981 (pb. in England as *Lantern Lecture, and Other Stories*, 1981)

The Darker Proof: Stories from a Crisis, 1987 (with Edmund White)

Monopolies of Loss, 1992

Other literary forms

Adam Mars-Jones's first novel, *The Waters of Thirst* (1993), received critical praise on both sides of the Atlantic; his second novel, *Pilcrow*, was published in 2008. He is the author of the nonfiction books *Venus Envy* (1990) and *Blind Bitter Happiness* (1997), the latter a selection of essays on gay issues and other topics. Mars-Jones also edited *Mae West Is Dead: Recent Lesbian and Gay Fiction* (1983).

Achievements

In 1982, Adam Mars-Jones was the recipient of the Somerset Maugham Award for *Lantern Lecture, and Other Stories*. He has received widespread praise for his fiction; writer Edmund White hailed him as England's most incisive and intelligent writer. He was elected a Fellow of the Royal Society of Literature in 2007.

Biography

Adam Mars-Jones was born in London, England, on October 26, 1954. His early education, which included instruction in Greek and Latin, shows in his impeccable prose style. He became aware of being gay at an early age. His stern father, a High Court judge who "anathematized" homosexuals, created his most serious adolescent crisis. It was many years before he finally admitted he was gay to his father and much longer before his father accepted it.

Mars-Jones caught critical attention with the publication of *Lantern Lecture, and Other Stories* in 1981, published in the United States as *Fabrications*. These stories were distinguished by the author's zany humor, imagination, and irreverence. When the acquired immunodeficiency syndrome (AIDS) epidemic hit England and began to decimate his gay friends, Mars-Jones realized that here was a subject worthy of his serious attention. In 1985, he discovered the work of the gay American writer Edmund White, and they became friends. They jointly published a collection of their stories dealing with the tragedies of lovers whose lives were destroyed by AIDS.

Mars-Jones has become a leading crusader for tolerance and better medical treatment for homosexuals. He earns part of his living by writing film and book reviews and is a regular contributor to *The Guardian*, *The Observer*, *The Times Literary Supplement*, and the British Broadcasting Company's (BBC) television program *Newsnight Review*. Mars-Jones is becoming increasingly popular as a fiction writer on both sides of the Atlantic.

Analysis

Most of Adam Mars-Jones's short stories deal with AIDS. The most striking feature about these stories is his humorous treatment of this tragic subject. In this respect he resembles the older American writer Edmund White, with whom he published an anthology of their stories about AIDS titled *The Darker Proof: Stories from a Crisis*. It is most helpful to read some of White's stories in order to appreciate the courage implicit in the lighthearted, campy tone both writers employ in recounting death and suffering.

One critic called Mars-Jones's fiction "discursive," another way of saying that he rambles, digresses, and never seems to be aiming at any particular point. The point, then, of a Mars-Jones story is often contained more in his tone and in what he decides *not* to say. The sensitive reader will recognize that his narrators deliberately avoid the painful truth and instead talk about everything else under the sun, as people sometimes do when distracted by grief. It is as if they are desperately searching for other things to talk about, including memories of brighter days, in order to avoid facing the horror haunting their lives. *The Times Literary Supplement* reviewer Peter Parker wrote of *Monopolies of Loss:* "Without in any way mitigating the catastrophe of AIDS, these grim, funny, touching, eloquent and brave stories demonstrate that it is possible to salvage something of lasting value from the wreckage."

Although Mars-Jones and White write about similar subjects, it should be noted that the characters in Mars-Jones's stories belong to a lower social class. His characters are forced to earn a living at semiskilled jobs and often lead rather precarious existences, whereas White's characters belong to an international gay society and are cultured, educated, and sophisticated.

The most comprehensive collection of Mars-Jones's short stories is *Monopolies of Loss*. This volume contains nine stories, including the four published in *The*

Adam Mars-Jones (Colin McPherson/Corbis)

Darker Proof: Stories from a Crisis. Monopolies of Loss also contains an illuminating introduction, in which Mars-Jones explains his purpose and rationale in writing about AIDS. He realized that the scourge killing his friends had ironically provided him with timely, internationally significant subject matter. "AIDS is a theme that won't let go of me," he wrote, "or else I won't let go of it. It isn't really a question of social responsibility. How often does a writer not have to go looking for a subject, but more or less have to barricade his door against it?"

"SLIM"

"Slim" is one of several stories written in the first person by a fictitious narrator, an approach with which Mars-Jones became comfortable. (His novel *The Waters of Thirst* is an unbroken monologue by an adopted persona.) This narrative device was popularized by the Victorian poet Robert Browning, well known for such dramatic monologues as "My Last Duchess," the device being very popular with contemporary fiction writers. "Slim" is a euphemism for "AIDS," a word Mars-Jones, like Edmund White and many other gay fiction writers, tends to avoid. "Slim" is the African word for AIDS; one common characteristic of victims is that they become emaciated because they cannot retain food. The narrator fantasizes that he has an unknown African family who were too poor to give him any other legacy but the disease that is decimating their unfortunate continent. Although the narrator is dying, he maintains a "gay," witty facade when visited by his friend Buddy so as not to distress him, as well as to avoid succumbing to the fear and hopelessness that lie just below the surface.

"AN EXECUTOR"

"An Executor" is one of Mars-Jones's most technically complex stories. The protagonist has the unwelcome responsibility of disposing of the belongings of his recently deceased lover. He also has to hide some conspicuously "gay" articles of clothing from his deceased lover's parents, who are still unaware that their son was a homosexual. He is forced to grapple with an aggressive acquaintance, who gives the story dramatic tension by claiming certain items with no proof he is entitled to them. Every personal item the dead man's executor handles brings back memories of the past, and there is a constant shifting from somber present to happy past and back again, which displays the author's literary talent to advantage.

"A Small Spade"

A gay couple visit the English seaside resort town of Brighton. Like many of Mars-Jones's characters, they are working-class people with limited incomes. The title refers to a little spade-shaped splinter that Neil, a hairdresser, picks up under a fingernail. An incident that most people would consider trivial is a matter of extreme importance to the lovers because Neil, who is suffering from AIDS, is highly susceptible to infections. This story is notable for its re-creation of the appearance and atmosphere of modern Brighton.

"Summer Lightning"

Only one of the nine stories, "Summer Lightning," does not deal with AIDS, but it blends in well with the others because it involves death and bereavement. "Summer Lightning," about the sudden death of a beloved aunt from a stroke or heart attack which she suffers at a nude beach, also has Mars-Jones's characteristic humorous treatment of tragedy and is told in the first-person narrative style he favors. Both aunt and nephew have brought along books by P. G. Wodehouse containing his famous Jeeves stories. The reader senses that Wodehouse's characteristically humorous approach to all subjects and strict avoidance of anything sad or serious must have influenced Mars-Jones, as well as other gay writers.

"Remission"

"Remission" is generally regarded as one of Mars-Jones's best short stories. As the title suggests, it concerns a man experiencing temporary relief from a serious disease. The narrator in this case is ostensibly dictating his random thoughts into a tape recorder, using his brief periods of freedom from suffering to collect "a hoard of positive moments" to which he can listen when his next attack occurs. This narrative device has the effect of conveying the terrible loneliness which so many AIDS victims endure because friends, relatives, and even professionals in the health field are afraid to be near them. The narrator has two "lovers" who come to visit him, do his housecleaning, run his errands, and take turns sleeping with him, although he has never been physically intimate with either of them.

As the story demonstrates, the AIDS epidemic has brought out the best in some individuals and the worst in others. It has created a subculture within the gay subculture, consisting of those gay males who are afflicted with the disease and those who stand by them to the inevitable end.

"Bears in Mourning"

"Bears in Mourning" deals with a group of men who are attracted to each other because of certain physical characteristics. "To be a Bear you need, let's see, two essential characteristics, a beard and a bit of flesh to spare, and preferably some body hair." This story contains one of the rare instances in which one of Mars-Jones's narrators refers to AIDS by name. "All of us were involved in the epidemic in some way, socially, politically, rattling collection buckets at benefit shows if nothing else. And of course we were all terrified of getting sick." The narrator introduces Victor, who was, "an absolute Bear" and the center of "the Bear community." When the fatherly Victor commits suicide, the community is dispersed. Throughout the story, the narrator maintains the campy, "discursive," fanciful, courageous, and ironically humorous tone that typifies Mars-Jones's fiction. The reader is frequently reminded of the wisdom William Shakespeare expressed in *King Lear* (pr. c. 1605-1606, pb. 1608):

> The lowest and most dejected thing of fortune
> Stands still in esperance, lives not in fear:
> The lamentable change is from the best;
> The worst returns to laughter.

Other major works

LONG FICTION: *The Waters of Thirst*, 1993; *Pilcrow*, 2008.

NONFICTION: *Venus Envy*, 1990; *Blind Bitter Happiness*, 1997.

EDITED TEXT: *Mae West Is Dead: Recent Lesbian and Gay Fiction*, 1983.

Bibliography

Canning, Richard. "Not Fade Away." *New Statesman and Society* 5 (September 25, 1992): 57. Discusses the stories in *Monopolies of Loss*, distinguishing between those previously published in *The Darker*

Proof and those written since, finding that the newer pieces are distinguished by "subtler gradations of character."

Keen, Suzanne. "Envisioning the Past: Alan Hollinghurst, Adam Mars-Jones, Robert Goddard, and Steve Davies." In *Romances of the Archive in Contemporary British Fiction*. Toronto: University of Toronto Press, 2001. Analyzes Mars-Jones's novel *The Waters of Thirst* and novels by three other contemporary British authors.

Mars-Jones, Adam. "I Was a Teenage Homophobe." *New Statesman* 11 (June 19, 1998): 23-25. Mars-Jones, an openly gay man, admits that he was homophobic himself during his teens. Explores attitudes of "straights" toward gays and the homophobia of his own father, who was a judge noted for his harsh sentencing of homosexuals. Mars-Jones concludes that there is little difference between gays' fear of straights and straights' fear of gays.

_____. "Then and Now." *The Times Literary Supplement* (March 28, 2008): 16. Mars-Jones comments on three of his stories: "Lantern Lecture," about an eccentric man named Philip Yorke; "Hoosh-Mi, a Farrago of Scurrilous Untruths," which focuses on the royal family; and "Bathpool Park." Mars-Jones says he "leveled everything" into the present tense to write about Yorke, and he included his own speculations on the character of Neilson in "Bathpool Park."

McCann, Richard. "Writing AIDS." *Lambda Book Report* 3 (July/August, 1992): 10-11. An interview with Adam Mars-Jones, who discusses the peculiar problems involved in writing about AIDS. He asserts that an understated style, such as his own, encourages readers to avoid emotional judgments and to treat AIDS-related issues rationally while being sympathetic to victims and those who care for them.

Murphy, Timothy F., and Suzanne Poirier, eds. *Writing AIDS: Gay Literature, Language, and Analysis*. New York: Columbia University Press, 1993. This excellent volume contains essays by fifteen authors on every aspect of writing about AIDS for the purpose of informing the public and demystifying the disease. Contains discussions of Mars-Jones's short stories and those of his highly influential friend and mentor Edmund White.

Wine, Pamela. "Fiction in the Plague Years: Writing in the Shadow of AIDS." *JAMA* 271 (March 2, 1994): 717-718. Compares and contrasts Mars-Jones and Dale Peck, both gay fiction writers, from a medical perspective. Such works of fiction, Wine contends, can help medical students understand the special problems facing the AIDS patients they are likely to encounter as medical professionals.

Wood, Gaby. "Something Fresh and Citric." *The Times Literary Supplement* (March 7, 1997): 36. This insightful article uses the publication of Mars-Jones's *Blind Bitter Happiness* as a springboard for a discussion of the author's entire career.

Bill Delaney

OWEN MARSHALL

Born: Te Kuiti, New Zealand; August 17, 1941
Also Known As: Owen Marshall Jones

PRINCIPAL SHORT FICTION

Supper Waltz Wilson, and
    Other New Zealand Stories, 1979
The Master of Big Jingles, and
    Other Stories, 1982
The Day Hemingway Died, and
    Other Stories, 1984
The Lynx Hunter, and Other Stories, 1987
The Divided World, Selected Stories, 1989
Tomorrow We Save the Orphans, 1992
The Ace of Diamonds Gang, and
    Other Stories, 1993
Coming Home in the Dark, 1995
The Best of Owen Marshall's Short Stories, 1997
When Gravity Snaps: Short Stories, 2002
Watch of Gryphons, and Other Stories, 2005
Owen Marshall, Selected Stories, 2008
Living as a Moon, 2009

OTHER LITERARY FORMS

Although Owen Marshall is best known as a writer of short stories, he also has published novels. His first *A Many Coated Man* (1995) was followed by *Harlequin Rex* (1999), which won the 2000 Deutz Medal for Fiction. *Drybread*, a third novel, was published in 2007. Marshall has written two books of poetry: *Sleepwalking in Antarctica, and Other Poems* (2001) and *Occasional: Fifty Poems* (2004). He edited *Burning Boats: Seventeen New Zealand Short Stories* (1994), *Letter from Heaven: Sixteen New Zealand Poets* (1995), *Beethoven's Ears: Eighteen New Zealand Short Stories* (1996), *Author's Choice* (2001), and *Essential New Zealand Short Stories* (2002).

ACHIEVEMENTS

Owen Marshall has been the recipient of numerous awards and prizes. He won the PEN Lillian Ida Smith Award for Fiction in 1986 and 1988, the *Evening Standard* Short Story Award in 1987, and the American Express short-story award that same year. In 2000, Marshall became an Officer of the New Zealand Order of Merit, for his services to literature. *When Gravity Snaps* was runner-up for the 2003 Deutz Medal for Fiction, and in 2003 Marshall was the first recipient of the $100,000 Creative New Zealand Writers Fellowship. In 2004, Marshall received the South Island Writers Award, in recognition of his contribution to New Zealand literature for more than two decades.

BIOGRAPHY

Owen Marshall Jones was born in the small North Island town of Te Kuiti, the third son of Alan Jones, a Methodist minister, and Jane Marshall. Despite the fact that his mother died when he was two and a half, Owen Marshall had a happy childhood. His father remarried when Marshall was five, and there were six more children. As a child, Marshall read a great deal and notes in an autobiographical article in *Sport* that books were a part of his home. Marshall was brought up in Blenheim, on the South Island, but when he was twelve, the family moved to Timaru, on South Canterbury's east coast. There he attended Timaru Boys' High School and continued to read voraciously. Following high school, he enrolled at the University of Canterbury, Christchurch, in 1960, and he graduated in 1964 with an M.A. in history. While at the university, he served two tours in the army at Waiouru, where Marshall notes it was his first time mixing with Maoris. After finishing his degree, he enrolled at Christchurch Teachers' College. It was then that he began to think about writing, but his attempt at a novel made him realize he was not yet ready. He earned his teaching degree in 1965.

In 1965, Marshall began teaching at Waitaki Boys' High School in Oamaru and remained there more than twenty years. He advanced to the deputy rector position before he resigned to write full time. One year later, however, he returned to teaching and served as deputy principal of Craighead Diocesan School in Timaru, from 1986 to 1991. Throughout his teaching career, he had continued to write, and in 1977 the *New Zealand Listener* published his story "Descent from the Flugelhorn." Other stories were published in various periodicals, and in 1979 he paid Pegasus Press to publish his first collection, *Supper Waltz Wilson, and Other New Zealand Stories*. The reviews were positive, and New Zealand short-story master Frank Sargeson praised the book. After this, Marshall was recognized as an author of note and was sought by publishers. Having successfully published several volumes of short stories, he tried another novel. *The Many Coated Man* was published in 1995; two more novels followed, and in 2001 he published the first of his poetry collections.

He married Jacqueline Hill in December, 1965; they had two daughters. Marshall settled in Timaru, where he writes full time and lectures at the University of Canterbury as an adjunct professor.

ANALYSIS

Owen Marshall, who has published more than two hundred stories, is known as New Zealand's finest short-story writer. His stories are highly descriptive of people and the natural world and often are shocking. Settings are important as to how characters live and range from cities and the countryside to the sea. Many of Marshall's stories are located on South Island, where he has spent most of his life, and illustrate his affinity with rural and small-town life. Most of the stories are told in first-person point of view, and generally the narrators are male. The tone of the stories varies from comic to sad, satiric to wistful. His style is generally straightforward storytelling, but he has experimented with new forms. One story, "The Divided World," is unique in that it has no plot but is rather an accumulation of the differences that make up the world, ranging from the philosophical to the mundane. The tone is somewhat cynical, but the story illustrates Marshall's

delight in playing with words. Marshall's style can also be poetic, as in "The Lynx Hunter," in which he creates, using a variety of mismatched images, a portrait of a man who looks fine on the outside but is dying emotionally inside.

Marshall is adept at drawing characters. In "The Charcoal Burner's Dream," he describes the Reverend Metcalf, visiting patients in the hospital, with his "look of infinite understanding and superiority" . . . who "would lay out his modulated laugh as a tapestry, while his eyes strayed to other beds, or the face of his digital watch." Marshall notes on his Web site that the "psychological landscapes of my fellow New Zealanders" are his major concern. He is more interested "in mood and character" than in "plot and action."

Particularly effective are his stories about boys growing into young men. Most of these stories are comic, such as "The Paper Parcel"; others are funny but with a hint of regret at time passing, such as "The Ace of Diamonds Gang," in which a group of thirteen-year-old boys play pranks, leaving an ace of diamonds as their calling card. Unfortunately, during one prank, the narrator, by mistake, leaves his library card. The gang is found out; it is an abrupt end to childhood. There are other coming-of-age stories, such as the title story of his first collection, *Supper Waltz Wilson*. At the beginning of the story the main character and his best friend Hugh, the narrator, are both schoolboys, but when Wilson's father assaults his wife and is taken to a mental hospital, Wilson leaves his friend, home, and boyhood behind, to go to sea: a sad ending to childhood.

At the other end of the age spectrum, Marshall's focus on older men who have lived rich lives has resulted in such memorable characters as Mr. Meecham, a World War I soldier, and Ted in "Takahe Man," one of the last of a breed of New Zealand farmers. In "A Day with Yesterman," Chatterton, dying of cancer, introduces his love of life and the beauty of the countryside to those he meets on that one day.

Marshall's stories tend to focus on the "drama of everyday life" and the day-to-day perils of living. His intent is to provide "some insight into the business of living." Besides the difficulties of growing up, Marshall revisits through a number of stories the dangers of marriage. He once stated that marriage is more interesting than murder. Some stories are a comic version of the changes that come about once people are married, such as Marshall's favorite, the satiric "Heating the World." Two bachelor farmers, typical of those living in the New Zealand heartland, who were once devoted to "rural simplicity" and thrift, are astounded by the changes resulting from marriages. Most marriages in his stories, however, are not a source of comedy: Some are simply unhappy; others result in violence. A reviewer for *New Zealand Books* in 1995 stated that the marriage of Mumsie and Zip, in the story of the same name, was "the blackest and most brilliantly sinister portrait of suburban marriage in New Zealand fiction." It tells the story of Zip, who has been doing the same job for twenty years, and Mumsie, whose joys in life are taking care of Zip and neighborhood gossip. Throughout the story, Marshall keeps referring to the rain on the windows as tears. However, their lives go beyond sadness. Trapped in suburbia, they are "like two rats in a dung hill," and their seemingly ordinary life is exposed to the reader when Zip repeatedly slams Mumsie's head against a wall.

THE MASTER OF BIG JINGLES

Marshall's second collection includes stories that have been anthologized heavily, such as "Mr. Van Gogh." Like several of Marshall's stories, this focuses on an old man who continues to live his life with a passion. In this instance, his passion is the artist Vincent Van Gogh. To most people the old man is an oddity, but Mr. Van Gogh, which is not his real name, has a secret. He collects glass and makes rather ordinary objects from it, but when Mr. Van Gogh is taken ill, the narrator and his father discover an astonishing world of cut-glass versions of Van Gogh's paintings in the old man's house. However, "progress" intrudes, and the house is condemned to make room for a two-lane bridge. Society, uncaring of what the house contains, dictates that Mr. Van Gogh relocate. When the house is finally destroyed, so is Mr. Van Gogh.

Another character defined by his conflicts with society is Mr. Meecham in "No Photos by Request." Mr. Meecham was a soldier during World War I. His brother was killed during the war, and every time he hears the bugle he is reminded of the harrowing battle of the Somme. Like many tribal people who feel a photo captures part of the soul, Mr. Meecham has a fear of photographs. At the annual Anzac (Australian and New Zealand Army) celebration, the narrator prevents a newspaperman from photographing Mr. Meecham, dressed in his uniform and wearing his war medals. Marshall captures the moment, equating the camera with a weapon: "like a sniper's rifle" aimed at Mr. Meecham. The story also includes a recurring theme in Marshall's stories: the differences between the generations. The narrator remarks that his generation "disparaged any convictions too firmly held; any codes of conduct in common," only believing "in subjective views, and compromise as an expectation."

In addition to those about older characters, some stories are about boys and young men. The title story "The Master of Big Jingles" details the end of a friendship between two young men because they go to different high schools. In "The Giving Up Party," the seventeen-year-old narrator, working as a grass cutter at the Jewell estate, meets Helen Jewell, the thirty-four-year-old daughter who has returned home from England. She is celebrating giving up her dream of becoming a poet: "I chose poetry as my husband." They share a passionate kiss that he will keep secret. Marshall's description of the gardens is memorable: "Magnolias tend to sulk . . . they'll sulk for years sometimes before they choose to flower." Helen has not flowered as a poet and has resigned herself to find a real husband.

The stories are also about other types of loss. In "Requiem in a Town House," a farmer, relocated into the city for his retirement, finds the new house a prison as he tries to adjust to his diminished world. In "The Charcoal Burner's Dream," the narrator loses a new friend when Chris chooses suicide rather than death by more rounds of surgery.

THE DAY HEMINGWAY DIED

Stories in Marshall's third collection continue his concerns with characters, particularly young and old men. "Kenneth's Friend" shows how young boys can be vicious to one another. In another story, "friendship" between two young men, developed through proximity of serving compulsory military service, results in a fight and estrangement. Difficulties of preadolescence are portrayed in "The Paper Parcel," when the twelve-year-old narrator, feeling good about himself because he is the second speediest runner, first in math, and attracting girls, is invited by a girl to his first dance, a costume ball. Unfortunately, his mother's idea of a costume is having him go as a parcel, complete with twine and stamps. The resulting humiliation and preteen angst show Marshall at his comic best.

Marshall's concern with the loss of expectations and the pains of marriage are illustrated in this volume. "Don't Blame Yourself at All" features an insensitive, priggish husband, who does not want a child at this point in his career. He persuades his wife to have an abortion, and he cannot understand why she cannot get over it and move on. In "A Test of Fire," the husband and wife hate each other, and no one, except their son, knows of the virulent atmosphere in the home. The fire that destroys their home and their lives is a metaphor for their hatred.

LIVING AS A MOON

Marshall's first collection was published in 1979; this collection, published thirty years later, shows the changes in his style and settings. The point of view in some stories is female; some settings go beyond New Zealand, ranging to Australia, Italy, and France. The effects of parents on children are still explored, as in "Michael," in which parents create a toxic atmosphere for their son, not with hate, as in "A Test of Fire," but with indifference. Questions of identity are raised. In the title story, the narrator, age twenty-nine and an assistant floor manager at Mademoiselle Coquette Fashions, is told she looks a lot like Estelle Page, a standup comic. She finds she has a talent for impersonation and begins to live her life as someone else. "It's like living your life as a moon," she declares, and she gives up her life and becomes a reflection of another person. However, in this instance, giving up her previous personality, career, and friends results in a different, better life.

In "No Stations of Remorse," Margaret, another female narrator, has lost her husband to cancer. She journeys to the past by visiting places that once were important to her and husband. Unlike many portrayed in Marshall's stories, Margaret's marriage was loving, and her discovery on the trip is that her

life will change without him, and people will see her in a different way. She will need to create her own identity. In the story "Howell," Marshall shows how identity can be discovered by digging into one's past. Although family legends are not exactly based on fact, as the narrator discovers, he also says, "Every family needs a hero," whether factual or fictional.

Sometimes one is mistakenly given the identity of a hero, such as in "Patrick and the Killer." Patrick has lost his white-collar position and is working in a dead-end job in a video store. However, his accidental encounter with a murderer has unexpected results. The press assumes he is a hero, and the media create the image of Patrick as a courageous man who has helped capture a killer. With his new identity, Patrick is sought after, rehired by his previous company, given a raise and promotion, and ends up with a girlfriend. Identity can also be awarded based on accomplishments. In "Head Butting," the narrator, a mentally disadvantaged young man, becomes an expert at head butting, and when asked why he does this, he replies, "You got to be best at something or cop out and die."

OTHER MAJOR WORKS

LONG FICTION: *A Many Coated Man*, 1995; *Harlequin Rex*, 1999; *Drybread*, 2007.

RADIO PLAY: *An Indirect Geography*, 1989.

POETRY: *Sleepwalking in Antarctica, and Other Poems*, 2001; *Occasional: Fifty Poems*, 2004.

EDITED TEXTS: *Burning Boats: Seventeen New Zealand Short Stories*, 1994; *Letter from Heaven: Sixteen New Zealand Poets*, 1995; *Beethoven's Ears: Eighteen New Zealand Short Stories*, 1996; *Author's Choice*, 2001; *Essential New Zealand Short Stories*, 2002.

BIBLIOGRAPHY

Marshall. Owen. "Tunes for Bears to Dance To." *Sport* 3 (1989): 56. An autobiographical account of Marshall's life and beginnings as a writer.

McLauchlan, Gordon. "Owen Marshall: *When Gravity Snaps*." *The New Zealand Herald*, August 10, 2002. Review includes material on Marshall's strengths as a writer. O'Sullivan, Vincent. "The Naming Parts: Owen Marshall and the Short Story." *Sport* 3 (Spring, 1989): 67. An overview of the art of writing a short story leads to a discussion of specific Marshall stories.

Watson, John. "From Sargeson to Marshall: The Male Hero in Recent Short Fiction by Male Writers." *Journal of New Zealand Literature* 9 (1991): 81-101. Discusses stories of male adolescence and old age.

Marcia B. Dinneen

W. Somerset Maugham

Born: Paris, France; January 25, 1874
Died: Nice, France; December 16, 1965

Principal short fiction

Orientations, 1899
The Trembling of a Leaf: Little Stories of the South Sea Islands, 1921
The Casuarina Tree: Six Stories, 1926
Ashenden: Or, The British Agent, 1928
Six Stories Written in the First Person Singular, 1931
Ah King: Six Stories, 1933
East and West: The Collected Short Stories, 1934
Cosmopolitans, 1936
The Favorite Short Stories of W. Somerset Maugham, 1937
The Round Dozen, 1939
The Mixture as Before: Short Stories, 1940
Creatures of Circumstances: Short Stories, 1947
East of Suez: Great Stories of the Tropics, 1948
Here and There: Selected Short Stories, 1948
The Complete Short Stories, 1951
The World Over, 1952
Seventeen Lost Stories, 1969
Collected Stories, 2004

Other literary forms

A dedicated professional, W. Somerset Maugham (mawm) earned more than three million dollars from his writing, a phenomenal amount for his day. Between 1897 and 1962, a career spanning eight decades, Maugham published twenty novels; four travel books; more than twenty stage plays; an autobiography of ideas; and innumerable essays, *belles-lettres,* and introductions; in addition to more than one hundred short stories, of which about ninety are readily accessible in different editions. Much of his work has been adapted for television and cinema.

Achievements

W. Somerset Maugham is best known for his urbanity, his wit, his controlled sense of writing, and his ability to describe not only objectively but also so realistically that he has been accused of lifting stories directly from life. Many of his stories do spring from real incidents or actual people, but the perceptions and surprise plot twists are always Maugham-inspired. In fact, Maugham is expressly known as a master of the surprise or twist ending to an inextricably woven plot in his short stories, many of which have been converted to film. His early work, under the influence of Oscar Wilde and his cult of aesthetes, shows a refined and civilized attitude toward life. Several of his novels illustrate the demanding sacrifices that art necessitates of life or that life itself can become, in turn, an art form, thereby demonstrating the "art of living" (*The Razor's Edge,* 1944).

Maugham was curiously denied many conspicuous honors (such as knighthood) usually conferred on a man of letters of his distinction, but he was awarded by the Royal Society of Literature the title of Companion of Literature, an honor given to "authors who have brought exceptional distinction to English letters." Furthermore, the occasion of his eightieth birthday was celebrated with a dinner at the Garrick Club, a distinction given to only three writers before him: Charles Dickens, William Makepeace Thackeray, and Anthony Trollope.

BIOGRAPHY

When William Somerset Maugham was eight, his mother died, and his father, a solicitor for the British embassy in Paris, died two years later. Shy and speaking little English, Maugham was sent to Whitstable in Kent to live with an uncle, the Reverend Henry MacDonald Maugham, and his German-born wife, and thence almost immediately to King's School, Canterbury. These wretched and unhappy years were later detailed in Maugham's first masterpiece, the novel *Of Human Bondage* (1915). A stammer which stayed with him for life seems to have originated about this time. At seventeen, Maugham went to Heidelberg and attended lectures at the university. His first play, *Schiffbrüchig* (*Marriages Are Made in Heaven*), was written during this year abroad and first performed in Berlin in 1902.

Returning to London, he began the study of medicine at St. Thomas' Hospital, where the misery of the nearby Lambeth slums profoundly impressed him. He took his medical degree in 1897, the same year *Liza of Lambeth*, his first novel, was published, and he then abandoned medicine. By 1908, Maugham had an unprecedented four plays running simultaneously in London, and by 1911, he had become successful enough to buy a fashionable house in Mayfair.

In 1915, he married Syrie Barnardo Wellcome. Divorced in 1927, they had one daughter, Liza, who became Lady Glendevon. During World War I, Maugham served as a medical officer in France and as an agent for the British Secret Service in Switzerland and Russia, where he was to prevent, if possible, the Bolshevik Revolution. During and after the war, he traveled extensively in Hawaii, Samoa, Tahiti, China, Malaysia, Indochina, Australia, the West Indies, various Central and South American countries, and the United States. In 1928, Maugham settled on the French Riviera, buying Villa Mauresque. Maugham died in Nice, France, on December 16, 1965.

ANALYSIS

W. Somerset Maugham first claimed fame as a playwright and novelist, but he became best known in the 1920's and 1930's the world over as an international traveler and short-story writer. Appearing in popular magazines such as *Nash's, Collier's, Hearst's*

International, The Smart Set, and *Cosmopolitan*, his stories reached hundreds of thousands of readers who had never attended a play and had seldom read a novel. This new public demanded simple, lucid, fast-moving prose, and Maugham's realistic, well-defined narratives, often set amid the exotic flora of Oceania or Indochina, were among the most popular of the day.

THE TREMBLING OF A LEAF

The Trembling of a Leaf: Little Stories of the South Sea Islands collected six of these first "exotic stories" and assured Maugham fame as a short-story writer on equal footing with his established renown as novelist and dramatist. It was actually his second collection, coming more than twenty years after *Orientations*, whose title clearly bespeaks its purposes. Apparently, Maugham had found no suitable possibilities for short fiction in the meantime until, recuperating from a lung infection between World War I assignments for the British Secret Service, he took a vacation to Samoa and Hawaii:

> I had always had a romantic notion of the South Seas. I had read of those magic islands in the books of Herman Melville, Pierre Loti, and Robert Louis Stevenson, but what I saw was very different from what I had read.

Although Maugham clearly differentiates life as he saw it in the South Seas from life as he had read about it in the writings of his "romantic" predecessors, his stories of British colonials, of natives and half-castes in exotic environments, are reminiscent of these authors and also of Rudyard Kipling. Maugham's assessment of Kipling, the only British short-story writer he thought comparable to such greats as Guy de Maupassant and Anton Chekhov, neatly clarifies their similar subject, as well as their ultimate stylistic differences. Kipling, Maugham writes,

> opened a new and fruitful field to writers. This is the story, the scene of which is set in some country little known to the majority of readers, and which deals with the reactions upon the white man of his sojourn in an alien land and the effect which contact with peoples of another race has upon him. Subsequent writers have treated this subject in their different ways, but . . . no one has invested it with more ro-

Critical Survey of Short Fiction

mantic glamour, no one has made it more exciting and no one has presented it so vividly and with such a wealth of colour.

Maugham's first South Sea stories are essentially criticisms of the "romantic glamour" of Kipling and his predecessors, especially Stevenson, his most immediate literary forefather in terms of location. Rather than repeat their illusions, Maugham tries to see the "alien land" as it really is, without poetic frills. "Red," which Maugham once chose as his best story, is a clear example of this process.

"Red"

A worldly, gruff, and overweight skipper of a bedraggled seventy-ton schooner anchors off one of the Samoan Islands in order to trade with the local storekeeper. After rowing ashore to a small cove, the captain follows a tortuous path, eventually arriving at "a white man's house" where he meets Neilson. Neilson seems a typical character out of Robert Louis Stevenson, a life deserter unable either to return to his homeland or to accommodate himself completely to his present situation. Twenty-five years ago he came to the island with tuberculosis, expecting to live only a year, but the mild climate has arrested his disease. He has married a native woman called Sally and built a European bungalow on the beautiful spot where a grass hut once stood. His walls are lined with books, which makes the skipper nervous but to which Neilson constantly and condescendingly alludes. Offering him whiskey and a cigar, Neilson decides to tell the skipper the story of Red.

Red was Neilson's romantic predecessor, Sally's previous lover, an ingenuous Apollo whom Neilson likes to imagine "had no more soul than the creatures of the woods and forests who made pipes from reeds and bathed in the mountain streams when the world was young." It was Red who had lived with Sally in the native hut, "with its beehive roof and its pillars, overshadowed by a great tree with red flowers." Glamorizing the young couple and the lush habitat, Neilson imagines them living on "delicious messes from coconuts," by a sea "deep blue, wine-coloured at sundown, like the sea of Homeric Greece," where "the hurrying fish were like butterflies," and the "dawn crept in among

W. Somerset Maugham (Library of Congress)

the wooden pillars of the hut" so that the lovers woke each morning and "smiled to welcome another day."

After a year of bliss, Red was shanghaied by a British whaler while trying to trade green oranges for tobacco. Sally was crestfallen and mourned him for three years, but finally, somewhat reluctantly, she acceded to the amorous overtures of the newcomer Neilson:

> And so the little wooden house was built in which he had now lived for many years, and Sally became his wife. But after the first few weeks of rapture, during which he was satisfied with what she gave him, he had known little happiness. She had yielded to him, through weariness, but she had only yielded what she set no store on. The soul which he had dimly glimpsed escaped him. He knew that she cared nothing for him. She still loved Red. . . .

Neilson, admittedly "a sentimentalist," is imprisoned by history. His books, a source of anxiety to the skipper, are a symbol of what Maugham believes he must himself avoid: useless repetition of and bondage to his forebears. As creation, Neilson does repeat Stevenson, but as character, he shows the absolute futility of this repetition. The dead romance assumes priority from the living one, and priority is everything. For the sentimentalist Neilson, tropical paradise has become living hell and the greatest obstacle preventing his own present happiness, the fulfillment of his own history, is his creation of an insurmountable predecessor, one whose "romantic glamour" is purer and simpler than his own reality.

The final irony, that the skipper, now bloated and bleary-eyed, is in fact the magnificent Red of Neilson's imagination and that when Sally and he meet they do not even recognize each other, snaps something in Neilson. The moment he had dreaded for twenty-five years has come and gone. His illusions disintegrate like gossamer; the "father" is not insurmountable:

> He had been cheated. They had seen each other at last and had not known it. He began to laugh, mirthlessly, and his laughter grew till it become hysterical. The Gods had played him a cruel trick. And he was old now.

In "Red," Neilson's realization of failure and waste do prompt some action, possibly an escape from the cell of his past. Over dinner, he lies to Sally that his eldest brother is very ill and he must go home. "Will you be gone long?" she asks. His only answer is to shrug his shoulders.

In its natural manner, Maugham's prose in these stories never strains for effect; each could easily be retold over coffee or a drink. Like Maupassant, Maugham is a realist and a merciless ironist, but while his narrator observes and his readers chuckle, characters such as Neilson grapple in desperate roles against the onrushing determination of their lives. In the style of the best "magazine" stories, incidents in Maugham inevitably build one on top of the other, slowly constraining his protagonists until, like grillwork, these incidents all but completely bar the protagonists from realizing their individual potential and freedom. Maugham's predilection for the surprise ending helps some find a final success, but not all; most end as readers have believed they would--like the cuckolded Scotsman Lawson in "The Pool" who, after losing job, friends' respect, wife,

and self, is "set on making a good job of it" and commits suicide "with a great stone tied up in his coat and bound to his feet."

Lawson, another "great coward" in the Stevenson mold, has married a beautiful half-caste and, naïvely assuming human nature the same the world over, has treated her as he would a white woman. By providing primarily in terms of his own culture's expectations, Lawson unwittingly shoulders "the white man's burden," that bequest of Kipling's, until he becomes himself a burden. Maugham implies, with great irony, that if Lawson had been less "a gentleman" and had taken the girl as a mistress, his tragedy might have been averted. As the reader must see the "alien land" for what it really is, so must they see its peoples.

"RAIN"

"Rain," Maugham's best-known short story, develops many of these same themes. Pago Pago is unforgettably described, but no one could confuse it with the romanticized "loveliness" of Neilson's island. When the rain is not falling in torrents, the sun is oppressive. Davidson, the missionary, and Sadie, the prostitute, act out their parts with the same furious intensity. Neither is banalized; Maugham neither approves nor condemns. Only the "mountains of Nebraska" dream foreshadows Davidson's lust. (With its overtones of sexual repression, this dream makes "Rain" a notable pioneer in Freudian fiction.) Other than that, however, Davidson's sincere religious fervor seems convincingly real, inspired though it is by his "mission," yet another example of "the white man's burden." In the ensuing struggle between spiritual and "heathen" sensuality, the ironic stroke is that the prostitute wins; up to the last few pages, the story's outcome looks otherwise. Finally, Davidson must admit that he cannot proscribe human nature, not even his own. Neither saint nor sinner, he is simply human. On a more universal level than either "The Pool" or "Red," "Rain" shows that, of human nature, only its unaccountability is predictable.

Maugham's detachment and moral tolerance, as well as assuring Davidson's and Sadie's vitality as characters, benefits his handling of the tale. The restraint exercised in *not* portraying for the reader either of the two "big scenes," Sadie's rape or Davidson's suicide, gives Maugham's story "Rain" an astounding dramatic power. The "real life" genesis of "Rain" is well known. Maugham jotted down his impressions of a few passengers aboard ship traveling with him in the winter of 1916 from Honolulu to Pago Pago; four years later he created a story from these notes. Of his prototype for Sadie Thompson he wrote:

> Plump, pretty in a coarse fashion perhaps not more than twenty-seven. She wore a white dress and a large white hat, long white boots from which the calves bulged in cotton stockings.

Six Stories Written in the First Person Singular

This practice of taking characters and situations directly from life is nowhere better elaborated in Maugham than in the volume entitled *Six Stories Written in the First Person Singular*. The personal touch--clear in the book's title--leaves a strong impression of reality. Whereas "Rain" seems a small classic in its theme, conflict, effective setting, and dramatic ending, it has one difficulty: The reader is unable to sympathize clearly with any one character, and this detracts from a greater, warmer effectiveness it might otherwise have. When the narrator-as-detached-observer is introduced as a character, however, there is no such problem with sympathy. This creation, the consistent and subsequently well-known cosmopolite, the story*teller* for his stories, is one of Maugham's finest achievements.

In "Virtue" the narrator--here differentiated as "Maugham"--browses at Sotheby's auction rooms, goes to the Haymarket, and dines at Ciro's when he has a free morning; he was once a medical student and is now a novelist. In "The Round Dozen," he is a well-known author whose portrait appears in the illustrated papers. He is at Elson, a tattered seaside resort "not very far from Brighton," recovering from influenza. There, "Maugham" coincidentally observes a well-known bigamist--whose portrait at one time had also graced the pages of the press--capture his twelfth victim. In "Jane," the versatile man-of-the-world is introduced as a writer of comedies, while in "The Alien Corn" he is a promising young novelist who has grown middle-aged, written books and plays, traveled and had

experiences, fallen in and out of love. Throughout *Six Stories Written in the First Person Singular*, "Maugham" is intermittently away from London, "once more in the Far East." Such frank appeals to verisimilitude (in other words, that "Maugham" is in fact Maugham) succeed extremely well.

"The Human Element"

In "The Human Element," the narrator is a popular author who likes "a story to have a beginning, a middle, and an end." He meets Carruthers, whom he does not much like, one night at the Hotel Plaza in Rome during the late summer "dead season." Carruthers is inhumanly depressed and tells Maugham why: He has found his life's love, the woman he would make his wife, Betty Weldon-Burns, living in Rhodes "in domestic familiarity" with her chauffeur.

Carruthers, also a short-story writer, has been praised by critics for "his style, his sense of beauty and his atmosphere," but when "Maugham" suggests he make use of his experience for a story, Carruthers grows angry: "It would be monstrous. Betty was everything in the world to me. I couldn't do anything so caddish." Ironically, the story ends with Carruthers's excuse that "there's no story there." That "Maugham" has in fact just made a story of it suggests that life can and does provide limitless possibilities for art if people are only ready to accept them.

Maugham specifically delineates these dual creative principles, life and art, in his introduction to the six stories in the collection. Defending the practice of drawing fictional characters from personal experience, Maugham cites Stendhal, Gustave Flaubert, and Jules Renard. "I think indeed," he writes, "that most novelists and surely the best, have worked from life." The concern of Maugham's South Sea stories, to convey what he "saw" rather than what he "had read," is continued here on a higher plane. Maugham qualifies that there must also be art:

> A real person, however eminent, is for the most part too insignificant for the purposes of fiction. The complete character, the result of elaboration rather than of invention, is art, and life in the raw, as we know, is only its material.

Illustrating the unaccountability of human behavior (for how could he endeavor to account for it?), "Maugham" remains a detached observer of life. Critics have wished for more poetry, loftier flights of imagination, more sympathy for his characters, and even occasional indirection; the lack of these things constitutes the limitation of Maugham's style. Rejecting both the atmospheric romanticism of his predecessors and the exhaustive modernism of his contemporaries, Maugham's short stories do not seek to penetrate either landscape or life. His reader, like his narrator, may experience admiration, annoyance, disgust, or pity for the characters, but he does not share or become immersed in their emotions. This point of view of a calm, ordinary man, so unusual for the twentieth century, is instructive, teaching careful and clear consideration of life's possibilities, its casualties and successes, banalities, and gifts. In this way, objective understanding is increased by reading Maugham much as intersubjective facilities are by reading James Joyce, D. H. Lawrence, or the other moderns.

OTHER MAJOR WORKS

LONG FICTION: *Liza of Lambeth*, 1897; *The Making of a Saint*, 1898; *The Hero*, 1901; *Mrs. Craddock*, 1902; *The Merry-Go-Round*, 1904; *The Bishop's Apron*, 1906; *The Explorer*, 1907; *The Magician*, 1908; *Of Human Bondage*, 1915; *The Moon and Sixpence*, 1919; *The Painted Veil*, 1925; *Cakes and Ale: Or, The Skeleton in the Cupboard*, 1930; *The Narrow Corner*, 1932; *Theatre*, 1937; *Christmas Holiday*, 1939; *Up at the Villa*, 1941; *The Hour Before Dawn*, 1942; *The Razor's Edge*, 1944; *Then and Now*, 1946; *Catalina*, 1948; *Selected Novels*, 1953.

PLAYS: *A Man of Honor*, wr. 1898-1899, pr., pb. 1903; *Loaves and Fishes*, wr.1903, pr. 1911, pb. 1924; *Lady Frederick*, pr. 1907, pb. 1912; *Jack Straw*, pr. 1908, pb. 1911; *Mrs. Dot*, pr. 1908, pb. 1912; *The Explorer*, pr. 1908, pb. 1912; *Penelope*, pr. 1909, pb. 1912; *Smith*, pr. 1909, pb. 1913; *The Noble Spaniard*, pr. 1909, pb. 1953; *Landed Gentry*, pr. 1910 (as *Grace*; pb. 1913); *The Tenth Man*, pr. 1910, pb. 1913; *The Land of Promise*, pr. 1913, pb. 1913, 1922; *Caroline*, pr. 1916, pb. 1923 (as *The Unattainable*); *Our Betters*, pr. 1917, pb. 1923; *Caesar's Wife*, pr. 1919, pb. 1922;

Home and Beauty, pr. 1919, pb. 1923 (also known as *Too Many Husbands*); *The Unknown*, pr., pb. 1920; *The Circle*, pr., pb. 1921; *East of Suez*, pr., pb. 1922; *The Constant Wife*, pr., pb. 1926; *The Letter*, pr., pb. 1927; *The Sacred Flame*, pr., pb. 1928; *The Breadwinner*, pr., pb. 1930; *The Collected Plays of W. Somerset Maugham*, pb. 1931-1934 (6 volumes; revised 1952, 3 volumes); *For Services Rendered*, pr., pb. 1932; *Sheppey*, pr., pb. 1933.

SCREENPLAY: *Trio*, 1950 (with R. C. Sherriff and Noel Langley).

NONFICTION: *The Land of the Blessed Virgin: Sketches and Impressions in Andalusia*, 1905 (also known as *Andalusia*, 1920); *On a Chinese Screen*, 1922; *The Gentleman in the Parlour: A Record of a Journey from Rangoon to Haiphong*, 1930; *Don Fernando*, 1935; *The Summing Up*, 1938; *Books and You*, 1940; *France at War*, 1940; *Strictly Personal*, 1941; *Great Novelists and Their Novels*, 1948; *A Writer's Notebook*, 1949; *The Writer's Point of View*, 1951; *The Vagrant Mood: Six Essays*, 1952; *Ten Novels and Their Authors*, 1954 (revision of *Great Novelists and Their Novels*); *The Partial View*, 1954 (includes *The Summing Up* and *A Writer's Notebook*); *The Travel Books*, 1955; *Points of View*, 1958; *Looking Back*, 1962; *Purely for My Pleasure*, 1962; *Selected Prefaces and Introductions*, 1963; *The Skeptical Romancer: Selected Travel Writing*, 2009 (Pico Iyer, editor).

MISCELLANEOUS: *The Great Exotic Novels and Short Stories of Somerset Maugham*, 2001; *The W. Somerset Maugham Reader: Novels, Stories, Travel Writing*, 2004 (Jeffrey Meyers, editor).

BIBLIOGRAPHY

Archer, Stanley. *W. Somerset Maugham: A Study of the Short Fiction*. New York: Twayne, 1993. An introductory survey of Maugham's short fiction, focusing on the style and technique of the stories and the frequent themes of how virtue ironically can cause unhappiness, how colonial officials come in conflict with their social and physical environment, and how people are often unable to escape their own cultural background. Reprints some of Maugham's own comments on short fiction and three previously published critical excerpts.

Burt, Forrest D. *W. Somerset Maugham*. Boston: Twayne, 1985. Argues that Maugham has long been an underestimated and neglected writer in terms of an assessment of his value and position in the literary canon and that there has been a more serious appraisal of his works since his death. Includes a chronology, a basic biography (in the early chapters), and a focus on the literary works from a critical standpoint.

Cordell, Richard A. *Somerset Maugham: A Writer for All Seasons*. 2d ed. Bloomington: Indiana University Press, 1969. Cordell, who was Maugham's friend and confidant, provides an in-depth examination of the writer's life and works. Cordell disputes the labeling of Maugham as "enigmatic" and "inscrutable," arguing instead that Maugham was just the opposite. Includes a substantial section devoted to a discussion of Maugham's short stories, along with chapters on three of the "autobiographical novels," plays, other fiction, and critical reception.

Curtis, Anthony. *Somerset Maugham*. Windsor, England: Profile Books, 1982. An excellent forty-seven-page pamphlet-sized volume that provides both an intensive and lucid overview of the writer, his genres, his life, and his themes. It also clearly distinguishes Maugham as preeminently a writer of short fiction. An insightful and brief introduction to the author that also includes an index of his available short stories.

Hastings, Selina. *The Secret Lives of Somerset Maugham: A Biography*. New York: Random House, 2010. Critically acclaimed biography focusing on the "hidden" aspects of Maugham's life. Hastings was the first biographer to receive permission to quote from Maugham's private papers and from the observations of his daughter Liza regarding a court case instigated by Maugham's homosexual lover. Hastings chronicles Maugham's homosexual relationships, his bitter marriage to his wife, and his work as an espionage agent in the two world wars.

Hitz, Frederick P. *The Great Game: The Myth and Reality of Espionage*. New York: Alfred A. Knopf, 2004. Hitz, the former inspector general of the Central Intelligence Agency, compares famous fictional spies and spy stories--including Maugham's *Ashenden: Or, The British Agent*--to real espionage agents and case studies to demonstrate that truth is stranger than fiction.

Holden, Philip. *Orienting Masculinity, Orienting Nation: W. Somerset Maugham's Exotic Fiction*. Westport, Conn.: Greenwood Press, 1996. Examines the themes of homosexuality, gender identity, and race relations in Maugham's works.

_____. "W. Somerset Maugham's 'Yellow Streak.'" *Studies in Short Fiction* 29 (Fall, 1992): 575-582. Discusses Maugham's story "The Yellow Streak" as a dialectical tale composed of the opposites of civilized/savage, male/female, and racial purity/miscegenation. Considers the treatment of the relationship between the two men in the story.

Jonas, Klaus W., ed. *The Maugham Enigma*. New York: Citadel Press, 1954. An informative background collection of articles, essays, biographical notes, and book reviews by numerous authors on Maugham. It covers the author as dramatist, novelist, "teller of tales," and essayist, and it also includes some interesting reminiscences and notes on writing from Maugham himself.

Loss, Archie K. *W. Somerset Maugham*. New York: Ungar, 1987. The chapter on short fiction in this general introduction to Maugham's life and art focuses largely on his most familiar story, "Rain," as the best example of his short-story technique and subject matter. Discusses Maugham as a tale-teller and argues that the voice of the narrator is the most important single element in a Maugham short story.

Malcolm, David. "W. Somerset Maugham's Ashenden Stories." In *A Companion to the British and Irish Short Story*, edited by Cheryl Alexander Malcolm and David Malcolm. Malden, Mass.: Wiley-Blackwell, 2008. Explicates Maugham's short stories about Ashenden, a British secret agent.

Meyers, Jeffrey. *Somerset Maugham*. New York: Alfred A. Knopf, 2004. Meyers's examination of Maugham's life and works provides comprehensive detail and new insights into his subject's creative process. Meyers defends Maugham's art and traces his influence on such writers as George Orwell and V. S. Naipaul.

Naik, M. K. *W. Somerset Maugham*. Norman: University of Oklahoma Press, 1953. Naik maintains there was a basic "conflict between the two strains of cynicism and humanitarianism" in Maugham's character. Naik defines this conflict, offers biographical data, and then examines Maugham's writing in various genres in the context of his premise.

Rogal, Samuel J. *A William Somerset Maugham Encyclopedia*. Westport, Conn.: Greenwood Press, 1997. Contains alphabetically arranged entries with information on Maugham's life; family members; friends; associates; written works; places where he lived and to which he traveled; and the cultural, social, and political contexts of his life and works.

Kenneth Funsten
Updated by Sherry Morton-Mollo

Cᴏʟᴜᴍ MᴄCᴀɴɴ

Born: Dublin, Ireland; February 28, 1965

PRINCIPAL SHORT FICTION
Fishing the Sloe-Black River, 1994
Everything in This Country Must: A Novella and Two Stories, 2000

OTHER LITERARY FORMS

The first published work of Colum McCann (kawlm muh-KAN) was short stories, and he has continued to write them; he is better known, however, as a novelist. It is a sad fact of the literary marketplace that collections of short stories do not sell as well as novels, and full-time fiction writers usually are novelists. Of McCann's five novels, four--*This Side of Brightness* (1998), *Dancer* (2003), *Zoli* (2006), and *Let the Great World Spin* (2009)--have been international best sellers. Like his short fiction, his novels explore otherness. The viewpoint character in *Zoli*, for example, is a Roma woman singer-poet, based on the Polish "Gypsy" (an ethnic slur to the Roma people) named Papuzsa, whose picture implored him to write her story. After many months of research in the New York Public Library and travel to the Czech Republic, Slovakia, Austria, and Hungary, McCann wrote the novel in part to counter prejudice against the Roma.

ACHIEVEMENTS

Colum McCann frequently has been acknowledged as a gifted author. In 1990, his short story "Tresses" won the Hennessey Award, and "Sisters" was included in *Best Short Stories* in England in 1993. His first collection, *Fishing the Sloe-Black River*, won the Rooney Prize in 1994. "Kingfishers Catch Fire" appeared in *Poetry* and won a Pushcart Prize in 1998. In 2004, McCann's novel *Dancer* won the Irish Novel of the Year Award. The film adaptation of his story "Everything in This Country Must" was nominated for an Academy Award in 2005. His novel *Let the Great World Spin* won the National Book Award for 2009.

BIOGRAPHY

Colum McCann was born February 28, 1965, into a middle-class Dublin family in which writing and reading were central. His father is a journalist and author of several books, and McCann recalls engaging his classmates with oral reports on his father's books for children. After working on *The Irish Press*, McCann came to the United States to pursue his writing career. Although his native land had more writers per capita than most countries, he feared he would end up writing about the middle-class Ireland he grew up in and sensed that the creative imagination would be stimulated by otherness. Several months after his arrival, when he noticed he still had the same blank sheet of paper in his typewriter, he set out to spend more than a year bicycling more than twelve thousand miles throughout the United States, finding work along the way to support himself. What he discovered was the profound need of people he met to tell their stories because they knew he would be moving on, just as strangers on an airplane will tell each other stories about themselves that they would never share with family and friends. Although he felt he could not violate the trust of those who told him stories by retelling them as his own, he was energized to become a storyteller to repay all those who had moved him with their stories. After marrying, he and his wife Allison lived for a year in Japan. They moved to New York, where they settled with their three children and where McCann has taught fiction writing at Hunter College.

ANALYSIS

Central to the stories in his first collection, *Fishing the Sloe-Black River*, is Colum McCann's fascination with the power generated by confronting the other. In his comments about *Dancer*, for example, he confessed how little he knew about ballet and even less about gay experience before he began his research. This first collection of stories may be read as McCann's explorations of confrontations with varieties of the "other" across the spectrum of gender, ethnicity, and sexual orientation. Referencing William Faulkner's Nobel Prize address, McCann called this collection "stories about family, about love and pride, pity, compassion, honesty, violence. All these things that go to making up the human spirit."

"SISTERS"

A case in point is "Sisters," in which the "other" is female. Sheona, the narrator, is a woman but not a "nice girl," who describes her early life of sexual promiscuity and her very different sister. The anorexic Brigid became religious after the death of their mother, "lifted from a cliff by a light wind while out strolling." As a young woman in the 1960's, Sheona came to the United States, attracted by the liberated lifestyle of San Francisco, so different from small-town Ireland, where she recalls her father sobbing in the night after hearing a man speaking of her as a "wee whore." In California, Sheona falls in love with Michael, a Native American, with whom she is arrested for involvement in the marketing of marijuana and for which she is deported to Ireland. In the present from which Sheona tells the

story, she has returned to the United States with the help of Michael, who smuggles her across the Quebec-Maine border to see her dying sister. In middle age, Sheona envisions a life with Michael in the New World.

"BREAKFAST FOR ENRIQUE"

In "Breakfast for Enrique," the confrontation with otherness is built into the story's structure. The storytelling is delegated to the Irishman O'Meara, who is taking care of his partner Enrique, an Argentine, who is suffering from some unidentified ailment, perhaps acquired immunodeficiency syndrome (AIDS) or substance abuse. O'Meara's task of making breakfast and, more generally, of taking care of Enrique's needs seems to be getting more difficult, and their money is running out. Two weeks earlier, Enrique and he had sold their car for $2,700, and the money is already gone, along with the trust fund Enrique's father presumably set up for him. Despite their growing need, Enrique has forbidden O'Meara to ask for more money, presumably because Enrique's father does not approve of his lifestyle. Because readers know only what O'Meara is willing to divulge, it is difficult to know if Enrique needs the cocaine to dull the pain of AIDS or if his "illness" is drug addiction. O'Meara hints at something like the former when he discloses that as "this goes on," Enrique will be at greater risk of bleeding from cuts. He also indicates Enrique's proteins are under attack. The story ends with an image of desire for the regenerative power of the starfish: when torn in two, each half can regrow what it has lost and become whole again.

"FISHING THE SLOE-BLACK RIVER"

The title story in McCann's first collection is less a story than an extended metaphor of a traditional Ireland mourning the loss of her sons to immigration. If the other stories frequently explore Irish discoveries of the empowering experience of confronting alterity, or otherness, this brief story focuses on the cost of that empowerment. It begins "The women fished for their sons in the sloe-black river . . . , while the fathers played football without their sons, in a field a half a mile away," and ends with the encounter of one couple. When the father returns from the football field and says "with a sad laugh: Well, f---k it anyway, we really need some new blood in midfield,'" the mother knows "he

Colum McCann (Press Association via AP Images)

too would go fishing that night, silently slipping out, down to the river to cast in vain." When asked if he writes poems, McCann has remarked that he is afraid of poetry, but his fiction demonstrates his incorporation of metaphor's power to "show forth" meaning in the midst of telling stories.

"Through the Field"

"Through the Field" offers an impressive encounter with the other, as McCann moves from his Irish roots into American culture. In fact, when this story appeared in Dermot Bolger's *The Picador Book of Contemporary Irish Fiction* (1994), Bolger positioned it last to foreground McCann's story as a "classic example of the diaspora" of Irish writers and a forecast of how future editors would "search out the new heart of Irish writing" outside Ireland.

The opening sentences of "Through the Field" set a distinctly un-Irish tone in the story's Texas setting. The narrator, for example, quotes his buddy Kevin's coinage as "hotter than a three-peckered goat," in the field of "klein grass" they are intent on harvesting "before we got ourselves a rain and lost all the nutrient to

seed." The two men have rented the land to grow hay as a weekend job, since their weekday jobs are at the state reform school for delinquents, about twenty of whom are "juvenile capital offenders." The story centers on one boy, Stephen Youngblood, sentenced to thirty years for murdering a man two years earlier, as he tells Ferlinghetti, a University of Texas student who provides counseling in a work-study project. The boy's story is what the narrator has overheard Stephen tell Ferlinghetti over several weeks and the narrator tells Kevin in the hayfield. The narrative strategically asserts the results of Kevin's having heard the murder story--he starts shivering and rushes "home to gather up mine and his family"--and then provides Stephen's story that provokes Kevin's response.

Ferlinghetti has pressed Stephen to tell the story of murdering Bill Harris to solve the mystery of why the boy surrendered to the police instead of fleeing with his victim's wife. The boy had happened in on Harris having sex with Stephen's mother while his father was away at work. Stephen goes at Harris with a baseball bat, but ends up in the hospital after Harris kicks him in the mouth. When Stephen later visits Harris's wife to expose her husband's infidelity she seduces the boy, who is fourteen, and they begin a sexual affair. His name, after all, is "Youngblood." After Harris finds Stephen in bed with his wife and beats him, the boy returns with a rifle and shoots Harris. At last Stephen admits to Ferlinghetti he surrendered to the police because he was afraid of the dark. Kevin, the reader learns, goes to get his children and the narrator's that night because Kevin does not want any of them to fear the dark. The two families end up dancing and laughing through the field. In the last sentences the narrator says he "knew right then and there what Kevin was doing," but he never tells the reader. As a storyteller, he knows that meaning is less to be explained than to be felt.

"Cathal's Lake"

McCann told interviewer Stephen Camelio that this is McCann's favorite story. He indicates its roots are in Irish mythology, particularly the myth of the Children of Lir, the sons and daughters of the sea god who were changed into swans. He tells Camelio that another source is the Jewish myth of the thirty-six saints who inhabit the world as working men--farmers, carpenters, shoemakers, and more. Cathal is one of those God forgot and who must bear the sorrows of his people.

Cathal seems to work in an infernal world, where it has become his burden to free the entrapped young swans from the earth and set them sailing on the lake. The old Irish myth of the Children of Lir provides the narrative with its metaphor of transformation, loss, and hope for freedom. The "Troubles" are turning Ireland's young, her hope for the future, into the victims of hatred and violence, and one can only hope that one day, like the swans in the myth, they will be set free.

Everything in This Country Must

Like "Cathal's Lake," these two stories and novella focus upon issues of an otherness closer to home, the "North," or "Northern Ireland." Even the name is contested: The Irish, especially in the "North," the old kingdom of Ulster, often reject the name "Northern Ireland" as an acknowledgment of British rule in their island. McCann wanted to write about "the Troubles" but struggled to find an approach until it came to him to write through the children's viewpoint. During the sectarian conflict in the 1980's, McCann was a teenager and recalls his mother, born in County Derry, watching the news and shaking her head at the sadness of the death and destruction in her homeland.

"Everything in This Country Must," the title story, focuses upon fifteen-year-old Katie, the narrator, who struggles to understand her father's feelings. Grieving the loss of Katie's mother and brother, accidentally hit by a truck occupied by British soldiers sent in to quell the Irish uprising, the father feels no gratitude when his favorite horse is saved from drowning by the "Brits." He shoots the horse, lifting his unexpected act of violence into a statement of the North's pain and anger against British rule.

"Wood" demonstrates that during the Troubles something much less significant than a horse could become "political." McCann noted that he overheard someone say that, in the North, "Even a piece of wood has politics." He added that this remark "had played itself in my imagination for years," while he puzzled over its meaning. Eventually he decided that even something as ordinary as wood could be associated with politics in the North. It took him four months to write the story, with all its "visions and revisions."

The impetus to the action is the visit of the "man with the big car," a leading "Orangeman," ordering forty poles to carry Ulster Unionist banners in a parade. Andrew, the boy-narrator, recalls this man with the "Union Jack in his lapel" from his (Presbyterian) "church," marking the family as Ulster Unionists, resisting the merging of "Northern Ireland" with the Republic. For the young teenager, the poles his mother cuts represent a political act, since his paralytic father is not to know about her activity. To the father they would represent an act of betrayal, since he has refused to support the Orangemen's marches, saying, "It's just meanness that celebrates other people dying."

Hunger Strike was written as a short story but revised as a novella, allowing the narrative to develop the viewpoint character, Kevin. At thirteen, Kevin struggles to deal with several major issues, not the least of which is the onset of puberty, with its evidence that biologically he has achieved manhood, while psychologically and socially he is still a boy. He seems a "typical" teenager in his irritable, pouty resentment against a mother who continues to treat him as the boy he is. Following his father's death in an accident six years earlier and the escalating sectarian violence in the North, she has moved him from Derry to Galway, in the Republic. Kevin, who feels the helpless prisoner of others and forces beyond his control, is drawn to his father's brother, incarcerated by the British government for violence against the state. Like other Irish (Catholic) internees, the uncle is demonstrating to achieve prisoner-of-war status through a hunger strike. This tactic has replaced the earlier strategies of internees who refused to wear prison garb and smeared the cell walls with their excrement to express outrage at their treatment as common criminals.

Kevin is drawn sympathetically toward his own "hunger strike." He tries to stop eating, but his growing body refuses to comply, and he attempts instead to resist the substance of his mother's love and his increasing affection for an old, impoverished Lithuanian couple who treat him as a grandson. The man, for example, teaches him how to paddle a kayak built for two. Ironically the old woman is a terrible cook, but when she kisses him on his head the hungry Kevin accepts her offering. Overnight the boy feels transformed into a man, beginning to put away childish things and to express love more freely for his mother and the old couple. The inevitable death of his uncle, after the false hope of his survival, turns Kevin temporarily into an "angry young man" again, attempting to smash the kayak, an emblem of his maturing capacity for love. Presumably it is a temporary setback, and the narrative radiates a restrained confidence that Kevin will survive this rite of passage.

Oᴛʜᴇʀ ᴍᴀᴊᴏʀ ᴡᴏʀᴋs

ʟᴏɴɢ ꜰɪᴄᴛɪᴏɴ: *Songdogs*, 1995; *This Side of Brightness*, 1998; *Dancer*, 2003; *Zoli*, 2006; *Let the Great World Spin*, 2009.

Bɪʙʟɪᴏɢʀᴀᴘʜʏ

Cusatis, John. *Understanding Colum McCann*. Columbia: University of South Carolina Press, 2011. Traces McCann's life, from his early days a sportswriter to his illustrious career as the author of international best sellers.

Mari, Catherine. "Tell-Tale Ellipsis in Colum McCann's *Everything in This Country Must*." *Journal of the Short Story in English* 40 (2003): 47-56. Demonstrates how McCann addresses the Troubles indirectly but powerfully in this collection.

Rich, Motoko. "Significant (Little) Moments Pulled from Obscurity." *The New York Times*, November 27, 2009. Interview with McCann after winning the National Book Award for his novel *Let the Great World Spin* reveals his methods of research and choice of themes, which are reflected as well in his short fiction.

Earl G. Ingersoll

Iᴀɴ MᴄEᴡᴀɴ

Born: Aldershot, England; June 21, 1948

Pʀɪɴᴄɪᴘᴀʟ sʜᴏʀᴛ ꜰɪᴄᴛɪᴏɴ

First Love, Last Rites, 1975

In Between the Sheets, and Other Stories, 1978

Oᴛʜᴇʀ ʟɪᴛᴇʀᴀʀʏ ꜰᴏʀᴍs

Ian McEwan (EE-ehn mehk-YEW-ehn) turned to longer forms after beginning his career as a writer of short fiction. He published his first novel, *The Cement Garden*, in 1978, and since then he has published ten other novels, including *The Child in Time* (1987), *Amsterdam* (1998), *Atonement* (2001), *Saturday* (2005), *On Chesil Beach* (2007), and *Solar* (2010). McEwan has also written plays for the stage, radio, and television, as well as the children's book *The Daydreamer* (1994).

Aᴄʜɪᴇᴠᴇᴍᴇɴᴛs

Ian McEwan has been the recipient of numerous awards in the United Kingdom, the United States, and elsewhere. His first collection of short fiction, *First Love, Last Rites*, won the Somerset Maugham Award in 1976. His novels have been short-listed for the Man Booker Prize several times, with *Amsterdam* receiving this prestigious honor in 1998. *The Child in Time* won the 1987 Whitbread Novel of the Year Award, the Prix Fémina Etranger (1993), and Germany's Shakespeare Prize (1999); *The Ploughman's Lunch* won the *Evening Standard* Award for best screenplay.

Atonement received the W. H. Smith Literary Award (2002), the National Book Critics' Circle Fiction Award (2003), the *Los Angeles Times* Prize for Fiction (2003), and the Santiago Prize for the European Novel (2004); the novel was also adapted for a film released in 2007. In 2006, McEwan won the James Tait Black Memorial Prize for his novel *Saturday*; *On Chesil Beach* received the Galaxy Book of the Year award at the 2008 British Book Awards ceremonies, at which McEwan was also named *Reader's Digest* Author of the Year. In addition, he became a Commander of the Order of the British Empire in 2000.

Biography

Ian Russel McEwan was born in Aldershot, England, on June 21, 1948, where his father, David McEwan, a career military man, was stationed. His mother, Rose Moore McEwan, the widow of a soldier killed in World War II, had two older children, and McEwan considered himself "psychologically, an only child." He spent his childhood at military bases in Singapore and Libya before returning to England in 1959 to attend a state-run boarding school and then enter the University of Sussex, from which he graduated with a B.A. honors degree in English in 1970.

During his third year at Sussex, he had begun to write fiction, and he decided to enter the M.A. program at the University of East Anglia because he could "submit a little fiction instead of writing a thesis." After graduating in 1971, he spent a year traveling before placing a story, "Homemade," with the *New American Review*. His first book, *First Love, Last Rites*, which developed out of his graduate thesis, was published in 1975. Explaining that he sometimes felt confined by fiction, McEwan began to write screenplays for television and films, and composed an oratorio, *Or Shall We Die?* (pr., pb. 1983), about nuclear annihilation, which was performed by the London Symphony Orchestra. His primary area of work, however, is the novel, and many of his novels have received both critical acclaim and popular success.

Analysis

Ian McEwan's short fiction was a significant element in the transformation of British literature during the 1970's from the gritty realism of the Angry Young Men and the still genteel social explorations of more traditional authors toward the anarchic, dystopic, neogothic postmodern writing of a generation responding to the fragmentation, fracture, and aggression of a postcolonial society in convulsive transition. Following the temporary euphoria of the "swinging London" of the 1960's, McEwan and contemporaries like Martin Amis, Angela Carter, J. G. Ballard, and Will Self completely

Ian McEwan (Press Association via AP Images)

removed and discarded a veneer of semirespectability to reveal and examine what they regarded as the essence of life in the British Isles. While some critics accused McEwan of dwelling in depravity, he has insisted that he is illuminating some of the most fundamental aspects of the human condition and that the base impulses to which his characters respond reveal essential aspects of human nature usually unacknowledged.

Like Ballard, McEwan has envisioned a late twentieth century world in which technological innovations have undermined human interaction; like Carter, he has explored the darkest regions of the human psyche in a style that recalls the almost delicious horror of the classic gothic genre; like Amis, he has looked with scathing contempt at the stupidity and opacity of people at their most selfish and narcissistic; and like Self, he has described with apparent relish the fullest range of the physical, examining the body with curiosity and an almost obsessive fascination. Nonetheless, McEwan has maintained, "I can't locate myself inside any shared, any sort of community taste, aesthetic ambition or critical position or anything else."

Aside from an understandable preference for avoiding categorization or superficial grouping, McEwan's expression of singularity is an attempt to provoke a discussion of his work that is not reduced to a reiteration of subjects like incest, sexual violence, and murder, which make his short fiction troubling for some readers. The shocking or macabre features of many stories are disturbing, attracting the initial attention a young writer might require, but the most successful stories use sensational detail and situation as a way to introduce questions about the societal norms that permit or encourage such behavior. McEwan, in his short fiction, seeks to understand without endorsing the characters he depicts and to convey the entropic turmoil that has resulted in the disintegration of the structure that supported relationships between people in earlier times.

First Love, Last Rites

A summary catalog of the central subjects of McEwan's first collection, *First Love, Last Rites*, suggests the sources of discomfort that produced uneasy responses from some commentators. The stories concern calculated, passionless incest ("Homemade"), compassionless control ("Solid Geometry"), exploitation and humiliation ("Disguises"), affectless murder ("Butterfly"), blatant sexual exhibitionism ("Cocker"), and a hideous rat as a symbol of pregnancy ("First Love, Last Rites"). The protagonists--frequently the narrators--of these stories range from the not particularly appealing to the pathetic and repulsive. McEwan explained his choices in 1979 by saying that he needed the tension of "what is bad and difficult and unsettling . . . to start me writing." His interest in the actions of his characters leads to an intense probing of the psychological basis for their motivation and derives from his desire to identify, describe, and, at least implicitly, condemn the social forces that have resulted in their isolation. McEwan's characters are outcasts or outsiders, marginal figures effectively beyond the reach of what social support might still be available, and only in the title story is there a suggestion of a personal relationship that might sustain and support a degree of hope for the future.

"In Between the Sheets"

Many of the protagonists of *First Love, Last Rites* are adolescents, in accordance with McEwan's feeling that this cohort is an

> extraordinary, special case of people; they're close to childhood, and yet they are constantly baffled and irritated by the initiations into what's on the other side.

He goes on to say that "short stories, and especially first-person narratives--can thrive on a point of view which is somehow dislocated, removed." One of the limitations of this position, however, is an almost total enclosure within the mind of the narrator, a factor which McEwan addressed in the title story of his next collection, *In Between the Sheets, and Other Stories*. The title story is about a single father, Stephen Cooke, who arranges a visit from his fourteen-year-old daughter Miranda and her strange close friend, the diminutive Charmian. The third-person narrative enables McEwan to remain slightly beyond the central characters while evoking their thoughts and feelings, especially Stephen's, through a persistent probing of their responses and reactions. The awkwardness that Stephen feels in his daughter's presence, an uncertainty growing out of separation and compounded by her growth toward young womanhood (and sexual echoes of Stephen's estranged wife) and by the mystery of Miranda's friendship with Charmian, is complicated but also ameliorated by his rediscovery of a deep care and concern for her. The title, taken from a popular rock song, is obviously designed to emphasize the sexual component of many of the stories, but the prior line "Don'cha think there's a place for you" is equally important as an indication of the need for a comfortable or safe place in any relationship.

"Dead as They Come"

"Dead as They Come" joins some of McEwan's prevalent concerns in a very compact, consistently intense narrative delivered by a wealthy middle-aged man who relates his obsessive fascination with a store-window mannequin. The story evolves as a kind of continuing present-tense confession that is clearly a record of progressive mental deterioration but which reads like a completely rational account of understandable behavior. The erudition, self-rational-ization, sexual absorption, increasingly violent re-sponses to frustration when will and desire are thwarted, and vividly graphic and explicit description of action are features of McEwan's writing at its most effective. The narrator is, characteristically, com-pletely removed from any social constraint and is be-reft of any human relationship which might alleviate his rage. The story almost functions as an allegory because the figure of desire has no mind or soul of her own and is seen only through the consciousness of a person who does not care about another's inner life. The fact that she is literally a model of a woman rather than a woman as supermodel is part of McE-wan's point.

"Psychopolis"

"Psychopolis" reaches beyond the limits of the short story toward the broader social and personal ex-plorations that have marked McEwan's novels. His narrator is a young Englishman, probably closer to McEwan's own sensibility than any other character in the short fiction. This story developed from McEwan's brief visit to Los Angeles, a city he uses as the template for the chaotic energy of a contemporary Western city in the last decades of the twentieth cen-tury. Adrift but exalted by the pulse of life in a strange land, open to experience, friendly with other self-ab-sorbed but not unpleasant young people, the narrator is alternately bemused and fascinated by what seems like the inexplicable but compelling behavior of his friends, or more accurately, social associates in what he calls "a city of narcissists." The bizarre situations, sexual latency, and lurking semiviolence that is common to McEwan's fiction is present in "Psychopolis," but instead of a feeling of dread, de-spair, or, even worse, benumbed indifference, the un-named narrator generally regards his own confusion and his friends' peculiarities with a degree of humor that widens the field of the story beyond the circum-scribed lives that are effectively prisons in other sto-ries. There are more distinct characters in this story than in any other one; these characters' vehement if somewhat incoherent arguments indicate a degree of complexity to their lives, and the narrator shares a few moments of exuberance and even temporary joy

with the others, which suggests his wayward quest for "something difficult and free" is not automati-cally doomed to failure.

Other major works

LONG FICTION: *The Cement Garden*, 1978; *The Comfort of Strangers*, 1981; *The Child in Time*, 1987; *The Innocent*, 1990; *Black Dogs*, 1992; *Enduring Love*, 1997; *Amsterdam*, 1998; *Atonement*, 2001; *Saturday*, 2005; *On Chesil Beach*, 2007; *Solar*, 2010.

PLAY: *Or Shall We Die?*, pr., pb. 1983 (oratorio; music by Michael Berkeley); *For You*, pr., pb. 2008 (libretto; music by Michael Berkeley).

SCREENPLAYS: *The Ploughman's Lunch*, 1983; *Soursweet*, 1988 (adaptation of Timothy Mo's novel *Sour Sweet*); *The Good Son*, 1993 (adaptation of Joseph Ruben's novel); *The Innocent*, 1995 (adaptation of his novel).

TELEPLAYS: *Jack Flea's Birthday Celebration*, 1976; *The Imitation Game*, 1980; *The Imitation Game: Three Plays for Television*, 1981 (also known as *The Imitation Game, and Other Plays*, 1981); *The Last Day of Summer*, 1983 (adaptation of his short story).

NONFICTION: *Conversations with Ian McEwan*, 2010 (Ryan Roberts, editor).

CHILDREN'S LITERATURE: *Rose Blanche*, 1985 (rewritten from translation of original by Roberto Innocenti); *The Daydreamer*, 1994.

Bibliography

Baxter, Jeannette. "Surrealist Encounters in Ian McEwan's Early Work." In *Ian McEwan: Contemporary Critical Perspectives*, edited by Sebastian Groes. New York: Continuum, 2009. Baxter's examination of McEwan's early works includes discussion of his two short-story collections and some of their indi-vidual stories.

Broughton, Lynda, "Portrait of the Subject as a Young Man: The Construction of Masculinity Ironized in 'Male' Fiction." *Subjectivity and Literature from the Romantics to the Present Day*. New York: Pinter, 1991. After a general survey of "feminist critical practice," Broughton presents an intellectually pow-erful and provocative discussion of the male narrator in "Homemade" as an exemplar of contemporary masculine concerns.

Childs, Peter, ed. *The Fiction of Ian McEwan*. New York: Palgrave Macmillan, 2006. A compilation of previously published reviews, essays, and articles about McEwan's fiction, organized in chronological order of his works' publication. The first two chapters focus on his two short-story collections and include articles that analyze the focus, theme, and scope of *First Love, Last Rites*; provide a feminist perspective of this collection; examine the representation of male sexuality, sadism, and masochism in *In Between the Sheets*; and explore how McEwan depicts the United States in "Psychopolis."

Hanson, Claire. *Short Stories and Short Fictions, 1880-1980*. New York: St. Martin's Press, 1985. Examines several of McEwan's short stories in terms of their explorations of the creative process, especially his innovative uses of form and structure.

Hunter, Adrian. "Angela Carter and Ian McEwan." In *The Cambridge Introduction to the Short Story in English*. Cambridge, England: Cambridge University Press, 2007. Places McEwan's work within the context of postmodern fiction. Analyzes several stories, including "Butterflies," "First Love, Last Rites," and "Pornography."

Malcolm, David. *Understanding Ian McEwan*. Columbia: University of South Carolina Press, 2002. Analyzes McEwan's work, placing it in the context of late-twentieth-century British literature and examining its relationship to feminism, concern with rationalism and science, and moral perspective.

Chapter 2 provides a close reading of the stories in McEwan's two short-fiction collections.

McEwan, Ian. *Conversations with Ian McEwan*. Edited by Ryan Roberts. Jackson: University Press of Mississippi, 2010. Reprints sixteen interviews with McEwan conducted during the past three decades. Among other subjects, McEwan discusses his writing process, the major themes in his fiction, and the state of literature in twenty-first-century society. Several of the interviewers are notable contemporary writers, such as Zadie Smith and Martin Amis.

Ricks, Christopher. "Adolescence and After: An Interview with Ian McEwan," *Listener* (April 12, 1979): 527. A characteristically candid and revealing conversation, with McEwan touching on many important aspects of his short fiction.

Slay, Jack. *Ian McEwan*. New York: Twayne, 1996. An excellent overview of McEwan's writing life, with detailed, incisive discussions of the short fiction.

Vannatta, Dennis. *The English Short Story, 1945-1980: A Critical History*. New York: Twayne, 1985. Identifies and explains the aesthetic strategies underlying McEwan's use of unconventional situations, which Vannatta claims are ultimately connected to concerns that are "determinedly traditional, unrelentingly moral," focusing on "Homemade," "Butterflies," "Disguises," "Dead as They Come," and "In Between the Sheets."

Leon Lewis

John McGahern

Born: Leitrim, Ireland; November 12, 1934
Died: Dublin, Ireland; March 30, 2006

PRINCIPAL SHORT FICTION

Nightlines, 1970
Getting Through, 1978
High Ground, 1985
The Collected Stories, 1992
Creatures of the Earth: New and Selected Stories,
   2007

OTHER LITERARY FORMS

After the publication of his first novel, *The Barracks* (1963), John McGahern (ma-GAH-ehrn) encountered trouble with the Catholic Church and the Irish Censorship Board because of his second novel, *The Dark* (1965); as a result of these experiences, McGahern decided to fictionalize the loss of his teaching job in *The Leavetaking* (1974, revised 1984) and parody the problems of writing about sex in *The Pornographer* (1979). *Amongst Women* (1990) is his most highly praised novel. In addition to his novels and short-fiction collections, McGahern also wrote a play, *The Power of Darkness* (pb. 1991), and his autobiography, *All Will Be Well: A Memoir* (2005). The collection *Love of the World: Essays* was published posthumously in 2009.

ACHIEVEMENTS

John McGahern's first novel, *The Barracks*, was the first prose work to win the A. A. Memorial Award in Ireland, and he was also awarded the Arts Council Macauley Fellowship for this work. *Amongst Women*, an international success, won the Aer Lingus Prize, was a finalist for the Man Booker Prize in 1990, was a bestseller in Ireland, and brought him wide recognition. McGahern received a Lannan Literary Award for Fiction in 2003.

BIOGRAPHY

John McGahern was born in Dublin in 1934, the son of a police officer. He was raised in County Roscommon, in the west of Ireland. He received his education at Presentation College in Carrick-on-Shannon, St. Patrick's Training College in Drumcondra, and University College in Dublin. For a brief time after receiving his degree, he worked as a laborer in London but soon returned to teach at St. John the Baptist Boys' National School in Clontarf. After seven years of teaching, he published *The Barracks* in 1963, which was well received and highly honored.

McGahern took a year's leave from teaching after the publication of *The Barracks* to go to London and write his second novel, *The Dark*. When the book was banned by the Irish Censorship Board because of its treatment of sexuality and child abuse, McGahern lost his teaching job. After appeals and legal action failed to reverse the board's decision, McGahern began a career as a visiting lecturer in the United States, England, and Europe. He later returned to settle in Ireland. McGahern published his autobiography, *All Will Be Well*, a year before his death from cancer on March 30, 2006.

ANALYSIS

John McGahern's writing career was plagued by controversy because he challenged many of Ireland's past religious, social, and sexual values. Although such abstract social issues are not at the center of his stories, there are no sentimental images of Ireland in them either. Many of the stories are darkly pessimistic, and they are not told in a garrulous, Irish storyteller voice. Instead, they are concise, controlled, and clipped--much more characteristic of Chekhovian writing than a folklorish oral style. It is not the speaking voice of Frank O'Connor that dominates these stories but the stylized tone of so-called modern minimalism.

John McGahern (Press Association via AP Images)

Because of the self-conscious control of McGahern's narrative technique, his short stories have received as much critical analysis as those of Mary Lavin and Edna O'Brien. These writers are both realistic and lyrical at once, as is typical of the modern Joycean tradition, pushing mere description of the material world to unobtrusive symbolic significance. McGahern was also typical of that tradition; although his stories have a recognizable social context, he was not interested in confronting his characters with the abstractions of social limitations. More often in his short stories, his characters face the universal challenges of responsibility, guilt, commitment, and death.

"KOREA"

"Korea" is a deceptively simple story with a seemingly misleading title. Although the story is quite brief, it contains within it another story, which a father tells, about being captured just after the revolution in 1919, when the British were shooting prisoners. The father describes a young man of sixteen or seventeen who, after being shot, plucked at the tunic over his heart as if to tear out the bullets, his buttons flying into the air. The father says that years later, while he was on his honeymoon, he saw bursting furze pods, which reminded him of the young man's buttons.

After the father urges his son to go to America, the boy overhears him excitedly telling a man that American soldiers' lives are insured for $10,000 and that, for the duration of a soldier's service, his parents receive $250 a month. Later when the boy tells his father he has decided he will not go to America, the father says it will be his own funeral if he refuses this chance and comes to nothing in "this fool of a country." Although this seems to be a story about a calculating father willing to sacrifice his own son for money, the boy does not see it that way, feeling closer to the father than ever before.

"PEACHES"

Both in terms of the clipped, repetitive syntax and the basic situation of a couple living in Spain, "Peaches" is McGahern's most Hemingwayesque story. It begins with a prevailing metaphor, also reminiscent of Ernest Hemingway, of a dead shark that lies stinking on the beach beneath a couple's house. The couple, referred to simply as "the man" and "the woman," have come to Spain, where they can live cheaply and where he can write and she can paint; however, the two do little more than quarrel, have sex, and talk about why they are unhappy, much as Hemingway's couples do.

The title metaphor of peaches brings the couple's lethargic and unproductive lifestyle to a head when the magistrate of the area invites them to his house to try his peaches, making it clear that it is the woman in whom he is interested by stuffing peaches into the breast pockets of her dress. When he urges them to come again so they can swim naked in his pool, the couple feel both shocked and bewildered. The story ends with the woman feeling somewhat responsible for what has happened, although she blames the man for not doing anything when the magistrate stuffed the peaches in her pockets. At the end, she says that the incident is no more than what she deserved.

"THE COUNTRY FUNERAL"

Described by several reviewers as McGahern's short-fiction masterpiece, this story has been compared to Joyce's "The Dead" (1914). The surface similarities are clear enough; the story approaches novella length, and it focuses on a social ritual, albeit a funeral instead of a dinner party, that ultimately leads to a kind of communal affirmation. The story centers on three brothers who go to the funeral of an uncle they never really liked. The focus is both on the discrepancy between their view of the uncle and others' views of him and on the relationship of the past to the present.

As in "The Dead," nothing much happens in this story except a routine, ritual meeting, common to Irish wakes, in which friends and relatives tell stories about the dead person. One of the brothers, Philly, who has come back home from the oil fields, is the most affected by the death, impressed by the respect everyone shows to his uncle's memory; Fonsie, who is confined to a wheelchair, is the most acerbic and sarcastic of the brothers, sneering that everyone is respected for a short time after he or she dies because he or she does not have to be lived with anymore. Philly, who says he cannot work in the oil fields forever, wants to buy his uncle's farm, where his mother was raised, and the story ends as undramatically as it has proceeded throughout.

"The Beginning of an Idea"

As the title suggests, this story actually begins with the idea that dominates it: the first sentences of Eva Lindberg's notebook, which describe how on a hot day the corpse of Anton Chekhov was carried home to Moscow on an ice wagon with the word "Oysters" chalked on the side of it. McGahern's story then describes, almost word for word, a brief Chekhov story, entitled "Oysters," about a young boy and his father who, begging on the street, are given oysters to eat by prosperous diners, who laugh when the boy also tries to eat the shells.

Eva Lindberg gives up her work as a theater director and her affair with a married man to go to Spain to write an imaginary biography of Chekhov beginning with the oyster story and ending with the story of the oyster wagon. The lines in her journal haunt her and are repeated several times throughout the story. However, when she arrives at the isolated house where she will be staying, she cannot write, taking on routine translation jobs instead. The only person she sees is a local police officer named Manolo, who visits her daily. When she agrees to get him some contraceptives, which are illegal in Spain, Manolo and the police chief tell her she

will go to jail unless she has sex with them. Repeating the Chekhov sentences in her mind like a mantra, she gives in and afterward packs up and leaves, feeling rage about her own foolishness. On the train she has the bitter taste of oysters in her mouth, and when a wagon passes she has a sudden desire to see if the word "Oysters" is chalked on it.

"All Sorts of Impossible Things"

The central metaphor of this story is a brown hat, which has been worn by a teacher, James Sharkey, for the past twenty years. The central event is his friend Tom Lennon's facing exams to determine whether he is eligible to become a permanent instructor; Lennon's anxiety about the exams is complicated by the fact that he is frail and has a weak heart.

As is frequently the case in McGahern's short fiction, the story has a story within it: Twenty years previously, when Sharkey's hair began to fall out, he felt his life slipping away and was desperate to moor it to a woman; however, from the day the woman rejected him, he has never taken off his brown hat. When he is warned that he must take off his hat in church, he tells the priest that his encroaching baldness has the effect on him of *timor mortis*, the fear of death, so he has decided to cover it up.

However, the more serious sign of mortality in the story is Lennon's weak heart, for when he goes to take his exams, he falls dead. Sharkey feels a certain amazement that it is Lennon lying there and not he. He keeps Lennon's dog and after the funeral experiences the same rush of feelings that occurred when his hair started to fall out. Now, however, he has a wild longing to throw away his hat, find a woman, and enter the dog in a race to win the silver cup. The story ends with his mind racing with a desire for "all sorts of impossible things."

Other major works

Long fiction: *The Barracks*, 1963; *The Dark*, 1965; *The Leavetaking*, 1974, revised 1984; *The Pornographer*, 1979; *Amongst Women*, 1990; *By the Lake*, 2002 (pb. in England as *That They May Face the Rising Sun*, 2002).

Play: *The Power of Darkness*, pb. 1991.

Nonfiction: *All Will Be Well: A Memoir*, 2005; *Dear*

Mr McLaverty--: The Literary Correspondence of John McGahern and Michael McLaverty, 1959-1980, 2006 (John Killen, editor); *Love of the World: Essays*, 2009 (Stanley van der Ziel, editor).

BIBLIOGRAPHY

Banville, John. "Big News from Small Worlds." *The New York Review of Books* 40 (April 8, 1993): 22-24. In this extended review of McGahern's *The Collected Stories*, fellow novelist Banville discusses a characteristic often criticized in the stories--their floating quality, resulting from the fact that they take place in no discernible place or time period.

Bradbury, Nicola. "High Ground." In *Re-Reading the Short Story*, edited by Clare Hanson. New York: Macmillan, 1989. Discusses "Parachutes" and "High Ground" as works that embody the short story's technique of being both involved and objectively distant at once. Briefly describes the historical and geographical contexts of McGahern's stories.

Brown, Terence. "John McGahern's *Nightlines:* Tone, Technique, and Symbol." In *The Irish Short Story*, edited by Patrick Rafroidi and Terence Brown. London: Colin, Smythe, 1979. Discusses McGahern's use of the Irish storytelling mode. Argues that he tries to exploit symbolist possibilities in physical properties without resorting to the traditional symbols of church and religion.

_____. "Redeeming the Time: The Novels of John McGahern and John Banville." In *The British and Irish Novel Since 1960*, edited by James Acheson. New York: St. Martin's Press, 1991. Discusses McGahern's literary realism, which has allowed him to treat subjects that have always been taboo in Irish fiction. Argues that in his novels the protagonist's world is explored with such obsessiveness that it reminds the reader of the short story.

Cahalan, James M. "Female and Male Perspectives on Growing Up Irish in Edna O'Brien, John McGahern, and Brian Moore." *Colby Quarterly* 31 (March, 1995): 55-73. Focusing primarily on McGahern's novel *The Dark* but providing a context for his short stories, Cahalan discusses McGahern's treatment of father-son relationships and the difficulty of trying to come of age in Ireland in the 1940's.

Ingman, Heather. "John McGahern and Éilís Ní Dhuibhne." In *A History of the Irish Short Story*. New York: Cambridge University Press, 2009. This chapter in Ingman's examination of the development of the Irish short story provides an overview of short fiction written from 1980 to the early twenty-first century, followed by detailed readings of some of McGahern's short stories.

Maher, Eamon. *John McGahern: From the Local to the Universal*. Dublin: Liffey Press, 2003. A guide to McGahern's fiction, analyzing his themes, scenes, scenarios, and characters. Argues that while McGahern's works on the surface seem to originate from a limited, local source, his writings actually present profound depictions of the entire scope of human experience.

Malcolm, David. Understanding John McGahern. Columbia: University of South Carolina Press, 2007. An introductory overview of McGahern's life, career, vision, and techniques. Devotes individual chapters to examinations of the short-story collections *Nightlines*, *Getting Through*, and *High Ground*.

Quinn, Antoinette. "Varieties of Disenchantment: Narrative Technique in John McGahern's Short Stories." *Journal of the Short Story in English* 13 (Autumn, 1989): 77-89. Describes McGahern's characters as obsessed with death but ill prepared for the infinite. Discusses how the characters are disappointed with the everyday, disillusioned by love, and in retreat from life.

Sampson, Denis. *Outstaring Nature's Eye: The Fiction of John McGahern*. Washington, D.C.: Catholic University of America Press, 1993. One of the most comprehensive treatments of McGahern's work. Traces his artistic development and the growth of his reputation in Ireland and France. Includes thorough bibliographies.

Van der Ziel, Stanley. "John McGahern: *Nightlines*." In *A Companion to the British and Irish Short Story*, edited by Cheryl Alexander Malcolm and David Malcolm. Malden, Mass.: Wiley-Blackwell, 2008. An examination of McGahern's short fiction, focusing on his first short-story collection and discussing many of his individual stories, including "Korea," "Peaches," and "The Recruiting Officer."

Charles E. May

           Critical Survey of Short Fiction

ROHINTON MISTRY

Born: Bombay (now Mumbai), India; July 3, 1952

PRINCIPAL SHORT FICTION

Tales from Firozsha Baag, 1987 (pb. in the United States as *Swimming Lessons, and Other Stories from Firozsha Baag,* 1989)
"*The Scream,*" 2008

OTHER LITERARY FORMS

Rohinton Mistry (roh-HIHN-tuhn MIHS-tree) is known primarily as a novelist. His three novels were written a number of years apart but will no doubt be added to in years to come. Like the short stories, they are set in Bombay (Mumbai), and deal largely with the Parsi community, though, as novels, their narrative spreads wider. They also make political comments in a way the short stories refrain from doing. *A Fine Balance* (1995) is critical of Indira Gandhi and the state of emergency that existed during her regime as prime minister of India.

ACHIEVEMENTS

Rohinton Mistry has added both to the corpus of Indian writing in English and to Canadian contemporary writing. His books are set almost entirely in India. A few deal with the immigrant experience of Indians, specifically in Canada. It is certainly easy to see why immigrants leave India, especially those who traditionally had been part of India's elite, such as the Parsis. Perhaps his main achievement has been to re-create an audience for Canadian literature in the United States following the popularity of Margaret Atwood's earlier work.

Such a Long Journey (1991) won the Governor-General's Literary Award for Fiction in 1991, a Canadian honor. The novel also won the Trillium Award, the Commonwealth Writers Prize, and the Books in Canada

Award for the best novel. It also was a Booker Prize finalist. *A Fine Balance* won a similar slew of prizes: the 1995 Giller Prize, the 1995 Royal Society of Literature's Winifred Holtby Prize, the 1995 Canada-Australian Literary Prize, the 1996 *Los Angeles Times* Book Award for fiction, and the 1996 Commonwealth Writers Prize. The novel also was shortlisted for the Booker Prize, as was *Family Matters* (2001). *Family Matters* won the Kiryama Pacific Rim Book Prize. *Tales from Firozsha Baag* was shortlisted for the Governor-General's Literary Award for fiction in 1988.

BIOGRAPHY

Rohinton Mistry was born in Bombay, India. His parents, Behram and Freny Mistry, were of Parsi origin. The Parsis belong to the ancient religion Zoroastrianism, which originated in Persia. In Indian society, the Parsis were considered a distinct group, separate from the Hindu caste system. Parsis tended to be better educated and often held professional posts. In British India they thrived; however, they could not hold an elite place in the new India after independence in 1947. The Parsis settled mainly around Bombay.

Rohinton Mistry attended Villa Theresa Primary School and St. Xavier High School, both Roman Catholic institutions. His parents embraced Indian and British culture, and Mistry was comfortable speaking in English, although he was fluent in Hindi, the national language, and Gujerati, the state language. As a high school student, he was in a folk rock band.

He took a B.S. in economics and mathematics at St. Xavier's College, part of the University of Bombay, graduating in 1975. That year he immigrated to Toronto, Canada, to join his fiancé, Freny Elavia. They were married that same year and later became Canadian citizens. At first Mistry worked as a clerk at the Canadian Imperial Bank of Commerce, becoming supervisor of the customer services department.

Up to this point, Mistry had exhibited few literary leanings. In 1978, he began studying literature and philosophy at the University of Toronto as a part-time student, obtaining a B.A. in 1983. In 1982, he began writing, soon winning success with a short story, "One Sunday," in 1983; he was awarded the $250 Hart House Literary Prize. The next year, another short story, "Auspicious Occasion," won the prize again. Both stories are in his first collection, *Tales from Firozsha Baag*, published in 1987.

A Canada Council grant in 1985 enabled him to give up his banking job and write full time. That year he also won the Canadian Fiction Magazine Annual Award. The next year he moved to the United States, where his wife had been offered a high school teaching post in Long Beach, California. However, the job did not prove satisfactory, and the couple soon moved back to Toronto.

Mistry's first collect won a good deal of attention, especially the stories dealing with Parsis leaving Bombay and their immigration to North America. The collection was reissued in 1989 in the United States and renamed *Swimming Lessons, and Other Stories from Firozsha Baag*. His first novel followed in 1991. It also centered on the Parsi community of Bombay but also traced the rise of the extreme right-wing Hindu nationalist group, the Shiv Sena. It was later made into a film, and Mistry helped to write the screenplay.

His next novel appeared in 1995; *A Fine Balance* is set during the national emergency imposed by Prime Minister Indira Gandhi, some twenty years earlier. It is a scathing attack on the political forces unleashed by the emergency and the needless disruption to ordinary citizens' lives. Mistry's scenario is far reaching, including Hindu and Muslim society as well as Parsi, and moves into the rural areas around Bombay and the shanty towns of the city. It became a best seller in North America, even making it to Oprah's Book Club list in August, 2001 It has been translated into five languages.

In 1996, Mistry was awarded an honorary doctorate from the University of Ottawa, and on the basis of just three books, he became a well-known Canadian writer. The appearance of *Family Matters* in 2001 further enhanced his reputation. Again, the book centered on the Parsi community of Bombay, but it also covered Hindu-Muslim relationships and gave rise to many insights of a historical and political nature. In 2006, he won the Timothy Findley Award of the Writers' Association of Canada. In 2008, *The Scream* appeared, a short story illustrated by Canadian artist Tony Urquhart. It first appeared as a limited art edition to raise funds, but then it was given a general print run, keeping the illustrations. Mistry has arranged for his papers to be kept at York University in Ontario.

ANALYSIS

Swimming Lessons, and Other Tales from Firozsha Baag, is a linked series of stories involving the inhabitants of an apartment complex in a Bombay suburb. Nearly all the inhabitants are from the Parsi community. Some are professional, but most are either retired or have fairly low-paying jobs, which means their lives are full of financial worries and restraints. The reader receives fragmented insights into the rituals and beliefs of the Parsis and a glimpse at typical life in the sprawling suburbs of India, with the heat, dust, and unsanitary conditions that typify them.

Some of the stories are told as first-person narratives; others are third person. One character is usually the focus of a story, but that character may then reappear as a minor character in another. There is some flow of time, so that a character may feature prominently in one story, only for the reader to be told in a later story he has died. Similarly, some of the children grow up to be students and even to have migrated to North America. One character in particular seems to be a persona for Mistry.

The plots are typical of ordinary lower middle-class urban family life. They contains events so universal that they appeal to any culture, while their difference, their Parsi-tincture, makes their flavor unique and fascinating. Mistry's eye for detail is unerring, though his style is generally plain, within the verbal range of his narrators.

"AUSPICIOUS OCCASION"

The first story in the collection deals with one of the professional families of Firozsha Baag, Rustom the lawyer. He is typically addressed as Rustomji, the "ji" suffix being the customary term of politeness given to professional men. The story deals with one of the Parsi holy days and how Rustom's wife, Mehroo, is looking forward to it. For her it brings happy memories, rather as Christmas does to other cultures. However, it also means certain things have to be done "just right." In fact, everything goes wrong, culminating in the murder of the Parsi priest by the temple caretaker.

Rustom is shown to be a "curmudgeon," often surly and bad-tempered, twenty years older than his wife and impatient with her. His ceremonial dress of pure white receives a red stain on it from chewed betel leaf, symbolically reenacting the red stain of the murdered priest's wound. In a sense, the white could represent the idealism of Mehroo and the meaning of the ritual itself, while the red represents the spoiling of this by the reality of everyday life. In the end, life goes on, a cup of tea representing as much happiness as people are likely to find.

"THE COLLECTORS"

A number of the stories center on the boys of the apartment complex; girls do not seem to exist there. The boys' adventures seem to mirror those of Mistry's

Rohinton Mistry (AP Photo/Alastair Grant)

boyhood. In "The Collectors," two boys stand out: Jehangir, the only son of the Bulsaras, something of a recluse, and very much dominated by his mother; and Pesi, the delinquent son of Dr. Murjor Mody, another of Firozsha Baag's professionals, the head of the Veterinarian College.

Mody has the hobby of stamp-collecting, but his son has no interest in it. Jehangir, a next-door neighbor, is persuaded to become interested, and for a number of Sunday mornings he visits the Modys' to be instructed in how to set about collecting stamps. Mrs. Mody is jealous of her husband's attention to Jehangir and his neglect of Pesi. In the end, it turns out she takes her husband's prize stamp and leads him to think that Jehangir stole it.

At the same time, Jehangir has been stealing stamps, in order to impress Mody. Inevitably this is discovered and he gives up the whole enterprise. Meanwhile, Pesi is sent away to boarding school to keep him out of trouble. At the end of the story, Mody dies suddenly, and his widow confesses to Jehangir her deception. By then, he has moved on in life.

"SQUATTER"

"Squatter" centers on the communal storyteller, Nariman Hansotia, who delights in telling the boys various stories, especially about a legendary Savukshaw, who is by turn a brilliant cricketer, hunter, and everything else. However, the main narrative is intended for Jehangir and any other boys planning to emigrate when they grow up . In a sense, this focuses on Mistry's immigration, the sense of guilt of leaving and the challenges of adaptation to a new culture.

Mistry chooses to treat the topic humorously, by dealing with the would-be immigrant, Sarosh, who promises his mother to return if within ten years he has not adapted totally to Canadian life. The bizarre failure to adapt deals with using the toilet. In India, he defecated by squatting--hence the title--and he cannot do it by sitting. However hard he tries, and he goes to bizarre lengths, he cannot manage it until he is on the airplane on the way back. However, by then, it is too late. Jehangir admires the storyteller's skills, not taking it personally. The reader senses underneath Mistry's anxieties as an Indian writer writing for Canadians.

"SWIMMING LESSONS"

The last story in the collection takes the Indian-in-Canada theme a lot further, by giving the perspective to Kersi, an immigrant to Toronto from Firozsha Baag. The reader has met Kersi and his older brother Percy in several previous stories, "One Sunday" and "Of White Hairs and Cricket." The family members are probably the most Westernized of all the community, and to some extent Kersi represents Mistry. Certainly Kersi sends a book of his published stories back to his parents, and the stories in the book are exactly the stories of *Swimming Lessons.* These stories within a story are perhaps Mistry's one gesture to a postmodernist stance.

The swimming lessons of the title symbolize Kersi's failure to learn to adapt to a different milieu. He has never learned to swim. However, the story suggests Kersi's learning to write is another way for him not only to adapt to a new culture but also to dissipate the guilt of leaving the old one. He is unable to communicate directly with his overprotective parents, but through writing, he conveys his feelings for the past, the family, and his present. The apartment block he lives in near Toronto is remarkably like Firozsha Baag itself. As a final story, it suggests Mistry can move on in his writing career.

"THE SCREAM"

"The Scream" was first published as a freestanding short story with lavish illustrations by Tony Urquhart in a limited edition. In a later general edition the illustrations were largely kept. The title is based on Edvard Munch's famous modernist painting with the same title.

The last story of *Swimming Lessons* involved an old man left stranded by life in an apartment block. Mistry's novel *Family Matters* also centers on an old man, and so does "The Scream." An old man, who has been left stranded in the front room of the apartment block in Bombay by his family, rants at his family and at life in general. His language is marvelous, and the illustrations are weird. It is difficult to know whether this indicates the future direction of Mistry's work or whether it is a once-off joke produced for a special occasion.

OTHER MAJOR WORKS

LONG FICTION: *Such a Long Journey*, 1991; *A Fine Balance*, 1995; *Family Matters*, 2001.

NONFICTION: "Passages," 1988; "The More Important Things," 1989.

BIBLIOGRAPHY

Cooke, Hope. "Beehive in Bombay." *The New York Times*, March 5, 1989. The compressed stories of *Swimming Lessons, and Other Stories from the Firozsha Baag* show Mistry's "antic humor" and his compassion for his characters trapped in an apartment block.

Leckie, Barbara. *Rohinton Mistry and His Works.* Toronto, Ont.: ECW Press, 1995. An early assessment of Mistry's writing until 1995.

Ross, Robert L. "Seeking and Maintaining Balance: Rohinton Mistry's Fiction." *World Literature Today* 73 (1999) 239-244. Based on a reading of *A Fine Balance*, Ross reviews Mistry's understanding of balance in all his fiction.

Singh, Amritjit. "Rohinton Mistry." In *Writers of the Indian Diaspora: A Bio-Bibliographic Critical Sourcebook*, edited by Emmanuel S. Nelson. Westport, Conn.: Greenwood Press, 1993. An early collection of essays and reviews of Mistry's fiction, including the short stories.

David Barratt

GEORGE MOORE

Born: Moore Hall, County Mayo, Ireland; February
24, 1852
Died: London, England; January 21, 1933

PRINCIPAL SHORT FICTION

Parnell and His Island, 1887
Celibates, 1895
The Untilled Field, 1903
Memoirs of My Dead Life, 1906
A Story-Teller's Holiday, 1918
In Single Strictness, 1922
Peronnik the Fool, 1924
Celibate Lives, 1927
A Flood, 1930
*In Minor Keys: The Uncollected Short Stories of
George Moore,* 1985 (David B. Eakin and Helmut
E. Gerber, editors)

OTHER LITERARY FORMS

George Moore began his career as a poet with
Flowers of Passion (1878) and was to go on to write
dramas and several novels, the most enduring and accomplished being *Esther Waters* (1894). He also wrote
art criticism, such as *Modern Painting* (1893), and autobiography, the best known being *Hail and Farewell:
A Trilogy* (1911-1914; *Ave,* 1911; *Salve,* 1912; *Vale,*
1914).

ACHIEVEMENTS

One of the most prolific of the Irish writers of the
late nineteenth and early twentieth centuries, George
Moore published numerous books, which included
seventeen novels, short-story collections, books of literary and art criticism, poetry, autobiography, and social criticism. On his eightieth birthday the London
Times praised his contribution to literature in an article,
signed by many of the major writers of the day, which

recognized his long and serious service to literature,
and his contribution, in particular, to the art of narrative. The Irish Academy was founded in 1932, and
Moore was included in the first list of members.

BIOGRAPHY

George Augustus Moore was born to a wealthy
family at Moore Hall, the family estate in County
Mayo, in the west of Ireland on February 24, 1852. The
family was originally Protestant but through marriage
had become Roman Catholic. He had a spotty education because of his health problems, spending some
time at Oscott, a Catholic boarding school in England.
When he was seventeen, he joined the family in
London, and his formal education ceased. In 1871, he
went to Paris to study painting and began his close association with the French painters and writers. By
1875, he gave up painting as a possible career but retained his interest in art as a critic of contemporary
French painters. He was an acquaintance of the artists
Édouard Manet and Edgar Degas, and the French naturalistic writer Émile Zola, who was a major influence
on him. In 1880, he returned to London and began to
write for a living. His first novel, *A Modern Lover,* appeared in 1883. Always concerned with the problems
of style and content in fiction, he was determined to
follow the French naturalistic writers and to bring their
simplicity and intellectual honesty to British fiction.
He also became a successful art critic and social man-
about-town in London. Lively and outgoing, he was an
outrageous self-promoter, often extolling his skills in
his various texts. He became more and more interested
in Irish letters and politics in the 1890's and became a
director of the Irish Literary Theatre, returning to live
in Ireland in 1901. He returned to London in 1911 and
lived there until his death, continuing his interest in Ireland and writing about Irish life in several genres. He
kept up his sometimes abrasive relationships with other
artists throughout these years, quarreling with William

Butler Yeats in 1902, with Æ (George Russell) in 1918, and later with Frank Harris. He died in London in 1933, and his ashes were deposited on Castle Island within sight of Moore Hall in Ireland.

ANALYSIS

George Moore brought to his short fiction the same theories and intentions that were the mark of all of his work. He wanted to write about ordinary people, and, in particular, about ordinary Irish people. He was determined to follow the late nineteenth century French writers, such as Zola and Gustave Flaubert, and the Russian writers, such as Ivan Turgenev, in attempting a realistic portrayal of life without artistic cleverness or dramatic heightening. His aim was to develop an "oral" style in which the reader would be presented with a sense of intimacy, as if the writer were talking to a friend.

The stories were chosen to avoid extravagant or violent action. The plots were simple and direct, with no intrusion of interior exploration of a character or of narratorial monologue. They were to be objective, not judgmental. It was a matter of showing, not telling the reader how to react. He followed Turgenev in using landscape to convey mood and to strive for a lyric simplicity, a flow of narrative with an avoidance of dramatic shaping, obvious climax, or clear conclusion.

He was to have a strong influence on the short story and particularly on the Irish writers. His determination to draw the short story away from eccentric, heightened behavior and incident to "real life" with a kind of subtle artlessness was to be an example followed by James Joyce in his collection *Dubliners* (1914). A further aspect of his career as a short-story writer appeared in his series of Irish folk tales, in which the fairy world comes into play and wherein he made a serious attempt to retrieve and reshape Irish literary heritage.

"WILFRID HOLMES"

Moore often published his stories in sets exploring a single theme. In his collection *In Single Strictness*, the characters live repressed lives, and Moore uses a minor incident to explore such unhappiness, very quietly, in stories leading to subdued, and often, inconsequential endings. Wilfrid Holmes is the youngest son of a middle-class family. He has a comfortable childhood but tends to be lazy and dreamy. The older children gradually go off to normal lives in business and marriage. It becomes obvious, however, that Holmes's aimlessness carries on into maturity. He tries a number of possible careers, but nothing quite works. He likes music and finally settles on composing operas, but he never attempts to learn the finer aspects of composition; his skill is in melody. He exists on a regularly paid allowance from an aunt.

Rubbing along, working on his opera, Wilfred is suddenly aware that his allowance has not come. Several days go by, and he becomes worried, not knowing if he should write his aunt. He gets a small amount of money from a brother. He attempts to get a job as a music critic, but it is obvious that he simply does not know enough for such work. The allowance comes. The aunt has simply forgotten to send it and to make up for her forgetfulness, she sends him considerably more than usual. He is happy again, continuing on his feckless, incompetent way with his opera.

Moore, who spoke and wrote often of his literary theories, liked to think that the arts had strong connections and could be helped by cross-reference; this story is an example of his use of "minor keys," a kind of story that goes nowhere but explores without comment a hopeless life. Aside from a very quiet heightening in the story when Wilfrid begins to fear that he will not be able to survive, the rest of the work is as lazily quiet as he is, an example of the idea that style is meaning.

"SARAH GWYNN"

In this story (from the collection *Celibate Lives*), Moore brings together his interest in the quiet desperation of humans and his admiration for the Irish working class. Sarah is taken on as a housekeeper by a Dublin doctor, who is moved by her story that after years of service as a lay sister in a convent, she was dismissed for complaining about the working conditions. She proves to be an excellent worker, and it looks as if she and the doctor's gardener will marry.

Suddenly she announces she must leave, and he discovers that she has a mission and cannot marry. Years earlier, alone and helpless in Dublin, she was befriended by a girl, Phyllis, who got her work in a biscuit factory. The pay was far too meager, however, and some of the girls also worked at night as prostitutes.

Phyllis does this and uses her extra money to keep both of them from starvation, refusing to let Sarah join her in the profession. When the chance comes for Sarah to enter an English convent, Phyllis raises the money for her passage.

Since then, Sarah has been searching for Phyllis. Now the chance of marriage is too much for her; it is not her right to have a decent life until she finds and rescues Phyllis, although she knows this is highly unlikely. The doctor tries to dissuade her, but she will not relent, and the story ends, as the doctor says, with three people unhappy, the doctor, Sarah, and her hopeless lover, the gardener.

"SO ON HE FARES"

Moore believed his best work as a short fictionist was in *The Untilled Field* and with characteristic immodesty said that "So on He Fares" was the best short story ever written by anyone. Moore was determined to avoid the caricature of the Irish peasant and the exaggerated plot in favor of the simplicity of the rambling tale, told quietly and intimately, about ordinary people. The style is strongly rhythmic, called by Moore his "melodic line."

Ulick Burke, with his father in the army, lives with his mother in rural Ireland. She dislikes him, and often punishes him severely. At the age of ten he runs away and almost drowns, but he is rescued by a passing barge. He becomes a sailor. In his twenties, he returns. His father is away again, and his mother has another son, also called Ulick. His mother is cool toward him but clearly has considerable affection for the brother. He senses her old dislike of him growing the longer he stays. He leaves, wondering if it might not have been better had he died when he fell in the river on first leaving home. He thinks of drowning himself but rejects the idea, since a man, unlike a child, cannot kill himself because his mother does not love him. He must get on with life. The quietly sombre conclusion, playing off the right of a child to die for lack of love against the adult's obligation to endure is the only touch of short-story cleverness in the work. It does, however, function as proof of Moore's idea of how life plays itself out, not in tricky endings but in sad acceptance.

A STORY-TELLER'S HOLIDAY

This work avoids one of the problems of the short-story collection--the fragmentary nature of one story following another. Here Moore solves that difficulty by immersing the stories in a wider, slightly novelistic tale of the writer (a fictional representation of Moore himself) going from London to Ireland, meeting travelers on the way, and gradually reaching the rural world of the old Irish tales. The stories come out of innocent conversations, allowing for different kinds of tales, individual characters offering them as modest entertainment. The Story-Teller tells some of the stories in educated English, but the locals use their native accent and sentence style. The frame is set slowly with the early material commenting upon the political, religious, and social problems of Ireland after the Easter Rebellion of 1916. When The Story-Teller gets into the country, the tales become closely related to rural life, and once he meets Alec Trusselby, a wandering storyteller, the stories shift into the genre of the Irish medieval tale, often with fairy connections.

George Moore (Library of Congress)

By 1918, depressed by World War I and the political troubles of Ireland, Moore had lost interest in modern life, and this collection marks a return to the solace of ancient Ireland, narrated by storytellers emotionally and intellectually connected to the bards, telling tales rather than writing them, which Moore, somewhat illogically, was attempting to duplicate in print. The love story of Liadin, the wandering singer, and Curithir, the wandering storyteller, doomed to fail since their gifts of enchanting the people must come before any private happiness, and their eventual reunion, side by side in death, is an example of the kind of tale Moore wanted to use to enrich the artistic and social fabric of a modern, violent Ireland.

OTHER MAJOR WORKS

LONG FICTION: *A Modern Lover*, 1883; *A Mummer's Wife*, 1884; *A Drama in Muslin*, 1886; *A Mere Accident*, 1887; *Spring Days*, 1888; *Mike Fletcher*, 1889; *Vain Fortune*, 1891; *Esther Waters*, 1894; *Evelyn Innes*, 1898; *Sister Teresa*, 1901; *The Lake*, 1905; *Muslin*, 1915; *The Brook Kerith*, 1916; *Lewis Seymour and Some Women*, 1917; *Héloise and Abélard*, 1921; *Ulick and Soracha*, 1926; *Aphrodite in Aulis*, 1930.

PLAYS: *Martin Luther*, pb. 1879 (with Bernard Lopez); *The Strike at Arlingford*, pr., pb. 1893; *The Bending of the Bough*, pr., pb. 1900; *Diarmuid and Grania*, pr. 1901 (with William Butler Yeats); *Esther Waters*, pr. 1911; *The Apostle*, pb. 1911; *Elizabeth Cooper*, pr., pb. 1913; *The Making of Immortal*, pb. 1927; *The Passing of the Essenes*, pr., pb. 1930 (revision of *The Apostle*).

POETRY: *Flowers of Passion*, 1878; *Pagan Poems*, 1881.

NONFICTION: *Confessions of a Young Man*, 1888; *Impressions and Opinions*, 1891; *Modern Painting*, 1893; *Hail and Farewell: A Trilogy*, 1911-1914 (*Ave*, 1911; *Salve*, 1912; *Vale*, 1914); *Avowals*, 1919; *Conversations in Ebury Street*, 1924; *Letters from George Moore to Edouard Dujardin, 1886-1922*, 1929; *The Talking Pine*, 1931; *A Communication to My Friends*, 1933; *Letters of George Moore*, 1942; *Letters to Lady Cunard*, 1957 (Rupert Hart-Davis, editor); *George Moore in Transition: Letters to T. Fisher Unwin and Lena Milman, 1894-1910*, 1968 (Helmut E. Gerber, editor).

TRANSLATION: *Daphnis and Chloë*, 1924 (of Longus).

BIBLIOGRAPHY

Averill, Deborah. *The Irish Short Story from George Moore to Frank O'Connor*. New York: University Press of America, 2002. A study of the Irish short story, with a historical and critical introduction and a chapter devoted to Moore.

Burkhart, Charles. "The Short Stories of George Moore." In *The Man of Wax: Critical Essays on George Moore*, edited by Douglas A. Hughes. New York: New York University Press, 1971. A clear and sensible discussion of the short stories in general terms without academic jargon. A good way to look at Moore's short fiction in the context of his other work. There is also an essay by Enid Starkie on Moore and French naturalism, which helps immensely in understanding the movement and how Moore adapted it to his work.

Dunleavy, Gareth W. "George Moore's Medievalism: A Modern Triptych." In *George Moore in Perspective*, edited by Janet Dunleavy. Totowa, New Jersey: Barnes & Noble, 1983. Moore used medieval themes in both his novels and short stories. Dunleavy offers a straightforward discussion of this kind of story, with *A Story-Teller's Holiday* receiving special attention. Another essay, written by Melvin J. Friedman, points out the similarities in the works of Moore and Samuel Beckett, which also brings the short stories into consideration.

Farrow, Anthony. *George Moore*. Boston: Twayne, 1978. A helpful study of Moore for the beginning reader, but somewhat restricted in format. An appreciative approach to Moore that places him at a high level of literary distinction, despite the fact that his novels remain largely unread. Includes a selected bibliography.

Frazier, Adrian. *George Moore, 1852-1933*. New Haven, Conn.: Yale University Press, 2000. A thorough biography, drawing on much previously unpublished material and emphasizing Moore's historical and cultural context.

Gramich, Katie. "Creating and Destroying the 'Man Who Does Not Exist': The Peasantry and Modernity in Welsh and Irish Writing." *Irish Studies Review* 17, no. 1 (February, 2009): 19-30. Gramich's examination of the depiction of peasants in Irish and Welsh fiction includes discussion of Moore's satirical view of peasants in *The Untilled Field*.

Heilmann, Ann. "'Neither Man nor Woman'? Female Transvestism, Object Relations, and Mourning in George Moore's 'Albert Nobbs.'" *Women* 14, no. 3 (Winter, 2003): 248-262. An analysis of "Albert Nobbs," first published in A Story-Teller's Holidayand later transferred to *Celibate Lives*. The story is about a female cross-gender transvestite who befriends another male impersonator. Provides a psychological analysis of Albert's character, arguing that the female transvestite is depicted as a "castrated, sexless and depressed 'perhapser,'" and "an outcast from both sexes."

Ingman, Heather. "The Modern Irish Short Story: Moore and Joyce." In *A History of the Irish Short Story*. New York: Cambridge University Press, 2009. Ingman's examination of the development of the Irish short story from the nineteenth century to the present includes an analysis of Moore's short fiction and an assessment of his contributions to the genre.

Jeffares, A. Norman. *George Moore*. London: Longmans, 1965. One of the volumes in the British Council series and the best short introduction to the author and his work, including his short stories. A good place to start.

Llewellyn, Mark, and Ann Heilmann. "George Moore and Literary Censorship: The Textual and Sexual History of 'John Norton' and 'Hugh Monfert.'" *English Literature in Transition, 1880-1920*, 50, no. 4 (2007): 371-392. Examines Moore's rewriting of his characters John Norton, who is featured in his novel *A Mere Accident*, and the title character in his short story "Hugh Monfert." Focuses on the characters and on Moore's portrayal of sexuality and masculinity in the two works.

Pierse, Mary, ed. *George Moore: Artistic Visions and Literary Worlds*. Newcastle, England: Cambridge Scholars Press, 2006. Collection of scholarly papers that were presented at a conference on Moore. Two of the papers focus on the short-story collection *The Untilled Field*, another discusses his story "Mildred Lawson," while other papers include analyses of individual stories; references to the individual stories are listed in the index.

Seinfelt, Frederick W. *George Moore: Ireland's Unconventional Realist*. Philadelphia: Dorrance and Company, 1975. A discussion of Moore's depiction of women. Includes comment upon his use of women in the short stories.

Charles Pull

ALICE MUNRO

Born: Wingham, Ontario, Canada; July 10, 1931
Also known as: Alice Anne Laidlaw

PRINCIPAL SHORT FICTION

Dance of the Happy Shades, 1968
*Something I've Been Meaning to Tell You: Thirteen
    Stories,* 1974
Who Do You Think You Are?, 1978 (pb. in U.S. as
    The Beggar Maid: Stories of Flo and Rose, 1979)
The Moons of Jupiter: Stories, 1982
The Progress of Love, 1986
Friend of My Youth: Stories, 1990
Open Secrets: Stories, 1994
Selected Stories, 1996
The Love of a Good Woman: Stories, 1998
*Hateship, Friendship, Courtship, Loveship, Mar-
    riage,* 2001
No Love Lost, 2003
Runaway: Stories, 2004
Vintage Munro, 2004
Carried Away: A Selection of Short Stories, 2006
The View from Castle Rock, 2006
Too Much Happiness, 2009

OTHER LITERARY FORMS

The line between long and short fiction is sometimes blurred in the work of Alice Munro (AL-ihs
muhn-ROH). Although principally a writer of short
fiction, she has also published a novel, *Lives of Girls
and Women* (1971), which she prefers to view as a
group of linked stories. On the other hand, some reviewers, including author John Gardner, have suggested that the stories in *The Beggar Maid* are so intricately related that the book could be viewed as a novel.
Most critics, however, treat it as short fiction.

ACHIEVEMENTS

Alice Munro has gained recognition as a consummate writer, principally of short, psychological fiction.
She received the Governor General's Award (Canada's
highest literary award) for *Dance of the Happy Shades*,
The Beggar Maid, and *The Progress of Love*. Her novel
Lives of Girls and Women won the Canadian Booksellers Association Award in 1972, as did *Open Secrets*
in 1995. In 1990, the Canada Council awarded her the
Molson Prize for her contribution to Canada's cultural
and intellectual life. In 1977 and 1994, she received the
Canada-Australia Literary Prize, and in 1995 *Open Secrets* won the W. H. Smith and Son Literary Award for
the best book published in the United Kingdom. Munro
received the National Book Critics Circle Award from
the United States in 1999 for *The Love of a Good
Woman*. In 2001, Munro received the Rea Award for
the Short Story. In 2009, she won the Man Booker International Prize, the first time a short-story writer has
won the award. She won Canada's Giller Prize in 2004
for *Runaway*. She was also nominated for the Giller
Prize again in 2009, but said she did not wish to be
considered.

BIOGRAPHY

Alice Munro was born July 10, 1931, in Wingham,
Ontario, Canada, where her father raised silver foxes. A
scholarship covering the years 1949 to 1951 to the University of Western Ontario led to her receiving her
bachelor's degree in 1952. Her marriage to bookstore
owner James Munro produced three daughters. After a
1976 divorce, Munro married geographer Gerald
Fremlin; they established homes in Clinton, Ontario,
and Comox, British Columbia.

ANALYSIS

Alice Munro has been compared to Ernest Hemingway
for the realism, economy, and lucidity of her style; to
John Updike for her insights into the intricacies of social

and sexual relationships; to Flannery O'Connor and Eudora Welty for Munro's ability to create characters of eccentric individualism; and to Marcel Proust in the completeness and verisimilitude with which she evokes the past. She is an intuitive writer, less likely to be concerned with problems of form than with clarity and veracity. Some critics have faulted her for a tendency toward disorganization or diffusion--too many shifts in time and place within a single story, for example. On her strengths as a writer, however, critics generally agree: She has an unfailing particularity and naturalness of style, an ability to write vividly about ordinary life and its boredom without boring her readers, a skill for writing about the past without being sentimental, and a profound grasp of human emotion and psychology. Chief among her virtues is her great honesty: her refusal to oversimplify or falsify human beings, their emotions, or their experiences. One of her characters states, "How to keep oneself from lying I see as the main problem everywhere." Her awareness of this problem is everywhere evident in her writing, certainly in the distinctive voices of her narrator-protagonists, who are scrupulously concerned with truth. Finally, her themes--memory, love, transience, death--are significant. To explore such themes within the limitations of the short-story form with subtlety and depth is Munro's achievement.

"DANCE OF THE HAPPY SHADES"

One of Munro's recurring themes is "the pain of human contact . . . the fascinating pain; the humiliating necessity." The phrase occurs in "The Stone in the Field" and refers to the narrator's maiden aunts, who cringe from all human contact, but the emotional pain that human contact inevitably brings is a subject in all of her stories. It is evident in the title story of her first collection, "Dance of the Happy Shades," in which an elderly, impoverished piano teacher, Miss Marsalles, has a "party" (her word for recital) for her dwindling number of students and their mothers, an entertainment she can ill afford. The elaborate but nearly inedible refreshments, the ludicrous gifts, and the tedium of the recital pieces emphasize the incongruity between Miss Marsalles's serene pleasure in the festivities and the grim suffering of her unwilling but outwardly polite guests. Their anxieties are intensified by the midparty arrival of Miss Marsalles's newest pupils, a group of mentally disabled children from a nearby institution. The other pupils and their mothers struggle to maintain well-bred composure, but inwardly they are repelled, particularly when one of the mentally disabled girls gives the only accomplished performance of a sprightly piece called "The Dance of the Happy Shades." The snobbish mothers believe that the idea of a mentally disabled girl learning to play the piano is not in good taste; it is "useless, out-of-place," in fact very much like Miss Marsalles herself. Clearly, this dismal affair will be Miss Marsalles's last party, yet the narrator is unable at the end to pity her, to say, "Poor Miss Marsalles." "It is the Dance of the Happy Shades that prevents us, it is the one communiqué from the other country where she lives." The unfortunate Miss Marsalles is happy; she has escaped the pain she would feel if she could know how others regard her, or care. She is living in another country, out of touch with reality; she has escaped into "the freedom of a great unemotional happiness."

Alice Munro (AFP/Getty Images)

"THE PEACE OF UTRECHT"

Few of Munro's characters are so fortunate. In "The Peace of Utrecht," for example, the inescapable emotional pain of human contact is the central problem. Helen, the narrator, makes a trip with her two children to Jubilee, the small town where she grew up, ostensibly to visit her sister Maddy, now living alone in their childhood home. The recent death of their mother is on their minds, but they cannot speak of it. Maddy, who stayed at home to look after their "Gothic Mother," has forbidden all such talk: "No exorcising here," she says. Exorcism, however, is what Helen desperately needs as she struggles with the torment that she feels about her sister's "sacrifice," her mother's life, and her own previous self, which this return home so vividly and strangely evokes. Mother was a town "character," a misfit or oddity, even before the onset of her debilitating and disfiguring illness (she seems to have died of Parkinson's disease). For Helen, she was a constant source of anxiety and shame, a threat to Helen's own precarious adolescent identity. (Readers who know Munro's novel *Lives of Girls and Women* will find a strong resemblance of Helen's mother to Del Jordan's bizarre mother. She also appears as recognizably the same character in the stories "The Ottawa Valley," "Connection," "The Stone in the Field," and perhaps "The Progress of Love.") Recalling the love and pity denied this ill but incorrigible woman, Helen experiences raging guilt, shame, and anger that she and her sister were forced into "parodies of love." Egocentric, petulant, this mother

> demanded our love in every way she knew, without shame or sense, as a child will. And how could we have loved her, I say desperately to myself, the resources of love we had were not enough, the demand on us was too great.

Finally, Helen and her sister withdrew even the pretense of love, withdrew all emotion:

> We took away from her our anger and impatience and disgust, took all emotion away from our dealings with her, as you might take away meat from a prisoner to weaken him, till he died.

Still, the stubborn old woman survived and might have lived longer except that Maddy, left alone with her mother and wanting her own life, put her in the hospital. After she tried to run away, restraint became necessary; she did not survive long after that.

Some critics believe that Munro's strongest works are those which draw on her own small-town origins in western Ontario, stories of Jubilee, Tuppertown, Hanratty, and Dalgleish. Munro has confessed in an interview that "The Peace of Utrecht" is her most autobiographical story and thus was difficult to write. Perhaps its emotional power derives in part from its closeness to her own experience, but it exhibits those qualities for which her writing has been praised: the effortless clarity of style, the psychological penetration of character, the evocation of time and place, the unfailing eye and ear that convey an impression of absolute authenticity--these are the hallmarks of Munro's finest fiction, and they are evident even in her earliest stories. For example, in "The Peace of Utrecht," Helen's visit to two memorable residents of Jubilee, her mother's sisters, Aunt Annie and Auntie Lou, demonstrates a deftness of characterization and a sureness of touch that are remarkable but typical of this writer at her best. Helen finds them

> spending the afternoon making rugs out of dyed rags. They are very old now. They sit in a hot little porch that is shaded by bamboo blinds; the rags and the half-finished rugs make an encouraging, domestic sort of disorder around them. They do not go out any more, but they get up early in the morning, wash and powder themselves, and put on their shapeless print dresses trimmed with rickrack and white braid.

Later, after tea, Aunt Annie tries to press on Helen a box of her mother's clothing (painstakingly cleaned and mended), seemingly oblivious to Helen's alarm and pain at the sight of these all-too-tangible reminders of her mother. To Aunt Annie, things are to be used up; clothes are to be worn. She is not insensitive, nor is she a fool. Revealing to Helen (who did not know) the shameful facts about her mother's hospitalization against her will, her pitiful, frantic attempt to escape one snowy January night, the board that was subsequently nailed across the bed to immobilize her, and

Maddy's indifference to it all, Aunt Annie begins "crying distractedly as old people do, with miserable scanty tears." Despite the tears, however, Aunt Annie is (as Helen is not) emotionally tough, "an old hand at grief and self-control." Just how tough she is conveyed by Aunt Annie's final, quietly understated words:'We thought it was hard,' she said finally. 'Lou and I thought it was hard.'"

Helen and Maddy, with less emotional resilience, try to come to terms with their own complex anguish through evasion, rationalization, and, finally, admonishment-- "don't be guilty"--but Munro is too honest to imply that they can be successful. In the final lines of the story, Helen urges her sister to forget the past, to take hold of her own life at last. Maddy's affirmation, "Yes I will," soon slips into an agonized question: "But why can't I, Helen? *Why can't I?*" In the "dim world of continuing disaster, of home," there is no peace of Utrecht, not for Munro's characters, perhaps not for Munro.

The preoccupation in Munro's fiction with family, usually as a "continuing disaster," is striking. Assorted eccentric aunts, uncles, and cousins appear and reappear; a somewhat miscreant brother appears in "Forgiveness in Families" and "Boys and Girls." Sometimes the family portraits are warmly sympathetic, as in the case of the grandmother in "Winter Wind" or especially the gentle father who calmly prepares for his death in "The Moons of Jupiter." Even the neurotic mother and father in "The Progress of Love" are treated sympathetically. There, the mother's fanatical hatred of her own father leads her to burn the desperately needed money she inherits from him at his death. Clearly, for Munro, family origins matter, sometimes as the source of humor and delightful revelation but more dependably as the source of endless mystery and pain. This is particularly true of "the problem, the only problem," as stated in "The Ottawa Valley": mother. At the story's conclusion, the narrator confesses that

> she is the one of course that I am trying to get; it is to reach her that this whole journey has been undertaken. With what purpose? To mark her off, to describe, to illumine, to celebrate, to *get rid,* of her; and it did not work, for she looms too close, just as

she always did. . . . She has stuck to me as close as ever and refused to fall away, and I could go on, and on, applying what skills I have, using what tricks I know, and it would always be the same.

Some relationships, some kinds of "fascinating pain," can be recorded or analyzed but not exorcized. Clearly, these may become the inspiration for significant literature. In Munro's fiction, the view of the emotional entanglements called "family" is unflinchingly honest, unsentimental, but always humane, at times even humorous.

"BARDON BUS"

Another important dimension of Munro's short stories is sexual relationships, particularly in the "feelings that women have about men," as she stated in an interview. In "Bardon Bus," the narrator, a woman writer spending time in Australia, meets an anthropologist (known as "X") and begins a deliberately limited affair, asking only that it last out their short time in Australia. Later, when both have returned to Canada, she is miserable, tortured by memory and need: "I can't continue to move my body along the streets unless I exist in his mind and in his eyes." Finally, she realizes her obsession is a threat to her sanity and that she has a choice of whether to be crazy or not. She decides she does not have the stamina or the will for "prolonged craziness," and further that

> there is a limit to the amount of misery and disarray you will put up with, for love, just as there is a limit to the amount of mess you can stand around a house. You can't know the limit beforehand, but you will know when you've reached it. I believe this.

She begins to let go of the relationship and finds "a queer kind of pleasure" in doing this, not a "self-wounding or malicious pleasure," but

> pleasure in taking into account, all over again, everything that is contradictory and persistent and unaccommodating about life. . . . I think there's something in us wanting to be reassured about all that, right alongside--and at war with--whatever there is that wants permanent vistas and a lot of fine talk.

This seeming resolution, however, this salvation by knowing and understanding all, is subtly undercut by the conclusion of the story. The narrator's much younger friend, Kay, happens to mention her involvement with a fascinating new "friend," who turns out to be X. The story ends there, but the pain (presumably) does not.

"TELL ME YES OR NO"

The female protagonist of "Tell Me Yes or No" is also sifting through the emotional rubble of an adulterous affair, which has ended, perhaps because of the death of her lover, or perhaps it has merely ended. In this story, it is difficult to distinguish reality from fantasy, and that may be the point. The other lives and other loves of her lover may be real, or they may be a fantasy (as defense mechanism) of the protagonist, but the central insight is the realization of how

> women build their castles on foundations hardly strong enough to support a night's shelter; how women deceive themselves and uselessly suffer, being exploitable because of the emptiness of their lives and some deep--but indefinable, and not final!--flaw in themselves.

For this woman, none of the remedies of her contemporaries works, not deep breathing, not macramé, and certainly not the esoteric advice of another desperate case: to live "every moment by itself," a concept she finds impossible to comprehend, let alone practice. The irony of her difficulty is evident, considering Munro's passionate concern throughout her fiction for "Connection" (the title of one of her stories). It seems that there is some connection between past choice and present desolation:

> Love is not in the least unavoidable, there is a choice made. It is just that it is hard to know when the choice was made, or when, in spite of seeming frivolous, it became irreversible. There is no clear warning about that.

"LABOR DAY DINNER"

Munro's clear-eyed, self-aware narrators are never easy on themselves. They constantly are requiring themselves to face reality, to be aware of and responsible for the consequences of their own choices. In "Labor Day Dinner," the narrator, forty-three-year-old Roberta, has for the past year been living on a run-down farm with George, a younger man and former art teacher. His ambitious plan is to restore the farm and create a studio in which do to his sculpture. Roberta's daughters Angela, seventeen, and Eva, twelve, are spending the summer with her. The atmosphere is emotionally charged, prickly, and tense. George does not approve of the way Roberta indulges her daughters, allowing them to practice ballet instead of doing any work. George does not approve of Roberta, who seems to be indulging herself with tears and moody idleness. On the other hand, Roberta (weeping silently behind her sunglasses) does not approve of George's cooling ardor, his ungallant awareness of her age as evidenced by his request that she not wear a halter top to his cousin's Labor Day dinner because she has flabby armpits. So far, this sounds like the unpromising stuff of the afternoon soaps. (In fact, some of Munro's short stories first were published in popular magazines.) The difference is in what Munro is able to do with her material, the way in which she prevents her characters from deteriorating into stereotypes or her theme into cliché.

Roberta (who has reduced her waist only to discover that her face now looks haggard) reflects mournfully:

> How can you exercise the armpits? What is to be done? Now the payment is due, and what for? For vanity. . . . Just for having those pleasing surfaces once, and letting them speak for you; just for allowing an arrangement of hair and shoulders and breasts to have its effect. You don't stop in time, don't know what to do instead; you lay yourself open to humiliation. So thinks Roberta, with self-pity--what she knows to be self-pity--rising and sloshing around in her like bitter bile. She must get away, live alone, wear sleeves.

The self-awareness, the complex mingling of humor and pathos, the comic inadequacy of the solution, to wear sleeves (rivaling Prufrock's momentous decision to wear his trousers rolled), these lend to the character and to the story a dimension that is generally missing in popular fiction.

Roberta's daughters are close observers of and participants in this somewhat lugubrious drama. Angela, watching the change in her mother from self-reliant woman to near wreck and viewing George as a despot who hopes to enslave them all, records in her journal, "If this is love I want no part of it." On the other hand, sensitive Eva, watching her older sister develop the unpleasant traits of a typical adolescent, wants no part of that-- "I don't want it to happen to me."

They all nearly get what they want, a way out of the emotional trauma in which they find themselves. On the way home from the Labor Day dinner, the pickup truck in which they are riding (the girls asleep in the back) comes within inches of being hit broadside by a car that careers out of nowhere, traveling between eighty and ninety miles an hour, no lights, its driver drunk. George does not touch the brake, nor does Roberta scream; they continue in stunned silence, pull into their yard and sit, unable to move.

> What they feel is not terror or thanksgiving--not yet. What they feel is strangeness. They feel as strange, as flattened out and borne aloft, as unconnected with previous and future events as the ghost car was.

The story ends with Eva, waking and calling to them, "Are you guys dead?" and "Aren't we home?"

The ending shocks everything in the story into a new perspective, making what went before seem irrelevant, especially Roberta's and George's halfhearted playing at love. For Munro, it seems that the thought of the nearness, the omnipresence, and the inevitability of death is the only thing that can put lives and relationships into true perspective. However, this (as Munro states at the conclusion of "The Spanish Lady") is a message that cannot be delivered, however true it may be.

THE LOVE OF A GOOD WOMAN

Munro continues at the top of her form in *The Love of a Good Woman*, where the pain of human contact, in its various guises, remains her central theme. In the title novella, Enid, a middle-aged, practical nurse, finds herself attending the dying Mrs. Quinn. Lonely, kind Enid strives to do good, resisting her dislike of the sick woman. As an intruder in a household that cannot function without her, she is unaware of her attraction to the husband, a former classmate, until his wife implicates him in the death of a local optometrist. If the dying woman's story is true, Enid must decide whether to confront the husband or to believe in his innocence as

she begins to lose hers. This complex, loosely structured work ends ambiguously, as do most of the stories, with Enid hesitating between motion and stillness.

"Cortes Island" is the most troubling story of this group, perhaps because of its ambiguity, perhaps because human lives have gone terribly wrong A newlywed couple rents a basement apartment from the elderly Gorries. When the young woman needs a job, Mrs. Gorrie asks her to sit with her wheelchair-bound husband. A stroke has rendered Mr. Gorrie virtually speechless, but by grunts he can make himself understood. He wants her to read scrapbook articles from Cortes Island, where long ago a house burned to the ground, a child escaped, and a man died. What happened on Cortes Island, where Mr. Gorrie operated a boat? Was the death an accident, suicide, murder?

This story is so subtly written that events are not immediately clear. Typically, Munro offers only hints, although the young woman realizes that the Gorries once had an intense relationship. With harsh noises, the crippled Mr. Gorrie demands, "Did you ever think that people's lives could be like that and end up like this? Well, they can." This marriage is a wreck of love, a ruin.

As always, Munro exhibits masterful use of irony. In "Jakarta," two young wives argue over D. H. Lawrence's assertion that a woman's happiness lies in a man and that her consciousness must be submerged in his. Kath is a proper Canadian wife and mother, but Sonje, her pot-smoking, commune-dwelling friend, is an American. Over the years, conservative Kath breaks away from her stuffy marriage to become strong and self-reliant. Sonje, who has routinely accepted her husband's wish to switch sexual partners, remains faithful to him, even after he disappears in Jakarta.

In other stories, a daughter seeks to ease a strained relationship with her abortionist father by revealing the birth of her child, but she is talking to a dead man. A young girl realizes that she is completely, utterly alone. In the best kind of horror story, one that will chill any parent's blood, a woman tries to entertain her grandchildren with a game that turns sinister as she glimpses the danger, as well as the pain, implicit in any human contact.

Munro stated in an interview that her need to write

> has something to do with the fight against death, the feeling that we lose everything every day, and writing is a way of convincing yourself perhaps that you're doing something about this.

Despite her characteristic concern for honesty and her determination to tell only the truth, it seems in this passage that she may be wrong about one thing: It seems clear that Munro's writing is destined to last for a long time.

HATESHIP, FRIENDSHIP, COURTSHIP, LOVESHIP, MARRIAGE

The nine stories in *Hateship, Friendship, Courtship, Loveship, Marriage* explore a set of common Munro themes--that truth can develop out of lies, that reality can derive from fantasy, and that good can result from bad. In the title story, a drab woman travels across Canada with a load of furniture to start a life with an ill man who has been sending her letters. The fact that the letters have been sent by two young girls as a practical joke little matters when it turns out that each is precisely what the other needs. When a man named Grant must put his aging wife Fiona in a rest home because of Alzheimer's symptoms in "The Bear Came Over the Mountain," she develops a relationship with a man who has had a stroke. After the man is taken out of the home by his wife, Fiona is so depressed that Grant goes to the man's wife to urge her to take him back for visits. What results is the wife's attraction to Grant, the return of the man to the home, and a bittersweet "happily ever after" ending for all.

The superiority of imaginative reality over the merely real energizes such stories as "What Is Remembered," in which woman has a single sexual encounter with a man that she "treasures" for the rest of her life as a hedge against disappointment and the merely everyday, and "Post and Beam," in which a woman fantasizes about her husband's student, although she does not really want to limit the fantasy by doing anything about it.

The desire to hold people only in the imagination is especially common in stories in which the female protagonist is a writer. In "Nettles," a woman "freed from domesticity" meets a man with whom she had an idealized childhood relationship. After being caught in a storm in which they cling together in a patch of stinging nettles, she feels childishly sheepish that they are covered with welts and blotches--innocent, asexual signs of an encounter with the ideal. The protagonist of "Family Furnishings" admires an older female cousin, Alfrida, who seems sophisticated and liberated. However, when she goes off to college and sees Alfrida as conservative and provincial, she transforms her into a character in a story. Ultimately, she feels it is a blessing to be surrounded by people she does not know and who do not know her, for this is how she wants her life to be.

The secret of Munro's short stories is that she is able to suggest universal, unspoken human desires--preferring meaningful fantasy to the insignificant actual, aesthetic disengagement to physical entanglement, the remembered past to the simple present--by describing what seems to be ordinary, everyday reality. Her stories are complex and powerful not so much because of what happens in them but because of what cannot happen except in the mysterious human imagination.

RUNAWAY

Munro understands brilliantly the mystery of what makes people do what they do. In the title story of *Runaway*, a young woman, in a "sudden inspiration," tells her husband a salacious "bedtime story" about an older, bedridden man trying to "nudge" her into intimacies. Later, with the help of the older man's widow, the young woman runs away from her husband, only to suddenly return and stay with him, even after she discovers he has secretly destroyed something she loves. In "Passion," a young woman, engaged to a caring man, goes to Thanksgiving dinner at his family's house, only to drive away with his alcoholic brother to get whiskey, in spite of being asked by his mother to help keep him sober.

The mystery of personality is also at the center of three stories-- "Chance," "Soon," and "Silence"-- linked by a single character named Juliet. In the first, as a young woman, Juliet takes an impulsive risk to visit a stranger she meets briefly on a train. In the second, she finds it impossible to make a simple caring reply to her dying mother's expression of need. In the third, her grown daughter disappears from her life for no apparent reason. Even as readers shake their heads in puzzlement over what makes people in Munro's stories do the things they do, readers simultaneously have a profound intuition that they fearfully understand.

These five stories are the strongest in the book. The remaining three, apparently previously unpublished, are somewhat weaker. In "Trespasses," a woman's attention to an adolescent girl is thought to be sexually dangerous but is finally explained in a secret that seems merely plot-based. Largely dependent on plot, too, is "Tricks," a clever bit of stagecraft with a Shakespearean twist of mistaken identity. The longest story in the collection, "Powers," which uses shifting points of view and covers some fifty years in the lives of its four central characters, is uncharacteristically lacking in the kind of tension typical of Munro's best work.

Although Munro's finest stories might initially appear to be novelistic, they are deceptive, lulling readers into a false sense of security, in which time seems to stretch out comfortably like everyday reality, only to tighten so subtly and intensely that readers are left breathless.

THE VIEW FROM CASTLE ROCK

In an introductory apologia for this, the most intimate book she has ever written, Munro notes that in old age, when personal futures close down, people cannot resist "rifling around in the past." When she was in her mid-sixties, Munro says, she began to take "more than a random interest" in the Laidlaw side of her family, which she traced back to Scotland. As she put this material together, it began to shape itself into "something like stories." In addition, Munro says, during this same period she was also writing a "special set of stories" that she did not include in her last four books of fiction, for they were so close to her own life. *The View from Castle Rock* is made up of these two separate sets--five family chronicles that Munro says are "something like stories" and six pieces drawn from her life that she emphatically declares are "stories." "No Advantages" is the most historical of the first group. The narrator, Munro, about sixty-two, is traveling alone in Scotland, where she finds the gravestone of her great-great-great-great-great grandfather, born at the end of the seventeenth century. She wonders, she opines, she draws conclusions, about him and generations that follow.

The title piece moves closer to fiction, its imaginative spark a received story of an ancestor whose father takes him up to Edinburgh Castle and points out a grayish-blue piece of land showing through the mist beyond the waves, pronouncing gravely, "America." Focusing on the journey the family makes to Nova Scotia, the narrator, now largely absent except as an omniscient voice, imagines their feelings and particularizes them. "Illinois" deals with an event that must have been irresistible to Munro, who has written previous stories of tricks and cross-purposes. A young male ancestor steals his baby sister and hides her; two silly young girls who like to play jokes steal the infant a second time to tease another boy. It is a comedy of errors that ends well when the father finds the baby.

"Fathers," the opening piece of the second part of the book, brings readers close to the kind of story that has made Munro famous. Describing the relationship two different girls have with their fathers, it is structured around theme rather than event. First, there is Dahlia, who hates her father for his brutality and would kill him if she could. Second, there is Frances, whose parents try to encourage their daughter's friendship with Munro. However, when Munro sees the father squeeze the mother's behind, she feels some sort of "creepy menace" about them.

All the stories in this second section point to Munro's future as a writer. In "Lying Under the Apple Tree," she has secret poetic ideas about looking up through apple blossoms, which has an irresistible formality for her, like kneeling in church. After an interruption of what was almost her first sexual encounter, Munro says over the next few years, sardonic, ferocious men in books, such as Heathcliff in *Wuthering Heights* (1847) and Rhett Butler in *Gone with the Wind* (1936), become her only lovers. In "Hired Girl," Munro, seventeen, takes a summer job with a family. Although she has erotic and romantic fantasies about them and the glamorous people who visit them, when the summer is over, the husband gives her a copy of Isak Dinensen's *Seven Gothic Tales.* (1934) As soon as Munro begins to read, she loses herself in the book, believing that this gift of literature has always belonged to her. These are Munro's most personal stories; they give readers a privileged portrait of a brilliant artist.

TOO MUCH HAPPINESS

Given Munro's advancing age, it is not surprising that many of the narrators in these ten stories are older women made to recall some crucial event from their past. In the story "Fiction," the past is the 1970's, when Joyce's husband leaves her for another woman. However, the primary action of the story takes place in the present, when, having remarried, she meets a woman at a party who seems familiar to her. Later, she sees the woman's picture on the back cover of a book and buys it. When Joyce reads the first story, she realizes that the author, Maggie, is the daughter of the woman for whom her husband left and that the story is about the daughter when she was a student in Joyce's music class. Joyce is chagrined to be reminded that she used the child's love and adoration for her as a means by which she could pry into the domestic life of her ex-husband and his new wife. However, at the story's end, Maggie's character comes to the realization that in spite of Joyce's selfish motives, if the great happiness she felt in her relationship with her teacher came out of Joyce's unhappiness, it is happiness nonetheless and not to be regretted.

The inextricability of happiness and unhappiness, a theme woven throughout many of these stories, is perhaps most obvious in the long title piece, which is about the nineteenth century Russian mathematician and novelist Sophia Kovalevsky. The story focuses on the last few days before Kovalevsky dies of pneumonia contracted during a cold, wet trip from Paris to Stockholm, where she held a chair in mathematics, the first woman to hold such a professorship in European history. Although the title of the story may suggest that Kovalevsky has so much happiness her death is a tragedy, it also may suggest her acceptance of the fact that happiness cannot be separated from unhappiness.

Fascinated by the fact that people do things for mysterious reasons, Munro uses "Deep Holes" as a metaphor for these subterranean motivations in one story, in which a young man cuts himself off from his family for no apparent cause, except his having fallen into a deep hole as a child from which he must be rescued by his father, whose subsequent indifference to his son may, or may not, be the cause of the young man's falling into an even deeper hole of alienation from family and society.

In "Wenlock Edge," when the central character, a young scholarship student, hears the story of the experiences of her roommate Nina--her pregnancy; her trip to Japan to get an abortion; the death of her child; her relationship with an older man, Mr. Purvis--it seems to her that Nina has the complex life of a fictional character, making the student feel like a simpleton. When at Nina's request the student goes to dinner at Mr. Purvis's home, she is taken aback when his housekeeper tells her to take her clothes off and calls her a bookworm when she hesitates. Determined to prove she is not simply a bookworm, but rather an enlightened woman fit to live in a sophisticated fiction, she sits naked throughout the meal and while she reads poetry to Purvis. Later, she decides to create a plot around the lives of Nina and Mr. Purvis, allowing whatever melodrama might occur next to go on as if in a wicked story of her own making.

In Munro's best work, the hidden story of emotion and secret life, communicated by atmosphere and tone, is always about something more enigmatic and unspeakable than a story generated merely by character and plot.

OTHER MAJOR WORK

LONG FICTION: *Lives of Girls and Women*, 1971.

BIBLIOGRAPHY

Blodgett, E. D. *Alice Munro*. Boston: Twayne, 1988. This volume provides a general introduction to Munro's fiction. Supplemented by a useful critical bibliography.

Canitz, A. E. Christa, and Roger Seamon. "The Rhetoric of Fictional Realism in the Stories of Alice Munro." *Canadian Literature*, no. 150 (Autumn, 1996): 67-80. Examines how Munro's stories portray and enact the dialectic between legend-making and demythologizing; discusses techniques that Munro uses to adapt the opposition between fiction and reality to the expectations and ethical beliefs of her audience.

Carrington, Ildikó de Papp. *Controlling the Uncontrollable: The Fiction of Alice Munro*. DeKalb: Northern Illinois University Press, 1989. A good critical study of Munro's fiction. Includes a bibliography.

_____. "Talking Dirty: Alice Munro's 'Open Secrets' and John Steinbeck's *Of Mice and Men.*" *Studies in Short Fiction* 31 (Fall, 1994): 495-606. Discusses Munro's foregrounding of language in three categories: spoken language, written language, and body language, primarily in "Open Secrets." Analyzes Munro's use of different kinds of language to interpret what has happened and to conceal secret, dirty meanings under innocuous surfaces. Traces the story's allusions to Steinbeck's Lennie in *Of Mice and Men* (1937).

Clark, Miriam Marty. "Allegories of Reading in Alice Munro's 'Carried Away.'" *Contemporary Literature* 37 (Spring, 1996): 49-61. Shows how the stories in Munro's *Friend of My Youth* and *Open Secrets* dismantle the foundations of realist narrative, figuring or disclosing the many texts in the one and so refiguring the linked practices of writing and reading; claims that "Carried Away" addresses allegorically the politics of the library and the ethics of reading.

Crouse, David. "Resisting Reduction: Closure in Richard Ford's 'Rock Springs' and Alice Munro's 'Friend of My Youth.'" *Canadian Literature*, no. 146 (Autumn, 1995): 51-64. Discusses how Ford and Munro deal with the problem of realistic closure and character growth in their short stories by manipulating time. Shows how they use various narrative devices to give more interpretive responsibility to the reader.

Goldman, Marlene. "Penning in the Bodies: The Construction of Gendered Subjects in Alice Munro's 'Boys and Girls.'" *Studies in Canadian Literature* 15, no. 1 (1990): 62-75. This essay presents a study of conflict between the adult voice and the child's idealistic perception of reality.

Heble, Ajay. *The Tumble of Reason: Alice Munro's Discourse of Absence.* Toronto, Ont.: University of Toronto Press, 1994. Includes a bibliography and an index.

Hiscock, Andrew. "'Longing for a Human Climate': Alice Munro's *Friend of My Youth* and the Culture of Loss." *The Journal of Commonwealth Literature* 32 (1997): 17-34. Claims that in this collection of stories, Munro creates complex fictional worlds in which character, narrator, and reader are involved in the business of interpreting versions of loss, tentatively attempting to understand their function and status in a mysteriously arranged reality.

Martin, Walter. *Alice Munro: Paradox and Parallel.* Edmonton: University of Alberta Press, 1987. An analysis of Munro's use of narrative techniques and language. Complemented by an excellent bibliography of her writings.

Mayberry, Katherine J. "'Every Last Thing . . . Everlasting': Alice Munro and the Limits of Narrative." *Studies in Short Fiction* 29 (Fall, 1992): 531-541. Discusses how Munro's characters use narrative as a means of coming to terms with the past, how they manage their pain by telling. Argues that most of Munro's narrators come to realize the imperfections of narrative because of the incongruence between experience and the story's effort to render it.

Murphy, Georgeann. "The Art of Alice Munro: Memory, Identity, and the Aesthetics of Connection." In *Canadian Women: Writing Fiction*, edited by Mickey Pearlman. Jackson: University Press of Mississippi, 1993. Discusses a number of recurring characters, themes, and concerns in Munro's short stories, such as writing as an act of magical transformation, familial connection, death as a violent upheaval, and sexual connection inflicting psychic pain.

Noonan, Gerald. "The Structure of Style in Alice Munro's Fiction." In *Probable Fictions: Alice Munro's Narrative Acts*, edited by Louis MacKendrick. Downsview, Ont.: ECW Press, 1983. A study of Munro's stylistic evolution from *Dance of the Happy Shades* to *Who Do You Think You Are?*

Nunes, Mark. "Postmodern Piecing': Alice Munro's Contingent Ontologies." *Studies in Short Fiction* 34 (Winter, 1997): 11-26. A discussion of Munro's postmodernist focus on narrative strategies. Argues that quilting and piecing in the stories are metaphors for narrative. Instead of suggesting a disruptive postmodernism, quilting in women's writing functions as an icon for the recuperation of fragmented traditions into a healed whole.

Rasporich, Beverly. *Dance of the Sexes: Art and Gender in the Fiction of Alice Munro.* Edmonton: University of Alberta Press, 1990. An interesting analysis focusing on male-female contrasts and relationships in Munro's fiction. Augmented by a critical bibliography.

Sheldrick Ross, Catherine. "'At Least Part Legend': The Fiction of Alice Munro." In *Probable Fictions: Alice Munro's Narrative Acts*, edited by Louis MacKendrick. Downsview, Ont.: ECW Press, 1983. A study of the way in which Munro's characters perceive legendary qualities in real-life experiences.

Smythe, Karen E. *Figuring Grief: Gallant, Munro, and the Poetics of Elegy*. Montreal, Que.: McGill-Queen's University Press, 1992. A generic study of Munro's stories based on the premise that her fiction, with its emphasis on loss and the importance of storytelling as a way of regaining knowledge of the past, enacts a poetics of elegy.

Thacker, Robert. *Alice Munro: Writing Her Lives*. Toronto, Ont.: McClelland, 2005. An extensive biography that provides new material about Munro's life, based on interviews Thacker had with her.

Valdes, Marcela. "Some Stories Have to Be Told by Me." *Virginia Quarterly Review* 82 (Summer, 2006): 82-92. A "literary history" that charts the development of Munro as a writer, focusing on how the writing of her story "The Peace of Utrecht" (1959) transformed the way she approached fiction.

Karen A. Kildahl; Kenneth W. Meadwell and
Joanne McCarthy
Updated by Charles E. May

O

Edna O'Brien

Born: Tuamgraney, County Clare, Ireland; December 15, 1930

PRINCIPAL SHORT FICTION

The Love Object, 1968

A Scandalous Woman, and Other Stories, 1974

Mrs. Reinhardt, and Other Stories, 1978 (pb. in U.S. as *A Rose in the Heart,* 1979)

Seven Novels, and Other Short Stories, 1978

Returning, 1982

A Fanatic Heart, 1984

Lantern Slides, 1990

OTHER LITERARY FORMS

Besides short stories, Edna O'Brien has written stage plays, screenplays, and teleplays; poetry (*On the Bone,* 1989); children's literature; and novels, including *The Country Girls* (1960), *The Lonely Girl* (1962), *Girls in Their Married Bliss* (1964), *Night* (1972), *House of Splendid Isolation* (1994), *Down by the River* (1996), *In the Forest* (2002), and *The Light of Evening* (2006). She has also published nonfiction, including autobiographical travel books such as *Mother Ireland* (1976), newspaper articles, and biographical and literary criticism such as *James and Nora: A Portrait of Joyce's Marriage* (1981), and *James Joyce* (1999). In addition, she edited the anthology *Some Irish Loving* (1979).

ACHIEVEMENTS

After a strong start in the early 1960's with three splendid short novels in the bildungsroman tradition of maturation and escape (*The Country Girls,* winner of the Kingsley Amis Award; *The Lonely Girl,* reprinted as *Girl with Green Eyes,* 1964; and *Girls in Their Married Bliss*), Edna O'Brien established herself publicly in a variety of television appearances. She became a most articulate spokeswoman for a not overly romantic view of Ireland, for women trapped in an eternal mother-daughter conflict, and for some feminists. The last-mentioned achievement is reached paradoxically in O'Brien's fiction by her frequent exploration and exploitation of an unsympathetic woman in the leading role--the Caithleen (Kate) of the early novels. O'Brien has very few male leads or narrators. Her Kate-women often are whiners and losers who make poor choices in their liaisons with men (often already married), which inevitably bring grief. However, her depiction of character, setting (particularly in Ireland--Philip Roth has praised her sense of place), and conflict is so strong, so graphic, and often in such memorable language, appealing to all the senses, that the negative point is made: This is not how a woman, or indeed any person, seeking happiness should go about the search "for love or connection."

At her best, O'Brien has another counterbalancing woman present as a foil, such as the ebullient Baba, the other heroine with Kate in her early novels; this confident voice is particularly strong in *Girls in Their Married Bliss* and *Night,* an extended "Baba" monologue in the fashion of Joyce's Molly Bloom in *Ulysses* (1922). O'Brien's achievement is to take her readers some distance along the road to realizing what it is to be an integrated, and therefore a happy, person. She is at her best when the setting of her fiction is rural Ireland, not the jet-setters' London or Mediterranean. O'Brien is most popular in the United States, where she has given frequent readings of her work. She is a gifted re-creator of the sights, smells, tastes, and feel of Ireland--with a vivid way of capturing what people might say, at their colorful best.

BIOGRAPHY

As the youngest child in a Roman Catholic family that included a brother and two sisters, Josephine Edna O'Brien was born on December 15, 1930, and grew up on a farm in the west of Ireland. She was educated at the local parochial school in Scarriff and was a boarder in the Convent of Mercy, Loughrea, County Galway. She went to Dublin to study pharmacy in the apprentice system then in vogue and began contributing to the *Irish Press*. In 1954, O'Brien married writer Ernest Gebler, author of *Plymouth Adventure* (1950); they had two sons, Carlo and Sasha.

The family moved to London, where O'Brien established her permanent residence and wrote *The Country Girls* in her first month there. She followed it quickly with the other parts of the trilogy, *The Lonely Girl* and *Girls in Their Married Bliss*. Though O'Brien and Gebler have argued in print over just how much help he gave her with the trilogy (the marriage was dissolved in 1964), O'Brien was launched on a successful, high-profile career. *The Lonely Girl* was made into a film, *The Girl with Green Eyes* (1977), starring Rita Tushingham.

Based in London, successfully bringing up her sons on her own, O'Brien had two most prolific decades of work, in a variety of genres. The novels accumulated: *August Is a Wicked Month* (1965); *Casualties of Peace* (1966); *A Pagan Place* (1970), her favorite work; *Zee and Co.* (1971); *Johnny I Hardly Knew You* (1977); and, after what was for O'Brien a long hiatus, *The Country Girls Trilogy and Epilogue* (1986), *The High Road* (1988), and other contemporary-setting novels, including *Wild Decembers* (1999). Between novels, she published short stories in a variety of magazines (*The New Yorker* in particular), the best of which have been collected. Along with prose fiction, journalism, and travel books, O'Brien also continued her interest in drama: *A Cheap Bunch of Nice Flowers* (pr. 1962), *Time Lost and Time Remembered* (1966), *X, Y, and Zee* (1971), and *Virginia* (pr. 1980).

O'Brien's biography provides the raw material for her fiction. "All fiction is fantasized autobiography," she affirms in the introduction to *An Edna O'Brien Reader* (1994). In 1984 and 1986, respectively, she published in New York a pair of matched volumes: *A*

Edna O'Brien (David Levenson/Getty Images)

Fanatic Heart, largely from the best of her previously collected stories, and, what many would consider her best work, *The Country Girls Trilogy and Epilogue*, of which a twenty-one-page last section is entirely new. For a while, it seemed that the well of inspiration was exhausted. In 1988, however, she was back again in New York with *The High Road*, published after a ten-year novel-writing hiatus. She also presented a reading in New York in 1990 of "Brother," from her short-story collection *Lantern Slides* and autographed her poem *On the Bone*.

ANALYSIS

Edna O'Brien has written short stories throughout her long career. "Come into the Drawing Room, Doris" (retitled "Irish Revel" in *The Love Object* collection) first appeared in *The New Yorker*, on October 6, 1962. "Cords," published as "Which of Those Two Ladies Is He Married To?" in *The New Yorker*, on April 25, 1964, adumbrates many of the aspects of loss and missed connections, which are O'Brien's constant themes. The missed connections are most frequently between mothers and daughters, and between women and men. O'Brien is at her most persuasively graphic when her protagonists are clearly Irish women, at home, in a vanished Ireland whose society as a whole she re-creates and often increasingly indicts most convincingly.

"CORDS"

The question "Which of Those Two Ladies Is He Married To?" which was the original title of "Cords," is posed in the story by Claire's scandalized, rural, Irish mother on a London visit to her sexually active, editor, lapsed Catholic, poet-daughter. The dinner guests are a husband, his pregnant wife Marigold, and his mistress Pauline--a grouping that elicits the mother's question. The newer title, "Cords," more aptly focuses attention on the constrictive mother-daughter bond, which is at the center of this story. The conflict is effectively rendered; no final judgment is made on who is to blame. The Catholic, self-sacrificing mother, who masochistically sews without a thimble, is a spunky traveler. The rather precious daughter, with her "social appendages" but no friends, "no one she could produce for her mother [or herself] and feel happy about," for her part means well. The two similarly looking women are deftly shown to be on a collision course, not just with their umbrellas or their differences over food. The detailed parts of the story all function smoothly. The mother looks at herself in a glass door; Claire sees herself reflected in a restaurant's mirrors. Each woman is herself and an image projected elsewhere. The constraint between them is vividly rendered from their moment of meeting until they are at the airport again, where both "secretly feared the flight number would never be called."

In the background here, in Claire's thoughts, is the father, "emaciated, crazed and bankrupted by drink," with whom the mother's unhealthy, symbiotic relationship continues: "She was nettled because Claire had not asked how he was." In "Cords," then, are many of the perennial, rush-of-memory themes: the family feuding; the malevolent church influence; the searing, almost flawlessly detailed exposé of the tie that binds many mothers and daughters. All is rendered here with the saving grace of good humor, and even old jokes are recalled, such as those about good grazing on the Buckingham Palace lawns, about Irish planes being blessed and therefore never crashing, and about an overly heavy suitcase-- "Have you stones in it?" Claire asks.

"A SCANDALOUS WOMAN"

"A Scandalous Woman" sets the tone for O'Brien's second collection, named after it, and reveals an increasingly gloomy view of the female predicament, whether in Ireland or elsewhere. The story, published in 1974, concludes, "I thought that ours indeed was a land of shame, a land of murder, and a land of strange, [to which is added in the stronger *A Fanatic Heart* version, 'throttled'] women." Here is an indictment of a family, its church, and society, very like that in *A Pagan Place* and to be seen again in "Savages." The anonymous narrator leads the reader through Eily's life from early courtship days until the moment when the narrator, now no longer a young girl but a mother herself, seeks out her childhood friend, to find her much changed: "My first thought was that they must have drugged the feelings out of her . . . taken her spark away." "They" and their "strange brews" are part of the "scandalous" environment of this pagan place.

The anonymous narrator graphically describes how, as a young girl, she admired and sought the company of Eily, who was a few years older and had the "face of a madonna." The narrator tells how she loved Eily and visited her home each Tuesday, even though this meant that she had to play, in the hospital game, the patient to Eily's sister's surgeon. Lying on the kitchen table, she saw "the dresser upside down" in a world whose values are far from upright either. It is Eily, however, who is hollowed out at the story's end: Her playing Juliet to her Protestant Romeo, a bank clerk named Jack, ends in Eily's sniveling at a shotgun wedding. The young narrator had acted as lookout and cover so Eily could meet her lover, "Sunday after Sunday, with one holy day, Ascension Thursday, thrown in." When Jack attempts to throw Eily over, the narrator reveals in herself the same confusion of pagan and Christian values of the others:

> I said . . . that instead of consulting a witch we ought first to resort to other things, such as novenas, putting wedding cake under our pillows, or gathering bottles of dew in the early morning and putting them in a certain fort to make a wish.

The combined forces of the family, church, and community, in a profusion of animal imagery, move events along to the marriage solution.

This is a dense, beautifully put together story, packed with details of the repressive effects of parents, school, and church on a lively girl, who is cowed into submission. From the symbolism of the upside-down world observed by the child on the kitchen table to the loaded "Matilda" term for the female genitalia (between "ma" and "da," there "I" am), everything in this story contributes to the indictment and ironic redefinition of what is "scandalous."

MRS. REINHARDT, AND OTHER STORIES

O'Brien's pessimism about much of the female condition shows little alleviation in the *Mrs. Reinhardt, and Other Stories* collection, heavily though erratically edited and renamed *A Rose in the Heart* in the American edition. The stories overall continue to chronicle the depressing, unsuccessful search of O'Brien's heroines for happiness in, but more often out of, marriage. Other perennial themes, such as loss, isolation, motherhood, and bigotry, are not neglected, especially when the setting is Ireland. The gothic story "Clara" has a rare male narrator.

The stories "Number Ten" and "Mrs. Reinhardt" fit together and were in fact dramatized as a unit in a 1981 drama prepared for the British Broadcasting Corporation. Tilly, in a failing marriage with her art-dealer husband, Harold, sleepwalks her way into misery. For the normally self-centered O'Brien woman who lives, especially when in England, in an economic and social vacuum (very unlike O'Brien's own successful career), Tilly's two afternoons a week teaching autistic children is unusual and helps her credibility. In her dreams, she sees the perfect "nest"--an apartment, with one entire bedroom wall a mirror, where she and her husband can come together at night. The apartment, surreally, does exist, she discovers, and her husband uses it in the daytime with another woman. It is a rending, no-communication stand-off; the unhappy O'Brien woman remains "an outsider looking in."

In the second tale, Mrs. Reinhardt heads off to color-splashed Brittany for a trial separation, determined to somnambulate no more. She resolves to forget the past and to "get even with life" by taking advantage of a brash Iowan in his mid-twenties whom she meets by the sea. It is an ugly picture that O'Brien paints of Tilly's sexual conduct, which is as predatory as that of the lobsters she observes in their tank. In this bleak tale, neither the love of the old patron at the hotel nor the arrival of Tilly's husband does much to alleviate: "What then does a Mrs. Reinhardt do? . . . One reaches out to the face that is opposite . . . for the duration of a windy night. And by morning who knows? Who knows anything anyhow?" Such is the pessimistic conclusion to this fiction; O'Brien's aging heroine's search continues.

RETURNING

O'Brien's sharp study of a certain kind of female psychology continues in the collection *Returning*, where the external topography in all nine stories is the west of Ireland and the craggy community there. A young girl is present in all the collection's stories, either as the ostensible narrator or as the subject of mature reflection on the part of the now-experienced woman. This then-and-now tension between the innocence of childhood and the experience of fifty years is isolated by Philip Roth, in his introduction to *A Fanatic Heart*, as the spring for these stories' "wounded vigor." There is no title story of the same name, but in a very real sense each of the tales here represents a return for O'Brien, a going home.

Another story in this collection, "Savages," represents O'Brien, often accused of careless, awkward, and too-rapid writing, at her careful, three-times-reworked best. The theme bears distinct similarities to "A Scandalous Woman" in its indictment of the community. The story deals with Mabel McCann's search for love in her village community, her false pregnancy, and ostracism. The three published versions of the story that exist (the version published in *The New Yorker* on January 18, 1982; the English edition; and the version in *A Fanatic Heart*) help reveal O'Brien's artistic development, which, though it is by no means a straight-line progression, nevertheless represents work and progress. A noticeable distancing and maturing in the narrator can be seen from the first version to the second one, where she is no longer a precocious twelve-year-old. The second version introduces the five-hundred-word addition of a lugubrious scene between a deaf-and-dumb brother and sister to underscore the gothic qualities of the environment. While all is not unequivocal, there is artistic progress in this second version, where Mabel is called a "simpleton" in the conclusion. In the third and final version, this term, removing her from the world of choices, is wisely dropped; readers are left to work out for themselves what happened. This emendation is a final improvement in the best overall version of an excellent story. The collection also includes the sensory-rich "Sister Imelda," which received the accolade of inclusion in the 1986 *Norton Anthology of English Literature*.

A Fanatic Heart

A Fanatic Heart includes twenty-five O'Brien stories previously anthologized and a quartet of stories initially published in *The New Yorker* and collected for the first time, in a splendidly produced volume introduced by Roth. The quartet is typical of O'Brien's writing when she is on the brittle high road outside Ireland and is generally much less satisfactory. The shallow, codependent Irish woman of these stories moves in three of them through bitter, first-person musings on a current, seemingly doomed affair of the heart with a married family man. Only in the second story, "The Call," is she observed in the third person as she does not answer the ringing telephone. It is time to cease to be strangers, she muses in "The Plan." In a later version of this tale, though, O'Brien cut the pessimistic note that follows immediately, "Though of course we would always be strangers." The "blue" narrator takes a geographical cure to forget, but that does not work, and readers are left with her wondering in "The Return" how much longer she will be able to endure.

"Another Time"

In "Another Time," in the collection *Lantern Slides*, the narrator, a single parent and glamorous former television announcer, gets away to her home in the west of Ireland. After a series of sharply observed encounters with and flashbacks to places and people, Nelly Nugent comes to terms with the present: "She felt as if doors or windows were swinging open all around her and that she was letting go of some awful affliction." At her best, O'Brien has the capacity in her fiction to give this release to her readers. The mirrors that appear so often in her work serve to alert not only her recurring characters but also her readers to the roller-coaster realities of love, loss, and endurance. This work was selected for *The Best New Yorker Stories of 1989*, and four other of the dozen stories in this collection also made their initial appearance in this magazine.

"Love's Lesson"

Whatever the question is, O'Brien's answer is love; this story, then, which appeared in *Zoetrope* (Summer, 1998) closes out a decade in which no collection appeared after *Lantern Slides*. The varieties-of-love theme continued in the 1990's to dominate O'Brien's short fiction, beginning with "No Place" (published in *The New Yorker* on June 17, 1991), where her well-off, ageless, lonely, Irish protagonist, her two boys still in boarding school, waits "on love" in North Africa; her man fails to show up from London's rougher-trade side. In "Sin" (appearing in *The New Yorker* on July 11, 1994), a now aging, lonely widow, the love of her children growing "fainter and fainter," her husband's "unloving love" now a memory, shows herself to be far from well as she pictures her paying guests' incestuous relations with their daughter: "What reached her ears could not be called silence."

In "Love's Lesson" a jagged, uneven, disconnected, and at times overwritten letter from an Irish woman in New York City reviews the course of her affair with a celebrated architect. Her relationship with him has magnified her feeling of being an outsider. Cosmopolitan and international in her experiences and sympathies, she is setting out for home, the mysteries of love still mysterious: "Now we will never know for sure." The lessons taught here by "love" in its various manifestations send the protagonist home to freedom, "to give up the habit of slavery." Freedom also has its costs; and love is not free, a lesson the narrator learns as she reviews her violent relationship with the architect, which she wishes was just physical. She shares her lesbian relationship with her friend Clarissa, who is greatly troubled by thoughts of her dead mother, as is the nameless narrator. People she meets and observes, all with their "connection" problems, cause her to book her flight home.

Given the personal-journal format here, reinforced by O'Brien's ongoing admiration for and work on master wordsmith James Joyce, the stream-of-consciousness technique is to be expected. O'Brien's best prior example of this technique is her novel *Night*. Here, in "Love's Lesson," she continues her alliterative reaching for metaphorical, verbal epiphanies through all the senses to establish the mood. Sometimes she is successful, sometimes not: "Skeins of sound sweetening the air." Here then O'Brien's Irish heroine, alone, courageously as ever, confronts life and the varieties and manifestations of love. The constraints of the Roman Catholic Church and rural society have no place here, but family pressures are not absent, nor is the gallant hope with which her secular heroines view life as they must live it.

OTHER MAJOR WORKS

LONG FICTION: *The Country Girls*, 1960; *The Lonely Girl*, 1962 (also known as *Girl with Green Eyes*, 1964); *Girls in Their Married Bliss*, 1964; *August Is a Wicked Month*, 1965; *Casualties of Peace*, 1966; *A Pagan Place*, 1970; *Zee and Co.*, 1971; *Night*, 1972; *Johnny I Hardly Knew You*, 1977 (pb. in U.S. as *I Hardly Knew You*, 1978); *The Country Girls Trilogy and Epilogue*, 1986 (includes *The Country Girls*, *The Lonely Girl*, *Girls in Their Married Bliss*, and *Epilogue*); *The High Road*, 1988; *Time and Tide*, 1992; *An Edna O'Brien Reader*, 1994; *House of Splendid Isolation*, 1994; *Down by the River*, 1996; *Wild Decembers*, 1999; *In the Forest*, 2002; *The Light of Evening*, 2006.

PLAYS: *A Cheap Bunch of Nice Flowers*, pr. 1962; *A Pagan Place*, pr. 1972 (adaptation of her novel); *The Gathering*, pr. 1974; *Virginia*, pr. 1980; *Flesh and Blood*, pr. 1985; *Triptych*, pr., pb. 2003; *Iphigenia*, pr. 2003, pb. 2003 (adaptation of Euripides' play).

SCREENPLAYS: *Girl with Green Eyes*, 1964 (adaptation of her novel); *Time Lost and Time Remembered*, 1966 (with Desmond Davis; also known as *I Was Happy Here*); *Three into Two Won't Go*, 1969; *X, Y, and Zee*, 1971 (also known as *Zee and Company*; adaptation of her novel).

TELEPLAYS: *The Wedding Dress*, 1963; *Nothing's Ever Over*, 1968; *Mrs. Reinhardt*, 1981 (adaptation of her short story); *The Country Girls*, 1983 (adaptation of her novel).

POETRY: *On the Bone*, 1989.

NONFICTION: *Mother Ireland*, 1976; *Arabian Days*, 1977; *James and Nora: A Portrait of Joyce's Marriage*, 1981; *Vanishing Ireland*, 1986; *James Joyce*, 1999; *Byron in Love: A Short Daring Life*, 2009.

CHILDREN'S LITERATURE: *The Dazzle*, 1981; *A Christmas Treat*, 1982; *The Expedition*, 1982; *The Rescue*, 1983; *Tales for the Telling: Irish Folk and Fairy Stories*, 1986.

EDITED TEXT: *Some Irish Loving*, 1979.

BIBLIOGRAPHY

Colletta, Lisa, and Maureen O'Connor, eds. *Wild Colonial Girl: Essays on Edna O'Brien*. Madison: University of Wisconsin Press, 2006. Wanda Balzano's essay, "Godot Land and Its Ghosts: The Uncanny Genre and Gender of Edna O'Brien's 'Sister Imelda,'" analyzes one of O'Brien's short stories. Other essays discuss the "love objects" in O'Brien's fiction and her biography of James Joyce.

Dunn, Nell. "Edna." In *Talking to Women*. London: Macgibbon and Kee, 1965. In this wide-ranging talk with O'Brien, the topics discussed range from the difficulties facing a single-parent writer to aging; she also shares her thoughts on family, love, and relationships.

Eckley, Grace. *Edna O'Brien*. Lewisburg, Pa.: Bucknell University Press, 1974. This excellent, eighty-eight-page study perceptively discusses the themes of love and loss in O'Brien's work.

Gillespie, Michael Patrick. "(S)he Was Too Scrupulous Always." In *The Comic Tradition in Irish Women Writers*, edited by Theresa O'Connor. Gainesville: University Press of Florida, 1996. Examines how O'Brien's humor is distinguished from that of Irish male writers; shows the relationship between her humor and that of James Joyce, particularly the relationship between her short stories and those in Joyce's *Dubliners* (1914).

Guppy, Shusha. "The Art of Fiction: Edna O'Brien." *The Paris Review* 26 (Summer, 1984): 22-50. The topics discussed include how O'Brien got started on her writing career; the writers, such as James Joyce, Marcel Proust, and Anton Chekhov, whom she admires; feminism, into which O'Brien fits uneasily;

religion; Ireland; and other areas, such as theater and film, in which O'Brien has worked. At fifty-four, O'Brien affirms that she is putting the themes of love, loss, and loneliness behind her. She recommends *A Pagan Place* as her best book.

Ingman, Heather. "Readings: William Trevor and Edna O'Brien." In *A History of the Irish Short Story*. New York: Cambridge University Press, 2009. This chapter in Ingman's examination of the development of the Irish short story provides an overview of short fiction written from 1960 to 1979, followed by detailed readings of some of O'Brien's short stories.

Laing, Kathryn, Sinéad Mooney, and Maureen O'Connor, eds. *Edna O'Brien: New Critical Perspectives*. Dublin: Carysfort Press, 2006. Collection of essays analyzing O'Brien's works. Although the primary emphasis is on her novels, there are discussions of O'Brien's relationship with her former husband, her use of epiphanies, and her depiction of "the female subject."

Moloney, Caitriona, and Helen Thompson. *Irish Women Writers Speak Out: Voices from the Field*. Syracuse, N.Y.: Syracuse University Press, 2003. O'Brien is one of the writers who were interviewed for this book, and she answers questions about her life and works.

O'Brien, Edna. "Interview." *The Paris Review* 26 (Summer, 1984): 22-50. O'Brien discusses the influence of Chekhov on her stories, the animosity of feminists to much of her writing, and the theme of Ireland and the focus on sexuality in many of her stories.

_____. "The Pleasure and the Pain." Interview by Miriam Gross. *The Observer* (April 14, 1985): 17-18. A provocative interview, interesting also in that, two weeks later, it drew from Ernest Gebler, O'Brien's former husband, a detailed rebuttal of her statements about him (*The Observer*, April 28, 1985) and an incendiary interview with him (*Sunday Independent*, April 28, 1985, p. 7).

_____. *Publishers Weekly* 239 (May 18, 1992): 48-49. O'Brien discusses her relationship with her mother, her calling to become a writer, her interest in the Gospels and the writings of Catholic mystics, and her relationship with her editors.

O'Brien, Peggy. "The Silly and the Serious: An Assessment of Edna O'Brien." *The Massachusetts Review* 28 (Autumn, 1987): 474-488. An overview of O'Brien's work, examining her central themes and critiquing the critical reception of her stories. Argues that her obsession with a father figure makes her portray sexually insatiable women in disastrous relationships with hurtful men.

O'Hara, Kiera. "Love Objects: Love and Obsession in the Stories of Edna O'Brien." *Studies in Short Fiction* 30 (Summer, 1993): 317-326. Discusses O'Brien's characters' obsession with love, which stands in the way of love's attainment. Analyzes "Irish Revel" from her 1968 collection *The Love Object* as the birth of the obsession and the title story of her 1990 collection *Lantern Slides* as the epitome of it.

Shumaker, Jeanette Roberts. "Sacrificial Women in Short Stories by Mary Lavin and Edna O'Brien." *Studies in Short Fiction* 32 (Spring, 1995): 185-197. Examines women characters in two stories by Lavin and two by O'Brien in which female martyrdom engendered by the Madonna myth has different forms, from becoming a nun to becoming a wife, mother, or "fallen woman."

Woodward, Richard B. "Edna O'Brien: Reveling in the Heartbreak." *The New York Times Magazine* (March 12, 1989): 42, 50, 52. An up-close and unsympathetic portrait, with a color photograph, of O'Brien, whom Woodward, after several meetings and much research, calls "a poet of heartbreak." This careful essay shows an off-putting, publicity-hunting, and difficult side of the deliberately apolitical O'Brien. Woodward does not find that her novel *The High Road* breaks any new ground, in contrast to the affirmation of critic Shusha Guppy; he believes her short fiction is more accomplished.

Archibald E. Irwin

FITZ-JAMES O'BRIEN

Born: County Limerick, Ireland; c. 1828
Died: Cumberland, Maryland; April 6, 1862

PRINCIPAL SHORT FICTION

The Poems and Stories of Fitz-James O'Brien, 1881, 1969

The Diamond Lens, with Other Stories, 1885
What Was It?, and Other Stories, 1889
Collected Stories by Fitz-James O'Brien, 1925
The Fantastic Tales of Fitz-James O'Brien, 1977
The Supernatural Tales of Fitz-James O'Brien, 1988
(2 volumes)

OTHER LITERARY FORMS

Fitz-James O'Brien's "Oh: Give a Desert Life to Me" in the Irish nationalist newspaper *The Nation* (1845) was the first of hundreds of his poems published in Irish, English, and American newspapers, journals, and literary magazines. Many poems can be read with pleasure by the modern reader; "The Finishing School," a long satiric poem on Madame Cancan's New York School for women, is one example. O'Brien wrote at least five plays; *A Gentleman from Ireland* (pr. 1854, pb. 1858), a two-act comedy, is the best known, having been staged at Wallack's Theatre in New York during his lifetime. He also wrote innumerable essays, dramatic reviews, articles on varied subjects, and narratives for periodicals, including *Atlantic Monthly, Knickerbocker, Putnam's Magazine, Harper's New Monthly Magazine, Harper's Weekly, Vanity Fair, American Whig Review, Lantern,* and *Home Journal.*

ACHIEVEMENTS

Although Fitz-James O'Brien was born in Ireland and began his literary career there and in England before emigrating to the United States, his short stories are more within the American than the Irish tradition of

that genre. Some critics have labeled O'Brien a minor Edgar Allan Poe. A figure of New York's bohemian literary scene in the 1850's, he wrote much poetry, several plays, and a number of short stories that appeared in many of the popular newspapers and magazines of the day. Although one of his plays was produced as late as 1895 and his verse was widely published in his own lifetime, his literary reputation had declined even before his death. Several of his short stories, however, possibly influenced later writers, such as Ambrose Bierce and Guy de Maupassant, and the application of his gothic imagination to science and pseudoscience, placed within a realistic setting, has influenced such modern practitioners of science fiction and fantasy as H. P. Lovecraft and Abraham Merritt.

BIOGRAPHY

Fitz-James O'Brien was the only child of an Irish attorney who died when Fitz-James was twelve years old. He lived better than most Irishmen. Educated at the University in Dublin, he never caught the rising political fever of his day, although he did contribute to *The Nation.* In 1849, on reaching twenty-one, he inherited his father's estate and immigrated to London. By 1851, he sailed to New York after squandering his fortune; in New York City he established himself as a journalist, a poet, and a soldier. O'Brien never married. In 1861, he joined the New York Seventh Regiment sent to the defense of Washington, D.C. Following a duel with a Confederate colonel in 1862, he died from tetanus after six weeks of intense pain.

ANALYSIS

The judgment of Fitz-James O'Brien's friends that "The Wondersmith" and "The Diamond Lens" were remarkable stories and pacesetters for other writers was a sound one; the two stories represent the best of O'Brien's short tales. The plots move quickly as the human characters interact with fantastic creatures, demons, and spirit mediums. Murder and mystery heighten the degree of horror evoked in the reader. The stories do not carry a message, moral, or meaning by which readers are to pattern their lives, although messages, morals, and meanings are evident. Written to entertain the readers of the *Atlantic Monthly*, these stories satisfied the desire for fictional horror. O'Brien held his audience by unfolding the plot through a series of dramatic episodes. By fusing fact with fiction, a blend of science and pseudoscience and good with evil, he created another world which came to life through vivid descriptive passages.

"THE DIAMOND LENS"

"The Diamond Lens," set in New York, is narrated by the protagonist, Linley, a master of deceit and cunning. This first deception involves his studying optics while telling his family that he is studying medicine. Setting up a laboratory in his apartment, he is a true scientist, experimenting, investigating, and theorizing about optics. Simon, a young French Jew then introduces the pseudoscientific element--Mrs. Vulpes, a spirit medium. She conjures up the spirit of scientist

Fitz-James O'Brien (Library of Congress)

Antoni van Leeuwenhoek, which instructs Linley on the mechanics of the perfect microscope. He learns that a one-hundred-and-forty-carat diamond is necessary to construct the universal lens for the perfect microscope. Coincidentally, Simon has such a diamond. Linley murders him, rationalizing that his act is a service to humankind, although when the perfect microscope is made, it is to serve Linley.

When Linley examines a common drop of water, the reader is hardly prepared for the vision he sees: a gaseous globule infused with supernatural light with clouds and forests of unbelievable hues. Through the colored clouds, a perfect female form emerges which Linley calls Animula--the "divine revelation of perfect beauty"--and he promptly falls in love with the phantom figure. The impossible nature of the relationship is later recognized by the lover, who tries to break the spell, to no avail.

Linley, frustrated by Animula's inability to return his passion, seeks the company of Signorina Caradolce, the most beautiful and graceful woman in the world; but he finds her ugly and her movements grotesque, and he hurries home. There he finds Animula suffering, convulsed in pain, her beauty fading; her multichromatic fantasy world is growing dim, and she is dying. Linley checks the water drop; it has evaporated. Haunted by his memories, he goes mad. Even in his madness, he shows no hint of repentance of his deeds; he only weeps for his lost love. The author leaves the reader to discover a moral for his tale.

"THE WONDERSMITH"

O'Brien's skill is again apparent in "The Wondersmith," which describes a deeper level of evil, cruelty, and terror than that seen in "The Diamond Lens." The story revolves around murder, science, pseudoscience, and an unusual love story, along with rituals which demonstrate that demonology is not dead. Everything takes place on Golosh Street, a ghetto off Chatham Street in New York. To the passerby, Herr Hippe and Madame Filomel are ordinary residents of Golosh Street. He is the wondersmith, a maker of lifelike toys, and she is a run-of-the-mill gypsy fortune-teller. In reality, they are bohemians; O'Brien uses the words "gypsy" and "bohemian" interchangeably, but there is no doubt that these bohemians are special gypsies.

Hippe is Duke Balthazar of Lower Egypt, possessor of the secrets of the ages; Filomel is one of his followers.

Hippe and Filomel are of a lower cast than Philip Brann of another tale, "The Bohemian." English by birth, Brann is a mesmerizer and operates alone. Confident of his supernatural powers, Brann chides Edgar Allan Poe, whom he identifies as a bohemian. Instead of using his powers, Poe simply writes about them. According to Brann, Poe should dig up buried treasures, as does Brann, rather than merely describe such things.

The Duke and the hag Filomel are joined by Kerplonne, a French gypsy, and Oaksmith, another English gypsy, to plan the slaughter of millions of innocent Christian children. By magical incantation, Madame Filomel, upon uncorking a black bottle of souls, animates a series of puppets, each of which, carrying a sword or dagger of some type, is an image of evil. A practice session is first arranged for the "Lilliputian assassins," during which they slaughter a roomful of caged birds. O'Brien describes this scene with vivid passages of blood and gore.

Counterbalancing this scene, O'Brien introduces a strange love affair between Solon, a hunchbacked bookseller of Golosh Street, and Zonela, Hippe's daughter (she is not really his daughter, having been kidnapped from a Hungarian nobleman). When Hippe accidentally discovers the lovers conversing in Zonela's room, he almost goes mad with rage against the cripple who dared to comfort his captive. Another unequal fight ensues, which O'Brien compares to the battle between Jove and the Titan; it ends when Hippe whiplashes the young man and binds him. Solon's life is spared so he can be the human target for the diminutive demonic army.

In another dramatic episode, the four gypsies meet in a religious rite for the anointing of the swords and daggers with a mysterious poison. Afterward, they drink to celebrate the success of their mission; but they drink too much wine and fall into a deep sleep. Solon, having been helped in his escape by Zonela, like his classical namesake, wisely looks through the keyhole of Hippe's door before planning any action. What he sees horrifies him. The black bottle falling from Filomel's pocket activates the manikins. With malice and pleasure, the incarnate fiends swarm over the

sleeping bodies, stabbing as they move from one region of the body to another. Hippe, the first to awaken, emits a frightful shriek. His body swollen and discolored, he is covered with his creations; the bodies of his followers are also grotesque masses. All four grab handfuls of the horde and fling them into the fire; but some of the puppets escape and run around the room, igniting it. All perish in the flames as Solon and Zonela flee into the night.

"WHAT WAS IT?"

In "What Was It?" Harry and Dr. Hammond are two opium smokers, living in a Twenty-sixth Street boardinghouse which is supposedly haunted. One night Harry is attacked by an invisible assailant. Hammond, discovering him in combat with the air, thinks he is experiencing an opium vision; but Harry is not hallucinating, as Hammond quickly discovers. Both men grapple with "The Thing," finally getting it controlled by tightly lacing it with rope. Although to the eye it appears as though the rope is encasing an empty space, a scientific investigation determines its weight and height. Physiologically, it breathes, has a pulsating heart, struggles to be free, and has a will and a human form. The men, curious to learn about the elemental being, have it chloroformed so that a plaster of paris mold can be cast. They are terrified by what they discover: It is a hideous ghoul capable of feeding on human flesh.

The fiend, actually starving to death because the pair cannot find the proper food for its survival, remains in Harry's room for a few weeks. Nobody knows what to do with it. When it dies, they bury it in the garden and give the cast to Doctor X as a memento of the link with the other world. To make the tale more credible, O'Brien introduces an interesting dialogue between Harry and Hammond in which Hammond recalls the voices in Charles Brockden Brown's *Wieland* (1798) and the pictures of terror in Henry Bulwer-Lytton's *Zanoni* (1842). Both the American and the British novelist were caught up in the nineteenth-century's preoccupation with the occult, which by that time had become a literary prop.

"DUKE HUMPHREY'S DINNER"

Not all of O'Brien's tales depict the transformation that mysticism and magic underwent in his lifetime,

Critical Survey of Short Fiction

when ancient science became a pseudoscience. His dramatic comic sense, for example, dominates in "Duke Humphrey's Dinner," which was adapted for the stage and produced at Wallack's Theatre in 1856. A starving couple with a vivid imagination pretend that they are dining with Duke Humphrey, enjoying the finest delicacies of the world. Fortunately, they are rescued by an old friend of the young husband and live happily ever after.

O'Brien's lasting fame rests upon his adherence to the Romance tradition, writing of the confrontation of the material world with its counterpart. Magic, the macabre, malevolent spirits, ritual, psychological phenomena, witchcraft, and spiritualism in its broadest definition are inherent parts of his fiction. Overall, there is more disharmony than harmony between humankind and the realm of the spirit. Modern science had not yet ordered the chaos, according to these tales, but the human spirit is not vanquished. On the contrary, it appears anxious to face the challenge and ready for the combat.

OTHER MAJOR WORKS

PLAYS: *My Christmas Dinner*, pr. 1852; *A Gentleman from Ireland*, pr. 1854, pb. 1858; *Duke Humphrey's Dinner*, pr. 1856; *The Sisters*, pr. 1856; *The Tycoon: Or, Young America in Japan*, pr. 1860 (with Charles G. Rosenberg).

POETRY: *Sir Basil's Falcon*, 1853.

BIBLIOGRAPHY

Franklin, H. Bruce. *Future Perfect*. 2d ed. New York: Oxford University Press, 1978. In his introduction to "The Diamond Lens," Franklin stresses O'Brien's great inventiveness as his major quality in becoming one of the seminal figures in the early era of science-fiction writing. He also discusses "How I Overcame My Gravity" and "What Was It?," which he argues influenced later stories by Ambrose Bierce, Guy de Maupassant, and H. P. Lovecraft's "The Color Out of Space."

Hoppenstand, Gary. "Robots of the Past: Fitz-James O'Brien's 'The Wondersmith.'" *Journal of Popular Culture* 27 (Spring, 1994): 13-30. Discussion of the way O'Brien blends realistic immigrant fiction with the nineteenth-century German fairy tale. Notes how O'Brien parodies Romantic conventions. Suggests that O'Brien helped to establish the robot as an important literary motif.

Moskowitz, Sam. *Explorers of the Infinite*. Cleveland: World, 1963. In a work that discusses writers of fantasy and science fiction from Cyrano de Bergerac to the mid-twentieth century, the author devotes one chapter to O'Brien, titled "The Fabulous Fantast--Fitz-James O'Brien." In Moskowitz's opinion, O'Brien was not only one of the significant early figures in the genre of fantasy but also one of the most important short-story writers of the nineteenth-century.

O'Brien, Fitz-James. *Selected Literary Journalism, 1852-1860*. Edited by Wayne R. Kime. Selinsgrove, Pa.: Susquehanna University Press, 2003. Reprints some of the articles that O'Brien wrote for *The New York Times* and other newspapers and magazines during the decade he spent in New York City; these pieces include his discussion of literature as a profession, his comments on Walt Whitman's *Leaves of Grass*, and his opinions of the work of the young Herman Melville. Kime's preface and introduction provide a great deal of information about O'Brien's life, literary career, and his writings.

Tremayne, Peter, ed. *Irish Masters of Fantasy*. Dublin: Wolfhound Press, 1979. In his introduction to O'Brien's "The Wondersmith," Tremayne discusses several of O'Brien's most important stories, including "The Diamond Lens," "Jubal the Ringer," "What Was It?," and "From Hand to Mouth." He also comments upon O'Brien's influence on Ambrose Bierce and Guy de Maupassant.

Wentworth, Michael. "A Matter of Taste: Fitz-James O'Brien's 'The Diamond Lens' and Poe's Aesthetic of Beauty." *American Transcendental Quarterly*, n.s. 2 (December, 1988): 271-284. Analysis of one of O'Brien's most famous stories, arguing that it manifests the transcendent theory of beauty articulated by Edgar Allan Poe in his aesthetic theory.

Wolle, Francis. *Fitz-James O'Brien: A Literary Bohemian of the Eighteen Fifties.* Boulder: University of Colorado, 1944. The first full biography of O'Brien's short but eventful life. Originally a doctoral dissertation, this study's approach and emphasis, which include a scholarly discussion of all O'Brien's writings, is suggested in the book's subtitle. Supplemented by a bibliography.

Eileen A. Sullivan
Updated by Eugene S. Larson

FRANK O'CONNOR

Born: Cork City, Ireland; 1903
Died: Dublin, Ireland; March 10, 1966
Also Known As: Michael Francis O'Donovan

PRINCIPAL SHORT FICTION

Guests of the Nation, 1931
Bones of Contention, and Other Stories, 1936
Crab Apple Jelly, 1944
Selected Stories, 1946
The Common Chord, 1947
Traveller's Samples, 1951
The Stories of Frank O'Connor, 1952
More Stories, 1954
Stories by Frank O'Connor, 1956
Domestic Relations, 1957
My Oedipus Complex, and Other Stories, 1963
Collection Two, 1964
A Set of Variations, 1969
Collection Three, 1969
Collected Stories, 1981

OTHER LITERARY FORMS

Frank O'Connor was a prolific writer who wrote in nearly every literary genre. His published books include poems, translations of Irish poetry, plays, literary criticism, autobiographies, travel books, and essays. His two novels--*The Saint and Mary Kate* (1932) and *Dutch Interior* (1940)--are interesting complements to the many short-story collections for which he is best known.

ACHIEVEMENTS

Frank O'Connor was a masterful short-story writer. He was a realist who closely observed his characters and their world. However, he was not a pitiless realist, for he always seemed to have great sympathy for his characters, even those who insisted on putting themselves in absurd situations. It follows that one of his major techniques was humor. There is a place for humor in nearly all of his works, including those that border on tragedy. His stories tend to deal with a domestic rather than a public world, and the characters make up what he has called a "submerged population."

Structurally, the stories are simple. O'Connor likes to use a sudden reversal to bring about the necessary change in the plot. The plots tend to be simple and the reconciliation of the conflict is always very clear. One of the special devices he employed to give the stories some distinction is his use of a narrator. Whether the narrator is a child or an old priest, there is always a distinctive voice telling the reader the story. This voice has some of O'Connor's special qualities: warmth, humor, sympathy, and a realistic appraisal of the circumstances.

BIOGRAPHY

Educated at the Christian Brothers College, Cork, Michael Francis O'Donovan (who would adopt the pseudonym Frank O'Connor) joined the Irish Volunteers and participated on the Republican side in the Irish Civil War (1922-1923), for which activity he was imprisoned. He supported himself as a librarian, first in Cork, and later in Dublin, where he met Æ (George Russell) and William Butler Yeats, and began his literary career on Æ's *Irish Statesman.* He was until 1939 a member of the board of directors of the Abbey Theatre. In 1940, he began coediting *The Bell,* a literary journal, with Seán O'Faoláin. In addition to his editorial work, O'Connor was writing the stories that ensured his fame. Beginning with his first collection, *Guests of the Nation*, O'Connor wrote a number of superb collections of short stories. In recognition of this feat, O'Connor was invited to teach at a number of prestigious American universities. In 1939 he married Evelyn Bowen, with whom he had two sons and a daughter. During part of World War II he lived in London, working for the Ministry of Information. In 1951, he took up a creative writing position at Harvard University, was divorced in 1952, and the following year married Harriet Randolph Rich, with whom he had one daughter. He returned to Ireland permanently in 1961. He received a Litt.D. from Dublin University in 1962, where for a time he held a special lectureship. He died in Dublin on March 10, 1966.

ANALYSIS

Although widely read in Western literature, Frank O'Connor's literary character is most profoundly influenced by tensions within the literature and life of Ireland, ancient and modern. He was a dedicated student of the literature of Ireland's native language, a keen observer of the life of the folk, intimately familiar with Ireland's topography, and an active participant in its revolutionary and literary politics. These interests shaped his art. His literary vocation, however, like so many others of his generation, begins with Yeats's literary nationalism and continues through a dialectic between his perceptions of that poet's idealism and James Joyce's early naturalism. O'Connor's predominantly realistic fiction attempts a fusion of these two influences, while also recalling the popular origin--in the oral art of the shanachie (the teller of tales and legends) --of the short story. He found that Yeats and Joyce were too "elitist" for the "common reader"; and with O'Faoláin, he is associated with the development of the realistic Irish short story, the most representative art of the Irish Literary Revival.

"GUESTS OF THE NATION"

"Guests of the Nation," the title story of O'Connor's first collection, is probably his single finest work. All the stories in this volume reflect his involvement in the War of Independence; and this one distinguishes itself by its austere transcendence of the immediate circumstances, which in the rest of the stories trammel the subjects with excessive patriotic enthusiasm. During the War of Independence, the protagonist's (Bonaparte's) cadre of Irish Volunteers has been charged with the task of holding hostage two British soldiers, Belcher and Hawkins; during their captivity, the forced intimacy of captors and hostages leads to a reluctantly admitted mutual respect, which develops through their card-playing, arguments, and sharing of day-to-day chores. As the reader observes the exchanges of sympathy, idiom, and gesture between Irish and English soldiers, the two Englishmen become distinct from their roles, and from each other. The narrative develops the issues of religion, accent, and political allegiances as only superficially divisive, so that when the order arrives from headquarters to execute the hostages in military reprisal, the moral conflict is joined.

The story nicely dramatizes the contrasting reactions to this order among the various figures, captors and hostages: Donovan's giving grim precedence to national duty over "personal considerations"; Noble's pious reflections, which short-circuit his comprehension of the enormity of his actions; and Bonaparte's reflective agony. The change in the attitudes of the Englishmen, once they know the truth of the directive, poignantly reveals new dimensions in these men's characters. The argument to the last of Hawkins, the intellectual, dramatizes the limitations of rational discussion; but the stoicism of the more effective Belcher, his unflappability in the face of his own annihilation, drives the story to its height of feeling, a height to which only Bonaparte is equal. Noble's moral earnestness and Donovan's objectivity provide contrasts and contexts for Bonaparte's tragic anagnorisis.

O'Connor achieves the inimitable effects of the fine conclusion by a combination of devices: the shreds of partisan argument about religion and politics, the range of attitudes embodied by the various characters, the carefully modulated speaking voice of the narrator--steady, intelligent, slightly uncouth, and bitter--the spare use of images (ashes, spades, light and dark), and the figure of the old woman who observes the whole affair. This woman, at once a representative of the "hidden powers" of the universe, the irrationality behind the appearances of coherence, and also a representative of the affinity between such forces in the human psyche and the justifiable cause of Mother Ireland, gives the story both historical and universal resonances. Thus as one considers the story as a tragic examination of the theme of duty (to self, friends, institutions, nation, and God) and of the tension between the claims of individual conscience and communal obligation, between commitments to the personal and the abstract, developed with psychological accuracy in a modern setting, one notes its roots in the soil of Irish literature and tradition. The political situation, the various elements of local color, the allusively named characters, the figure of the old woman, the precedence of the ancient Celtic ritual of bog-burial, and the echoes of the tension in Celtic society between the obligations to provide hospitality to strangers and at the same time to protect the clan's rights through the insurance of hostage-taking: all these elements blend the modern with the archaic. Taken in combination, they achieve the result of casting these English soldiers as "guests" of the nation as an imaginative entity.

The restrained lyricism of the last paragraph, coming as it does on the heels of a rather colloquial narrative, shows how moved is the storyteller by his recollections. The bathetic solecism of the summary comment, however-- "And anything that happened to me afterwards, I never felt the same about again"--certifies that the narrator's education is unfinished. This sentence mirrors the dislocation of his feelings, while it also preserves the integrity of O'Connor's characteristic fictional device, the speaking voice.

"IN THE TRAIN"

The story "In the Train" (included in *Bones of Contention, and Other Stories*) dramatizes the reactions of a group of South-of-Ireland villagers toward an accused murderer in their midst, as they all return homeward by train from the Dublin criminal court. They have all conspired to prevent the woman's conviction, planning to punish her in their own manner when they return home. By a series of interconnected scenes, observed in a sequence of compartments of the train as it traverses the dark countryside, the story develops the theme of the villagers' common

Frank O'Connor (Library of Congress)

opposition to the law of the state and, by implication, their allegiance to the devices of their ancient community. From the bourgeois pretensions of the sergeant's wife to the dialogue that reveals the tensions and boredom among the policemen, to the stoicism of the peasants, to the huddled figure of the accused herself, the focus narrows from the humor of the opening scenes to the brooding interior monologue of the isolated woman in the final scene. The various parts of the story are interconnected by the characters' common motion west; their agreed attitude toward the legal apparatus of the Free State; by the Chaplinesque rambling drunk; and by the fated, defiant pariah. The story proceeds by indirection: Its main action (the murder and trial) is over and revealed only in retrospect; and its focus (the accused) is not fully identified until the final section. O'Connor develops these suspensions, however, in a resourceful manner, by focusing on the secondary tension in the community occasioned by the presence of the sergeant's carping wife and by having the shambling drunk lead the reader to the transfixed woman.

The apparent naïveté of the narrator's voice--colloquial, amused, relishing the folksy scenes--is belied by the complex structure of the piece. Moreover, the narrative is rich with echoes of Anton Chekhov, touches of melodrama and vaudeville, and devices from folktales and folkways, as it portrays the residue of the ancient legal unit of Celtic society, the *derb-fine*, persisting under the "foreign" order of the Irish Free State. In these contexts, the ambiguities of the sergeant's position and that of the local poteen manufacturer are richly developed, while readers discern that the woman's guilt is never firmly established. The story ends with a choric circle around the tragic complaint of the woman, whose community has preserved her only to impose their own severe penalty: ostracism from the only community she knows. O'Connor shares and enlarges her despair. The initial amusement of his story yields to chagrin at the loss both of the ideals of the Irish revolution in the Free State and of humaneness in the dying rural communities of Ireland.

"The Long Road to Ummera"

"The Long Road to Ummera" concerns an old woman's conflict with her son over her desire for burial in the ancestral ground in the remote West Cork village of Ummera. Abby, Batty Heig's daughter, has followed her son Pat to the city of Cork, but feeling the approach of death, desires to be returned to Ummera, not by the modern highway but by the ancient "long road." A tragicomic test of wills between mother and son ensues, pitting the desires for established ritual against modern efficiency, uncouth rural mannerisms against polite town manners, and homage to ancestors against modern progressivism. Because of her son's insensitivity, the old woman is forced to engage in comic subterfuge to achieve her last wish, and by grotesque turns of events involving a cobbler, a jarvey, and a priest, she has her way in all its details: Her body is transported along the prescribed road and announced ritually to the desolate countryside.

This is a moving portrait of an old woman, dignified by a lively sense of the presence of the dead and by lyrical evocations of the scenery of West Cork. In contrast to these qualities is the philistinism of her businessman son. The story itself has a ritual quality, woven as it is with repeated phrases, scenes, arguments,

events, recurrent images of death, various addictions, and the rehearsals of rituals themselves. The story represents O'Connor's criticism of bourgeois Ireland and the triumph of profit and respectability, major themes of his sweet-and-sour stories from the 1930's and 1940's contained in this, perhaps his best collection, *Crab Apple Jelly*. Although the speaking voice remains the norm, the tone here is more knowing than in the earlier stories. O'Connor, like Abby, is keeping promises to ancient values, including the language, family loyalty, community, and rootedness. If the old woman's loyalty to her circuitous way is bypassed by Ireland's new one, however, the narrator's sad lyricism suggests that he can tread neither.

"First Confession"

Of O'Connor's childhood stories, "First Confession," "My Oedipus Complex," and "The Drunkard," developed over the 1940's, are his most famous, although not his most distinguished, works. The much-anthologized "First Confession" humorously exploits the mildly exotic Catholic rite, as the little boy finds that the image of religion fostered by his female educators is not borne out in the encounter with the priest-confessor. Hearing that the boy's chief sin is his desire to murder his ill-mannered grandmother, the priest humors the impenitent child by having him articulate the fantasy and sends him back to the sunny street. The idiom of an Irish child carries the narration here, although with the injection of some adult irony directed at the boy's naïve literalism. The story might be faulted for its slapstick and cuteness, as if O'Connor indulges too liberally in the mood of his creation. Many of O'Connor's stories portray insensitive and repressive priests, but not this one. Rather, it is the women who are the agents of terrifying, dogmatic religiosity, in contrast with the priest's personification of a paternal, forgiving, and humorous God.

"My Oedipus Complex" and "The Drunkard"

"My Oedipus Complex" and "The Drunkard" are charming examples of O'Connor's mastery of the narrator-as-child. In them, the themes of marital tension, domestic evasiveness, and the dependence of Irish males on their mothers are treated with light irony. By means of an unexpected turn of events, the severe social controls on incest and alcoholism are toyed with as the jealous conspiracies of women; thus moral awareness commences with male bonding. In each of these three childhood stories, the antagonist at first appears as male--priest, bed-rival, drunken father--until the possessiveness of women emerges as the substantial moral antagonist. In these much-revised stories, O'Connor has refined the instrument of the speaking voice to a point that is perhaps too ingratiating, too calculatedly smooth, so that the spontaneity of the "rough narrative voice" is lost, and with it, some of his cold and passionate isolation. The attraction of these stories, however, is readily apparent in their author's recorded versions, which he narrates with considerable relish.

"A STORY BY MAUPASSANT"

O'Connor's tendency to reread his own work with disapproval led to constant revisions, so that there are two, three, or more variants of many of his most popular works. A case in point is "A Story by Maupassant," which first appeared in *The Penguin New Writing* (no. 24, 1945) and in a significantly revised version in *A Set of Variations*. This story of the corruption of an Irish intellectual, observed by his more concrete-minded friend, climaxes when Terry Coughlan admits to the narrator that his appreciation of Maupassant's grasp of "what life can do to you" came during a sleepless night in the bed of a Parisian prostitute. A comparison of the two versions shows several changes: O'Connor expands the proportion of more precise and graphic details and reduces dialectal, self-conscious, and repetitive elements; he achieves a more complex ironic effect by a stronger investment in double perspective; he condemns more forthrightly the hypocrisy of the Catholic school, as he renders more deft the function of religious metaphor; and he enlarges the sympathy for Terry Coughlan by an expansion of oblique cultural references and a softening of the narrator's moralizing. O'Connor's own view of Maupassant--that the mainspring of his art lay in the mixture of creative and destructive tendencies interacting as perversity--is brought to bear on the bitter conclusion of the story: Maupassant, at least, has not abandoned these self-destructive characters. In his revisions, O'Connor strengthens Maupassant's perspective, focusing in the end on the prostitute's baby, a symbol of the naïveté of new life. O'Connor bitterly notes that nature, like Maupassant's fiction, without an ideal that is

informing, seeks the lowest level. Here is a story that, by the intervention of O'Connor's matured hand, gains considerably in power and perspective, subtlety and professionalism.

"INTROVERTED" IRELAND

The general subject of O'Connor's fiction is a critique of the "introverted religion" and "introverted politics" of bourgeois Ireland--sectarian obscurantism, the abuses of clerical power, class snobbery, family rivalries, disingenuous piety, Anglophobia, and thwarted idealism--although these criticisms are usually modified by warm portraits of energetic children, humane clerics, and unpretentious peasants. His central object in these stories is "to stimulate the moral imagination" by separating his characters from their assumed social roles and having them stand, for a moment, alone. In many of his most distinguished works, and indeed throughout his whole career as a writer of short fiction, one may discern such a movement from the depiction of the comfortably communal to that of the isolated, enlightened individual. He proposes a nexus between such a contrast of perspectives and the short-story form.

THE LONELY VOICE

In his study entitled *The Lonely Voice* (1963), O'Connor holds as central that "in the short story at its most characteristic [there is] something not often found in the novel--an intense awareness of human loneliness." This collection of essays on selected practitioners of the modern short story (Ivan Turgenev, Anton Chekhov, Rudyard Kipling, James Joyce, Katherine Mansfield, D. H. Lawrence, Ernest Hemingway, A. E. Coppard, Isaac Babel, and Mary Lavin) draws on seminar notes from O'Connor's classes at various universities in the 1950's. The discussions are genial, opinionated, and not academic, and they afford brilliant comments on individual artists and works, although they suffer from diffuseness and overextension at certain points in the argument. The study rests on the theory that the distinction of the short story from the novel is less a formal than an ideological one: It is the expression of "an attitude of mind that is attracted by submerged population groups . . . tramps, artists, lonely idealists, dreamers, and spoiled priests . . . remote from the community--romantic, individualistic, and intransigent."

From this position, O'Connor argues that "the conception of the short story as a miniature art is inherently false," holding that, on the contrary, "the storyteller differs from the novelist in this: he must be much more of a writer, much more of an artist . . . more of a dramatist." From the same vantage point he evaluates his selected authors as they severally identify with some "submerged population group," finding that as these writers compromised or found less compelling the vision of their subjects as outsiders or social or political minorities, they either failed as short-story writers or found another form more expressive of their visions.

While O'Connor's claims for these theories are maintained in the face of easily adduced contrary evidence, they have limited, and in some ways startling, application to certain authors and works. As a critic, O'Connor possessed brilliant intuitions, although he did not have the power to systematize. In *The Lonely Voice* his remarks on Joyce and Hemingway's rhetorical styles, his contrasting Chekhov and Mansfield, and his accounting for Kipling's artistic failure, and in *The Mirror in the Roadway* (1956), his discussion of Joyce's "dissociated metaphor," have useful application to the contribution of each of these authors to the literature of the short story.

From various accounts by former students and colleagues, as well as from these critical works, it is quite clear that O'Connor was a brilliantly successful teacher of fiction-writing. His seminars were guided with authority and seriousness, and he placed great emphasis on the perfection of technique. He trained his students to begin with a "prosaic kernel" which the "treatment" takes to its crisis. The finished work takes its power from the cumulation of the drama, poetry, and emotion developed throughout the narrative, finally resolving itself in universalizing mystery. The short story is not concerned with the passage of time or with particularities of character; ideally it is based on an incident and a briefly stated theme, which technique elaborates to the final formula; it should not proceed on technique alone (Hemingway's fault) or follow a preconceived symbolic pattern (Joyce's fault), but ideally it is a fusion of the opposites of naturalism and symbolism.

Other MAJOR WORKS

LONG FICTION: *The Saint and Mary Kate*, 1932; *Dutch Interior*, 1940.

PLAYS: *In the Train*, pr. 1937 (with Hugh Hunt); *The Invincibles: A Play in Seven Scenes*, pr. 1937 (with Hunt); *Moses' Rock*, pr. 1938 (with Hunt); *The Statue's Daughter: A Fantasy in a Prologue and Three Acts*, pr. 1941.

POETRY: *Three Old Brothers, and Other Poems*, 1936.

NONFICTION: *Death in Dublin: Michael Collins and the Irish Revolution*, 1937; *The Big Fellow*, 1937; *A Picture Book*, 1943; *Towards an Appreciation of Literature*, 1945; *Irish Miles*, 1947; *The Art of the Theatre*, 1947; *The Road to Stratford*, 1948; *Leinster, Munster, and Connaught*, 1950; *The Mirror in the Roadway*, 1956; *An Only Child*, 1961; *The Lonely Voice*, 1963; *The Backward Look: A Survey of Irish Literature*, 1967; *My Father's Son*, 1968; *The Happiness of Getting it Down Right: Letters of Frank O'Connor and William Maxwell, 1945-1966*, 1996.

TRANSLATIONS: *The Wild Bird's Nest*, 1932 (of selected Irish poetry); *Lords and Commons*, 1938 (of selected Irish poetry); *The Fountain of Magic*, 1939 (of selected Irish poetry); *Lament for Art O'Leary*, 1940 (of Eileen O'Connell); *The Midnight Court: A Rhythmical Bacchanalia from the Irish of Bryan Merryman*, 1945 (of Brian Merriman's *Cuirt an mheadhoin oidhche*); *Kings, Lords, and Commons*, 1959 (of selected Irish poetry); *The Little Monasteries*, 1963 (of selected Irish poetry); *A Golden Treasury of Irish Poetry*, 1967 (with David Greene).

MISCELLANEOUS: *A Frank O'Connor Reader*, 1994; *The Best of Frank O'Connor*, 2009 (Julian Barnes, editor).

BIBLIOGRAPHY

Alexander, James D. "Frank O'Connor in *The New Yorker*, 1945-1967." *Eire-Ireland* 30 (1995): 130-144. Examines how O'Connor changed his narrative style during the more than twenty years he was writing for *The New Yorker*, contracting the presence of a narrator to a voice and developing a double-leveled view of "experienced innocence" in his young boy stories. Argues that O'Connor created a genial persona in his stories that diverted attention from his more serious subject matter of Irish social problems.

Bordewyk, Gordon. "Quest for Meaning: The Stories of Frank O'Connor." *Illinois Quarterly* 41 (Winter, 1978): 37-47. Discusses O'Connor's concern with fundamental qualities of everyday life and his sense of wonder in the mundane in four major groups of stories of war, religion, youth, and marriage. Examines how the search for meaning changes the lives of characters in these four groups.

Davenport, Gary T. "Frank O'Connor and the Comedy of Revolution." *Eire-Ireland* 8 (Summer, 1973): 108-116. Davenport analyzes some of O'Connor's early stories on the Irish Civil War and points out the persistence of comedy even in tragic situations. He claims that O'Connor sees revolution as farcical.

Evans, Robert C., and Richard Harp, eds. *Frank O'Connor: New Perspectives*. West Cornwall, Conn.: Locust Hill Press, 1998. A collection of essays providing varied and thoughtful interpretations of O'Connor's works.

Hunter, Adrian. "Frank O'Connor and Seán O'Faoláin." In *The Cambridge Introduction to the Short Story in English*. Cambridge, England: Cambridge University Press, 2007. An overview of the two authors' short fiction, providing analyses of some of the individual stories.

Ingman, Heather. "1920-1939: Years of Transition." In *A History of the Irish Short Story*. New York: Cambridge University Press, 2009. This chapter in Ingman's examination of the development of the Irish short story provides an overview of short fiction written from 1920 through 1939, followed by detailed readings of some of O'Connor's short stories.

Lennon, Hilary, ed. *Frank O'Connor: Critical Essays*. Dublin: Four Courts Press, 2007. The essays examine O'Connor's works from a variety of perspectives and include discussions of O'Connor and critical memory, O'Connor and a vanishing Ireland, O'Connor's reception in America, a working theory of the Irish short story, and analyses of his stories "Guests of the Nation" and "Lonelyrock."

Matthews, James H. *Frank O'Connor*. Lewisburg, Pa.: Bucknell University Press, 1976. This book is an excellent introduction to O'Connor's fiction since it deals with the social context of the stories and the critical theory underlying them.

McKeon, Jim. *Frank O'Connor: A Life*. Edinburgh: Mainstream, 1998. A brief, readable biography of O'Connor. Comments on the biographical sources of some of the short stories and discusses O'Connor's literary career.

Neary, Michael. "The Inside-Out World in Frank O'Connor's Stories." *Studies in Short Fiction* 30 (Summer, 1993): 327-336. Discusses O'Connor's use of smallness to accent the collision between the world of the self and the vast world outside. Discusses "The Story Teller" as the most emphatic embodiment of this tension in O'Connor's stories, for the protagonist confronts characters who refuse to take her quest for magic and meaning seriously.

Renner, Stanley. "The Theme of Hidden Powers: Fate Versus Human Responsibility in 'Guests of the Nation.'" *Studies in Short Fiction* 27 (Summer, 1990): 371-378. Argues that the story's moral design emphasizes the existence of mysterious "hidden powers" or forces of chance and fate that control human lives. Suggests that the moral judgment of the story is against the protagonist-teller Bonaparte, who contributes to the world's brutality by mistakenly believing people have no choice.

Steinman, Michael. *Frank O'Connor at Work*. Syracuse, N.Y.: Syracuse University Press, 1990. Examines how O'Connor created some of his short stories, comparing unpublished and published versions and discussing how and why he made revisions. "First Confession," "Judas, "The Genius," "Orpheus and His Lute," "The Cornet Player Who Betrayed Ireland," and "The Little Mother" are among the stories studied.

Tomory, William M. *Frank O'Connor*. Boston: Twayne, 1980. An introduction to O'Connor that briefly sketches his life and gives an overview of his work. Tomory touches on a few stories, but most of the analysis is on themes and character types.

Winston, Greg. "Frank O'Connor: 'Guests of the Nation' and 'My Oedipus Complex.'" In *A Companion to the British and Irish Short Story*, edited by Cheryl Alexander Malcolm and David Malcolm. Malden, Mass.: Wiley-Blackwell, 2008. An explication of the two stories, which helps place them in the larger context of the Irish short story.

Wohlgelernter, Maurice. *Frank O'Connor: An Introduction.* New York: Columbia University Press, 1977. The fullest critical study on O'Connor's fiction available. The author is especially good at articulating O'Connor's theory of the story and in applying those concepts to individual short stories.

Cóilín Owens
Updated by James Sullivan

SEÁN O'FAOLÁIN

Born: Cork City, Ireland; February 22, 1900
Died: Dublin, Ireland; April 20, 1991
Also Known As: John Francis Whelan

PRINCIPAL SHORT FICTION

Midsummer Night's Madness, and Other Stories, 1932
A Purse of Coppers, 1937
Teresa, and Other Stories, 1947
The Man Who Invented Sin, and Other Stories, 1948
The Finest Stories of Seán O'Faoláin, 1957
I Remember! I Remember!, 1961
The Heat of the Sun: Stories and Tales, 1966
The Talking Trees, and Other Stories, 1970
Foreign Affairs, and Other Stories, 1976
The Collected Stories of Seán O'Faoláin, 1980-1982 (3 volumes)

OTHER LITERARY FORMS

Seán O'Faoláin (shawn oh-fay-LAWN) wrote novels, biographies, travel books, social analysis, and literary criticism. He produced a number of well-received novels and several biographies of prominent Irish political figures. O'Faoláin's most notable work of literary criticism is his study of the short story, *The Short Story*, published in 1948. O'Faoláin also wrote a memorable autobiography, *Vive Moi!* (1964).

ACHIEVEMENTS

Seán O'Faoláin is one of the acknowledged Irish masters of the short story. His stories are realistic and closely dissect the social world of the ordinary Irishman of the twentieth century. His protagonists are usually forced to accept the limitations and defeats that life in modern Ireland enforces. O'Faoláin, however, is not a social critic or satirist. Such an accommodation with society is often seen as welcome and necessary. The central theme in many of O'Faoláin's stories is the defeat of rigid principle and idealism by social and individual compromise. O'Faoláin seems to resist any appeal to pure principle and to celebrate a healthy realism and recognition of the limits that life imposes.

Seán O'Faoláin's most important structural device is the reversal, in which a character's situation is suddenly altered. These reversals may be embarrassing or even humiliating, but O'Faoláin often softens the ending to show something human and positive even in the defeat that the reversal effects. O'Faoláin progressed as a writer of short fiction from his early autobiographical stories, focusing on the Irish troubles and civil war, to stories dealing with a variety of Irish people in different sections and social situations. The autobiography became a more flexible and distanced art as O'Faoláin approached the ideal of his master, Anton Chekhov.

BIOGRAPHY

Seán O'Faoláin was born John Francis Whelan in Cork City, Ireland, in 1900. His parents led an untroubled conventional life; his father was a constable for the Royal Irish Constabulary and his mother a pious Roman Catholic. By the time that John grew up, however, the problems of Ireland and England were becoming acute. The 1916 uprising in Dublin declared an Irish Republic, and a war broke out between Irish revolutionaries and British soldiers. John Whelan knew on which side he had to be and joined the Irish Volunteers in 1918 and later the Irish Republican Army. He changed his name to its Gaelic form of Seán O'Faoláin in 1918 to signal his new identity.

During the Irish troubles, O'Faoláin was educating himself; he received his B.A. and M.A. from University College, Cork, and a fellowship to Harvard University in 1928. In 1932, he published his first collection of short stories, *Midsummer Night's Madness, and Other Stories*. After that O'Faoláin became a prolific writer, as he produced novels, travel books, biographies, and studies of the national character of Ireland. Above all, however, he was a masterly writer of short stories.

O'Faoláin's *Midsummer Night's Madness, and Other Stories* contains a number of stories dealing with the Irish Civil War. Most of these treat broken promises and the destruction of idealism and romantic dreams. The later collections contain a considerable amount of irony, as the ordinary Irishman, with little hope of engaging in a historic event, tries to find some distinction in a bleak society. O'Faoláin, however, often modulates his irony and finds some compensatory victory even in defeat.

After having found his style and subject matter, O'Faoláin published a number of excellent collections of stories, culminating in *The Collected Stories of Seán O'Faoláin*. O'Faoláin became one of the finest Irish writers of the twentieth century and a master in his chosen genre, the short story.

ANALYSIS

Seán O'Faoláin's stories are varied. The earliest ones deal with the immediate political concerns of the Irish Civil War. Others use irony, although the irony tends to be gentle rather than harsh. O'Faoláin never merely mocked or made fun of his characters; there is always affection and sympathy for those he created. Another group of stories expose idealism or abstract principles. O'Faoláin had little use for such general principles; he was consistently on the side of the specific case and the

demands of realism and life. The later stories deal with sexuality and relationships between men and women, especially the problems of husbands and wives.

A few constants do exist, however, in the stories. O'Faoláin's strength is in the portrayal and development of character and world. Each of his major characters fully exists in a well-defined environment. Ireland, as portrayed by O'Faoláin, is nearly a character in the story, and the limitations created by that world are significant. Whether it be religion or a narrow-minded social system, Ireland often restricts in various ways the opportunities for expression and a fuller and freer life.

"THE OLD MASTER"

"The Old Master," from *A Purse of Coppers*, is an early story that punctures the claims of a character to a privileged position; it uses a sudden and surprising reversal to bring about its resolution. The use of irony in this story is direct and amusing, if not very sophisticated. The protagonist, John Aloysius Gonzaga O'Sullivan, spends his time mocking the provincialism and lack of culture in his small Irish town. He has a sinecure as a law librarian and refuses to practice law; he spends his time, instead, berating the locals for their lack of sophistication. He is "the only man left in Ireland with a sense of beauty . . . the old master deserted in the abandoned house."

One day, the Russian Ballet comes to town, and he is ecstatic. A conflict arises, however, from the presence of the Russian Ballet. When O'Sullivan attempts to see a performance, he is stopped by men from the Catholic Church who oppose "Immoral Plays." O'Sullivan holds his sinecure from the county council, and he can lose his job if he offends the Catholic Church. Therefore, he compromises and walks away from the door; he apparently failed to live up to his ideals. He tries, however, to make amends by sneaking in the back way and reassuring the Russian performers that he is with them.

O'Sullivan returns to the front of the theater and is immediately involved in a march against the ballet company. If he is seen by the people at the courthouse, he will be ruined, but if he is seen abandoning the march, he may lose his job. He tries to resolve his conflict by escaping to an outhouse and cursing the local leaders, as he has done so often in the past. He remains in the outhouse all night and catches pneumonia from this exposure and soon dies. The people in the town had seen him earlier as a "public show" and only at his death did they see him as a "human being." "The Old Master" is a typical O'Faoláin story. The unnatural idealism and pomposity of the main character have to be exposed. He is not mocked, however, for his fall; he has instead joined a fallible human community and rid himself of false pretensions.

"CHILDYBAWN"

"Childybawn" was published in *The Finest Stories of Seán O'Faoláin*, and it is a delightful study of the Irish character in which O'Faoláin reverses the usual view of the Irishman's dominance by his mother. The story is simple in its structure, and its effect depends on a reversal of expectations. O'Faoláin is not really a comic writer in the traditional sense; in later stories, the humor is much more subtle and becomes a part of the story, not the only element as it is here. The plot begins when Benjy Spillane's mother receives an anonymous note telling her that her son, fat and forty, is carrying on with a bank teller. Her strategy to retain the dedication and presence of her son is to remind him incessantly of Saint Augustine's love for his mother, Monica. This has little effect until Benjy becomes seriously ill and begins to read religious texts and change his life.

Suddenly the relationship is reversed; the religious Benjy begins complaining about the drinking and excessive betting of his mother. His mother now wishes that he would get married and leave her alone. The climax of the story is another reversal, as Benjy returns to his riotous ways and finally gains the promise of the bank clerk to wed him. There is a five-year engagement until his mother dies. After all, Benjy notes, "a fellow has to have *some* regard for his mother!"

"Childybawn" is a comic story and plays on many Irish stereotypes. There is the dominating mother and the middle-aged son who worships his mother. O'Faoláin gives the story and the types an original twist when he shows what would happen if a middle-aged son actually behaved the way a mother wished him to behave. Mrs. Spillane realizes that she has not had a peaceful moment since her son took up religion; she longs for the old, irreverent, and natural relationship that works on conflict and confrontation.

"THE FUR COAT"

"The Fur Coat" is a poignant story taken from *The Man Who Invented Sin, and Other Stories*. It is concerned with social class, a somewhat unusual area for an O'Faoláin story. Most of his characters seem to live in a static environment, and such social change in Ireland is very different from the earlier stories. The plot is very simple, since it emphasizes character rather than action. Paddy Maguire receives an important promotion, so his wife, Molly, immediately determines that she must have a fur coat to go with her new status. She immediately becomes defensive over such a purchase, however, asking her husband if he thinks that she is "extravagant." The conflict grows between husband and wife as they discuss the fur coat, but it is really within Molly. Her own doubts about such a purchase are projected onto her husband, and they end up fighting, with her accusing him of being "mean." The climax of the story comes when Paddy gives Molly a check for 150 pounds and she rips it up. She wants the coat desperately, but she cannot afford it. "I couldn't, Paddy. I just couldn't." The story ends with Paddy asking her why she cannot purchase what she most desires and receiving the despairing answer, "I don't know."

"The Fur Coat" is a social story as well as a character study. The sudden rise in class and position leaves Molly between the old ways that have sustained her and the new ones that she cannot embrace. O'Faoláin has found a new subject for Irish fiction. The focus is no longer the enduring and unchanging peasant but an urban middle-class character who must deal with changes in his or her social position and personal life.

"THE SUGAWN CHAIR"

"The Sugawn Chair," from *I Remember! I Remember!*, is a perfect example of O'Faoláin's gentle irony; the story pokes fun at the illusions of an ideal rural life with economy and humor. O'Faoláin seems dedicated to exposing the various illusions that are endemic in Ireland. The chair, as the story opens, is abandoned and without a seat in the attic of the narrator. He associates the chair with memories of a yearly sack of apples that would be delivered, smelling of "dust, and hay, and apples. . . ." The sack and the chair both signify another world, the country.

The chair also has a history. It was an object of comfort in which "my da could tilt and squeak and rock to his behind's content." One night while rocking, his father went through the seat of the chair, where he remained stuck and cursing, much to the amusement of his wife and son. The father decides to repair his chair with some straw that he bought in a market. He enlists the aid of two of his country comrades. They soon, however, begin to argue about the different regions that they came from in rural Ireland. These arguments subside, but a new argument erupts about the type of straw needed to repair the chair. One claims that this straw is too moist, while another says that it is too short. Finally, they abandon the project and return to their earlier pursuits.

The story ends with the father symbolically admitting defeat by throwing a potato back into the sack and sitting on one of the city-made "plush" chairs. The Sugawn chair remains as it had been, shattered without a seat. The narrator comes upon the chair one day when he is cleaning out the attic after his mother has died. It recalls to his mind not only the country smells but also his mother and father embracing and "laughing foolishly, and madly in love again." "The Sugawn Chair" modulates its irony at the very end, so that the mocking at the illusions of an ideal rural life are tempered by the real feelings and memories that they share. O'Faoláin is by no means a James Joyce who fiercely indicts the false dreams of his Dubliners; O'Faoláin has a place even in his irony for true affections and relationships.

"DIVIDENDS"

"Dividends," from *The Heat of the Sun: Stories and Tales*, is a more ambitious story than many of the earlier ones, and it shows both a greater tolerance for the foibles of the characters and a subtlety in structure. Its primary subject is the clash between principle and reality, a favorite O'Faoláin theme. The story begins with the narrator's Aunt Anna coming into a legacy of 750 pounds. The narrator advises her to invest her legacy in secure stocks, so that she will receive a steady income. An old friend of the narrator, Mel Meldrum, arranges the transaction. The conflict arises when Aunt Anna sells her shares and continues to demand her dividends from Mel. Mel finally gives in and pays her the money, even though it is against his principles.

In order to resolve the dispute, the narrator is forced to return to Cork from Dublin. He finds that Mel is very well situated, with a country cottage and a beautiful young girl as a servant. Mel reveals that Aunt Anna has sold the shares not for a chair and some masses for her soul but for a fancy fur coat. Mel now refuses to compromise and pay Anna her dividends. This intensifies the conflict, as the narrator urges Mel to be his old self and take a chance on life, abandon his principles, pay Aunt Anna the dividends, and marry the young girl. Mel, however, is unable to change; if he marries the girl, he may be unhappy; if he pays the dividends, he is compromised and is no longer his ideal self.

Mel resolves the problem by abandoning his relationship with the young girl and hiring Aunt Anna as a servant. He will remain logical and consistent. The ending of the story, however, is not an indictment of Mel's principled consistency but a confession by the narrator that he has done something terrible by demanding that Mel remain the Mel that he had known as a boy at school. He had "uncovered his most secret dream and destroyed it by forcing him to bring it to the test of reality." He also has been narrow-minded in demanding a consistency of character and exposed a life-giving illusion no less than Mel had. "Dividends" is a complex narrative and a psychological study of how characters live upon illusions rather than principles. There is no neat exposure of illusions as in "The Old Master" but instead an unmasking of those who are all too eager to uncover dreams.

"HYMENEAL"

"Hymeneal" is a story from O'Faoláin's latest period, and it is one of the fullest explorations of marriage, as O'Faoláin scrutinizes the relationship between husband and wife. "Hymeneal" covers the many years of a couple's marriage, but it focuses on the period of retirement. It is one of O'Faoláin's best plotted stories, with a sudden and surprising reversal. It begins peacefully, detailing the enduring relationship of a married couple, Phil and Abby Doyle, who have been rooted in one spot in the North Circular section of Dublin. They have lived in this section for some thirty-five years. Phil, however, is to retire in a year, and he knows that Abby needs some help with the house, but he cannot afford it on his pension. He then decides--without consulting his wife--to sell their house and move to West Clare, where he can hire a servant and have the peace and time to write the book that he has been planning to write for years, which will expose the Education Department and Ministry.

The conflict between Phil and Abby develops quickly. She hates the isolation of West Clare, especially since it means moving away from her Dublin-based sister, Molly. Phil is also unhappy, although he refuses to admit it. He does none of the things that he has talked about for years; he does not fish or hunt, and he makes no progress on his book, although he continues to talk about it. Phil talks incessantly about exposing the department, where he has worked for such a long time, and the current minister, Phelim Quigley, the husband of Molly, Abby's sister. He sees Phelim as the perfect example of a man who has sacrificed principle to sentiment and convenience. When Phelim refuses to fire a teacher who drinks and quarrels with his wife, Phil Doyle is outraged at this lack of action. The book will reveal all.

The plot turns when Phelim Quigley suddenly dies in a car crash and Phil and Abby return to Dublin to console Molly and set her affairs in order. Phil assigns himself to work alone to sort out Phelim's papers. In those papers, Phil finds a number of surprising documents that alter his life. First of all, he finds that Phelim has acquired a decent sum of money and has recently purchased Phil's old house in Dublin. He then finds a sequence of poems that Phelim has written about his love for Abby rather than his wife, Molly. Phil is enraged at this soiling of his own love for Abby. Phil changes once more, however, when he comes upon some letters of Abby to Phelim that tell of Phelim's advice to Abby to stick to Phil and not divorce or leave him. Phelim also praises Phil's great ability as a civil servant; it is just those rigid qualities, however, that have made it so difficult to live with him. The whole tone and attitude of the last part of the story changes. The weather changes from stormy to sunny and clear. Molly announces that she would like to rent the Dublin house that she and Phelim had bought recently to Phil and Abby. Phil has become more accommodating. He will abandon his book and his inhuman principle for a fuller and less rigid life.

"THE PATRIOT"

O'Faoláin's fiction shows clear lines of development. The early stories that focus on the Irish Civil War are filled with bitterness at the failure of leaders to live up to the republican ideal. They also tend to lack the smooth narrative surface, and some, such as "The Patriot," are quite simple and undemanding in their structure. The collections that followed showed an increasing mastery of the short-story form. They also avoid the simple structure and tiresome bitterness at the failures of ideals. "The Old Master," for example, shows an exposure of ideals that can deepen a character's humanity.

By the time of *I Remember! I Remember!*, O'Faoláin had mastered the short story; the stories from this period demonstrate a subtlety of characterization, plot, and theme that was not found in the earlier works. In addition, O'Faoláin changes his attitude toward the world of his fiction. He now was able to distance himself and find amusement in the dreams of his characters, as "The Sugawn Chair" makes clear. The last phase of O'Faoláin's development can be seen in the stories of *The Heat of the Sun: Stories and Tales* and *The Talking Trees, and Other Stories*. He began more fully to investigate the place and role of sexuality in Ireland. Stories such as "One Man, One Boat, One Girl" and "Falling Rocks, Narrowing Road, Cul-de-Sac Stop" are humorous explorations of human relationships. The Irishman's fear of women is handled with grace and sympathy, while at the same time acknowledging its absurdity. One other aspect of human relationships in O'Faoláin's fiction needs to be mentioned. "Hymeneal" is a haunting portrayal of marriage in which the main character's illusions are punctured so that he might recreate and strengthen his relationship with his wife.

OTHER MAJOR WORKS

LONG FICTION: *A Nest of Simple Folk*, 1933; *Bird Alone*, 1936; *Come Back to Erin*, 1940; *And Again?*, 1979.

PLAY: *She Had to Do Something*, pr. 1937.

NONFICTION: *The Life Story of Eamon De Valera*, 1933; *Constance Markievicz: Or, The Average Revolutionary*, 1934; *King of the Beggars: A Life of Daniel O'Connell*, 1938; *An Irish Journey*, 1940; *The Great O'Neill: A Biography of Hugh O'Neill, Earl of Tyrone*,

1550-1616, 1942; *The Story of Ireland*, 1943; *The Irish: A Character Study*, 1947; *The Short Story*, 1948; *A Summer in Italy*, 1949; *Newman's Way*, 1952; *South to Sicily*, 1953 (pb. in U.S. as *An Autumn in Italy*, 1953); *The Vanishing Hero*, 1956; *Vive Moi!*, 1964.

EDITED TEXT: *The Silver Branch: A Collection of the Best Old Irish Lyrics Variously Translated*, 1938.

BIBLIOGRAPHY

Arndt, Marie. *A Critical Study of Sean O'Faolain's Life and Work*. Lewiston, N.Y.: E. Mellen Press, 2001. Examines O'Faoláin's life and writings, placing them in the historical and political context of contemporary Irish issues, such as Gaelic heritage, Catholicism, nationalism, and the Anglo-Irish and English presence in Ireland .

Bonaccorso, Richard. *Seán O'Faoláin's Irish Vision*. Albany: State University of New York Press, 1987. An excellent study that places O'Faoláin and his work in a social and literary context. The readings of O'Faoláin's stories are thorough and ingenious, if not always convincing.

Butler, Pierce. *Seán O'Faoláin: A Study of the Short Fiction*. New York: Twayne, 1993. An introduction to O'Faoláin's short fiction in which Butler claims that O'Faoláin shifts from an early focus on individuals in conflict with repressive Irish forces to more universal human conflicts. Examines O'Faoláin's realistic style and narrative voice as it changes throughout his career. Includes O'Faoláin's comments on the short story, some contemporary reviews, and three previously published critical studies.

Davenport, Guy. "Fiction Chronicle." *The Hudson Review* 32 (1979): 139-150. Davenport has high praise for O'Faoláin's ability as a writer of short fiction. He finds the central themes of O'Faoláin's stories to be the Irish character and Irish Catholicism.

Delany, Paul. "The Desie for Clarity: Seán O'Faoláin's 'Lovers of the Lake.'" In *A Companion to the British and Irish Short Story*, edited by Cheryl Alexander Malcolm and David Malcolm. Malden, Mass.: Wiley-Blackwell, 2008. Provides an explication of this short story.

Doyle, Paul A. *Sean O'Faoláin*. New York: Twayne, 1968. A life and works study of O'Faoláin in the Twayne series. Discusses the novels, the short fiction, and the literary context in which O'Faoláin wrote.

Hanley, Katherine. "The Short Stories of Seán O'Faoláin: Theory and Practice." *Eire-Ireland* 6 (1971): 3-11. An excellent introduction to O'Faoláin's stories. Hanley briefly sketches the theoretical base of the stories and then traces the development of O'Faoláin from the early romantic stories to the more sophisticated ones.

Harmon, Maurice. *Seán O'Faoláin*. London: Constable, 1994. Harmon first analyzes O'Faoláin's biographies on Irish figures to provide a social context and then examines briefly each book of short stories. Useful for an understanding of the Irish political and social scene.

Hunter, Adrian. "Frank O'Connor and Seán O'Faoláin." In *The Cambridge Introduction to the Short Story in English*. Cambridge, England: Cambridge University Press, 2007. An overview of the two authors' short fiction, providing analyses of some of the individual stories.

Ingman, Heather. "1940-1959: Isolation." In *A History of the Irish Short Story*. New York: Cambridge University Press, 2009. This chapter in Ingman's examination of the development of the Irish short story provides an overview of short fiction written from 1940 through 1959, followed by detailed readings of some of O'Faoláin's stories.

Neary, Michael. "Whispered Presences in Seán O'Faoláin's Stories." *Studies in Short Fiction* 32 (Winter, 1995): 11-20. Argues that O'Faoláin confronts his Irishness in his stories in a way that refuses closure or the comfort of the telling detail. Asserts that many of his stories create a feeling of characters being haunted by some event from the past of which they cannot make sense.

James Sullivan

LIAM O'FLAHERTY

Born: Inishmore, Aran Islands, Ireland;
   August 28, 1896
Died: Dublin, Ireland; September 7, 1984

PRINCIPAL SHORT FICTION

Spring Sowing, 1924
Civil War, 1925
Darkness, 1926
The Tent, and Other Stories, 1926
The Terrorist, 1926
The Mountain Tavern, and Other Stories, 1929
The Ecstasy of Angus, 1931
The Short Stories of Liam O'Flaherty, 1937
Two Lovely Beasts, and Other Stories, 1948
Dúil, 1953
The Stories of Liam O'Flaherty, 1956
The Pedlar's Revenge, and Other Stories, 1976
The Wave, and Other Stories, 1980
Liam O'Flaherty: The Collected Stories, 1999 (A.A.
   Kelly, editor)

OTHER LITERARY FORMS

Liam O'Flaherty (LEE-ohm oh-FLAHRT-ee) wrote four regional novels, of which *Thy Neighbour's Wife* (1923), *The Black Soul* (1924), and *Skerrett* (1932) are set on Inishmore, the largest of the Aran Islands; the fourth, *The House of Gold* (1929), is set in Galway City. His four novels of Dublin city life are *The Informer* (1925), *Mr. Gilhooley* (1926), *The Assassin* (1928), and *The Puritan* (1931). Another novel, *The Return of the Brute* (1929), concerns O'Flaherty's World War I experiences in trench warfare; *The Martyr* (1933), *Famine* (1937), *Land* (1946), and *Insurrection* (1950) are Irish historical novels for the years 1845-1922. O'Flaherty wrote three books of autobiography; a biography, *The Life of Tim Healy* (1927); several essays on social conditions and on literature; poems; and stories in Gaelic.

ACHIEVEMENTS

The source of many of Liam O'Flaherty's achievements is his birthplace off the coast of the west of Ireland. The Aran Islands's remoteness and stark natural beauty, the dependence of their scattered population on the vagaries of wind and sea, the inhabitants' preservation of the Irish language as their primary means of communication, and the virtually mythological status accorded such phenomena by leading figures in the Irish Literary Revival, such as William Butler Yeats and John Millington Synge, all exerted a crucial influence on the development of O'Flaherty's work.

Both his short fiction and novels are noteworthy for their unsentimental treatment of island life, the vivid directness of their style, and their attention to natural detail. While by no means all, or even all the best, of O'Flaherty's work draws on his Aran background, the marked degree to which all of his work emphasizes the spontaneity and volatility of all living things is the product of his formative exposure to the life forces of Aran. One of the consequences of this background's influence is plots that deal with the problematical socialization of natural energy. These plots tend to take on a melodramatic or expressionistic coloration that can mar the overall balance and objectivity of the work. However, such coloration also unwittingly reveals O'Flaherty's essential opposition to the aesthetic and cultural codes of the Irish Literary Revival and lends his work an often overlooked but crucial, critical dimension.

O'Flaherty won the James Tait Black Memorial Prize in 1926 for his novel *The Informer*. That same novel won him several other awards and honors in France and England, and the book was adapted for a film directed by John Ford and released in 1935. O'Flaherty was honored with a doctorate in literature from the National University of Ireland in 1974 and with the Irish Academy of Letters Award for literature in 1979.

BIOGRAPHY

Liam O'Flaherty was educated in seminaries and at University College, Dublin, from which in 1915 he joined the British army. He served in France and Belgium and, shell-shocked, became an invalid in 1918. He traveled to the United States and Canada and returned to Ireland in 1920 and became a communist and socialist activist. Forced to escape to England in 1922, he began writing steadily. He married Margaret Barrington in 1926 but they separated in 1932, the same year he helped to found the Irish Academy of Letters. During World War II he lived in Connecticut, the Caribbean, and South America. Despite his controversial participation in the Irish struggle for independence and the general political militancy of his twenties, and despite his active contribution to the establishment of the Irish Academy of Letters, O'Flaherty absented himself from public involvement for virtually the last forty years of his life. Unlike most Irish writers of his generation, O'Flaherty did not continue to develop. The widespread public congratulations that greeted his eightieth birthday in 1976 and the republication of many of his best-known novels during the last decade of his life did nothing of significance to break the immense silence of his later years.

ANALYSIS

To experience the full range of Liam O'Flaherty's stories, one must deal with the exceptions in the collection *The Stories of Liam O'Flaherty*, notably "The Mountain Tavern," which, like his historical novels, treats the revolutionaries in the 1920's, and "The Post Office," a humorous account of visitors' attempts to send a telegram from a small Irish town. The bulk of his stories, however, deal with nature and with people close to nature. In his nonfiction book *Joseph Conrad* (1930), O'Flaherty distinguishes himself from Joseph Conrad and other novelists, saying, "I have seen the leaping salmon fly before the salmon whale, and I have seen the sated buck horn his mate and the wanderer leave his wife in search of fresh bosoms with the fire of joy in his eye." Such firsthand observance characterizes twelve of the forty-two stories in the collection, for all twelve are animal stories with little or no intrusion of a human being.

The raw guts of nature, its tenderness and its viciousness, appear in these stories, with both wild and domesticated animals. A cow follows the trail of its stillborn calf to where it has been thrown over a cliff, the maternal instinct so strong that, when a wave washes the calf's body away, the cow plunges to her death in pursuit. A rockfish fights for its life against a fisherman's hook, winning the battle by leaving behind a torn piece of its jaw. A proud black mare overruns a race and falls to her death; a huge conger eel tears up a fisherman's net in making his escape; a wild goat, protecting its kid, attacks and kills a marauding dog. In "Birth," the people watch through the night for a newborn calf. Among several bird stories, a blackbird, proud of his song, barely escapes the claws of a cat; a baby seagull conquers fear and learns to fly; a wild swan's mate dies and, forlorn and desperate, he woos, fights for, and flies away with another mate. A wounded cormorant, outcast from its flock, tries to gain acceptance, but the others tear at it and destroy it. A hawk captures a lark to feed his mate and by his very presence, drives peaceful birds out of the territory; but then

Liam O'Flaherty (AP Photo)

the hawk loses his life in attacking a man climbing up to his nest, and the man captures the mate and takes the eggs.

The objective study of nature, impassioned alike with tenderness and viciousness, yields a delicate study of erotica. The laws of nature are so closely observed in primitive living conditions and so necessary to the barren efforts of survival that any slight aberration seems marked by a higher intelligence. In O'Flaherty's stories, this phenomenon seems to take two directions. Ordinary living conditions become bound by rigid customs so that anything not traditional, the peasants say, has "the law of God" against it. Some creatures, however, respond to a different divinity. In these cases the law of nature may permit more individuality than does social custom or the Church. Caught between these baffling natural and socioreligious forces, the people may switch their allegiances with remarkable speed and use the same kind of logic to support two different kinds of action. Some of O'Flaherty's best stories-- "The Fairy Goose," "The Child of God," "Red Barbara," "Two Lovely Beasts"--deal with the reaction of the people not so much to adversity as to difference. "The Red Petticoat" and "The Beggars" deal with people who are different.

"THE FAIRY GOOSE"

The title creature of "The Fairy Goose" from before its birth evokes undue emotion; sitting on the egg with two others, an old woman's pet hen dies. Of the three eggs, only one hatches, into a scrawny, sickly thing obviously better off dead. The woman's husband intervenes with his admonition of "the law of God" not to kill anything born in a house. The goose's subsequent behavior is so "ungooselike" that the people begin to treat it as a fairy, adorn it with ribbons, and bestow other favors. Regarding it as sacred, O'Flaherty writes, "All the human beings in the village paid more respect to it than they did to one another." On the basis of its supernatural powers, its owner becomes a wise woman sought far and near, but jealousy intervenes: A woman who herself casts spells informs the local priest. He destroys the goose's nest and calls its admirers idolators. Confronted with the powers of the Church, the former adherents of the goose now denounce it and threaten to burn the old

woman's house. Only those villagers hitherto unconcerned manage to restrain the threatened violence, but eventually young men during the night approach and kill the goose. The old woman's only defense, a traditional curse, seems to linger in the air, for thereafter the villagers become quarrelsome drunkards.

"THE CHILD OF GOD"

No doubt based on his own disaffection with the Church, O'Flaherty's stories do not present priests as dispensers of benevolence or wisdom. For the people themselves, religion, custom, and superstition equally comprise the law of God. Tradition, moreover, curbs the active intelligence and promotes baleful ironies; a thing may be blessed and cursed in rapid succession. Such is the career of Peter O'Toole in "The Child of God." The farmer O'Toole and his wife, in their forties, have an embarrassing "late from the womb" child, Peter. The baby's uncommon ill health provokes the first accusation that he is a fairy child, but the mother maintains that he is a child of God. The wife's unusual attention to the child seems in itself to be a miracle and alters the conduct of the father, who gives up his drinking bouts. The mother believes the child will bring prosperity to the house, and she makes the older children take jobs and save. At age ten, as if to confirm the mother's faith, Peter announces his ambition to become a priest--an honor higher than his parents could have dreamed for him. After six years, however, with the family driven into debt to support his education, Peter is expelled because, as he explains later, he does not believe in God. Further, they learn upon his return home at age nineteen that he has become an artist. To their horror, his books of pictures show "naked women . . . like French postcards." Peter's difference becomes a threat, and the artist, like the satirists of old, becomes feared for sketching people in unflattering poses.

After some six months, an "orgy" occurs at a wake. It would be bad enough for Peter as a participant, but it is much worse for him when the people discover that he is stone sober. As if spellbound, they watch while he sketches the entire shameful scene; afterward outraged, they call his art sacrilege and threaten to stone him. His mother now believes he has brought a curse with his birth, and his father believes God will strike all the villagers dead for what Peter has done. The priest intervenes and dispels a stone-throwing mob; but exhibiting no more compassion, benevolence, or enlightenment than do the people, he denounces Peter for having brought a curse on the parish and banishes him. The mother, left alone, weeps for her lost child, not aware of the irony that her son's creativity indeed makes him a child close to God.

"RED BARBARA"

Between the alternatives of a blessing or a curse, one who thrives--provided he is not too different--surely must be blessed. Barbara's second husband in "Red Barbara," although a weaver and a flower grower, gains acceptance until his marriage proves unfruitful; then he proves himself limited to the prevailing viewpoint. Barbara, accustomed to beatings and violent lovemaking by a frequently drunken husband, shrinks from Joseph's gentle touch and soon despises him as a "priestly lecher." Sharing the people's belief in the importance of a family, he grows fearful of his own failure to father a child; becomes strange, solitary, and emaciated; and eventually dies deranged. Barbara returns to her wild ways with her third husband, and Joseph is remembered only as "a fable in the village."

"TWO LOVELY BEASTS"

A small Aran community is so closely knit that the owner of a cow shares its milk, free, with his neighbors. Thus a crisis occurs in "Two Lovely Beasts" when Colm Derrane consents to buy a motherless calf from a poor widow and feed it alongside his own calf. The widow, Kate Higgins, assures Colm that he is different from everybody else. The difference in his decision to raise a calf on the people's milk definitely breaks the law of God and of the community, and the family becomes outcast. Kate herself cannot find another cow to buy, uses the sale money to feed her children, and turns against Colm with the accusation that his money was cursed. Forcing his family to live frugally in order to feed both calves, Colm beats his wife into submission; this evidence of male sanity restores her confidence in him. Hereafter all the children work hard to save, the tide of public opinion turns as the family prospers, and now the people say that God has blessed the family's efforts to rise in the world.

Two of the Higgins children die without proper nourishment; the distraught mother, removed to an asylum, leaves behind a plot of grassland which Colm rents through a difficult winter. He demands of his starving and threadbare family another year of sacrifice while the two beasts grow into bullocks and he can save money to open a shop. At last, with the community's belief that God blesses those who prosper, the shop brings financial success, and the calves become champions on fair day. Envy intrudes, but as Colm and his family drive away to open a shop in the town, he appears unaware of the people's hostility and derision. "Two Lovely Beasts" in this way shows the possible rise of a merchant class, who as money lenders became known as the hated gombeen men--those who live off the peasants by buying their produce at low prices and selling it elsewhere for a profit, a topic O'Flaherty treated in *The House of Gold*.

"THE RED PETTICOAT"

Most of the stories relate the peasants' situation at home--their contention with the forces of nature, their primitive living conditions, and their sensitivity to social order and ideals. Often conditions seem to be fixed at the close of a story, but occasionally good wit or good fortune alters the circumstances, at least temporarily, as in "The Red Petticoat" and "The Beggars." The ankle-length skirt of red or blue wool called a petticoat is a colorful part of the native costume of women of the Aran Islands. Often paired with a heavy, long shawl, it stands out against a somber background of rocks and grey houses. "The Red Petticoat" begins with Mrs. Mary Deignan and her four children, with no food in the house, trying to think of a way to obtain provisions. This unusual family does not work consistently, although all work valiantly when they have work; they enjoy laughing together and composing poems, some of them satires against their enemies. Unlike most residents of Aran, they can laugh in the midst of near-starvation. Out of such a background and the family's rehearsals come the expediency that Mrs. Deignan contrives to relieve their want--a melodrama spawned in her own brain, using the stock character of a witch or "wise woman," and acted out against the village storekeeper.

Mrs. Deignan, known as "Mary of the bad verses" because her poems are "scurrilous and abusive, and at times even indecent and in a sense immoral," is not powerless when she sets forth wearing her shawl and her new check apron to visit Mrs. Murtagh, the local storekeeper who has somewhat the character of a gombeen. In her "wise woman" role Mrs. Deignan terrifies Mrs. Murtagh with a hissing account of Mrs. Murtagh's sins in the traditional style of name-calling, out of which eventually Mrs. Deignan shoots a question: "Where is the red petticoat you were wearing last Sunday night, when you went to visit the tailor?" Tricking Mrs. Murtagh into denying it was red and admitting it was a black skirt, Mrs. Deignan now has what she wanted--the means of blackmail. Mrs. Murtagh launches into a vicious battle with Mrs. Deignan and knocks her into a corner but attracts passersby. Mrs. Deignan only pretends to be unconscious and, at the propitious moment, she changes character and becomes a pitiful beggar, blessing Mrs. Murtagh for having agreed to provide whatever she wants on six-months' credit. The neighbors understand that something is wrong, but they are totally mystified. Mrs. Deignan returns home with her shawl turned into a grocery sack slung over her shoulder; Mrs. Murtagh knows she will be subject to further blackmail but comforts herself with thoughts of spending more time with the tailor.

"THE BEGGARS"

"The Beggars" features as protagonist a blind man who with "priestly arrogance" exhorts people to beware the hour of their deaths, although he knows from experience that a church is not a place to beg alms; cemeteries and missions are better. His repeated cry, totally incongruous with his surroundings, earns him nothing near the gateway to a racetrack. Changing to angry curses when he thinks a man jeers at him, the beggar gains the sympathy and the aid of other beggars--a tipster, a singing woman, and an accordionist. The honor and generosity he finds among beggars seem sufficient to confirm his dream that he would find good fortune in a strange place on this day; but then the formerly cursed man returns to count into his hand five one-pound banknotes, part of two hundred pounds earned from an intuitive flash at the sight of the blind man and the memory of a horse named "Blind Barney."

"THE MOUNTAIN TAVERN"

In "The Mountain Tavern" O'Flaherty records some of the political upheaval caused by the Act of Partition in 1921. Three Republican revolutionaries trudge through a night snowstorm to reach a tavern and obtain aid for their wounded. When they arrive, the tavern is a smoking ruin, destroyed in a shootout between the Republicans and the Free Staters. Their incredulity on finding that the destitute survivors can do nothing for them parallels the anger of the tavern owner's wife, who tongue-lashes them for the three years she has suffered in their war. The wounded man dies and the other two are taken prisoner.

"THE POST OFFICE"

In an opposite and humorous vein, O'Flaherty in "The Post Office" assembles on old-age pension day the most traditional elements of a small Gaelic town; to them, the telephone, a newfangled gadget, complicates former lives of simplicity which relied on donkeys, carts, and rowboats. Three tourists speaking French and arriving in a New York Cadillac have a tourist's reason for sending a telegram to California--a friend's ancestor is from this town--and create great humor and confusion because the postmaster considers telegrams the bane of his existence. Even a priest forgets to be scandalized by the two women's clothing when he learns the visitors' purpose. The local old people take the male visitor to be a government spy because of his fluent Gaelic, consider that the women's painted toenails are a disease on their feet, believe the Spanish girl to be a duke's daughter, and appraise the American girl for her obvious reproductive capacities. The postmaster refuses to send a telegram in Spanish because it may be obscene, relents upon a recitation of Federico García Lorca's poetry, and tries to place a call to Galway; but he finds himself on the telephone at first cursed as a fishmonger, then receives news of a neighbor's operation and death, and finally hears a wrong-number grievance from a schoolteacher. "We are all in it," say some of the natives upon pronunciation of their town's name, Praiseach, which in Gaelic means confusion, disorder, and shapelessness.

The best character, the mocking young man who has graduated from his native background, lends himself to the confusion for the humor of it, reads a letter to oblige an old soldier, and with quick wit constructs tales appropriate for the native credulity. O'Flaherty's depiction of the clash of two cultures, his ear for the local diction, and his intelligence for the local logic and laughter here show him at his very best.

OTHER MAJOR WORKS

LONG FICTION: *Thy Neighbour's Wife*, 1923; *The Black Soul*, 1924; *The Informer*, 1925; *Mr. Gilhooley*, 1926; *The Assassin*, 1928; *The House of Gold*, 1929; *The Return of the Brute*, 1929; *The Puritan*, 1931; *Skerrett*, 1932; *The Martyr*, 1933; *Hollywood Cemetery*, 1935; *Famine*, 1937; *Land*, 1946; *Insurrection*, 1950.

NONFICTION: *The Life of Tim Healy*, 1927; *Joseph Conrad*, 1930; *Two Years*, 1930; *I Went to Russia*, 1931; *Shame the Devil*, 1934; *The Letters of Liam O'Flaherty*, 1996 (A.A. Kelly, editor).

CHILDREN'S LITERATURE: *All Things Come of Age and the Test of Courage*, 1984.

BIBLIOGRAPHY

Cahalan, James M. *Liam O'Flaherty: A Study of the Short Fiction*. Boston: Twayne, 1991. An introduction to O'Flaherty's stories by an expert in Irish literature. Discusses the peasant consciousness in the stories, as well as the stories' relationship to the Irish language. Comments on issues of gender and politics raised by the stories. Includes many comments by O'Flaherty from letters and articles, as well as secondary sources.

Costello, Peter. "Land and Liam O'Flaherty." In *Famine, Land, and Culture in Ireland*, edited by Carla King. Dublin: University College Dublin Press, 2000. Focuses on O'Flaherty's story "Land" to demonstrate the influence the land on O'Flaherty's writings.

_____. *Liam O'Flaherty's Ireland*. Dublin: Wolfhound Press, 1996. Explores O'Flaherty's life and times, describing how his environment influenced his writings.

Daniels, William. "Introduction to the Present State of Criticism of Liam O'Flaherty's Collection of Short Stories: *Dúil*." *Eire-Ireland* 23 (Summer, 1988): 122-134. A summary of criticism of O'Flaherty's stories in *Dúil*. Takes issue with a number of the critiques, such as the argument that the stories fail to focus on setting, plot, and point of view. Maintains that the stories deserve much better analysis than they have received from critics in both Irish and English.

Doyle, Paul A. *Liam O'Flaherty*. Boston: Twayne, 1972. The first comprehensive overview of O'Flaherty's life and work. The author's reading of O'Flaherty's short fiction tends to be more illuminating than that of the novels. Although superseded by later studies, this volume is still helpful as a means of orientating the newcomer to O'Flaherty's work. Contains an extensive bibliography.

Jefferson, George. *Liam O'Flaherty: A Descriptive Bibliography of His Works*. Dublin: Wolfhound Press, 1993. A useful tool for the student of O'Flaherty. Includes bibliographical references and an index.

Kelly, A. A. *Liam O'Flaherty: The Storyteller*. London: Macmillan, 1976. An exhaustive treatment of the themes and techniques of O'Flaherty's short fiction. Although somewhat disjointed in organization, this study ultimately makes a convincing case for the distinctiveness of O'Flaherty's achievements in the genre. Particular emphasis is placed on the range and variety of his stories. Supplemented by an excellent bibliography.

Kilroy, James R. "Setting the Standards: Writers of the 1920's and 1930's." In *The Irish Short Story: A Critical History*, edited by James F. Kilroy. Boston: Twayne, 1984. An introduction to O'Flaherty's stories, emphasizing their ethical implications and naturalism. Discusses his simple narrative technique and style and how the short story suits his single-minded vision.

O'Brien, James H. *Liam O'Flaherty*. Lewisburg, Pa.: Bucknell University Press, 1973. A brief introduction to O'Flaherty's life and work. Its longest chapter is devoted to O'Flaherty's short stories, but the study also contains biographical information and analyses of the novels. O'Flaherty's achievements as a short-story writer are considered in the context of those of his Irish contemporaries. The stories' themes and motifs are also discussed.

O'Hare, Shawn. "The Short Stories of Liam O'Flaherty." In *A Companion to the British and Irish Short Story*, edited by Cheryl Alexander Malcolm and David Malcolm. Malden, Mass.: Wiley-Blackwell, 2008. An overview of O'Flaherty's short fiction, including discussion of some individual stories and some of the collections, including *Two Lovely Beasts* and *The Mountain Tavern*.

Phillips, Terry. A Study in Grotesques: Transformations of the Human in the Writing of Liam O'Flaherty." *Gothic Studies* 7, no. 1 (May, 2005): 41-52. Examines the "sometimes monstrous" characters and other grotesque elements in O'Flaherty's short stories and historical novels. Argues that he uses the grotesque to express the tension between "disappointed idealism and lingering romanticism."

Sheeran, Patrick J. *The Novels of Liam O'Flaherty: A Study in Romantic Realism*. Dublin: Wolfhound Press, 1976. This study contains more than its title suggests. It is both a comprehensive study of O'Flaherty's novels and an investigation of their cultural context. The author's knowledge of, and original research into, O'Flaherty's background provides invaluable information about his formative experiences. The critique of O'Flaherty's longer works may be usefully adapted by students of his short fiction. In many ways, the most satisfactory study of O'Flaherty's work.

Thompson, Richard R. "The Sage Who Deep in Central Nature Delves: Liam O'Flaherty's Short Stories." *Eire-Ireland* 18 (Spring, 1983): 80-97. A discussion of the central themes in O'Flaherty's stories, focusing primarily on the moral lessons inherent in his nature stories, which urge a turning away from intellectualism.

Zneimer, John. *The Literary Vision of Liam O'Flaherty*. Syracuse, N.Y.: Syracuse University Press, 1970. An ambitious approach to O'Flaherty's work. Zneimer sees a strong religious component in O'Flaherty's novels and stories and a tension between the two forms; he argues that the novels are despairing, while the stories offer a redemptive alternative.

Grace Eckley
Updated by George O'Brien

P

WILLIAM PLOMER

Born: Pietersburg, Transvaal (now South Africa);
    December 10, 1903
Died: Hassocks, Sussex, England;
    September 21, 1973

PRINCIPAL SHORT FICTION
I Speak of Africa, 1927
Paper Houses, 1929
The Child of Queen Victoria,
    and Other Stories, 1933
Four Countries, 1949

OTHER LITERARY FORMS

Electric Delights (1978), a posthumously published collection of "scattered pieces" by William Plomer (PLEW-mehr), reveals the breadth of his interests. During his long career, Plomer published many volumes of poetry and many novels, as well as biographies and autobiographies. He also wrote librettos for operas and cantatas composed by the prominent British composer Benjamin Britten.

ACHIEVEMENTS

William Plomer received the Queen's Gold Medal for Poetry in 1963 and was made a Commander of the Order of the British Empire in 1968. He was corecipient with Alan Aldridge of the Whitbread Literary Award for best children's book (*The Butterfly Ball and the Grasshopper's Feast*) in 1973.

BIOGRAPHY

William Charles Franklyn Plomer was born of English parents in Transvaal (now South Africa) on December 10, 1903. He was educated at Rugby in England and St. John's College in Johannesburg. In South Africa he worked on farms and later operated a trading store with his father in Zululand. He became sensitized both to the beauty of the country and the injustice of white colonialism. He left South Africa when outrage on the part of his fellow white colonists forced the closure of his antiracist journal *Voorslag* (Whiplash). He had already scandalized the white elite minority with his first novel, *Turbott Wolfe* (1925), because of its condoning of intermarriage between whites and blacks and criticism of the multiple ways in which blacks were exploited and in some instances brutalized by whites. He traveled extensively--notably in Japan, Greece, and Italy--before finally settling in England in 1932, where he eventually became a prominent British man of letters. During World War II he served in British Naval Intelligence. He was noted for his wide range of literary interests, which included short stories, poems, novels, memoirs, essays, travel sketches, translations, musical librettos, and a children's book. He knew many of the most important writers of his time. For more than thirty years he was senior editor at the London publishing firm of Jonathan Cape. He died in Hassocks, England, on September 21, 1973.

ANALYSIS

Most of William Plomer's short stories were written in his twenties. His best stories deal with Africa, where he was born and spent much of his early life. His claim to literary fame is that he was one of the first white colonists to sympathize with the exploited natives of South Africa and to foresee the time--which has since arrived--when they would demand democracy and equality.

Plomer was a poet, as well as a polished fiction and nonfiction writer. His poetic sensibility is evident in his remarkably mature powers of description. He has the ability to make the reader see, smell, hear, and feel--so that the reader is drawn into a three-dimensional setting.

Plomer was a world traveler for many years, like other famous British writers, such as Joseph Conrad, Rudyard Kipling, W. Somerset Maugham, and Graham Greene. The two short-story writers who influenced him most strongly were Guy de Maupassant and Ivan Bunin. Plomer's remarkable sensitivity made him an accurate recorder of the differences and similarities of humans everywhere--a gift indispensable to a fiction writer. It also made him aware of the social unrest that would lead to such dramatic social and political changes after World War II.

Plomer's stories are characterized by polished prose, poetic sensitivity to impressions, modesty, sincerity, and freedom from prejudice. In the preface to *Four Countries*, a collection of stories set in South Africa, Japan, Greece, and England, Plomer wrote: "In their way I think most of my stories reflect the age by isolating some crisis caused by a change of environment or by the sudden and sometimes startling confrontation of different races and classes."

"ULA MASONDA"

Ula Masonda is the name of a young South African native who, like many of his contemporaries, leaves his village to go to Johannesburg to work in the mines. Torn from family, friends, and native soil, Ula Masonda undergoes a character change. He becomes more and more like the dissolute, proletarianized natives who arrived before him. Evil companions lure him into committing robberies in order to support their corrupt lifestyle. He falls in love with a black prostitute. His dangerous occupation leads to his being injured in a rock fall. He is sent back home wearing European clothing which makes him look ridiculous. He no longer feels a sense of belonging and even rejects his own mother as a "heathen." He is a man without a country, despised by the whites, a stranger among his own people.

This story displays Plomer's creative imagination, as well as his social and political awareness. "Ula Masonda" is unique because it incorporates a long poem prophesying revolution and liberation, presented as part of the hero's delirium while lying under the rubble. John Robert Doyle, the best explicator of Plomer's stories, writes: "Clearly Ula Masondo is a symbol, and William Plomer is here concerned not with one human being but with millions."

"THE CHILD OF QUEEN VICTORIA"

"The Child of Queen Victoria" is one of Plomer's best and best-known short stories. Like all of Plomer's South African fiction, it draws heavily on his personal experience. It was written when he was quite young and reflects a young man's libido. The viewpoint character, Frant, a young Englishman with a good education and genteel manners, goes to South Africa to "find himself," as so many young Englishmen did in the days when the British Empire girdled the globe. He is employed by an ignorant, materialistic, and racist couple named MacGavin, who operate a trading station in Lembuland selling cheap manufactured goods to the natives. Unlike his employers, Frant finds himself in sympathy with the natives and recognizes them as individuals rather than "niggers" who have to be kept in their place.

Frant feels lonely. He has nothing in common with the MacGavins and is unable to make friends among the natives. As a member of the white ruling class, he has to maintain a certain distance, and the natives regard him as a strange alien whom they call "the child of Queen Victoria." Then Frant falls in love with a beautiful young native woman named Seraphina, who also seems attracted to him. He is torn with desire but cannot establish an intimate relationship. Marriage is out of the question, even illegal. She would not consider anything less--although sexual relations between white men and black women are hardly unknown in the region. Ultimately, Frant's dilemma is resolved when Seraphina and her family are wiped out in a flash flood.

"The Child of Queen Victoria" resembles Joseph Conrad's famous long story *Heart of Darkness* (1899, serial; 1902, book) in its ability to evoke the sights, sounds, and atmosphere of Africa. Plomer makes the reader feel he is actually in South Africa and even right inside the crowded, noisy trading station. His story also resembles Conrad's in dealing with the impact of environment on human character. Frant, like Conrad's Kurtz, is gradually and irrevocably changed and--as MacGavin repeatedly warns him--is in danger of "going native." The story's only flaw is its deus-ex-machina ending. Frant's internal conflict is unresolved, and perhaps unresolvable; Plomer is forced to end his story by arbitrarily killing the object of his hero's obsession.

"WHEN THE SARDINES CAME"

This story is told through the viewpoint of a minor character, but the dramatic events concern his hostess Mrs. Reymond and her husband. Charles Edwards, a young medical student, is staying at their home near the coast. They promise a thrilling spectacle when the annual sardine run takes place in June. Life is uneventful until the huge shoals of sardines appear, pursued by bigger fish and diving gulls and gannets. This creates a sort of mass hysteria among the human population. People of all races and all social classes rush to gather beached sardines and catch the bigger fish pursuing them. One young man named Boris is badly injured while trying to haul his five-foot-long catch ashore. Mrs. Reymond, excited by the blood sport and Boris's animal magnetism, has him carried to her bedroom, where she nurses him back to health. They become lovers. After Boris recuperates, Mr. Reymond confides to Edwards that he was aware of what was going on and felt jealous but did nothing. He saw this affair for what it was: a middle-aged woman's last taste of romance before accepting the boredom and sexlessness of old age.

This ostensibly simple story, like "Black Peril," is fraught with implications. It reflects Plomer's belief in the supremacy of the life force, the hypocrisy of middle-class values, his antipathy for the repression of women everywhere, and the indelible influence of environment on human character.

"BLACK PERIL"

This is another story of adultery but was even more daring for its time than "When the Sardines Came" because it involves a white woman and a black native African. Vera Corneliussen is a sensual woman married to a man who takes her for granted and is preoccupied with his own affairs, like George Tessman in Henrik Ibsen's play *Hedda Gabler* (pb. 1890, pr. 1891; English translation, 1891) or Leonce Pontellier in Kate Chopin's novel *The Awakening* (1899). Vera takes advantage of her husband's extended absence to seduce Charlie, a young black house servant who exudes sexuality and "the lure of the forbidden." This avant-garde, impressionistic story is told mostly through the rambling thoughts and memories of Vera while in a delirium. Eventually she dies, but Plomer leaves the cause of her death unclear. At any rate, Charlie is automatically considered a rapist and murderer because of his race. He will inevitably be captured and lynched by white colonials.

OTHER MAJOR WORKS

LONG FICTION: *Turbott Wolfe*, 1925; *Sado*, 1931 (also pb. as *They Never Came Back*, 1932); *The Case Is Altered*, 1932; *Cecil Rhodes*, 1933; *The Invaders*, 1934; *Ali the Lion: Ali of Tebeleni, Pasha of Jannina, 1741-1822*, 1936.

PLAYS: *Gloriana*, pr., pb. 1953 (libretto); *Curlew River: A Parable for Church Performance*, pb. 1964 (libretto); *The Burning Fiery Furnace: Second Parable for Church Performance*, pb. 1966 (libretto); *The Prodigal Son: Third Parable for Church Performance*, pb. 1968 (libretto).

POETRY: *The Family Tree*, 1929; *The Fivefold Screen*, 1932; *Visiting the Caves*, 1936; *Selected Poems*, 1940; *The Dorking Thigh, and Other Satires*, 1945; *Borderline Ballads*, 1955 (pb. in England as *A Shot in the Park*, 1955); *Collected Poems*, 1960 (enlarged edition, 1973); *Taste and Remember*, 1966; *Celebrations*, 1972.

NONFICTION: *Notes for Poems*, 1927; *Double Lives: An Autobiography*, 1943 (revised 1956); *Museum Pieces*, 1952; *At Home: Memoirs*, 1958; *The Autobiography of William Plomer*, 1975.

CHILDREN'S LITERATURE: *The Butterfly Ball and the Grasshopper's Feast*, 1973.

EDITED TEXTS: *Japanese Lady in Europe*, 1937 (of Haruko Ichikawa); *Kilvert's Diary, 1870-1879*, 1938-1940 (of Robert Francis Kilvert; 3 volumes; revised, 1961); *Selected Poems*, 1943 (of Herman Melville); *Curious Relations*, 1945 (of William D'Arfey); *A Message in Code: The Diary of Richard Rumbold, 1932-1961*, 1964 (of Richard Rumbold).

MISCELLANEOUS: *Electric Delights*, 1978 (essays, poems, stories, and travel sketches).

BIBLIOGRAPHY

Allen, Walter. *The Modern Novel in Britain and the United States*. New York: E. P. Dutton, 1964. Allen includes Plomer in this discussion of the most important modern fiction writers, hailing him as the ancestor of South African fiction. Allen states that

Plomer's theme "has always been that of the Displaced Person in the larger and literal sense of the phrase."

Doyle, John Robert. *William Plomer*. New York: Twayne, 1969. Part of the distinguished Twayne World Authors Series, this is one of the best studies of Plomer available. Doyle, an authority on Plomer's writings, taught at many South African universities and published essays in a number of South African periodicals. Chapter 2 describes and analyzes Plomer's short stories in depth. Contains a chronology, copious reference notes, a bibliography, and an index.

Georganta, Konstantinal. "'And So to Athens': William Plomer in `The Land of Love.'" *Journal of Modern Greek Studies* 28, no. 1 (May, 2010): 49-71. Analyzes Plomer's short stories and poems about Greece, arguing that in these works he combined "homosexual themes and an ironical look at history's essential heroes" to depict the country's "cultural plurality."

Spender, Stephen. "A Singular Man." *New Statesman* 86 (November 9, 1973): 690. Spender, a leading English poet and influential literary figure, published this tribute shortly after his friend Plomer's death. Spender writes: "All his qualities were wind-blown, sun-saturated, sparkling, and in his writing the language shines and curls like waves animated by a strong breeze on a clear day."

Tucker, Martin. *Africa in Modern Literature: A Survey of Contemporary Writing in English*. New York: Frederick Ungar, 1967. This interesting and authoritative discussion of all modern literature about the African continent contains many pages about Plomer in various contexts. Tucker hails him as the first white South African writer to treat miscegenation and interracial fraternization from the viewpoint of social and political protest rather than as something forbidden and shameful.

Van der Vlies, Andrew Edward. "'Hurled by What Aim to What Tremendous Range': Roy Campbell, William Plomer. and the Politics of Reputation." In *South African Textual Cultures: White, Black, Read All Over*. Manchester, England: Manchester University Press, 2007. Analyzes the work of Plomer and other south African writers to describe the effects of local and global networks on the publication, promotion, and reception of these writers' works.

Bill Delaney

V. S. PRITCHETT

Born: Ipswich, England; December 16, 1900
Died: London, England; March 20, 1997
Also Known As: Victor Sawden Pritchett

PRINCIPAL SHORT FICTION

The Spanish Virgin, and Other Stories, 1930
You Make Your Own Life, and Other Stories, 1938
It May Never Happen, and Other Stories, 1945
Collected Stories, 1956
The Sailor, The Sense of Humour, and Other Stories,
  1956 (also known as *The Saint, and Other Stories,*
  1966)
When My Girl Comes Home, 1961
The Key to My Heart, 1963
Blind Love, and Other Stories, 1969
The Camberwell Beauty, and Other Stories, 1974
Selected Stories, 1978
The Fly in the Ointment, 1978
On the Edge of the Cliff, 1979
Collected Stories, 1982
More Collected Stories, 1983
A Careless Widow, and Other Stories, 1989
Complete Collected Stories, 1990

OTHER LITERARY FORMS

Apart from his many short stories, in his sixty-year career as a writer V. S. Pritchett (PRIHCH-iht) produced several novels (not well received); two autobiographies (*A Cab at the Door,* 1968, and *Midnight Oil,* 1972); several travel books (the noteworthy ones include *The Spanish Temper,* 1954, and *The Offensive Traveller,* 1964); volumes of literary criticism; literary biographies (*George Meredith and English Comedy,* 1970; *Balzac,* 1973; *The Gentle Barbarian: The Life and Work of Turgenev,* 1977); essays (among them *New York Proclaimed,* 1965, and *The Working Novelist,* 1965); and journalistic pieces from France, Spain, Ireland, and the United States that remain in the literary canon, so well are they written.

ACHIEVEMENTS

In his long and distinguished career, V. S. Pritchett, who preferred the abbreviation V. S. P., produced an impressive number of books in all genres--from novels and short stories, on which rests his fame, to literary criticism, travel books, and journalistic pieces written for *The Christian Science Monitor* when he covered Ireland, Spain, and France. His most successful genre was the short story, which resulted from his razor-sharp characterizations of all classes, both in England and on the Continent; his focus on the moment of epiphany; his graceful writing; and his ironic, bittersweet wit. Pritchett has the uncanny ability to select a commonplace moment and through imagery, wit, and irony lift it to a transfiguration. He focuses on the foibles of all people without malice, anger, or sentimentality but rather with humor, gentleness, and understanding. In his preface to *Collected Stories,* Pritchett states that although some people believe that the short story has lost some of its popularity, he does not think so: "[T]his is not my experience; thousands of addicts still delight in it because it is above all memorable and is not simply read, but re-read again and again. It is the glancing form of fiction that seems to be right for the nervousness and restlessness of contemporary life."

BIOGRAPHY

Victor Sawden Pritchett was born in Ipswich, England, of middle-class parents. His father, Walter, a Yorkshireman, espoused a strict Congregationalism. He married Beatrice of London, whom he had met when both worked in a draper's shop. Enthralled by wild business schemes, Walter often left his family for months as he pursued dreams that shattered and left the family destitute, forcing it into innumerable moves and frequent sharing of flats with relatives. Often a traveling salesman, Pritchett's father, despite his long absences, caused the family unmitigated misery when he returned. Pritchett's dictatorial father is reflected in many of his stories and novels, and Pritchett is completely frank in his autobiography about his father's brutality.

Most remarkable, Pritchett received only the barest of formal training at Alleyn's Grammar School, which he left when he was only sixteen to enter the leather trade. Clever with languages, he soon showed proficiency in French. He read omnivorously. In his stories, he reflects a cerebral ability, perceptiveness, and imagism. Despite his lack of formal training in literature, he is considered to be one of the best writers of the short story in twentieth-century England. In 1975, he was knighted as Sir Victor for his contributions to literature.

After working in the leather trade for several years as a tanner, he left for a two-year interlude in Paris. Those years as a tanner were fruitful, he has declared, for he encountered all classes of people in England, a factor noted in his short stories, depicting the monied aristocrats and the working classes, together with the middle classes that he fixes in amber. In Paris, he worked in a photography shop as clerk and letter writer but soon wearied of the routines and determined to become a writer. His connection with *The Christian Science Monitor* became the key transitional phase, for he wrote and published for this newspaper a series of articles. When there was no longer a need for these articles written in Paris, *The Christian Science Monitor* sent him to Ireland, where the civil war raged. Pritchett soaked up experiences from his wide travels as he journeyed from Dublin to Cork, Limerick, and Enniskillen. A year later the newspaper editors informed him that they needed him in Spain, and he left for that country with Evelyn Maude Vigors, whom he married at the beginning of 1924. There are virtually no details about his first wife, except that she was an actress. Their marriage, however, turned out not to be a happy one; the couple was divorced in 1936, and during that same year, Pritchett married Dorothy Roberts. His wife continued to assist him in his literary work, and he has invariably dedicated his work to her, one inscription reading "For Dorothy--always."

The years in Spain were productive, with Pritchett writing novels, short stories, travel books, and journalistic pieces. While there, he learned Spanish easily and immersed himself in Spanish literature, especially being influenced by Miguel de Unamuno y Jugo, whose philosophic themes often concern the intensity of living near the jaws of death, and by Pío Baroja, whose books often focus on atheism and pessimism. Pritchett especially was influenced by Baroja's empathy for character. After two years in Spain, Pritchett visited Morocco, Algeria, Tunisia, the United States, and Canada, travels that further shaped his contours of place and people. In the 1930's, his writing approached the luminous. In the second volume of his autobiography, *Midnight Oil*, Pritchett wrote to this point:

> If I began to write better it was for two reasons: in my thirties I had found my contemporaries and had fallen happily and deeply in love. There is, I am sure, a direct connection between passionate love and the firing of the creative power of the mind.

V. S. Pritchett (Getty Images)

Critics agree that Pritchett reached a high level of achievement in the short story in the 1930's. He continued writing on a high level until all was interrupted, as it was for many other writers, by the onset of World War II, during which he served in the Ministry of Information.

Pritchett became literary editor of *New Statesman* in 1945, resigning this position in 1949 to become its director from 1951 to 1978. Along the way, he had been given lectureships at Princeton University (1953, Christian Gauss Lecturer) and the University of California, Berkeley (1962, Beckman Professor), and he was appointed as writer-in-residence at Smith College in 1966. Brandeis University, Columbia University, and the University of Cambridge also invited him to teach.

Honors poured on Pritchett. He was elected Fellow by the Royal Society of Literature, receiving a C.B.E. in 1969. Two years later he was elected president of the British PEN and was made Honorary Member of the American Academy of Arts and Letters. In 1974, he was installed as international president of PEN for two years. One of his greatest honors came from Queen Elizabeth II as she received him into knighthood in 1975 for his services to literature. Pritchett through the years also received academic honors from several universities in the Western world, including honorary D.Litt. degrees from Leeds (1972) and Columbia University (1978).

Pritchett continued to contribute to journals both in the United States and Europe and England. Not wishing to rest on his innumerable laurels, this grand master of the short story continued to write and to select stories for his collections. By many, he is thought to be a writer's writer. He died on March 20, 1997, at the age of ninety-six, in London, England.

ANALYSIS

V. S. Pritchett writes in *Midnight Oil*:

I have rarely been interested in what are called "characters," i.e., eccentrics; reviewers are mistaken in saying I am. They misread me. I am interested in the revelations of nature and (rather in Ibsen's fash-

ion) of exposing the illusions or received ideas by which they live or protect their dignity.

An approach to the short stories reveals that Pritchett is projecting comic incongruities. He captures the moment of revelation when his men and women recognize an awareness of their plight. His panoply of people ranges from sailors, divers, clerks, blind men, and shop girls to piano accompanists, wastrels, and the penurious wealthy. Pritchett concentrates on selected details with tart wit and irony in dialogue that characterizes those who people his short stories. Two highly discrete characters often interrelate to their despair or to their joy. With such irony, the reader may conclude that in reading a Pritchett story, nothing is but what is not.

One of the earliest collections of short stories by Pritchett, *You Make Your Own Life, and Other Stories*, already reflects the mature touch of the writer. Although showing some slight inconsistency, the tales attest variety in narrative, theme, tone, and style. Some stories are stark and Kafkaesque, especially "The Two Brothers," in which a nightmarish suicide is the central concern. The longest story in this group is "Handsome Is as Handsome Does," set on the French Mediterranean.

"HANDSOME IS AS HANDSOME DOES"

The focus is on Mr. and Mrs. Coram, an English couple, both of whom are unusually ugly. Their ugliness is their only similarity. He is rude, inarticulate, and slow-witted, and he quarrels with everyone. He is especially rude to M. Pierre, the proprietor of the hotel, insulting him in English, which he does not understand. Mrs. Coram is left to play the role of diplomat and apologist. Soon after the English couple's arrival, Alex, whose forebears are flung throughout Europe, also vacations at the inn. He is young and handsome and delights in swimming. Childless, Mrs. Coram views Alex as the son she might have had. One day, she attempts to seduce him while he watches unfeelingly, and she, scorned, feels ridiculous. On another day, the Corams, Alex, and M. Pierre go to a deserted beach that is known for its dangerous undertow. M. Pierre dives in, and before long it is apparent to all that he is drowning. Alex rescues him while Mr. Coram looks on, never even thinking of saving the innkeeper. His wife is silently furious at him. Later, as M. Pierre brags at the hotel about his narrow escape, Mrs. Coram blandly tells some recent English arrivals that her husband saved M. Pierre's life.

Clearly, the Corams are loathsome people, but through Pritchett's portrayal of them as wounded, frustrated, and vindictive, even grotesque, they emerge as human beings, capable of eliciting the reader's empathy. Alex, protected by his "oily" youth, remains the catalyst, rather neutral and asexual. The aging couple, in Pritchett's lightly satirical portraiture, in the end claim the reader's sympathy.

"Sense of Humour"

Another well-known and often-quoted story in this collection is "Sense of Humour." Arthur Humphrey, a traveling salesman, is the narrator. On one of his trips, he meets Muriel MacFarlane, who is dating a local boy, Colin Mitchell, who always rides a motorcycle. Colin is obsessively in love with Muriel. Arthur courts Muriel, who stops dating Colin. Nevertheless, the motorcyclist compulsively follows the couple wherever they go. Muriel says that she is Irish, and she has a sense of humor, although she never exhibits this so-called Irish trait. When Colin, who is also an auto mechanic, announces that he cannot repair Humphrey's car and thereby hopes to ruin the couple's plan, they take the train to Humphrey's parents' house. Shortly after their arrival, Muriel receives a call from the police: Colin has been killed in a motorcycle crash nearby. That night, Muriel is overwhelmed with grief for Colin; Arthur begins to comfort her, and they eventually, for the first time, have sex. All the while, Muriel is crying out Colin's name. To save Colin's family the expense, Colin's body is returned to his family in a hearse belonging to Arthur's father. Both Muriel and the obtuse Arthur feel like royalty when the passing drivers and pedestrians doff their hats in respect. Arthur says, "I was proud of her, I was proud of Colin, and I was proud of myself and after what happened, I mean on the last two nights, it was like a wedding." Colin is following them for the last time. When Arthur asks Muriel why she stopped seeing Colin, she answers that he never had a sense of humor.

Critics believe that Pritchett in this story exerts complete control in keeping the reader on tenterhooks between crying and guffawing. The narrator, like the reader, never concludes whether Muriel is marrying Arthur for his money or for love or whether she loves Colin or Arthur. The story underscores one of Pritchett's favorite techniques: peeling away at the character with grim irony and even then not providing enough details to see the character's inner self. As Pritchett declared, however, his interest is in the "happening," not in overt characterization. In death, Colin after all does seem to win his love; however, in the conclusion it appears that all three people have been deluded. Some of the grim gallows humor in this story reminds the reader of Thomas Hardy, whom Pritchett acknowledged as an important influence.

"When My Girl Comes Home"

More than a decade after the end of World War II, *When My Girl Comes Home* was published. The mature style of Pritchett is readily discernible in this collection. The stories become somewhat more complex and difficult in morality, in situations, and in the greater number of characters. The moral ambiguities are many. The title story, "When My Girl Comes Home," is Pritchett's favorite short story.

Although World War II is over, the bankruptcy of the war ricochets on many levels. The "girl" coming home is Hilda Johnson, for whom her mother has been working and scrimping to save money. Residents of Hincham Street, where Mrs. Johnson lives, had for two years implored the bureaucracies of the world to obtain news about the whereabouts and the condition of Hilda, who was believed to be wasting away in a Japanese concentration camp. Now Hilda has come home, not pale and wan but sleek and relaxed. Only gradually does the story emerge, but never completely. In fact, because Hilda's second husband was a Japanese officer, she survived the war comfortably. She does not need the money that her mother saved from years of sewing. En route home, Hilda met two men, one of whom, Gloster, a writer, wished to write Hilda's story. The narrator observes, when he first sees her, that her face was vacant and plain. It was as vacant as a stone that has been smoothed for centuries in the sand of some hot country. It was the face of someone to whom nothing had happened; or, perhaps, so much had happened to her that each event wiped out what had happened before. I was disturbed by something in her--the lack of history, I think. We were worm-eaten by it.

Hilda sleeps with her mother in a tiny bedroom while she waits for help from Gloster, who never appears. She seems to become involved with a real prisoner of the Japanese, Bill Williams, who survived through the war, as he terms it, with "a bit of trade." Some of the neighbors begin to understand that Hilda, too, survived by trading as well. At one point in the tale, Hilda begs her friends to save her from Bill Williams, and she stays away from her apartment that night. When she returns to her flat, she discovers that Bill Williams has robbed her flat completely and has disappeared. Soon after, Hilda leaves London and surfaces only in a photograph with her two boyfriends, Gloster and someone else. Gloster does publish a book, not about Hilda's war experiences but about the people on Hincham Street.

The story's subtext may suggest that it might have been better for Hincham Street had the "girl" not come home, for then they would have retained their illusions about her. The illusion versus reality theme is one often used by Pritchett. Mrs. Johnson, now dead, seemed to have kept the street together in a kind of moral order, now destroyed on Hincham Street. After her death, Hilda and Bill were involved in seamy happenings. In the Hincham Street pubs, the war is discussed but only fitfully and inconclusively because "sooner or later, it came to a closed door in everybody's conscience." Hilda and Bill, surviving the Japanese camps through moral bankruptcy, form a mirror image of those Englishman who became black marketers, malingerers, ration thieves, and hoodlums. Moral codes were shattered by Englishmen--whether at home or abroad. Pritchett is deliberately murky in theme and relationships, but the story suggests that just as the Japanese disturbed the civil and moral order thousands of miles away, the disruption caused a moral decay at home at the same time that the war was fought to reestablish the world order. Perhaps Pritchett is suggesting that England during the war and after was a microcosm. Despite the disillusionment that touches the entire street and the gravity of the theme, Pritchett never fails to use the restorative of humor and subtle satire, watchwords of the writer.

Blind Love, and Other Stories appeared in 1969. This collection reflects Pritchett's admiration of Anton Chekhov and Ivan Turgenev, whose bittersweet irony enfolds the characters as they experience, at the end, self-revelation. In his later years, Pritchett continued to grow as an artist in many ways. The story lines are compelling, and no matter what the theme, Pritchett's wit provides humor and pathos. The transition between time present and time past is accomplished with laser-beam precision.

"THE SKELETON"

"The Skeleton," concerning George Clark, fleshes out a skinny man who has never loved. Cantankerous, selfish, perfectionistic, and thoroughly narcissistic, George is painted to perfection with satirical brushes. His encounter with Gloria Archer, whom George accuses of corrupting his favorite painter, transforms him. The comic becomes almost caricature and is flawless. Pritchett shows him guarding his whiskey bottle like a Holy Grail, but his valet finds it mistakenly left on the table, drinks a bit, and then dilutes the bottle with water. Dean R. Baldwin, who wrote the excellent Twayne biography of Pritchett, wrote, "George is the skeleton, until Gloria puts a bit of meat on his emotional bare bones."

"BLIND LOVE"

Like many of Pritchett's best stories used as title stories, "Blind Love" is a masterful portrait of two people who are scarred by nature but who succumb to pride before their fall. Mr. Armitage, a wealthy lawyer living in the country and blind for twenty years, has been divorced because of his affliction. He interviews Mrs. Johnson by feeling her face and hands, and he hires her as a secretary and housekeeper. As Thomas Gray would say, nothing disturbed the even tenor of their ways for a few years. One day, Armitage, walking in his garden, loses his balance when a dog chases a rabbit, and he falls into his pool. Mrs. Johnson sees the fall but before she can rush out to help him, he is rescued. When Mrs. Johnson tries to help him change his clothes in his room, she breaks the cardinal rule of never changing the physical order of things because Armitage has memorized the place for every item. He screams at her to get out and leave him alone. This verbal attack stimulates a flashback that reveals that Mrs. Johnson had heard "almost exactly those words, before. Her husband had said them. A week after the wedding." She recalls that he was shocked and disgusted at

> a great spreading ragged liver-coloured island of skin which spread under the tape of her slip and crossed her breast and seemed to end in a curdle of skin below it. She was stamped with an ineradicable bloody insult.

After Armitage's rudeness, Mrs. Johnson decides to leave, for in addition to those scorching words, she disliked the country. Armitage apologizes and begs her to stay. Soon thereafter, he gropes toward her and kisses her, and they make love. Mrs. Johnson, initially motivated by the pleasure of revenge against her husband, begins in time to enjoy Armitage's lovemaking. Religion is woven into the story when Armitage mocks Mrs. Johnson for going to church, and at one time, he insists that she use spittle and dirt on his eyes to mock a miracle of Christ: "Do as I tell you. It's what your Jesus Christ did when he cured the blind man."

Armitage then goes to Mr. Smith, an expensive faith healer, actually a charlatan-manqué, to regain his sight. Once, Mrs. Johnson accompanies him. As she leaves, Armitage hears her telling Smith that she loves Armitage as he is. Earlier, Smith appeared when Mrs. Johnson had been sunbathing nude at the pool. After wondering whether he saw her, Mrs. Johnson concludes that he did not. When Armitage later asks her whether Smith had seen her at the pool, Mrs. Johnson explodes and says that Smith saw everything. Unzipping her dress, she cries, "You can't see it, you silly fool. The whole bloody Hebrides, the whole plate of liver."

Later, when Mrs. Johnson for some strange reason is found lying face down in the pool, she, like Armitage earlier, is rescued. Both have had their "fall." This

parallel happening seems to be a moment of epiphany, and the story ends with the couple living in Italy, where Mrs. Johnson describes churches and gallery pictures to her "perhaps" husband. In the last paragraph, Mrs. Johnson proclaims her love for her husband as she eyes the lovely Italian square below. She says that she feels "gaudy," leaving the reader wrestling over her selection of the word. Long after the reading, the poignancy of the story resonates.

This title story, an intensely poignant one, forthright and absorbing, shows the handicaps bringing people together and almost tearing them apart. They are both anointed by their "fall" from pride, and in their moment of epiphany, they see their need of each other and the love accompanying the need. Through each other and by self-analysis, they transcend their limitations and experience the joy of seeing themselves anew. Again, this revelatory process is a mainstay of Pritchett.

"THE DIVER"

Five years later, Pritchett continued his consistent stream of productivity by publishing *The Camberwell Beauty, and Other Stories*. This volume particularly focuses on the eccentric foibles of the middle class. "The Diver," set in Paris, is an enjoyable tale of a diver who is a metaphor for sexual encounters. This diver is sent to retrieve bundles of leather goods that a Dutch ship accidentally spews into the Seine. A young clerk for the leather tannery is assigned to count the sodden bales. Quite by chance, he himself falls into the Seine and is fished out by the onlookers. His boss takes him across the street to a bar and expects the lad to pay for his own brandy. Mme Chamson, feeling sorry for the youth, takes him to her shop for a change of clothing. Later, she calls him into her bedroom, where he finds her nude, and she initiates a sexual encounter. The youth, yearning to become a writer, feels inarticulate. This encounter with Mme Chamson, his first sexual experience, has released his creative wellsprings. A simple tale, "The Diver" is rib-tickling in its theme of innocence lost and creativity gained. Pritchett elsewhere has written of the link between sexuality and creativity.

"THE CAMBERWELL BEAUTY"

Again, the long title story, "The Camberwell Beauty," is one of the most arresting. The ambience is that of the antique dealers of London, a cosmos of its own. Each antique dealer has his own specialty, and "within that specialty there is one object he broods on from one year to the next, most of his life; the thing a man would commit murder to get his hands on if he had the nerve."

The narrator is a former antique dealer. A current art dealer, Pliny, an elderly man, has married a beautiful woman, and the narrator is determined to get hold of the Camberwell beauty, who is essentially a work of art. Once more, Pritchett writes of illusion, this time using the art world and the gulf between the greed of the dealers and the loveliness of the art and the artifacts. Isabel, the Camberwell beauty, is exploited by being held captive, like any objet d'art. The narrator fails in his attempt at seduction, which might have replicated another sexual exploitation. Isabel insists that Pliny is a good lover, but Pritchett strongly suggests that there is no intimacy between them. She, like William Blake's Thel, seems not to descend into generation (or sexuality). Remaining under the illusion that she is safe and protected in her innocence, and content to be in stasis and in asexuality, she never does reach a moment of self-awareness. She might just as well have been framed and hung on a wall.

"THE ACCOMPANIST"

Another collection of original stories, *On the Edge of the Cliff*, was published in 1979, and it contains stories wrought with a heightened sensibility and subtlety. The humor and technical brilliance are very much in evidence. Marital infidelity is the theme of several tales, especially in "The Fig Tree" and "A Family Man." A well-carved cameo, "The Accompanist" also portrays an unfaithful mate. William, the narrator, on leave from his Singapore job, is having an affair with Joyce, a piano accompanist, married to Bertie, impotent but particularly likable by a circle of friends who gather for dinner in his flat. The furnishings, Victorian monstrosities, obsess Bertie, since they are a link to the past. For undisclosed reasons, the furniture may almost affirm his asexuality. Critics invariably remark on a Henry James-like subtlety of

sensitivity and particularity of detail. This texture surfaces when Bertie, accompanied by his wife, sings a French bawdy song about a bride who was murdered on her wedding night. Despite Bertie's problems with sex, he seems not to be aware of the irony in singing this song and in being anchored in the protected illusion of bygone Victorian days. His wife, Joyce, may emerge from the decadence of her marriage if, as the narrator says at the end, she will hear her tune: "And if she heard it, the bones in her legs, arms, her fingers, would wake up and she would be out of breath at my door without knowing it." William is saying that *if* she arrives out of a sexual impulse, there will be hope for her liberation from Bertie and from the historical frost symbolized by the Victorian furnishings.

"ON THE EDGE OF THE CLIFF"

The centerpiece story, "On the Edge of the Cliff," unravels the tale of a May-December liaison. Harry, a botanist in his seventies, and Rowena, an artist and twenty-five, have a happy affair in his house on the edge of a cliff. Driving down to a nearby village fair, they engage in role-playing. The omniscient narrator declares, "There are rules for old men who are in love with young girls, all the stricter when the young girls are in love with them. It has to be played as a game." The game stimulates the love affair. At the fair, Harry meets Daisy Pyke, who was a former mistress and who has a young man in tow, mistakenly thought by Harry and Rowena to be her son but actually her lover. Daisy subsequently visits Harry, not to resume any romance but to beg Harry to keep the two young people apart so that her own love life will not be jeopardized. She cries, "I mean it, Harry. I know what would happen and so do you and I don't want to *see* it happen."

Ironically, both Harry and Rowena rarely venture into society. When Harry denies that Rowena is being kept prisoner, Daisy shrewdly insists, "You mean *you* are the prisoner. That is it! So am I!" Harry replies, "Love is always like that. I live only for her." In this tale, as in many of Pritchett's stories, there are contrasting sets of people who are often foils for each other. Both Daisy and Rowena are jealous of their lovers and want their May-December relationships to continue. Pritchett is undoubtedly concerned with the aging process and the capacity to sustain love. Both Daisy and Harry find their capacity to love undiminished with age. Although their love affairs are viable, Pritchett's metaphor of the house on the cliff may suggest that the lovers are aware of inherent dangers because of the differences in ages. At the same time, Pritchett may be implying that even with no age differences between lovers, there is an element of risk. Illusion in this and many other of Pritchett's tales plays an important role. As Harry and Daisy discuss their younger lovers, illusion is implicit. In their confronting the reality of age differences, they become intensely aware of their predicament, and it is at this moment that they experience a Pritchett epiphany. This realization will help them to savor the time spent on the edge of the cliff.

In his short fiction, Pritchett fashions a host of unique characters, uses witty and humorous dialogue, employs a variety of "happenings," and leaves readers with the sense that they themselves have been mocked not with bitterness or caustic wit but with gentleness and love.

OTHER MAJOR WORKS

LONG FICTION: *Claire Drummer*, 1929; *Shirley Sanz*, 1932 (also known as *Elopement into Exile*); *Nothing Like Leather*, 1935; *Dead Man Leading*, 1937; *Mr. Beluncle*, 1951.

NONFICTION: *Marching Spain*, 1928; *In My Good Books*, 1942; *The Living Novel and Later Appreciations*, 1946; *Why Do I Write? An Exchange of Views Between Elizabeth Bowen, Graham Greene, and V. S. Pritchett*, 1948; *Books in General*, 1953; *The Spanish Temper*, 1954; *London Perceived*, 1962; *The Offensive Traveller*, 1964 (also known as *Foreign Faces*); *New York Proclaimed*, 1965; *Shakespeare: The Comprehensive Soul*, 1965; *The Working Novelist*, 1965; *Dublin: A Portrait*, 1967; *A Cab at the Door*, 1968; *George Meredith and English Comedy*, 1970; *Midnight Oil*, 1972; *Balzac: A Biography*, 1973; *The Gentle Barbarian: The Life and Work of Turgenev*, 1977; *The Myth Makers: Literary Essays*, 1979; *The Tale Bearers: Literary Essays*, 1980; *The Other Side of the Frontier: A V. S. Pritchett Reader*, 1984; *A Man of Letters*, 1985; *Chekhov: A Spirit Set Free*, 1988; *Lasting Impressions*, 1990; *The Complete Essays*, 1991.

MISCELLANEOUS: *The Pritchett Century*, 1997.

BIBLIOGRAPHY

Angell, Roger. "Marching Life." *The New Yorker* 73 (December 22-29, 1997): 126-134. In this biographical sketch, Angell, who was Pritchett's editor at *The New Yorker*, contends that, although Pritchett was called First Man of Letters, the title never fit properly because he was neither literary nor a stylist, and he liked to say he was a hack long before he was a critic.

Baldwin, Dean. *V. S. Pritchett*. Boston: Twayne, 1987. This slim book of 133 pages contains a superb short biography of Pritchett, followed by a clear-cut analysis of his novels, short stories, and nonfiction. One caution is to be noted: Baldwin says there is no article analyzing any of Pritchett's short stories, yet the *Journal of the Short Story in English* devoted an entire volume as a special Pritchett issue. It may be that Baldwin's book was already in the process of publication when the journal issue was completed.

Bloom, Jonathan. *The Art of Revision in the Short Stories of V. S. Pritchett and William Trevor*. New York: Palgrave Macmillan, 2006. Charts the development of the two writers' short stories from their initial ideas through the stories eventual publication. Describes how they transformed incidents and people in their lives into fictional events and characters and discusses their relationships with editors. Compares their published stories to demonstrate their different approaches to common themes and analyzes the role of fantasy in their works. The chapter "V. S. Pritchett's Ministering Angell," based on an article published in *Sewanee Review* (Spring, 2004), focuses on Pritchett's close and sympathetic relationship with Roger Angell of *The New Yorker*; Angell edited all but four of Pritchett's twenty-seven stories that were published in this magazine from 1949 to 1989.

Gąsiorek, Andrzej. "The Short Fiction of V. S. Pritchett." In *A Companion to the British and Irish Short Story*, edited by Cheryl Alexander Malcolm and David Malcolm. Malden, Mass.: Wiley-Blackwell, 2008. An overview of Pritchett's short fiction, including his stories "Handsome Is as Handsome Does," "The Camberwell Beauty," and "When My Girl Comes Home."

Hunter, Adrian. "Elizabeth Bowen and V. S. Pritchett." In *The Cambridge Introduction to the Short Story in English*. Cambridge, England: Cambridge University Press, 2007. Pritchett is one of the "post-modernist" writers whose short stories are analyzed in this volume. "The Fall," "The Sailor," "Handsome Is as Handsome Does," "Satan Comes to Georgia," "Things as They Are," and "When My Girl Comes Home" are among the stories examined.

Johnson, Anne Janette. "V(ictor) S(awdon) Pritchett." In *Contemporary Authors, New Revision Series*, edited by James G. Lesniak. Vol. 31. Detroit: Gale Research, 1990. This article includes general material on Pritchett's life and work, with a wide range of critical comments by magazines and literary journals, such as *The Times Literary Supplement, The New York Times*, and *The New Republic*. Contains a listing of Pritchett's writings divided into genres and biographical and critical sources, especially those articles that appeared in newspapers, magazines, and literary journals. Geared for the general reader, with the variety of quotes appealing to a specialist.

Oumhani, Cecile. "Water in V. S. Pritchett's Art of Revealing." *Journal of the Short Story in English* 6 (1986): 75-91. Oumhani probes the immersion motif in the pattern of water imagery in Pritchett's short stories, especially in "On the Edge of a Cliff," "The Diver," "The Saint," and "Handsome Is as Handsome Does." Oumhani believes that Pritchett's views about sensuality can be intuited from the stories she analyzes. The article will appeal to the introductory reader of Sigmund Freud.

Pritchett, V. S. "An Interview with V. S. Pritchett." Interview by Ben Forkner and Philippe Sejourne. *Journal of the Short Story in English* 6 (1986): 11-38. Pritchett in this interview reveals a number of salient details about writing in general and the influences of writers like H. G. Wells and Arnold Bennett. He talks at length about the Irish predilection for storytelling and Irish ideas about morality and the art of concealment. Pritchett reveals his penchant for the ironic and pays homage to writer Anton Chekhov, one of his models. He believes that the comic is really a facet of the poetic. The interview is written in a question-answer style and is a straightforward record of Pritchett's views.

Stinson, John J. *V. S. Pritchett: A Study of the Short Fiction*. New York: Twayne, 1992. An introduction to Pritchett's short fiction. Suggests that Pritchett's stories have been largely ignored by critics because they do not have the symbolic image pattern favored by formalist critics. Provides interpretations of a number of Pritchett's stories. Includes Pritchett's own comments on writers who have influenced him, as well as essays on his short fiction by writers Eudora Welty and William Trevor.

Theroux, Paul. "V. S. Pritchett." *The New York Times Book Review*, May 25, 1997, 27. A biographical tribute, claiming that Pritchett was probably the last man who could be called a man of letters. Notes that Pritchett worked slowly and with confidence.

Tracy, Karen. "Victor Sawdon Pritchett." In *A Reader's Companion to the Short Story in English*, edited by Erin Fallon, et al., under the auspices of the Society for the Study of the Short Story. Westport, Conn.: Greenwood Press, 2001. Aimed at the general reader, this essay provides a brief biography of Pritchett followed by an analysis of his short fiction.

Treglown, Jeremy. *V. S. Pritchett: A Working Life*. New York: Random House, 2004. An admiring and engaging biography of Pritchett that examines both the breadth of his literary production and the highs and lows of his personal life.

Julia B. Boken

R

JEAN RHYS

Born: Roseau, Dominica Island, West Indies;
   August 24, 1894
Died: Exeter, England; May 14, 1979
Also Known As: Ella Gwendolen Rees Williams

The Left Bank, and Other Stories, 1927
Tigers Are Better-Looking, 1968
Sleep It Off, Lady, 1976
The Collected Short Stories, 1987

OTHER LITERARY FORMS

Jean Rhys (rees) wrote five novels: *Postures* (1928), which was published in the United States in 1929 under the title *Quartet; After Leaving Mr. Mackenzie* (1930); *Voyage in the Dark* (1934); *Good Morning, Midnight* (1939), which was dramatized for radio by the British Broadcasting Corporation (BBC) in 1958; and *Wide Sargasso Sea* (1966), which many consider to be her masterpiece. She also wrote *Smile Please: An Unfinished Autobiography* (1979). Her letters were published in 1984.

ACHIEVEMENTS

During the first decade of her writing career, Jean Rhys achieved only limited success. Although her books were well received by critics, they attracted only a small readership. After years of neglect, however, interest in her work increased dramatically following the publication of *Wide Sargasso Sea.* She was elected a Fellow of the Royal Society of Literature; her novel won the W. H. Smith Literary Award and the Award for Writers from the Arts Council of Great Britain. Throughout the 1970's, her reputation grew, and she holds a secure place in the first rank of twentieth-century novelists. Her work is notable for its unsparing exploration of a particular character type: the dispossessed, dependent, exploited single woman, struggling to survive in a society in which she has no roots, no money, no power, and often no hope.

BIOGRAPHY

Jean Rhys was born Ella Gwendolen Rees Williams on August 24, 1894, in Roseau, Dominica Island, in the West Indies. Her father was a Welsh doctor and her mother a white Creole (a native West Indian of European ancestry). In 1910, she was sent to England to live with an aunt in Cambridge, and she later studied acting at the Royal Academy of Dramatic Art. When her father died, she was forced to make her living as a chorus girl in touring musical companies. In 1919, she married a French-Dutch poet and journalist and went to live on the Continent, where the couple led a bohemian life. The marriage ended in divorce in 1927. In 1938, she married again and settled in Cornwall, England. Following her second husband's death in 1945, she married for the third time in 1946. Her literary career flourished moderately in the late 1920's and 1930's, but she disappeared entirely from the literary scene during World War II and did not reappear until 1958, when the BBC adapted *Good Morning, Midnight* for radio. Encouraged by the new interest in her work, she began writing again, and her reputation was still growing at her death in 1979, at the age of eighty-four.

ANALYSIS

The range of Jean Rhys's stories, as of her novels, is narrow. She focuses on the world of the lonely, the outcast, the vulnerable. Her central characters are all women who live in a world they cannot control and which regards them with indifference and cruelty. Communication is often found to be impossible, and the protagonists' fragmented, tormented world is perpetually on the verge of falling apart.

The dominant note is of isolation, dependency, and loss, with more than a smattering of self-pity.

THE LEFT BANK, AND OTHER STORIES

Rhys's first collection, *The Left Bank, and Other Stories*, consists of twenty-two stories, most of them short sketches, of life on the Parisian Left Bank. A few stories, "In the Rue de l'Arrivée," "A Night," and "Learning to Be a Mother," end on an optimistic note, as does "Mannequin," in which a young girl, at the end of her first day as a mannequin, feels a surge of happiness as she steps into the street and merges into the vibrant life of the city. She is one of the few heroines in Rhys's fiction who discover a sense of belonging. The dominant mood of the collection, however, is one of helplessness and troubled uncertainty, and as such it sets the tone for Rhys's later work. The stories focus on characters who inhabit the fringes of society: artists, exiles, misfits, and deprived women. "Hunger," for example, is a despairing, first-person monologue of an English woman who is down and out in Paris. She takes the reader, day by day, through her experience of five days without food.

"LA GROSSE FIFI"

"La Grosse Fifi" is a more ambitious story, one of a group at the end of the collection that is set outside Paris--in this case, on the French Riviera. Fifi is a huge, vulgar woman who keeps a gigolo half her age in a sleazy hotel. The other main character is a young woman named Roseau. The name, she explains, means "reed," and her motto in life is "a reed shaken by the wind" (a motto that might adequately describe virtually all Rhys's helpless and vulnerable heroines). Roseau can survive, she says, only as long as she does not think. Unhappy and lonely, without home, friends, or money, she is comforted one night by Fifi, who reveals herself to be infinitely kind and understanding. Fifi knows the foolishness of her own situation, yet she genuinely loves her man, however irregular and unhappy the relationship appears. When her lover abruptly leaves her, she faces the hostile world with dignity, still attracting men and still cheerfully defying the darker elements in her life. Roseau feels protected by her presence, which is so full of life that she cannot help but feel gladdened by it. The story reaches a climax when Roseau learns that Fifi has been stabbed to death in a quarrel with her lover.

Fifi's almost tragic grandeur serves as a measure of Roseau's inadequacy. She knows that she can never love with such full abandon or live so wholeheartedly. She decides to leave the hotel, and the story ends with her packing (a typical activity for the rootless Rhys heroine) while the yellow sunshine--yellow always carries negative connotations for Rhys--streams through the window.

"THE LOTUS"

Rhys wrote no more short stories until the early 1960's, and then eight of them were published in *Tigers Are Better-Looking*. These stories are longer and more complex, and the characters are more fully realized than those in *The Left Bank, and Other Stories*, but Rhys's vision has become even more bleak and despairing. "The Lotus," told with a taut economy and a ruthless fidelity to what Rhys saw as reality, is one of the bleakest. Lotus Heath is an eccentric middle-aged poet and novelist. Ronnie Miles invites her for drinks one evening, since they live in the same apartment building. His wife Christine dislikes Lotus, however, and her frequent cruel insults sabotage Ronnie's attempts to be polite and sociable. When Ronnie helps Lotus down to her own small, ill-smelling apartment, her cheerful guise suddenly drops and she reveals her own despair and frustration. Later, Ronnie sees Lotus running naked and drunk (she is one of many Rhys heroines who drink too much) down the street, soon to be escorted away by two policemen. When one of the policemen inquires at the Miles' apartment about Lotus, Ronnie denies that he knows much about her, and no one else in the building will admit to knowing her either. An ambulance takes her to the hospital. Christine, who found her own insults highly amusing, ignores the whole affair, lying in bed smiling, as if Lotus's eclipse has somehow made her own star rise. The story ends when Ronnie, his kindness revealed as shallow and ineffectual, begins to make love to Christine--cruelty has its reward, and compassion is snuffed out without a trace. There cannot be any escape or consolation through art, which is represented, however inadequately, by Lotus and mocked by Christine. In this story, the only arts which flourish are popular songs preserved on secondhand gramophone records.

"TILL SEPTEMBER PETRONELLA"

The best-known story in the collection is probably "Till September Petronella." It opens with the heroine and narrator, Petronella Grey, performing a typical action--packing. She dislikes London, with its gray days and heartless people, a recurring theme in Rhys's fiction. Typically also, Petronella has no money and has cut herself off from her family. She admits to herself that she has never lived in a place that she liked, and the story chronicles the directionless drift of her life. She goes to the country to visit her boyfriend Marston and his guests Frankie and her lover Julian. During a lunch loosened by drink, they fall to pointless quarreling. Petronella decides to return to London, and Marston says that he will see her in September. The date of their parting is significant: July 28, 1914, because it coincides with the start of World War I.

In London, she is befriended by an eager young man, Melville, and during their evening together she recalls that her career as a chorus girl failed because she could not remember the only line she had to speak. The incident keeps coming back to her; it is a parable of her life. She has lost her connections, the threads which bind her to the rest of life and society. She cannot fit smoothly into the flow of life. When Melville tells her that he, too, is going away until September, their lighthearted farewell does not disguise for the reader the dangerous period of loneliness which Petronella is about to enter. Not only does the story emphasize her dependence on men, who provide her with distractions but not fulfillment, but also it makes clear that Petronella enters her private wasteland just as Europe begins to tear itself apart in World War I. Her aimlessness is somehow linked to a wider spread of chaos. There will be no September reunions.

Much of the story's power comes through Rhys's gift for subtle suggestion rather than overt statement. The reader is forced to penetrate beyond the apparently trivial nature of the dialogue, which makes up nine-tenths of the story, to the darkness which lies behind it and threatens to engulf it. When the story ends with Petronella sitting quietly, waiting for the city clock to strike, the moment has acquired an ominous quality, as if the striking clock will inaugurate some dreadful Day of Judgment which she, waiting passively, can do nothing to avert.

SLEEP IT OFF, LADY

Sleep It Off, Lady consists of sixteen stories. They are predominantly tales of regret and loss and fall into a rough chronological sequence which resembles the chronology of Rhys's own life. The first five take place in the West Indies at the beginning of the twentieth century. Two of these ("Pioneers, Oh, Pioneers," and "Fishy Waters") deal with the difficulties of white settlers in the West Indies, isolated in the land they were responsible for colonizing. A strongly autobiographical middle group centers on a young female protagonist who goes to school in Cambridge, England; trains as an actress; and becomes a member of the chorus in a touring company. Three stories toward the end of the collection ("Rapunzel, Rapunzel," "Who Knows What's Up in the Attic?" and "Sleep It Off, Lady") feature elderly female protagonists.

"SLEEP IT OFF, LADY"

There is probably no more quietly horrifying story in English literature than "Sleep It Off, Lady." Told with an unsentimental, almost clinical precision, it centers on an elderly heroine, Miss Verney, a spinster who lives in one of the poorer parts of the village, where she does not really belong. The central action consists of her attempts to rid herself of a dilapidated old shed which stands next to her cottage, but she cannot persuade any of the local tradesmen to pull it down. She feels increasingly helpless, and the shed begins to acquire a sinister power over her. She dreams of it as a coffin.

One day, she sees a rat in the shed, and the powerful rat poison which Tom, her neighbor, puts down seems to have no effect. The rat walks unhurriedly across the shed, as if he is in charge of everything, while she feels herself to be in charge of nothing. Tom suggests that the rat must be a pink one, the product of her excessive drinking. She feels trapped and misunderstood and retreats into a closed world of her own. She stops going for walks outside. Letters remain unanswered, and she rejects the good-neighborliness of Tom.

What makes the story so poignantly effective is that just before her inevitable demise she undergoes a form of rebirth. On her birthday, she awakes feeling refreshed, happy, and young again. It is a windless day, with a blue sky overhead. Poised between one year and the next, she feels ageless, and she makes plans to reach out to other people once more when her new telephone is installed. Her optimism, however, is misplaced. Later in the day, as she struggles to move a garbage container back to the shed, she falls and loses consciousness. When she awakes it is nearly dark, and she is surrounded by the contents of the trash can, including broken egg shells (symbolizing the failure of her rebirth). When she calls to some passing women for help, the wind drowns out her cries. Even nature has turned against her. A local child named Deena finds her but refuses to help and makes it clear that Miss Verney is despised in her own neighborhood. The next morning, Miss Verney is discovered by the postman, who is carrying a parcel of books for her. The parcel--like the telephone, a symbol of communication with the outside world--comes too late. She dies that evening. Her individual will to live proves useless in the face of the hostility and indifference of her neighbors. Regarded as trash, she dies surrounded by trash. Her feeling of renewal was only the last and the cruellest trick that life was to play upon her.

"I Used to Live Here Once"

The last story in the collection, only one-and-a-half pages, serves as an appropriate epitaph for all of Rhys's stories. "I Used to Live Here Once" features an unnamed protagonist who in later life returns to her childhood home in the West Indies. She crosses a stream, using the stepping stones she still remembers well, and approaches her old house. In the garden, she sees a young boy and a girl under a mango tree and calls to them twice, but they do not answer. When she says hello for the third time, she reaches out, longing to touch them. The boy turns to her, looks her directly in the eye, and remarks how cold it has suddenly become, and he and the girl run back across the grass into the house. The story ends with the pregnant sentence "That was the first time she knew."

She knows that she cannot return to the freshness and vitality of her youth. She also knows that the coldness emanates from her, and therefore she must have frozen into a kind of living death. Beyond this, it is as if she knows everything that Rhys's stories have depicted, time after time: the pain of final separation, the loneliness of exile, the failure of people to connect with

one another, and the horrible realization of what life can become. Several critics have seen the woman as posthumously returning to the scenes of her childhood and achieving no emotional accommodation or reconciliation even after death.

Jean Rhys's stories do not elevate the spirit but rather reveal the gradual strangulation of the life force. They do not make easy or comfortable reading. Rhys's merit lies in her quiet but devastating presentation of the hopeless and the forgotten. She looks on despair and futility with an unblinking eye; she does not flinch or sentimentalize, and she does not deceive.

Other major works

LONG FICTION: *Postures*, 1928 (pb. in U.S. as *Quartet*, 1929); *After Leaving Mr. Mackenzie*, 1930; *Voyage in the Dark*, 1934; *Good Morning, Midnight*, 1939; *Wide Sargasso Sea*, 1966.

NONFICTION: *Smile Please: An Unfinished Autobiography*, 1979; *The Letters of Jean Rhys*, 1984 (also known as *Jean Rhys: Letters, 1931-1966*).

Bibliography

Angier, Carole. *Jean Rhys*. New York: Viking, 1985. A biography of Rhys that treats her fiction as essentially autobiographical. Far from being seen as a feminist, Rhys is presented as an intensely lonely individualist and solipsist without a program or external loyalties. Her lifelong attempt to understand herself was governed by a tragic and pessimistic view of human nature and the world.

_____. *Jean Rhys: Life and Work*. Boston: Little, Brown, 1990. This monumental work of Rhys scholarship combines detailed biographical study with sections devoted to interpretations of her fiction. Unfortunately, chapters specifically examining the short stories were deleted because of length considerations. The book contains voluminous notes and an extensive bibliography.

Czarnecki, Kristin. "Jean Rhys's Postmodern Narrative Authority: Selina's Patois in 'Let Them Call It Jazz.'" *College Literature* 35, no. 2 (Summer, 2008): 20-37. Focuses on Selina Davis, the first-person mulatta narrator of this short story. Argues that Davis is "a departure in characterization for

Rhys and a new narrative response to patriarchal assaults upon women and the poor."

Davidson, Arnold E. *Jean Rhys*. New York: Frederick Ungar, 1985. Drawing heavily on a number of critical sources, Davidson supports a feminist interpretation of the texts and provides a useful approach to the major works, including the stories.

James, Louis. *Jean Rhys*. London: Longman, 1978. Although concentrating on *Wide Sargasso Sea*, James provides a good short introduction to Rhys's life and work.

Kineke, Sheila. "'Like a Hook Fits an Eye': Jean Rhys, Ford Maddox Ford, and the Imperial Operations of Modernist Mentoring." *Tulsa Studies in Women's Literature* 16 (Fall, 1997): 281-301. Discusses how the fatalism, submission, and masochism of Rhys's main female characters are a side effect of the female condition in white Western culture and specifically of the operation of male mentorship by Ford Madox Ford.

Kotrodimos, Paul. "Jean Rhys." In *A Reader's Companion to the Short Story in English*, edited by Erin Fallon, et al., under the auspices of the Society for the Study of the Short Story. Westport, Conn.: Greenwood Press, 2001. Aimed at the general reader, this essay provides a brief biography of Rhys, discusses the critical reception of her work, and analyzes her short fiction.

Lonsdale, Thorunn. "Literary Allusion in the Fiction of Jean Rhys." In *Caribbean Women Writers*, edited by Mary Condé and Thorunn Lonsdale. New York: St. Martin's Press, 1999. Discusses the many critically neglected, intertextual references to nineteenth- and twentieth-century European and American literature in Rhys's novels and short stories. Examines such stories as "Again the Antilles" and "Let Them Call It Jazz."

Malcolm, Cheryl Alexander. "Jean Rhys: 'Let Them Call It Jazz.'" In *A Companion to the British and Irish Short Story*, edited by Cheryl Alexander Malcolm and David Malcolm. Malden, Mass.: Wiley-Blackwell, 2008. Provides an explication of this short story.

Malcolm, Cheryl Alexander, and David Malcolm. *Jean Rhys: A Study of the Short Fiction*. New York: Twayne, 1996. This book makes up for what Angier's biography--and most critical assessments of Rhys--lacks. After a section devoted to their assessment of Rhys's short fiction, the Malcolms provide a chapter on Rhys's own views of herself--conveyed in excerpts from her letters and an interview--and conclude with a section that reprints a wide range of critical opinion about Rhys's fiction.

Morrell, A. C. "The World of Jean Rhys's Short Stories." *World Literature Written in English* 18 (1979): 235-244. Rhys's stories are seen as having a unity of vision achieved through the expression of a consistent center of consciousness and sensibility no matter what the narrative point of view. Critical analysis is provided and demonstrates that Rhys's stories can be categorized as either episodes or completed experiences.

Pizzichini, Lilian. *The Blue Hour: A Life of Jean Rhys*. New York: W. W. Norton and Company, 2009. Rhys's mostly unhappy life is depicted in this biography, which sheds light on her three marriages, her experiences as a mother, and her love affair with Ford Maddox Ford. From Rhys's childhood in the West Indies to her death in 1979, Pizzichini traces the highs and lows of Rhys's life, including her days as a chorus girl and a prostitute and her struggle with alcoholism and depression. Includes twenty photos.

Savory, Elaine. *The Cambridge Introduction to Jean Rhys*. New York: Cambridge University Press, 2009. A concise overview of Rhys's life and works. One section devotes several pages to all her texts, including her short-story collections. Another section places her work in the contexts of cultural identity, modernist literature, women artists outside polite society, colonialism, and postcolonialism; a final section assesses the critical reception of her works.

Bryan Aubrey
Updated by Douglas Rollins

MORDECAI RICHLER

Born: Montreal, Quebec, Canada; January 27, 1931
Died: Montreal, Quebec, Canada; July 3, 2001

PRINCIPAL SHORT FICTION

The Street: Stories, 1969

OTHER LITERARY FORMS

Although primarily a novelist, Mordecai Richler (MOR-deh-ki RIHK-lur) wrote in many genres, including essays, articles, screenplays, journalism, television plays, and children's literature. He is perhaps best known for his novel *The Apprenticeship of Duddy Kravitz* (1959), which he adapted as a screenplay for a film of that name released in 1974. Two of his novels, *Cocksure: A Novel* (1968) and *St. Urbain's Horseman* (1971), won Canada's foremost literary prize, the Governor-General's Award. In 1997, he published his last novel, *Barney's Version*; a film based on this novel was released in 2010.

ACHIEVEMENTS

Mordecai Richler's achievements over the course of his writing career were considerable. He was awarded both a John Simon Guggenheim Memorial Foundation Fellowship in creative writing and a Canada Council Senior Arts Fellowship. His literary awards include the President's Medal for Nonfiction from the University of Western Ontario (1959), a humor prize from the *The Paris Review* (1967), two Governor-General's Awards for Fiction (1969 and 1972), the *London Jewish Chronicle* literature award (1972), a Book of the Year for Children Award from the Canadian Library Association and a Ruth Schwartz Children's Book Award (both 1976), an H. H. Wingate award for fiction from the *London Jewish Chronicle* (1981), a Commonwealth Writers Prize (1990), the Giller Prize (1997), a Hugh MacLanna Prize, and the Stephen Leacock Prize (both 1998). The screenplay

based on his novel *The Apprenticeship of Duddy Kravitz* earned him a Screenwriters Guild of America Award in 1974; the film itself garnered a Golden Bear Award at the Berlin Film Festival in 1974.

After his return to Canada in 1972, after twenty years in England and continental Europe, Richler's journalistic writing on Canada, widely published both in Canada and the United States, chronicled his crotchety love and growing sadness for the fate of Canada, his home and native land. His subjective, often savagely funny and derisive depictions of Canadian political and cultural life made Americans in particular aware of a Canada they had never known or contemplated; his adroit skewering of Canadian pretensions has both entertained and enraged his Canadian readers. His later essays, which appeared regularly in major American and Canadian periodicals, concentrated with increasing vitriol on Quebec's nationalist aspirations.

Perhaps his major achievement was the group of fictional works that explores so thoroughly and captures so vividly the lives and fractious spirit of Jewish-Canadian immigrants in a Montreal community now largely dispersed. As Richler said, "That was my time and my place, and I have elected myself to get it exactly right."

BIOGRAPHY

Mordecai Richler was born on January 27, 1931, in the Jewish ghetto of east Montreal. His parents Moses and Lily made sure their son received a solid Jewish education, first at United Talmud Torah and then at Baron Byng High School in Montreal. He attended Sir George Williams University from 1949 to 1951 but left school to work as a writer in London, England, and later worked briefly as a news editor for the Canadian Broadcasting Company. For almost twenty years he resided in London, publishing much of his work there. In 1972, Richler returned to Montreal, where he settled with his wife and children. For ten years Richler was a member of the editorial board of the Book-of-the-Month Club. After his return to Canada, he published works whose spiritual center was still Montreal, though their scope is broader. Otherwise, his writing was devoted to essays, articles, and reviews; many of these--funny, biting, and wearily resigned--were collected in his book *Broadsides: Reviews and Opinions* (1990). Richler died in Montreal on July 3, 2001.

ANALYSIS

George Woodcock says of Mordecai Richler, "The worlds he creates are not autonomous entities re-made each time. Rather, they belong to a fictional continuum that perpetually overlaps the world in which Richler himself lives and feels, thinks and writes." The reader receives a distinct impression of the primacy of memory over imagination in Richler's work. Most of his stories and novels deal with the characters and situations of the Montreal ghetto of his early years; the stories in his collection *The Street* and the scenes of many of the novels examine with compassion and realism the lives of Canadian and immigrant Jews in this restricted and variegated environment. Most of the author's work functions within this frame of reference, with only an occasional change of focus. A peripheral character in one story comes under more thorough scrutiny in another. Often a new character will be introduced to interact with the established ones. The reader is given a continuity of the values and traditions of the old world as they evolve in the setting of their new Canadian world. There seems to be, then, no clear distinction between the fictional and the autobiographical elements of Richler's narrative. In fact, *The Street*, his only episodic collection that can be considered to comprise stories, has been more accurately described as "a lightly fictionalized memoir."

The importance of Richler's work, consequently, is the analysis of age-old human problems found in familiar situations. He saw things with little sentimentality; life is filled with illusions, poverty, despair, and selfishness. Richler reacted positively in spite of these negative aspects, despite showing how limiting they are. This view is emphasized by a keen sense of the ridiculous which sharpens readers' perceptions and evaluations. Absurd as his characters sometimes are,

however, Richler still had a tender attitude toward them. Despite their moral and social blindness, they are human beings, desperately trying to control their own lives, and Richler wanted the reader to understand them rather than love them. Although their environment is a Jewish neighborhood with its own laws, legends, and language, these characters speak to all readers; in fact, they become even more authentic by belonging to a particular social setting. Their external circumstances only show more clearly that their reactions are human and universal.

"THE SUMMER MY GRANDMOTHER WAS SUPPOSED TO DIE"

The story "The Summer My Grandmother Was Supposed to Die" is perhaps Richler's best. Here the author forces the reader to confront lingering death and its implications for a family. The story is graphically realistic. Since life must go on, even in tragedy, the reader is shown the absurd black comedy of ordinary existence. As are all the stories in *The Street*, this one is in the format of a recollection by old Malka's grandson, Jake Hersh. Dr. Katzman discovers that Malka has gangrene, and he says she will not last a month; he says the same thing the second, third, and fourth months. Malka remains bedridden for seven years; hers is a common story of the courageous person with an incredible will to live. The grotesque nature of the situation is dramatized very quickly when Jake says, "When we sat down to eat we could smell her." While Mr. and Mrs. Hersh wait for her to die, saying it will be for the best, the neighborhood children wait to peek up the nurse's dress. The grotesque and the ridiculous are simply integral parts of life--and death.

Malka, the widow of Zaddik, one of the Righteous, is described as beautiful, patient, shrewd, and resourceful. When she was married to Zaddik, these qualities were necessary since he often gave his money away to rabbinical students, immigrants, and widows. As Jake says, this "made him as unreliable a provider as a drinker." The couple's sons are prominent men, a rabbi, a lawyer, and an actor, but it is left to Jake's mother to take care of Malka. No one, it seems, wants the old woman, despite all that she has done for them; she becomes an inconvenience, "a condition in the house, something beyond hope or reproach, like a leaky ice-box." Jake can no longer kiss her without a feeling of revulsion, and he wonders if she knows that he covets her room. The shock of her tragic illness over a period of time gives way to resignation. Malka becomes only a presence, no longer recognizable as a human being. Instead of love being engendered by the grandmother's plight, there is resentment.

After the fourth year of her illness the strain begins to show. Mrs. Hersh is openly scornful of her husband and finds fault with her two children; she also takes to falling asleep directly after supper. Hersh seeks escape more often to Tansky's Cigar and Soda, and people tell him that he might as well be a bachelor. Malka's children finally take her, against her will, to the Jewish Old People's Home. With the reminder of death gone from the home, family relationships improve. Mrs. Hersh no longer needs the comfort of her bed, her cheeks glow with health, and she even jokes with her children. Mr. Hersh begins to come home early, no longer finding it necessary to go to Tansky's. Malka is seldom mentioned.

When Jake asks if he can move back to his room, however, his mother's caring instinct returns, and she decides to bring Malka home. The cycle of despair starts again, and the family returns to their habits of escape. Mr. Hersh says, "I knew it, I was born with all the luck." For two more years there is no change in Malka's condition; she seems to gain her strength at the expense of the family. The tension is almost unbearable for the Hershes. The fatigue and morbidity are most noticeable in Mrs. Hersh, but they are also evident in each member of the household.

Finally, in the seventh summer, Malka dies. When Jake returns home from a baseball game, he is not allowed to see her; he is only told what he and his sister will receive from their grandmother's belongings. When Jake's sister Rifka tells him that he can now have Malka's room, he changes his mind, saying "I couldn't sleep in there now." Rifka, sensing his discomfort, approaches his bed with a sheet over her head to frighten him. When all the family members gather together, cousin Jerry is skeptical of their reactions, claiming that now everyone will be sickeningly sentimental. Mr. and Mrs. Hersh, however, are openly scornful of these relatives, especially the rabbi, who did very little to

Mordecai Richler (Getty Images)

comfort Malka during her illness. Ironically, Dr. Katzman tries to console this religious man. The rabbi can be pensive, but he does not feel the emotions of being involved. The comfort and simple decency of being allowed to die at home gave Malka the courage and strength to live, but the demands of caring for her have sapped the strength of the family.

"SOME GRIST FOR MERVYN'S MILL"

Richler also examines the problem of involvement when an outsider, Mervyn Kaplansky, moves to the St. Urbain area. Within the borders of his Montreal ghetto, peopled with established families and the Jewish immigrants, there is an exaggerated emphasis on getting ahead, most forcefully presented by Richler in his novel *The Apprenticeship of Duddy Kravitz*. Any display of talent is treated with admiration, especially if that talent is recognized in the United States. There is a considerable amount of difference between the pressure to succeed and actual success, and expectations are often greater than achievement itself. "Some Grist for Mervyn's Mill" illustrates this point and its consequences.

Mervyn, a short, fat man from Toronto, about twenty-three years of age, rents a room in the Hersh household. When he says that he is a writer, Mrs. Hersh is enraptured. Mervyn even carries with him a check for $14.50, which he received from the *Family Herald & Weekly Star*. This small check has given Mervyn a great ego; he says, "I try not to read too much now that I'm a wordsmith myself. I'm afraid of being influenced, you see."

Mervyn is now writing a novel entitled *The Dirty Jews* "about the struggles of our people in a hostile society"; he spends much time discussing this book and other literary matters with Mrs. Hersh. Again, Mr. Hersh is alienated from the family and goes to Tansky's to play cards. In order to finish the novel, Mervyn rarely leaves his room. Thinking that this is bad for him, Mrs. Hersh arranges a date for him with Molly Rosen, the "best looker" on St. Urbain Street. The match is unsuccessful, but Mervyn writes to her anyway. All the letters, however, come back unopened. Mervyn's love-life seems to parallel his unattained success as a writer.

Ironically, roles begin to reverse when Mr. Hersh sees a story, "A Doll for the Deacon," supposedly published under Mervyn's pseudonym. For Mr. Hersh this is proof that Mervyn is a writer, and he overlooks his faults, as well as his overdue rent, now treating the budding wordsmith as an author in full flower. He clips out material from newspapers for him, takes him to meet the boys at Tansky's, and talks more tenderly to him than he does to his own children. Mervyn soon becomes more important to Molly, even though she knows that a publisher has rejected his novel. Winning the praise of Mr. Hersh and the fancy of Molly puts a great deal of pressure on Mervyn. He knows that he has gained recognition on false pretenses, although he never doubts his talent as a writer.

To prove something to the locals, Mervyn concocts a lie about receiving an advance from a United States publisher. Unfortunately, Mr. Hersh proclaims a celebration including the men from Tansky's and the Rosens, and at the party Molly announces her engagement to Mervyn. Mervyn can only drink heavily and suffer the pain caused by his deceit. Later he tells Jake that Molly only wanted his fame; before the rumors of

his success, he was an object of ridicule, but with established fame, everyone feels possessive. Mervyn is now accepted for what they think is his achievement, and to save face, Mervyn perpetuates the illusion by showing Mr. Hersh a telegram with an offer from Hollywood. He leaves immediately, saying that he must check out the offer. A few days later the Hershes receive a bill for the telegram, and no one sees Mervyn again. The boys at Tansky's are scandalized, and Molly is disgraced. After a month Mr. Hersh starts to receive money from Toronto for the unpaid rent, but Mervyn never answers any of his letters.

Richler was at his best satirizing the subtle human relationships that make up the social fabric. The consequences of almost insignificant and innocent efforts have a kind of ripple effect until a number of people become involved; the microcosm around St. Urbain Street is only a focus for broader social problems. Personal human contact creates deception, pain, family alienation, and only very rarely a sense of joy. Individuals struggle in a social context with only a hope that things will get better. Richler's characters, then, are survivors who exist not as victims of a cruel, impersonal fate but as victims of their own actions. There is no significant harm done when Mervyn is exposed as a fraud. Life resumes at Tansky's, and Mr. Hersh has merely to take a severe ribbing from his friends. For most of Richler's people, this is what life is all about--a comedy of bearable suffering in which only minor victories, at best, are won.

"PLAYING BALL ON HAMPSTEAD HEATH"

Perhaps Richler's best-known short story is "Playing Ball on Hampstead Heath," which was first published in the August, 1966, issue of *Gentleman's Quarterly*, a men's fashion magazine which contains advertisements for expensive men's clothing. These advertisements express the subliminal message that men who wear such clothing will succeed in business and appear attractive to women. At first glance, it may seem odd that a serious writer like Richler would publish in such a vain and superficial magazine, but the characters in this short story would be at ease in the fantasy world of *Gentleman's Quarterly*.

The characters in this short story are middle-aged Americans and Canadians who work in the entertainment industry in London. Some are actors but most are producers of financially successful but superficial films. They have not adapted at all to English culture, and their popular summer activity is to play baseball on Hampstead Heath, a park in London. As their game begins, the players have difficulty concentrating because their eyes wander. Some players ogle attractive young women and for this reason they commit several errors. Most of the players are divorced and both their present and former wives are watching this game. Perspectives keep changing. Sometimes the men look at their new and young wives, who married them for their money, and at other times, they look at their old wives, who are on the opposite side of the field. The men refer to their former wives as the "Alimony Gallery." Their former wives are understandably still very bitter. They sacrificed and worked at menial jobs while their husbands were struggling to succeed. Richler tells his readers that these women have not changed, whereas their former husbands have. An extraordinarily selfish man named Ziggy Alter justifies his divorce from his first wife and his marriage to a much younger woman by saying that he wanted to grow old with a younger woman whom he "can now afford" and not with a woman his own age.

These men are not just insensitive and selfish, they are also racist. In a clear effort to improve the quality of his mediocre team, Lou Caplan persuades an African American actor named Tom Hunt to join. Readers soon realize that if Hunt had refused this request to join Caplan's team, he would not have been hired for future films. Hunt is very polite, but the other male characters refer to him as "a surly Negro actor" because he is not subservient. "Playing Ball on Hampstead Heath" is a witty short story that satirizes the vanity and mental cruelty of these superficial men.

OTHER MAJOR WORKS

LONG FICTION: *The Acrobats*, 1954 (also pb. as *Wicked We Love*); *Son of a Smaller Hero*, 1955; *A Choice of Enemies*, 1957; *The Apprenticeship of Duddy Kravitz*, 1959; *The Incomparable Atuk*, 1963 (also pb. as *Stick Your Neck Out*); *Cocksure: A Novel*, 1968; *St.*

Urbain's Horseman, 1971; *Joshua Then and Now*, 1980; *Solomon Gursky Was Here*, 1989; *Barney's Version*, 1997.

SCREENPLAYS: *No Love for Johnnie*, 1961 (with Nicholas Phipps); *Young and Willing*, 1964 (with Phipps); *Life at the Top*, 1965; *The Apprenticeship of Duddy Kravitz*, 1974 (adaptation of his novel); *Joshua Then and Now*, 1985 (adaptation of his novel).

NONFICTION: *Hunting Tigers Under Glass: Essays and Reports*, 1968; *Shovelling Trouble*, 1972; *Notes on an Endangered Species and Others*, 1974; *The Great Comic Book Heroes, and Other Essays*, 1978; *Home Sweet Home*, 1984; *Broadsides: Reviews and Opinions*, 1990; *Oh Canada! Oh Quebec! Requiem for a Divided Country*, 1992; *This Year in Jerusalem*, 1994; *Belling the Cat: Essays, Reports and Opinions*, 1998; *Dispatches from the Sporting Life*, 2001; *On Snooker: The Game and the Characters Who Play It*, 2001.

CHILDREN'S LITERATURE: *Jacob Two-Two Meets the Hooded Fang*, 1975; *Jacob Two-Two and the Dinosaur*, 1987; *Jacob Two-Two's First Spy Case*, 1997.

EDITED TEXTS: *Canadian Writing Today*, 1970; *Writers on World War II: An Anthology*, 1991.

MISCELLANEOUS: *Mordecai Richler Was Here: Selected Writings*, 2007 (Jonathan Webb, editor).

BIBLIOGRAPHY

Arsenault, Michel. "Mordecai Richler Was Here." *World Press Review* 37 (June, 1990): 74-75. A brief biographical sketch, noting how Richler satirized the experiences of the French, the Canadians, Jews, and women. Contends that, although Richler is often accused of presenting an extremely critical view of Canada, he believes it his right to do so.

Brenner, Rachel Feldhay. *Assimilation and Assertion: The Response to the Holocaust in Mordecai Richler's Writings*. New York: P. Lang, 1989. Examines the role of Jewishness in Richler's writing and his portrayal of the Holocaust. Includes a bibliography and an index.

Came, Barry. "A Magical Craftsman." *Maclean's* 103 (December 31, 1990): 18-19. Discusses the universal appeal of Richler's fiction; provides a biographical sketch, emphasizing his most famous works.

Craniford, Ada. *Fiction and Fact in Mordecai Richler's Novels*. Lewiston, N.Y.: E. Mellen, 1992. A good study of Richler's Jewishness and his identity as a Canadian. Includes a bibliography and an index.

Darling, Michael, ed. *Perspectives on Mordecai Richler*. Toronto: ECW Press, 1986. In eight richly footnoted articles by eight different writers, the reader encounters different analyses of Richler's craft and the especially moral vision expressed in his fiction. Some of the articles provide an illuminating overview of Richler's themes, while others concentrate on his style.

Iannone, Carol. "The Adventures of Mordecai Richler." *Commentary* 89 (June, 1990): 51-53. Notes that Richler is among those Jewish writers who take an interest in the shadier side of Jewish experience, challenging the stereotype of the "good Jewish boy."

Kramer, Reinhold. *Mordecai Richler: Leaving St. Urbain*. Montreal: McGill-Queen's University Press, 2008. Comprehensive biography, in which Kramer demonstrates how Richler's personal experiences, his "uneasy Jewishness," and his "reluctant Canadianness," were central to his writing.

Maclean's 115, no. 25 (June 24, 2002). This issue of the Canadian magazine features several articles about Richler, including discussions of his relationship with his wife and his place in the Canadian literary tradition, his daughter's description of his funeral, and reminiscences from people who knew him.

McSweeney, Kerry. "Mordecai Richler." In *Canadian Writers and Their Works*, edited by Robert Lecker, Jack David, and Ellen Quigley. Vol. 6. Toronto: ECW Press, 1985. McSweeney provides an orderly, lucid, and insightful analysis of Richler's fiction through *Joshua Then and Now*. The notes and the select bibliography document a wealth of reference material.

Quennet, Fabienne C. "The Social Critic at Work: Mordecai Richler, 'Benny, the War in Europe, and Myerson's Daughter Bella' (1956)." In *The Canadian Short Story: Interpretations*, edited by Reingard M. Nischik. Rochester, N.Y.: Camden House, 2007. An analysis of this story, which also discusses Richler's collection *The Street*.

Ramraj, Victor J. *Mordecai Richler*. Boston: Twayne, 1983. This six-chapter study of Richler's fiction to *Joshua Then and Now* is enriched by a preface, a useful chronology of Richler's writing life, and a thorough select bibliography. *The Street*, the only one of Richler's fictional works that can be considered a work of short fiction, is examined in the context of Richler's vision and stance toward the Jewish community that he depicts so vividly in all of his fiction.

Richler, Mordecai. Interview by Sybil S. Steinberg. *Publishers Weekly* 237 (April 27, 1990): 45-46. Richler discusses the difficulty of writing the novel *Solomon Gursky*, partly because it was the first time he had to rely on research to authenticate his story and partly because of the complexity of the time sequences.

Sheps, G. David, ed. *Mordecai Richler*. Toronto: McGraw-Hill Ryerson, 1971. The seventeen articles and essays in this book treat Richler's fictional works both specifically and in more general contexts, such as their place in Jewish fiction in English. The authors of the pieces are among the preeminent names in Canadian literary criticism. Includes a thoughtful introduction by Sheps.

Woodcock, George. *Mordecai Richler*. Toronto: McClelland and Stewart, 1970. Woodcock has a talent for presenting analyses in a down-to-earth prose style accessible to student readers. In this early work on Richler's fiction, the concluding seventh chapter includes a short assessment of *The Street*.

James MacDonald
Updated by Jill Rollins and Edmund J. Campion

LEON ROOKE

Born: Roanoke Rapids, North Carolina; September
  11, 1934

PRINCIPAL SHORT FICTION

  Last One Home Sleeps in the Yellow Bed, 1968
  The Broad Back of the Angel, 1977
  The Love Parlour, 1977
  Death Suite, 1981
  The Birth Control King of the Upper Volta, 1982
  A Bolt of White Cloth, 1984
  Sing Me No Love Songs I'll Say You No Prayers:
    Selected Stories, 1984
  Muffins, 1995
  Who Do You Love?, 1992
  Oh! Twenty-seven Stories, 1997
  Last Shot: A Novella and Seven Stories, 2009

OTHER LITERARY FORMS

Leon Rooke has produced a number of novels, including *Fat Woman* (1980), *Shakespeare's Dog* (1983),
A Good Baby (1989), *Who Goes There* (1998), *The Fall
of Gravity* (2000), and *The Beautiful Wife* (2005). He
also has published poetry and plays, including *Krokodile* (1973), *Sword Play* (1973), and *Ms. America*
(1974). His work, including many stories that have had
only magazine publication, has been translated into
French, Italian, Spanish, Dutch, and Croatian, con-
firming his international reputation. A film version of *A
Good Baby* was released in 2000.

ACHIEVEMENTS

Leon Rooke's "If Lost Return to the Swiss Arms"
was one of the O. Henry Prize Stories for 1965. In
1981, he received the Canada-Australia Literary Prize,
and in 1983 he collected the Governor General's Award
for Fiction in English for the novel *Shakespeare's Dog.*
The Pushcart Prize was given to Rooke in 1988, and

the following year he was the cofounder of the Eden
Mills Writers' Festival. In 1990, he earned the North
Carolina Award for Literature. Rooke took the W. O.
Mitchell Prize, the ReLit Short Fiction Award, and the
Canadian Broadcasting Corporation Fiction Prize in
2002 and the Order of Canada in 2007.

BIOGRAPHY

Leon Rooke was born in Roanoke Rapids, North
Carolina, in 1934 and was raised in straitened circumstances by his single mother, who worked as a
weaver at the local textile mill. In high school, he
was a sportswriter for the school paper and published poetry in local newspapers. After working
one year in a Charlotte bank, he attended Mars Hill
College near Asheville, North Carolina, and from
1955 to 1958 he attended the University of North
Carolina at Chapel Hill, starting in the journalism
program and finally majoring in dramatic art, where
he took awards in writing.

In 1958, Rooke was drafted, and after training at
Fort Benning he served two years in Alaska as a
mail clerk. Throughout his university years and his
Army service, he continued to write and publish poetry and to perform in a drama group, acting the lead
in a production of *Under Milk Wood* (1953). Released from the service in 1960, he lived in San
Francisco and New Orleans for several years before
returning to North Carolina, where he worked on social initiatives designed by John Ehle (founder of
the North Carolina School of the Arts) and as a
writer for the UNC News Bureau before becoming
writer-in-residence at Chapel Hill. His "If Lost Return to the Swiss Arms" was selected as one of the
1965 O. Henry Prize stories. He met Constance
Raymond, a Ph.D. student, in 1967, and they were
married in 1969. His first story collection, *Last One
Home Sleeps in the Yellow Bed*, was published by
Louisiana State University Press in 1968.

In 1969, Constance took a teaching position at the University of Victoria, British Columbia, and the Rookes moved to Canada. They lived in Victoria until 1987, during which time their son Jonathan was born in 1971. They became Canadian citizens, and Rooke produced seven collections of short stories, three novels, and several plays. His work was rewarded with the Canada-Australia Literary Prize (1981) and the Governor General's Award for Fiction in English (1983) for his novel *Shakespeare's Dog*.

In 1987, the Rookes moved to Eden Mills, Ontario, where Constance became chair of the University of Guelph's English Department. They cofounded the Eden Mills Writers' Festival in 1989, with help from their friends Rohinton Mistry, Michael Ondaatje, Jane Urquhart, and Linda Spalding. The festival has attracted such eminent writers as P. K. Page, Margaret Atwood, Richard Ford, Alice Munro, Audrey Niffenegger, and John Irving, and it has introduced many new writers. Six more volumes of short stories followed, and Rooke, often in conjunction with Canadian writer-academic John Metcalf, has played a major role in the publication of anthologies of Canadian short stories. Rooke settled in Toronto and Mexico.

Leon Rooke (Getty Images)

Analysis

Leon Rooke's craft is rhetorical in the true sense. In a body of more than 350 short stories plus novels and plays, he finds the words and the styles that precisely convey the differing intents of each piece. His youth, spent in straitened circumstances in North Carolina in the 1930's and 1940's, provided him with a view of human nature rich in a mixture of the ironic, the comic, the gothic, the angry (at racism and human brutality), and a sense of the weird (or uncanny). He transposes this understanding into words--his metaphors chosen with infinite care, his details weighed for their contribution to the whole story, and his dialogue freighted with realism to define the characters. His stories are performances and, as a result of several summers of theater work early in his career, he is noted as a marvelous performer of them. Most of his stories do not hide their fictionality and often display, in structure and narration, a mythic or miraculous quality reminiscent of dark fairy tales. Just as often his stories parody the

mythic, leaving the reader unsure whether Rooke is tongue-in-cheek about his miracles. He is at heart a comic writer: an observer who makes readers laugh as he reveals human weaknesses and the strangeness that life can present.

His work contains a dizzying panorama of characters and situations. In "Magi Dogs," a painter completes a painting of a cottage, and a dog walks into his studio and into the painting, settling on the cottage steps. In "Why Agnes Left," Mr. Banks refuses to leave a party that has ended and finally settles down in his hosts' (whom he does not know) bathtub for a long soak. In "The Bucket Brigade," a wife puts on the head of her complaining husband a bucket, into which he can moan his woes. In "Hanging Out with the Magi," a bitter Southern country couple bicker with each other, then see spirits, and finally have a baby (delivered in a box), to which the wife gives immediate suckle. His stories to some extent follow the arc of his life, starting in the South, moving to his military and wandering years, and then to Canada and family life. Southern motifs and country folk recur, as he uses simple situations to probe human emotions and the strangeness of reality.

The Southern Man

Rooke's most intensely evocative Southern story (and many of his stories fit such a group) is "Who Do You Love?" Like many of his stories, its shape is as important as its content. It begins by saying there was a time in North Carolina when nothing happened, and there are other times that the narrator could tell about and he does not know which to tell. Then it switches back and forth through a life's memories, rebounding again and again to his mother, asking him as a child whether he loves her or his father more (his father has abandoned them). In vignettes from childhood, he remembers losing through a crack in floorboards a nickel that he had stolen from his mother, seeing a fat couple in a lit room having sex, watching his mother dress up to go drinking and dancing, observing a blue baby with a swollen head, and a myriad of other events that impressed and often puzzled him as a child. The story ends in the present, where he sits, holding his comatose mother's hand in the hospital and regretting that he never answered the title question. In that unanswered and never-again-to-be-asked question lies the poignant silence of a childhood that was confusing and the pain of a love unexpressed and uncertain.

In contrast to the delicacy of "Who Do You Love?" is the raucous creation of Mama Tuddi, a small-time southern African American radio and television personality, who attends the living-room funeral of one of her fans, the child Reno Brown, who became her fan when he was dying and saw her on television. In "Mama Tuddi Done Over," she has come for publicity reasons and looks down on these primitive crackers, but the reader in turn looks down on her monstrous ego. Rooke depicts the full glory of a gospel funeral with wailing and hymns and a long break for food before the Reverend Teebone comes to preach Reno into his grave. Beneath the vivid and often comic details (Reno's twin brother is Lasvegas, his mother is lusting after her man moments after she is wailing for her child), Rooke weaves a darker line. When Mama Tuddi is alone briefly in the parlor in the opening, she takes the black cloth off a mirror to look at herself, and

moments later she is warned by a mourner that Satan comes for those who do this for their vanity. Later there is casual mention that Reno did the same thing at his father's funeral and then sickened. Mama Tuddi makes a show of kissing the dead boy and throwing her fox fur into the coffin, but the reverend, arriving late because of a traffic jam, lights into her in his roaring sermon. She does not care much, because at this point she is bored, but the last paragraphs speak of the thing inside her that makes her comfortable and will drive her to success. Suddenly the story, redolent with Southern atmosphere, peels her back, and the reader realizes that in her pride she belongs to the devil.

Mythic, Gothic, Weird

"A Bolt of White Cloth" is Rooke's most beautiful and elegant mythic story. A man carrying a heavy bolt of white cloth comes to an isolated and poor farmer (the narrator) and his wife. After talk about price, the man says only love can buy it, and, in fact, after some discussion of the kinds of love and human suffering and after ascertaining that the wife is kind and caring, he gives them fifty yards of the beautiful white cloth. The wife urges the man to take some cloth to poorer neighbors, and after he leaves she discovers the cloth virtually makes itself into curtains, sheets, and finally a beautiful white dress for her. The husband and wife speculate in bed that night about who the man is and from where he came.

The simple beauty and plain language of this story elevate it into the realm of myth. The whiteness of the cloth represents love, purity, and kindness in a single image; the farmer and his wife are plain speaking but far from foolish; the dipperful of sweet water the wife gives the peddler stands for all simple kindness. In a Christian context, this would be a parable of grace, but Rooke makes it one in which the universe seems to reward love and goodness.

The darker side of Rooke's imagination is evident in stories such as "The Shut-In Number," in which Mr. Charles, an independent evangelist, explains how he "collects" children by picking them off the streets and keeping them. He rejects queries about how other well-known preachers would view this and says he has assured himself of its rightness through prayer and being born again. It emerges that he is a member of conservative organizations and a biblical literalist, facts interspersed between his boasts that he has "collected" a whole minibus full of children. His friends are awed by his achievements and his ambition to find a way to capture shut-ins, and they are impressed when he shows them an obviously cowed, mumbling child named Samson, one of his current captives. They leave, promising to support his work, and as he settles in his easy chair, with a drink and dressed only in a dressing gown, he calls for a girl and boy to be sent up to him.

The horror of this story is in its ordinariness. None of his guests sees anything wrong with what this self-justifying, egotistical monster, hiding the guise of a religious man, is doing. For a monster he surely is, a hypocrite of hypocrites surrounded by those who would dare not challenge his horrible acts. Rooke chooses a patient and apparently reasonable and civilized discussion format to present a truly horrifying vignette of modern religious blindness.

DOMESTIC IRONIES

Some of Rooke's stories make use of his magical imagination and his ear for dialogue to interrogate the worlds of the mundane and the domestic. In the hilarious "Some People Will Tell You the Situation at the Henny Penny Nursery Is Getting Intolerable," a group of parents protest the conditions in a nursery school to the owner. They begin with the fact that the teacher is mentally challenged, and soon the story escalates to the wildest nightmares of any parents who have ever entrusted children to a nursery: children always kept inside, no furniture or cots, lack of heat, presence of rats, absence of toys (the teacher is playing with them), and a babysitting television with one channel, no sound, and a shaky picture. The owner, who is the narrator, then offers the parents the option of going to the competition, but mention of whippings and barbed-wire fences ends that. The parents consider starting their own nursery, and the owner, who admits how much he hates small children, warns them that he did that fifty-three years ago and that, indeed, he is a Henny Penny graduate.

The comic exaggeration that drives a story such as this is delightfully ambiguous, for while it is wildly ironical it contains the seeds of such truths as the fact that, once one's children grow up, one stops worrying about the quality of nursery schools. It also expresses the home and school mentality of parents who may protest but will not protest too much, for fear of having nowhere to park their children.

"Some People Will Tell You the Situation at the Henny Penny Nursery Is Getting Intolerable" is domestic reality with a nasty bite, but in "Typical Day in a Desirable Woman's Life" the domestic is infused with a lyrical outburst of joy. In it, a wife is ordering a husband about, demanding first that he think of sparrows, so he describes five hundred in her bedroom. She is constantly riled with him, blaming him for all that men have ever done, for admiring her body as they walk together, for not being quick enough. However, when they come into a beautiful grassy meadow, she stands on a rocky outcrop, has him think "bird," and suddenly she is soaring, "She was a beautiful woman bird." After this extraordinary epiphany, they walk back to the house, and she takes a warm bath, as he sits and wonders what else she can do. There is sheer magic in these moments, as a situation of verbal jousting turns suddenly into one of the most tender and delicate statements of love in all of prose, one which, though in a very different key, reminds the reader of James Joyce's birdlike girl on the strand. Rooke sees that the lover's imagination must combine with the woman's will to make her fly. Rooke is a teller of stories that sing in the unique voices over which he has absolute control and which highlight, through simplicity or burning images and through eccentric visions of human behavior, the wonder and strangeness contained in everyday life.

OTHER MAJOR WORKS

LONG FICTION: *Vault, a Story in Three Parts: Conjugal Precepts, Dinner with the Swardians, and Break and Enter*, 1973; *Fat Woman*, 1980; *The Magician in Love*, 1981; *Shakespeare's Dog*, 1983; *A Good Baby*, 1989; *How I Saved the Province*, 1989; *Who Goes There*, 1998; *The Fall of Gravity*, 2000; *The Beautiful Wife*, 2005.

PLAYS: *Lady Physhie's Café*, pr. 1960; *Krokodile*, pb. 1973; *Sword Play*, pr. 1973; *Ms. America*, pr. 1974; *Of Ice and Men*, pr. 1985; *Shakespeare's Dog*, pr. 1985 (adaptation of his novel); *The Good Baby*, pr. 1987; *Evening Meeting of the Club of Suicide*, pr. 1991.

NONFICTION: *Writer's Path: An Introduction to Short Fiction*, 1998 (with Constance Rooke).

BIBLIOGRAPHY

Gorjup, Branko, ed. *White Gloves of the Doorman*. Toronto, Ont.: Exile, 2004. A major collection of articles, biographical vignettes, interviews, and commentary on Rooke. It also has a meticulous bibliography of all his work to 2004 and to further sources of scholarship.

Manguel, Alberto. "Protean and Surreal." *The New York Times*, April 1, 1984. This review of *Sing Me No Love Songs, I'll Say You No Prayers* praises the differing voices and textures Rooke achieves in the collection of stories.

Sabatini, Sandra. "The Wider Truth: Infants in the 1980's and 1990's." *Making Babies: Infants in Canadian Fiction*. Waterloo, Ont.: Wilfrid Laurier Press, 2004. This chapter treats infants in Rooke's fiction.

Peter Brigg

S

SAKI

Born: Akyab, Burma (now Myanmar);
December 18, 1870
Died: Beaumont Hamel, France; November 14, 1916
Also known as: Hector Hugh Munro

PRINCIPAL SHORT FICTION

Reginald, 1904
Reginald in Russia, 1910
The Chronicles of Clovis, 1911
Beasts and Super-Beasts, 1914
The Toys of Peace, 1919
The Square Egg, 1924
The Short Stories of Saki (H. H. Munro) Complete,
1930

OTHER LITERARY FORMS

The fame of Saki (SAH-kee) rests on his short stories, but he also wrote novels, plays, political satires, a history of imperial Russia, and journalistic sketches.

ACHIEVEMENTS

The brilliant satirist of the mind and manners of an upper-crust Great Britain that World War I would obliterate, Saki operates within a rich national tradition that stretches from the towering figure of Jonathan Swift well into the present, in which fresh wits such as Douglas Adams have obtained a certain stature. An intelligent, perceptive, and uncannily unsentimental observer, Saki focuses many of his deeply sarcastic pieces, which fill six volumes, on the criminal impulses of a privileged humanity. In his tightly wrought stories, for which surprise endings, ironic reversals, and practical jokes are de rigueur, Saki's mischievous protagonists thus arrive on the scene to wreak havoc on victims who have invited their tormentors out of folly or a streak of viciousness of their own. The frequent inclusion of intelligent, independent, and improbable animal characters further betrays Saki's fondness for the supernatural as a powerful satirical device.

BIOGRAPHY

Born in colonial Burma (now Myanmar) to a family that had for generations helped to rule the British Empire, Hector Hugh Munro grew up in a Devonshire country house where, reared along with his brother and sister by two formidable aunts, he had the secluded and strictly supervised sort of childhood typical of the Victorian rural gentry. This upbringing decisively shaped--or perhaps warped, as some sources suggest--his character. After finishing public school at Bedford, Munro spent several years studying in Devonshire and traveling on the Continent with his father and sister. In 1983, he went to Burma to accept a police post obtained through his father's influence. Much weakened by recurrent malaria, he returned to Devonshire to convalesce and write. In the first years of the twentieth-century he turned to journalism, wrote political satires, and served as a foreign correspondent in Eastern Europe and Paris. At this time he adopted the pseudonym "Saki," which may refer to the cup-bearer in *The Rubáiyát of Omar Khayyám* (1859), or may be a contraction of "Sakya Muni," one of the epithets of the Buddha. After 1908, Saki lived and wrote in London. Despite being overage and far from robust, he volunteered for active duty at the outbreak of World War I. Refusing to accept a commission, to which his social position entitled him, or a safe job in military intelligence, for which his education and experience equipped him, Munro fought as an enlisted man in the trenches of France. He died in action.

ANALYSIS

Saki is a writer whose great strength and great weakness lie in the limits he set for himself. Firmly rooted in the British ruling class that enjoyed "dominion over palm and pine," Saki wrote about the prosperous Edwardians among whom he moved. His stories, comedies of manners, emphasize the social side of the human animals as they survey the amusements, plots, and skirmishes that staved off boredom for the overripe leisure class whose leisure ended in August, 1914, with the onset of World War I.

Just as Saki wrote about a particular class, so he aimed his stories at a comparatively small and select readership. Although he was indifferent to wealth, Saki subsisted by his pen; he was, therefore, obliged to write stories that would sell. From the first, he succeeded in producing the "well-made" story savored by literate but not necessarily literary readers of such respected journals as the liberal *Westminster Gazette* and the conservative *Morning Post*. His debonair, carefully plotted stories full of dramatic reversals, ingenious endings, and quotable phrases do not experiment with new literary techniques but perfect existing conventions. Without seeming to strain for effect, they make of Hyde Park an enchanted forest or treat the forays of a werewolf as an ordinary country occurrence. Like the Paris gowns his fictional duchesses wear, Saki's stories are frivolous, intricate, impeccable, and, to some eyes, obsolete.

If Saki's background, subjects, and techniques were conventional, however, his values and sympathies certainly were not. As a satirist, he mocked the people he entertained. His careful portraits of a complacent ruling class are by no means flattering: They reveal all the malice, pettiness, mediocrity, and self-interest of people intent on getting to the top or staying there. His heroes--Reginald, Clovis, Bertie, and the like--are aristocratic iconoclasts who share their creator's distaste for "dreadful little everyday acts of pretended importance" and delight in tripping the fools and hypocrites who think themselves exceptional but walk the well-worn path upward. "Cousin Theresa," a variation on the theme of the Prodigal Son, chronicles the frustration of one such self-deluder.

"COUSIN THERESA"

In Saki's version of the parable, the wandering brother--as might be expected in an age of far-flung Empire--is the virtuous one. Bassett Harrowcluff, a young and successful bearer of the "white man's burden," returns from the colonies after having cheaply and efficiently "quieted a province, kept open a trade route, enforced the tradition of respect which is worth the ransom of many kings in out of the way regions." These efforts, his proud father hopes, might earn Bassett a knighthood, as well as a rest.

The elder brother Lucas, however, a ne'er-do-well London bachelor, claims to have his own scheme for certain success--a refrain that, appended to a song and embodied in a musical revue, should catch the ear of all London: "Cousin Theresa takes out Caesar,/ Fido, Jock, and the big borzoi." Fate bears out Lucas's prophecy. Theresa and her canine quartet enthrall the city. Orchestras acquire the four-legged accessories necessary for proper rendition of the much-demanded melody's special effects. The double thump commemorating the borzoi rings throughout London: Diners pound tables, drunks reeling home pound doors, messenger boys pound smaller messenger boys. Preachers and lecturers discourse on the song's "inner meaning." In Society, the perennial mystifications of politics and polo give way to discussions of "Cousin Theresa." When Colonel Harrowcluff's son is knighted, the honor goes to Lucas.

Saki's parable offers two lessons: an obvious one for the "eminent," a subtler one for the enlightened. If the reader takes the story as an indictment of a foolish society that venerates gimmicks and ignores achievements, that rewards notoriety rather than merit, he classes himself among the Bassett Harrowcluffs. For the same delicate irony colors Saki's accounts of both brothers' successes: Whether this treatment whimsically elevates the impresario or deftly undercuts the pillar of empire is problematic. As Saki sees it, administering the colonies and entertaining the populace are equally trivial occupations. To reward Lucas, the less self-righteous of two triflers, seems just after all.

Saki, then, does not profess the creed of the society he describes; both the solid virtues and the fashionable attitudes of the adult world come off badly in his stories. In contrast to other adults, Saki's dandy-heroes and debutante-heroines live in the spirit of the nursery romp; and when children and animals appear (as they often do) he invariably sides with them. "Laura," a fantasy in which a mischievous lady dies young but returns to life first as an otter and then as a Nubian boy to continue teasing a pompous fool, is one of many stories demonstrating Saki's allegiance to *Beasts and Super-Beasts* at the expense of men and supermen.

Saki's favorites are never sweetly pretty or coyly innocent. The children in "The Lumber-Room," "The Penance," and "Morlvera" are cruel, implacable, and the best of haters. The beasts, almost as fierce as the children, tend to be independent or predatory: wolves and guard dogs, cats great and small, elk, bulls, and boars figure in Saki's menagerie. Embodied forces of nature, these animals right human wrongs or counterpoise by their example the mediocrity of humanity throughout Saki's works, but nowhere more memorably than in the chilling tale of "Sredni Vashtar."

"SREDNI VASHTAR"

In "Sredni Vashtar," Conradin, a rather sickly ten-year-old, suffers under the restrictive coddling of his cousin and guardian, Mrs. De Ropp, a pious hypocrite who "would never, in her honestest moments, have confessed to herself that she disliked Conradin, though she might have been dimly aware that thwarting him 'for his good' was a duty which she did not find completely irksome." Conradin's one escape from her dull, spirit-sapping regime is the toolshed where he secretly cherishes Sredni Vashtar, the great ferret around whom he has fashioned a private religious cult. Offering gifts of red flowers, scarlet berries, and nutmeg that "had to be stolen," Conradin prays that the god Sredni Vashtar, who embodies the rude animal vitality the boy lacks, will smite their common enemy the Woman. When Mrs. De Ropp, suspecting that the toolshed harbors something unsuitable for invalids, goes to investigate, Conradin fears that Sredni Vashtar will dwindle to a simple ferret and that he, deprived of his god, will grow ever weaker under the Woman's tyranny.

Eventually, however, Conradin sees Sredni Vashtar the Terrible, throat and jaws wet with a dark stain, stalk out of the shed to drink at the garden brook and slip away. Mrs. De Ropp does not return from the encounter, and Conradin, freed from his guardian angel, helps himself to the forbidden fruit of his paradise--a piece of toast, "usually banned on the ground that it was bad for him; also because the making of it 'gave trouble,' a deadly offense in the middle-class feminine eye."

"THE OPEN WINDOW"

The brutal vengeance of "Sredni Vashtar" demonstrates that Saki's preference is not founded on the moral superiority of children and animals. "The Open Window," probably Saki's most popular story, makes the point in a more plausible situation, where a "self-possessed young lady of fifteen" spins from the most ordinary circumstances a tale of terror that drives her visitor, the nervous and hypochondriacal Mr. Frampton Nuttel, to distraction. In Saki's world the charm and talent of the liar makes up for the cruelty of her lie; the readers, cut adrift from their ordinary values, admire the unfeeling understatement of Saki's summing up: "Romance at short notice was her specialty." The readers join in applauding at the story's end not injustice--the whimpering Nuttel gets no worse than he deserves--but justice undiluted by mercy, a drink too strong for most adults most of the time.

What Saki admires about the people and animals he portrays is their fidelity to absolutes. They follow their natures single-mindedly and unapologetically; they neither moralize nor compromise. Discussing the preferences of a character in his novel *When William Came* (1913), Saki indirectly explains his own austere code: "Animals . . . accepted the world as it was and made the best of it, and children, at least nice children, uncontaminated by grown-up influences, lived in worlds of their own making." In this judgment the satirist becomes a misanthrope. Saki endorses nature and art but rejects society.

It is this moral narrowness, this refusal to accept compromise, that makes Saki, despite the brilliance of his artistry, an unsatisfying writer to read in large doses. His dated description of a vanished world is really no flaw, for he does not endorse the dying regime but clearly shows why it ought to die. His lack of sentiment is refreshing; his lack of emotion (only in such rare stories as "The Sheep," "The Philanthropist and the Happy Cat," and "The Penance" does Saki credibly present deep or complex feelings) does not offend present-day readers long inured to black comedy. Saki's defect is sterility. He refuses to be generous or make allowances as he considers society, that creation of adults, and he sends readers back empty-handed to the world of compromise where they must live.

O<small>THER MAJOR WORKS</small>

LONG FICTION: *The Unbearable Bassington*, 1912; *When William Came*, 1913.

PLAYS: *Karl-Ludwig's Window*, pb. 1924; *The Death-Trap*, pb. 1924; *The Square Egg, and Other Sketches, with Three Plays*, pb. 1924; *The Watched Pot*, pr., pb. 1924 (with Cyril Maude).

NONFICTION: *The Rise of the Russian Empire*, 1900; *The Westminster Alice*, 1902.

B<small>IBLIOGRAPHY</small>

Birden, Lorene M. "Saki's 'A Matter of Sentiment.'" *The Explicator* 5 (Summer, 1998): 201-204. Discusses the Anglo-German relations in the story "A Matter of Sentiment" and argues that the story reflects a shift in Saki's image of Germans.

Byrne, Sandie. "The Short Stories of Hector Hugh Munro (Saki)." In *A Companion to the British and Irish Short Story*, edited by Cheryl Alexander Malcolm and David Malcolm. Malden, Mass.: Wiley-Blackwell, 2008. Provides a comprehensive overview of Saki's short-fiction collections and individual stories, including "Sredni Vashtar," *Beasts and Super-Beasts*, *The Chronicles of Clovis*, and *Reginald in Russia*.

_____. *The Unbearable Saki: The Work of H. H. Munro*. Oxford, England: Oxford University, 2007. Discusses how Munro used his unhappy childhood as inspiration for themes in his short stories and other fiction. Draws on a biography written by Saki's sister to reveal details about his life. His political views and his participation in World War I are also key subjects.

Gillen, Charles H. *H. H. Munro (Saki)*. New York: Twayne, 1969. A comprehensive overview of the life and work of Saki, with a critical discussion of his literary output in all its forms. Balanced and readable, Gillen's work also contains an annotated bibliography.

Lambert, J. W. Introduction to *The Bodley Head Saki*. London: Bodley Head, 1963. A perceptive, concise, and persuasive review of Saki's work. Written by a biographer who enjoyed a special and productive working relationship with Saki's estate.

Langguth, A. J. *Saki*. New York: Simon & Schuster, 1981. Probably the best biography, enriching an informed, analytical presentation of its subject with a fine understanding of Saki's artistic achievement. Eight pages of photographs help bring Saki and his world to life.

Munro, Ethel M. "Biography of Saki." In *The Square Egg, and Other Sketches, with Three Plays*. New York: Viking, 1929. A warm account of the author by his beloved sister, who shows herself deeply appreciative of his work. Valuable for its glimpses of the inner workings of Saki's world and as a basis for late twentieth-century evaluations.

Queenan, Joe, ed. *The Malcontents: The Best Bitter, Cynical, and Satirical Writing in the World*. Philadelphia: Running Press, 2002. This anthology of cynicism and satire includes five of Saki's stories, as well as Queenan's commentaries on Saki and the other authors.

Salemi, Joseph S. "An Asp Lurking in an Apple-Charlotte: Animal Violence in Saki's *The Chronicles of Clovis*." *Studies in Short Fiction* 26 (Fall, 1989): 423-430. Discusses the animal imagery in the collection, suggesting reasons for Saki's obsessive interest in animals and analyzing the role animals play in a number of Saki's major stories.

Spears, George J. *The Satire of Saki*. New York: Exposition Press, 1963. An interesting, in-depth study of Saki's wit, which combines careful textual analysis with a clear interest in modern psychoanalysis. The appendix includes four letters by Saki's sister Ethel M. Munro to the author, and the bibliography lists many works that help to place Saki in the context of the satirical tradition.

Peter W. Graham
Updated by R. C. Lutz

WILLIAM SANSOM

Born: London, England; January 18, 1912
Died: London, England; April 20, 1976

PRINCIPAL SHORT FICTION
Fireman Flower, 1944
Three, 1946
Something Terrible, Something Lovely, 1948
South, 1948
The Passionate North, 1950
A Touch of the Sun, 1952
Lord Love Us, 1954
A Contest of Ladies, 1956
Among the Dahlias, 1957
The Stories of William Sansom, 1963
The Ulcerated Milkman, 1966
The Marmalade Bird, 1973

OTHER LITERARY FORMS

The works of William Sansom (SAN-suhm) include literary criticism; biography, especially *Proust and His World* (1973); essays, such as *The Birth of a Story* (1972); travel articles; and literary commentaries, such as *The Icicle and the Sun* (1958) and *Blue Skies, Brown Studies* (1961). He also wrote three children's books, with illustrations, and nine novels, with the three outstanding ones being *The Body* (1949), *The Loving Eye* (1956), and *The Cautious Heart* (1958).

ACHIEVEMENTS

Known by many critics as the quintessential short-fiction stylist, William Sansom evoked high praise from Elizabeth Bowen, who called him a "short-storyist par excellence; the short-storyist by birth, addiction and destiny." His stories display a keen interest not only in surrealism and grotesque horror but also in fantasy, comedy, and downright playfulness.

Influenced by music and art and by his work in film, Sansom wrote cameo portrayals of all social classes, both English and continental. Two of his short-story collections, *South* and *The Passionate North,* are innovations in travel stories, a blending of the travel article and fiction. Rather than following the traditional pattern of character and plot, Sansom favored the aesthetic of places, objects, and people, not the emphasis on conflicts and feelings. Sansom said this of his literary ethos:

> A writer lives best, in a state of astonishment. Beneath any feeling he has of the good or evil of the world lies a deeper one of wonder at it all. To transmit that feeling, he writes.

Sansom received the Society of Authors Award in 1946 and 1947. The Royal Society of Literature elected him as Fellow in 1951.

BIOGRAPHY

William Sansom was born in London, the only child of Ernest Brooks, a naval architect, and Mabel Clark. His father encouraged him to enter the banking profession and, with this career in mind, Sansom, after preparatory school, lived in Bonn, Germany, for three years, learned German and other foreign languages, and traveled throughout Europe. On his return to London, he trained and later worked in the Anglo-German Bank for five years. From the ages of seventeen to twenty-three, he was stricken with an odd vocal problem in not being able to control his modulation, speaking only in whispers or shouts. This nightmarish experience eventually resonated in a number of the short stories.

Following a stint in banking, Sansom became an advertising copywriter; while working at the advertising agency, he met a fellow worker, Norman Cameron, a poet and a translator, who strongly influenced Sansom's life. These kindred spirits discussed literature, politics, and art. A visit to a Surrealist exhibition became a turning point in Sansom's life. He said, "I was immediately addicted forever." Indeed, there are countless reverberations of Surrealism in his short stories and novels. Cameron encouraged Sansom to read Arthur Rimbaud, Rainer Maria Rilke, and Ernest Hemingway, all of them impinging in theme and style on Sansom's writing. Along with his work in advertising, Sansom composed jazz at night, played the piano at a nightclub, and also participated in running this same nightclub. Unfit for military service during World War II, Sansom joined the National Fire Brigade and continued to serve until the end of the war. This fortuitous experience became a rich mine for future stories and novels. Many of the National Fire Brigade firefighters lost their lives or limbs and became the unsung heroes of the war. This terrifying and dangerous work provided Sansom with Kafkaesque situations, which he used in *Fireman Flower*, a collection of short stories that received instant critical acclaim and catapulted Sansom to literary fame.

Following his advertising career, Sansom joined a film company and wrote screenplays. Shortly thereafter, he assumed the risk of writing fiction full time and did so until the end of his life. Sansom published travel articles in various magazines and eventually developed a unique genre--a combination of travel and short stories--particularly exemplified in such well-known books as *South* and *The Passionate North*.

At forty-two, Sansom married for the first time. His wife, Ruth Grundy, an actress and a literary agent, had two sons from a previous marriage. The family settled in St. John's Wood, a suburb of London; Sansom lived there for the rest of his life. This environment provided him with much material for his writing. A frequent pub patron, Sansom met there many workers and other people from the vicinity; these relationships were woven into his fiction. He particularly absorbed the dialects and the rhythms of his neighbors and fellow pub patrons.

Sansom's early allegorical fiction gave way to romance and eventually to comedy. *Lord Love Us*, one of his favorite collections of short stories, reflects fancy run riot, and its joyous mélange is portrayed in a virtual arabesque of magical language, according to many critics and general readers. It is noteworthy that the publication date of *Lord Love Us* and his work on *The Loving Eye*, one of his most comic and irresistible novels, together with *A Contest of Ladies*, published the same year as *The Loving Eye*, coincided with the first years of his happy marriage.

Sansom particularly read and reread the work of the Russian writer Ivan Bunin, the stories of Edgar Allan Poe, and the work of Marcel Proust. In 1976, the year of his death, Sansom was involved in writing an introduction to the short stories of Bunin. Always an experimentalist in his approach to the short story, Sansom often explored the Blakeian contrarieties. His approach is neither social nor political nor even psychological, but in the final analysis, it is aesthetic. His language, often akin to a kind of Joycean brio, is elegant and musical. The themes in his stories are often the search for an essence and a meaning of life, a reconciliation of opposites, or a balance and harmony in existence. His vision, although at times reflecting the surrealism of Franz Kafka and the morbidity of Poe, remains strangely something at the same time terrifying and beautiful, these last words almost a literary axiom in the writings of the short stories of Sansom.

ANALYSIS

William Sansom is distinct in the writing of short stories in England from the 1940's onward, since he does not focus necessarily on plot or character but is rather interested in setting and situation or a moment of revelation, a rendering of the visual. His concern is primarily aesthetic, and he emphasizes the very process of writing. Most significant, his short fiction presents a Seeing Eye that renders the visual as an ideal. He often speaks of a canvas, and, like the artist/writer, he concentrates on process as development. Often, Sansom focuses on a moment of Joycean epiphany, a significant opportunity lost, or an awareness too late for reconciliation.

"THE WALL"

The course of Sansom's short fiction began with the Fireman stories (*Fireman Flower*), which are often characterized by a Kafkaesque stream of consciousness. Many of these stories seem to be reportage blended with art, since they stem from

Sansom's actual experiences as a firefighter in London during the nightmare of the German buzz bombs and heavy blitzing of the city. The first collection of short stories about firefighters contains "The Wall," the first story Sansom wrote about the tireless men who extinguished the London blazes. This story, a hallucinatory and apocalyptic fantasy of a wall that collapses on the firefighters, stuns the reader. It begins with, "It was our third job that night. . . . I suppose we were worn down and shivering." Suddenly, a five-story wall started collapsing on the firefighters. The narrator says, "I was thinking of nothing at all and then I was thinking of everything in the world." Time stopped as the narrator waited for the wall to smash into the four men. He was hypnotized, arrested in time and space. One man was killed and three survived with severely burned faces because the three crouching men had been framed by a window space. The action lasts for a few seconds, but the frozen moment in time keeps resonating. Sansom achieves this effect in four pages.

These Fireman stories are often allegories. The men search for the source of fire as if for the Holy Grail. The fire, smoke, and steam symbolize obstacles. In the title story, Fireman Flower remarks that he has at last "come face to face with the essence of things." The firefighters encounter odd and strange businesses--coffee warehouses, clothing stores, even candy storages. Awestruck at the convulsion of man and nature, the workers are struck dumb.

"THE WITNESS"

One of the most harrowing of the tales is "The Witness," set in a coffee bean warehouse in flames. The steam of the water used to fight the fire creates an eeriness when the air is filled with the pungency of roasting, boiling coffee beans. The men see a fireman poised on the wall far above; he is panic-stricken because he has had an earlier argument with the hose operator. Believing that he sees the operator smile (and it could have been only a grimace), "a yellow snarl of delight," he jumps into the boiling furnace of beans and perishes. The story, horrifying in its mere telling, reflects the untrustworthiness of sense perceptions. The men who witness the horror cannot verify that the hose operator really would or did increase the water pressure. The

steam obscured their vision. Bombed London becomes a microcosm of the world. The men who extinguish fires or search through debris for bodies, living or dead, become crusaders and knights of the Apocalypse.

"SOMETHING TERRIBLE, SOMETHING LOVELY"

Published in 1948, *Something Terrible, Something Lovely* is a kaleidoscope of twenty-one memorable stories, narratives and sketches depicting not only traditional realism but also surreal landscapes, pathological personalities, satirical comedy, and weird tales. Sansom displays himself as a magus of landscape and a facile raconteur. The title story, "Something Terrible, Something Lovely," leads the reader along the garden path as Nita, who is nine, and her younger cousin talk about the boys. "It was a boy done it . . . we'll do it back on the boys." The reader is led to believe that some catastrophe has occurred and that the girls will exact an awful revenge. The secret is revealed only at the end of the story. The boys had written on a hospital wall in spidery, capital letters, "NITA HOBBS LOVES STAN CHUTER." The charming and naïve girls exact their pound of flesh sweetly and humorously. They cross out the five-word message and write their seven words, "THE PERSON WHO WROTE THIS IS DAFT." The charming artlessness reminds the reader of Jane Austen's heroine Catherine Morland in *Northanger Abbey* (1818) when she looked for gothic mystery and found only a laundry list. Sansom succeeds in his theme of revenge, a favorite subject that he explored in later stories, such as "A Contest of Ladies," that entailed neither children nor unadulterated charm.

"THE VERTICAL LADDER"

In this same collection, *Something Terrible, Something Lovely*, are two Sansom cameos. One is the harrowing tale "The Vertical Ladder," portraying Flegg, a young boy, who is dared by his friends to climb a vertical ladder on an ancient gasometer. A young girl, perhaps showing sexual awareness, particularly urges him to mount the ladder. As he climbs upward with growing vertigo, he loses a sense of familiarity and feels endangered and defenseless. He begins to descend but discovers that his friends, who have left, removed the ladder below. As he climbs back upward toward the platform, he finds that the top rungs are missing. Flegg is arrested in space, unable to climb to safety either above or below. The tale ends as "Flegg stared dumbly, circling his head like a lost animal . . . then he jammed his legs in the lower rungs and his arms past the elbows to the armpits in through the top rungs and there he hung shivering and past knowing what more he could ever do." The story does not probe character but delineates simply what happened. Readers can conclude what they will--a moral; pride; sexual awakening; exploration into the unknown; desertion of friends; risk-taking; or, as a final possibility, the terrible aloneness of the individual.

"DIFFICULTY WITH A BOUQUET"

"Difficulty with a Bouquet," a two-page story, is one of Sansom's best-known anthologized pieces. The protagonist, Seal, has picked in his garden a bouquet of flowers that he wishes to give to a Miss D., a neighbor, but after a few moments he is aware that the gift might be considered an affectation. Miss D. watches the discarding of the flowers from an adjacent window (Sansom was preoccupied with windows, especially in the novel *The Loving Eye*, depicting an almost compulsive voyeurism). Miss D. wishes that Seal had given her the flowers, but at the same time, she is glad that he did not. "I should have been most embarrassed. It's not as if he wanted me. It would have been just too maudlin for words." Anthologists dearly favor this short-short story because in a neat nutshell, Sansom, on a deeper level, is articulating the difficulty of two persons' interrelating on a simple level--any gift given unsolicited and a simple explanation of appreciation in return. The marvel of the story is its simplicity. "Difficulty with a Bouquet" is an ironic vignette of quiet tone and is painted with a few deft brush strokes.

"TUTTI-FRUTTI"

In the next few years, Sansom's creativity flowered. *South* and *The Passionate North* both introduced a unique genre that formed a transition from the early Poesque and Kafkaesque stories. This new genre combines a distinct sense of place with that of a short-story form. *South* includes a bittersweet story "Tutti-Frutti," set in Nice, a concept of place as important as Egdon Heath in Thomas Hardy's *The Return of the Native* (1878). These two places are as important as the characters. The main character, Ohlsson, a Swede and a romantic, is overpowered by the unexpected attention of

a woman and is equally overpowered by the beauty of this Mediterranean port. Spending the entire day with this mystery woman, Ohlsson, having the prospect of seeing her again, goes onto the balcony to smoke a cigarette, which he drops, and in attempting to retrieve it, reaches out too far and falls several stories below. He is seriously injured and will never walk again. He remains in Nice to become a writer. Romance fatalistically turns to a tragedy manqué, and Ohlsson, losing the woman, whom he does not tell of his accident and who probably would have gone off with another man, becomes the writer that he would not have become if the accident had not occurred. However, it is the account at Nice that the readers remember and that interacts with Ohlsson. Sansom blends the tale with the city, a new genre that succeeds with the reader.

"THREE DOGS OF SIENA"

In *South* appears another memorable story, "Three Dogs of Siena." The tale again features a place: Siena, with all of its history, *palios*, and *Sbandierata* (a flag-waving ceremony). The story unfolds from the standpoint of three dogs from Naples, Genoa, and Venice. As the animals run around the city searching for new experiences (a favorite theme of Sansom--risk-taking is life-affirming), the animals are cruelly mistreated. Since the Italians love their dogs as they love life, this attitude appears strange, but the people also love ceremony. Sansom writes, "in all ceremony there is the touch of death." The pomp and circumstance become more important than the dogs, who after being kicked and beaten, slink back into the shadows. Just as important as the dogs is Siena, whose observances of history and religion are rich and traditional. The reader sees the subtext: The Italians, who ignore the mistreatment of dogs, are contrasted to the English, who observe and are horrified at the mistreatment. The story appeals to the reader for many reasons, but the interest is maintained from the story's projection of animals as the perceivers.

"THE GIRL ON THE BUS"

Many stories from *The Passionate North*, also combining the travel and short-story technique, are concerned with love or its absence. Elizabeth Bowen calls this craving or the absence of love the resignation-reconciliation theme. In this collection, the story element becomes a shade more significant than place. The "place" obviously is the North. In "The Girl on the Bus," Sansom writes, "Since to love is better than to be loved, unrequited love may be the finest love of all." The protagonist, Harry, sees a beautiful woman skiing by; he is breathless at her loveliness, but he feels that he will never see her again. She sets a standard that will never be met by another woman. Lamenting over his chance meeting at Haga Park, he curses himself for having gone there. In Denmark, he boards a train that will eventually take him to England. There, he encounters the woman but lacks the courage to speak to her--an opportunity lost. Happily for him, however, the woman eventually talks to him, and they are finally married. Harry was resigned to his loss, yet the "reconciliation" eventually occurs. Critics generally agree that there is a better integration of story and locale in this collection.

Sansom's oeuvre strikes out in another direction with *A Touch of the Sun*. Although again Sansom blends his travel experiences with the short story, these tales reflect the protagonist's encounter with nightmare. These stories show the influence of Ivan Bunin, who is known for comic portrayals and whom Sansom greatly admired. "Episode at Gastein" is set in a German spa where Ludwig De Broda, forty but distinctly older in demeanor, aristocratic and wealthy, meets Fräulein Laure, distinctly inferior in education and social advantage. Both have marriage in mind. De Broda is immersed in the history of Gastein and its geography; Laure is interested in the cinema. De Broda intends to be Pygmalion to her Galatea, and it all backfires. Because Laure initiates a kiss in a *Weinstube*, De Broda feels that his proposal might be attributed to the excitement of the evening, and his rationality is the obstacle that ruins the possibility of marriage with Laure, who finds a younger, more physical Swiss and becomes immediately engaged to him. This story, nearly forty pages long, is almost a novella. The theme is a frequent one: Action delayed is action defeated. The pace is leisurely, and the nightmare is sudden. De Broda attempts suicide. His sense of failure is overpowering and Sansom depicts him in a bathtub contemplating suicide with a razor blade in each hand.

"LIFE, DEATH"

There is a shift in the collection *Lord Love Us*, especially since the year it was published was the year of Sansom's marriage. The technique is experimental--the tones ranging from the seriocomic to even the frivolous, charming, amusing, and yet tragic and sorrowful. Sansom claimed that this collection was his favorite. A particularly appealing story is "Life, Death." In this tale, a fishmonger is a veritable artist as he sculpts the display of fish. Eventually, he meets a damsel whom he courts with free fish, and they marry. This delightful tale ends in tragedy when his wife and child die. No explanation is given: They simply die, and the fishmonger laments at the end, "Why, if *you* can tell me, such happy days? Why with happy days such shade?" At the end, even the slab that was his canvas no longer attracts him. His slide into sorrow is reminiscent of Samuel Taylor Coleridge's *Ancient Mariner*, who must keep repeating his tale. The meaning is implicit: Fate rules, bestowing bliss and sorrow. The story ends with questions but no answers.

"A CONTEST OF LADIES"

A *Contest of Ladies* gathers stories written over a period of years, and the terrain ranges from the ludicrous to the grotesque, from the melodramatic to the humorous. The title story, almost a novella, presents a retired actor who has designed his house like a hotel. Six international beauty contestants search for a hotel, and the local pranksters direct these lovelies to Morley's house. Morley entertains them and soon tells them that his home is not an inn. Most attracted to the Danish Miss Great-Belt, Morley becomes angry with her because she stands him up one evening, and he convinces his fellow jurors not to vote for her. She loses, but she wins Morley. Some critics called this tale a morality play, comically rendered.

"AMONG THE DAHLIAS"

Among the Dahlias is not a memorable collection except for the title story, wryly amusing and somewhat farcical. Mr. Doole loves animals and often visits the zoo. One day, he encounters a full-maned lion in a path, and he is frozen in terror. They stare at each other, and Doole almost begs the lion to let him live. When the lion obliges by walking away, the protagonist spends a good part of his life wondering why the lion turned away. The absurdity of Doole's narcissistic concern with his physique underscores theme, technique, and tone. Clara, in "Various Temptations," another tale in this collection, becomes the victim of an insane murderer, who falls in love with his victim until she preens herself to become more attractive, the very trait that the strangler seeks out, since he finds beauty akin to prostitution. Both Doole and Clara are rejected--one survives and the other perishes.

"THE MARMALADE BIRD"

Sansom's final collection, *The Marmalade Bird*, contains less comedy and more ironic humor. Especially absorbing is the title story, set in Marrakech. Sansom echoes disenchantment in this final volume. "The Marmalade Bird" focuses on a married couple who, though content, find that they must have conflict. A bird enjoys their marmalade pot and visits them daily. One day, they believe that the bird is gone, and they put some facial tissue over the pot. When the bird returns and dives into the pot, his beak is stuck in the tissue. The tragedy of the bird brings the couple together. Sansom delighted in this story, aware that marriage means strife but that reconciliation follows, and this becomes the human condition, the bittersweetness of life.

These last stories in *The Marmalade Bird* vividly contrast with Sansom's early Fireman stories, when the characters survive through illusion. His final short fiction reflects a disillusionment and a disenchantment with fantasy. Especially in his stories of marriage in this final volume, Sansom confronts the challenges and the bare realities of life to be lived now, not in some never-never land of an enchanted forest. However, this final vision is not a dour one: Human beings facing the struggle to survive in an industrialized world will prevail and find their own identity.

OTHER MAJOR WORKS

LONG FICTION: *The Body*, 1949; *The Face of Innocence*, 1951; *A Bed of Roses*, 1954; *The Loving Eye*, 1956; *The Cautious Heart*, 1958; *The Last Hours of Sandra Lee*, 1961; *Goodbye*, 1966; *Hans Feet in Love*, 1971; *A Young Wife's Tale*, 1974.

NONFICTION: *Jim Braidy: The Story of Britain's Firemen*, 1943 (with James Gordon and Stephen Spender); *Pleasures Strange and Simple*, 1953; *The Icicle and the Sun*, 1958; *Blue Skies, Brown Studies*, 1961; *Away to It All*, 1964; *Grand Tour Today*, 1968; *The Birth of a Story*, 1972; *Proust and His World*, 1973.

CHILDREN'S LITERATURE: *It Was Really Charlie's Castle*, 1953; *The Light That Went Out*, 1953; *Skimpy*, 1974.

BIBLIOGRAPHY

Allen, Walter. *The Short Story in English*. New York: Oxford University Press, 1981. Discusses Sansom's "Old Man Alone," "The Wall," and "How Claeys Dies." Argues that Sansom transmits a Poe-Bierce horror in a Defoesque way.

Beachcroft, T. O. *The Modest Art: A Survey of the Short Story in English*. New York: Oxford University Press, 1968. A brief discussion of Sansom's prose style. Claims he is a master of sensuous and atmospheric effects. Comments on his being influenced by Franz Kafka and the similarity of his comic stories to those of V. S. Pritchett.

Bernard, Jeffrey. "Low Life: Very Much in Love." *The Spectator* 274 (June, 1995): 54. In this tribute, Bernard remembers meeting Sansom.

Chalpin, Lila. *William Sansom*. Boston: Twayne, 1980. This short volume is a clear approach to Sansom's life and work, particularly tracing the development of his fictional techniques. Contains a comprehensive treatment of the early fiction, the novels, the travel books, and the later short stories. Chalpin stresses the influence of Edgar Allan Poe rather than Franz Kafka on Sansom's work. Like many other commentators, Chalpin laments the critical neglect of a first-class short-story writer. Includes a chronology of Sansom's life and works and a bibliography.

Hanson, Clare. *Short Stories and Short Fictions, 1880-1980*. New York: St. Martin's Press, 1985. Discusses "Fireman Flower" and "The Wall" as stories that are concerned with the relationship between illusion and reality, chance and design.

Mason, Ronald. "William Sansom." In *Modern British Writing*, edited by Denys Val Baker. New York: Vanguard Press, 1947. A provocative commentary on Sansom's symbolism and realism used in the early fiction. Mason traces the writer's development from the Fireman stories and evaluates his growth from a miniaturist to a seasoned artist.

Michel-Michot, Paulette. *William Sansom: A Critical Assessment*. Paris: Société d'Édition, 1971. This doctoral dissertation was published as a thorough analysis and examination of all Sansom's work, except for the last five years of his productivity. It is an exhaustive account of his short fiction, novels, and essays. Michel-Michot, like most critics of Sansom, believes that his penchant is for the short story, not the novel. The author interviewed Sansom and provides in-depth material concerning theme, symbolism, technique, and criticism.

Peden, William H. "The Short Stories of William Sansom: A Retrospective." *Studies in Short Fiction*, no. 4 (1988): 421-431. Since there is little contemporary criticism on Sansom, this article, although brief, is a high-density approach to his short fiction. Peden's concludes that all Sansom's fiction is enjoyable to read and reread. He particularly commends Sansom's short stories as "alive with excitement" and considers his fictional world unforgettable.

Reeve, N. H. "Away from the Lighthouse: William Sansom and Elizabeth Taylor in 1949." In *The Fiction of the 1940's: Stories of Survival*, edited by Rod Mengham and Reeve. New York: Palgrave, 2001. Focuses on Sansom's novel *The Body*, but includes a brief discussion of his short story "The Wall." Argues that *The Body* is characterized by the pressure of experiences during World War II, even though the war itself has been deleted from the characters' lives.

Trussler, Michael. "Suspended Narratives: The Short Story and Temporality." *Studies in Short Fiction* 33, no. 4 (Fall, 1996): 557. Analyzes Sansom's short story "The Vertical Ladder" to explain its use of temporality.

Vickery, John B. "William Sansom and Logical Empiricism." *Thought* 36 (Summer, 1961): 231-245. Sansom's early fiction is discussed in terms of his surrealistic phase. Although Sansom is not a university graduate of Cambridge or Oxford, Vickery believes that these educational centers exerted a philosophical influence on Sansom instead of the continental influence of rationalism or of the later existentialism.

Julia B. Boken

SIR WALTER SCOTT

Born: Edinburgh, Scotland; August 15, 1771
Died: Abbotsford, Scotland; September 21, 1832
Also known as: First Baronet Scott

PRINCIPAL SHORT FICTION

"Wandering Willie's Tale," 1824
Chronicles of the Canongate, 1827 (2 volumes)
"Death of the Laird's Jock," 1828
"My Aunt Margaret's Mirror," 1828
"The Tapestried Chamber," 1828
The Shorter Fiction, 2009 (Graham Tulloch and Judy King, editors)

OTHER LITERARY FORMS

A giant of European Romanticism, Sir Walter Scott made important contributions to many literary forms. He wrote the Waverley novels (1814-1831), a series that virtually created the historical novel. Particularly admired are the Scottish novels, including *Waverley: Or, 'Tis Sixty Years Since* (1814), *Old Mortality* (1816), *Rob Roy* (1817), *The Heart of Midlothian* (1818), *The Bride of Lammermoor* (1819), and *Redgauntlet* (1824). Scott also wrote extremely popular poetry, including *The Lay of the Last Minstrel* (1805), *Marmion: A Tale of Flodden Field* (1808), and *The Lady of the Lake* (1810). He also collected ballads in the three-volume *Minstrelsy of the Scottish Border* (1802-1803); published critical editions of the works of John Dryden (1808) and Jonathan Swift (1814); and wrote histories, essays, reviews, criticism, and plays.

ACHIEVEMENTS

Sir Walter Scott's life was a series of remarkable achievements. In literature, he was a pioneer whose works still stand on their own merits. He collected ballads for the *Minstrelsy of the Scottish Border*, a milestone in the study of Scottish antiquities. From 1805 to 1810, Scott wrote the most popular poetry in Great Britain, setting unprecedented sales records. In 1813, he was offered the poet laureateship, which he refused. His greatest achievement came in the field of fiction. The Waverley novels virtually created a new genre, the historical novel, and made Scott one of the two most popular novelists of the century. He was knighted in 1819. Scott was also an accomplished writer of short fiction, and three of his stories are generally acknowledged to be among the best in the genre. Finally, Scott wrote a series of literary prefaces, criticisms, and reviews that made him an important literary theorist.

BIOGRAPHY

Sir Walter Scott was born in Edinburgh, Scotland, on August 15, 1771, and attended Edinburgh Royal High School and Edinburgh College. In 1786, he signed indentures to become a Writer to the Signet, and in 1792 he became a Scottish advocate. In 1797, he married Charlotte Carpenter, with whom he had four children. He became sheriff-deputy of Selkirkshire in 1799 and clerk to the Scottish Court of Session in 1806. From 1805 to 1810, he published best-selling poetry. In 1812, he bought Abbotsford, his home for life. Two years later, Scott published *Waverley*, the first in the series of remarkably successful and influential Waverley novels. He became a baronet in 1819, and later, in 1822, he arranged and managed the visit to Scotland of King George IV. Four years following this peak in his social career, Scott's wife died and he suffered bankruptcy, which he struggled to overcome during the remainder of his life. In 1827, he acknowledged publicly his authorship of the Waverley novels, and, in 1829, he began publication of the "Magnum Opus," a forty-eight-volume edition of the Waverley novels. He died at Abbotsford on September 21, 1832.

ANALYSIS

Sir Walter Scott is known primarily as a novelist and secondarily as a poet. He wrote comparatively little short fiction. Nevertheless, he remains an important figure in that genre, too. In *The Short Story in English* (1981), the distinguished critic Walter Allen begins his survey of the genre with Scott's story "The Two Drovers," which he calls "the first modern short story in English." In addition, three of his stories are generally acknowledged to be among the masterpieces of the form.

Scott uses the same methods and explores the same subjects in his stories as in his novels. He places his characters in concrete historical situations; they are social beings rooted in a particular time and place. Conflicts between individuals symbolize larger issues--the conflict between past and present, the conflict between national traditions and temperaments, and the tragedy of cultural incomprehension. Scott presents these themes more starkly, however, in his stories. The demanding form of the short story forced him into a directness and concision often lacking in his novels. Thus, to many readers, Scott's short stories may be the most satisfactory works he ever wrote.

"WANDERING WILLIE'S TALE"

Scott's first short story, "Wandering Willie's Tale," appeared in the novel *Redgauntlet*. Although it attains its full significance only in the context of that larger work, this universally admired tale stands on its own merits. It presents a comic version of serious Scott themes. Steenie Steenson, the grandfather of the narrator, goes on a strange odyssey. When he brings his rent to his landlord, Sir Robert Redgauntlet, the old persecutor dies in burning agony just before giving Steenie a receipt. The silver disappears. Sir John Redgauntlet, the son and successor, threatens to evict Steenie from his hereditary home unless he can produce either rent or receipt. Poor Steenie, tossing off a mutchkin of brandy, makes two toasts: the first to "the memory of Sir Robert Redgauntlet, and might he never lie quiet in his grave till he had righted his poor bond-tenant"; the second, "a health to Man's Enemy, if he would but get him back the pock of siller." Immediately afterward, riding through the dark wood of Pit-murkie, Steenie is accosted by a strange gentleman

Sir Walter Scott (Library of Congress)

who takes him to Redgauntlet Castle, where dead Sir Robert is reveling with a set of ghastly persecutors. Avoiding various temptations, Steenie demands and obtains his receipt. When Sir Robert insists that he return every year to pay homage, Steenie cries, "I refer myself to God's pleasure, and not to yours." Losing consciousness, he awakens in this world. He brings the receipt to Sir John and, acting upon a hint from Sir Robert, unlocks the mystery of the missing silver.

This comic tale of demonism has a serious side. The portrayal of Sir Robert and his cohorts from "the killing times" is a grim reminder of Scotland's bloody past. Like other Scott heroes, Steenie cannot evade the past but must come to terms with it. When the past demands his unconditional loyalty, however, he struggles to retain his freedom, and the present time is not idealized. Sir John, the advocate, can be just as tyrannical as his father. As wartime Scotland evolves into civil peace, physical coercion gives way to legal. Scott balances the evils of the past against those of the present. In like manner, he balances the natural against the supernatural. He suggests the possibility of a rational explanation for the extraordinary events; perhaps Steenie was having a drunken dream. Where did the receipt come from, though, and how did Steenie know where to recover the silver? As usual, Scott suggests something at work beyond the rational.

"Wandering Willie's Tale" is a gem of formal art. The onward rush of events is played off against the balanced structure. For example, Steenie's first meeting with Sir Robert is contrasted with his first meeting with Sir John. Scott highlights the contrast by focusing on the account book in each scene. The second meeting with Sir Robert also necessitates a second meeting with Sir John. The short-story form allows Scott to achieve a superb structure that is lacking in his novels. Finally, it is generally acknowledged that Scott writes his freest, raciest, most humorous prose when he is writing in Scots dialect. His only story related wholly in the vernacular, "Wandering Willie's Tale" is his one sustained masterpiece of prose.

"THE HIGHLAND WIDOW"

"The Highland Widow" first appeared in *Chronicles of the Canongate*. It is the tragedy of Elspat MacTavish, who must live with the guilt of having caused the death of her only son. She is compared to Orestes and Oedipus, and the inevitability and starkness of her drama are indeed Sophoclean. However, the method is unmistakably Scott's. The tragedy arises out of particular historical circumstances.

Scott's narrator declares that his object is "to throw some light on the manners of Scotland as they were, and to contrast them, occasionally, with those of the present day." Elspat MacTavish grew to womanhood in the years before the rebellion of 1745, when the Highlands was a law unto itself. She became the wife and faithful companion of the famous MacTavish Mhor, who did not hesitate to take anything, lawfully or not, that he desired to have. The morality of husband and wife is that of the old Highland, one of "faithful friends and fierce enemies." In Scott, however, the old order changes, yielding place to new. MacTavish Mhor is killed by soldiers, the rebellion of 1745 is foiled, the Highlands are pacified, and military violence is replaced by civil order. Only Elspat MacTavish, dwelling in the wildest recesses of the Highlands, remains unconscious of the great change. Even her son, Hamish

Bean, mingling more with people in this world, understands that his father's trade of cateran is now dangerous and dishonorable. To provide for his mother and himself, he enlists in a new Scottish regiment. Living in the past, Elspat finds Hamish's actions incomprehensible--to be a soldier; to fight under a Campbell, their hereditary enemies; and to support the government of Hanover. Conditioned by her historical environment, acting by her own best lights, she determines to save Hamish from dishonor.

The tragic climax comes inexorably. Elspat drugs Hamish's parting drink, preventing him from returning to his regiment in time. She knows that her son retains enough of the old Highland traditions to consider the promised scourging for lateness as appropriate only for dogs. Caught between his duty to his new masters and his old Highland dread of dishonor, and urged on by his mother, Hamish kills the sergeant sent to secure him. He himself is speedily apprehended, found guilty, and executed. Hamish's fate is sad, but that of Elspat is tragic. She continues to live with the knowledge that she has killed her only child. The parallels with Orestes and Oedipus suggest not only the mental torment that results from such epic crimes but also the deep love between mother and son.

Once again, the strict demands of the short-story form compelled Scott into a concentration of effort and intensity of effect that are absent from his novels. Everything is directed toward the tragic end. The opening description of old Elspat and her crime eliminates all suspense about what happened but stimulates wonder as to how it happened. It also gives the following story of long ago a sense of inevitability. In like manner, although there are occasional references to Fate, the action develops inevitably out of the characters of the two major figures, who are themselves products of their historical environments. Finally, Scott raises the language of Elspat to the heroic level, partly to suggest her Gaelic speech but mostly to give her the tragic tone.

"THE TWO DROVERS"

"The Two Drovers" also appeared in *Chronicles of the Canongate*. Whereas "The Highland Widow" is based on a conflict between different times, "The Two Drovers" is based on a conflict between different places. Robin Oig M'Combich is a Highlander, Harry

Wakefield a Yorkshireman. The two are best of friends, but because neither understands the national traditions or temperament of the other, tragedy results.

The story begins with an ominous instance of second sight. Robin's aunt warns him not to undertake the cattle drive because she sees Saxon blood on his dirk. Robin's reply, "All men have their blood from Adam," indicates that he is unaware of the great national differences between men. He gives his weapon to Hugh Morrison, but the sense of doom hangs over him.

The story modulates into the realistic mode. Scott quickly establishes the genuine friendship between the two drovers. However, when Robin unintentionally gains possession of the very field that Harry had been seeking for his own cattle, the simple Yorkshireman suspects the canny Scot of duplicity. Even when Robin offers to share the field, Harry's hurt pride makes him refuse. His anger is increased by his drinking, the wretchedness of the pasturage he finally obtains, and the taunts of his English cronies "from the ancient grudge against the Scots." Consequently, when Robin arrives at the inn, Harry challenges him in characteristic English fashion, "a tussle for love on the sod . . . and we shall be better friends than ever." To a Highlander, however, to be beaten with fists stains a man with irremovable dishonor. When Robin tries to leave, Harry knocks him down.

The story hastens to its inevitable climax. Despite the sense of doom, the tragedy can be understood entirely in terms of the actors and their backgrounds. Robin walks ten miles to obtain his dirk from Hugh Morrison, tells Harry, "I show you now how the Highland dunnièwassel fights," and plunges his dagger into Harry's heart. Throwing the fatal weapon into the turf-fire, he exclaims, "take me who likes--and let fire cleanse blood if it can." His aunt's vision was accurate: The imagery of blood, prominent from the start, ends here. Before leaving, though, Robin looks "with a mournful but steady eye on the lifeless visage" of his friend and remarks, "He was a pretty man!" Scott's capacity for expressing the most intense dramatic emotions in the simplest language, his realistic eloquence, justifies his title of the most Shakespearean of prose writers.

The story ends with the trial judge's lengthy summation, which reflects Scott's own view of historical tragedy. No villains are involved. The crime arose from an "error of the understanding . . . men acting in ignorance of each other's national prejudices." The judge also points out that, if Robin had had his dirk and killed Harry immediately, he would have been guilty of manslaughter. Ironically, his aunt's second sight caused him to commit murder. Robin acknowledges the justice of the death sentence, and the story closes on his simple but resonant monosyllables: "I give a life for the life I took, and what can I do more?"

Scott's last three short stories were published in the 1828 edition of *The Keepsake*, a Christmas gift book published annually. "My Aunt Margaret's Mirror" and "The Tapestried Chamber" are ghost stories; "Death of the Laird's Jock" is a sketch of "a subject for the pencil" of an artist. None is significant literature. These stories were subsequently reprinted in *The Shorter Fiction*, a collection of eight short stories which Scott originally wrote for periodicals from 1811 through 1831. In addition, this compilation featured five stories made readily available for the first time: "The Inferno of Altisodora," "Christopher Corduroy," "Alarming Increase of Depravity Among Animals," "Phantasmagoria," and "A Highland Anecdote."

Three of Scott's stories set the highest standards for the newly emerging genre. "Wandering Willie's Tale," a marvelous comic story, was regarded by Dante Gabriel Rossetti and Andrew Lang as the finest short story in English. "The Highland Widow" and "The Two Drovers" triumph on a nobler plane, reaching the heights of tragedy. All three stories exemplify Scott's major contribution to British fiction: the portrayal of individuals as social and historical beings.

OTHER MAJOR WORKS

LONG FICTION: *Waverley: Or, 'Tis Sixty Years Since*, 1814; *Guy Mannering*, 1815; *Old Mortality*, 1816; *The Antiquary*, 1816; *The Black Dwarf*, 1816; *Rob Roy*, 1817; *The Heart of Midlothian*, 1818; *A Legend of Montrose*, 1819; *Ivanhoe*, 1819; *The Bride of Lammermoor*, 1819; *The Abbot*, 1820; *The Monastery*, 1820; *Kenilworth*, 1821; *The Pirate*, 1821; *The Fortunes of Nigel*, 1822; *Peveril of the Peak*, 1823; *Quentin*

Durward, 1823; *St. Ronan's Well*, 1823; *Redgauntlet*, 1824; *The Betrothed*, 1825; *The Talisman*, 1825; *Woodstock*, 1826; *The Fair Maid of Perth*, 1828; *Anne of Geierstein*, 1829; *Castle Dangerous*, 1831; *Count Robert of Paris*, 1831; *The Siege of Malta*, 1976.

PLAYS: *Halidon Hill*, pb. 1822; *Macduff's Cross*, pb. 1823; *The House of Aspen*, pb. 1829; *Auchindrane: Or, The Ayrshire Tragedy*, pr., pb. 1830; *The Doom of Devorgoil*, pb. 1830.

POETRY: *The Eve of Saint John: A Border Ballad*, 1800; *The Lay of the Last Minstrel*, 1805; *Ballads and Lyrical Pieces*, 1806; *Marmion: A Tale of Flodden Field*, 1808; *The Lady of the Lake*, 1810; *The Vision of Don Roderick*, 1811; *Rokeby*, 1813; *The Bridal of Triermain: Or, The Vale of St. John, in Three Cantos*, 1813; *The Ettrick Garland: Being Two Excellent New Songs*, 1815 (with James Hogg); *The Field of Waterloo*, 1815; *The Lord of the Isles*, 1815; *Harold the Dauntless*, 1817.

NONFICTION: *The Life and Works of John Dryden*, 1808; *The Life of Jonathan Swift*, 1814; *Lives of the Novelists*, 1825; *The Life of Napoleon Buonaparte: Emperor of the French, with a Preliminary View of the French Revolution*, 1827; *Religious Discourses by a Layman*, 1828; *Tales of a Grandfather*, 1828-1830 (12 volumes); *The History of Scotland*, 1829-1830; *Letters on Demonology and Witchcraft*, 1830; *The Journal of Sir Walter Scott*, 1890.

TRANSLATIONS: *"The Chase," and "William and Helen": Two Ballads from the German of Gottfried Augustus Bürger*, 1796; *Goetz of Berlichingen, with the Iron Hand*, 1799 (of Johann Wolfgang von Goethe).

EDITED TEXTS: *Minstrelsy of the Scottish Border*, 1802-1803 (3 volumes); *A Collection of Scarce and Valuable Tracts*, 1809-1815 (13 volumes); *Chronological Notes of Scottish Affairs from the Diary of Lord Fountainhall*, 1822.

BIBLIOGRAPHY

Allen, Emily. "Re-Marking Territory: *Redgauntlet* and the Restoration of Sir Walter Scott." *Studies in Romanticism* 37 (Summer, 1998): 163-182. A discussion of the generic politics of the Romantic literary marketplace and how the laws of genre become established. Argues that the novel *Redgauntlet* encodes an elaborate allegory of its generic history and of its forecasted reception.

Cockshut, A. O. J. *The Achievement of Walter Scott*. London: Collins, 1969. Combines a biographical sketch and a discussion of Scott's most famous and highly regarded novels--*Waverley*, *Old Mortality*, *Rob Roy*, *The Heart of Midlothian*, and *Redgauntlet*.

Cusac, Marian H. *Narrative Structure in the Novels of Sir Walter Scott*. The Hague, Netherlands: Mouton, 1969. The focus of this book is on structure, separating Scott's fiction into three classifications: romances, chronicles, and the mediocre hero history. Contains helpful appendixes, including classifications of novels and significant recurring elements, and a bibliography.

Dennis, Ian. *Nationalism and Desire in Early Historical Fiction*. New York: St. Martin's Press, 1997. Discusses works by Scott, James Fenimore Cooper, Jane Porter, and Lady Sydney Morgan.

Ferns, Chris. "Look Who's Talking: Walter Scott, Thomas Raddall, and the Voices of the Colonized." *Ariel* 26 (October, 1995): 49-67. Argues that although both Scott and Raddall are concerned with portraying the interaction between conflicting political and social forces within an essentially similar historical context, the manner in which they do so is very different; whereas Scott allows an unusually free interplay of voices, Raddall subordinates the dialogic interplay of voices to the monologic discourse of the narrator.

Harvey Wood, Harriet. *Sir Walter Scott*. Tavistock, England: Northcote House/British Council, 2006. An introductory overview of Scott's life and work, placing both within the historical, political, and social contexts of late eighteenth century Scotland. Charts his development as a novelist and a poet.

Hussein Ali, Zahra A. "Adjusting the Borders of Self: Sir Walter Scott's *The Two Drovers*." *Papers on Language and Literature* 37, no. 1 (Winter, 2001): 65. Analyzes the "poetics of space" and the "politics of nationalism" in Scott's story.

Lauber, John. *Sir Walter Scott*. Boston: Twayne, 1989. A good starting point for a study of Scott. The first three chapters provide an overview of Scott's career, the rest provide discussions of the novels, and the final chapter discusses the Waverley novels and their literary reputation. Includes a chronology and a select bibliography.

Lee, Yoon Sun. "A Divided Inheritance: Scott's Antiquarian Novel and the British Nation." *ELH* 64 (Summer, 1997): 537-567. Argues that the antiquarian mode of thought determines the historical novel's political ambivalence and provides the most effective means of understanding how this genre's popularity sprang from its literary nature.

Lincoln, Andrew. *Walter Scott and Modernity.* Edinburgh: Edinburgh University, 2007. Fourteen of Scott's novels and poems are examined here to give readers an understanding of his conservative politics and their impact on his writing.

Scott, Sir Walter. *The Shorter Fiction.* Edited by Graham Tulloch and Judy King. Edinburgh: Edinburgh University Press, 2009. Compilation of eight short stories originally written for periodicals, beginning with a satirical piece published in 1811. This collection is one of the twenty-eight volumes in the Edinburgh Edition of the Waverly novels, for which a team of scholars unearthed and subsequently published Scott's original writings, aiming to produce his work as he intended, without the errors that were generated in previous publications.

Todd, William B. *Sir Walter Scott: A Bibliographical History.* New Castle, Del.: Oak Knoll Press, 1998. A useful tool for students of Scott. A comprehensive listing of all Scott's separate publications through 1832, the year of his death; of editions of every genre from 1806 to 1833; of the final magnum opus in full; and of everything from Scott's legal papers to tributes and dedications.

Zimmerman, Everett. "Extreme Events: Scott's Novels and Traumatic History." *Eighteenth-Century Fiction* 10 (October, 1997): 63-78. Discussion of extreme events in history and fiction. Argues that descriptions of these events are a rhetorical device to assert an unanalyzed perspective, implying that analysis would erode the clear boundaries that divide humanity from the inhumane.

Mark A. Weinstein
Updated by Kimberley L. Jacobs

RACHEL SEIFFERT

Born: Oxford, England; January, 1971

PRINCIPAL SHORT FICTION
The Dark Room, 2001 (three novellas)
Field Study, 2004

OTHER LITERARY FORMS

Known primarily for short fiction, Rachel Seiffert (RAY-chehl SEE-furt) published a novel, *Afterwards* (2007), which is a study about the repercussions of post-traumatic stress disorder on an already fragmented psyche and the people surrounding that psyche. The story concentrates on the evolution and devolution of the romance between Joseph, a man unable to deal with the guilt of killing a man during a military maneuver in Northern Ireland, and Alice, his lover, who is not informed of Joseph's past and who is baffled by his emotional distance and erratic behavior. His relationship with Alice eventually ends, and Joseph continues to avoid professional help. The reader necessarily focuses on the brutality of sending people into war-torn situations with little or no preparation for integrating their war self into their civilian self when they return home.

ACHIEVEMENTS

Rachel Seiffert has been winning accolades for her writing for more than a decade. Her first professional recognition came in the Macallan/Scotland on Sunday Short Story Competition, where her short story "Blue" was shortlisted for the prize in 1999. Seiffert's writing is distinctive for its paucity of detail and its reliance on emotion to carry the story. Her writing exploded on the literary field in 2001, when she won the PEN David T.

K. Wong Award for her short story "The Crossing," was shortlisted for the Booker Prize for Fiction for *The Dark Room*, and then won the Betty Trask Award for *The Dark Room*. The *Los Angeles Times* Book Prize/ Art Seidenbaum Award for First Fiction soon followed in 2002 for *The Dark Room*. She was named one of the *Granta* Best of Young British Novelists in 2003.

BIOGRAPHY

Rachel Seiffert was born to a German mother and an Australian father and raised in Oxford, England, and Glasgow, Scotland. Fluent in both German and English since infancy, Seiffert was inundated with German culture from her mother and from her numerous trips through Germany, and this has had a significant impact upon her fiction. While Seiffert is almost two generations removed from World War II, she still faced bullying and was called a "Nazi" by schoolmates because of her German heritage. Seiffert was working as a film editor, writer, and director when *The Dark Room* was published in 2001, but she also has worked as an educator. She settled in London, England, with her husband and two children.

ANALYSIS

At the heart of Rachel Seiffert's fiction is the search for identity, whether it is personal, political, societal, or emotional. The need for definition that her characters seek may stem, in small part, from Seiffert's own questioning of identity as a half German, half Australian woman. All of her characters exist on the periphery of society because of age, race, economic circumstance, or self-imposed isolation, but they share the desire for inclusion. Further, almost all of her characters have difficulty sustaining meaningful relationships with others outside the family and suffer from an inability to communicate effectively. *The Dark Room* focuses on the feelings experienced by average Germans regarding National Socialism prior to and during World War II (Helmut), at the very end of the war (Lore), and two generations removed (Micha). *Field Study* consists of eleven short stories that revolve around the search for meaning and the conflict with identity, while *After-wards* details the devastation of post-traumatic stress disorder on the sufferer and everyone in that person's

sphere. All three works focus on the difficulty of finding a sense of balance in the midst of absence and loss.

Seiffert's minimalist writing style, reminiscent of that of Ernest Hemingway, stresses both the importance of what is and what is not stated. She trusts the reader--without much guidance from the author--to intuit meaning in the story. Indeed, Seiffert's emphasis on essentials demands a great level of concentration from the reader to imagine what is usually supplied by the author. This writing style can be jarring to those used to more detail-saturated fiction. Because of the paucity of detail, some critics have accused Seiffert of writing with a lack of emotion, creating a stilted feeling in her work, while others attribute this to a photographic style of writing. However devoid of excessive detail, Seiffert's work does not lack depth. Perhaps because of the focus on the emotions of the scene rather than the specifics of the visual element, the reader has a better sense of the narrative arc of the piece; an intricate understanding of plot and theme is privileged over setting and emphasizes, rather than detracts from,

Rachel Seiffert (Getty Images)

character. For example, Helmut, the main character in the novella *Helmut* from *The Dark Room*, is a challenging character because Seiffert refuses to romanticize his faults. Indeed, his attributes, both positive and negative, are detailed in an objective manner and show him to be less than heroic. However, because Helmut is not sentimentalized, the reader clearly can see him becoming more insulated as a coping mechanism to deal being labeled as "different." As Helmut becomes more marginalized, his character becomes less emotionally accessible to readers, which emphasizes the depression and loneliness experienced by this character as he searches for meaning in his culture. However, not all of Seiffert's characters come off as abrasive. Indeed, many of her characters, like Ewa in "Field Study" and "Second Best" from the collection entitled *Field Study*, become more compelling and multidimensional because of Seiffert's extremely objective and minimalist writing style.

THE DARK ROOM

Consisting of three novellas, *The Dark Room* concentrates on the impact of World War II from the average German perspective. The first section, *Helmut*, follows a young man deemed unfit for military service because of a muscle abnormality. Because he is "different," Helmut is unable to assimilate into the society surrounding him. As he grows older, Helmut slowly removes himself more and more from the world and becomes obsessed with stationary objects. In his youth and adolescence, Helmut obsessively documents the departures and arrivals at the Berlin train station, and in young adulthood, he takes pictures of random places and people in the city. While Helmut has friends in his early years, he grows more and more insular as time goes by, even distancing himself from his father and eventually his mother as the war drags on. Photography becomes a perfect medium for Helmut because it enables him to document without participating in any of the life around him. Helmut's depression marginalizes and alienates him to the point of obscurity. Even his parents abandon him, leaving him totally and utterly alone in Berlin. Helmut realizes that if he is to survive, he must adapt, and he does this in a resourceful manner. With the end of the war comes occupation by the Russians, but the final vision of Helmut is a man with a

smile on his face becoming the subject of a photograph instead of the unnoticed entity behind the camera taking the picture.

Lore, the second novella, follows the journey of a group of siblings attempting to reach their grandmother's house in Hamburg at the very end of the war. In fact, the reader is privy to the moment when Lore's mother informs her, tearfully, that the Fuhrer is dead. Lore is the oldest child of a Nazi soldier father and patriotic mother, both convinced of the legitimacy of the Nazi cause and eventually sent to camps run by Americans. Lore, then, must shepherd her younger brothers and sister (the youngest is an infant) in the midst of the total devastation of the governmental system and landscape (including the transportation system, which means that they must walk all the way to Hamburg, a trip that they normally would take by train). Lore and her siblings endure fatigue, starvation, illness, and the loss of one of the boys, but they continue onward with little more than the belief that their grandmother will still be alive with an intact house. When Lore is almost devoid of hope, a guardian angel named Tomas appears to help the children get to their grandmother's house. Amazingly, the grandmother is there and can take the children in, but Tomas remains in the background, a secret hidden in a dank, bombed-out house on the edge of town. When Lore finds out Tomas's secret, she no longer goes to visit him and one day he vanishes, leaving the children abandoned once again. The key to this story is the realization that nothing is what it seems.

Micha, the final section of the book, follows the quest of a young man two generations removed from Nazism, who is trying to find out "the truth" about his grandfather's actions during World War II. At the start of the story, Micha begins to think about his deceased grandfather and, more particularly, the role that he played in the Nazi army during the war. He begins to question his grandmother, who regards Micha's questions with excitement because she believes that Micha is showing an interest in his grandfather's life, although Micha's mother and sister are suspicious of his motives. As the story unravels, Micha finds that his grandfather was in the Waffen-SS, the military force of the Third Reich, in Belorussia and remained there for years after the war (not returning home until the

1950's), because he was held in a prisoner camp. Micha believes that there must be a reason his grandfather was held captive for so long, that it must point to some sort of guilt on his grandfather's part. Micha eventually journeys to Belorussia twice, to the same town that his grandfather was stationed in, and finds out the grisly truth that he both wanted to know and was afraid to find out. As Micha becomes overwhelmed by the guilt of his grandfather's past, he finds that all of his relationships are strained to the breaking point. Micha cannot reconcile his family's past, and this becomes even more difficult for him when his daughter Dilan is born. What legacy will he leave her? What does family mean? Micha comes to an uneasy compromise at the end of the story when he brings his daughter to visit his grandmother, suggesting that acceptance is the first step to healing.

The title *The Dark Room* obviously refers to the dark room Helmut uses to develop photographs, but in all three stories, it is a place of refuge from the world, where the inhabitants can find respite for a few precious hours. Further, the dark room is a place where perception can be distorted, playing upon the idea that one can manipulate the images of photographs in a dark room with chemicals and lighting techniques. Finally, the dark room is a place where images, or the truth, slowly develops (like a photograph), if the viewer is patient enough to wait for it. In all three stories, the characters slowly move from despair to places of acceptance (albeit in differing levels) and force the reader to rethink the problematic consequences of black-and-white thinking.

FIELD STUDY

This collection consists of eleven short stories, including "Blue," which was shortlisted for the Macallan/Scotland on Sunday Short Story Competition in 1999, and "The Crossing," which won the PEN David T. K. Wong Award in 2001. All eleven revolve around identity and connection, demonstrating barriers that people face when negotiating both issues. Two of the most compelling stories, the first, "Field Study," and the last, "Second Best," focus on Ewa, a young Polish woman dealing with emotional devastation and confusion in the face of a new relationship and an old one, after her husband has deserted her. "Reach," "The Late

Spring," and "Dog-Leg Lane" feature parent-guardian figures making complicated and uncomfortable realizations about their feelings for their child, while "Dimitroff" shows an adult child (daughter-in-law) discovering complicated emotions about her father figure. "Tentsmuir Sands" is a snapshot of a day in the life of a relatively happy family, while "Architect" watches a man reconfigure his identity as he realizes that he is not an architect any longer. Finally, "The Crossing" is the first version of an episode that will figure largely in the *Lore* novella in *The Dark Room*, while both "Blue" and "Francis John Jones, 1924" are reminiscent of issues of emotional distancing and veterans' guilt that will later control the narrative of *Afterwards*.

This story collection is a primer to the work of Seiffert because it explores all of the issues inherent in the longer pieces, but it does so in a way that is accessible for general readers. Forefronted in each story is the idea of identity and how a shift in identity causes incomprehensible anguish for the individuals. For example, in "Reach," Alice, Kim's mother, knows that she should care more deeply for her daughter, and the realization that she does not causes her both guilt and irritation, which do not subside even after her daughter is hospitalized for meningitis. The woman's inability to bond with her daughter in "the way that she should," the way that she has with her son, needles her, but she feels that she cannot change what is. Written in a fragmented manner, with short statements creating layers of meaning, "Reach" reads like Kim's daily journal written from a third-person perspective. It is the objectivity of that third-person narrator that makes this story masterful. Toward the middle of the story, it reads, "An unwieldy dead weight with limbs, Alice carries her daughter to the bathroom." The brilliance of this seemingly throwaway line is that it is key to the reader's understanding of the main characters and the underlying message of the story: The reader knows that the "the unwieldy dead weight" should be a reference to Kim, the daughter, because this how Alice feels about her, but as written, it is a reference to Alice, the mother. The reader wonders whey Alice will not yield or be for her daughter what her daughter needs. The story concentrates on Alice, but, in doing so, it brings the plight of Kim into sharper focus. Each story in this collection is written in a different style, yet each forces the reader to be engaged, to put all of the clues in the texts together, rather than being told by the author "what the story means." Because of this engagement with the text, the themes of disconnection, confusion, and anguish resonate more deeply, almost hauntingly.

OTHER MAJOR WORKS

LONG FICTION: *Afterwards*, 2007.

BIBLIOGRAPHY

Horstkotte, Silke. "Transgenerational Mediations of Identity in Rachel Seiffert's *The Dark Room* and Marel Beyer's *Spies*." *Thamyris/Intersection: Place, Sex and Race* 15, no. 1 (2007): 149-160. Considers how identity is created in the space of the family unit and what happens when that identity is lost, shifted, or somehow violated.

Pividori, Cristina. "Out of the Dark Room: Photography and Memory in Rachel Seiffert's Holocaust Tales." *Atlantis* 30, no. 2 (2008): 79-94. A fascinating discussion of the photographic elements inherent in *The Dark Room* and the effectiveness of this style of writing when dealing with stories of trauma.

Tollance, Pascale. "Freezing Emotion: The Impersonality of 'Photographic Writing' in Rachel Seiffert's *The Dark Room*." In *Impersonality and Emotion in Twentieth-century British Literature*, edited by Christine Reynier and Jean-Michel Ganteau. Montpellier, France: Université Montpellier III, 2005. Speaks to Seiffert's writing style and addresses the notion that her lack of detail translates into a lack of emotion, proving the exact opposite to be the case.

Zeitlin, Froma. "Imaginary Tales in the Land of the Perpetrators." *Journal of Modern Jewish Studies* 5, no. 2 (2006): 213-228. Discusses three novels, including *The Dark Room*, that showcase the viewpoints of "average Germans" during the Holocaust and considers how each novel, written by authors far removed from the events of the stories, attempts to gain an understanding of German society's seeming apathy to what was happening to the "undesirables."

Valerie A. Murrenus Pilmaier

CAROL SHIELDS

Born: Oak Park, Illinois; June 2, 1935
Died: Victoria, British Columbia, Canada; June 16, 2003

PRINCIPAL SHORT FICTION

Various Miracles, 1985
The Orange Fish, 1989
Dressing Up for the Carnival, 2000
Collected Stories, 2004

OTHER LITERARY FORMS

Though Carol Shields is probably best known for her novels, of which she published ten, she enjoyed an extensive and varied career, publishing in addition three volumes of poetry, five plays, two works of nonfiction, and numerous short stories. Her work remains widely published and has been translated into many different languages.

ACHIEVEMENTS

Carol Shields's novels have garnered much acclaim, often nominated and receiving and winning various Canadian, British, and American awards. *Small Ceremonies* (1976), her first novel, won the Canadian Author's Association Award for Best Novel. *Swann: A Mystery* (1987) received the Arthur Ellis Award for Best Canadian Mystery; it was later adapted into a screenplay. Shields's most celebrated novel, *The Stone Diaries* (1993), received multiple awards: the U.S .National Book Critics Circle Award, the Canadian Booksellers Association Prize, the McNally Robinson Award for Manitoba Book of the Year, and the Pulitzer

Prize for Fiction in 1995. *Larry's Party* (1997) received the Orange Prize and France's Prix de Lire. Her last published novel, *Unless* (2002), won the Ethel Wilson Prize for Best British Columbian Fiction.

Shields's short stories have appeared in various publications and anthologies. "Flitting Behavior" won the Canadian Broadcasting Corporation (CBC) Literary Award for Short Fiction, second prize, in 1984, and "Mrs. Turner Cutting the Grass" received the Canadian National Magazine Award in 1985. Shields was honored for her contributions to drama for *Women Waiting* (1983), winning the CBC's first prize for the Annual Literary Competition, and for her nonfiction, as biographer for *Jane Austen* (2001), receiving the Charles Taylor Award for Literary Non-Fiction.

For her lifelong work as author and educator, Shields received many distinguished honors, including the Writer's Development Trust's Marian Engel Award in 1990, numerous honorary doctorates. In 2002, Shields accepted Canada's highest honor and was named as a Companion of the Order of Canada.

Carol Shields (Getty Images)

BIOGRAPHY

Carol Shields was born Carol Ann Warner in Oak Park, Illinois, in 1935 to father Robert and mother Inez, the youngest of three children. Shields's passion for reading and writing began at an early age, and by the time she reached Oak Park High School she was making her first attempts at writing poetry.

In 1953, Shields attended Hanover College in Indiana, where she earned a scholarship to study abroad at Exeter University in England. During the exchange program, she met Donald Shields, an engineering graduate student from Canada, who would later become her husband. Carol Shields returned to the United States in 1957 to graduate magna cum laude in history and education and to be married in her hometown. Shortly thereafter, Shields moved with her husband to Vancouver, Canada, where they settled and began a family. Shields became a Canadian citizen in 1971.

Shields's first child, John Douglass, was born in 1959, and in the coming years daughters Anne, Catherine, Margaret, and Sara followed. Shields concentrated on motherhood during her children's early years, but she set aside a small amount of time for writing

daily. Shields eventually completed her M.A. in literature at the University of Ottawa in 1975, later publishing her thesis on Susanna Moodie in 1976. During her graduate education, Shields worked part time as an editorial assistant for a scholarly quarterly and published a number of poems for various periodicals, which were later collected and published as *Others* (1972) and *Intersect* (1974).

At the age of forty, Shields published her first novel, *Small Ceremonies*, and several novels followed, all of them critically well received. Often as byproducts of her novels, Shields began publishing short fiction with *Various Miracles*, *The Orange Fish*, and *Dressing Up for the Carnival*. In 1983, Shields became a playwright with *Women Waiting*; its success inspired her to continue as a dramatist, and she later created four more plays.

As she wrote and raised a family, Shields was an educator as well. She taught creative writing at the University of Ottawa and the University of British Columbia. In 1982, Shields moved to Winnipeg and taught at the University of Manitoba, where she was made full professor in 1995. She was later appointed chancellor of the University of Winnipeg from 1996 to 2000. Shields was diagnosed with advanced breast cancer in 1998, which caused her death in 2003; in spite of her illness, in 2001 Shields published her biography of Jane Austen, and *Unless*, a novel, soon followed to critical acclaim. Since Shields's death, there have been numerous tributes to her outstanding legacy.

ANALYSIS

Carol Shields's primary concerns are the "everydayness" of human existence and the examination of human relationships, subjects that permeate both her novels and her short fiction. Her work often reveals the unseen significance of the commonplace and the ordinary occurrences that punctuate human lives, investigating how those moments expose certain truths and subdued revelations. Core themes include an examination of love (in its joys and failings), marriage, loss, grief, and strange coincidences that illuminate the interconnectedness of human experience and compose the scope of a life.

Shields's short fiction--especially *Dressing Up for the Carnival*, perhaps her most unorthodox collection--also has been noted for its whimsical, playful nature. Many of the stories are brief vignettes that portray unexplained, self-contained flashes of seemingly insignificant moments in characters' lives. As trivial as they may seem, these moments point toward a meaning that often cannot be described entirely or fully. In Shields's fiction, these moments in their simplicity frequently lead her characters, and readers, to strange and sometimes profound discoveries.

"MRS. TURNER CUTTING THE GRASS"

One of Shields's best-known stories, "Mrs. Turner Cutting the Grass" portrays an aging widow who, while wearing inappropriately youthful apparel, is seen cutting her grass one afternoon in June. Passing schoolgirls gape in shock and embarrassment; her neighbors scoff and whisper. Mrs. Turner has a somewhat scandalous past: As a girl, she was caught in an affair with a married farmer. She fled to New York, where she met Kiki, am African American man, with whom she mothered a child out of wedlock. After Kiki disappeared, she abandoned the child, leaving it in a carriage on the front porch of a house, and never looked back. She later

married a good man and settled in Winnipeg. After her husband died, Mrs. Turner traveled the world with her sisters. During one such trip to Japan, she was observed by a professor and struggling poet, who, affronted by her garish dress and vulgar speech, was inspired to write a poem about the unfortunate encounter; the poem would later, ironically, launch his career.

Shields paints a portrait of a woman who has lived her life fully and, in the process, unknowingly left her mark on all those around her. Mrs. Turner wholly believes that, despite her sordid past, she always "did the best she could under the circumstances"; there is no reason to question or to look back in guilt or uncertainty. It is this quality of living without reservations and inhibitions that makes her very existence beautiful, though unconventionally so. In the end it is not what Mrs. Turner did or did not do, what her neighbors think about her, or what she does or does not know that defines her, but rather merely that she lived, without regrets. For that, Shields insists, Mrs. Turner must be admired.

"FLITTING BEHAVIOR"

Meershank, a writer, cares for his wife Louise in her final days, as she suffers from terminal cancer. He is paid a visit by his attractive friend and editor, Maybelle Spritz, a woman with whom he had slept only once after learning of his wife's illness. As the two share brandy on the veranda, Meershank ponders kissing her, but he is startled by the sudden bursting of fireworks in honor of Victoria Day. The explosion of lights overhead conjures for Meershank images of the malignant cells that, at that very moment, ravage his wife's body. Overcome with the sudden urge to attend to his wife, he hurries upstairs to her.

He reflects on his thirty-five years of marriage and is stung by the irony that he, a man so "widely known as a professional misogynist," had managed to love one woman for so many years. He recalls with great clarity and tenderness his young bride, who had once promised to stay by his side forever. Now it seems she will leave him after all. He ruminates on how she permeates every moment of his existence: typing his novels in those early years, cooking his meals, cutting his hair, and never laughing at his books, a trait for which he respected her most.

Finding his wife has taken a turn for the worse, Meershank asks Maybelle to phone the children. After she does, sitting alone in the darkened kitchen, Maybelle imagines herself as each of the daughters on her way home to her mother, then as the doctor hurrying to his patient, and finally as Louise as she lay dying. As Meershank and the children surround her bed, Louise utters her final words, and each person present hears them differently. Maybelle alone is able to interpret them; in so doing, she delivers the comfort Meershank and his daughters will need to carry on without Louise.

Similar to many of Shields's short stories, "Flitting Behavior" features a long-married couple that must come to terms with a great transition, and it details the various, seemingly insignificant moments that have made up their life together. Meershank must cope with his own grief and loss during his wife's final moments, and does so in unconventional ways. The story explores the reactions of loved ones facing the inevitable and the vulnerability of human nature, examples of which can be seen in Meershank's brief affair with Maybelle and his flitting desire to kiss her on the veranda while his wife is dying upstairs, actions which at first may seem abominable to readers. Ultimately, though, these desires are not born of passion or disrespect but are an attempt to cope with grief and even anger; they are Meershank's way of staving off the sense of abandonment that ultimately would overtake him, evident in his rumination of how his wife swore to never leave his side and his admitting "what a joke she [had] played on him in the end."

"The Orange Fish"

"The Orange Fish" is another story that explores the ups and downs of married life. The unnamed narrator admits to having been unhappily married to Lois-Ann for twelve years. They are a couple "deep in their thirties" and are struggling to cope with the reality of growing older and accepting middle age. Both admit to have given up on their life's dreams (hers of raising dahlias and his of running a dude ranch), for more practical vocations, decisions that perhaps have made their aging more difficult to bear.

The couple, finally agreeing upon something, decides to buy a lithograph of a fish. Upon hanging it above their breakfast table, a sense of calm and tranquillity overtakes them. They find the intimacy they had once enjoyed is restored. They soon learn that the people who bought the remaining prints have established a group; all of them want to share how the miraculous power of the orange fish has changed their lives and given them a sense of direction and happiness. They all share their story, expressing their fears aloud and putting them to rest. Simultaneously, in another part of town, thousands of the orange fish are being printed (on posters, on stamps, and even on a Sears flyer), but with its mass publication, the powers of the fish begin to die.

Typical of Shields's short fiction, a married couple struggle to deal with the central conflict of being unsatisfied in their relationship and unfulfilled in their individual lives. However, by making what seems to be an arbitrary decision to purchase a lithograph, they are changed; the mysterious object possesses a transformative power to bring them the happiness they seek, a theme similar to that found in "Dressing Up for the Carnival." There is no real sense of closure in this story (and in much of Shields's work); the reader is left to decide what will happen to the couple, and to the others, once the fish loses its power. Will they be able to maintain their happiness? The mysterious occurrence cannot ever be fully explained.

"Dressing Up for the Carnival"

"Dressing Up for the Carnival" is a series of brief vignettes depicting the lives of various characters as they go about their day and the small, revealing choices they make. The story opens with Tamara, whose favorite part of the day is choosing what she will wear. She never dresses for the weather outside, for "her clothes *are* the weather," and she is careful to choose just the right accessories; through her clothes, she is no longer just a clerk-receptionist, but "A Passionate, Vibrant Woman About to Begin Her Day. Her Life." Next is Roger, who suddenly decides to buy a mango rather than an apple, and, strolling the street, fruit in hand, finds himself no longer a man divorced, but something new, exotic: a man carrying a mango. Wanda, a bank teller, is asked to retrieve a baby carriage for her manager. Having obtained it, she feels herself changed, imagining herself a mother and uttering "there, there, now," to the empty carriage. An elderly man, deciding to buy flowers for his disagreeable daughter-in-law, suddenly experiences the weight of friendlier, warmer eyes upon him. On and on the stories go, and in each the character feels transformed by somehow altering his or her outward appearance with physical objects.

"Dressing Up for the Carnival" explores the basic human desire to create and project illusions, fantasies that allow a temporary escape or a hiding place from reality. These unrelated characters share the same urge to transform themselves, an act accomplished by changing their outward appearances. By so doing they are no longer themselves; what they wear and carry with them determines how they see themselves and how they are seen by others. Ultimately, through their illusions, they are able to become, more or less, whoever they want to be. In contrast to "Dressing Up for the Carnival," the collection's concluding story, "Dressing Down," brings the premise full circle and deals with the difficulty many have dispelling illusions and coming to terms with what lies underneath: truth or true identity.

OTHER MAJOR WORKS

LONG FICTION: *Small Ceremonies*, 1976; *The Box Garden*, 1977 (later published with *Small Ceremonies* as *Duet*, 1996); *Happenstance*, 1980; *A Fairly Conventional Woman*, 1982; *Swann: A Mystery*, 1987; *A Celibate Season*, 1991 (with Blanche Howard); *The Republic of Love*, 1992; *The Stone Diaries*, 1993; *Larry's Party*, 1997; *Unless*, 2002.

PLAYS: *Departures and Arrivals*, pr., pb. 1990; *Thirteen Hands*, pr., pb. 1993; *Fashion, Power, Guilt, and the Charity of Families*, 1995 (with Catherine Shields); *Anniversary: A Comedy*, pr., pb., 1998 (with Dave Williamson); *Thirteen Hands, and Other Plays*, pb. 2002.

RADIO PLAY: *Women Waiting*, 1983.

POETRY: *Others*, 1972; *Intersect*, 1974; *Coming to Canada*, 1992.

NONFICTION: *Susanna Moodie: Voice and Vision*, 1976; *Jane Austen*, 2001.

EDITED TEXTS: *Scribner's Best of the Fiction Workshops*, 1998; *Dropped Threads: What We Aren't Told*, 2000 (with Marjorie Anderson); *Dropped Threads Two: More of What We Aren't Told*, 2003 (with Anderson and Catherine Shields).

BIBLIOGRAPHY

Fellman, Anita Clair. "A World Made of Words." *Women's Review of Books* 7, no. 3 (December, 1989): 16. Provides concise yet thoughtful analysis of central themes in "Various Miracles" and a brief investigation of form in "Swann."

Glover, Douglas. "Amiably Elegant Shields, Raw and Passionate York." *Canadian Forum* 79, no. 890 (2000): 39-41. Reviews "Dressing Up for the Carnival", analyzing several stories in particular.

Nelson, Ronald J. "Inconclusive Closure in Carol Shields's 'The Orange Fish.'" *Postscript* 22 (Spring, 2005): 21-28. Investigates narrative closure in "The Orange Fish."

Oates, Joyce Carol. "An Endangered Species." *New York Review of Books* 47, no. 11 (June, 2000): 38-41. Reviews "Dressing Up for the Carnival" and analyzes several of the collection's standout stories.

Wachtel, Eleanor. "Telling It Slant." *Books in Canada* 18, no. 4 (May, 1988): 9-14. Offers helpful biographical information and a thematic overview of Shields's works.

Danielle A. DeFoe

ALAN SILLITOE

Born: Nottingham, England; March 4, 1928
Died: London, England; April 25, 2010

PRINCIPAL SHORT FICTION

The Ragman's Daughter, 1963
A Sillitoe Selection, 1968
Guzman Go Home, and Other Stories, 1968
Men, Women, and Children, 1973
The Second Chance, and Other Stories, 1981
The Far Side of the Street, 1988
Collected Stories, 1995
Alligator Playground: A Collection of Short Stories,
    1997
New and Collected Stories, 2003

OTHER LITERARY FORMS

Alan Sillitoe (SIHL-ee-toh) has published more than three dozen books, which include novels, collections of poetry, stories for children, travel literature, essays, and plays. Four of his books, including *The Loneliness of the Long-Distance Runner* (1959) and *The Ragman's Daughter*, have been made into films. His first novel, *Saturday Night and Sunday Morning* (1958), was also produced in a stage adaptation, and his second, *The General* (1960), carried the film title *Counterpoint* (1967).

ACHIEVEMENTS

Alan Sillitoe's early novels and stories fall within the tradition of British working-class fiction established by Charles Dickens and Elizabeth Gaskell in the 1840's and carried on by George Gissing, Arthur Morrison, and Walter Greenwood. Sillitoe's work has gone on to be seen as part of English provincial or regional writing, echoing D. H. Lawrence's work in representing Nottinghamshire in fiction. *Saturday Night and Sunday Morning* won the Author's Club Prize as the

best English novel in 1958, and Sillitoe's best-known story, *The Loneliness of the Long-Distance Runner,* won the Hawthornden Prize in 1959 and is widely accepted as a modern classic on proletarian life. *The General,* which began as a short story in 1950, won the Nottingham Writers' Club competition in 1960. It is said that Sillitoe refused to have his work submitted for prizes, which may explain the absence of other large literary awards to his name. Sillitoe's later work was perceived to be less political, although he was still prolific into his eighties, and the work he produced showed a willingness to experiment in form and style. He was elected as a fellow of the Royal Society of Literature in 2007. In 2008, Sillitoe received the Freedom of the City of Nottingham. His large body of writing was commemorated within his lifetime with numerous local, national, and international literary festival events. His stories have been frequently anthologized and have been translated into more than twenty languages.

BIOGRAPHY

Born into a working-class family in the English industrial city of Nottingham, Alan Sillitoe was educated to the age of fourteen at Radford Boulevard School for Boys and worked in the local Raleigh bicycle factory before he joined the Royal Air Force in 1946. Missing service during the war because of his age, he served in Malaya for two years before returning, having been diagnosed with tuberculosis. He spent the following sixteen months recuperating in a sanatorium at Royal Air Force Wroughton in Wiltshire. It was during this period he read voraciously and began to write. From 1952 to 1958, he lived in France and Spain, where he became friends with Robert Graves. On the publication of *Saturday Night and Sunday Morning*, he returned to England, and he settled in Kent. He traveled frequently and widely and made extended visits to North Africa, Israel, and the Soviet Union. He married American poet

Ruth Fainlight in 1959. The couple had two children, David and Susan. His avocations were wireless telegraphy and collecting maps. Sillitoe died of cancer in London on April 25, 2010, at the age of eighty-two.

ANALYSIS

"The Loneliness of the Long-Distance Runner," the title story of Alan Sillitoe's first collection of short fiction, quickly became one of the most widely read stories of modern times. Its basic theme, that one must be true to one's own instincts and beliefs despite intense social pressure to go against them, is echoed in many of his best-known stories, including "On Saturday Afternoon," "The Ragman's Daughter," "The Good Women," and "Pit Strike." Such an attitude strikes a responsive chord in modern readers who feel hemmed in by the dictates of "official" bureaucracies and by government interference in their personal lives. It is important for Sillitoe's characters to establish their independence in a conformist world, yet at the same time they often subscribe to a class-oriented code of values that pits the disadvantaged working class against the rest of society. Sillitoe went on to revisit the characters of the Seaton family, introduced in *Saturday Night and Sunday Morning*, in two subsequent novels, *Key to the Door* (1961) and *The Open Door* (1989). The fourth and final book to focus on the Seatons, *Birthday*, was published in 2001. Sillitoe's 2003 volume of *New and Collected Stories* serves as an anthology of a remarkable body of work, adding three previously unpublished stories, "Brothers," "The Caller," and "Spitfire."

"UNCLE ERNEST"

Many of Sillitoe's stories are located in urban working-class slums and reflect the environment he knew himself. In story after story, these ghetto-dwellers are seen as society's underdogs, as victims of a series of injustices, real or imagined, which undermine their sense of personal dignity and self-esteem. Ernest Brown, for example, the protagonist in "Uncle Ernest," is a lonely, aging upholsterer who befriends Alma and Joan, two young schoolgirls he meets at a local café. In a series of encounters, always at the café and in public view, he buys them food and small gifts and takes pleasure in learning something of their lives. He asks

nothing of the girls in return, and they come to think of him affectionately as "Uncle Ernest." After a few weeks, however, he is accosted by two detectives who accuse him of leading the girls "the wrong way" and forbid him to see them again. Unable to cope with this "official" harassment, Ernest retreats into alcohol and despair.

In one sense "Uncle Ernest" is an anomaly in Sillitoe's short fiction, for although it illustrates the victimization his characters often face, it chronicles a too-ready acceptance of the larger society's interference and power. For the most part his characters remain defiant in the face of directives from those in positions of authority.

"ON SATURDAY AFTERNOON"

"On Saturday Afternoon," the story of an unnamed working-class man's attempt to commit suicide, offers a sardonic example of this defiance. The man first tries to hang himself from a light fixture, but before he can succeed the police arrive and arrest him. In response to his bitter comment, "It's a fine thing if a bloke can't tek his own life," the police tell him "it ain't your life." They take him to a psychiatric hospital and imprudently put him in a sixth-floor room and fail to restrain him. That night he jumps from the window and succeeds in killing himself.

"On Saturday Afternoon" is typical of Sillitoe's stories in its assumed attitude to social authority: Although "they" interfere and place controls on an individual's right to act as he pleases, they can usually be outwitted. Here and in other stories Sillitoe's workers place great stress on "cunning," the ability to preserve individual freedom of action in a restrictive or oppressive social environment.

"THE LONELINESS OF THE LONG-DISTANCE RUNNER"

This attitude of cunning is well illustrated in Sillitoe's best-known story, "The Loneliness of the Long-Distance Runner." The protagonist in this story is called simply Smith, the modern equivalent of Everyman. He is a seventeen-year-old boy who has been put in a Borstal, a reform school, for theft from a baker's shop. He is also an accomplished long-distance runner and has been chosen by the governor, or warden, to represent the Borstal in a competition for the

All-England Championship. As the reader meets Smith, he is running alone over the early-morning countryside, and as he runs he considers his situation. It soon becomes apparent that he has rejected the warden's platitudes ("if you play ball with us, we'll play ball with you") and has seen through the hypocrisy of his promises as well. Smith recognizes the difference between his brand of honesty, which allows him to be true to his own instincts, and the warden's, which rejects the needs of the individual in favor of social expediency. Smith's only counter to the warden's attempt to use him for his own ends is cunning. As he sees it, the warden is "dead from the toenails up," living as he does in fear of social disapproval and manipulating the inmates of his Borstal to gain social prestige. Smith, however, resolves to fight against becoming swallowed up in social convention, to be true to his own concept of honesty. Adopting such a stance means recognizing "that it's war between me and them" and leads to his decision to lose the upcoming race.

In the second part of the three-part story the reader shares Smith's reminiscences about his boyhood in a Nottingham slum. He first engages sympathy by telling how he impulsively took part in the theft for which he was sent to Borstal, and then moves quickly to describe the confrontations with police who investigated the robbery. In this section Sillitoe manages a difficult feat by maintaining support for his protagonist, even though readers know the boy is guilty of theft. Sillitoe does this by turning the investigation into a series of skirmishes between Smith and the authorities, which allow the reader to be caught up in admiration of the boy's ability to outwit for a time a vindictive, slow-thinking policeman. Not unexpectedly, persistence pays off for the investigators, and in a highly original and amusing climax the stolen money is found and Smith is taken into custody. The facts are less important here, however, than Sillitoe's narrative skill in sustaining the reader's sympathetic involvement with his protagonist. Having manipulated the reader into becoming Smith's ally by allowing conventional notions of right and wrong to be suspended, he also paves the way for the acceptance of Smith's dramatic gesture in the final section of the story.

Alan Sillitoe (Press Association via AP Images)

The third part brings the reader back to the present and the day of the race. The warden, anticipating Smith's win and the reflected glory it will bring to the warden, has invited numbers of influential friends to witness the competition. Ironically, none of the boys' parents is present, their invitations having been worded so that they would be likely to mistrust or misunderstand them. Details such as this add to the impression of the callousness of the Borstal authorities and help to confirm Smith's conviction that they are using the boys as pawns in a selfish social game. The purity of Smith's intentions, however, is underscored during the race by his sense of communication with the natural surroundings through which he runs and his Edenic perception of himself as "the first man ever to be dropped into this world." As he runs, his thoughts alternate between lyrical commentary on the physical satisfaction of running well and consideration of his decision to lose the race and the punitive consequences this will bring him. Nevertheless he remains firm in his decision, committed to showing the warden "what honesty means if it's the last thing I do." In the end, he does lose the race and makes his point, but in a much more dramatic manner than he had foreseen. Arriving at the finish line well in advance of the other runners, he is forced to mark time in front of the grandstand until one of his competitors passes him and crosses the line. Smith has made his point: Like so many other of Sillitoe's protagonists, he refuses to be manipulated.

"The Good Women"

The fierce independence espoused by Sillitoe's working-class characters, and the rejection of what they see as unwarranted interference by society's authority figures in their personal affairs, is also evident in "The Good Women." The heroine of this story is Liza Atkin, a vital and earthy woman one critic called "a Nottingham Mother Courage." Liza's life, like that of Bertolt Brecht's protagonist, is plagued by economic hardship and marked by injustice and the stupidity of war. Although the story has no real plot, readers are shown a series of disconnected events that take place over a period of years. Readers are caught up in the problems of Liza's life and come to applaud her feisty, tough-minded manner of coping with them.

Dogged by poverty, she ekes out a precarious existence, supporting her out-of-work husband and two boys by filling a decrepit baby carriage with old rags and bits of metal from local dumps and selling them to scrap dealers and by taking in washing from troops stationed nearby. When the means-test man attempts to deny her welfare payments because of her "business," she shouts him down so the whole street can hear. She makes her gesture of protest against war by harboring a deserter; standing up for workers' rights in the factory where she eventually finds work, she quickly becomes known to management as "the apostle of industrial unrest." Later, when her son dies because Allied planes bombed his unit by mistake, she is devastated. She recovers, however, to become a passionate advocate of violent revolution at a time in life when most women would be settling into comfortable grandmother roles.

"The Good Women," like many of Sillitoe's stories, has strong didactic overtones. Liza Atkin, along with Smith, Ernest Brown, and the unnamed protagonist in "On Saturday Afternoon," finds herself in a world in which the dictates of society at large often contradict her personal convictions. Nevertheless, she is able to

resist the pressure to conform, partly because of her strong belief in what is right (harboring the deserter to protest against war, for example), partly because she shares the habitual working-class mistrust of "them" (the authority figures who come from outside and above her own social station) and their motives. From her perspective, and from Sillitoe's, society is badly flawed, and it is up to the individual to strive for a new order in which the unjust exercise of power and the suffering it can cause are eliminated. Memorable characters such as Atkin are meant to show the reader how to begin.

"Pit Strike"

In "Pit Strike," which was filmed for British Broadcasting Corporation Television, Sillitoe offers yet another working-class hero, a champion of fairness and integrity. Joshua, a fifty-year-old Nottingham miner, journeys to the south of England with a number of his friends to support a strike by fellow colliers. In a well-organized program of action, the men race from one coal-powered generating station to another to form picket lines and halt deliveries of coal. In a number of cases they are confronted by police whose job it is to see that deliveries are uninterrupted. Clashes between the workers, who feel they are being treated unjustly, and the police, representing the power of society as a whole, are inevitable in such circumstances. Although Joshua acts to restrain his more belligerent companions in these confrontations, he makes his own mark in a dramatic and courageous manner. When a fully loaded coal truck is seen crawling up an incline away from a picketed power station to make its delivery at another, Joshua daringly and at great personal risk runs after it and forces open the rear gate safety catches, allowing tons of coal to fall on the highway. Although he narrowly escapes death, the gesture seems worth making, and soon after this the strike is settled in the miners' favor.

Like Joshua, the characters in Sillitoe's stories are usually agitators, passionately and defiantly reaffirming the value of the individual spirit in a world that too often encourages unthinking conformity to social norms. Sillitoe's audience may not always concur with the views his characters express, nor wish to accept the methods they use to further their aims, but their stories nevertheless touch readers and stay tenaciously with them, disturbing, provoking, and making them more aware of the imperfect world and of themselves.

"BROTHERS"

"Brothers," a short character study of two brothers, is one of Sillitoe's last published short stories. In it, Sillitoe dwells on time passing, familial ties, and lives deeply embedded in the Nottingham setting. The main protagonist Ken has just lost his job and spends a tea break at his brother's house, reflecting on a life that has passed him by. The style of narration deftly shifts between speech and the interior lives of the brothers as readers witness two figures with complex mental portraits of each other. Political tensions are subtly suggested, with Ken wondering what Tony's Conservatives might have to conserve, but are dispelled by an agreement uttered in a noticeable Nottingham dialect that they have "allus," or always, shared a motto. Tony's daydreaming that Ken looks certain to fall socially mirrors Ken's own daydreaming about suicide. At the story's end Ken is left surveying the city from the castle top. Seeing fit to comment on the city's improved air, he briefly imagines plunging to his death in bodily detail before turning to go home. The wry reflection that on buying the local paper there will be no stories about those who resist such suicidal impulses unravels to reveal Ken alone talking to his budgerigar. The poignancy and muted heroics that live in the mundane are classic Sillitoe themes that recur here, distilled in a stylistically complex short story.

OTHER MAJOR WORKS

LONG FICTION: *Saturday Night and Sunday Morning*, 1958; *The Loneliness of the Long-Distance Runner*, 1959 (novella); *The General*, 1960; *Key to the Door*, 1961; *The Death of William Posters*, 1965; *A Tree on Fire*, 1967; *A Start in Life*, 1970; *Travels in Nihilon*, 1971; *The Flame of Life*, 1974; *The Widower's Son*, 1976; *The Storyteller*, 1979; *Her Victory*, 1982; *The Lost Flying Boat*, 1983; *Down from the Hill*, 1984; *Life Goes On*, 1985; *Out of the Whirlpool*, 1987; *The Open Door*, 1989; *Last Loves*, 1990; *Leonard's War*, 1991; *Snowstop*, 1993; *The Broken Chariot*, 1998; *The German Numbers Woman*, 1999; *Birthday*, 2001; *A Man of His Time*, 2004.

PLAYS: *All Citizens Are Soldiers*, pr. 1967 (adaptation of Lope de Vega; with Ruth Fainlight); *Three Plays*, pb. 1978.

SCREENPLAYS: *Saturday Night and Sunday Morning*, 1960 (adaptation of his novel); *The Loneliness of the Long-Distance Runner*, 1961 (adaptation of his novella); *Che Guevara*, 1968; *The Ragman's Daughter*, 1974 (adaptation of his novel).

POETRY: *Without Beer or Bread*, 1957; *The Rats, and Other Poems*, 1960; *A Falling out of Love, and Other Poems*, 1964; *Love in the Environs of Voronezh, and Other Poems*, 1968; *Shaman, and Other Poems*, 1968; *Poems*, 1971 (with Ted Hughes and Ruth Fainlight); *Barbarians, and Other Poems*, 1974; *Storm: New Poems*, 1974; *Snow on the North Side of Lucifer*, 1979; *More Lucifer*, 1980; *Sun Before Departure*, 1984; *Tides and Stone Walls*, 1986; *Collected Poems*, 1993.

NONFICTION: *The Road to Volgograd*, 1964; *Raw Material*, 1972; *Mountains and Caverns: Selected Essays*, 1975; *The Saxon Shore Way: From Gravesend to Rye*, 1983 (with Fay Weldon); *Nottinghamshire*, 1986 (with David Sillitoe); *Every Day of the Week*, 1987; *Leading the Blind: A Century of Guidebook Travel, 1815-1914*, 1996; *Life Without Armor*, 1996; *A Flight of Arrows: Opinions, People, Places*, 2003; *Gadfly in Russia*, 2007.

CHILDREN'S LITERATURE: *The City Adventures of Marmalade Jim*, 1967; *Big John and the Stars*, 1977; *The Incredible Fencing Fleas*, 1978; *Marmalade Jim at the Farm*, 1980; *Marmalade Jim and the Fox*, 1984.

BIBLIOGRAPHY

Atherton, Stanley S. *Alan Sillitoe: A Critical Assessment*. London: W. H. Allen, 1979. This study primarily emphasizes the revolutionary spirit of Sillitoe's first novels, but it deals with short fiction and lesser works as well.

Hanson, Gillian Mary. *Understanding Alan Sillitoe*. Columbia: University of South Carolina Press, 1999. A useful volume of Sillitoe criticism and appreciation.

Hensher, Philip. "Radical Sentiments." *Sunday Telegraph*, July 23, 1995, p. B9. A discussion of the life and works of Sillitoe, focusing on his autobiography *Life Without Armour* and his *Collected*

Stories; discusses briefly "The Loneliness of the Long-Distance Runner" and the political nature of some of Sillitoe's short stories.

Hitchcock, Peter. *Working-Class Fiction in Theory and Practice: A Reading of Alan Sillitoe*. Ann Arbor, Mich.: UMI Research Press, 1989. A good examination of the writer's themes and execution.

Leonardi, Susan J. "The Long-Distance Runner (the Loneliness, Loveliness, Nunliness of)." *Tulsa Studies in Women's Literature* 13 (Spring, 1994): 57-66. An intertextual examination of how Grace Paley's "The Long-Distance Runner" and Sara Maitland's "The Loveliness of the Long-Distance Runner" rewrite Sillitoe's "The Loneliness of the Long-Distance Runner."

Penner, Allen Richard. *Alan Sillitoe*. Boston: Twayne, 1972. A useful midcareer overview of Sillitoe's work. Penner offers a short biography and a helpful bibliography. The discussion covers Sillitoe's poetry and fiction.

Rothschild, Joyce. "The Growth of a Writer: An Interview with Alan Sillitoe." *Southern Humanities Review* 20 (Spring, 1986): 127-140. This interview sheds light on Sillitoe's career and the irrelevance of class on his artistic sensibility. Sillitoe stresses the importance of character in his fiction.

Skovmand, Michael, and Steffen Skovmand, eds. *The Angry Young Men*. Aarhus, Denmark: Akademisk Forlag, 1975. Hans Hauge's essay on Sillitoe considers *Saturday Night and Sunday Morning* as a representative novel from an angry generation of young writers that included John Osborne, John Wain, John Braine, and Kingsley Amis.

Taylor, D. J. "The Common Touch." *The Guardian*, March 1, 2008, p. 21. Celebrating the reissue of *A Start in Life*, Taylor reflects on Sillitoe's writing career and his place in British literary history.

Stanley S. Atherton; Jerry Bradley
Updated by Will Smith

MURIEL SPARK

Born: Edinburgh, Scotland; February 1, 1918
Died: Florence, Italy; April 13, 2006
Also known as: Muriel Sarah Camberg; Evelyn Cavallo

PRINCIPAL SHORT FICTION

The Go-Away Bird, and Other Stories, 1958
Voices at Play, 1961 (with radio plays)
Collected Stories I, 1967
Bang-Bang You're Dead, and Other Stories, 1981
The Stories of Muriel Spark, 1985
Open to the Public: New and Collected Stories, 1997
All the Stories, 2001 (also pb. as *The Complete Short Stories*)

OTHER LITERARY FORMS

Muriel Spark was known primarily for her novels and short fiction, but her body of work also includes nonfiction, children's literature, poetry, film adaptations, and radio plays. She began her career writing news articles as a press agent. Later she expanded her range to include works of poetry and literary criticism, contributing poems, articles, and reviews to magazines and newspapers, occasionally using the pseudonym Evelyn Cavallo. Spark published her first short story in 1951 and in 1954 began writing novels, her best known being *The Prime of Miss Jean Brodie* (1961).

ACHIEVEMENTS

Muriel Spark's honors and awards include the Prix Italia (1962) for her radio play adaptation of her novel *The Ballad of Peckham Rye* (1960); the *Yorkshire Post* Book of the Year Award (1965) and the James Tait Black Memorial Prize (1966), for *The Mandelbaum Gate* (1965); Commander, Order of the British Empire (1967); the Booker McConnell Prize nomination (1981) for *Loitering with Intent* (1981); the Scottish Book of the Year Award (1987) for *The Stories of*

Muriel Spark; *Officier de l'Ordre des Arts et des Lettres* (1988); the Ingersoll T. S. Eliot Award (1992); Dame, Order of the British Empire (1993); Honorary Fellowship, Royal Society of Edinburgh (1995); the David Cohen British Literature Prize for Lifetime Achievement (1997); Arts Council of Scotland Spring Book Prize (1997) for *Reality and Dreams* (1996); and honorary citizenship, Arezzo commune, Italy (2005).

BIOGRAPHY

Muriel Sarah Camberg was born and educated in Edinburgh, Scotland, the daughter of Bernard and Sarah Elizabeth Camberg. In 1937, Spark went to live in the British colony of Southern Rhodesia (now Zimbabwe). During her stay in Africa she married S. O. Spark but was divorced a short time later. The couple had one child, a son named Robin.

After spending several years in Africa, Spark returned to England in 1944. During the war years she wrote news articles for the political intelligence department of the British government. Afterward she held various posts in the publishing field, including a position as founder of the short-lived literary magazine *The Forum*. Spark began producing serious works of literary criticism and poetry in the early 1950's, and Hand and Flower Press published her first volume of poetry in 1952. At the same time she was involved in editing and researching critical and biographical works on several nineteenth-century literary figures, including William Wordsworth, Mary Wollstonecraft Shelley, and Emily Brontë.

Spark received considerable attention when her initial attempt at fiction, "The Seraph and the Zambesi," won top honors in a contest in 1951. She was encouraged to expand the scope of her fiction in 1954 when her publisher, Macmillan, persuaded her to write a full-length novel. The result was *The Comforters* (1957), which examines theological issues and reflects a religious struggle that she had undergone.

Although Spark maintained that her father was Jewish while her mother was Presbyterian, her son Robin and several residents of Edinburgh later insisted that both parents were Jewish. In any case, Spark practiced the Anglican faith until her interest in the writings of John Henry Newman, a nineteenth-century Catholic

theologian, convinced her to convert to Catholicism in 1954. Her personal search for spiritual belief would be reflected not only in *The Comforters* but also in many of her subsequent stories and novels.

Spark described her early life and the beginnings of her writing career in her autobiography *Curriculum Vitae* (1992), a volume that led to a bitter public feud with her son. She lived in Italy from the late 1960's until her death in Florence on April 13, 2006.

ANALYSIS

Muriel Spark was an adept storyteller with a narrative voice that was often distant or aloof. Her tales are psychologically compelling because she was reluctant to reveal all that her characters think and feel; in consequence, readers are forced to evaluate the stories, think about issues from a different perspective, and try to fill in the gaps. Critics regard Spark's novels as her strongest genre, but her short stories are also well constructed and intriguing. Published over more than four decades, her collections reprint many of the same stories, with new ones added to each new edition.

Muriel Spark (AP Photo/Jerry Bauer)

Spark's tales are generally set in England, British Africa, and mainland Europe. Her works reflect a sense of moral truth, which some critics view as the influence of her conversion to Catholicism in 1954. Her narrative is rarely wordy. The story line relies on the impressions and dialogue of the characters or narrator to convey the plot. Spark made frequent use of first-person narrative, but none of her voices "tells all." One of the distinguishing elements of her style was her penchant for leaving gaps that her readers must fill for themselves.

"THE SERAPH AND THE ZAMBESI"

Spark's first short story, "The Seraph and the Zambesi," won an award in a Christmas contest sponsored by *The Observer* in 1951. In characteristic Spark style, this story does not mince words but focuses on action and sparse dialogue. Set in Africa at Christmastime, it describes the events surrounding preparations for a Christmas pageant. Besides sweltering temperatures, curious natives, and preoccupied performers, the presentation is "hindered" by the presence of a heavenly Seraph, complete with six wings and a heat-producing glow. The writer of the nativity play is incensed when this real angel appears. He expresses rage rather than awe and destroys the stage in his attempts to banish the Seraph. Though Spark refuses to offer a moral at the close of "The Seraph and the Zambesi," the story resembles a parable, illustrating the egocentrism of human beings, especially "artists." The narrative also serves as a metaphor for the definition of genuine "art."

A related story dealing with art and creativity is entitled "The Playhouse Called Remarkable." Published several years after "The Seraph and the Zambesi," it features a character named Moon Biglow. Moon confesses to the narrator that he is really a native of the moon who migrated to Earth on the "Downfall of [the] Uprise" sometime in the distant past. His primary mission was to save Earth's residents from suffocating aesthetic boredom. It seems human beings had no form of recreation other than that of gathering in groups to chant "Tum tum ya" each evening. The moon migrants organize the "playhouse called Remarkable" to offer alternative entertainment and also to give earthlings a creative outlet for their imaginations.

"THE PAWNBROKER'S WIFE"

Often Spark's short fiction depicts varied types of female personalities. These stories, narrated in first person and set in Africa, tell little about the narrators themselves but focus on the manipulative power of the central female characters. The narrator of "The Pawnbroker's Wife" relates the story of Mrs. Jan Cloote, who is never identified by her first name. Her pawnbroker husband has disappeared, and Mrs. Cloote carries on the business herself but denies the slightly sordid reputation of her vocation by claiming that she is only the pawnbroker's wife. Thus, in her name and her speech, she tries to separate her actions from her image. Such "distancing" allows Mrs. Cloote freedom in refusing to accept responsibility for her conduct, no matter how cruel or petty, as she performs the duties of a pawnbroker. Ironically, she is far more successful at the business than her husband had been. She uses a show of politeness to remain corrupt without having to admit fault or make concessions. She breaks her promises to customers and sells the pawned items of her friends at the first opportunity. Mrs. Cloote's poor taste, grasping manipulation, and innocent pretense give her character an insidious cast. However, the narrator who reveals these facts refuses to pass judgment regarding Mrs. Cloote's morality. That matter is left to the reader.

"THE CURTAIN BLOWN BY THE BREEZE"

In a similar story, Sonia Van der Merwe, the female protagonist of "The Curtain Blown by the Breeze," gains power over her domain in the absence of her husband. Mr. Van der Merwe, who lives in the remote territory of Fort Beit, is imprisoned for fatally shooting a young native boy who was a peeping Tom. While her husband's conviction and imprisonment might have prompted a feeling of tragedy, the opposite occurs. Sonia finds that she has considerable financial resources at her disposal with her husband gone. Like Mrs. Cloote, Sonia takes charge, encouraged by the female British medical workers serving in the colony. She soon learns to use her feminine wiles to access power and control in Fort Beit. The male workers seek her attention, captivated by her "eccentric grandeur." Much to the chagrin of the British women who helped to create the "new Sonia," she gains influence over even government officials. However, just as the English nurse narrating the story can never truly decide what she wants, the same applies to Sonia. At the close of the story, Mr. Van der Merwe returns from prison unexpectedly. When he discovers his wife Sonia in the company of another man, he shoots them both. Thus, Sonia and her image are quickly eliminated. In her stories, Spark explores the roles of greedily ambitious females, the irony of their plight, and their cloaks of politeness.

Spark also deals with themes of childhood or adolescent memories in her short fiction. She may contrast the innocent but terrifyingly real fears of children with the more serious cruelty of adults, or she may reverse the irony and explore the cruelty of "devilish" children who are shielded by a guise of adult politeness. For example, "The Twins" describes two seemingly polite children who exercise some invisible but insidious control over their parents and other adults who enter their household.

"THE PORTOBELLO ROAD" AND "BANG-BANG YOU'RE DEAD"

"The Portobello Road" and "Bang-Bang You're Dead" juxtapose the childhood memories of two girls with their lives as "grown-ups." These stories explore the serious ramifications of situations in which childish conceptions or antagonisms are transferred into adulthood. Both stories are examples of Spark's ability to create unique narrative forms. "The Portobello Road" is narrated by Needle, a girl whose childhood nickname was given to her because she found a needle in a haystack. When the story opens, Needle is dead and her ghostly voice chronicles the events that led to her murder--when she becomes the "Needle" who is murdered and buried in a haystack by a childhood friend.

"Bang-Bang You're Dead" connects the present and the past in a complex narrative using a series of flashbacks. In the present, represented in the story's opening scene, Sybil's friends gather to view four reels of eighteen-year-old films from Sybil's past years spent in Africa. As the group views the "silent movies," the third-person narrative reveals Sybil's memories--not those seen by the spectators of the film but as Sybil remembers them. As each reel ends, Sybil's mental narrative is interrupted by the surface chatter of her friends, who are impressed by the appearance of the people and exotic scenes revealed in the film. At the conclusion of

the final reel, the reader finds, through Sybil's mental recollections, that two murders were committed shortly after the scenes were recorded on film. As the acquaintances agree to view the last reel again because it is their "favorite," Sybil remains stoically unmoved by the memories of the tragedy. Her indifference and objectivity regarding the memories of her deceased friends reveal a chilling aspect of her personality. Coldly intellectual and detached, Sybil remains unmoved by the recorded memories, even though she was largely responsible for the murders.

"THE GO-AWAY BIRD" AND "THE FIRST YEAR OF MY LIFE"

"The Go-Away Bird" is one of the longest of Spark's stories. It is also about a woman and murder. Daphne, the central female figure, is reared in a British colony in Africa. Caught between two cultures, those of the Dutch Afrikaaners and the English colonists, Daphne searches for her identity--for a world in which she can not only belong but also find safety. Set in Africa and England during World War II, "The Go-Away Bird" presents characters who reflect diverse backgrounds, personalities, motivations, and societies. Daphne's struggles and her relationship with the African Go-Away Bird illustrate the individual's difficulty in trying to fulfill his or her need for love and identity within diverse cultural and social structures.

At the opposite end of the spectrum, "The First Year of My Life" does not struggle with maturing in society but presents the first-person commentary of an infant, born during World War I. The adults who care for the baby treat the child as an "innocent infant," unaware of the newborn's ability to grasp the tragedy of war. Such diversity in narrative voice, subject, and style is a trademark of Spark. As a writer, she avoids classification and is unafraid of experimentation.

OPEN TO THE PUBLIC: NEW AND COLLECTED STORIES

Spark's collection *Open to the Public* reprints the contents of *The Stories of Muriel Spark* (1985) and adds ten new works. One of the earlier stories, "The Fathers' Daughters," centers on a thirty-year-old intellectual named Ben who pursues the daughters of famous writers in order to meet the authors themselves. When the young, beautiful Carmelita is unable to gain an audience for Ben with her father, a successful novelist, Ben abandons her to marry Dora, the forty-six-year-old daughter of an aged author whose popularity has faded. Spark creates an ironic situation in which the characters use one another for their own purposes. Ben wants to write essays based on another author's work, Dora's father craves an audience for his forgotten books, and Dora needs someone to provide income for their impoverished household.

The story "Open to the Public" is a sequel to "The Fathers' Daughters" and presents Ben and Dora five years later. Dora's father dies, but Ben's promotion of the father's works restores the family's fortune. However, the dead man's memory is not enough to sustain the relationship; the couple separate. Their plans to open the writer's house and personal documents to the public are abandoned when both Ben and Dora realize that museums "have no heart." In a humorous turn, they burn the father's archives instead. The story demonstrates the hopelessness of trying to maintain perpetual fame and the futility of attempting to build one's future on another's achievements.

In a story with similar elements, "The Executor," the protagonist Susan, who is a middle-aged spinster like Dora, must dispose of her uncle's literary estate. She sells his papers to a university foundation but retains an unfinished manuscript, which she hopes to complete and publish as her own. However, her plans are thwarted when her uncle's ghost returns to write warning messages to her. Thus Susan, like the women in "The Fathers' Daughters," must abandon her schemes of finding success vicariously and learn to build her own future.

The remaining additions in the *Open to the Public* collection are stylized and brief. Some plots turn on a single ironic twist, as in "The Girl I Left Behind Me," whose narrator finds her own body "lying strangled on the floor." Other stories feature the troubling imposition of the supernatural into the natural world. For example, a shady specter haunts the staff and patients of a medical clinic in "The Pearly Shadow." The specter finally disappears when doctors begin dispensing sedatives to his "stressed-out" victims. "Going Up and Coming Down" is a poetic vignette about a man and woman who ride to work in the same elevator every

day. Once the two actually meet, their speculations about each other disappear in the face of "plain real facts."

All the Stories

The last collection published during the author's lifetime, *All the Stories*, adds a brief foreword and four stories to *Open to the Public*. One of the latter, "The Young Man Who Discovered the Secret of Life," is a whimsical ghost story that few readers will find memorable. The others, however, are worthy additions to Spark's oeuvre, and while they do nothing to broaden her fictional world, they display her customary wit and economy of means.

As is the case in several of her works, "The Snobs" is narrated by a writer who sounds much like Spark herself. Visiting friends at a château that they have inherited in France, she is surprised when a couple she had known decades before are brought to the château by its new owner, who has discovered them hopelessly lost nearby. All too soon the couple reveal themselves as snobbish nuisances who believe that they should be invited to stay the night, and it is left to the narrator to invent a subterfuge--that the château's owner is merely the cook--in order to eject them from the premises.

"Christmas Fugue" describes a young woman's somewhat lackadaisical search for identity, first in England and then in Australia. Finding her new home and her new friends increasingly empty, she decides to fly back to England on Christmas Day. She enjoys a romantic afternoon aboard the plane with a pilot during a long layover in Thailand, and the two agree to live together. When she reaches England and finds herself surrounded by her family, however, her experience aboard the plane begins to seem--like so much else in her life--unreal. She realizes that she does not have the pilot's address, and when she calls the airline, she discovers that there was no pilot matching his description on the flight. Did the liaison really occur, or did she only imagine it? Spark leaves it for the reader to decide.

An exercise in nostalgia leavened with irony, "A Hundred and Eleven Years Without a Chauffeur" is the most substantial of the new stories and again features a writer as narrator. In this case, the writer is assisting her biographer (as Spark initially would assist her biographer Martin Stannard) in research but is puzzled to find that many of her photographs are missing. In the process, she recalls an old friend, an ersatz baron named Damian de Dogherty. Charming and attractive, he was an amateur genealogist and was particularly good at "discovering" noble ancestors for his many friends. Much later the narrator discovers that the late baron had stolen her photographs and altered them to look like portraits of his own aristocratic ancestors. Unexpectedly, the narrator admits to loving the doctored photographs, which she has run across in a bookshop and purchased. As readers learn from Stannard's *Muriel Spark: The Biography* (2010), de Dogherty was modeled on Spark's close friend "Baron" Brian de Breffny.

All the Stories showcases Spark's mastery of the short-story form. Her plots expose human foibles with an ironic, mysterious, or sarcastic tone. She was adept at illustrating the slightly macabre or deceitful nature of human actions. Her characters may be subtly malevolent or sinisterly civilized, but evil is punished and hypocrisy is exposed in her comic tales.

OTHER MAJOR WORKS

LONG FICTION: *The Comforters*, 1957; *Robinson*, 1958; *Memento Mori*, 1959; *The Bachelors*, 1960; *The Ballad of Peckham Rye*, 1960; *The Prime of Miss Jean Brodie*, 1961; *A Muriel Spark Trio*, 1962 (contains *The Comforters, Memento Mori*, and *The Ballad of Peckham Rye*); *The Girls of Slender Means*, 1963; *The Mandelbaum Gate*, 1965; *The Public Image*, 1968; *The Driver's Seat*, 1970; *Not to Disturb*, 1971; *The Hothouse by the East River*, 1973; *The Abbess of Crewe: A Modern Morality Tale*, 1974; *The Takeover*, 1976; *Territorial Rights*, 1979; *Loitering with Intent*, 1981; *The Only Problem*, 1984; *A Far Cry from Kensington*, 1988; *Symposium*, 1990; *The Novels of Muriel Spark*, 1995; *Reality and Dreams*, 1996; *Aiding and Abetting*, 2000; *The Finishing School*, 2004.

PLAY: *Doctors of Philosophy*, pr. 1962.

POETRY: *The Fanfarlo, and Other Verse*, 1952; *Collected Poems I*, 1967; *Going up to Sotheby's, and Other Poems*, 1982; *All the Poems of Muriel Spark*, 2004.

NONFICTION: *Child of Light: A Reassessment of Mary Wollstonecraft Shelley*, 1951 (revised as *Mary Shelley*,

1987); *Emily Brontë: Her Life and Work*, 1953 (with Derek Stanford); *John Masefield*, 1953; *Curriculum Vitae*, 1992 (autobiography); *The Essence of the Brontës: A Compilation with Essays*, 1993.

CHILDREN'S LITERATURE: *The Very Fine Clock*, 1968; *The Small Telephone*, 1993.

EDITED TEXTS: *Tribute to Wordsworth*, 1950 (with Derek Stanford); *My Best Mary: The Selected Letters of Mary Shelley*, 1953 (with Stanford); *The Brontë Letters*, 1954 (pb. in U.S. as *The Letters of the Bröntes: A Selection*, 1954); *Letters of John Henry Newman*, 1957 (with Stanford).

BIBLIOGRAPHY

Aly, Abdel-Moneim. "The Theme of Exile in the African Short Stories of Muriel Spark." *Scottish Studies Review* 2, no. 2 (Autumn, 2001): 94-104. Consideration of Spark's African stories in the light of her own experiences and subsequent career. Aly suggests that the stories represent a breakthrough that allowed Spark to develop more fully as a writer.

Gardiner, Michael, and Willy Maley, eds. *The Edinburgh Companion to Muriel Spark*. Edinburgh: Edinburgh University Press, 2010. Collection of original essays addressing the entire range of Spark's fiction and nonfiction and considering her alongside such masters as James Joyce and Vladimir Nabokov. Comprehensive primary and secondary bibliography.

Hynes, Joseph, ed. *Critical Essays on Muriel Spark*. New York: G. K. Hall, 1992. A comprehensive collection of reviews, essays, and excerpts from books on Spark's fiction by both detractors and admirers. Includes autobiographical essays and a survey and critique of past criticism.

Randisi, Jennifer Lynn. *On Her Way Rejoicing: The Fiction of Muriel Spark*. Washington, D.C.: Catholic University of America Press, 1991. Argues that Spark's vision is metaphysical, combining piety and satire, deception and anagogical truth. Discusses the tension between mysticism and satire in Spark's novels and stories.

Richmond, Velma B. *Muriel Spark*. New York: Frederick Ungar, 1984. Richmond explores Spark's writing in terms of content and emphasis. Spark's novels, poetry, and short stories are discussed in relation to their themes rather than their chronology. The closing chapter includes a discussion of Spark's "comic vision." Richmond includes biographical material along with a detailed chronology, a bibliography, and an extensive index.

Richmond, Velma B., Jeanne Devoize, and Pamela Valette. "Muriel Spark." *Journal of the Short Story in English* 41 (2003): 243-254. A 1989 interview in which Spark discusses her early life, identifies

writers who have influenced her, and names "The Portobello Road" and "The Executor" as being her best stories.

Stannard, Martin. *Muriel Spark: The Biography.* New York: Norton, 2010. Comprehensive, fair-minded biography written with Spark's cooperation over a period of fifteen years. Photographs, select primary and secondary bibliography.

Paula M. Miller
Updated by Grove Koger

SIR RICHARD STEELE

Born: Dublin, Ireland; March 12, 1672 (baptized)
Died: Carmarthen, Wales; September 1, 1729
Also known as: Isaac Bickerstaff

PRINCIPAL SHORT FICTION

The Tatler, 1709-1711 (with Joseph Addison)
The Spectator, 1711-1712, 1714 (with Addison; also known as *The Sir Roger de Coverly Papers*)
The Guardian, 1713 (with Addison)
The Englishman, 1713-1714, 1715
The Reader, 1714 (with Addison)
The Lover, 1714 (with Addison)
The Spectator, 1965 (Donald Bond, editor)

OTHER LITERARY FORMS

Sir Richard Steele is well known for his four plays, his prose work, *The Christian Hero* (1701), and his later periodicals. His plays are strongly didactic in purpose and tone, and this intention carries over to his short fiction published in his periodicals. Perceived as a reformer of the stage, Steele was named governor of the Drury Lane Theatre in order to improve the moral tone of the playhouse. His last play, *The Conscious Lovers* (pr. 1722; pb. 1723), is often identified as "sentimental" drama whose influence changed the course of the English theater.

ACHIEVEMENTS

Sir Richard Steele enjoyed a well-rounded and successful writing career. He was well known as "Mr. Spectator" and enjoyed a tremendous success with his daily. Nearly all fashionable London knew about *The Spectator*, and its influence on the taste, fashion, and opinions of the well-to-do is hard to discount. Steele was also widely influential when he began his dramatic career. His play *The Conscious Lovers* was touted as a new genre, the domestic comedy. It was controversial because it broke the dramatic rules of the day, but the controversy merely improved its popularity. Steele increased his influence on Londoners yet again when he became stage manager of Drury Lane, one of the leading theaters. He became responsible for deciding the very plays theatergoers would see in an era when the theater was the major source of entertainment. In 1714, Steele was knighted, having served the government's cause through his writing.

BIOGRAPHY

Educated at the Charterhouse and the University of Oxford, Sir Richard Steele lived in England and made his living first as a soldier and later as a writer and a politician. Although his plays and periodicals earned him some money, he always seemed to be in debt. He married Margaret Ford Stretch in 1705, but she died the following year. In 1707, he married Mary Scurlock, owner of a small estate in Wales, where he ultimately retired. He became the major propagandist for the

Whigs from 1710 to 1714, when they were the opposition, and after the Whigs regained power under King George I in 1714, he was knighted as a reward for his industriousness in the Whig cause. His later life was filled with financial difficulties, family problems, and political discouragement; after a stroke, he retired to Wales in 1724, where he died in 1729.

ANALYSIS

Sir Richard Steele's short fiction appears in *The Tatler*, *The Spectator*, and *The Guardian*, as well as in some shorter periodicals. There is a double level of fiction in all three of these periodicals: The first is the fictional creation of the narrator and his family or club, with all the telling details that make Steele's narrators interesting; the second is the storytelling of the narrator himself. The narrator of *The Tatler* is Isaac Bickerstaff, a name made popular by Jonathan Swift in his attack on the astrologer John Partridge. Bickerstaff is an elderly, benevolent astrologer who enjoys relating humorous stories about his family and friends while good-naturedly poking fun at himself. In contrast, *The Spectator* has as its narrator Mr. Spectator, the most taciturn member of the Spectator Club and the undisputed master observer of human nature and human foibles. Because of his careful observation of those around him, Mr. Spectator is also an excellent storyteller. Finally, the narrator of *The Guardian* is Nestor Ironside, the feisty protector of the Lizard family and adviser to the British nation. To a large degree, *The Tatler* and *The Spectator* are the mutual creation of Steele and his friend and schoolfellow Joseph Addison, although Steele alone signed his name to the final issue of both periodicals; in contrast, *The Guardian* is largely Steele's and is generally recognized as inferior to the two earlier works. Steele's contribution to these works is a lively imagination and a facile wit; he promotes benevolence as the proper response to the sorrows and sufferings of one's fellow humans, and he satirizes slavish adherence to fashion. Plain-dealing honesty and kindly benevolence are Steele's major moral themes in both *The Tatler* and *The Spectator*; Steele's didactic purpose is always foremost, in both his fiction and his plays.

Sir Richard Steele (Library of Congress)

THE TATLER

In *The Tatler*, Isaac Bickerstaff enjoys teaching the correct way to treat one's spouse by describing his sister's marital problems. Poor Jenny Distaff has more than her share of difficulties to overcome with her spouse, Tranquillus; Isaac's bachelor wisdom helps them both to achieve happiness. The essential problem is Jenny's desire for domination over her husband, and Isaac teaches her to accept her husband's superior position in marriage. At first glance, it appears that Steele is preaching a very reactionary attitude toward marriage; however, this is not quite the case. Steele believes that women are people, not objects, and that they must be treated as thinking human beings by their husbands. Such an attitude was not universally held by men in the early eighteenth century, and although Steele's attitude may seem conservative by modern standards, he deserves to be credited with some advancement of women's situation in his own century. For example, he decries the double standard of sexual morality and the marriage contract based solely on financial considerations. Women were losers in both situations, and

Steele saw and spoke against what he considered serious social evils. In *The Tatler*, Steele is master of the dramatic scene, nowhere better exemplified than in the reconciliation between Jenny and Tranquillus through the efforts of Isaac Bickerstaff.

THE SPECTATOR

It is reasonable to assert that Steele was fascinated by all the various pleasures and problems in domestic relationships. Primary are courtship, marriage, and married life, but the parent-child relationship was also important to Steele. Mr. Spectator enjoys almost nothing more than a didactic story about the improvement of marital relations, parent-child relations, or a study of the potential for happiness in an impending marriage. *The Spectator* proved the ideal vehicle for these short, succinct stories, providing a different story daily and a need for constant reinforcement of central themes. One of Steele's often reinforced themes is the difficulty caused by parents who insist on choosing a spouse for their child. In *The Spectator* 533, in a letter appealing to Mr. Spectator's sense of justice, a male correspondent describes his unhappy situation as his elderly family insist that they choose their son's wife. This twenty-two-year-old is pleading for assistance: "You have often given us very excellent Discourses against that unnatural Custom of Parents, in forcing their Children to marry contrary to their Inclinations." The same theme in a different setting appears in *The Spectator* 220, in a letter from a twenty-one-year-old woman to an elderly suitor who is appealing to her father and not to her. She complains stridently of the injustice foisted upon her by a father and a suitor who believe that she must accept the suitor because her father does. Steele lets the letter communicate its message without additional comment, but it is clear that he wholly supports the unjustly treated young woman.

Steele enjoyed using the letter device as a mode of developing his short fictions; he used letters, for example, much more often than did Addison. Letters helped him to develop various perspectives, which are more effectively presented through various points of view than through Steele's voice alone. A parallel example might be the epistolary format in Samuel Richardson's *Clarissa: Or, The History of a Young Lady* (1747-1748), where four perspectives are well developed through letters. Steele is interested in brevity as well as perspective, and yet his need as an author to create perspectives other than his own is similar to Richardson's. Steele presents another of his favorite themes in a letter to Mr. Spectator from an admirer in *The Spectator* 268, wherein the correspondent laments the tragedy of so many people marrying for the wrong reasons. What are these wrong reasons? They are: money, position, power. What then are proposed as the right reasons to marry? They are: virtue, wisdom, a person's good qualities, good humor, similar manners and attitudes. In this letter--and throughout Steele's writings--marriage is spoken of reverently, as the state which may "give us the compleatest Happiness this Life is capable of." For this to happen, however, Steele warns repeatedly through precept and example, men and women must be free to choose their spouses on the basis of lasting and endearing qualities.

One of the most famous stories in *The Spectator*, "Inkle and Yarico," depicts the suffering and misery of a less than circumspect love. In *The Spectator* 11, Steele describes the selfish and mean treatment by Mr. Thomas Inkle of a Native American maiden who trusted him completely. Inkle, having landed with a group of Englishmen in America, was attacked by Native Americans and retreated into the woods, where he was found and protected by Yarico, the Native American maid. They fell in love, he made great promises of wealth and comfort, and when the ship came, Yarico left her people to go with Inkle. Shortly thereafter and safe once again with his own people, Inkle sold Yarico to a Barbadian merchant as a slave. The story is a warning to both sexes, but especially to women, to be circumspect in choosing a mate. Although the potential for great happiness does exist in marriage, numerous traps for the unwary, Steele warns, may also make marriage a source of great unhappiness.

On another narrative level, two members of Mr. Spectator's club, Sir Roger de Coverley and Sir Andrew Freeport, provide a continuing story line and numerous little anecdotes. Sir Roger is an old-fashioned country squire, while Sir Andrew is a vigorous, intelligent merchant. Whereas loveable Sir Roger's ideas are as out of date as his clothing, Sir Andrew's clear concepts on the role of trade in England's future are of the utmost importance. Usually these two club members get along well, but when an argument develops on the relative value of merchants to the British nation, Sir Andrew proves his superiority. Many of these little stories subtly identify the Tories with Sir Roger and the Whigs with Sir Andrew. Both Steele and Addison were wholeheartedly committed Whigs, and despite their assurances that *The Spectator* was nonpolitical, their political beliefs inevitably surfaced. Their propaganda is delightfully subtle, as it slowly proves Sir Roger's ineffectiveness and Sir Andrew's undeniable capability.

THE GUARDIAN

As one might suppose, Steele remained consistent in his attitudes on marriage, parent-child relationships, and politics as he discontinued writing for *The Spectator* in order to begin *The Guardian*. Although in some places the tone does become more stern and foreboding, there are still delightful stories in *The Guardian* that promote the values of charity, benevolence, and love rather than authority, and unselfishness rather than self-centeredness. For example, Nestor Ironside himself, although he would like to appear stern and crusty, exemplifies in his own story an overriding concern with the joys and sufferings of those about him. Nestor accepts the responsibility of guiding the Lizard family upon the death of his good friend, Sir Marmaduke Lizard. The lessons he inculcates in the family are based on love of neighbor rather than of self; he leads the daughters away from vanity and pride, while he admonishes the eldest son against keeping a mistress.

Steele's approach to moral issues remained essentially fixed from 1701, the date of his lengthy explication of moral values in his prose tract *The Christian Hero*. Steele argued there that reason is incapable of guiding the passions to virtue, that only religion is capable of aiding reason sufficiently to guide the passions effectively, and that once so directed the passions may become an additional impetus to virtue. Steele posits in *The Christian Hero* a fundamentally irrational view of human nature. For this reason, perhaps, he teaches morality in his periodicals not by precept and argument but by example and story.

The influence of *The Tatler* and *The Spectator*, and to a lesser degree *The Guardian*, was extraordinary. When one realizes that each periodical lasted less than two years, the fact of such widespread influence is all the more remarkable. In both England and America, *The Spectator* was revered in many families as a repository of moral teaching, as well as an entertaining book, and one may imagine that there were many, such as Benjamin Franklin, who developed a polished writing style through imitation of *The Spectator*. Although some topics contemporary to the eighteenth century may appear of little interest to the modern reader, many of the stories still prove enjoyable.

OTHER MAJOR WORKS

PLAYS: *The Funeral: Or, Grief-à-la-Mode*, pr. 1701, pb. 1702; *The Lying Lover: Or, The Ladies' Friendship*, pr. 1703, pb. 1704 (adaptation of Pierre Corneille's play *Le Menteur*); *The Tender Husband: Or, The Accomplished Fools*, pr., pb. 1705 (adaptation of Molière's play *Le Sicilien*); *The Conscious Lovers*, pr. 1722, pb. 1723 (adaptation of Terence's play *Andria*); *The Plays of Richard Steele*, pb. 1971 (Shirley Strum Kenny, editor).

POETRY: *The Procession*, 1695; *Prologue to the University of Oxford*, 1706; *Epilogue to the Town*, 1721; *The Occasional Verse of Richard Steele*, 1952 (Rae Blanchard, editor).

NONFICTION: *The Christian Hero*, 1701; *The Importance of Dunkirk Considered*, 1713; *The Englishman*, 1713-1714, 1715 (periodical essays);*The Plebieian*, 1718; *The Theatre*, 1720 (later as *Richard Steele's "The Theatre,"* 1920, 1962; John Loftis, editor); *The Correspondence of Richard Steele*, 1941 (Rae Blanchard, editor); *Tracts and Pamphlets by Richard Steele*, 1944 (Blanchard, editor).

BIBLIOGRAPHY

Calhoun, Wineton. *Captain Steele: The Early Career*. Baltimore: Johns Hopkins University Press, 1964. Primarily a biographical study, this book discusses *The Tatler* and *The Spectator* but focuses primarily on the circumstances surrounding them rather than on actual analysis.

Connely, Willard. *Sir Richard Steele*. New York: Charles Scribner's Sons, 1934. The standard biography of Steele. While it is old, it is relatively useful. The chapters on *The Tatler* and *The Spectator* are helpful, including information on the business aspects of producing the two periodicals.

Cowan, Brian. "The Curious Mr. Spectator." *Media History* 14, no. 3 (December, 2008): 275-292. Examines Steele and Joseph Addison's aesthetic ideas in relation to the "virtuoso culture" of their era. Argues that the two sought to reform and redefine virtuoso culture, promoting a neoclassical aesthetic "that rejected and ridiculed a supposedly indiscriminate virtuoso aesthetic of curiosity."

Dammers, Richard H. *Richard Steele*. Boston: Twayne, 1982. A good overview of Steele's work. Discusses his essays and plays and includes two excellent chapters on his short fiction in *The Tatler* and *The Spectator*. Contains a chronology and a select bibliography.

Ketcham, Michael G. *Transparent Designs: Reading, Performance, and Form in "The Spectator" Papers*. Athens: University of Georgia Press, 1985. Provides a detailed analysis of *The Spectator* by examining its readers; its treatment of time, family, and language; and its social and historical context.

Knight, Charles A. *Joseph Addison and Richard Steele: A Reference Guide, 1730-1991*. New York: G. K. Hall, 1994. A comprehensive listing of the works of both writers, as well as the numerous studies of the two undertaken from 1730 through 1991.

_____. *A Political Biography of Richard Steele*. Brookfield, Vt.: Pickering and Chatto, 2009. Focuses on Steele's checkered political career, including his stint as a leading Whig propagandist, his expulsion from Parliament for "seditious libel" during the reign of Queen Anne, and his return to Parliament during the reign of George I.

_____. "The Spectator's Moral Economy." *Modern Philology* 91 (November, 1993): 161-179. Examines principles of moral economy presented by Addison and Steele in *The Spectator* to control dreams of endless gains. Argues that Addison and Steele found in the economic order a secular basis for moral behavior that emphasized the common good over individual gain. Suggests that they connected commercial values to values of politeness and restraint.

Loftis, John. *Steele at Drury Lane*. Berkeley: University of California Press, 1952. Details Steele's theatrical career and provides a good understanding of the eighteenth century stage and business management. Includes a useful appendix.

McCrea, Brian. *Addison and Steele Are Dead: The English Department, Its Canon, and the Professionalization of Literary Criticism*. Newark: University of Delaware Press, 1990. Examines the legacy of Steele and Addison.

Pollock, Anthony. "Formalist Cultural Criticism and the Post-Restoration Periodical." *Philological Quarterly* 86, no. 3 (Summer, 2007): 227-250. Analyzes the formalist style of Addison and Steele's periodicals. Argues that these journals, which had a strong sense of political and cultural inquiry, are being neglected by literary and rhetorical critics.

Rounce, Adam. "Fame and Failure in *The Spectator*." *Media History* 14, no. 3 (December, 2008): 309-322. Examines the contradictions between *The Spectator*'s content and its ideas in order to understand the journal's appeal and the nature of its cultural and historical politics. Among these contradictions are the manner in which Sir Roger de Coverley is "both venerated for representing a nostalgic form of pastoral, and gently satirized as a symbol of a way of life that is necessarily in the past."

Richard H. Dammers
Updated by Kimberley L. Jacobs

ROBERT LOUIS STEVENSON

Born: Edinburgh, Scotland; November 13, 1850
Died: Vailima, near Apia, Samoa; December 3, 1894

PRINCIPAL SHORT FICTION

The New Arabian Nights, 1882
More New Arabian Nights, 1885
The Merry Men, and Other Tales and Fables, 1887
Island Nights' Entertainments, 1893

OTHER LITERARY FORMS

Despite poor health, Robert Louis Stevenson was a prolific writer, not only of juvenile fiction but also of poetry, plays, and essays. He is best known for adventure romances such as *Treasure Island* (1881-1882, serial; 1883, book), *Kidnapped: Being memoirs of the Adventures of David Balfour in the Year 1751* (1886), and the horror-suspense novel *The Strange Case of Dr. Jekyll and Mr. Hyde* (1886), works that appeal principally to youthful readers. A habitual voyager, Stevenson also wrote travelogues and sketches recounting his personal experiences. His children's poems, published in *A Child's Garden of Verses* (1885), remain perennial favorites, as do several of his beautiful family prayers.

ACHIEVEMENTS

For clarity and suspense, Robert Louis Stevenson is a rarely equaled raconteur. He reveals his mastery of narrative in his economical presentation of incident and atmosphere. Despite his sparse, concise style, many of his tales are notable for dealing with complex moral ambiguities and their diagnoses. Although influenced by a host of romantic writers, including Charles Lamb, William Hazlitt, William Wordsworth, and Nathaniel Hawthorne, Stevenson's theories of prose fiction were most directly provoked by Henry James's *The Art of Fiction* (1884). Stevenson placed himself in literary opposition to James and the "statics of

character," favoring instead an action-fiction whose clear antecedents are allegory, fable, and romance. His tales of adventure and intrigue, outdoor life and old-time romance, avidly read by children and young adults, have had a continuous and incalculable influence since their first publication in the 1880's.

BIOGRAPHY

The only child of a prosperous civil engineer and his wife, Robert Louis Balfour Stevenson was a sickly youth, causing his formal education to be haphazard. He reacted early against his parents' orthodox Presbyterianism, donning the mask of a liberated bohemian who abhorred the hypocrisies of bourgeois respectability. As a compromise with his father, Stevenson did study law at Edinburgh University in lieu of the traditional family vocation of lighthouse engineer. In 1873, however, he suffered a severe respiratory illness, and although he completed his studies and was admitted to the Scottish bar in July, 1875, he never practiced. In May, 1880, Stevenson married Fanny Van de Grift Osbourne, a divorcée from San Francisco and ten years his senior. The new couple spent most of the next decade in health resorts for Stevenson's tuberculosis: Davos in the Swiss Alps, Hyéres on the French Riviera, and Bournemouth in England. After his father's death, Stevenson felt able to go farther from Scotland, and so he went to Saranac Lake in the Adirondack Mountains of New York, where treatment arrested his disease. In June, 1888, Stevenson, his wife, mother, and stepson sailed for the South Seas. During the next eighteen months they saw the Marquesas, Tahiti, Australia, the Gilberts, Hawaii, and Samoa. In late 1889, Stevenson decided to settle and bought "Vailima," three miles from the town of Apia, Upolu, Samoa, and his home until his death. His vigorous crusading there against the white exploitation of native Samoans almost led to expulsion by both German and English authorities. Stevenson's tuberculosis remained quiescent, but he suddenly died of a cerebral hemorrhage on December 3, 1894, while working on the novel *Weir of Hermiston* (1896), a fragment that many modern readers think to be his best writing. Known to the natives as "Tusitala," the Storyteller, Stevenson was buried on the summit of Mount Vaea.

ANALYSIS

Robert Louis Stevenson has long been relegated to either the nursery or the juvenile section in most libraries, and his mixture of romance, horror, and allegory seems jejune. In a century where narrative and well-ordered structure have become the facile tools of Harlequin paperbacks and irrelevant to high-quality "literature," Stevenson's achievement goes quietly unnoticed. To confine this technique of "Tusitala" solely to nursery and supermarket, however, is to confuse Stevenson's talents with his present audience.

Stevenson's crucial problem is the basic one of joining form to idea, made more difficult because he was not only an excellent romancer but also a persuasive essayist. In Stevenson, however, these two talents seem to be of different roots, and their combination was for him a lifelong work. The aim of his narratives becomes not only to tell a good story, constructing something of interest, but also to ensure that all the materials of that story (such as structure, atmosphere, and character motivation) contribute to a clear thematic concern. Often Stevenson's fictional talents alone cannot accomplish this for him, and this accounts--depending in each instance on whether he drops his theme or attempts to push it through--for both the "pulp" feel of some stories and the "directed" feel of others.

"A LODGING FOR THE NIGHT"

Appearing in the *Cornhill Magazine* for May, 1874, an essay on Victor Hugo was Stevenson's very first publication. The short stories he began writing soon after demonstrate a strong tendency to lapse into the more familiar expository techniques either as a solution to fictional problems or merely to bolster a sagging theme. A blatant example of this stylistic ambiguity is the early story "A Lodging for the Night."

Robert Louis Stevenson (Library of Congress)

The atmosphere of the first part of the story is deftly handled. It is winter, and its buffets upon the poor are reemphasized in every descriptive detail. Paris is "sheeted up" like a body ready for burial. The only light is from a tiny shack "backed up against the cemetery wall." Inside, "dark, little, and lean, with hollow cheeks and thin black locks," the medieval poet François Villon composes "The Ballade of Roast Fish" while Guy Tabard, one of his cronies, sputters admiringly over his shoulder. Straddling before the fire is a portly, purple-veined Picardy monk, Dom Nicolas. Also in the small room are two more villains, Montigny and Thevenin Pensete, playing "a game of chance." Villon cracks a few pleasantries, quite literally gallows humor, and begins to read aloud his new poem. Suddenly, between the two gamesters:

> The round was complete, and Thevenin was just opening his mouth to claim another victory, when Montigny leaped up, swift as an adder, and stabbed him to the heart. The blow took effect before he had time to utter a cry, before he had time to move. A tremor or two convulsed his frame; his hands opened

and shut, his heels rattled on the floor; then his head rolled backward over one shoulder with the eyes wide open; and Thevenin Pensete's spirit had returned to Him who made it.

Tabard begins praying in Latin, Villon breaks into hysterics, Montigny recovers "his composure first" and picks the dead man's pockets. Naturally, they must all leave the scene of the murder to escape implication, and Villon departs first.

Outside, in the bitter cold, two things preoccupy the poet as he walks: the gallows and "the look of the dead man with his bald head and garland of red curls," as neat a symbol as could be for the fiery pit of hell where Villon eventually expects to find himself. Theme has been handled well, Stevenson's fiction giving readers the feeling of a single man thrown by existence into infernal and unfavorable circumstances, being pursued by elements beyond his control, the gallows and Death, survival itself weaving a noose for him with his own trail in the snow, irrevocably connecting him to "the house by the cemetery of St. John." The plot is clear and the situation has captured the reader's interest. On this cold and windy night, after many rebuffs, Villon finally finds food and shelter with a "refined," "muscular and spare," "resonant, courteous," "honorable rather than intelligent, strong, simple, and righteous" old knight.

Here, the structure of "A Lodging for the Night" abruptly breaks down from fiction, from atmospheric detail, plot development, and character enlargement, to debate. What Stevenson implied in the first part of his story, he reasserts here in expository dialogue, apparently losing faith in his fictional abilities as he resorts back to the directness of the essay.

Villon takes the side of duty to one's own survival; he is the first modern skeptic, the prophet of expediency. In contrast, the knight stands for honor, *bonne noblesse*, with allegiance always to something greater than himself. The moral code of the criminal is pitted against the hypocrisy of the bourgeoisie. One's chances in life are determined by birth and social standing, says Villon. There is always the chance for change, implores the knight. In comparison to Stevenson's carefully built atmosphere and plot, this expository "solution" to his story is extremely crude.

"MARKHEIM"

"Markheim," a ghost story that deals with a disturbing problem of conscience, also contains a dialogue in its latter half. This dialogue, however, is a just continuation of the previous action. Different from "crawlers" such as "The Body-Snatcher," "Markheim" reinforces horror with moral investigation. Initial atmospherics contribute directly to Stevenson's pursuit of his thematic concern, and the later debate with the "visitant" becomes an entirely fitting expression for Markheim's own madness.

An allegory of the awakening conscience, "Markheim" also has the limits of allegory, one of which is meaning. For readers to understand, or find meaning in, an allegory, characters (or actors) must be clearly identified. In "Markheim" this presents major difficulties. Not only is an exact identity (or role) for the visitant finally in doubt, but also the identity of the dealer is unclear. It can be said that he usually buys from Markheim, not sells to him, but exactly what the dealer buys or sells is a good question. Whatever, on this particular occasion (Christmas Day), Markheim will have to pay the dealer extra "for a kind of manner that I remark in you today very strongly."

Amid the "ticking of many clocks among the curious lumber" of the dealer's shop, a strange pantomime ensues. Markheim says he needs a present for a lady and the dealer shows him a hand mirror. Markheim grows angry:

"A glass," he said hoarsely, and then paused, and repeated it more clearly. "A glass? For Christmas? Surely not!"

"And why not?" cried the dealer. "Why not a glass?"

Markheim was looking upon him with an indefinable expression. "You ask me why not?" he said. "Why, look here--look at it--look at yourself! Do you like to see it? No! nor I--nor any man."

After damning the mirror as the "reminder of years, and sins, and follies--this hand-conscience," Markheim asks the dealer to tell something of himself, his secret life. The dealer puts Markheim off with a chuckle, but as he turns around for something more to show, Markheim lunges at him, stabbing him with a "long, skewerlike dagger." The dealer struggles "like a hen" and then dies. The murder seems completely gratuitous until Markheim remembers that he had come to rob the shop: "To have done the deed and yet not to reap the profit would be too abhorrent a failure."

Time, "which had closed for the victim," now becomes "instant and momenteous for the slayer." Like Villon, Markheim feels pursued by Death, haunted by "the dock, the prison, the gallows, and the black coffin." The blood at his feet begins "to find eloquent voices." The dead dealer extracts his extra payment, becoming the enemy who would "lift up a cry that would ring over England, and fill the world with the echoes of pursuit." Talking to himself, Markheim denies that this evil murder indicates an equally evil nature, but his guilt troubles him. Not only is Markheim pursued by Death, but also he is pursued by Life. He sees his own face "repeated and repeated, as it were an army of spies"; his own eyes meet and detect him. Although alone, he feels the inexplicable consciousness of another presence:

> Ay, surely; to every room and corner of the house his imagination followed it; and now it was a faceless thing, and yet had eyes to see with; and again it was a shadow of himself; and yet again beheld the image of the dead dealer, reinspired with cunning and hatred.

Eventually, Markheim must project an imaginary double, a doppelgänger or exteriorized voice with which to debate his troubles. Here, action passes from the stylized antique shop of the murdered to the frenzied mind of the murderer. The visitant, or double, is a product of this mind. Mad and guilty as Markheim appears to be, his double emerges as a calm-sounding sanity who will reason with him to commit further evil. Thus, the mysterious personification of drives buried deep within Markheim's psyche exteriorizes evil as an alter ego and allows Markheim the chance to act against it, against the evil in his own nature. Stevenson's sane, expository technique of debate erects a perfect foil for Markheim's true madness.

In the end, although Markheim thinks himself victorious over what seems the devil, it is actually this exteriorized aspect of Markheim's unknown self that conquers, tricking him into willing surrender and then revealing itself as a kind of redemptive angel:

> The feature of the visitor began to undergo a wonderful and lovely change; they brightened and softened with a tender triumph; and, even as they brightened, faded and dislimned. But Markheim did not pause to watch or understand the transformation.

Material and intention are artistically intertwined in "Markheim," but the moral ambiguities of Stevenson's theme remain complex, prompting various questions: Is Markheim's martyrdom a victory over evil or merely a personal cessation from action? Set on Christmas Day, with its obvious reversal of that setting's usual significance, is "Markheim" a portrayal of Christian resignation as a purely negative force, a justification for suicide, or as the only modern solution against evil? What is the true nature and identity of the visitant? Finally, can the visitant have an identity apart from Markheim's own? Even answers to these questions, like Markheim's final surrender, offer only partial consolation to the reader of this strange and complex story of psychological sickness.

"THE BEACH OF FALESÁ"

With Stevenson's improved health and his move to the South Seas, a new type of story began to emerge, a kind of exotic realism to which the author brought his mature talents. "The Bottle Imp," for example, juxtaposes the occult of an old German fairy tale (interestingly enough, acquired by Stevenson through Sir Percy Shelley, the poet's son) with factual details about San Francisco, Honolulu, and Papeete. These settings, however, seem used more for convenience than out of necessity.

The long story "The Beach of Falesá" fulfills Stevenson's promise and gives evidence of his whole talents as a writer of short fiction. Similar to Joseph Conrad's *Heart of Darkness* (1899, serial; 1902, book), Stevenson's story deals with a person's ability or inability to remain decent and law-abiding when the external restraints of civilization have been removed. Action follows simply and naturally a line laid down by atmosphere. Stevenson himself called it "the first realistic South Sea story," while Henry James wrote in a letter the year before Stevenson's death, "The art of 'The Beach of Falesá' seems to me an art brought to a perfection and I delight in the observed truth, the modesty of nature, of the narrator."

In this adventure of wills between two traders on a tiny island, Stevenson is able to unify fitting W. Somerset Maugham would further perfect this technique using the same exotic South Sea setting.

Stevenson's "The Beach of Falesá," along with the incomplete *Weir of Hermiston* and perhaps the first part of *The Master of Ballantrae* (1889), rests as his best work, the final integration of the divergent roots of his talents. If he had lived longer than forty-four years, "Tusitala" might have become one of the great English prose writers. As history stands, however, Stevenson's small achievement of clear narrative, his victory of joining form to idea, remains of unforgettable importance to students and practitioners of the short-story genre.

OTHER MAJOR WORKS

LONG FICTION: *Treasure Island*, 1881-1882 (serial), 1883 (book); *Prince Otto*, 1885; *Kidnapped: Being Memoirs of the Adventures of David Balfour in the Year 1751*, 1886; *The Strange Case of Dr. Jekyll and Mr. Hyde*, 1886; *The Black Arrow: A Tale of the Two Roses*, 1888; *The Master of Ballantrae*, 1889; *The Wrong Box*, 1889; *The Wrecker*, 1892 (with Lloyd Osbourne); *Catriona*, 1893; *The Ebb-Tide*, 1894 (with Osbourne); *Weir of Hermiston*, 1896 (unfinished); *St. Ives*, 1897 (completed by Arthur Quiller-Couch).

PLAYS: *Deacon Brodie*, pb. 1880 (with William Ernest Henley); *Admiral Guinea*, pb. 1884 (with Henley); *Beau Austin*, pb. 1884 (with Henley); *Macaire*, pb. 1885 (with Henley); *The Hanging Judge*, pb. 1887 (with Fanny Van de Grift Stevenson).

POETRY: *Moral Emblems*, 1882; *A Child's Garden of Verses*, 1885; *Underwoods*, 1887; *Ballads*, 1890; *Songs of Travel, and Other Verses*, 1896.

NONFICTION: *An Inland Voyage*, 1878; *Edinburgh: Picturesque Notes*, 1878; *Travels with a Donkey in the Cévennes*, 1879; *Virginibus Puerisque*, 1881; *Familiar Studies of Men and Books*, 1882; *The Silverado*

Squatters: Sketches from a Californian Mountain, 1883; *Memories and Portraits*, 1887; *The South Seas: A Record of Three Cruises*, 1890; *A Footnote to History*, 1892; *Across the Plains*, 1892; *Amateur Emigrant*, 1895; *Vailima Letters*, 1895; *In the South Seas*, 1896; *The Letters of Robert Louis Stevenson to His Family and Friends*, 1899 (2 volumes), 1911 (4 volumes); *The Lantern-Bearers, and Other Essays*, 1988; *The Letters of Robert Louis Stevenson*, 1994-1995 (8 volumes); *R. L. Stevenson on Fiction: An Anthology of Literary and Critical Essays*, 1999 (Glenda Norquay, editor).

BIBLIOGRAPHY

Ambrosini, Richard, and Richard Dury, eds. *Robert Louis Stevenson: Writer of Boundaries*. Madison: University of Wisconsin Press, 2006. A collection of essays that seek to establish Stevenson's reputation as a significant writer. Some of the essays analyze his short fiction, and the pages of these discussions can be found in the comprehensive index.

Bell, Ian. *Dreams of Exile: Robert Louis Stevenson: A Biography*. New York: Henry Holt, 1992. Bell, a journalist rather than an academic, writes evocatively of Stevenson the dreamer and exile. His study of Stevenson's brief but dramatic life does a fine job of evoking the man and the places he inhabited. It is less accomplished in its approach to the work.

Bevan, Bryan. "The Versatility of Robert Louis Stevenson." *Contemporary Review* 264 (June, 1994): 316-319. A general discussion of Stevenson's work, focusing on his versatility in a number of genres. Discusses early influences on his writing and comments on his essays and his fiction.

Calder, Jenni. *Robert Louis Stevenson: A Life Study*. New York: Oxford University Press, 1980. This excellent study is richly documented with Stevenson's letters. Less a biography than a study of the writer's mind, it focuses on the personal values and attitudes informing Stevenson's work.

Chesterton, G. K. *Robert Louis Stevenson*. London: Hodder & Stoughton, 1927. An older but distinguished critical study of Stevenson that is still highly regarded for its insights, as well as for its wit and lucidity.

Daiches, David. *Robert Louis Stevenson.* Norwalk, Conn.: New Directions, 1947. Along with J. C. Furnas, Daiches is credited with pioneering a positive reappraisal of Stevenson. His study is urbane and penetrating in the tradition of G. K. Chesterton.

Furnas, J. C. *Voyage to Windward.* New York: William Sloane, 1951. Furnas, who briefly lived in Stevenson's home in Samoa, traced the author's steps backward to his native Scotland. This work is a popular and sympathetic biography documented with unpublished letters. It contains an elaborate works-consulted bibliography.

Goh, Robbie B. "Stevenson's Financial Gothic: Money, Commerce, Language, and the Horror of Modernity in 'The Isle of Voices.'" *Gothic Studies* 10, no. 2 (November, 2008): 51-66. Analyzes Stevenson's short story "The Isle of Voices" in the context of his comments on money. Argues that this story is one of the few fictional texts which uses certain characteristics of money to create a "financial Gothic narrative."

Harman, Claire. *Myself and the Other Fellow: A Life of Robert Louis Stevenson.* New York: HarperCollins Publishers, 2005. A comprehensive biography, covering Stevenson's early family life, his writing and travels, and his curious but successful marriage. Includes bibliography and index.

Hayes, Timothy S. "Colonialism in R. L. Stevenson's South Seas Fiction: 'Child's Play' in the Pacific." *English Literature in Transition, 1880-1920* 52, no. 2 (2009): 160-181. Discusses Stevenson's essay "Child's Play," in which describes the differences between stories told by children and those told by adults. Uses this essay to analyze two subsequent works of fiction: his story "The Beach of Falesá" and his novel *The Ebb-Tide.*

McLaughlin, Kevin. "The Financial Imp: Ethics and Finance in Nineteenth-Century Fiction." *Novel* 29 (Winter, 1996): 165-183. Examines the key issue of finance that can be found at the center of some works of British fiction during this time, focusing particularly on Stevenson's treatment of these issues in his short story "The Bottle Imp."

McLynn, Frank. *Robert Louis Stevenson: A Biography.* New York: Random House, 1995. Argues that Stevenson's wife was a negative influence on his life and work. Discusses Stevenson's struggle with agnosticism and his conflicted attitude toward women. Tries to counter the critical view of Stevenson as an unimportant writer of boys' literature by discussing the moral seriousness of his work.

Meyer, Michael. "Robert Louis Stevenson: 'The Bottle Imp,' 'The Beach of Falesá,' and 'Markheim.'" In *A Companion to the British and Irish Short Story*, edited by Cheryl Alexander Malcolm and David Malcolm. Malden, Mass.: Wiley-Blackwell, 2008. An explication of the three stories, which helps situate them in the larger context of the British short story.

Orel, Harold. "Robert Louis Stevenson: Many Problems, Some Successes." In *The Victorian Short Story: Development and Triumph of a Literary Genre.* 1986. Reprint. New York: Cambridge University Press, 2010. Analyzes Stevenson's short fiction, placing it in the context of the growing popularity of the short story during the Victorian era.

Reid, Julia. *Robert Louis Stevenson, Science, and the Fin de Siècle.* New York: Palgrave Macmillan, 2006. Examines the role of science, especially the theory of evolution, in Stevenson's works and in the fin-de-siècle culture that produced them. Some of the works discussed are "The Beach of Falesá" and other short stories.

Saposnik, Irving S. *Robert Louis Stevenson.* New York: Twayne, 1974. A useful critical survey of Stevenson's major works and the best starting point for serious study of Stevenson's fiction. Supplemented by a helpful annotated bibliography.

Kenneth Funsten
Updated by John W. Fiero

GRAHAM SWIFT

Born: London, England; May 4, 1949

PRINCIPAL SHORT FICTION

Learning to Swim, and Other Stories, 1982

OTHER LITERARY FORMS

Graham Swift is best known for his novels: *The Sweet Shop Owner* (1980), *Shuttlecock* (1981), *Waterland* (1983), *Out of This World* (1988), *Ever After* (1992), *Last Orders* (1996), *The Light of Day* (2003), and *Tomorrow* (2007).

ACHIEVEMENTS

Graham Swift's best-known novel, *Waterland*, was a finalist for the British Commonwealth's Man Booker Prize and was named best English novel of 1983 by the newspaper *The Guardian*. His novel *Last Orders* won the Booker Prize in 1996, as well as the James Tait Black Memorial Prize.

BIOGRAPHY

Graham Colin Swift was born in London, England, on May 4, 1949. His mother's family, prosperous Jewish tailors, emigrated from Poland around the beginning of the nineteenth-century; his father was a civil servant in the National Debt Office. Swift attended Dulwich College in London, after which he graduated from Cambridge University with a B.A. in 1970 and an M.A. in 1975. He taught for one year in Greece and was a part-time English instructor in London until the success of his third novel *Waterland* in 1983.

ANALYSIS

Because of his experimental novels, which examine the relationship between history and fiction, Graham Swift is often cited as one of the most important British postmodernists. Although he published only a small number of short stories--the eleven included in his collection *Learning to Swim, and Other Stories*--both his importance in contemporary British fiction and the fact that the British short story is often ignored make them deserving of attention.

Whereas Swift deals with the large social and cultural issues of history in his novels, his short fiction focuses more sharply on the nature of story, which, in an interview, he argued is always a "magical, marvelous, mysterious, wonderful thing." Because of Swift's belief that telling stories is a therapeutic means of coming to terms with the past, his stories, in which characters must try to come to terms with their personal pasts, form the core of his novels, in which the personal past becomes cultural history.

"LEARNING TO SWIM"

The focus of "Learning to Swim" begins with Mrs. Singleton, lying on a beach in Cornwall, watching her husband try to teach their six-year-old son Paul how to swim. However, most of the story takes place in her memory as she recalls having thought about leaving her husband three times in the past, primarily because of his lack of passion. The story then shifts to the two times Mr. Singleton has thought of leaving his wife-- once when he considered jumping into the water and swimming away.

Indeed, swimming is a central metaphor in the story, for Mr. Singleton had been an excellent swimmer in school, winning titles and breaking records; in the Spartan purity of swimming he feels superior to others who will "go under" in life, unable to "cleave the water" as he did. Mr. Singleton dreams of swimming; even when he makes love to his wife, he feels her body gets in the way, and he wants to swim through her.

The undercurrent of marital conflict between Mr. and Mrs. Singleton comes to a head at the end of the story. Mrs. Singleton is indifferent to her husband and wants the kind of close relationship with her son typical of women who have rejected their husbands; she thinks that when he is grown he will become a sculptor and she will pose naked for him. At the same time, Mr. Singleton thinks that if Paul could swim he would be able to leave his wife. The story shifts finally to the boy, who fears that his mother will swallow him up and that he will not win the love of his father if he fails to swim; even though he is terrified of the water, he knows if he swims his mother will be forsaken. The story ends with Paul swimming away both from his father and his mother, finding himself in a strange new element that seems all his own.

"HOFFMEIER'S ANTELOPE"

The title refers to a rare, almost extinct, pygmy antelope discovered by a German zoologist named Hoffmeier. However, the focus of the story is the relationship of the narrator to his uncle, an animal keeper at a London zoo, after the uncle's wife dies. The story centers on the fact that the two surviving antelopes are placed together in the zoo under the uncle's care. The narrator, who teaches philosophy part time in London, argues with his uncle that, if an unknown species exists, it is the same as if it did not exist at all; therefore, if something known to exist ceases to exist, it is the same as something that exists but is not known to exist. The idea that there may be animals existing in the wilds still unknown to humans is exciting to the protagonist; he notes that, even given the variety of known species, humans still like to dream up such mythical creatures as griffins, dragons, and unicorns.

The nature of reality is a central issue in the story; the narrator even begins to doubt the reality of Hoffmeier, for his actual life seems as elusive as that of the antelope he rescued from anonymity. The story comes to a climax when the male antelope dies and the uncle feels more closely bound to the surviving female, suffering from the illusion, common among children, that mere loving brings babies into the world and that she could conceive by the strong affection he has for her. When the antelope disappears from the zoo, the uncle disappears also.

"THE TUNNEL"

Typical of Swift's stories, "The Tunnel" begins broadly and narrows its focus near the end. The story centers on a young male narrator and his girlfriend Clancy during a spring and summer, when they live together in an old tenement after having run away

from the girl's parents. Underlying their idyllic, albeit shabby, retreat is the girl's confidence that her seventy-three-year-old crippled uncle, who has a soft spot for her, will leave her everything when he dies.

A motif that runs throughout the story is the life of the painter Paul Gauguin, which fascinates the boy and causes the girl to buy him paints and brushes and urge him to paint the walls of their tenement apartment. Their romantic escape turns sour when, just as the boy felt he was transforming their little hole into a miniature Tahiti, they begin to become aware of the filth surrounding them. As they both get laboring jobs, the tenement area where they live begins to be demolished, and they start to see the paintings and the place as worthless, sentimental trash.

The crisis in their lives becomes more acute when the boy severely burns his hands in a kitchen accident and is confined to the apartment alone to think, particularly about the crippled uncle, with whom he now identifies; he begins to wonder if the uncle is a fiction Clancy invented. The title metaphor of the tunnel is evoked near the end of the story when below his

Graham Swift (Getty Images)

window five boys begin to dig a tunnel out of a fenced-in playground into which they have climbed. He thinks that in their minds the boys have transformed the playground into a prison camp and are trying to escape from a place they had entered and could leave at their own free will. He wants them to succeed because he sees their situation as that of his own. The story ends when the boys break through and when Clancy arrives to say that her uncle has died and left her everything. What the couple will do with this windfall, however, is left unresolved.

"THE WATCH"

Because "The Watch" is based on a thematic premise, it is fabulistic rather than realistic. The premise is announced in the first sentence, with the narrator musing that nothing is more magical and sinister, yet more consoling and expressive of the constancy of fate than a clock. The narrator has descended from a family of clock makers who once had the primitive faith that clocks not only recorded time but also caused it, that without clocks the world would vanish into oblivion.

The central metaphor governing the story is a magical watch, invented in 1809 by the narrator's great-grandfather, which not only could function perpetually without winding but also had a magnetic charge that infected its wearer with its longevity. Thus, his great-grandfather lived to be 133 years old and his grandfather lived to be 161. Although his father died young in the war, the narrator, Adam Krepski, is now the owner of the watch.

The final event in the story occurs one week before the time of the telling, when Krepski hears a female cry in the room below him and discovers a woman in childbirth. He recognizes that the cries come from a region ungoverned by time and thus are as poisonous to him as fresh air to a fish. When the baby is born close to death, Krepski understands that time is not something that exists outside human beings but rather that all people are the distillation of all time, and that each human being is the sum of all the time before him. He dangles the watch near the baby, and when the child grasps it, it is brought back to life and simultaneously the watch stops. The narrator stumbles out into the street and is struck by an internal blow, which he says

topples family trees. The story ends with doctors bending over him to lift his wrist to check his pulse against their own ordinary watches, and he knows that his breaths are numbered.

OTHER MAJOR WORKS

LONG FICTION: *The Sweet Shop Owner*, 1980; *Shuttle-cock*, 1981; *Waterland*, 1983; *Out of This World*, 1988; *Ever After*, 1992; *Last Orders*, 1996; *The Light of Day*, 2003; *Tomorrow*, 2007.

NONFICTION: *Making an Elephant: Writing from Within*, 2009.

EDITED TEXT: *The Magic Wheel: An Anthology of Fishing Literature*, 1985 (with David Profumo).

BIBLIOGRAPHY

Broich, Ulrich. "Muted Postmodernism: The Contemporary British Short Story." *Zeitschrift für Anglistik und Amerikanistik* 41 (1993): 31-39. Discusses the market conditions of the contemporary British short story and surveys three major types of British short fiction: the feminist story, the cultural conflict story, and the experimental, postmodernist story. Discusses Swift's "Seraglio" as a story in which postmodernist narrative strategies are used in a muted way.

Higdon, David Leon. "Double Closures in Postmodern British Fiction: The Example of Graham Swift." *Critical Survey* 3 (1991): 88-95. A theoretical discussion of the lack of closure in British postmodern fiction, using Swift as an example of a writer who successfully combines the postmodern sense of a lack of certainty with the aesthetic demands of some type of boundary. Argues that Swift has created a kind of double closure, maintaining the ambiguity of postmodern narratology while at the same time providing a firm, clear response.

_____. "'Unconfessed Confessions': The Narrators of Graham Swift and Julian Barnes." In *The British and Irish Novel Since 1960*, edited by James Acheson. New York: St. Martin's Press, 1991, 174-191. Argues that the fiction of Swift and Barnes defines what is meant by British postmodernism. Claims they share themes of estrangement, obsession, and the power of the past. Examines their creation of what Higdon calls "the reluctant narrator," who, although quite perceptive, has experienced something so traumatic he must tell it through indirections, masks, and substitutions.

Lea, Daniel. *Graham Swift*. Manchester, England: Manchester University Press, 2005. Offers a close reading of all Swift's work through his 2003 novel *The Light of Day*, with one chapter devoted to an examination of the novel *Shuttlecock* and the short-story collection *Learning to Swim*. Argues that Swift's work repeatedly examines how human beings can find solace in a world in which the traditional markers of identity have become destabilized.

Malcolm, David. *Understanding Graham Swift*. Columbia: University of South Carolina Press, 2003. Devotes a chapter to an examination of *Learning to Swim* in addition to chapters about individual novels. Describes how Swift explores family conflict and emotional disturbance, uses complex narrative technique and combined genres, and expresses interest in metafictional issues, among other aspects of Swift's fiction.

Swift, Graham. "A Conversation with Graham Swift." Interview by Lewis Burke Frumkes. *The Writer* 111 (February, 1998): 19-21. Swift discusses the plot of his highly praised novel *Last Orders*, talks about the symbolic value of water in his fiction, comments on how he evolved as a writer, and gives some advice to young, beginning authors.

_____. "An Interview with Graham Swift." Interview by Catherine Bernard. *Contemporary Literature* 38 (Summer, 1997): 217-231. Swift discusses the importance of voice in his fiction, his use of repetition for thematic and aesthetic effect, his relationship to the tradition of nineteenth-century English fiction, his rejection of formalism that is mere artifice and cleverness, his literary theory that writers are either defensive or vulnerable, and his respect for the magic and mystery of storytelling.

_____. Interview by Amanda Smith. *Publishers Weekly* 239 (February 17, 1992): 43-44. Swift talks about his background, his entrance into publishing, his experiences with American publishers, novel writing, and his most recent fiction. He says he sees the structure of his fiction in terms of rhythm, movement, pace, and tension; it is a musical thing, rather than an intellectual thing. He notes that he is very concerned about the ambiguities of knowledge.

Widdowson, Peter. *Graham Swift*. Tavistock, Devon, England: Northcote House, 2006. An overview of Swift's works, providing analyses of his first seven novels.

_____. "Newstories: Fiction, History, and the Modern World." *Critical Survey* 7 (1995): 3-17. A theoretical discussion of the relationship between history and story in postmodernist fiction, using Swift as the most self-conscious and sophisticated British writer concerned with the interface between history and story. Although the essay is primarily about Swift's novel *Out of This World*, which Widdowson calls a "historiographic metafiction," the focus is on a thematic/narrative tactic, which Swift uses in other fiction.

Charles E. May

T

ELIZABETH TAYLOR

Born: Reading, Berkshire, England; July 3, 1912
Died: Penn, Buckinghamshire, England; November 19, 1975
Also known as: Elizabeth Coles

PRINCIPAL SHORT FICTION

Hester Lilly, and Twelve Short Stories, 1954 (pb. in England as *Hester Lilly, and Other Stories*, 1954)
The Blush, and Other Stories, 1958
A Dedicated Man, and Other Stories, 1965
The Devastating Boys, and Other Stories, 1972
Dangerous Calm: The Selected Stories of Elizabeth Taylor, 1995 (Lynn Knight, editor)

OTHER LITERARY FORMS

Elizabeth Taylor is best known for her "genteel novels" of social comedy. However, because critics have viewed them as relatively lightweight entertainments, they are often more appreciated by general readers than by university scholars. Critics have noted that much of her longer fiction focuses on how people become victims of their own self-delusion. Her career as a novelist extends from the postwar *At Mrs. Lippincote's* (1945) to the posthumously published *Blaming* (1976).

ACHIEVEMENTS

Elizabeth Taylor's fiction was reissued in paperback in the 1980's, reaching a wider audience; her stories have been praised by critics, but her novels have been more popular with general readers. Her 1957 novel *Angel* was selected by the Books Marketing Council in 1984 as one of the "Best Novels of Our Time."

BIOGRAPHY

Elizabeth Taylor was born Elizabeth Coles in Reading, England, on July 3, 1912. She became a governess after attending the Abbey School and then a librarian at the public library at High Wycombe. In 1936, she married John William Kendell Taylor, a manufacturer, and began writing full time, publishing stories in popular journals both in England and America. After World War II, she and her husband settled in the village of Penn, in Buckinghamshire, where she wrote most of her fiction. Taylor said that she loved England and would find it painful to live any place else, commenting, "I should like to feel that the people in my books are essentially English and set down against a truly English background." She died in Penn on November 19, 1975.

ANALYSIS

Elizabeth Taylor said that one basic difference between the short story and the novel is that, whereas the novel is a work of conscious scheming, short stories are inspired, "breathed in a couple of breaths." For them to succeed, she argued, there must be an immediate impact resulting from suggestiveness and compression. Indeed, critics have suggested that what makes Taylor's stories so fascinating is her ability to crystallize a particular "moment of being."

Great short stories, said Taylor, are so charged with a sense of unity, they are like lyric poetry, thus giving a "lovely impression of perfection, of being lifted into another world, instead of sinking into it, as one does with longer fiction." Many of Taylor's stories are social comedies that satirize class distinctions and social expectations; however, the best of them begin as social comedies, only to become subtle evocations of characters caught in elusive psychological conflicts.

"THE FIRST DEATH OF HER LIFE"

This popular anthology piece is so short and slight that many readers may feel it is not a story at all, but rather a simple emotional reaction to, as the title suggests, the first death the central character has experienced. Although the story starts with tears, it immediately moves to writing, in this case, the protagonist's writing a letter in her mind telling her boss why she will not be in to work for the next four days.

The basic method the story uses to communicate emotion is Chekhovian, for instead of focusing on feelings, it focuses on concrete details--either in the present or in the past--that evoke emotion. The thoughts of the protagonist shift first to an image of her father riding through the streets on his bicycle and then to images of her mother, most of which recall the boredom, drabness, and denial of her life. The detail at the end of the story--when the protagonist opens the window and thinks that it is like the end of a film, but without music rising up and engulfing the viewer--suggests that the story is about one of those experiences that is such a disruption of everyday reality it seems unreal. The final image of the father propping his bicycle against the wall and running across the wet gravel completes in actuality what the protagonist earlier imagined.

"A RED-LETTER DAY"

The story opens with a gothic ominousness--leaves "dripping with deadly intensity, as if each falling drop were a drop of acid." The "malevolent" landscape is redolent with the horrors of family life: rotting cabbages, rakish privies, rubbish heaps, and gray napkins drooping on clotheslines. The central female character, Tory Foyle (a figure from Taylor's novel *A View of the Harbour*, 1949), is attending Visiting Day at her son's school, but without a husband. Because Tory's husband has asked for a divorce, her own life is frail and precarious; she feels she and her son are amateurs without tradition and no gift for the job. On Tory's arrival at the school, the point of view shifts to her son Edward, age eleven. When the mother and son go to the Guildhall Museum to see Roman remains, Tory flirts with the attendant and Edward feels unsafe with her; thoughts of the future and death disturb him, as they would not do if he were at school, "anonymous and safe." At the end of the story, when Tory leaves, her son waves at her, "radiant with relief." When she disappears around the curve of the drive, he runs "quickly up the steps to find his friends, and safety."

The relief that both mother and son feel at the end of the story when the required visit is completed suggests that this is not simply a story about a woman who is not comfortable as a mother; rather it is about the depressing fall into reality from the ideal of what society says a mother/son relationship should be. It is a story about the loss of the ideal of marriage, family, and motherhood, and one woman's halting and uncertain efforts to cope with that loss.

"A DEDICATED MAN"

In this combination social comedy and psychological drama, a stereotypical, stiff-necked British waiter, Silcox, enters into a "partnership" with a reserved waitress, Edith, pretending they are husband and wife in order to procure a more prestigious position in a fancy hotel restaurant; however, they sleep in twin beds, maintaining strict decorum. The focus of the story is on Edith, a woman who has known from childhood that she is not attractive to men and thus exaggerates her gracelessness to such an extent that she becomes sexless. Her attitude toward Silcox is that he is always a waiter and nothing else; the two are "hardly even human beings" in each other's eyes.

The story is complicated by the fact that the pretense Silcox creates includes a fictional son, complete with a photograph placed prominently in the couple's room. However, Edith begins to believe more and more in the reality of the fictional son, bragging to the other employees about his successes. Although Silcox thinks she is losing her mind, she says she has never been so happy.

The ruse crashes when Edith finds a photograph in Silcox's drawer that reveals the boy is his son by a previous marriage; because the picture also includes the boy's real mother, Edith feels she has been displaced; her hatred for Silcox's deception increases when he laughs at her disappointment. This shift from social comedy to domestic poignancy makes a final turn at the end of the story when Edith spreads rumors that her "son" has been disgraced as a thief. When she packs and leaves the hotel, Silcox is left to confront a loss of prestige in the eyes of the staff because of his son's disgrace.

"THE BLUSH"

In this short, highly compressed story, Taylor once again combines social comedy with psychological drama. The story centers on two women of the same age--Mrs. Allen and the woman who comes to do her housework every day, Mrs. Lacey. The domestic drama element of the story stems from Mrs. Allen's sadness at not being able to have children. She imagines them in fleeting scenes, like snatches of a film, even crying when she dreams of the day her eldest boy will go off to boarding school.

Mrs. Allen's sadness is contrasted with Mrs. Lacey's complaints about her own children, who make demands of her and treat her disrespectfully. The life in Mrs. Lacey's house fascinates Mrs. Allen, and Mrs. Lacey's children are vivid in her imagination, although she has never actually seen them. Mrs. Lacey, however, envies Mrs. Allen her pretty house and clothes, her figure, and her freedom. The central conflict of the story occurs when Mrs. Lacey misses work because of nausea, suggesting that she might be pregnant again.

The story's climactic scene centers on Mrs. Lacey's husband coming to Mrs. Allen's house, concerned about his wife working too hard. When he tells Mrs. Allen that Mrs. Lacey can no longer come to the house in the evenings to care for Mrs. Allen's children while she and her husband go out to parties, Mrs. Allen knows that Mrs. Lacey has been lying to her husband and has been sneaking out to the pub in the evenings to drink with other men. She does not tell Mr. Lacey this, only promising not to ask his wife to babysit in the evenings again. When Mr. Lacey leaves, Mrs. Allen begins to blush and she goes to the mirror to study "with great interest this strange phenomenon."

OTHER MAJOR WORKS

LONG FICTION: *At Mrs. Lippincote's*, 1945; *Palladian*, 1946; *A View of the Harbour*, 1947; *A Wreath of Roses*, 1949; *A Game of Hide and Seek*, 1951; *The Sleeping Beauty*, 1953; *Angel*, 1957; *In a Summer Season*, 1961; *The Soul of Kindness*, 1964; *The Wedding Group*, 1968; *Mrs. Palfrey at the Claremont*, 1971; *Blaming*, 1976.

CHILDREN'S LITERATURE: *Mossy Trotter*, 1967.

BIBLIOGRAPHY

Baldwin, Dean. "The English Short Story in the Fifties." In *The English Short Story, 1945-1980*, edited by Dennis Vannata. New York: Twayne, 1985. Argues that "shaming nature," which is what the Matron does at the beginning of "A Red-Letter Day," is a good description of the story's theme, for Tory is unable to connect with her son; she is the prototype of the modern parent--alienated, awkward, divorced--unable to say where she has failed.

Beauman, Nicola. *The Other Elizabeth Taylor*. London: Persephone Books, 2009. Although most of Taylor's personal papers and letters have been destroyed, Beauman located five hundred letters, an unpublished novel, and several unpublished stories, and she used these materials to produce a literary biography of Taylor. Beauman recounts the events of Taylor's life and describes the writer's literary influences, her milieu, her working methods, and the critical reception of her work.

Gillette, Jane Brown. "'Oh, What a Something Web We Weave': The Novels of Elizabeth Taylor." *Twentieth-century Literature* 35 (Spring, 1989): 94-112. Discusses Taylor's fiction in three stages: the early period, in which she is critical of the distortion of the imagination; the middle period, in which she moderates her criticism; and the later years, when she celebrates the creative imagination. Argues that Taylor struggles with two major paradoxes: the novelist's use of fiction to depict the real and the novelist's condemnation of egotistical isolation.

Grove, Robin. "From the Island: Elizabeth Taylor's Novels." *Studies in the Literary Imagination* 9 (1978): 79-95. Discusses the critical neglect of Taylor's work. Argues that her books claim that watching the mind's ironies and reflections on itself is a natural and nourishing activity. Maintains that she is the funniest and the most poignant writer of her generation. Analyzes the comic nature of her work.

Hicks, Granville. "Amour on the Thames." *Saturday Review* 44 (January 21, 1961): 62. Compares Taylor to Jane Austen. Includes brief comments about Taylor's work generally, with more extended comments on her novel *In a Summer Season*.

Hosmer, Robert Ellis, Jr. "The Short Stories of Elizabeth Taylor." In *A Companion to the British and Irish Short Story*, edited by Cheryl Alexander Malcolm and David Malcolm. Malden, Mass.: Wiley-Blackwell, 2008. Provides a comprehensive overview of Taylor's short-story collections, as well as some of the individual stories.

Kingham, Joanna. Introduction to *A Dedicated Man, and Other Stories*. London: Virago Press, 1993. An article based on an interview with Taylor in 1971, in which she talks about when and why she started to write, her writing habits, her reactions to feminism, and the things that give her pleasure. Taylor's daughter talks about her childhood and her relationship with her mother.

Leclercq, Florence. *Elizabeth Taylor*. Boston: Twayne, 1985. In this general introduction to Taylor's work, Leclercq devotes one chapter to Taylor's short stories. Leclerq argues that what makes Taylor's stories so fascinating is her "crystallization of one particular 'moment of being.'" She maintains that Taylor's craft is more clearly defined in her stories than in her novels. Discusses her stories in three categories: small psychological dramas, social comedies, and anecdotes detached from social context.

Reeve, N. H. "Away from the Lighthouse: William Sansom and Elizabeth Taylor in 1949." In *The Fiction of the 1940's: Stories of Survival*, edited by Rod Mengham and Reeve. New York: Palgrave, 2001. Focuses on Taylor's novel *A Wreath of Roses*, discussing how it reflects World War II and its aftermath and comparing it to the work of writer Virginia Woolf.

_____. *Elizabeth Taylor*. Tavistock, England: Northcote House, 2008. A critical introduction to Taylor's short stories and novels. Discusses her themes of memory, dispossession, bereavement, and her generation's experience of World War II. Describes how she uses wit to deflate her characters' egotism and self-satisfaction.

Taylor, Elizabeth. "England." *Kenyon Review*, 1969, 469-73. In her contribution to this symposium on the short story, Taylor says some stories are nearer to poetry than the novel; others are like paintings, full of suggestion and atmosphere; the unity of the short story gives an impression of perfection, of being lifted into another world, instead of sinking into it, as one does with the novel.

Charles E. May

WILLIAM MAKEPEACE THACKERAY

Born: Calcutta, India; July 18, 1811
Died: London, England; December 24, 1863
Also known as: M. A. Titmarsh; Ikey Solomons, Jr.;
  George Savage Fitz-Boodle

PRINCIPAL SHORT FICTION

The Yellowplush Papers, 1837-1838
Some Passages in the Life of Major Gahagan,
  1838-1839
Stubb's Calendar: Or, The Fatal Boots, 1839
Barber Cox and the Cutting of His Comb, 1840
The Bedford-Row Conspiracy, 1840
Comic Tales and Sketches, 1841 (2 volumes)
Men's Wives, 1843 (as George Savage Fitz-Boodle)
A Legend of the Rhine, 1845 (as M. A. Titmarsh)
Jeames's Diary: Or, Sudden Wealth, 1846
The Snobs of England, by One of Themselves,
  1846-1847 (later as *The Book of Snobs,* 1848,
  1852)
Mrs. Perkin's Ball, 1847 (as Titmarsh)
A Little Dinner at Timmins's, 1848
"Our Street," 1848 (as Titmarsh)
Doctor Birch and His Young Friends, 1849 (as
  Titmarsh)
The Kickleburys on the Rhine, 1850 (as Titmarsh)
*The Confessions of Fitz-Boodle, and Some Passages
  in the Life of Major Gahagan,* 1852
A Shabby Genteel Story, and Other Tales, 1852
*The Rose and the Ring: Or, The History of Prince
  Giglio and Prince Bulbo,* 1855 (as Titmarsh)
*Memoirs of Mr. Charles J. Yellowplush [with] The
  Diary of C. Jeames De La Pluche, Esqr.,* 1856

OTHER LITERARY FORMS

William Makepeace Thackeray (THAK-uh-ree)
published ten novels during his lifetime, two under
pseudonyms, and the unfinished *Denis Duval* was
printed posthumously in 1864. *Vanity Fair: A Novel*
Without a Hero (1847-1848, serial; 1848, book) and
*The Luck of Barry Lyndon: A Romance of the Last Cen-
tury* (1844, serial; 1852, book) are considered his masterpieces, both of them featuring memorable protagonists who exhibit both heroic and venal qualities.
Thackeray was a prolific contributor to periodicals of
parodies, satires, humorous sketches, essays, reviews,
and articles. He was a correspondent for many newspapers and an editor of several magazines. He also issued
popular Christmas annuals for many years.

ACHIEVEMENTS

In the last decade of his life, William Makepeace
Thackeray was considered one of Great Britain's most
powerful novelists. His novels, taken together, form an
appraisal of English social history and morals between
1690 and 1863. The lasting value of both the novels
and his shorter works, however, rests in their huge cast
of vivid characters, ranging from despicable, amoral
scoundrels through attractive rascals to truly noble heroes, male and female, from every class. What brings
these characters to energetic life is Thackeray's command of style and narrative technique and his gift for
satire. Thackeray experimented with every sort of first-
person narration. By manipulating his various
personae, he created subtle distinctions in tone. Even
when Thackeray employed an omniscient narrator, he
was always a mask, distinct from the author. For his
Victorian audience, this mediating voice was one of the
pleasures of reading Thackeray, who built on the oral
nature of storytelling. To moderns, however, the tendency to tell rather than to dramatize can seem an intrusive disruption of illusion, and thus, they sometimes do
not appreciate the very commentary that made him so
popular in his own time.

Almost as valuable is the impression that remains of
Thackeray's personality. He was a man of good will
and a loving father, financially improvident but generous and kindly. Even the difficult times in his own

life he reshaped in his works into positive experiences. As a writer and talented caricaturist, he deftly skewered pretension and folly where he found them; as a man, he seemed to view human nature with charity and tolerance, above all affirming what he saw as its inherent good sense.

Biography

Born in India, William Makepeace Thackeray was the only son of Richmond and Ann Becher Thackeray. His grandfathers on both sides of the family had been with the Indian civil service, and after his father died in September, 1815, he was sent to school in England. He attended schools in Southampton, Chiswick, and Charterhouse; the bullying he received there was later fictionalized. One of his first pen names was Michael Angelo Titmarsh, adopted because his nose was broken by a classmate, as Michelangelo's had been three centuries earlier. He called his school "Slaughter House" for the brutality he endured there. His mother remarried, and he spent 1828 in Devon with her and Major-General Henry Carmichael-Smythe. From February, 1829, to July, 1830, he attended Trinity College, Cambridge. He traveled in Germany until May, 1831, and met Johann Wolfgang von Goethe in Weimar. He briefly studied law in England. In 1832, he spent four months in Paris, and in 1834 he began training as a professional artist since he had always had a talent for drawing. On August 20, 1836, he married Isabel Shawe, whose neurotic, domineering mother became the model for all the terrible mothers-in-law in Thackeray's fiction. Their daughter Anne was born in June, 1837; she later became a novelist and the editor of her father's letters to Edward Fitzgerald, and of his complete works. She married Sir Richmond Ritchie of the India office. His daughter Jane was born in July, 1838, and died eight months later; Harriet, born in May, 1840, was to marry Sir Leslie Stephen in 1867. In 1840, Isabel became so depressed that she attempted suicide, and in 1846 she was declared incurably insane. The fortune Thackeray had inherited was dissipated by 1833, and the professional gamblers who swindled him out of his money figure in several of his stories. His stepfather invested in a newspaper so that Thackeray could write for it, but it failed, leaving them financially ruined. He wrote for twenty-four different periodicals between 1830 and 1844 trying to support his family, even applying to Charles Dickens for the job of illustrating the *Pickwick Papers* (1836-1837). Finally, the publication of *Vanity Fair* in 1848 made him a public figure. He began a series of public lectures, which took him twice to the United States, from 1852 to 1853 and from 1855 to 1856. He died at the age of fifty-two on Christmas Eve, 1863.

Analysis

William Makepeace Thackeray's "Yellowplush," a footman, was first introduced in *Fraser's* in November, 1837, and was republished in the United States and translated into German. In 1845, the character was revived in *Punch*, having been promoted to Charles James De La Pluche, Esq., through successful speculation in railway shares.

"Miss Shum's Husband"

On his first appearance in "Miss Shum's Husband," Yellowplush tells how he got his name. His mother, who always introduced him as her nephew, named him for the livery of a famous coachman, Yellowplush. Although he was illegitimate, he has gentlemanly tastes, and his cockney speech is spiced with affectations. His employer, Frederic Altamont, takes rooms in a crowded house in John Street. The footman reports that they breakfast from his master's tea leaves and dine on slices of meat cut from his joints, but Frederic endures this to be near his loved one Mary. In the next episode and with his next employer, Yellowplush has descended to petty thievery (which he calls his "perquisites") himself. During his courtship, Altamont refuses to reveal where he works but assures Mary that he is honest and urges her never to question him about what it would cause her misery to learn.

After their marriage, Frederic and Mary move to an elegantly furnished house in Islington, from which he mysteriously disappears each day. After their baby is born, Mrs. Shum becomes a daily visitor. This mother of twelve daughters who spends her time reading novels on the drawing room sofa, scolding, screaming, and having hysterics is the first of the terrible mothers-in-law so prominent in Thackeray's fiction, including Mrs. Gam, Mrs. Gashleigh,

William Makepeace Thackeray (Library of Congress)

Mrs. Cuff, Mrs. Crum, Lady Kicklebury, and Mrs. Baynes. They are always snobbish, interfering, and domineering. Mrs. Shum undermines the mutual affection in her daughter's household by implanting suspicions: "Where does his money come from? What if he is a murderer, or a housebreaker, or a forger?" When Mary answers that he is too kind to be any of those things, Mrs. Shum suggests that he must be a bigamist. At this moment, as Mary faints, Mrs. Shum has hysterics, the baby squalls, the servants run upstairs with hot water, and Frederic returns. He expels Mrs. Shum, double-locks the door, and tries to appease his wife without exposing his secret. His in-laws set up a spy network and finally discover that he is a crossing sweeper. Frederic sells his house and starts his new life abroad. His footman renders his snobbish judgment of the whole affair:

> Of cors, I left his servis. I met him, a few years after, at Badden-Badden, where he and Mrs. A. were much respectid, and pass for pipple of propaty.

The satire depends for its effect on the dissonance between the social pretensions and the misspellings in which they are conveyed. In Victorian England, a gentleman did not work for a living, and a footman conscious of his position could not work for a laborer. He could "pass" abroad because foreigners were unable to tell the difference between inherited and earned money. Obviously, only income from property qualified one to enter society.

"DIMOND CUT DIMOND"

"Dimond Cut Dimond" is about Yellowplush's next master, who is penniless but titled. He is the Honorable Algernon Percy Deuceace, fifth son of the earl of Crabs. If he had been a common man, he would have been recognized as a swindler, but since he is a gentleman, with his family tree prominently displayed in his sitting room, his gambling is considered acceptable. Dawkins, just out of Oxford, moves in with his entire fortune of six thousand pounds to establish himself as a barrister. Deuceace manipulates an introduction by tripping the servant carrying Dawkins's breakfast tray. He substitutes a pastry he has purchased for this purpose with an elaborate letter, claiming it had been sent to him by an aristocratic friend. Once they are acquainted, he suggests a game of cards, which he deliberately loses as a setup.

The scheme is complicated by a second con man, Richard Blewitt, who tells Deuceace that Dawkins is his pigeon to pluck and that he means to strip this one alone since he already has him securely in his claws. Deuceace makes a deal to split the gains; after he wins, however, he coldly announces to Blewitt, who has come for his share, that he never had any intention of keeping his promise. Blewitt, "stormed, groaned, bellowed, swore" but gets nothing, and the villain escapes to Paris, telling Yellowplush that he can come too, if he likes.

Thackeray, as a student, had lost large sums to such gamblers. The insolent criminality with which Deuceace robs both Dawkins and Blewitt is not condemned by his footman, who is engaged in robberies of his own. "There wasn't a bottle of wine that we didn't get a glass out of . . . we'd the best pickens out of the dinners, the livvers of the fowls, the forcemit balls out of the soup, the egs from the sallit . . . you may call this robbery--nonsince--it's only our rights--a suvvant's purquizzits." In the eyes of the footman, the cold-blooded malice of his master is superior to the blustering passion of Blewitt.

"FORING PARTS"

The next episode, "Foring Parts," tells how Deuceace has posted a sign on his door, "Back at seven," and departed, owing the laundress. The footman learns that to gain respect in France, one must be rude. His master had abused the waiters, abused the food, and abused the wine, and the more abusive he was, the better service he got; on his example, the footman also practices insolence because people liked being insulted by a lord's footman. Deuceace writes to Lord Crabs for his allowance, but the answer comes back that, since all London knows of Deuceace's winnings, could he instead lend Lord Crabs some money. He encloses clippings from the newspapers about the transaction. Shortly afterward, a retraction appears in the newspaper for which Deuceace had sent a ten-pound note, with his compliments. The narrator comments that he had already sent a tenner before it came out, although he cannot think why.

"CONFESSIONS OF FITZ-BOODLE"

"Dorothea," "Miss Loewe," and "Ottilia" appeared in *Fraser's* in 1843 as part of "Confessions of Fitz-Boodle." Since their narrator is a leisured gentleman, these stories differ in pace and tone from the Yellowplush series; Fitz-Boodle's aristocratic birth and classical education enable him to make social commentary of a different sort. The story turns on his failure to have learned dancing at Slaughter House school, where he learned little that was useful. He adds ruefully, however, that such is the force of habit that he would probably send his sons there, were he to have any. In a series of semiscenes typical of Thackeray's style, Fitz-Boodle describes the many dancing lessons he has taken from various instructors in London, in Paris, and finally in Germany, from Springbock, the leader of the Kalbsbraten ballet.

The continual shifting of temporal perspectives is also typical of Thackeray. He interrupts chronology for an amiable digression which meanders back to the starting point and also digresses into the future consequences of an action, or presents retrospective memories even from years later. For example, the discursive soliloquy on dancing is suddenly interrupted by, "The reader, perhaps, remembers the brief appearance of his Highness, the Duke." This is followed by an elaborate description of the Duke's pump, the whole point of which is that Speck, who designed it, is Dorothea's father. He ingratiates himself into the family by sketching the pump and is consequently introduced to the beauty, whose charms inspire him to classical allusions. Then the narrative redoubles again:

> In thus introducing this lovely creature in her ball-costume, I have been somewhat premature, and had best go back to the beginning of the history of my acquaintance with her.

Next follows a history of the Speck family leading up to the narrator's first glimpse of her, and the narrative resumes.

The next semiscene, midway between summary and dramatization, is characteristic of Thackeray's refusal to disguise his fictions, to mount them dramatically. His narrators set the stage but do not retire from it; they remain to pose alternatives, suggest possibilities, speculate, and muse expatiatingly. Thackeray constructs a model which the reader must then fill in; by concealing as much as he discloses, he forces the reader's participation in completing his paradigm, using a pronoun shift to the second person which asks "you" to participate. Thackeray appeals to universality (an eighteenth-century device probably derived from his study of Henry Fielding, whom he had both imitated and parodied), and the interjected "I have often said" is a strategy found throughout his work. *Vanity Fair* contains countless "Captain Rawdon often said" interspersings, a technique that allows the author to interpolate commentary and to leave the rest to the reader's imagination. The story concludes with the ball at which Fitz-Boodle has managed to sign up Dorothea for a waltz, and his subsequent fall on the dance floor.

"MR. AND MRS. FRANK BERRY"

"Mr. and Mrs. Frank Berry" is part of the story sequence called *Men's Wives*, which first appeared in *Fraser's* in March, 1843. In two parts, it shows Frank as a boy bravely battling the school bully and being hero-worshiped by the narrator; then, in a later en-counter, he is seen as a uxorious husband who has shaved off his mustache and grown fat and pale. Part 1 is called "The Fight at Slaughter House." After the pre-liminaries, as the air resounds with cries of "To it, Berry!" there is a typical Thackerayan footnote: "As it is very probable that many fair readers may not ap-prove of the extremely forcible language in which the combat is depicted, I beg them to skip it and pass on to the next chapter."

This chapter is entitled "The Combat at Versailles," and this time the heroic Frank is not the victor. Mrs. Berry has "a rigid and classical look" and wears a min-iature of her father, Sir George Catacomb, around her thin neck. Her genteel coldness is aptly caught in her maiden name, Miss Angelica Catacomb. She spends her time making notes in the baronetage on her pedigree, and she entertains her guest with an icy silence. After several pages about the other guests, Thackeray pro-vides the apostrophe that, if there had been anything in-teresting, "I should have come out with it a couple of pages since, nor have kept the public looking for so long a time at the dishcovers and ornaments of the table. But the simple fact must now be told, that there was nothing of the slightest importance at this repast."

The narrator then tells how Angelica controlled her husband's smoking, drinking, and conversation. The narrator decides to rescue Frank from his captivity and orders claret, which, after sufficient quantity has been consumed, leads to riotous singing. He feels free enough to complain, when he is inebriated, about having to spend his evenings reading poetry or missionary tracts out loud, about having to take physics whenever she in-sists, about never being allowed to dine out, and about not daring even to smoke a cigar. In a moment of daring, the narrator accepts an invitation for the next night, but he is not permitted to keep the appointment, and the next time he meets Frank, the latter sheepishly crosses over to the other side of the street; he is wearing galoshes. The boy who was courageous enough to beat the school bully has turned into a henpecked husband.

OTHER MAJOR WORKS

LONG FICTION: *Catherine: A Story*, 1839-1840 (as Ikey Solomons, Jr.); *The History of Samuel Titmarsh and the*

Great Hoggarty Diamond, 1841 (later as *The Great Hog-garty Diamond*, 1848); *The Luck of Barry Lyndon: A Ro-mance of the Last Century*, 1844 (serial), 1852 (book) (commonly known as *Barry Lyndon*); *Vanity Fair: A Novel Without a Hero*, 1847-1848 (serial), 1848 (book); *The History of Pendennis: His Fortunes and Misfortunes, His Friends and His Greatest Enemy*, 1848-1850 (serial); 1849, 1850 (book); *Rebecca and Rowena: A Romance upon Romance*, 1850 (as M. A. Titmarsh); *The History of Henry Esmond, Esquire, a Colonel in the Service of Her Majesty Q. Anne*, 1852 (3 volumes); *The Newcomes: Memoirs of a Most Respectable Family*, 1853-1855 (se-rial), 1855 (book); *The Virginians: A Tale of the Last Cen-tury*, 1857-1859 (serial); 1858, 1859 (book); *Lovel the Widower*, 1860; *The Adventures of Philip on His Way Through the World, Shewing Who Robbed Him, Who Helped Him, and Who Passed Him By*, 1861-1862 (se-rial), 1862 (book); *Denis Duval*, 1864.

PLAY: *The Rose and the Ring*, pb. 1854.

POETRY: *The Chronicle of the Drum*, 1841.

NONFICTION: *The Paris Sketch Book*, 1840 (2 vol-umes; as M. A. Titmarsh); *The Irish Sketch Book*, 1843 (2 volumes; as Titmarsh); *Notes of a Journey from Cornhill to Grand Cairo, by Way of Lisbon, Athens, Constantinople and Jerusalem, Performed in the Steamers of the Penninsular and Oriental Company*, 1846 (as Titmarsh); *The English Humourists of the Eighteenth-century*, 1853; *Sketches and Travels in London*, 1856; *The Four Georges: Sketches of Man-ners, Morals, Court and Town Life*, 1860.

BIBLIOGRAPHY

Bloom, Harold, ed. *William Makepeace Thackeray*. New York: Chelsea House, 1987. A collection of es-says on various aspects of Thackeray's fiction, in-cluding such issues and concepts as humor, realism, characterization, point of view, and irony.

Carey, John. *Thackeray: Prodigal Genius*. London: Faber & Faber, 1977. Carey's appreciation of Thac-keray's "imaginative vitality," particularly as it is ex-pressed in his earlier, shorter, largely satirical literary and journalistic work, provides the focus for this ab-sorbing study. Many of Thackeray's major short works are discussed and analyzed in their chrono-logical context.

Clarke, Michael M. *Thackeray and Women*. DeKalb: Northern Illinois University Press, 1995. Examines Thackeray's treatment of female characters. Includes a bibliography and an index.

Dodds, John Wendell. *Thackeray: A Critical Portrait*. New York: Oxford University Press, 1941. This scholarly, twelve-chapter study of Thackeray's genius and the art of his fiction includes, particularly in chapter 3, "The Early Humorist and Story-Teller: 1838-1840," an assessment of his short satirical sketches and stories. A thorough index is useful. An important book in the canon of Thackeray criticism.

Harden, Edgar F. *Thackeray the Writer: From Journalism to "Vanity Fair."* New York: St. Martin's Press, 1998.

_____. *Thackeray the Writer: From Pendennis to "Denis Duval."* New York: St. Martin's Press, 2000. Analyzes all of Thackeray's works--including the short fiction--in chronological order to trace his development as a writer.

Mudge, Isadore Gilbert, and M. Earl Sears. *A Thackeray Dictionary: The Characters and Short Stories Alphabetically Arranged*. 1910. Reprint. New York: Humanities Press, 1962. An essential reference book for students of Thackeray's works. The "Chronological List of Novels and Stories" clarifies and lists the individual and collected works by the titles under which many of Thackeray's short sketches and stories were published and republished; "Synopses" provides invaluable annotations on the contents of all Thackeray's fiction, short and long. The main "Dictionary" section is an alphabetical reference book about Thackeray's characters.

Peters, Catherine. *Thackeray's Universe: Shifting Worlds of Imagination and Reality*. New York: Oxford University Press, 1987. The purpose of this thorough, fresh, intelligent, and readable twelve-chapter study is, in the author's words, "to identify the raw materials, but to be aware that the finished work is a work of art, and not a covert autobiography." In defining what Thackeray's writings owe both to his life and to his particular genius, Peters provides invaluable insights. Short-fiction works, such as *Men's Wives* and *The Yellowplush Papers*, are analyzed, and individual short pieces are discussed in context. A thorough index helps readers search out the discussion of individual works.

Salmon, Richard. *William Makepeace Thackeray*. Tavistock, England: Northcote House, 2005. Examines a wide range of Thackeray's works, including short fiction, novels, journalism, and criticism, to discuss his common themes and writing style.

Shillingsburg, Peter. *William Makepeace Thackeray: A Literary Life*. New York: Palgrave, 2001. An introduction to Thackeray's life and work, focusing on his major novels. Analyzes why Thackeray's popularity declined in the twentieth and twenty-first centuries. Examines the narrative voice, subtle allusions, and complex characters in Thackeray's novels.

Taylor, D. J. *Thackeray: The Life of a Literary Man*. New York: Carroll and Graf, 2001. A lengthy biography that argues for Thackeray's preeminence among nineteenth-century English novelists. A relatively comprehensive study of the man that sheds much light on his work.

Welsh, Alexander, ed. *Thackeray: A Collection of Critical Essays*. Englewood Cliffs, N.J.: Prentice-Hall, 1968. These thirteen essays by a selection of the foremost Thackeray scholars are a useful introduction to the student of Thackeray, although discussion of the short works is included only in the analyses of Thackeray's narrative techniques and style.

Wheatley, James H. *Patterns in Thackeray's Fiction*. Cambridge, Mass.: MIT Press, 1969. Lucid, readable study of the development of Thackeray's techniques and concerns as a fiction writer. Follows his literary career from chapter 1, "Early Parody," through chapter 6, "Later Fiction: The Sentiment of Reality." Two works of short fiction, *The Yellowplush Papers* and *A Shabby Genteel Story, and Other Tales*, are discussed at some length in chapter 2, "Developments from Parody." The "Works Cited" section guides the reader to other relevant critical sources.

Ruth Rosenberg
Updated by Jill Rollins

DYLAN THOMAS

Born: Swansea, Wales; October 27, 1914
Died: New York, New York; November 9, 1953

PRINCIPAL SHORT FICTION

Portrait of the Artist as a Young Dog, 1940
Selected Writings of Dylan Thomas, 1946
A Child's Christmas in Wales, 1954
A Prospect of the Sea, and Other Stories, 1955
Adventures in the Skin Trade, and Other Stories,
    1955
Early Prose Writings, 1971
The Followers, 1976
The Collected Stories, 1984

OTHER LITERARY FORMS

In addition to his short fiction, Dylan Thomas published several collections of poetry, including *Eighteen Poems* (1934), *Twenty-five Poems* (1936), *New Poems* (1943), and *Collected Poems: 1934-1952* (1952). *Under Milk Wood: A Play for Voices* (pr. 1953, public reading; pr. 1954, radio play; pb. 1954; pr. 1956) is a verse drama that affectionately portrays a day in the life of the inhabitants of a tiny Welsh fishing village. Thomas also wrote many screenplays, most notably *The Doctor and the Devils* (1953). and a comic detective novel *The Death of the King's Canary* (1976).

ACHIEVEMENTS

The lyricism of Dylan Thomas's poetry probably constitutes his most powerful contribution to twentieth-century verse and is also a notable characteristic of his prose. One source of that lyric quality is surely Thomas's Welsh origins and his awareness of the depth and richness of Welsh poetic traditions. He also paid homage to Wales in his short fiction, lovingly, if sometimes satirically, describing it in works such as *A Child's Christmas in Wales* and in the stories that make up *Portrait of the Artist as a Young Dog* and

Adventures in the Skin Trade. In these works appear characters and events from his childhood in Swansea and his early work as a news reporter.

His poetry won the "Poet's Corner" Prize of the *Sunday Referee* in 1934, the Blumenthal Poetry Prize in 1938, the Levinson Poetry Prize in 1945, and Foyle's Poetry Prize for *Collected Poems: 1934-1952* in 1952. Thomas also received a grant from The Authors' Society Traveling Scholarship Fund in 1947.

BIOGRAPHY

Dylan Marlais Thomas's father, John David Thomas, was an embittered schoolmaster, emotionally remote from his son, but he possessed a fine library of contemporary fiction and poetry in which his son was free to read. His father's distance and unhappiness may have made Thomas more susceptible to the indulgences of his mother, Florence Williams Thomas. It is her family who appears in Thomas's work as the chapel-going farmers, and it is her oldest sister whose husband owned the farm near Llangain where the young Thomas often spent summer vacations. Thomas also had a sister, Nancy, nine years older than he. The family home at 5 Cwmdonkin Drive, Swansea, was across the street from the park which sometimes appears in his poems ("The Hunchback in the Park," for example). Likewise the beautiful Gower peninsula and his aunt's farm appeared in his adult work as subjects for his poetry and memoirs (most notably in "Fern Hill"). Thomas's early life in Wales furnished him with material that surfaced in his work for the rest of his life.

Thomas was a lackadaisical student at Swansea Grammar School. Talented in English, he edited the school magazine while he was there, and he began to keep the notebooks that reveal his early attempts to form his style, but he gave little attention to subjects that did not interest him. It was at school that he began his friendship with Dan Jones, with whom he composed poems and played elaborate word games. In adulthood, Jones became Dr. Daniel Jones, musical composer and editor of Thomas's work.

Thomas left school in 1931 to work--not very successfully--as a reporter for the *South Wales Evening Post*, a job that gave him material for many of his stories. During the next three years, he also experienced a period of exciting poetic growth, learning about Welsh poets of the past and producing much work of his own. Late in 1934, he moved to London where he cultivated a conscious bohemianism and began to gain a reputation as drinker, brilliant conversationalist, and poet of merit. Through the rest of his life, the two parts of his personality--the serious poet who cared about his craft and the hard-drinking bohemian--were at odds in dominating his behavior.

In 1937, he married Caitlin Macnamara, a strong-willed, passionate dancer with whom he was intensely in love. They had three children--Llewelyn, Aeron, and Colm. During World War II, Thomas, a conscientious objector, wrote mostly prose. Afterward, his life alternated between London and the Welsh fishing village of Laugharne, where he lived with his family and did his most profitable work. In London, when he was in need of money (as he usually was), he often worked for the British Broadcasting Corporation, but there, too, his drinking began to cause him more and more troubles.

In 1950, he made the first of four tours to the United States, reading his work at colleges and universities. It was an enormous success, but it documented his reputation as an "outlaw" poet--a hard drinker and womanizer who spent the proceeds of his readings on women and whiskey while his family went without necessities. The subsequent tours intensified that legend. He died of alcohol poisoning in St. Vincent's Hospital in New York City in 1953.

ANALYSIS

Dylan Thomas's ten stories in *Portrait of the Artist as a Young Dog* are charming reminiscences of his relatives, school friends, and neighbors in the town where he grew up. Their wit and accessibility made them immediately popular, in contrast to the dark, subjective stories he had written prior to 1938, for which he had difficulty finding a publisher. In March, 1938, he wrote to Vernon Watkins that "A Visit to Grandpa's" was "the

first of a series of short, straightforward stories about Swansea." Published on March 10, 1939, in the *New English Weekly*, it told of a boy's waking up on a mild summer night to the sounds of "gee-up and whoa" in the next room where his grandfather, wearing his red waistcoat with its brass buttons, is reining invisible horses. On their morning walks, the grandfather has expressed his wish not to be buried in the nearby churchyard. When he is missing a few days later, the entire village is summoned to go in search of him, and they find him on Carmarthen Bridge in his Sunday trousers and dusty tall hat on his way to Llangadock to be buried. They try to persuade him to come home to tea instead.

"THE PEACHES"

In "The Peaches," first published in the October, 1938, issue of *Life and Letters Today*, the naïve narrator tells of his spring holiday on a farm in Gorsehill. His uncle Jim drives him there in a green cart late one April evening, stopping for a drink at a public house. The squeal coming from the wicker basket he takes inside with him prepares the reader for the fact that cousin Gwilym will note that one of the pigs is missing the next day. The terror of being abandoned in a dark alley is assuaged by Aunt Annie's warm welcome of him later that night at the farmhouse. He enters, small, cold, and scared, as the clock strikes midnight, and is made to feel "among the shining and striking like a prince taking off his disguise." Next morning, Gwilym takes him to see the sow, who has only four pigs left. "He sold it to go on the drink," whispers Gwilym rebukingly. The boy imagines Jim transformed into a hungry fox: "I could see uncle, tall and sly and red, holding the writhing pig in his two hairy hands, sinking his teeth in its thigh, crunching its trotters up; I could see him leaning over the wall of the sty with the pig's legs sticking out of his mouth." Gwilym, who is studying to be a minister, takes him to the barn, which he pretends is his chapel and preaches a thunderous sermon at him, after which he takes up a collection.

Next, the complication begins. Gwilym and Jim are told to dress up for Jack Williams, whose rich mother will bring him in an automobile from Swansea for a fortnight's visit. A tin of peaches has been saved from Christmas; "Mother's been keeping it for a day like

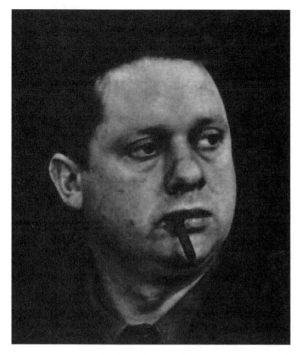

Dylan Thomas (Library of Congress)

this." Mrs. Williams, "with a jutting bosom and thick legs, her ankles swollen over her pointed shoes," sways into the parlor like a ship. Annie precedes her, anxiously tidying her hair, "clucking, fidgeting, excusing." (The string of participles is typical of Thomas's prose style; one sentence in "Return Journey" contains fifteen.) The rich guest declines refreshments: "I don't mind pears or chunks, but I can't bear peaches." The boys run out to frolic, climb trees, and play Indians in the bushes. After supper, in the barn, Gwilym demands confessions from them, and Jack begins to cry that he wants to go home. That night in bed, they hear Uncle Jim come in drunk and Annie quietly relating the events of the day, at which he explodes into thunderous anger: "Aren't peaches good enough for her!" At this, Jack sobs into his pillow. The next day Mrs. Williams arrives, sends the chauffeur for Jack's luggage, and drives off with him, as the departing car scatters the hens and the narrator waves good-bye.

Two aspects of the point of view are significant. The first, its tone, is what made all the stories so immediately beloved. The genial Chaucerian stance, which perceives and accepts eccentricities, which notes and blesses all the peculiarities of humanity, is endearing without being sentimental because the acuteness of the observations stays in significant tension with the non-judgmental way in which they are recorded. This combination of acuity and benevolence, of sharpness and radiance, is the special quality of Thomas's humor. The second aspect of the author's style is its expansion and contraction, which indicates the view of a visionary poet. The narrator is both a homesick, cold, tired little boy, and "a royal nephew in smart town clothes, embraced and welcomed." The uncle is both a predatory fox and an impoverished farmer, as he sits in "the broken throne of a bankrupt bard." The splendid paradise where the narrator romps is simultaneously a poor, dirty "square of mud and rubbish and bad wood and falling stone, where a bucketful of old and bedraggled hens scratched and laid small eggs." The "pulpit" where Gwilym's inspired sermon is "cried to the heavens" in his deepest voice is a dusty, broken cart in an abandoned barn overrun with mice; but this decrepit building on a mucky hill becomes "a chapel shafted with sunlight," awesome with reverence as the "preacher's" voice becomes "Welsh and singing." The alternate aggrandizement and diminution of the perceptions energize the style as the lyric impulse wars with the satiric impulse in the narrator's voice.

"PATRICIA, EDITH AND ARNOLD"

The naïve narrator of the third of the *Portrait of the Artist as a Young Dog* stories, entitled "Patricia, Edith and Arnold," is totally engrossed in his imaginary engine, whose brake is "a hammer in his pocket" and whose fuel is replenished by invisible engineers. As he drives it about the garden, however, he is aware of his maid, Patricia, plotting with the neighbor's servant, Edith, to confront Arnold with the identical letters he wrote to both of them. The girls take the child to the park as it begins to snow; Arnold has been meeting Edith there on Fridays, and Patricia on Wednesdays. As the girls wait for Arnold in the shelter, the boy, disowning them, pretends he is a baker, molding loaves of bread out of snow.

Arnold Matthews, his hands blue with cold, wearing a checked cap but no overcoat, appears and tries to bluff it out. Loudly he says, "Fancy you two knowing each other." The boy rolls a snowman "with a lop-sided dirty head" smoking a pencil, as the situation grows more tense. When Arnold claims that he loves them both, Edith shakes her purse at him, the letters fall out all over the snow, and the snowman collapses. As the boy searches for his pencil, the girls insist that Arnold choose between them. Patricia turns her back, indignantly. Arnold gestures and whispers to Edith behind Patricia's back and then, out loud, chooses Patricia. The boy, bending over his snowman, finds his pencil driven through its head.

Later, during a discussion of lying, the boy tells Patricia that he saw Arnold lying to both of them, and the momentary truce, during which Patricia and Arnold have been walking arm in arm, is over. She smacks and pummels him as he staggers backward and falls. The boy says he has to retrieve the cap that he left near his snowman. He finds Arnold there, rereading the letters that Edith dropped, but does not tell Patricia this. Later, as his frozen hands tingle and his face feels on fire, she comforts him until "the hurting is gone." She acknowledges his pain and her own by saying, "Now we've all had a good cry today." The story achieves its effects through the child's detachment. Totally absorbed in his play, he registers the behavior of the adults, participating in their sorrows without fully comprehending them. In spite of his age-appropriate egocentricity and his critical remarks about her girth (her footprints as large as a horse's), he expresses deep affection for her and such concern as he is capable of, given the puzzling circumstances.

"THE FIGHT"

The narrator of "The Fight" is an exuberant adolescent. Although he is fourteen, he deliberately adds a year to his age, lying for the thrill of having to be on guard to avoid detection. The self-conscious teenager is continually inventing scenarios in which he assumes various heroic postures. The story tells of his finding an alter ego, as gifted as he, through whom he can confirm his existence, with whom he can share his anxieties, collaborate imaginatively, and play duets. The opening incident illustrates Dylan's testing himself against the adults about him. He is engaged in a staring contest with a cranky old man who lives beside the schoolyard when a strange boy pushes him down. They fight.

Dylan gives Dan a bloody nose and gets a black eye in return. Admiring each other's injuries as evidence of their own manliness, they become fast friends.

Dylan postures, first as a prizefighter, then as a pirate. When a boy ridicules him at school the next day, he has a revenge fantasy of breaking his leg, then of being a famous surgeon who sets it with "a rapid manipulation, the click of a bone," while the grateful mother, on her knees, tearfully thanks him. Assigned a vase to draw in art class, the boys sketch inaccurate versions of naked girls instead: "I drew a wild guess below the waist." This boyish sexual curiosity leads him mentally to undress even Mrs. Bevan, the minister's wife, whom he meets later at supper at Dan's house, but he gets frightened when he gets as far as the petticoats.

Dan shows Dylan the seven historical novels he wrote before he was twelve, plays the piano for him, and lets him make a cat's noise on his violin; Dylan reads Dan his poems out of his exercise book. They share feelings, such as their ambivalences toward their mothers, a love tinged with embarrassment. They decide to edit a paper. Back upstairs, after supper, they imitate the self-important Mr. Bevan and discuss the time Mrs. Bevan tried to fling herself out the window. When she joins them later, they try to induce her to repeat this by pointedly opening the window and inviting her to admire the view. When he has to leave at 9:30, Dan announces that he "must finish a string trio tonight," and Dylan counters that he is "working on a long poem about the princes of Wales." On these bravura promises, the story closes.

"A PROSPECT OF THE SEA"

Thomas called these luminous remembrances of his youth "portions of a provincial autobiography." The stories he wrote earlier, drafts of which exist in "The Red Notebook" which he kept from December, 1933, to October, 1934, were not published until later. Considered obscure, violent, and surrealistic, the stories are difficult because of the use of narrative devices borrowed from lyric poetry. In "A Prospect of the Sea," for example, the scenery seems to contract and expand. A boy lying in a cornfield on a summer day sees a country girl with berry-stained mouth, scratched legs, and dirty fingernails jump down from a tree, startling the birds.

The landscape shrinks, the trees dwindle, the river is compressed into a drop, and the yellow field diminishes into a square "he could cover with his hand." As he masters his fear and sees she is only "a girl in a torn cotton frock" sitting cross-legged on the grass, things assume their proper size. As she makes erotic advances, his terror rises again, and everything becomes magnified. Each leaf becomes as large as a man, every trough in the bark of the tree seems as vast as a channel, every blade of grass looks as high as a house. This apparent contraction and expansion of the external world is dependent upon the protagonist's internal state.

Thomas uses another device commonly employed in lyric poetry, the literalized metaphor. Because a thing seems like another, it is depicted as having been transformed into that other thing. For example, the "sunburned country girl" frightens the lonely boy as if she were a witch; thus, in his eyes, she becomes one. "The stain on her lips was blood, not berries; and her nails were not broken but sharpened sideways, ten black scissorblades ready to snip off his tongue." Finally, not only space and character are subject to transformations but also time. As the narrator fantasizes union with this girl, he attains a mystical vision of history unrolling back to Eden. The story ends as it began; she disappears into the sea. He had imagined, at the beginning, as he dabbled his fingers in the water, that a drowned storybook princess would emerge from the waves. The apparent obscurities are resolved by seeing the plot of this story as simply the daydreams of a lonely boy on a summer's day.

"THE ORCHARDS"

"The Orchards" is another prose-poem about a man's attempt to record a vision in words. Marlais has a repetitive dream about blazing apple trees guarded by two female figures who change from scarecrows to women. He tries and fails to shape this into a story, and finally sets out on a quest. Striding through eleven valleys, he reaches the scene he has dreamed of, where he reenacts the kissing of the maiden as the orchard catches fire, the fruit falls as cinders, and she and her sister change to scarecrows. These smoldering trees may be related to the sacrificial fires of the Welsh druids on Midsummer Day. The woman figure might be connected with Olwedd, the Welsh Venus,

associated with the wild apple. Marlais's adventure, however, is a mental journey undertaken by the creative writer through the landscape of his mind, and the temporal and spatial fluctuations are the projections of that mind, mythicized.

"THE TREE"

"The Tree" illustrates this same process. A gardener tells a boy the story of Jesus, reading the Bible in his shed by candlelight. While he is mending a rake with wire, he relates the twelve stages of the cross. The boy wants to know the secrets inside the locked tower to which the bearded gardener has the key. On Christmas Eve, the gardener unlocks the room through whose windows the boy can see the Jarvis Hills to the east. The gardener says of this "Christmas present" in a tone which seems prophetic: "It is enough that I have given you the key."

On Christmas morning, an idiot with ragged shoes wanders into the garden, "bearing the torture of the weather with a divine patience." Enduring the rain and the wind, he sits down under the elder tree. The boy, concluding that the gardener had not lied and that the secret of the tower was true, runs to get the wire to reenact the crucifixion. The old man's obsessive religiosity has been transmitted to the boy, who takes it literally: "A tree" has become "The Tree," "a key" has become "The Key," and a passive beggar stumbling from the east has become Christ inviting his martyrdom.

"THE VISITOR"

"The Visitor" is the story of a dying poet, Peter, tended lovingly by Rhiannon, who brings him warm milk, reads to him from William Blake, and at the end pulls the sheet over his face. Death is personified as Callaghan, whose visit Peter anticipates as his limbs grow numb and his heart slows. Callaghan blows out the candles with his gray mouth, and, lifting Peter in his arms, flies with him to the Jarvis Valley where they watch worms and death-beetles undoing "brightly and minutely" the animal tissues on the shining bones through whose sockets flowers sprout, the blood seeping through the earth to fountain forth in springs of water. "Peter, in his ghost, cried with joy." This is the same assurance found in Thomas's great elegies: Death is but the reentry of the body into the processes of nature. Matter is not extinguished, but transformed into other shapes whose joyous energies flourish forever.

OTHER MAJOR WORKS

LONG FICTION: *The Death of the King's Canary*, 1976 (with John Davenport; wr. c. 1940).

PLAY: *Under Milk Wood: A Play for Voices*, pr. 1953 (public reading), pr. 1954 (radio play), pb. 1954, pr. 1956 (staged; musical settings by Daniel Jones).

SCREENPLAYS: *No Room at the Inn*, 1948 (with Ivan Foxwell); *Three Weird Sisters*, 1948 (with Louise Birt and David Evans); *The Doctor and the Devils*, 1953; *The Beach at Falesá*, 1963; *Twenty Years A'Growing*, 1964; *Me and My Bike*, 1965; *Rebecca's Daughters*, 1965.

RADIO PLAYS: *Quite Early One Morning*, 1944; *The Londoner*, 1946; *Return Journey*, 1947; *Quite Early One Morning*, 1954 (twenty-two radio plays).

POETRY: *Eighteen Poems*, 1934; *Twenty-five Poems*, 1936; *The Map of Love*, 1939; *New Poems*, 1943; *Deaths and Entrances*, 1946; *Twenty-six Poems*, 1950; *Collected Poems, 1934-1952*, 1952; *In Country Sleep*, 1952; *The Poems of Dylan Thomas*, 1971, rev. ed. 2003 (Daniel Jones, editor).

NONFICTION: *Letters to Vernon Watkins*, 1957 (Vernon Watkins, editor); *Selected Letters of Dylan Thomas*, 1966 (Constantine FitzGibbon, editor); *Poet in the Making: The Notebooks of Dylan Thomas*, 1968 (Ralph Maud, editor); *Twelve More Letters by Dylan Thomas*, 1969 (FitzGibbon, editor); *The Collected Letters*, 1985 (Paul Ferris, editor).

MISCELLANEOUS: *"The Doctor and the Devils," and Other Scripts*, 1966 (two screenplays and one radio play).

BIBLIOGRAPHY

Ackerman, John. *Dylan Thomas: His Life and Work*. New York: St. Martin's Press, 1996. Analyzes Thomas's poetry and prose works to trace his development as a writer.

Cox, C. B., ed. *Dylan Thomas: A Collection of Critical Essays*. Englewood Cliffs, N.J.: Prentice-Hall, 1966. Of the thirteen essays in this collection, only Annis Pratt's deals specifically with Thomas's prose; three others analyze *Under Milk Wood*.

Davies, James A. *A Reference Companion to Dylan Thomas*. Westport, Conn.: Greenwood Press, 1998. A user-friendly guide to Thomas's life and works, including the short fiction. Includes bibliography and index.

Emery, Clark M. *The World of Dylan Thomas*. Coral Gables, Fla.: University of Miami Press, 1962. Contains explications of ninety of Thomas's poems with some brief commentary on the short fiction.

FitzGibbon, Constantine. *The Life of Dylan Thomas*. London: J. M. Dent & Sons, 1965. The standard biography, this work includes a list of Thomas's screenplays, itineraries of his reading tours, and a detailed index that gives the reader access to references to individual works.

Goodby, John, and Chris Wigginton, eds. *Dylan Thomas*. New York: Palgrave, 2001. Ten critical essays that analyze Thomas's works, many focusing on his poetry. Jeni Williams examines Thomas's short fiction in her essay "'Oh, for Vanished Youth': Avoiding Adulthood in the Later Stories of Dylan Thomas," and the index lists many references to the short-story collections and individual stories.

Hardy, Barbara Nathan. *Dylan Thomas: An Original Language*. Athens: University of Georgia Press, 2000. Examines how Thomas re-creates language, including his use of Welsh-derived terms, in his poems and short stories. The short-story collection *Portrait of the Artist as a Young Dog* is among the works discussed. Includes bibliography and index.

Korg, Jacob. *Dylan Thomas*. Boston: Twayne, 1965. Korg includes a long chapter on Thomas's prose and analyzes several stories. Supplemented by a bibliography.

Lycett, Andrew. *Dylan Thomas: A New Life*. Woodstock, NY: Overlook Press, 2004. A thorough, exhaustively detailed account of Thomas's life, including many of the seamier aspects of his character.

Mayer, Ann Elizabeth. *Artists in Dylan Thomas's Prose Works*. Montreal: McGill-Queen's University Press, 1995. In this detailed study of the image of the artist in Thomas's prose, Mayer provides a close analysis of "The Peaches" and "One Warm Saturday." Discusses the folktale basis of "The Peaches" and the child-as-artist figure who places himself within the stories he tells. Argues that "The Peaches" sets up many themes further explored and developed in the other stories in *Portrait of the Artist as a Young Dog*.

Peach, Linden. *The Prose Writings of Dylan Thomas*. Totowa, N.J.: Barnes & Noble Books, 1988. Shows how Thomas's prose rather than his poetry demonstrates his concern with Wales. Examines Thomas's focus on a backward, rural Wales and discusses how the early stories examine the restrictions of close-knit communities, which act as straitjackets on the emotional development of the Welsh people.

Sinclair, Andrew. *Dylan the Bard: A Life of Dylan Thomas*. New York: Thomas Dunne Books, 2000. Sinclair's biography describes how the division and tensions of Thomas's Welsh background influenced his writing.

Tindall, William York. *A Reader's Guide to Dylan Thomas*. Syracuse, N.Y.: Syracuse University Press, 1996. Although primarily offering analyses of the poems, Tindall includes some biography, as well as some discussion of Thomas's themes and interests in the introduction.

Ruth Rosenberg
Updated by Ann Davison Garbett

Colm Tóibín

Born: Enniscorthy, County Wexford, Ireland;
May 30, 1955

PRINCIPAL SHORT FICTION
Mothers and Sons, 2006
The Empty Family, 2010

OTHER LITERARY FORMS

Until the publication of *Mothers and Sons* in 2006, Colm Tóibín (CAHL-uhm toh-BEEN) had an international literary reputation based primarily on his six novels, published between 1990 and 2009. Praised for their linguistic brilliance and consummate craftsmanship, his novels are far-ranging in setting, from Ireland and Spain to Argentina and the United States. His characters are as diverse as a man dying of acquired immunodeficiency syndrome (AIDS), a judge struggling with the death of his wife, immigrants, and Henry James. However, all his novels share a preoccupation with isolated people struggling to find lasting connections yet often trapped in their inarticulateness, which Tóibín contrasts with evocations of their complex interior lives.

Since the 1970's, he also has been a prolific nonfiction writer, editor, journalist, and book reviewer.

ACHIEVEMENTS

From the publication of his first novel, *The South*, in 1990, Colm Tóibín has been acknowledged as a major talent, incisive and complex in his characterizations, quintessentially Irish in his preoccupations and international in his reach. Having won the *Irish Times*/Aer Lingus First Fiction Award for *The South*, Tóibín earned a raft of literary prizes, including the Encore Award (for 1992's *The Heather Blazing*), the Ferro-Grumley Prize (for 1996's *The Story of the Night*), the IMPAC Prize and *Prix du Meilleur Livre Étranger* (for 2004's *The Master*, which also was named *Los Angeles Times* Novel of the Year), the Costa Novel of the Year (for 2009's *Brooklyn*), and the Edge Hill Prize (for *Mothers and Sons*). His fiction also has been shortlisted for the Whitbread First Novel Award, the IMPAC Prize, and twice for the Booker Prize; he was the winner of the E. M. Forster Prize from the American Academy for Arts and Letters.

The recipient of honorary doctorates from the University of Ulster and University College Dublin, Tóibín was elected to Aosdána, appointed to the Arts Council of Ireland, was twice named Stein Visiting Writer at Stanford University, and served as visiting writer at the Michener Center at the University of Texas at Austin and the Leonard Milberg Lecturer in Irish Letters at Princeton University He was a fellow at the Center for

Scholars and Writers at New York Public Library. His writing has been translated into thirty languages.

BIOGRAPHY

Born in Enniscorthy, County Wexford, a market town of long historical significance, Colm Tóibín was the second youngest of five children. His father's death when Toíbín was only twelve has had a lifelong impact on the author, finding its way into his fiction in the autobiographical *The Heather Blazing* and woven throughout his portrayals of fragmented families. After studying literature and history at University College Dublin, Tóibín spent several years in Spain in the 1970's, where he developed a strong sympathy for the Catalan people and culture. Returning to Ireland in 1978, he worked as a journalist for *In Dublin* (for which he became features editor in 1981), *Hibernia*, and *The Sunday Tribune*. In 1985, he left after two years as editor of *Magill* and traveled in Africa and South America, engaging in journalistic and travel writing.

Tóibín's career as a novelist began with the publication of *The South* in 1990; his other novels include *The Heather Blazing*, *The Story of the Night*, *The Blackwater Lightship* (1999), *The Master*, and *Brooklyn*. He is the author of two collections of short stories, *Mothers and Sons* and *The Empty Family*. Starting with his journalistic and travel writing in the 1970's, he has been a prolific nonfiction writer.

ANALYSIS

Colm Tóibín had already established an international reputation as a novelist when he published his first book of short stories, *Mothers and Sons*, in 2006 to immediate critical acclaim. With the appearance of his second collection, *The Empty Family*, in 2010, he made it clear that he was a master practitioner of the short-story genre as well.

As in his novels, characters vacillate between lush interior awareness and public inarticulateness; the historical, political, and familial past haunts the present; people ache with poetically rendered isolation while recalling past connections and contemplating future ones. As with his novels, Tóibín's short stories reveal a journalist's talent for revealing diverse settings and cultures; his skill as a fiction writer renders him at ease

Colm Tóibín (Reuters /Landov)

in a variety of points of view, lengths of story; he proves himself a lyrical chronicler of the natural world and a keen anthropologist of urban life. Though often disappointed, his characters are stoic rather than self-pitying; though often immersed in dark nights of the soul, their author neither abandons his wry, sometimes outrageous sense of humor nor the perennial human hope that, heartbreak notwithstanding, love--or at least a rueful self-awareness--waits around the corner.

MOTHERS AND SONS

Not surprisingly, the stories in *Mothers and Sons* explore a familial relationship that has inspired countless works of Irish literature: the possessive Irish matriarch, a stereotype of long standing, with Ireland often personified as "Mother." The stories in this collection are anything but predictable, however; diverse in setting, tone, and style, they subtly explore the complexities of relationships whose deepest emotions are more often than not unspoken. In "A Song," a young Irish musician whose mother, a traditional singer, had abandoned him and his father many years earlier, leaves the pub where she is performing without speaking to her or even knowing whether or not she recognized him. Ironically, his own flawless ear for music positions him uniquely to appreciate her performance, and in the listening lies their most intimate connection. "A Priest in the Family" makes an unexpected turn on a familiar path: Having a priest in an Irish family was once counted a special blessing; in this story, the priest's mother must contend with the revelation that her son is also a pedophile. In "A Summer Job," a woman whose relationship with her mother is strained manages vicariously her son's much closer relationship with his grandmother. Indulged by his grandmother and thwarted by his mother, the son chafes against a complex psychological game, in which he has become a resentful pawn and in which his ultimate checkmate is his self-containment.

Interviewers and reviewers have commented frequently on the seeming contradiction between Tóibín's gregarious humor and the somberness of his fiction, yet the humor is in evidence in this collection, particularly in those stories in which mothers and sons are locked in epic battles of wills. Widowed Nancy in "The Name of the Game," shocked to discover that her husband's death has left the family finances in ashes, engages in some financial skulduggery to open up a fish-and-chips shop, a move deplored by her neighbors, friends, and even her son, all of whom see the enterprise as being beneath her husband's family's long-held respectability. When her son realizes that the business is a financial boon, he immerses himself in it, assuming himself to be the heir apparent, but is shocked to discover that his mother has other plans.

Perhaps the most affecting story in the collection is set not in Ireland but in the Catalan region of Spain, an area for which Tóibín has long had a deep affection and respect. A tour de force of authorial restraint, "A Long Winter" quietly evokes the emotional turmoil beneath the surface of a hardworking but largely uncommunicative family. Grieving over the departure of their younger son, Jordi, for mandatory military service, the parents displace their emotions: the father by annoying the store clerks during a family shopping trip, the mother by succumbing to her unacknowledged but long-standing alcoholism. When the father disposes of all the alcohol in the house in a ham-handed attempt to

break his wife's addiction, the mother sets off on a catastrophic journey, only to disappear in a snowstorm. Tóibín subtly evokes the unraveling of a family in the wake of the mother's disappearance, a process at once emotional and palpable, for each member performs tasks essential to the family's existence. The father and older son, Miquel, have no domestic skills; in a rural community where cooperation is a matter of survival, the father has alienated his neighbors, who nevertheless grudgingly help him search for his wife, a life-threatening enterprise. When the father employs a young man to do the "women's work" he reviles but cannot do without, the older son finds in Manolo a sympathetic companion and perhaps a future lover. With consummate skill, Tóibín adheres to the writer's directive to "show, don't tell": gestures, glances, and physical details peel back these multilayered characters and their fraught alliances, as with the final image of the two young men covertly embracing in the wake of a shocking scene of violence. These two damaged people have found mutual comfort, but they will have to tread carefully in this place of aggressive masculinity, where nature's brutality lives close to the surface of both man and beast.

THE EMPTY FAMILY

Tóibín's second collection of stories, *The Empty Family*, is middle-aged in its sensibility, even though only some of its characters are middle-aged. Reflective, melancholy, filled with longing and regret, the stories are sometimes autobiographical, set in Enniscorthy, Tóibín's hometown; in Catalunya, where the author lived as a young man; in Dublin, where Tóibín has spent much of his adult life; in the United States, where he has been a visiting professor and writer at several universities. Able to remember a time when poverty was endemic to Ireland and emigration a foregone conclusion for many, Tóibín conjures an Ireland to which expatriates return, either to bury their dead or to resume their lives, as in "One Minus One" and "The Empty Family." It is a place where people rediscover home and wrestle with family secrets, where former lovers and friends realign themselves, as in "The Pearl Fishers," in which the wife of the narrator's former lover, herself a conservative journalist, reveals her intention to publish an exposé of the priest who seduced her. Taking its title from Georges Bizet's opera, a performance of which marked a turning point in the trio's lives when they were still teenagers, the story is a sly commentary on contemporary upper-middle-class Dublin. Bizet's affecting aria "Au fond du temple saint," with its intricate interweaving voices, serves as an ironic metaphor for the two former lovers' life choices: Donnacha, now married and conventionally respectable; the narrator solitary, openly gay, a successful writer of violent thrillers.

A former love affair likewise haunts the elderly protagonists of "Two Women" and "Silence." The former depicts an expatriate Irish film set dresser who returns to Ireland for a short-term assignment only to encounter the widow of her former lover. The latter features Lady Gregory and Henry James, two historical figures appearing elsewhere in Tóibín's writing, as the publicly irreproachable Gregory recalls an extramarital affair and the ways in which art not so much imitates life as offers it up in self-protective camouflage.

Mortality infiltrates these stories, some of which deal with deaths, others with contemplating the shades of former selves. In the exquisitely written "One Minus One," an expatriate Irishman addresses a second-person narrative to a former lover in Ireland as he revisits his mother's death six years earlier, a mother who remained emotionally elusive to the last. In the title story, another second-person narrative that may in fact employ the same narrator and the same lover, an Irishman contemplates returning home to live in the place where his dead are buried. In "The Colour of Shadows," a Dublin-dwelling man returns to Enniscorthy as the aunt who raised him sickens and dies. The emotional pull of the dead upon the living is very much in evidence, sometimes even when the death is metaphorical, as in ended love affairs.

Similar preoccupations inform the three stories set in the Catalan region of Spain, for, as critics have noted, Tóibín's fictional renderings of Catalunya share much of the psychological geography of Ireland. "Barcelona, 1975" recalls the narrator's twenty-year-old self, a newly arrived Dubliner sexually liberated by his introduction to the gay scene in Barcelona. In "The New Spain," a Catalan woman, whose communist, anti-Francisco Franco politics alienated her from her family and her homeland, returns from a long absence in London to assume her new, ironic role as a property owner.

The concluding story of the collection, "The Street," subtly melds Irish, Catalan, and Pakistani preoccupations. Malik, a Pakistani Muslim, shares with many Irish the lonely, frightening experience of being an immigrant in an alien city. Unable to speak the language, learning that his religion and ethnicity render him a possible target for persecution, aware that should his precarious employment collapse that his father would not welcome him home, Malik is poignantly rendered. Looking surreptitiously at the frightening pictures of American soldiers torturing Muslim prisoners, warned not to stray far from his job or the small flat he shares with other immigrants, he struggles to find some sense of rootedness. Tóibín with great restraint and tenderness unfolds Malik's growing love for Abdul, a fellow immigrant, in a relationship facing formidable odds: a vicious beating by their boss when he discovers them making love; the unexpected revelation that Abdul has a wife and children at home; the realization that they are continually scrutinized by authority figures within and outside their immigrant community. With an insight into the immigrant experience worthy of one of Bharati Mukherjee's stunning stories, Tóibín concludes the story--and the collection--as the couple enjoys a carefully choreographed afternoon in Barcelona, where they can be anonymous, where a casual touch will go unremarked, and where they can fantasize about going home to Pakistan someday and living a hidden life in Abdul's large extended family.

Mournful but not bleak, preoccupied with the past but not nostalgic, these are mature stories not only in their subtlety and their command of language but also in the courage of their characters, who face their regrets without wallowing in them and who recognize that meaning resides in flashes of insight or clarity rather than in momentous revelations.

OTHER MAJOR WORKS

LONG FICTION: *The South*, 1990; *The Heather Blazing*, 1992; *The Story of the Night*, 1996; *The Blackwater Lightship*, 1999; *The Master*, 2004; *Brooklyn*, 2009.

PLAY: *Beauty in a Broken Place*, pb. 2004.

NONFICTION: *Walking Along the Border*, 1987 (with photographs by Tony O'Shea; later reissued with text alone as *Bad Blood: A Walk Along the Irish Border*, 1984); *Homage to Barcelona*, 1990; *The Trial of the Generals: Selected Journalism, 1980-1990*, 1990; *The Sign of the Cross: Travels in Catholic Europe*, 1994; *The Irish Famine*, 1999 (expanded version with Diarmaid Ferriter pb. as *The Irish Famine: A Documentary History*, 2001); *Lady Gregory's Toothbrush*, 2002; *Love in a Dark Time: Gay Lives from Wilde to Almodóvar*, 2002; *All a Novelist Needs: Essays on Henry James*, 2010.

EDITED TEXTS: *The Modern Library*, 1999 (with Carmen Callil); *The Penguin Book of Irish Fiction*, 1999.

BIBLIOGRAPHY

Delaney, Paul, ed. *Reading Colm Tóibín*. Dublin: Liffey Press, 2008. The first book-length study of Tóibín's writing, this collection of essays analyzes Tóibín's writing career up through *Mothers and Sons*. Topics include the author's treatment of history and memory, gay sexuality, his travel writing, and studies of individual works, such as *The Heather Blazing*, *The Master*, and *Mothers and Son*. The latter essays treat the short stories' transformation of mother-son relationships in Irish literature and Tóibín's reworking of Oedipal themes. An in-depth interview with Irish journalist Fintan O'Toole and a comprehensive bibliography are also included.

Iyer, Pico. "A Strangers in the Family." *The New York Times*, December 31, 2006. This review provides an in-depth analysis of *Mothers and Sons* and places it in the context of Tóibín's writing career.

Lee, Hermione. "*The Empty Family* by Colm Tóibín." *The Guardian*, October 9, 2010. Connecting *The Empty Family* to the novels that most recently preceded it, Lee praises Tóibín's use of diverse literary techniques in a collection unified by its theme of regret.

Mary Fitzgerald-Hoyt

ROSE TREMAIN

Born: London, England; August 2, 1943

PRINCIPAL SHORT FICTION

The Colonel's Daughters, and Other Stories, 1984
The Garden of the Villa Mollini, and Other Stories, 1987
Evangelista's Fan, and Other Stories, 1994
Collected Short Stories, 1996
The Darkness of Wallis Simpson, and Other Stories, 2005
"The Jester of Artapovo," 2009

OTHER LITERARY FORMS

Rose Tremain is known mainly as a novelist, though she began her career writing radio scripts. Her novels range widely over time and place, but her reputation has rested with two historical novels, *Restoration* (1989) and *Music and Silence* (1999), both set in the seventeenth century. She has claimed that her historical fiction is not costume drama but serious fiction with contemporary insights, using literary constructions.

ACHIEVEMENTS

Rose Tremain's main achievement has been to raise the status of the historical novel, which had been debased by popular writers into what has been called "costume drama" and "bodice rippers." She claims that her historical novels have used sophisticated literary techniques to convey universal themes and make contemporary comments. She has maintained also the British tradition of short-story writing with the use of unusual places and plots for her characters.

Awards have been many. For her radio play *Temporary Shelter* (1984) she won the Giles Cooper Award. Her novel *Restoration* won the *Sunday Express* Book of the Year for 1984 and also was shortlisted for the Booker Prize. *Music and Silence* won Whitbread Novel of the Year in 1999. In between, she won the James Tait Black Memorial Prize and the *Prix Femina Étranger* from France. She has been a Fellow of the Royal Society of Literature (FRSL) since 1983.

BIOGRAPHY

Rose Tremain was born Rosemary Jane Thomson to Keith and Viola Thomson in London during World War II. Tremain attended Francis Holland School, a prestigious girls' high school, and the Sorbonne, the ancient university of Paris, where she obtained a Diploma in Literature in 1963. On returning to England, she enrolled at the newly formed University of East Anglia, at Norwich, graduating with honors in English in 1967.

Her first job was as an elementray school teacher, where she specialized in French and history. This lasted only a short time, until she obtained the post of editor of British Printing Corporation (BPC) Publications in London. In 1971, she married Jon Tremain, by whom she had one daughter; they were divorced in 1978. By then she had branched out into writing, first for the BPC, with an account of the women's emancipation movement and a biography of Joseph Stalin. She wrote a novel, *Sadler's Birthday* (1976), which was well received.

From there she got into radio work for the British Broadcasting Company (BBC), and did a number of radio plays for them, from 1976 till the end of the century. Later, she did some television writing. Again, these were well-received. Two more novels followed, as she devoted her life to full-time writing.

In 1982, Tremain married Jonathan Dudley, a marriage that did not last long. In 1984 came her first collection of short fiction, *The Colonel's Daughter, and Other Stories*. For this she won the Dylan Thomas Prize. Another collection followed in 1987, *The Garden of the Villa Mollini, and Other Stories*, firmly establishing her as a leading short-story writer in England.

Restoration, however, was the work that propelled her into literary fame. It was a historical novel that sought to rise above "costume drama" and say something to Tremain's contemporary world, at that time under the regime of British prime minister Margaret Thatcher, in which social cohesion was under great strain. There was a 1995 film adaptation of the book, and it was shortlisted for the Booker Prize.

In 1992, she began to live with a new partner, biographer Richard Holmes, near Norwich, the home of the University of East Anglia, whose creative-writing courses she sometimes taught. Her third volume of short stories, *Evangelista's Fan, and Other Stories*, was published in 1994. Her short stories were then republished as *Collected Short Stories* in 1996. A second major historical novel, *Music and Silence*, followed in 1999. She continued to produce novels and short stories, including *The Darkness of Wallis Simpson, and Other Stories* in 2005.

ANALYSIS

Rose Tremain's short fiction lies well within the traditional British short story, following on from Virginia Woolf, E. M. Forster, and V. S. Pritchett. The majority deal with twentieth-century English middle-class life, with the many nuances of British class life well caught and handled. Some stories deal with historical subjects, but these are in the minority. Others deal with foreign cultures, either European or American. The mode of narration is simple, more in the style of a story than a literary fiction. Postmodern and structuralist techniques and constructions are generally avoided.

While there is no overriding concern uniting the stories, a number of topics do emerge, and an overall gently satiric pessimism pervades most. Male sexuality as expressed in adolescenec and homosexuality are particular topics. Tremain seems to understand boys rather better than girls, in fact. Female sexuality is confined to the desire for marriage, usually unhappily fulfilled, and is seen to work against personal freedom in women. Marriage is thus another topic. It is seen as either dull and depersonalizing or as an unhappy power struggle, with the woman usually emerging as a victim of the husband's unfaithfulness or violence. Happy resolutions are the exception. There is little attempt at political statement.

THE COLONEL'S DAUGHTER, AND OTHER STORIES

That Tremain is in many ways a popular rather than an academic writer can be seen from the magazines in which these short stories appeared. Three appeared in popular women's magazines; only one appeared in a serious literary journal. This accents Tremain's ability to tread in both popular and serious literature, which

Rose Tremain (Colin McPherson/Corbis)

was acknowledged by Dylan Thomas Award of 1984 for the volume. The opening story, "The Colonel's Daughter," is the longest and most complex. It takes up an early interest in the women's movement and casts its heroine, Charlotte, as an antiestablishment aristocrat who ends up causing the death of an elderly butler at her parents' house and also the suicide of her lower-middle-class lover, all in an attempt to promote the women's movement.

Tremain uses a technique she later employed more skillfully in *Music and Silence*, of laying various subplots side by side as they unfold in time. It is hardly a modern technique, but it suggests the inter-connectedness of human relationships, despite their seeming disconnectedness. On the one hand are the incomprehending colonel and his stately wife, gliding through a Swiss vacation in wealth and leisure; on the other hand is their daughter Charlotte, in her self-chosen squalor with her lover, who, as in Forster's *Howards End* (1910), has become her project. In the middle is an American journalist, who by the end of the book has decided to make Charlotte his project as she goes to

prison. Both he and Charlotte think they are in love with their projects. Tremain suggests it is their own egoistic desires that have infatuated them. Tremain's characterization is strong, apart from the journalist-Charlotte relationship, which remains contrived.

"Wedding Night" deals with adolescent male sexuality, and, as are a number of Tremain's stories, is set largely in Paris. "Dinner for One" deals with a gay relationship that ends unhappily. The last story in the volume, "My Love Affair with James I," deals with a similar topic but much more wittily. It is told in the first person; the male actor who is the speaking voice is undertaking a writing course and frequently draws attention to the rules he is breaking. As Tremain herself taught creative- writing courses, there is a good deal of tongue in cheek. It would seem that the protagonist's writing and his homosexuality are a joke. Sex does not lead to passion but to bathos.

THE GARDEN OF THE VILLA MOLLINI, AND OTHER STORIES

The title story, "The Garden of the Villa Mollini," is placed, for no apparent reason, second in the volume. It is set in late nineteenth-century Tuscany and centers on a famous opera singer, Antonio Mollini. He is a somewhat stereotyped Italian tenor. At first he buys a dilapidated villa and promises to be the patron to the village lying downstream from his grounds. However, after each new affair, when a mistress supplants a wife, the plans for the villa's garden gets more and more elaborate. He deprives the villagers of their water by damming the stream; he takes away their common land to add to his grounds; in the end cannot even remember the villagers' names.

Only the gardener has any conscience about the social implications, but he cannot rally the villagers to act. The story appears unfinished at the end, but only because the reader knows exactly what is going to happen: The pattern will repeat itself inexorably. Tremain suggests strongly the antisocial nature of egotistical love and the lack of social conscience in the successful artist. Everything gets trampled on, yet brings no fulfillment to the artist. There is barely anything positive to be salvaged from this fable, just as there was little good to salvage from "The Colonel's Daughter."

The women's movement theme from that story is continued in "The Kite Flyer." The vicar's Christianity is of such an odd variety that it is best seen as an allegory of power, which flows away from him into his wife. She turns from being vicar's wife to an ardent Campaign for Nuclear Disarmament (CND) campaigner, aligning herself with the women of Greenham Common, the site of a well-known feminist protest. However, her emancipation is short-lived: In a fit of jealousy, her husband strangles her with kite wire, just as Charlotte's gestures put her in prison. They are both seen as having Joan of Arc complexes, and Tremain's attitude to women's emancipation remains ambivalent and even contradictory.

EVANGELISTA'S FAN, AND OTHER STORIES

This volume came out between Tremain's best two historical novels and reflects more of her historical interest than any of the other stories hitherto, most of which had been set in the mid-twentieth-century. "Evangelista's Fan" is set in the post-Napoleonic era (1815 onward) in Piedmont, Italy, and London. Tremain opens up a number of allegorical interpretions as her protagonist, Cavalli, sets up as a "Repairer of Time" in London, turning away from his vocation as a watch-maker. In fact, he sacrifices his love and then his name to become a famous barometer maker in London, but he lives under a false name and married to a wife he did not intend to marry. Time, Tremain seems to suggest, cannot be repaired; rather it takes away one's ideals. One either pines away for those ideals or one just gets on with life by taking what chances time offers.

"The Candle-Maker" was the result of a commission from the Cheltenham Literature Festival, a prestigious British event. The story is set in nineteenth-century Corsica and deals with survival in life, rather than a lying down and dying for what cannot be restored. Its survivor is Mercedes, a poor laundress, jilted in a long-ago love affair. Both these stories allow some sort of resolution but for a life far from what was desired.

"Two of Them" is more typical of Tremain's stories: concerning a middle-class family in mid-twentieth-century England. The father's madness, rather than the father's marriage, as in "Wedding Night," helps bring about the adolescent boy's sexual initiation. Again, Tremain avoids exploring the female equivalent, though two girls are brought into the story. What emerges is just how insane British middle-class life is, or was. Tremain presumably is commenting on her own upbringing.

THE DARKNESS OF WALLIS SIMPSON, AND OTHER STORIES

The title story, "The Darkness of Wallis Simpson," is a fascinating historical construct based on old age. A number of Tremain's stories dealt with the problems of aging. Tremain's problem is with aging rather than with death, and the old woman's helplessness in the face of her "carers" bears this out. Wallis Simpson was the wife of Edward VIII of England, on whose account he famously abdicated shortly before World War II. The problem was not so much she was an American and not of noble blood, but that she had been twice divorced.

The ironic twist to the whole story is that the dying Wallis, widowed and adrift in Paris, cannot remember Edward but only her first two husbands. She can remember her abusive first husband, but she remembers Edward only as a sad-faced, nameless little man, whose relationship to herself she cannot place. She even remembers Adolf Hitler better than the man who gave up the throne for her. Tremain is thus reducing to nothing a famous twentieth-century love affair. Tremain seems to question, is love worth anything?

The other story of interest in the volume is "The Beauty of the Dawn Shift," which was selected as the best example of Tremain's work for the prestigious *Oxford Book of British Short Stories* (1998), edited by A. S. Byatt. It has a contemporary setting in East Germany, just after the Berlin Wall came down and the Communist regimes in Eastern Europe fell. Its protagonist, Hector, remains a loyal Communist and sets off east rather than west. He perishes on the way in the freezing winter cold of Poland. An incestuous affair with his sister is the sexual subplot. Again, the theme seems to be the futility of ideals and the vanity of human wishes, to use Samuel Johnson's famous phrase.

OTHER MAJOR WORKS

LONG FICTION: *Sadler's Birthday*, 1976; *Letter to Sister Benedicta*, 1979; *The Cupboard*, 1981; *The Swimming Pool Season*, 1985; *Restoration: A Novel of Seventeenth Century England*, 1989; *Sacred Country*, 1992; *The Way I Found Her*, 1997; *Music and Silence*, 1999; *The Colour*, 2003; *The Road House*, 2007; *Trespass*, 2010.

TELEPLAYS: *Hallelujah, Mary Plum*, 1979; *Findings on a Late Afternoon*, 1981; *A Room for the Winter*, 1981.

RADIO PLAYS: *The Wisest Fool*, 1976; *Dark Green*, 1977; *Blossom*, 1977; *Don't Be Cruel*, 1978; *Leavings*, 1978; *Down the Hill*, 1979; *Half Time*, 1980; *Temporary Shelter*, 1984; *The Kite Flyer*, 1989; *Music and Silence*, 1992; *Who Was Emily Davison?*, 1996; *The End of Love*, 1999.

NONFICTION: *The Fight for Freedom for Women*, 1973; *Stalin*, 1975.

CHILDREN'S LITERATURE: *Journey to the Volcano*, 1985.

BIBLIOGRAPHY

Brownrigg, Sylvia. "Talking with Rose Tremain: Making It All Up." *Newsday*, July 12, 1998. An interview that discusses Tremain's view of fiction and gives useful insights into her approaches to writing.

Colvin, Clare. "The Books Interview: Chance of a Lifetime." *The Independent*, September 4, 1999. In this interview, Tremain claims the historical novel should be taken as seriously as the contemporary one.

Sceats, Sarah. "Appetite, Desire, and Belonging in the Novels of Rose Tremain." In *The Contemporary British Novel Since 1980*, edited by James Acheson and Sarah Ross. New York: Palgrave Macmillan, 2005. Looks at Tremain's writing from a feminist perspective, focusing on the concepts of desire and longing.

David Barratt

WILLIAM TREVOR

Born: Mitchelstown, County Cork, Ireland;
  May 24, 1928
Also Known As: William Trevor Cox

PRINCIPAL SHORT FICTION

The Day We Got Drunk on Cake, and Other Stories,
  1967
The Ballroom of Romance, and Other Stories, 1972
The Last Lunch of the Season, 1973
Angels at the Ritz, and Other Stories, 1975
Lovers of Their Time, and Other Stories, 1978
Beyond the Pale, and Other Stories, 1981
The Stories of William Trevor, 1983
The News from Ireland, and Other Stories, 1986
Family Sins, and Other Stories, 1990
Collected Stories, 1992
Ireland: Selected Stories, 1995
Marrying Damian, 1995 (limited edition)
Outside Ireland: Selected Stories, 1995
After Rain, 1996
The Hill Bachelors, 2000
A Bit on the Side, 2004
The Dressmaker's Child, 2005
Cheating at Canasta, 2007
Collected Stories, 2009 (2 volumes)

OTHER LITERARY FORMS

Though probably best known as a writer of short stories, William Trevor (TREH-vuhr) has also written television and radio scripts, plays, and numerous novels. Among Trevor's novels, *The Old Boys* (1964), *Miss Gomez and the Brethren* (1971), *Elizabeth Alone* (1973), *The Children of Dynmouth* (1976), *Fools of Fortune* (1983), *Felicia's Journey* (1994), and *Death in Summer* (1998) have been particularly praised. He has also written two nonfiction works, *A Writer's Ireland: Landscape in Literature* (1984) and *Excursions in the*

Real World (1993). Trevor's novel *The Story of Lucy Gault* was published in 2002, and his novel *Love and Summer* came out in 2009.

ACHIEVEMENTS

William Trevor is widely regarded as one of the finest storytellers and craftsmen writing in English. In Great Britain, his work has long been reviewed widely and favorably and has frequently been adapted for radio and television broadcast by the British Broadcasting Corporation. In 1964, Trevor's second novel, *The Old Boys*, was awarded the Hawthornden Prize; his fourth collection, *Angels at the Ritz, and Other Stories*, was hailed by writer Graham Greene as "one of the finest collections, if not the best, since James Joyce's *Dubliners*." In addition, Trevor has won the Royal Society of Literature Award, the Allied Irish Banks' Prize for Literature, and the Whitbread Literary Award; he is also a member of the Irish Academy of Letters. In 1979, "in recognition for his valuable services to literature," Trevor was named an honorary Commander, Order of the British Empire and in the same year received the Irish Community Prize. In 1980 and 1982, he received the Giles Cooper Award for radio plays; in 1983, he received a Jacob Award for a teleplay. He received D.Litt. degrees from the University of Exeter, Trinity College in Dublin, the University of Belfast, and the National University of Ireland in Cork. Trevor received the Sunday Express Book of the Year Award in 1994 for *Felicia's Journey*. In the United States, knowledge of Trevor's work increased markedly when *The Stories of William Trevor*, an omnibus collection, was published in 1983 and received highly enthusiastic reviews.

BIOGRAPHY

Born William Trevor Cox in Ireland's County Cork, William Trevor, the son of a bank manager, spent much of his childhood living in small Irish towns and attending a series of boarding and day schools that included St. Columba's in Dublin. After earning a B.A. in history from Dublin's Trinity College, Trevor, a Protestant, began work as a sculptor and schoolmaster, taking his first job as an instructor of history in Armagh, Northern Ireland. In 1952, Trevor married Jane Ryan and moved to England, where he spent the next eight years teaching art at two prestigious public schools--first at Rugby and then at Taunton. Between 1960 and 1965, Trevor worked as a copywriter at an advertising agency in London; he simultaneously began devoting an increasing portion of his free time to the writing of fiction. By the early 1970's, following the appearance of several novels and a steady stream of stories in such publications as *Encounter*, *The New Yorker*, and *London Magazine*, Trevor's reputation was secure. The father of two sons, Trevor settled in Devon and continued to write full time.

William Trevor (AP Photo/Alastair Grant)

ANALYSIS

Like his novels, William Trevor's short stories generally take place in either England or the Republic of Ireland. For the most part, Trevor focuses on middle-class or lower-middle-class figures whose lives have been characterized by loneliness, disappointment, and pain. His stories feature tight organization and lean but detailed prose. Their very "average" characters are made interesting by Trevor's careful attention to the traits and quirks that make them individuals, to the memories and regrets they have of the past. Trevor, often wry and always detached, refuses to sentimentalize any of them; he does not, however, subject them to ridicule. Their struggles reveal the author's deep curiosity about the manifold means by which people foil themselves or, more rarely, manage not to do so. Many of Trevor's characters are trapped in jobs or familial circumstances that are dull or oppressive or both; many retreat frequently to fond memories or romantic fantasies. Trevor rarely mocks the men and women who inhabit his fiction, nor does he treat them as mere ciphers or automatons. In fact, like Joyce, to whom he is often compared, Trevor assumes a detached authorial stance, but occasionally and subtly he makes it clear that he is highly sympathetic to the plight of underdogs, self-deluders, and the victims of abuse and deceit. Invariably, his principal characters are carefully and completely drawn--and so are the worlds they inhabit. Few contemporary writers of short fiction can render atmosphere and the subtleties of personality as precisely and as tellingly as William Trevor. Few can capture so accurately and wittily the rhythms and nuances of everyday speech. Though its themes can be somber and settings quite bleak, Trevor's brilliantly paced and carefully sculpted fiction consistently moves, amuses, and invigorates.

"THE GENERAL'S DAY"

One of Trevor's earliest stories, "The General's Day," illustrates with particular clarity the dark side of his artistic vision. Contained in *The Day We Got Drunk on Cake, and Other Stories*, "The General's Day" centers on a decorated and now-retired military man, who, at seventy-eight, has never quite come to grips with his retirement and so spends his days wandering around the local village looking for something to do. On the day of the story, a sunny Saturday in June, General Suffolk greets the day with energy and resolution but ends by simply killing time in the local tea shop, where he musters what is left of his once-celebrated charm and manages to convince a woman-- "a thin, middle-aged person with a face like a faded photograph"--to join him for drinks at the local hotel. There, fueled by gin, General Suffolk flirts so blatantly and clumsily with the woman that she flees, "her face like a beetroot." Fueled by more gin, the lonely man becomes increasingly obnoxious. After suffering a few more rejections and humiliations, he finally stumbles back home, where he is mocked further by his "unreliable servant," Mrs. Hinch, a crude woman who habitually cuts corners and treats herself to secretive swigs of the general's expensive South African sherry. In the story's final scene, General Suffolk, "the hero of Roeux and Monchy-le-Preux," is shown leaning and weeping on his cleaning woman's fat arm as she laughingly helps him back to his cottage. "My God Almighty," General Suffolk, deflated, mutters, "I could live for twenty years."

"AN EVENING WITH JOHN JOE DEMPSEY"

Trevor often portrays older men and women who make stoic adjustments to the present while living principally in the past. He also sometimes focuses on children and adolescents who use vividly constructed daydreams as a means of escaping dreary surroundings or obtuse parents who are themselves sunk in the deadness of their cramped and predictable lives. In "An Evening with John Joe Dempsey," from *The Ballroom of Romance, and Other Stories*, Trevor's central figure is a boy of fifteen who lives in a small house in a small Irish town, where, daily, he sits in a dull classroom in preparation for a dead-end job at the nearby sawmills. John Joe lives with his widowed mother, a wiry, chronically worried woman, whose principal interest in life is to hover protectively about her only son. John Joe escapes his mother's smothering solicitations by wandering about the town with Quigley, an elderly dwarf reputed to be, as one local puts it, "away in the head." Quigley likes to fire John Joe's already active imagination by regaling the boy with detailed descriptions of the sexual vignettes he claims to have witnessed while peeping through area windows. In his own daydreams, John Joe dallies with many of the same sizable matrons whom Quigley likes to portray in compromising positions. One of them, Mrs. Taggart, "the wife of a postman," is a tall, "well-built" woman who in John Joe's fantasies requires repeated rescuing from a locked bathroom, in which she stands unblushingly nude. Like many of Trevor's characters, John Joe is thus a convincing mix of the comic and the pathetic. If his incongruous sexual fantasies are humorous, the rest of his life looks decidedly grim. In the story's particularly effective closing scene, Trevor portrays John Joe in his bed, in the dark, thinking again of impossible erotic romps with wholly unobtainable women, feeling

> more alive than ever he was at the Christian Brothers' School . . . or his mother's kitchen, more alive than ever he would be at the sawmills. In his bed he entered a paradise: it was grand being alone.

"NICE DAY AT SCHOOL"

In "Nice Day at School," from the same collection, Trevor's principal character is a girl of fourteen, Eleanor, who lives on a housing estate with her cranky, chain-smoking mother and her father, a former professional wrestler who now works as a nightclub bouncer and likes to claim that his work has made him the trusted friend of many celebrities, including Rex Harrison, Mia Farrow, Princess Margaret, and Anthony Armstrong-Jones. Though Eleanor is embarrassed by her father's obviously exaggerated accounts of his encounters with the rich and famous, she is much given to vivid imaginings of her own. Bombarded daily by saccharine pop songs and the blatantly sexual chatter of her friends, Eleanor thinks obsessively of her ideal lover:

> a man whose fingers were long and thin and gentle, who'd hold her hand in the aeroplane. Air France to Biarritz. And afterwards she'd come back to a flat where the curtains were the colour of lavender, the same as the walls, where gas fires glowed and there were rugs on natural-wood floors, and the telephone was pale blue.

Subtly, however, Trevor indicates that Eleanor is not likely to find a lover so wealthy and suave. Like her friends and most girls of the same social class, this daughter of a bloated bouncer and a bored, gin-sipping housewife will instead settle for someone like Denny Price, the young butcher's apprentice with "blubbery" lips, who once moved his rough hand up and down her body "like an animal, a rat gnawing at her, prodding her and poking."

"OFFICE ROMANCES"

Trevor often focuses on women who find themselves pursued by or entangled with insensitive or calculating males. In "Office Romances," from *Angels at the Ritz, and Other Stories*, Trevor's central character is Angela Hosford, a typist who works quite anonymously in a large London office appointed with "steel-framed reproductions" and "ersatz leather" sofas and chairs. At twenty-six, Angela is pleasant but plain and myopic: She wears contact lenses that give her eyes a slightly "bulgy look." Her pursuer, Gordon Spelle, is, at thirty-eight, tall and "sleek," but his left eyelid droops a bit, and the eye it covers is badly glazed. While watching old films on television when she was fourteen, Angela developed a crush on the American actor Don Ameche and had imagined "a life with him in a cliff-top home she'd invented, in California." Now, she finds herself drawn to the deliberately "old-fashioned" Spelle and at one point imagines herself "stroking his face and comforting him because of his bad eye." One day, after his flatteries succeed in rendering Angela both "generous and euphoric," Spelle manages to lure her into a dark and empty office, where--muttering "I love you" repeatedly--he makes love to her, inelegantly, on the floor. Angela finds this experience "not even momentarily pleasurable, not once," but afterward she basks in the memory of Spelle's heated professions of love. Angela eventually takes a job elsewhere, convinced that Spelle's passion for her "put him under a strain, he being married to a wife who was ill." Like many of Trevor's characters, she understandably decides not to look past her comforting delusions; she refuses to accept the well-known fact that Spelle was "notorious" and "chose girls who were unattractive because he believed such girls, deprived of sex for long periods of time, were an easier bet."

"LOVERS OF THEIR TIME"

The vast gulf that often separates romantic fantasy from unsavory fact is similarly revealed in the title story of *Lovers of Their Time, and Other Stories*. In this piece, set in the 1960's, Trevor's lovers are Norman Britt, a mild-mannered travel agent with "a David Niven moustache," and a young woman, Marie, who tends the counter at Green's the Chemist's. Norman and Marie meet regularly in one of Trevor's favorite fictional locations--a dark pub filled with a wide array of drinkers, talkers, and dreamers.

"THE DRUMMER BOY"

In that same place, in "The Drummer Boy," the two listen to Beatles songs and talk of running away with each other to some romantic foreign country--an event they realize is not likely to materialize. Marie is single, but Norman is married to the loud and bawdy Hilda, who spends the better part of her life sipping cheap wine and watching police dramas on the television and who has previously hinted that she is quite content in the odd marital arrangement that Norman loathes. Thus, at Norman's instigation, the two lovers begin to rendezvous more intimately at the nearby hotel, the Great Western Royal. Specifically, they begin to sneak into a large, infrequently used bathroom, "done up in marble," on the hotel's second floor. Here, luxuriating in an enormous tub, they talk hopefully of happier days that, unfortunately, never arrive. Hilda dismisses her husband's request for a divorce by telling him, "You've gone barmy, Norman"; Marie, tired of waiting, weds "a man in a brewery." Thus, as the years pass, Norman is left with a nostalgic longing not only for Marie but also for that brief period in the 1960's when playful risk-taking was much in the air. Often, while riding "the tube" to work, Norman

> would close his eyes and with the greatest pleasure that remained to him he would recall the delicately veined marble and the great brass taps, and the bath that was big enough for two. And now and again he heard what happened to be the sound of distant music, and the voices of the Beatles celebrating a bathroom love, as they had celebrated Eleanor Rigby and other people of that time.

"FLIGHTS OF FANCY"

This allusion to a popular and bittersweet Beatles song is especially appropriate in yet another Trevor story about two thoroughly average and lonely people whose lives have not often been marked by episodes of great passion. In "Flights of Fancy," also from *Lovers of Their Time, and Other Stories*, Trevor's principal character, Sarah Machaen, is yet another Rigby-like character destined, one assumes, to spend the rest of her life uneasily alone. Sarah, a clergyman's daughter, is an executive secretary in a large London firm that manufactures lamps; she visits museums, sings in a Bach choir, and is "a popular choice as a godmother." Well into middle age, Sarah is quite content with the externals of her life and gradually has become "reconciled to the fact that her plainness wasn't going to go away." Sometimes, however, she gets lonely enough to daydream of marriage--perhaps to an elderly widower or a blind man. Ironically, the one person who does express a romantic interest in Sarah is another woman, a young and pretty but unschooled factory worker called Sandra Pond. Sarah is shocked at the very idea of lesbianism, yet she cannot stop her mind from "throwing up flights of fancy" in which she pictures herself sharing her flat with Sandra and introducing her to London's many cultural delights. Though her shyness and acute sense of propriety prompt her to reject Sandra's clumsy but clearly genuine professions of love, Sarah is haunted by the sense that she has perhaps passed up her last chance for passion and romance.

"BROKEN HOMES"

"Broken Homes," also from *Lovers of Their Time, and Other Stories*, is one of Trevor's most powerful stories. Its principal character, Mrs. Malby, lives with her two budgerigars in a little flat that is scrupulously neat and prettily painted. Mrs. Malby, a widow, lost both of her sons thirty years earlier during World War II; now, at eighty-seven, she has come to terms with her own impending death and wants nothing more than to spend her remaining days in familiar surroundings, her faculties intact. Unfortunately, Mrs. Malby's flat is destroyed and her serenity threatened by a squad of loud and insensitive teenagers from a nearby comprehensive school-- "an ugly sprawl of glass and concrete buildings," Mrs. Malby recalls, full of "children swinging along the pavements, shouting obscenities." As part of a community relations scheme, the teenagers have been equipped with mops and sponges and brushes and sent out into the neighborhood in search of good deeds to perform. Mrs. Malby politely asks these obnoxious adolescents to do nothing more than wash her walls, but they treat her with condescension and contempt, and while she is out, they proceed to make a complete mess of her apartment, splattering its walls

and floors with bright yellow paint. The students' "teacher," an obtuse and "untidily dressed" bureaucrat, patronizingly assures Mrs. Malby that the damage is slight. He reminds her that, in any event, one must make allowances for the children of "broken homes."

Perhaps more than any of his other stories, "Broken Homes" reveals Trevor's sympathy for the plight of the elderly and his acute awareness of the infirmities and insecurities that accompany old age. The story certainly reveals a strong suspicion that, by the mid-1970's, the British welfare state had become both inefficient and rudely intrusive. Indeed, "Broken Homes" is informed by the subtly expressed sense--not uncommon in Trevor's later fiction--that contemporary Great Britain and Ireland have grown increasingly crass and tacky and that the old social fabric is rapidly and perhaps deleteriously unraveling.

"THE PARADISE LOUNGE"

Arguably, "The Paradise Lounge," from *Beyond the Pale, and Other Stories*, is Trevor's most representative story. Set principally in the small bar of Keegan's Railway hotel, in "a hilly provincial town" in the Republic of Ireland, "The Paradise Lounge" shifts its focus between two recognizably Trevor-esque figures. One of them, Beatrice, is thirty-two; the other, Miss Doheny, is in her eighties. Beatrice--who wanted to be an actor once--drives often to Keegan's and its adjoining Paradise Lounge to rendezvous with her lover, a middle-aged businessman already married. Miss Doheny, one of the locals, goes regularly to the lounge for a bit of company and several good, stiff drinks. The two have never formally met. However, Beatrice--observing Miss Doheny from across the room--is convinced that the old woman is an intriguing figure with a fascinating and no doubt satisfyingly romantic past; Beatrice does not realize that Miss Doheny is not only lonely but also full of anger and regret. Miss Doheny, in turn, envies Beatrice's freedom--her ability, in a more liberated and enlightened age, to enter into a friendly sexual affair without running the risk of paralyzing guilt and ostracism. She does not realize that the younger woman's affair has grown stale and mechanical and that by her own estimation Beatrice is about to engage in nothing more than a "mess of deception and lies."

AFTER RAIN

The twelve stories of *After Rain* concern how marriage and family ties constrain, bewilder, confound, or, occasionally, help their characters. For instance, a woman's attempt to invigorate the life of her best friend by encouraging an affair ends the friendship; a young man refuses to visit his parents for his birthday because he is jealous of their deep love for each other; a pregnant young woman is forced to marry a man she hardly knows to save the family reputation; a barren wife spends her days drinking herself insensate while fantasizing about her husband's mistress; a Protestant family shrinks in shame when one son claims that a dead Catholic saint has visited him; a retired couple is helpless and dismayed when an old friend, a hopeless reprobate, courts their daughter. As in Trevor's earlier volumes, the central characters, however muddled in their behavior, usually learn some truth about themselves or recognize a fundamental change in their lives. The tone is taut but not judgmental; the reader is invited to share their emotions rather than laugh at or deplore their plight. The imagery of home, religion, and occupation frequently invests commonplace dramas with broad moral power.

In "The Piano Tuner's Wife," the opening story, a blind piano tuner remarries after his first wife dies. Violet, the second wife, was rejected decades earlier when the piano tuner married her rival, Belle. Now Violet at last succeeds but finds that Belle's memory and style of managing the husband's affairs haunts the marriage at every turn. Violet sets out to efface Belle by contradicting many of the things the first wife told the husband about the countryside and people around them. The piano tuner recognizes Violet's conduct for what it is, self-assertion, and accepts it calmly. In his marriages, as in his work, he seeks harmony. In the title story, "After Rain," Harriet has fled to an Italian resort because of a failed love affair, the same resort that her parents took her to as a child. In the sweltering heat, she feels oppressed by her life. The reader learns of her astonished shock, still disturbing her more than a decade later, at her parents' divorce; she has had previous promising love affairs that all fizzled inexplicably; she cannot be other than distant to her fellow vacationers. To relieve her tedium, she visits a nearby church. There

a painting of the Annunciation, vividly colored and showing a rain-swept landscape in the background, lifts her out of her self-absorption. Meanwhile, a hard rain has broken the afternoon heat. Returning to the resort in the refreshing coolness, she suddenly sees her life in a new light, as if she has had an annunciation of her own. She realizes that she has frightened away her lovers by needing too much from love, a reaction to her parents' failed marriage. The annunciation is of her own solitude.

A BIT ON THE SIDE

The twelve stories in this collection, seven of which appeared in *The New Yorker*, reaffirm that Trevor has a profound understanding of the complexity of what makes people do what they do and an unerring ability to use language to suggest that intimate intricacy. For example, in the title story, a mature couple having an affair reaches that moment of terrible relief when it must end. Explanations are exchanged, excuses made, and it all seems so apparent. However, it is not.

"Big Bucks" seems like a traditional Irish emigration story. The young man goes to the United States to get work, while the young woman waits for him to send for her. As usual, work is hard to find, communication is difficult, and it seems the man has forgotten. However, it is not that conventional. She begins to realizes that what held them together was not love, whatever that is, but the shared goal of going to the United States. In "Sitting with the Dead," a woman, whose cold and uncaring husband has just died, must entertain two professional comforters, to whom she confesses her secret hatred for the man. However, it is not that straightforward, and they know that the dead they have been sitting with is the woman herself. In "Sacred Statues," a woman whose husband has some artistic talent but must get by as a simple laborer cannot understand why she, who has children easily, cannot sell her unborn baby to a childless neighbor to give her husband a chance. Although the reason seems obvious, as usual in Trevor's stories, it is not.

These stories are not cultural examinations of either the old Ireland of legend or the new Ireland of the European Union, but rather profoundly wise explorations of individual, yet universal, secrets and mysteries of the heart. Even when Trevor writes a story with a social or historical context, it is levered on the personal. In "Justina's Priest," the loosening hold of the Catholic Church on modern Ireland is revealed in an old priest's clinging to the simple-minded devotion of one young woman. In "The Dancing-Master's Music," the whole history of peasant Ireland's dreadful dependence on England's Big House mastery is suggested by a young scullery maid's romantic memory of distant music. These are luminous, restrained stories that fill the reader with awe at the complexity of the human experience and the genius of Trevor.

CHEATING AT CANASTA

As in all great short stories, from those of Anton Chekhov to Carver, there is mystery and not a little menace in those of Trevor, secrets so tangled and inexplicable that efforts to explain them with the language of psychology, sociology, or history are either futile or absurd. A classic example is Trevor's "The Dressmaker's Child," in which Cahill, a nineteen-year-old Irish man, takes a couple of young Spanish tourists, seeking a blessing on their marriage, to a statue that was once thought to shed miraculous tears. However, the miracle of the statue has since been discredited, and the Dublin man who told them about it was only lying to get them to buy him drinks. Cahill knows all this, but he wants the fifty euro he charges to drive the couple out to the statue. On the way back, a young female child, who has a habit of doing such things, runs out in the road and into his car. Cahill does not stop. When the child's body is found in a quarry half a mile from her home, the mother, a dressmaker, who has borne the child out of wedlock, begins to stalk Cahill, hinting that she saw him hit the girl. Cahill imagines that he walked back to the site of the accident and carried the body of the child to the quarry, but he knows that it was the mother who did this. The mother urges Cahill to leave his girlfriend and invites him to come home with her. Cahill, afraid, but without knowing what he fears, cannot dismiss the connection between him and the dressmaker. When he tries to understand this, he is bewildered, but he knows that one day he will go to her. The story suggests that it is possible that death and guilt, as well as birth and love, can unite two people.

The mystery of motivation and the secrets of the past also energize "The Room." A forty-seven-year-old woman named Katherine is having an affair, perhaps in revenge, for her husband's involvement with a prostitute, who was murdered nine years before. Katherine's husband was a suspect in the case, and Katherine lied for her husband then, in partial repayment for her inability to have children, providing him with an alibi, although it seems quite clear that he did not kill the woman. When the man with whom she is having an affair asks Katherine why she loves her husband, she says that no one can answer that question and, in a statement central to Trevor's success with the short story, asserts that, most often, people do not know why they do things. For the nine years since the murder, she has not asked her husband about the girl, but she knows that her alibi for him has given her release from any restraint. The story ends with her knowledge that the best that love can do is not enough, for what holds people together is often guilt, debt, and secrets.

The title story opens with Mallory, an Englishman in his middle years, at Harry's Bar in Venice, famous as a hangout of Ernest Hemingway. It has been four years since he was last here with his wife Julia, who is now afflicted with Alzheimer's disease. As a last request, she has made him promise to go back to Harry's, but he is not sure if this trip is really meaningful. However, when he hears an American man ask his wife why she is crying, Mallory becomes interested in their quarrel. When they leave, he tells them the reason for his trip, feeling ashamed that he has come close to deploring this tiresome, futile journey. He recalls letting his wife win at canasta, even though she was not sure why she was happy when she won. As the couple leave, the man smiles, hearing his wife's voice say that shame is not bad, nor is humility, which is shame's gift.

OTHER MAJOR WORKS

LONG FICTION: *A Standard of Behaviour*, 1958; *The Old Boys*, 1964; *The Boarding-House*, 1965; *The Love Department*, 1966; *Mrs. Eckdorf in O'Neil's Hotel*, 1969; *Miss Gomez and the Brethren*, 1971; *Elizabeth Alone*, 1973; *The Children of Dynmouth*, 1976; *Other People's Worlds*, 1980; *Fools of Fortune*, 1983; *Nights at the Alexandra*, 1987; *The Silence in the Garden*,

1988; *Juliet's Story*, 1991; *Two Lives*, 1991; *Felicia's Journey*, 1994; *Death in Summer*, 1998; *The Story of Lucy Gault*, 2002; *My House in Umbria*, 2003; *Love and Summer*, 2009.

PLAYS: *The Elephant's Foot*, pr. 1965; *The Girl*, pr. 1967 (televised), pr., pb. 1968 (staged); *A Night with Mrs. da Tanka*, pr. 1968 (televised), pr., pb. 1972 (staged); *Going Home*, pr. 1970 (radio play), pr., pb. 1972 (staged); *The Old Boys*, pr., pb. 1971; *A Perfect Relationship*, pr. 1973; *Marriages*, pr. 1973; *The Fifty-seventh Saturday*, pr. 1973; *Scenes from an Album*, pr. 1975 (radio play), pr., pb. 1981 (staged).

RADIO PLAYS: *Beyond the Pale*, 1980; *Autumn Sunshine*, 1982.

NONFICTION: *A Writer's Ireland: Landscape in Literature*, 1984; *Excursions in the Real World*, 1993.

EDITED TEXT: *The Oxford Book of Irish Short Stories*, 1989.

BIBLIOGRAPHY

Bonaccorso, Richard. "William Trevor's Martyrs for Truth." *Studies in Short Fiction* 34 (Winter, 1997): 113-118. Discusses two types of Trevor characters: those who try to evade the truth and those who gravitate, often in spite of themselves, toward it. Argues that the best indicators of the consistency of Trevor's moral vision may be his significant minority, those characters who find themselves pursuing rather than fleeing truth.

Firchow, Peter, ed. *The Writer's Place*. Minneapolis: University of Minnesota Press, 1974. In this volume, the editor has interviewed a number of contemporary authors from the British Isles, including Trevor, Kingsley Amis, Roald Dahl, Margaret Drabble, John Wain, and Angus Wilson. Trevor discusses such things as writing for radio, his interest in Ireland after living in England, and the then-current British literary scene.

Gitzen, Julian. "The Truth-Tellers of William Trevor." *Critique: Studies in Modern Fiction* 21, no. 1 (1979): 59-72. Gitzen claims that most critics of Trevor's work have found it in the comedic tradition, sometimes dark and at other times more compassionate in its humor. He argues that, if it is comic, it is also melancholic in its journey from "psychological truth" to "metaphysical mystery."

Haughey, Jim. "Joyce and Trevor's Dubliners: The Legacy of Colonialism." *Studies in Short Fiction* 32 (Summer, 1995): 355-365. Compares how Joyce's "Two Gallants" and Trevor's "Two More Gallants" explore the complexities of Irish identity; argues that Trevor's story provides an updated commentary on the legacy of Ireland's colonial experience. Both stories reveal how Irish men, conditioned by colonization, are partly responsible for their sense of cultural alienation and inferiority.

MacKenna, Dolores. *William Trevor: The Writer and His Work*. Dublin: New Island, 1999. Offers some interesting biographical details; includes a bibliography and an index.

Morrison, Kristin. *William Trevor*. New York: Twayne, 1993. A general introduction to Trevor's fiction, focusing on a conceptual "system of correspondences" often manifested in Trevor's work by a rhetorical strategy of "significant simultaneity" and a central metaphor of the Edenic garden. Through close readings of Trevor's major works, including such short stories as "Beyond the Pale" and "The News from Ireland," Morrison examines the overall unity of his fiction.

Paulson, Suzanne Morrow. *William Trevor: A Study of the Short Fiction*. New York: Twayne, 1993. This introduction to Trevor's stories examines four common themes from Freudianism to feminism: psychological shock, failed child-parent relationships, patriarchal repressiveness, and materialism in the modern world. Also contains an interview with Trevor and a number of short reviews of his stories.

Rhodes, Robert E. "William Trevor's Stories of the Troubles." In *Contemporary Irish Writing*, edited by James D. Brophy and Raymond D. Porter. Boston: Twayne, 1983. Rhodes claims that, although most of Trevor's fiction had until the 1980's revolved around English characters, his Anglo-Irish stories and protagonists, because of their environment and historical experience, are of greater significance in exploring the complexities of the human condition.

Schirmer, Gregory A. *William Trevor: A Study in His Fiction*. London: Routledge, 1990. One of the first full-length studies of Trevor's fictional writings. Schirmer notes the tension in Trevor's works between morality and the elements in contemporary society that make morality almost an impossibility, with lonely alienation the result. He also discusses Trevor as an outsider, both in Ireland and in England. An excellent study. Includes bibliographical references.

Trevor, William. "A Clearer Vision of Ireland." *The Guardian*, April 23, 1992, p. 25. A personal account of what it means to be an Irish writer. Trevor talks about when he first began consciously to feel Irish and when he first realized what Ireland was really like. Talks about his childhood and youth and his decision to become a writer.

_____, ed. *The Oxford Book of Irish Short Stories*. Oxford, England: Oxford University Press, 1989. In this collection of Irish short stories from the earliest times through the second half of the twentieth-century, Trevor in his introduction makes insightful comments about the significance and context of that literary form to Irish letters and, by implication, discusses his own work.

Brian Murray; Roger Smith; Eugene S. Larson
Updated by Charles E. May

FRANK TUOHY

Born: Uckfield, Sussex, England; May 2, 1925
Died: Shepton Mallet, Somerset, England;
    April 11, 1999

PRINCIPAL SHORT FICTION

The Admiral and the Nuns, with Other Stories, 1962
Fingers in the Door, and Other Stories, 1970
Live Bait, and Other Stories, 1978
The Collected Stories, 1984

OTHER LITERARY FORMS

In addition to his short stories, Frank Tuohy (TOO-ee) wrote three novels, a biography of William Butler Yeats, a travel book on Portugal, numerous articles for British newspapers, and teleplays for British public television.

ACHIEVEMENTS

Frank Tuohy never had a wide general audience, nor did he find favor with academic critics. Still, his writing received high praise from reviewers and from prominent fiction writers. C. P. Snow, Muriel Spark, and Graham Greene all praised Tuohy's fiction.

The high praise from reviewers and fellow writers is reflected in the honors that were bestowed on Tuohy. His first short-story collection, *The Admiral and the Nuns, with Other Stories*, received the Katherine Mansfield-Menton Prize (1960), and *Live Bait, and Other Stories* won the William Heinemann Memorial Award (1979). Tuohy's third novel, *The Ice Saints* (1964), received both the James Tait Black Memorial Prize and the Geoffrey Faber Memorial Prize. In England, Tuohy was elected a Fellow of the Royal Society of Literature in 1965. Two major awards demonstrate the high standing his fiction holds among the literati in the United States. In 1972, the American Institute of Arts and Letters bestowed on him the E. M. Forster Award. In 1995, Tuohy came to New York City to receive the 1994 Bennett Award of twenty thousand dollars from the *Hudson Review*. Eight years earlier, in 1987, he was awarded an honorary doctorate from Purdue University.

BIOGRAPHY

John Francis Tuohy's father was Irish, and his was mother Scottish. Tuohy was educated at Stowe School and at King's College, Cambridge. He traveled widely and lived for extended periods in Finland, Brazil, Poland, Japan, Portugal, and the United States. The contrast and conflict of manners and cultures became the chief subject of his fiction.

Tuohy was ineligible for military service during World War II because of a defective heart valve, a condition later corrected by surgery. After the war, he spent six years in Brazil as a professor of English language and literature at the University of São Paulo and two years as a visiting professor in Poland at the Jagiellonian University. In the United States he was a visiting writer at various universities, including Purdue University and Texas A&M University. He also lectured at two universities in Tokyo, Rikkyo University from 1983 to 1989 and Waseda University in the 1990's.

ANALYSIS

An initial impression of Frank Tuohy's short stories is likely to be that they are the observations of a sharp-eyed and widely traveled reporter who is filling in the reader on life in such diverse places as Japan, Poland, South America, London, rural England, New England, and New York. Tuohy does have a remarkable talent for direct observation, for bringing before the eyes of his reader the look and feel, the sound, and even the smell of actual places. The gestures of his characters, their speech, and their actions all ring true. Tuohy's accuracy of observation and precision of language, although doubtless a reflection of his own interest in being literally truthful to the physical realities of the places about which he writes, are all part of his strategy for supporting and making real his underlying view of life.

Despite the variety of locales, of character types, and even of subjects, Tuohy's short-story collections are bound together by an overriding vision of the world as a place of moral confusion. Here and there one finds in unlikely places remnants of an older, more civilized way of life, but generally one finds, also in unsuspected places, moral baseness of the sort that would have made a decent man of former times put his hand firmly on his sword. At their most poignant, Tuohy's stories expose the raw nerves of conflicting cultures, the below-the-surface gnawing of social lesions bloodied by sudden rupture, the confinements within the self caused by differences of custom, of language, of status, and of religion.

"THE ADMIRAL AND THE NUNS"

The best people in Tuohy's stories are usually women. In the title story of his first collection, *The Admiral and the Nuns, with Other Stories*, an English woman, the daughter of an English admiral, is living in the interior of a South American country with her Polish husband. The place is a company town; the husband is employed as an engineer at a nearby factory; the neighbors, who are nationals of the country, have developed a deep dislike for the English woman and her husband and have, in effect, instituted a community-wide boycott. The grounds of dislike are these: The English woman is a dreadful housekeeper and cannot discipline her children; her husband drinks too much and pursues women. Tuohy's point is made clear by his narrator, also English, who sees that the woman is charming and valiant, having been formed by her father (the admiral) and trained by the nuns in her convent school. She remains loyal to her husband and, throughout her ordeal (which concludes with their deciding to return to Poland), keeps her chin firmly up.

There is a dreariness, however, in this kind of life and more dreariness ahead, and the narrator's admiration is tempered by what he regards as the woman's limitations: "She was one of those people whom experience leaves untouched. But she was durable. After all, she was an Admiral's daughter." As for the nuns, the narrator "cannot decide whether they had given her the worst, or the best education in the world."

"A SURVIVOR IN SALVADOR"

A more clearly admirable character is the young mulatto woman in "A Survivor in Salvador," the last story in his first collection. The protagonist of this story is an exiled Polish prince who has arrived in San Salvador without money but with a packet of cocaine, which he is attempting to sell. Without friends, liable to deportation if caught with the drug, without food or shelter, he is befriended by a girl who herself has been a victim of various kinds of exploitation, including sexual abuse by the chief of police. The girl, Antonieta, befriends the prince, becomes his mistress, keeps him from starving, and when he is seriously ill from exposure, nurses him back to health. In return, Christophe, the prince, does what he can to show his love for Antonieta.

At thirty-two pages, "Survivor in Salvador" is easily the longest story in Tuohy's first collection and perhaps his most virtuoso performance in the genre. Always in his three novels and frequently in his stories, he adopts the narrative viewpoints of perceptive European outsiders who are trapped between the shallowness of what they have abandoned and the poverty (in all senses) of what exile has wrought. In "Survivor in Salvador," Tuohy takes on as naturally as if he were born to it the central intelligence of a down-but-not-quite-out, dispossessed Pole, Prince Krzysztof Wahorski, who has fled Poland after "promises, his title, his bridge game" have all failed. He sees the heroine as his passport back to the noblesse oblige his title, if not his circumstances, ought to bestow. In Tuohy's handling, Antonieta is neither brutalized nor romanticized as she throws the prince a lifeline. This story crosses Joseph Conrad with Guy de Maupassant but ends as pure Frank Tuohy.

"FINGERS IN THE DOOR"

Frequently in Tuohy's stories the main character or characters are exiled Europeans living in a simpler or more integrated culture, in which even the poor are bound together by some mutually shared consciousness. For example, the prince in "Survival in Salvador" perceives that even the most despised are not as alone as he is. The prince is unusual in Tuohy's fiction, however, for most of Tuohy's exiles are unaware of their loneliness and alienation and are likely to regard those from simpler, more integrated cultures as inferiors to be exploited.

Exploitation of the weak or innocent and the snobbery that appears to be one of its causes are treated in the title story of his second volume of short stories, *Fingers in the Door, and Other Stories*. The story takes place on a train traveling to London; the occupants of a first-class carriage are Andrew Ringsett, a successful real estate agent who has moved up in the world, his overdressed wife, their spoiled, teenage daughter, Caroline, and for a time, an elderly woman in an ancient fur, whom the agent's wife Merle recognizes as someone from a higher social class who (she believes) will always snub her (although, as Tuohy remarks, the snobbery is all in Merle's head). The train stops at a station, the husband alights for a few moments, and when he reenters the carriage through an outside door the train lurches suddenly, and the steel door slams shut on his fingers. The husband is in terrific pain, but his wife, embarrassed before someone whom she regards as her social better, apologizes for him to the old woman. The daughter merely stares out the window, outraged that her trip to London has been ruined by her father's accident. The old woman rises from her place in the carriage and addresses the wife, telling her to look after her husband; to the man, she offers her sympathy and the advice to seek immediate medical assistance. It is the husband, however, who exhibits the most admirable behavior. He sees immediately that his wife is embarrassed and humiliated and puts his arm around her and tries to make light of his injury. He has something in common with other Tuohy characters who have not lost the power to feel affection.

LIVE BAIT, AND OTHER STORIES

In Tuohy's third collection, *Live Bait, and Other Stories*, the theme of exploitation becomes predominant, and as his camera eye moves closer to home, to New England and New York and then to England itself, the sense of moral confusion becomes more acute, the remoteness from human feeling even more profound. In "Summer Pilgrim," a young Japanese teacher visits an elderly English pastoral poet who has been her ideal. At dinner, while his wife is in the kitchen, the venerable poet runs his hand up her leg. The girl, who has been reared to behave dutifully, is too timid and self-effacing either to protest or move away. At a loss what to do, she simply sits there, feeling "rather deaf: . . . like a change in the atmospheric pressure, high up a mountain."

In "Evening in Connecticut" an English visitor is attending a dinner party in the home of a very rich old man, an important benefactor of Barford College, and finds himself in a world which seems detached from reality, a kind of battered Eden in which things are plentiful but life abstract. What the visitor discovers, at last, under the banter and expensive food and drink, is the kind of exploitation Tuohy has found in other times and places but not in so odious a form: The elderly white-haired host informs his English guest that he regularly makes trips to England, where an English doctor, who shares his tastes, has found him a suitable girl of the lower classes, whose parents do not object. The English visitor is outraged but paralyzed by the social conventions and his own timidity. Later he believes that he was on the point of rising to his feet and attacking, but that "surely, was self-delusion." In this kind of society, the sexual exploitation of children appears to be indistinguishable from any other kind of gratification.

The assault on innocence is also the subject of the title story of *Live Bait, and Other Stories*. Here, a twelve-year-old boy, a scholarship pupil at a school attended mainly by the rich, accompanies a school acquaintance on a fishing expedition to a lake on the property of an elderly rich aunt and her eccentric son, Major Peverill. The boy is asked about his father's profession and is treated insultingly by both the old woman and her son, who advises the boy, Andrew, to be grateful for being invited into the society of his betters and then, when the boy admits that he is a scholarship student, laughs in his face. Andrew's interest, however, is in the fishing; what in particular excites him is the gardener's account of a twenty-pound pike that inhabits the lake. He contrives to haul off his father's fishing gear and a boat that is usually kept locked away at the lake. His upper-class friend quarrels with him and makes insulting remarks about Andrew's mother; Andrew then fishes for the pike by himself. He hooks the big fish but it breaks his line, and while he is rolling around on the ground in anger, he is watched by Major Peverill, who then attempts to molest him. Andrew escapes but is drawn back to the lake by the hope of catching the pike; this time he is visited by Major Peverill's granddaughter, a strange girl who tries to be friendly until she discovers that Andrew is using a live frog for bait; she then runs off to denounce him to her family. Andrew lands the pike but is chased by Major Peverill and his laborers, and, from the other side of the lake, by his mother. Andrew is obliged to surrender.

What Tuohy does is to catch, without sentimentalizing, the way a twelve-year-old boy at this particular time and place is himself "live bait" to those about him, who use him to get some strange pleasure, social superiority, adventure, or sensual indulgence. One is made to feel, rather than merely to understand, the meaning of what has happened.

It is impossible to summarize the kind of pleasure afforded by Tuohy's fiction. Each of his stories is like a miniature novel of manners, in which persons of different classes, nationalities, races, religions, political persuasions, and ages are brought into a conflict that also reveals an underlying moral conflict. There is nothing depressingly cynical or fashionably despairing about Tuohy's stories. Life should be better than this-- that is the assumption behind his fiction--and Tuohy is simply an observer-commentator, a truth-teller whose scalpel-like cutting away of pretense reveals the rottenness underneath. His stories are neither about innocents at home nor about innocents abroad, and although they are often about the kind of social incarceration that people impose on human relationships in an alien country, one need not go abroad to find oneself imprisoned. His stories say, in effect, that this is the way life is: awful, incredible, confusing, painful, but, at the same time, fascinating when seen for what it is. The act of experiencing the "bite down on the rotten tooth of fact," is what gives Tuohy's stories their characteristic pleasure. That is the kind of pleasure the best fiction has always given.

Asked by novelist Anthony Burgess which contemporary writers he liked, Graham Greene answered, "I used to read Frank Tuohy" (*Newsweek*, February 4, 1985). Greene's implicit regret that Tuohy had stopped writing novels twenty years earlier with *The Ice Saints* must bow to praise--again implied--from the master of intrigue--political and religious--in foreign outposts. Did Greene hail his younger contemporary for declining to exploit his experiences in widely differing cultures for exotic effect but rather to illustrate the humiliations that blur human communication on any level and in any milieu? Tuohy's last published story, "A Rainy Season" appearing in *London Magazine* one year before he suffered a fatal coronary attack in the spring of 1999, conveys the unwitting betrayal by local customs in an unnamed country (surely Brazil) of a Miss Bond, an American, a sincere do-gooder on a U.S. State Department mission. The viewpoint character is Marsden, a bystander distinguished in Great Britain but reduced by the provincialism he finds abroad. The only evolving character is a Canadian, who becomes, via Marsden's account of Miss Bond's disaster, someone who might be saved from his predecessor's folly.

In presenting Tuohy the 1994 Bennett Award in New York, critic Dean Flower observed that "it has become politic . . . these days to speak warmly of Diversity and Multi-Cultural enrichment. Let Frank Tuohy's stories expose the sentimentality and hypocrisy of all that."

OTHER MAJOR WORKS

LONG FICTION: *The Animal Game*, 1957; *The Warm Nights of January*, 1960; *The Ice Saints*, 1964.

NONFICTION: *Portugal*, 1970; *Yeats*, 1976.

BIBLIOGRAPHY

Flower, Dean. "Frank Tuohy and the Poetics of Depression." *The Hudson Review* 49 (Spring, 1996): 87-96. Suggests that such collections of Tuohy's short stories as *Fingers in the Door, and Other Stories* and *The Admiral and the Nuns, with Other Stories* may be out of print because most readers probably found them too depressing. Concludes that what makes all of Tuohy's works worth reading is their anguished and inconsolable tone.

Hazzard, Shirley. Review of *Fingers in the Door, and Other Stories*, by Frank Tuohy. *The New York Times Book Review*, September, 1970, 5. Hazzard maintains that Tuohy writes with Chekhovian simplicity about "the violence we do to others and ourselves," and she discusses several of the stories in light of this opinion.

King, Francis. "Obituary: Frank Tuohy." *The Independent*, April 15, 1999, p. 6. A biographical sketch of Tuohy's life and literary career, commenting on his early fiction, his resemblance to W. Somerset Maugham in his attitude toward sex, and his receiving the Katherine Mansfield-Menton Prize for his first volume of short stories.

Prescott, Peter S. "The Whiplash Effect." Review of *The Collected Stories*, by Frank Tuohy. *Newsweek*, February 4, 1985, p. 78. Prescott argues that Tuohy's stories are "extremely pessimistic" but powerful in their portrayal of human pain. Particularly effective, he says, is the "whiplash effect," by means of which Tuohy, having caused the reader to sympathize with a character, suddenly reverses direction and shows the character in an unfavorable light.

Snow, C. P. "Snapshot Album." Review of *Fingers in the Door, and Other Stories*, by Frank Tuohy. *Financial Times*, May 14, 1970. Snow remarks that Tuohy's "great gifts" are concentration, "intensive exactness," and a language that is "as firm and limpid as English can be." He discusses the "sociology" of Tuohy's stories and demonstrates how in three stories Tuohy's characteristic theme of pain and loneliness is effectively presented.

Wilson, Jason. "Foreigners Abroad: Frank Tuohy's Three Novels." *London Magazine*, July, 1992. Although Wilson is writing mostly about Tuohy's long fiction, which he praises as still perceptive about "Britons abroad" even though it is thirty years out of print, he finds Tuohy's novels "episodic, linked short stories." He says, "The stories cover the same area of exploration [but, because compressed] . . . offer a greater sense of the mystery of people, for there is less need for a plot."

W. J. Stuckey
Updated by Richard Hauer Costa

V

GUY VANDERHAEGHE

Born: Esterhazy, Saskatchewan, Canada;
April 5, 1951

PRINCIPAL SHORT FICTION
Man Descending, 1982
The Trouble with Heroes, and Other Stories, 1983
Things as They Are?, 1992

OTHER LITERARY FORMS

Guy Vanderhaeghe (VAHN-dehr-hehg) has written the novels *My Present Age* (1984), *Homesick* (1989), *The Englishman's Boy* (1996), and *The Last Crossing* (2002) and the plays *I Had a Job I Liked Once,* (1992) and *Dancock's Dance* (1996). *My Present Age* was a finalist for the Man Booker Prize and has been translated into several languages; *Homesick* won the City of Toronto Book Award. Despite these honors, Vanderhaeghe's short stories were generally more critically esteemed than his novels. This changed when, in 1996, Vanderhaeghe's novel *The Englishman's Boy*, set in Saskatchewan in the 1870's and Hollywood in the 1920's, won the coveted Governor-General's Award for Fiction. In the late 1990's, international publishers became more interested in Canadian novels, especially in the wake of the success of the film version of Michael Ondaatje's novel *The English Patient* (1992). It was hoped that *The Englishman's Boy*, with its similar title, would become both a popular and critical success. This did not happen, though the novel sold moderately well. Vanderhaeghe's next novel, *The Last Crossing*, was critically well received and was a best seller in Canada, and by the beginning of the twenty-first century, critics increasingly referred to him as a "historical novelist."

ACHIEVEMENTS

Man Descending, Guy Vanderhaeghe's first collection of short stories, won the Geoffrey Faber Memorial Prize in 1982. His longer fiction won the Governor-General's Award, the City of Toronto Book Award, and five Saskatchewan Book Awards, as well as being nominated for the Man Booker Prize. In 2003, Vanderhaeghe was a recipient of the Saskatchewan Order of Merit; the following year, he was made an Officer of the Order of Canada, and he won the Writers' Trust of Canada Timothy Findley Award.

BIOGRAPHY

Guy Clarence Vanderhaeghe was born in Esterhazy, Saskatchewan, about 150 kilometers from the city of Regina. He received his B.A. (1971) and M.A. (1975), both in history, from the University of Saskatchewan; he also received a bachelor's degree in education from the University of Regina in 1978. He worked in various academic jobs, as well as doing occasional writing, editing, and archival work until the publication of his first story collection, *Man Descending*. During the mid-1980's, he was a writer-in-residence at the Saskatchewan Public Library. Despite holding a part-time teaching job in the national capital of Ottawa, Vanderhaeghe for the most part continued to reside, teach, and write in his native Saskatchewan.

ANALYSIS

Guy Vanderhaeghe is a Canadian prairie writer, the prairie provinces being those of Alberta, Saskatchewan, and Manitoba. Prairie writing tends to be largely realistic, though not without symbolic and experimental overtones. Vanderhaeghe's social realism is given heft by both a sense of place and a sense of style. He is particularly known for his portrayal of male characters living in contemporary times.

Vanderhaeghe's stories have some similarities to those of American writers a decade or so senior to him, such as Richard Ford and Raymond Carver. Like Ford and Carver, Vanderhaeghe often focuses on alienated male protagonists who are bewildered by the contemporary universe in which the time-honored rules of masculinity seem no longer operative. He differs from them, though, in that his perspective is more comic, less gritty than theirs. Vanderhaeghe's stories are more philosophical than the norm, even if the philosophy is more practical than theoretical. For instance, in the story "Sam, Soren, and Ed," Vanderhaeghe uses the thought of the Danish philosopher Søren Kierkegaard to illuminate issues in his protagonist's development, though this reference is in the spirit of fun as much as erudition. Also, Vanderhaeghe does not affect the artlessness possessed at times by American writers; his stories are finely crafted, and, despite their often contemporary Canadian setting, are in the twentieth-century tradition of the short story as art form. Vanderhaeghe's gently humorous tone and his agility at making wry comments and observing odd details assist him in putting his own stamp upon the form.

"MAN DESCENDING"

"Man Descending" is about a married couple, Ed and Victoria. Ed is monopolizing the bathroom, smoking and drinking, and generally trying to maintain traditional male modes of excess. Victoria is distressed by this and is generally upset about the state of her marriage, especially because Ed is unemployed. Ed feels his wife's love for him has been diminished by what should be the external factor of his present joblessness, and he strongly suspects she is having an affair with Howard, a pompous professional man.

Using the example of a child prodigy, whose life ended at four and a half basically because he had no more worlds to conquer, Ed hypothesizes that everyone's life follows the same curve, after a certain point descending from its peak. Ed feels that, though only thirty, he is losing out to less manly, more negotiable men, such as Howard. Ed is not a blue-collar worker; indeed, he is intellectual enough to use words like "innuendo" and to work in an adult education program, but he is skeptical of the bureaucratic jargon bandied about in his workplace, and this seems to represent a general

Guy Vanderhaeghe (Getty Images)

dissent from the overly formalized living conditions of postmodern humanity.

Ed and Victoria go to a party, where Ed sees that Victoria and Howard are obviously flirtatious. He gets involved in a physical fight with Howard, in which Howard bests him. Howard is about to beat Ed to a pulp when Victoria suddenly intervenes on Ed's behalf. Moved by Victoria's gesture, Ed pledges to reform himself, to get a job, and to treat his wife better. Victoria, though, seems skeptical of these promises, and, it is implied, the reader should be as well.

Vanderhaeghe skillfully balances the reader's sympathies between husband and wife. Ed is shown to be self-pitying; he acts as if Howard, though "superior" to him in being employed, is less of a "man's man" than is Ed himself, but the fact that Howard wins the fight demonstrates that this is not so. Victoria at first seems to be callously not sticking by her husband, but her intervention in Ed's favor makes her more sympathetic. The overall impression is that the problems in this marriage have grown too large for these two flawed people to solve.

It is interesting that, even though Vanderhaeghe is often seen not only as a male writer but also as one who is sympathetic with the plight of contemporary men, he nonetheless shows neither Ed nor Howard in a positive light. Indeed, Vanderhaeghe comes across as much as a "male feminist" as a defender of archaic gender roles, although the concrete predicaments of his characters make either generalization seem fatuous.

"THE WATCHER"

"The Watcher" begins with a classic short-story premise: the young child as observer, onlooker, both failing to understand the adults around him and providing a perspective on them. Charlie is a sickly boy in the late 1950's, who often is bedridden from bronchitis, enabling him to hear a lot of gossip about his family's friends and neighbors. Charlie moves in with his grandmother, who is the only rock of stability in an otherwise dysfunctional family; Grandma Bradley is a strong, self-reliant woman. A new element is introduced by the arrival of Charlie's aunt, Evelyn, and her lover, an eccentric, disreputable intellectual named Robert Thompson. Aunt Evelyn is a cocktail waitress who is always criticized by the overbearing Grandma Bradley. She finds self-definition in her relationship with Thompson, a graduate student from British Columbia, who admires the American Beat writers, even though Thompson beats her and exploits her sexually. Charlie, too, has a weird fascination with the raffish Thompson, who provides a model of virility lacking in his immediate family. Charlie even gratuitously strangles his grandmother's chicken in emulation of Thompson's sadistic control of Aunt Evelyn, underscoring how Thompson's masculine self-expression is characterized by violence and abuse. Grandma Bradley tries everything to keep the sponging Thompson from becoming a permanent resident of her home. After a particularly obtrusive display of lovemaking on the couple's part, Grandma decides that Thompson must go. She hires two local thugs from the auto body shop to beat up Thompson; at first, he is supposed to come to them, but when Thompson does not fall to the ruse, the attackers come to the Bradley house and assault him. Later on, Thompson is taken into custody by the police, who tell him to leave town, both because Grandma Bradley is a local and because Thompson has, after all, beaten his girlfriend. Evelyn does not come with him, not because she does not want to but because she sees that the forces of authority are on her mother's side.

More interesting to the reader is the evolving stance of Charlie. Asked by the police if he witnessed the assault, Charlie lies and says he did not because he is still too young to be deprived of his grandmother's protection. As a child, Charlie is in the category of vulnerable women like Evelyn, whose life choices are controlled by others. If maturing as a man entails becoming like Thompson, however, the transition from watching to acting, which Charlie will make as an adult male, will not necessarily be benign.

"THE EXPATRIATES' PARTY"

"The Expatriates' Party" starts with a fifty-seven-year-old Canadian man visiting his adult son in London in 1977. Joe has not seen his son Mark in two years. Upon meeting him at the airport, he is disconcerted not only by his son's changed demeanor but also by the way England itself does not conform to his stereotype of it, acquired in his years of teaching English poetry to generations of Canadian schoolchildren. (Vanderhaeghe here is commenting upon Canada's residual colonial posture toward Great Britain.) Joe's wife, Marie, has just died, and, traumatized by his recent loss, Joe punches one of his students, a boy named Wesjik, representative of the slack youth whom he cannot reach and who do not appreciate the sacrifices made by his generation. Joe is forced to resign from the school for this incident but is not prosecuted. After talking about current politics with his son and his London friends, most of whom are Canadian expatriates, Joe remembers his wife's final decaying years and what he sees as his own pointless, unrewarding career as a schoolteacher. Though Mark and his friends are expatriates in a literal sense, perhaps, Joe thinks, he is one as well, having never found a true "home" in his life, even though he has lived all the time in one place. The last words of the story are Joe's as he muses, "Je me souviens." This phrase means "I remember" in French, but in a Canadian context it is the national motto of the province of Quebec. Joe's personal memories cannot be separated from the condition of his country. Other allusions to the monarchy and to the ethnic diversity of contemporary Britain and Canada contribute to Vanderhaeghe's interweaving of past and present, universal feeling and Canadian content.

OTHER MAJOR WORKS

LONG FICTION: *My Present Age*, 1984; *Homesick*, 1989; *The Englishman's Boy*, 1996; *The Last Crossing*, 2002.

PLAYS: *I Had a Job I Liked Once*, 1992; *Dancock's Dance*, 1996.

BIBLIOGRAPHY

Dunning, Stephen. "What Would Sam Waters Do? Guy Vanderhaeghe and Søren Kierkegaard." *Canadian Literature* 198 (Autumn, 2008): 29-45. Examines how Vanderhaeghe's works have been influenced by the existential philosophy of Søren Kierkegaard. Demonstrates how this influence is particularly evident in the struggles of Ed, the protagonist in the stories "Man Descending" and "My Present Age."

Gray, Alasdair. "Varieties of Contempt." In *The New York Times Book Review* (October 13, 1985): 28. Vanderhaeghe was fortunate to have his first public exposure to American readers mediated through this distinguished Scottish novelist, who praises his Canadian counterpart for the "variety of voices" and "special sort of rage and hatred" evoked by his characters.

Keahey, Deborah. *Making It Home: Place in Canadian Prairie Literature*. Winnipeg: University of Manitoba Press, 1998. This critical comment on Vanderhaeghe is divided into specialized articles in academic journals and brief mentions in overall surveys on Canadian literature. This is a good example of the latter category, importantly situating Vanderhaeghe in his regional milieu and considering later as well as earlier work.

Kruk, Laurie. "Guy Vanderhaeghe: A Vernacular Richness." In *The Voice Is the Story: Conversations with Canadian Writers of Short Fiction*. Niagara Falls, N.Y.: Mosaic Press, 2003. Vanderhaeghe discusses his short fiction.

Prober, Kenneth G. *Writing Saskatchewan: Twenty Critical Essays*. Regina: University of Regina, 1989. Includes several comments on Vanderhaeghe's early stories.

Sorensen, Sue. "Don't Hanker to Be No Prophet: Guy Vanderhaeghe and the Bible." *Canadian Literature* 191 (Winter, 2006): 32-46. Analyzes the religious themes and the influence of the Bible on Vanderhaeghe's long and short fiction.

Vanderhaeghe, Guy. "An Interview with Guy Vanderhaeghe." Interview by Doris Hillis. *Wascana Review* 19, no. 1 (1984): 11-28. This interview of Vanderhaeghe by a respected local critic is largely taken up with discussion of the stories in *Man Descending*.

Van Herk, Aritha. Review of *Man Descending*, by Guy Vanderhaeghe. *Western American Literature* 18, no. 3 (November, 1983). This early review by a major contemporary of Vanderhaeghe is a valuable consideration of his themes and techniques.

Nicholas Birns

W

John Wain

Born: Stoke-on-Trent, Staffordshire, England; March
14, 1925
Died: Oxford, England; May 24, 1994

PRINCIPAL SHORT FICTION
Nuncle, and Other Stories, 1960
Death of the Hind Legs, and Other Stories, 1966
The Life Guard, 1971
King Caliban, and Other Stories, 1978

OTHER LITERARY FORMS

John Wain built his reputation as a novelist in the
1950's, his first novel being *Hurry on Down* (1953),
which was published in the United States as *Born in
Captivity*. He subsequently published twelve other
novels, including *Where the Rivers Meet* (1988), *Comedies* (1990), and *Hungry Generations* (1994). In addition, Wain published several volumes of poetry, criticism, and literary biography; his plays include *Johnson
Is Leaving: A Monodrama* (pb. 1994). He also wrote
Sprightly Running: Part of an Autobiography (1962),
in which he declared, "I would be a short-story writer
[over being a novelist] if it weren't so impossible to
make a living at it." An influential essayist, editor,
critic, and literary biographer, Wain believed his poetry
to be his most important literary contribution.

ACHIEVEMENTS

John Wain won the Somerset Maugham Award in
1958 for *Preliminary Essays* (1957), the James Tait
Black Memorial Prize and Heinemann Bequest Award
in 1975 for *Samuel Johnson* (1974), and the Whitbread
Literary Award in 1985 for *Young Shoulders* (1982;
published in the United States as *The Free Zone Starts
Here*). In 1973, he was elected the twenty-seventh professor of poetry at the University of Oxford. He held
honorary degrees from the University of Keele and the
University of Loughborough and became an honorary
fellow of St. John's College, Oxford University, in
1985.

BIOGRAPHY

John Barrington Wain was born in Staffordshire,
England, in 1925, the son of a dentist. After he was
found unfit to join the armed forces because of poor
eyesight, he went in 1943 to St. John's College, Oxford, being graduated in 1946 and staying on for three
years as a Fereday Fellow. At Oxford he began to publish his first verse and met Kingsley Amis and Philip
Larkin, both of whom spoke both respectfully and venomously of him in conversation and memoir. He left
teaching and became a full-time writer in 1955. In
1953, he hosted the British Broadcasting Corporation's
"First Reading" program, which became a springboard
for the British movement poets.

Because Wain, Amis, and John Osborne, all near
thirty years old, were writing social protest and caustic
humor, they were inevitably--if artificially--grouped by
critics as the "Angry Young Men." Although Wain objected to this classification, the label stuck. Despite the
authors' individual differences, the "Angry Young
Men" did have the collective effect of sharpening England's social sensibility and invigorating its literature.
Wain and his second wife Eirian James had three sons;
she died in 1988. He married Patricia Dunn the next
year. Wain died of a stroke in 1994.

ANALYSIS

Though frequently categorized as one of the "Angry
Young Men" of the 1950's, John Wain claimed that his
work was not decidedly bitter. Still, his reputation as a
debunker of rigid English society and an apologist for
the alienated young man has persisted. While Wain's
short stories are disciplined and energetic, he was at
times an acerbic social critic and frequently wrote with

a strong moral cast. Typically, Wain's stories concern the internal conflict of a first-person narrator. The narrator usually is not very perceptive, whether for lack of intelligence or maturity. A frequent effect of Wain's stories is that a conflict is well developed, human narrowness is scourged with satire, and a thematic irony is made unmistakably clear. His early stories reflected his "angry" mood of the 1950's but also show concern for a wide range of topics.

"MASTER RICHARD" AND "A MESSAGE FROM THE PIG-MAN"

Two stories from Wain's first collection *Nuncle, and Other Stories* provide insight into his early short fiction. Both "Master Richard" and "A Message from the Pig-Man" are dominated by the perceptions of their child-protagonists. Richard, a five-year-old prodigy, is the narrator of his story. It develops by means of the diary convention, with Richard recording his observations secretly in a notebook. The boy gauges his maturity of mind at roughly thirty-five because the conversation of adults is easily comprehensible. Such a voice puts considerable strain on the narrative credibility of the story.

Richard reads, writes, and types with the facility of an adult. Wain makes a few concessions to the age of his narrator: He faces pain and cries like any other child and throws china cups to get attention. At the other extreme, the boy has a sense of perspective that belies that of the most precocious child. He carries out a long conditioning process to prepare his parents gradually for the realization that he has learned to read on his own. The very notion of patience over a long period of time is alien to the mind of even a very bright child. Further, Richard makes jokes and uses a vocabulary of slang that cannot be accounted for, since these abilities come almost entirely from experience. The greatest breach of credibility occurs when Richard speaks of the absurd and of insanity, constructs that only time and experience--not precocity--can bring to the consciousness. The problem is that no clear frame of reference is established for the reader. The narrator's situation, environment, and comments are based on the presumption of conventional reality as the norm of the story; Richard's unique perception, however, forces the reader to view the story as somewhat surrealistic. The

narrative exhibits both realism and surrealism but is committed consistently to neither, and the ambivalence is disconcerting.

Richard's crisis comes with the birth of a younger brother, whom he hates jealously. As a result of his contempt for his own cruelty to his brother and for his parents, who cannot understand him, he coolly decides to commit suicide. This conclusion, which has not been prepared for in the development of the story, is more convenient than satisfying.

Unlike "Master Richard," "A Message from the Pig-Man" is thoroughly believable. Eric, the viewpoint character, is also five years old, but the narrative is third-person, giving Wain more room to maneuver in disclosing the story. The thematic function of the boy's sensibility in the story is to comment on the need to confront fear. Eric finally faces the Pig-man, whom he assumes to be a grotesque creature rather than an old man simply collecting scraps for his pigs. He goes out with some scraps at his mother's insistence and tells himself, "It was the same as getting into icy cold water. If it was the end, if the Pig-man seized him by the hand and dragged him off to his hut, well, so much the worse."

Although Eric's fear has a comic effect, it teaches the central lesson of the story. Once he has faced the Pig-man and found him harmless, he returns home to be put off when he asks his mother and his new stepfather why his father cannot live with them. Lacking Eric's courage to face up to problems, they hedge instead of answering. The viewpoint of the child generates humor and provides insight into the deeper weaknesses of adults; still the concluding irony is too heavy.

"KING CALIBAN"

This powerful story may well be Wain's most widely read on both sides of the Atlantic. Originally published in *The Saturday Evening Post*, it leads off *Death of the Hind Legs, and Other Stories*, his second collection, just as it does his fourth, *King Caliban, and Other Stories*. Despite a predictable outcome, the story is effective because of the flashback narration of the cocky, street-smart Bert, who takes on caretaker duties for Fred, his older brother ("as strong as three men and as honest as daylight"). "Short of grey matter," Fred works as a handyman in the same office managed by his wife Dorene. To make more money, brother and wife inveigle the gentle Fred into professional wrestling as King Caliban ("some kind of monster on a desert island"). Neither can understand Fred's simple moral outrage at the gratuitous violence and bloodthirsty taunting. First, the anguished Fred injures an opponent and later nearly kills a heckler. Bert walks away from the situation unscathed and uncomprehending, leaving his bewildered brother to face the consequences. The strength of "King Caliban" is its deft interlocking of two major themes, corruption of innocence and innocence of corruption, within the narrative without commentary.

DEATH OF THE HIND LEGS, AND OTHER STORIES

Death of the Hind Legs, and Other Stories also contains two stories of adultery-- "Come in Captain Grindle" and "Further Education"--in which Wain captures the casual, amoral sordidness of contemporary mores. The issue is not simply sexual. At their core--and in "King Caliban" too--is the willingness to manipulate people for personal ends. In "Giles and Penelope," a young woman comes to realize that her lover uses her as a pawn. In the end she demands to be treated as what she in fact is--a kept woman. At first appalled, Giles finally accepts, excited by the prospect of using, then discarding, Penelope when it suits him.

The stories in *The Life Guard*, Wain's third and last important collection, are more sophisticated than the earlier ones. In the title story there is overdone irony in the death of Hopper, who actually drowns when he is supposed to be pretending to drown in order to make Jimmy look necessary as a lifeguard. Despite the unrestrained turn of plot, the story achieves substance and interest as the narrative lets the reader see Jimmy's desperation. As a dull boy, he is in his element when he gets the job of lifeguard at the beach. He fears the future and lacks ambition, but he has skill and confidence in the water. Eager to prove that he is useful on the calm shore, Jimmy decides to win attention by appearing to save Hopper's life. When he sees that Hopper really is in trouble, he is faced with exactly the kind of test he had been waiting for all summer, only he fails, and Hopper dies. In Jimmy's moral and physical agony as he brings Hopper to land, there is considerable dramatic energy--almost enough to make the reader overlook the predictable conclusion.

"WHILE THE SUN SHINES"

Another story from the collection, "While the Sun Shines," shows considerable control and is one of Wain's best stories by far. The conflict here between the tractor driver, the unnamed first-person narrator, and Robert, the son of the absent farm owner, is well drawn. First-person narration is particularly appropriate because the external conflict of the story is secondary to what goes on in the narrator's mind. Another man was seriously injured when the tractor overturned as he tried to mow a dangerously steep hill. When Robert orders the narrator to try the same task, he refuses more out of spite than fear. Later, however, he takes on the challenge, not for Robert's sake, but for his own, and possibly to impress Robert's roving wife Yvonne. The appeal she holds for the narrator adds a subtle dimension to the story. Although he knows she is a woman who uses men, she appeals to him more than he will admit. Thus in retrospect there is a question as to whether the narrator mastered the hill entirely for himself, as he thinks, or for Yvonne as well. Because he professes contempt for her throughout the story, his yielding to her at the end is a surprise, but a very effective one. The man who tells the story is ironically unaware of his own motives. He concludes, "What could I do? Another time, I'd have gone straight back to Mary and the kids. But today I was the king, I'd won and it was a case of winner take all." He goes from the tractor to her bed, and there is some question as to who has really won the day. The strength of the piece lies in what Wain does not say outright.

There is no doubt that Wain's concern as a writer is well placed; the problems he chooses to present are significant. The weakness in his short stories is a lack of restraint. When he makes the necessary effort to say less explicitly and more implicitly, his stories gain the light touch and resonance that mark good writing.

OTHER MAJOR WORKS

LONG FICTION: *Hurry on Down*, 1953 (pb. in U.S. as *Born in Captivity*); *Living in the Present*, 1955; *The Contenders*, 1958; *A Travelling Woman*, 1959; *Strike the Father Dead*, 1962; *The Young Visitors*, 1965; *The Smaller Sky*, 1967; *A Winter in the Hills*, 1970; *The Pardoner's Tale*, 1978; *Young Shoulders*, 1982 (pb. in

U.S. as *The Free Zone Starts Here*); *Where the Rivers Meet*, 1988; *Comedies*, 1990; *Hungry Generations*, 1994.

PLAYS: *Harry in the Night: An Optimistic Comedy*, pr. 1975; *Johnson Is Leaving: A Monodrama*, pb. 1994.

TELEPLAY: *Young Shoulders*, 1984 (with Robert Smith).

RADIO PLAYS: *You Wouldn't Remember*, 1978; *A Winter in the Hills*, 1981; *Frank*, 1982.

POETRY: *Mixed Feelings*, 1951; *A Word Carved on a Sill*, 1956; *A Song About Major Eatherly*, 1961; *Weep Before God: Poems*, 1961; *Wildtrack: A Poem*, 1965; *Letters to Five Artists*, 1969; *The Shape of Feng*, 1972; *Feng: A Poem*, 1975; *Poems for the Zodiac*, 1980; *Thinking About Mr. Person*, 1980; *Poems, 1949-1979*, 1981; *Twofold*, 1981; *Open Country*, 1987.

NONFICTION: *Preliminary Essays*, 1957; *Gerard Manley Hopkins: An Idiom of Desperation*, 1959; *Sprightly Running: Part of an Autobiography*, 1962; *Essays on Literature and Ideas*, 1963; *The Living World of Shakespeare: A Playgoer's Guide*, 1964; *Arnold Bennett*, 1967; *A House for the Truth: Critical Essays*, 1972; *Samuel Johnson*, 1974; *Professing Poetry*, 1977; *Samuel Johnson, 1709-1784*, 1984 (with Kai Kin Yung); *Dear Shadows: Portraits from Memory*, 1986.

CHILDREN'S LITERATURE: *Lizzie's Floating Shop*, 1981.

EDITED TEXTS: *Contemporary Reviews of Romantic Poetry*, 1953; *Interpretations: Essays on Twelve English Poems*, 1955; *International Literary Annual*, 1959, 1960; *Fanny Burney's Diary*, 1960; *Anthology of Modern Poetry*, 1963; *Selected Shorter Poems of Thomas Hardy*, 1966; *Selected Stories of Thomas Hardy*, 1966; *Thomas Hardy's "The Dynasts,"* 1966; *Shakespeare: Macbeth, a Casebook*, 1968, revised 1994; *Shakespeare: Othello, a Casebook*, 1971; *Johnson as Critic*, 1973; *The New Wessex Selection of Thomas Hardy's Poetry*, 1978 (with Eirian James).

BIBLIOGRAPHY

Amis, Kingsley, *Kingsley Amis: Memoirs*. New York: Summit Books, 1991. Gives a vivid glimpse of infighting among aspiring writers. Amis hints wryly that Wain envied the best-sellerdom of *Lucky Jim* that placed his own first novel, *Hurry on Down*, into the shade.

Bayley, John. "Obituary: John Wain." *The Independent*, May 25, 1994, p. 14. In this biographical sketch of Wain's life and literary career, Bayley compares him with Kingsley Amis and praises his biography of Samuel Johnson.

Burgess, Anthony. *The Novel Now: A Guide to Contemporary Fiction*. New York: W. W. Norton, 1967. Expanded from an earlier study, Burgess's work groups Wain with other class-conscious British fiction writers.

Gerard, David E. *John Wain*. Westport, Conn.: Meckler, 1987. Contains a comprehensive annotated bibliography of Wain's work. Lists materials of critical and biographical interest, including radio, television, and sound recordings.

Gindin, James J. *Postwar British Fiction: New Accents and Attitudes*. Berkeley: University of California Press, 1962. Gindin's chapter "The Moral Center of John Wain's Fiction" discusses Wain's use of morality as a thematic and structural device and claims that each novel contains a central statement of the moral worth of the individual.

Heptonstall, Geoffrey. "Remembering John Wain." *Contemporary Review* 266 (March, 1995): 144-146. A brief discussion of Wain's central themes of faithlessness and the assumption that there are no assumptions. Discusses Wain's rejection of realism and his intention to speak imaginatively.

Parini, Jay, ed. *British Writers*. Supplement 16. Detroit: Charles Scribner's Sons, 2010. Includes an overview of Wain's life, literary career, and works.

Pickering, Jean. "The English Short Story in the Sixties." In *The English Short Story, 1945-1960*, edited by Dennis Vannatta. Boston: Twayne, 1985. The most comprehensive study of Wain as a writer of short fiction.

Salwak, Dale. *John Wain*. Boston: Twayne, 1981. Part of Twayne's English Authors series, this work is the first book-length study of Wain and is a useful introduction to Wain's career.

Schlüssel, Angelika Gelika. "Making a Political Statement or Refusing to Grow Up: Reflections on the Situation of the Academic Youth in Postwar British Literature." *American Journal of Psychoanalysis* 65, no. 4 (December, 2005): 381-403. Applies the psychoanalytic concept of "prolonged adolescence" to Wain's novel *Hurry on Down* and John Osborne's *Look Back in Anger*, two literary works which reflect England's social and political mood in the years after World War II.

Walzer, Michael. "John Wain: The Hero in Limbo." *Perspective* 10 (Summer/Autumn, 1958): 137-145. In his consideration of Wain's first three novels, Walzer maintains that Wain develops a new kind of picaresque hero.

James Curry Robison
Updated by Jerry Bradley and
Richard Hauer Costa

SYLVIA TOWNSEND WARNER

Born: Harrow, Middlesex, England;
December 6, 1893
Died: Maiden Newton, Dorset, England;
May 1, 1978

PRINCIPAL SHORT FICTION

"Some World Far from Ours," and "Stay, Corydon, Thou Swain," 1929
Elinor Barley, 1930
Moral Ending, and Other Stories, 1931
The Salutation, 1932
More Joy in Heaven, and Other Stories, 1935
Twenty-four Short Stories, 1939 (with Graham Greene and James Laver)
The Cat's Cradle Book, 1940
A Garland of Straw, and Other Stories, 1943
The Museum of Cheats, 1947
Winter in the Air, and Other Stories, 1955
A Spirit Rises, 1962
A Stranger with a Bag, and Other Stories, 1966 (pb. in U.S. as *Swans on an Autumn River: Stories,* 1966)
The Innocent and the Guilty: Stories, 1971
Kingdoms of Elfin, 1977
Scenes of Childhood, 1981
One Thing Leading to Another, and Other Stories, 1984
Selected Stories of Sylvia Townsend Warner, 1988
The Music at Long Verney: Twenty Stories, 2001 (Michael Steinman, editor)

OTHER LITERARY FORMS

In addition to the short stories for which Sylvia Townsend Warner is best known, she wrote seven novels: *Lolly Willowes: Or, The Loving Huntsman* (1926), *Mr. Fortune's Maggot* (1927), *The True Heart* (1929), *Summer Will Show* (1936), *After the Death of Don Juan* (1938), *The Corner That Held Them* (1948), and *The Flint Anchor* (1954). She also wrote several collections of poetry, which were published as *Collected Poems* (1982) and *New Collected Poems* (2008); a biography; a travel guidebook; and a volume of literary criticism, and she translated two books from French into English.

ACHIEVEMENTS

In 1926, Sylvia Townsend Warner's first novel, *Lolly Willowes*, was the first Book-of-the-Month Club selection; her second novel, *Mr. Fortune's Maggot*, was a selection of the newly formed Literary Guild. Her later novels did not attain the same popularity, but her short stories, 144 of which were published in *The New Yorker* over a period of four decades, gained for her a wide readership.

In 1967, she became a Fellow of the Royal Society of Literature (she wryly commented that it was the first public acknowledgment she had received since she was expelled from kindergarten) and in 1972, an honorary member of the American Academy of Arts and Letters. Her short story "The Love Match" was awarded the Prix Menton for 1968.

No full-length critical monograph of Warner's achievement as novelist, short-story writer, and poet has been produced, although in 2006 a collection of essays analyzing a wide range of her writings was published. John Updike noted in a favorable review that her "half century of brilliantly varied and superbly self-possessed literary production never won for her the flaming place in the heavens of reputation that she deserved." As far as her achievement in the short story is concerned, however, she certainly ranks alongside H. E. Bates and V. S. Pritchett, her two British contemporaries, whose work most resembles her own.

BIOGRAPHY

Sylvia Townsend Warner was born in Harrow, Middlesex, on December 6, 1893. She was educated mostly at home (her father was a schoolmaster), having been considered a disruptive influence in kindergarten. Her early talent was for music, and in 1914 she was set to travel to Vienna to study under Arnold Schönberg, but the outbreak of World War I prevented it. In 1916, after the death of her father, she moved to London and was a member of the editorial committee that compiled the ten-volume *Tudor Church Music* (1922-1929). Her first publication was a collection of poetry, *The Espalier*, in 1925, a time when she thought of herself primarily as a poet. In the 1920's, she met the novelist T. F. Powys, who proved to be influential on her early poetry and fiction. In 1930, Warner moved to the country and lived with her friend Valentine Ackland in a Dorset village. During the 1930's, she and Ackland became involved in left-wing politics, joining the Communist Party and serving with the Red Cross in Barcelona during the Spanish Civil War. In subsequent years, Warner lived the quiet life of an English gentlewoman in rural Dorset, managing to sustain her literary output up to her final years. She died in 1978.

ANALYSIS

One of the notable features of Sylvia Townsend Warner's short stories is her elegant, precise, epigrammatic, and witty prose. These qualities are particularly noticeable when she focuses on what she knows best: the niceties of English middle- and upper-class life as they reveal themselves in day-to-day domestic

and social routines, and the sudden disruption of those routines. As in the novels of her British contemporary, Barbara Pym, Warner's detached and humorous observance of the oddities of humanity is one of the chief pleasures to be gained from her stories. She has a sharp but sympathetic eye for eccentricity of all kinds, and her stories cover a wide range of situations and points of view.

Perhaps because of the variety of her fiction, it would be misleading to pinpoint specific themes or leading ideas. Warner's stories do not reveal a consistent or dominant mood or atmosphere. She does not espouse a philosophy or champion a cause. Her subject matter is the infinite variety of human nature: its follies, regrets, hopes, deceits, compromises, small defeats and victories, and the tidy chaos of the average human life. The stories frequently develop out of an apparently insignificant event or chance encounter or an incident or memory from the protagonist's past, which resurfaces to affect the present. A sudden rift is produced in the otherwise smooth fabric of daily life, and often an ironic twist at the end will reveal a new dimension to a relationship or to the inner life of the protagonist.

Warner is a traditionalist. She does not experiment with modern techniques (her chief technical device is the flashback); her stories succeed through strong characterization and plotting. There is an old-fashioned quality about her and her fictional world. Almost all of her stories are set in England, with a carefully evoked spirit of place (perhaps this accounts in part for her success in *The New Yorker*, since she usually portrays a timeless, civilized England that popular American culture has tended to idealize).

"HEE-HAW!"

Warner has a Thomas Hardy-like awareness of the ironies of fate (Hardy was a major influence on her early poetry) and of the tricks that time plays. Many of her stories, for example, "The Sea Is Always the Same," "Johnnie Brewer," and "A Second Visit," center on the protagonist's return, after a gap of many years, to a former home or place of memories. In "Hee-Haw!" from *Winter in the Air, and Other Stories*, Mrs. Vincent returns to the village in Cornwall, where for three years, thirty years previously, she had lived turbulently with her first husband, Ludovick, a young artist who was later to gain eminence. The first sound she hears on her return is the unchanging, regular sound of the foghorn from the lightship ("Hee-Haw, Hee-Haw!"), which seems to span the thirty years of her absence, giving a sense of permanence and familiarity to the external environment. What of her internal environment? She is introduced to an old man in the hotel bar, who needs little prompting to recall the famous artist. His recollections, however, shock her. He tells her that Ludovick and his wife (or girlfriend, he did not know which) were the happiest couple he had ever seen, and he relates several incidents in which they were playing and laughing together. Mrs. Vincent, however, knowing how stormy her relationship with Ludovick was, assumes without question that the old man must be referring to another woman. In a wave of jealousy, she realizes that she has discovered, thirty years after the event, her husband's infidelity. She is left to her anger and her melancholy; an old wound has been reopened in a way that she would not have imagined possible.

The strength of "Hee-Haw!" is in the contrast between the ease with which the reader guesses the truth (although the truth is never overtly established) and the inability of Mrs. Vincent to recognize that her relationship with Ludovick might have looked quite different from the outside. It is at once a poignant tale of reminiscence and a reminder of the subjectivity of the experience of life. Appearances are not what they seem, and memory is only shifting sand.

"WINTER IN THE AIR"

"Winter in the Air" also focuses on a return. A middle-aged woman, Barbara, returns to live in London after a twelve-year absence following the breakup of her marriage. The story consists of a series of flashbacks to the final stages of her marriage two months previously, interspersed with Barbara's thoughts as she arranges the furniture in her new apartment. The reader is given a minimum of clues regarding the reasons for the divorce, and the chief interest of this otherwise slight, although typical, story lies in the fact that nine-tenths of its emotional force lies below the surface. Deep emotions surface only momentarily.

What Barbara really feels, though, is contained in the half-remembered snatches of a quotation from William Shakespeare's *The Winter's Tale* (pr. c.

1610-1611, pb. 1623) which flash into her mind: the dignified, despairing speech of Hermione, the wronged wife, whose chief comfort in life, the favor of her husband, has gone, though she does not know how or why it went. As Barbara sits down to write to her former husband Willie, she knows that in real life one does not say such things, and all she is prepared to commit to paper is a platitude about her new charwoman; this, however, is as unsatisfactory to her as confessing her true feelings and she tears up the letter and throws it away. Neither truth nor platitude can be uttered, and the deeper emotional terrain of her life must remain as silent as the silence that she notices enveloping her new apartment. Silence will hide secrets and heal pain, and life will go on. The story finishes with Barbara projecting herself into the mundane thoughts of the charwoman about the weather: Winter is in the air. This final thought has a slightly ominous connotation; whether it hints at Barbara's future loneliness, old age, or simply the demise of emotional honesty and communication, Warner rightly leaves it to the reader to decide.

"A LOVE MATCH"

Swans on an Autumn River contains what is often regarded as Warner's finest story, "A Love Match." It centers on a quiet conservative couple, Justin Tizard and his elder sister Celia. Justin returns on leave after the 1916 Battle of the Somme, in which Celia's fiancé has been killed. He stays at her apartment in London, but during his sleep he relives the terrible scenes of battle, raving incoherently. Celia, sleepless, listens in horror in the adjoining room. The following day, as they stroll casually around London, an old woman mistakes them for man and wife. The incident is one of several foreshadowings of what is to come. Two nights later, Celia is again awakened by Justin's ravings. She goes to his side to comfort him, and the combination of her compassion and his distress drives them into the physical expression of love.

Afterward, they feel no regret, and as the years go by they find happiness together. They possess an intuitive insight into each other's feelings, feel no need to impress each other, and are not particularly concerned with each other's likes and dislikes. Their common childhood memories act as a bond between them. They also become practiced at shielding their true relationship from their neighbors in Hallowby, the English village to which they move in 1923, and soon become one of the most respectable of couples.

Their lives are upset in the 1930's when Celia, who has become bored with local society and has developed a reputation for supporting unusual causes, receives a series of anonymous letters which claim that her secret is common knowledge in the village. The letters turn out to be only idle gossip from one of Justin's disappointed female admirers, and he soon puts a stop to them. Nothing has changed, and the secret remains intact.

The final outcome is carefully developed to produce the maximum effect. During World War II, Hallowby is bombed. Rescue workers entering a bombed house find a bedroom floor deep in rubble. Slates from the roof have fallen on the bed, crushing the two bodies that lay there. One of the villagers at the scene offers the opinion that Justin went into Celia's bedroom to comfort her. Others agree, and the coroner accepts this hypothesis as truth.

Warner's comment that the story's success was a victory for "incest and sanity" was only partly tongue-in-cheek. Rarely has incest been so sympathetically portrayed. Warner places subtle emphasis on the ease with which the lovers communicate and the depth of their love. The very criminality of their liaison adds to its preciousness for them. The ambiguity of the conclusion is also important. It is not made explicit whether the villagers genuinely believe their own explanation, whether they simply cannot comprehend the implications of what they see, or whether they guess the truth but, out of common human decency, desire to shield the lovers from shame. The open-endedness of this conclusion reflects the necessary mixture of emotions which the story has raised and left unresolved. The image of the two lovers in death, locked together in the tenderness of their illegal union and surrounded by the debris of their ruined house, remains vividly in the reader's mind.

"SWANS ON AN AUTUMN RIVER"

"Swans on an Autumn River" also culminates in a strong visual image, which juxtaposes opposites to suggest the unattainable nature of an ideal. Norman

Repton, an engineer in his late sixties, visits Ireland for the first time on a business trip. It is a country for which he has always felt a romantic longing, fueled by the poetry of William Butler Yeats. The country does not meet his expectations, however, and he soon discovers that he is an alien in an unfamiliar land.

Repton is attracted to the river, which is one of two central symbols in the story. It is as if the river has power to compensate him for his old age, his weak physical condition, and the dissatisfaction with life that he feels. At night, he leaves the curtain of his room undrawn in order to see the river, which also casts its lightly dancing reflection on the ceiling. In spite of this, he is aware of neither, being alternately sunk heavily in sleep or at the mercy of his bladder and digestion. His low vitality is a strong contrast to everything that the flowing river and its reflection suggests. In its ease, serenity, and sparkling movement, the river represents another realm of being, but it is a realm which is forever closed to him, however much he longs for it.

This theme is restated and developed by another powerful symbol in the climax of the story. When he wakes in the morning, he sees a gathering of swans on the river. He looks at them enraptured, as if they were his own treasure. He grabs some bread and rushes out of the hotel, by which time eighteen swans have collected. The swans come flocking toward him as he excitedly tosses them the bread. He notes how skillfully they swim "without check or collision," unlike his own troubled and unsatisfactory life. When the feeding is interrupted by a swarm of gulls competing for the bread, Repton strikes at one of them and becomes so angry that he loses all thought of where he is. He only succeeds in making a fool of himself, falling down and hitting his head on the pavement. To two passersby, he is nothing more than a corpulent old Englishman behaving eccentrically, and the story ends with a policeman arranging for an ambulance to take him away.

The poetry of Yeats may well have been in Warner's mind when she wrote this story. The swans resemble those in "The Wild Swans at Coole" which "drift on the still water,/ Mysterious, beautiful." In their effortlessness, they seem to belong to a realm of eternity, and they are contrasted in the story with the frequent emphasis on the limitations and restrictions of ordinary bodily life. Repton himself calls to mind the lines from Yeats's "Sailing to Byzantium": "An aged man is but a paltry thing,/ A tattered coat upon a stick, unless/ Soul clap its hands and sing! . . . ." Repton cannot clap his hands and sing, however, and he cannot be gathered into the "artifice of eternity" which the swans on the river symbolize. "Swans on an Autumn River" thus becomes a tragic story of the disparity between the infinity of human desire and the finite realities within which it must operate.

THE INNOCENT AND THE GUILTY

The Innocent and the Guilty is the only one of Warner's collections to be organized under a specific theme. She had confessed to an "obsessive" concern with this theme, but the title is wholly ironic ("Perhaps one day, I shall . . . write a story where the innocent are charming and the guilty nauseating"). The ironic purpose is clear from "Truth in the Cup," in which a group of self-righteous villagers, celebrating in the local hotel on a stormy night, lament the moral decay of the young. Like sinful man in Genesis, however, they become victims of a catastrophic flood. Warner's purpose is also clear in "The Quality of Mercy," in which a drunken young woman and the local toughs who help her home are more virtuous than the "respectable" sister who greets them with abuse and recrimination.

"BUT AT THE STROKE OF MIDNIGHT"

The distinctions between innocence and guilt become blurred in "But at the Stroke of Midnight," one of Warner's most ambitious stories. It is a mysterious tale, with a hint of the supernatural, and it centers on the motif of rebirth. The protagonist is Lucy Ridpath, an undistinguished middle-aged woman who escapes from her dull marriage to seek a new life. Adopting the name Aurelia, she goes through a number of adventures in London and becomes like "a nova--a new appearance in the firmament, the explosion of an aging star." She has a powerful effect on everyone she meets. A clergyman sees her as a tranquil, spiritual woman; others find themselves curiously attracted to her and do her unexpected favors.

Leaving London to stay at a guesthouse, she adopts a stray cat and calls it Lucy. (Cats appear with somewhat alarming frequency in Warner's fiction.) She moves to a country cottage and successfully tries her hand at being a landscape artist. It seems that her rebirth is accomplished. The title, however, with its Cinderella connotations, suggests that it will not last, and that is how it turns out. One cold wet night, Lucy returns late, mortally injured, and the moment the cat dies, she realizes that she is no longer Aurelia but Lucy Ridpath once more. When morning breaks, she goes outside to bury the cat, but she finds herself immersed in floodwater. Walking toward the road, she has a half-conscious desire to drown, and as she wades deeper in the water, she falls and is swept away by the current.

This curious but stimulating story, a mixture of realism and fantasy, is one of Warner's very few attempts to deal with an archetypal theme. It does not entirely succeed. The ending is abrupt and the reason for Lucy's death is unexplained. The cat, it seems, mysteriously embodies her former self, to which she must return when the cat dies. It is quite possible that Warner intended such a supernatural implication. In one of her early stories, "Early One Morning," from the collection *The Salutation*, an old woman dies and her soul immediately passes into one of the local greyhounds. Perhaps the tragedy of "But at the Stroke of Midnight" is that having once known rebirth, Lucy cannot lapse back into a former state. Caught between two selves, the old and the new, she can be neither.

"OXENHOPE"

In "Oxenhope," Warner returns to a favorite theme, the effects of the passing of time, as experienced by a protagonist who returns to former haunts. As the story develops, it becomes a subtle meditation on the presence of mortality and the longing for immortality.

William, a man in his sixties, returns to the village where he had stayed for a month when he was seventeen. As he drives through, he recognizes everything in the landscape. He thinks about the old shepherd he had known, with his prodigious memory that seemingly would never die, and he wants to know all the changes that the unchanging valley has seen. As he reminisces, the narrative passes freely between present event and past remembrance; past and present seem to merge. He finds the gravestone of the woman who had befriended him and cleans it so that the name stands out, just as he had done with the other family gravestones so many years previously. He notices, however, that the most recent name is the least visible, as if the woman had not expected to be remembered.

Fully aware of the imprint of mortality, he decides that the past is irrecoverable and that there is no purpose in staying. Then comes the ironic twist in the tale, so characteristic of Warner. He meets a local boy, who talks to him about local legends. One story is of a man who "set fire" to the loch and sent flames leaping up around his boat. William immediately realizes that the man was him--out in a rowing boat he had taken a match to bubbles of marsh gas as they rose to the surface of the water, and the fire had been the result. He leaves the village satisfied, with no need even of a backward glance, realizing that he is lodged in the collective memory of the locality, which lends him a kind of immortality. The subtlety of the observed paradox and its implications reveal Warner's fiction at its best. Human life remains embedded in the past even when the past has seemed to vanish or to be vanishing, and yet the knowledge of this fact paradoxically frees the present from the past's stifling grip.

KINGDOMS OF ELFIN

Two more collections are worthy of comment. *Kingdoms of Elfin* is a collection of fantasies about fairy kingdoms. The product of Warner's final creative years, these stories display considerable ingenuity (and Warner clearly relishes the telling of them), but few rank with her best work. The fantasy setting does not supply the moral bearings necessary in order to feel and respond fully to the odd adventures of the fairy protagonists. Warner invents her own fairy lore with considerable aplomb, but the kingdoms she describes are not mythical or otherworldly. On the contrary, they tend to parallel human institutions, particularly the hierarchical structure of medieval or Renaissance society. In consequence, much of the pleasure to be gained from them is in the occasional acid comment about the superstitions of religion, or in the gentle mocking of the social pretenses and snobbery and the political plotting and maneuvering that bedevil both human and fairy worlds.

SCENES OF CHILDHOOD

Scenes of Childhood is a posthumous collection of Warner's reminiscences about her upbringing in Edwardian England, a time "when there was a Tzar in Russia, and scarcely an automobile or a divorced person in Mayfair." Impressionistic sketches rather than fully developed stories, they display her epigrammatic style to best advantage. Extracting much harmless fun from the eccentricities of upper-middle-class English life, she parades an assortment of odd characters ranging from her parents to great-aunts, nannies, retired majors, French teachers, and a butler whose smile was so ghastly that he had to be got rid of (he revenged himself by joining the fire brigade and ruining the Warner's kitchen while putting out a minor fire).

At their best, Sylvia Townsend Warner's short stories constitute a quiet exploration of the oddities and ironies of the human condition as it unfolds itself in time, fate, and circumstances. She is an acute observer, but she is careful not to judge. Her humor, always tart, is never malicious. She is a realist, and few of her stories end in unqualified optimism. She is aware of the pain of loss and the mockery that time makes of human ideals. She notes the human capacity for self-deceit but also the ability to make peace with limitations. Rarely faltering in the smoothness of her controlled, elegant, economical prose, she is a craftswoman whose finely wrought stories entertain and delight.

OTHER MAJOR WORKS

LONG FICTION: *Lolly Willowes: Or, The Loving Huntsman*, 1926; *Mr. Fortune's Maggot*, 1927; *The True Heart*, 1929; *Summer Will Show*, 1936; *After the Death of Don Juan*, 1938; *The Corner That Held Them*, 1948; *The Flint Anchor*, 1954.

POETRY: *The Espalier*, 1925; *Time Importuned*, 1928; *Opus 7*, 1931; *Whether a Dove or a Seagull: Poems*, 1933; *Boxwood*, 1957; *Azrael, and Other Poems*, 1978; *Twelve Poems*, 1980; *Collected Poems*, 1982; *New Collected Poems*, 2008 (Claire Harman, editor).

NONFICTION: *Jane Austen*, 1951; *T. H. White: A Biography*, 1967; *Letters*, 1982; *The Diaries of Sylvia Townsend Warner*, 1994 (Claire Harman, editor); *I'll Stand by You: Selected Letters of Sylvia Townsend Warner and Valentine Ackland*, 1998 (Susanna Pinney, editor); *The Element of Lavishness: Letters of Sylvia Townsend Warner and William Maxwell, 1938-1978*, 2001.

BIBLIOGRAPHY

Ackland, Valentine. *For Sylvia: An Honest Account.* New York: W. W. Norton, 1985. A brief but poignant autobiography by Warner's lover, detailing the years with Warner and the painful separation caused by Ackland's struggle with alcoholism. Bea Howe's lengthy foreword discusses her firsthand understanding of the influence of Ackland on Warner's personal and professional life.

Brothers, Barbara. "Through the 'Pantry Window': Sylvia Townsend Warner and the Spanish Civil War." In *Rewriting the Good Fight: Critical Essays on the Literature of the Spanish Civil War*, edited by Frieda S. Brown, et al. East Lansing: Michigan State University Press, 1989. Places Warner in the context of her contemporaries regarding the period of the Spanish Civil War. Includes bibliography.

Davies, Gill, David Malcolm, and John Simons, eds. *Critical Essays on Sylvia Townsend Warner, English Novelist, 1893-1978.* Lewiston, N.Y.: Edwin Mellen Press, 2006. John Simons's essay examines the "compositional genetics" of *Kingdoms of Elfin*, one of Warner's works of short fiction. Other essays discuss the importance of place in Warner's writing, analyze two of her novels, and demonstrate how Warner's works reflect her relationship with Valentine Ackland.

Dinnage, Rosemary. "An Affair to Remember." *The New York Times*, March 7, 1999. A review of *Selected Letters of Sylvia Townsend Warner and Valentine Ackland*. Comments on Warner's offbeat short stories from *The New Yorker*, arguing that the short story was well suited to her whimsy. Discusses her lesbian relationship with Valentine Ackland.

Garrity, Jane. *Step-Daughters of England: British Women Modernists and the National Imaginary.* Manchester, England: Manchester University Press, 2003. Examines the work of four British women modernists--Warner, Virginia Woolf, Dorothy Richardson, and Mary Butts--to determine how their works situated them within the British Empire. The chapter on Warner focuses on her novels.

Harmon, Claire. *Sylvia Townsend Warner: A Biography.* London: Chatto & Windus, 1989. An even and thorough biography that deals openly and prominently with the relationship between Warner and Valentine Ackland. Gives a biographical and historical context of Warner's work but offers little critical detail.

Hauser, Freda S. "Worldly Chickens in a Homely Empire: Accounts of Colonialism in Sylvia Townsend Warner's *The Salutation*." In *At Home and Abroad in the Empire: British Women Write the 1930's*, edited by Robin Hackett, Freda S. Hauser, and Gay Wachman. Newark: University of Delaware Press, 2009. Focuses on Warner's depiction of the British empire in *The Salutation*, her novella written as a sequel to her novel *Mr. Fortune's Maggot*. Hauser maintains that whereas *Mr. Fortune's Maggot* is a "lighthearted critique" of the empire, *The Salutation* reflects Warner's "somber misgivings" about the empire's "insidious inheritance."

Loeb, Marion C. "British to the Core." *St. Petersburg Times*, August 6, 1989, p. 7D. A review of *The Selected Stories of Sylvia Townsend Warner*. Notes that her stories deal with the world of civil servants, vicars' wives, and pensioners. Comments on her graceful, lyrical style.

Maxwell, William, ed. Introduction to *Letters*. New York: Viking, 1982. Maxwell, a novelist and editor for *The New Yorker* and Warner's longtime personal friend, shows great admiration for Warner's work. He notes her historical astuteness, her "ironic detachment," and her graceful formalism of language. Maxwell also considers Warner's letters as being a writer's "left-over energy" and as written without the inhibition of editorial or critical judgment. Includes a brief biographical sketch.

Perenyi, Eleanor. "The Good Witch of the West." *The New York Review of Books* 32 (July 18, 1985): 27-30. Argues that Warner's literary reputation has suffered from the inability of critics to categorize her writings, which include dozens of short stories and seven novels. Notes that the publication of her letters has sparked new interest and that their talk of dreams and visitations suggests that Warner harbored "more than a touch of the witch."

Strachan, W. J. "Sylvia Townsend Warner: A Memoir." *London Magazine* 19, no. 8 (November, 1979): 41-50. An overview of Warner's fiction, with a close look at its elements of fantasy and realism. Strachan argues that *Kingdoms of Elfin* and *Lolly Willowes* seem incongruent given Warner's activity during World War I, but such realistic works as *The Flint Anchor* demonstrate her earthy, pragmatic quality. Maintains that even her most fantastic works reveal reason "firmly in control."

Tomalin, Claire. "Burning Happiness." *The New York Times*, February 18, 1996. A review of *The Diaries of Sylvia Townsend Warner*. Discusses the nature of Warner's feminism and her communism. Notes the passion of her grief for Valentine Ackland after Ackland's death.

Wachman, Gay. *Lesbian Empire: Radical Cross-writing in the Twenties*. New Brunswick, N.J.: Rutgers University Press, 2001. Wachman's examination of sexually radical fiction written by British women during the interwar years places Warner as the central figure in the creation of a modernist literary tradition. Discusses how Warner overcame the inhibitions confronted by authors who wanted to write about lesbian love. Demonstrates how Warner "crosswrote" about homosexuality by depicting "unrepresentable" lesbian characters as gay men. The many references to Warner's works, including the short fiction, are listed in the index.

Bryan Aubrey
Updated by Lou Thompson

DENTON WELCH

Born: Shanghai, China; March 29, 1915
Died: Crouch, Kent, England; December 30, 1948

PRINCIPAL SHORT FICTION

Brave and Cruel, 1948
A Last Sheaf, 1951
The Stories of Denton Welch, 1985

OTHER LITERARY FORMS

Besides his short-story collections, Denton Welch published two novels, an unfinished novel, journals, and uncollected poems. Both the unfinished novel and the short-story collections were published after his death.

ACHIEVEMENTS

Denton Welch's fiction has been favorably compared to that of Jean Cocteau, Marcel Proust, André Gide, Christopher Isherwood, and Truman Capote. Few writers began their career with the kind of precocious brilliance and searing honesty that characterized the early works of Welch. Dead at age thirty-three after thirteen years of debilitating pain resulting from a bicycle accident in 1935, Welch had been known primarily as a painter until he began writing only six years before his death. His first work garnered high critical praise from a number of respected and established British literary figures, such as Edith Sitwell, Sir Herbert Read, and Cyril Connolly, to name but a few. His direct narrative manner, sexual openness, and dazzling prose style contrasted greatly with the highly realistic war fiction that was being produced throughout the 1940's. Much of his short fiction documents the fall from innocence to experience that oversensitive young boys undergo when they lose a parent or a friend through death or misunderstanding. A number of his later stories are also superb portraits of the initial stirrings of artistic impulse and demonstrate how creative adolescents learn to trust their imaginations and begin to become artists. An authentically original voice, Welch writes in a style that appears completely nonderivative. Few writers have dramatized so precisely the agony of adolescence, a phase he labeled as "sordid and fearful."

BIOGRAPHY

Maurice Denton Welch was born in Shanghai, China, into a family of wealth and privilege. His father was a prosperous rubber merchant, and his American-born mother a devoted Christian Scientist. He spent much of his youth traveling back and forth between Asia and Europe in the company of his mother, to whom he was inordinately devoted because of his father's absence. To his great disappointment, he was enrolled in one of England's finest boarding schools, Repton, which his two older brothers attended. The typical lifestyle of an English boys' school brought traumatic change in the young boy's life, especially in the wake of the casual days spent with his mother traveling throughout the world. He so detested Repton that he ran away, preferring to visit well-known cathedrals at Salisbury and Exeter. He finally found satisfaction at the Goldsmith School of Art in London, where he was able to develop his considerable talent as a painter and where he enjoyed the relaxed and open atmosphere of an art school.

Two experiences profoundly altered Welch's relatively secure and happy life: The first was the death of his beloved mother when he was eleven years old, and the second, at age twenty, was a catastrophic bicycle accident that left him a permanent invalid and contributed to his early death at the age of thirty-three. The last thirteen years of his life were spent in great pain and discomfort but were, ironically, his most artistically productive years.

From his early published writings, Welch found great and encouraging praise from Edith Sitwell, who called him "a born writer." Renowned literary editors such as Cyril Connolly and Sir Herbert Read found his work fresh and completely original. In an age that rarely allowed mention of sexual matters, Welch's candor about his homosexuality disturbed a number of England's conservative literary intelligentsia. More disturbing to them, however, was the originality of his writing style and its apparent artlessness and absence of any discernible literary influences.

ANALYSIS

Denton Welch's early stories deal with the recurrent theme of the loss of an innocent vision of the world. There is usually a fall of some kind in which an innocent young boy learns some devastating information that alters, or will soon alter, the way he feels about his life thereafter.

"THE COFFIN ON THE HILL"

One of Welch's finest stories, "The Coffin on the Hill," documents an eight-year-old boy's first serious confrontation with mortality. The story concerns an Easter voyage of a family on a boat up a river in China. The story is told through the eyes of the eight-year-old as he experiences the mysteries of the Orient. The ship is, obviously, a symbol of an ark floating on the river of life, and life on the ship is Edenic. Welch is an unashamedly symbolic writer.

The cooks on the ship playfully tease the young boy with stories about drowned people in the river who, if he fell into the water, would pull him down to the bottom. His response is to return to his cabin, assume the fetal position, and hug his strange doll, which he has named "Lymph Est." The family then visits an ancient Chinese graveyard, where the boy sees, while off on his own, an open grave with a rotting corpse in it. He is so stunned by the sight that he returns to his family but is unable to separate the lesson of death from the fear and the sure knowledge that even his dear mother will someday become mere dust and ashes. Though he is only eight, his sensitive nature already has begun to torment him: "For I knew that she would come to it at last; and that knowledge was unbearable." His last act is to throw his favorite doll into the river as a sign of his growing maturity but also as a kind of propitiatory sacrifice that might somehow appease the gods of necessity and fate.

"AT SEA"

"At Sea" can be viewed as a further development of the same themes found in "The Coffin on the Hill." Again, there is a sea journey of a young boy, Robert, with his mother, but in this story the boy is pathologically attached to her to such an extent that their relationship becomes the major focus of the story. There is no father in the story at all. There is, however, a male character named Mr. Barron, who expresses some interest in Robert's mother and asks her to dance at a party. Robert's Oedipal jealousy so enrages him that he wets himself and publicly humiliates himself and his embarrassed mother. The reader discovers that his mother is showing signs of some eventual illness that seems fatal and, as in "The Coffin on the Hill," the youthful protagonist is forced to face the inevitable death of his mother.

Welch introduces a princess and her little dog, who tries repeatedly to break his leash and gain freedom, characters presenting fairly obvious mirror images of Robert chained to his mother's love. Some critics see Mr. Barron's name as a pun on Charon, the mythical guide and personification of death, who is leading Robert's beloved mother in a dance of death. The title of the story also foreshadows the plight of the boy after his mother's death, when he will surely be "at sea" or alone and lost. One of the strange rituals that the boy practices is writing elaborate letters in spite of the fact that he can neither read nor write, so that the reader sees him as someone who also cannot "read" or interpret the signs or portents of the catastrophe of his mother's impending death.

The narrative ends with a highly emotional loss of innocence as the boy realizes that his mother is ill. As he views her in a semiconscious state, he says: "He wanted to sing something so consummate and wonderful that his mother would turn over and smile and be happy forever; but he knew that she was dying and that she could not save herself." It is fairly clear that both of these extremely well-crafted stories are, if not blatantly autobiographical, at least fictive expressions of the deep and abiding loss that Welch experienced during his mother's lingering illness and eventual death when he was eleven years old.

His mother was a strict Christian Scientist and refused medication throughout her fatal illness, a fact that embittered Welch against the beliefs and practices of that religion. Indeed, he quotes hymns and some of Mary Baker Eddy's writings at the conclusion of "At Sea." Not only does this story and several of his novels record young children's loss of innocence, but also it particularly records the disappearance of the core of his emotional being, the love of his mother.

"WHEN I WAS THIRTEEN"

"When I Was Thirteen" is, unquestionably, one of Welch's most accomplished stories; it certainly is his most famous and most frequently anthologized one. The reader sees only the beginning of a fall from innocence to knowledge. The major character experiences a violent beating from his brother after spending a day and night with an older lad named Archer. He has absolutely no understanding of the names his brother is calling him: "Bastard, Devil, Harlot, Sod!"--except "Devil."

The story details a holiday trip that the unnamed narrator and his older brother, William, a student at Oxford, spend in Switzerland. William prefers the company of his fellow Oxford students and virtually abandons his young brother, who rather enjoys his solitude. Shortly after his brother leaves for an extended ski trip, the thirteen-year-old meets the handsome, charming, and friendly Archer, who is the same age as William. The younger boy is flattered by the attention of the attractive Archer, and they spend time together eating, skiing, and drinking. The younger boy is exhilarated by the contact and states quite honestly: "I had never enjoyed myself quite so much before. I thought him the most wonderful companion, not a bit intimidating, in spite of being rather a hero . . . and thought that, apart from my mother, who was dead, I had never liked anyone so much as I liked Archer." They get somewhat drunk together, bathe in the same water, and give each other body rubs. Nothing overtly sexual takes place, and though the language describing their contact is highly sensual, even sexual, innocence prevails. Indeed, the evening ends with Archer singing "Silent Night" in German and: "I began to cry in the moonlight with Archer singing my favorite song; and my brother far away up in the mountain."

Though the boy sleeps at Archer's that night, he awakens with a hangover the next morning and goes back to his hotel just as his brother, William, returns from his ski trip. Once William hears about the boy's escapades, he assumes that Archer has sexually seduced his brother and proceeds to beat his innocent brother, plunging his head in a basin of ice water and plunging his fingers down his brother's throat forcing him to vomit. Welch has so brilliantly constructed the story that the reader, not the boy, experiences the fall from innocence to knowledge, anticipating the boy's fall when he discovers what those words mean in the future. What the thirteen-year-old will find out is that what he experienced as genuine love, affection, and care from Archer is labeled, by the world, as sodomy and prostitution. Welch also cleverly uses the name "Archer" as a possible mythic echo of Cupid whose arrows cause people to fall in love.

Welch has further indicted types, such as William and his friends, who hate and fear Archer but do not know why. Robert Phillips, the most reliable critic on Welch, theorizes that William may be projecting his own fear of his homosexual feelings toward Archer. This fear, in turn, causes him to read homosexual undertones in perfectly innocent relationships. Archer is probably homosexual, but he is also rich, independent, and comfortable in his sexuality. It could also simply be that William's violent response to his brother's friendship is jealousy. The story is so rich in its construction that Welch enables the reader to interpret it in many equally valid ways. This story is one of his first to document various steps in a young boy's rite of passage from childhood to the more manly ceremonies of smoking and drinking with an older male whom he admires and wants to imitate.

"THE JUDAS TREE"

"The Judas Tree" is another story that is thematically related to "The Coffin on the Hill" and "At Sea" insofar as all three show how young people perceive the pain and loneliness of old age and begin to feel within themselves foreshadowings of their own dwindling powers. Specifically, this story concerns a young art student who is pursued by Mr. Clinton, a retired schoolmaster. They meet on the street of an English town as the older man offers to let the younger man sniff the bouquet of hyacinths, narcissus, and daffodils that he is carrying. The figure of Mr. Clinton carries echoes of Oscar Wilde, who frequently carried flowers, and the ominous pervert from James Joyce's "An Encounter," who persisted in trying to engage a boy in sexual conversation. There is also a suggestion of the strangers that the closeted Aschenbach from Thomas Mann's *Der Tod in Venedig* (1912; *Death in Venice*, 1925) kept encountering on his trip south.

The obviously lonely retired schoolmaster begs the art student to paint for him a picture of Judas actually hanging on the tree where he committed suicide, since of all the pictures that he has collected of Judas, none portrays him actually in the throes of death. He also proposes that he give the young man voice lessons as payment for the picture. The young man promises to paint the picture but then decides that there is something deeply disturbing in their relationship and tells the man that he has no time. The desperate older man immediately rejects the art student's friendship, treating him as one who has "betrayed" his promise, a Judas figure, and the story concludes on a despairing note as the art student declares: "How old and mad and undesirable he must be feeling!" The reader is left with the distinct impression that he is also describing himself in his inevitable later years.

Welch's next story, "The Trout Stream," could certainly be considered a novella, since it is divided into three major sections and runs to about twenty-six pages. In this well-constructed piece, a young boy sets out on another voyage of discovery with his sensitive and beautiful mother. This time it is a land voyage to an Edenic setting of an English manor presided over by Mr. Mellon. It is also a story of the fall of a great house, a genre that was particularly popular in British and American fiction throughout the nineteenth century.

The central character, Mr. Mellon, is the lord of his manor but is also paralyzed from the waist down and must be confined to a wheelchair. The large house is strangely sterile and lifeless, and the young narrator keeps finding artifacts, such as a beautifully carved ivory piece of a beggar covered with rats, an object that symbolizes the servant class that surrounds Mr. Mellon and attends to his needs. The name Mellon is also used to suggest the American family of the same name known for their fabulous wealth. The young boy becomes friendly with the housekeeper, Mrs. Slade, and her daughter, Phyllis. An unattractive, blunt girl, Phyllis takes the young boy on a tour of the grounds to show him the artificial trout stream that Mellon has built. The trout, like the characters in the story, are controlled and trapped by Mellon's pervasive power and wealth. The story concludes with Mellon building a more impressive estate, which is even more sterile than the first. Part 3 shows the narrator, now a young man, returning to the ruins of the estate after Mrs. Slade has drowned herself in the trout stream because Mellon rejected her, and after Phyllis has run away with the handsome chauffeur, Bob. All Mellon's effort to create his own little human "trout stream" or regenerated Eden has failed, and he is left lonely and helpless at the story's conclusion. Welch's novella has become another parable of the ravages of time even on the rich and powerful.

"BRAVE AND CRUEL"

"Brave and Cruel," the title story of Welch's first short-story collection, is one of his most compelling creations. The major characters are both artists of a sort. David, the narrator, is a painter, but Micki Beaumont is a con artist par excellence. Micki claims to be a returning hero after World War II and entertains the local crowd with fascinating tales of his bravery as a fighter pilot. Everyone believes him because of his charm and good looks. He asks the quiet Katherine Warde to marry him, and she accepts. The major theme of the story is appearance versus reality, or how normal people see what they want to see even though the artist, David, suspects Micki's stories from the beginning. As the story unfolds, the community discovers that Micki's real name is Potts, not Beaumont--that is, a little pot rather than a "beautiful mountain" (the literal translation of the French *beau mont*). Though everyone knows that Micki is a charming con artist, the Warde family, strangely enough, stays in contact with him throughout his embarrassing arrest and disgrace. The snobbish David sees him years later on a bus, dressed in expensive clothes and seemingly prosperous. "Brave and Cruel" is certainly one of Welch's best constructed stories and also discusses on a very sophisticated level how people need their fictions, even though they know them to be fictions, to vivify their banal lives. The necessity of art and illusion becomes, in this story, one of Welch's most serious themes.

"THE FIRE IN THE WOOD"

Many critics consider the short story "The Fire in the Wood" to be Welch's finest work. Again, the main character, Mary, a virgin, is an artist who cannot seem to find a subject that engenders enthusiasm or "fire" in her imagination. Her name obviously evokes the Blessed Virgin but also suggests "sea," or the primordial repository of archetypes that artists use for inspiration. The plot also shows strong affinities with a number of D. H. Lawrence's tales in which dried-up artist types meet sexually charged primitive innocents whose naturalness and physical energy revitalize their artistic powers. *Lady Chatterley's Lover* (1928) is the prototype of such stories. Mary, the artist, meets Jim, the woodsman or Adam figure, in an artificial woods that a wealthy man had designed to surround his proposed mansion but died before it could be completed. Like the trout stream in the story of the same name, the "wood" becomes a human-made, regenerated Eden in which Mary tempts the innocent Jim into an adulterous affair. Jim, however, has saved Mary not only by becoming her lover but also, more important, by becoming a model for her reawakened artistic energies. At the story's conclusion, reality intrudes as Mary discovers that what appeared to be innocent and noble is merely another sordid tale of madness, greed, and retribution. The important "fall" in the tale is Mary's coming into reality and leaving her adolescent dream-world. The fall then is a *felix culpa*, or "happy fall," because Mary may now be able to ground her imagination in reality rather than fantasy.

"THE HATEFUL WORD" AND "THE DIAMOND BADGE"

Two stories in Denton Welch's second collection stand out as exceptionally well wrought: "The Hateful Word" and "The Diamond Badge." "The Hateful Word" bears a strong resemblance to "The Fire in the Wood": Both stories use a female narrator, or what several critics call an Albertine voice--that is, the female voice through which Marcel Proust speaks in much of his fiction even though the speaker in the actual story is a male. Both Proust and Welch used this device as a method of covering their homosexuality. In "The Hateful Word," an aging woman offers a gardening job to a young German prisoner named Harry Diedz. Her name, Flora Pinkston, symbolizes her passionate (pink) nature and her desire that Harry "till" her garden. Her first name means "flower." The obvious Freudian overtones are difficult to overlook. The plot is also very Laurentian insofar as it describes a frustrated but passionate woman married to a dull lawyer who has not been able to satisfy her sexual needs. The young, handsome German gardener is paid to come each day and revive her neglected garden. Flora momentarily loses control of herself and passionately kisses the sensuous but polite young man. Though embarrassed by her pass, he tries, nevertheless, to explain that he feels to-ward her the way he feels toward his mother. He states: "You are like mother to me--my English mother." The word "mother"--the hateful word--devastates Flora and simultaneously awakens her to the harsh reality of her middle years, ushering away any residual illusions of appealing to young males.

The final story in the collection *A Last Sheaf*, "The Diamond Badge." is one of Welch's most sophisticated psychological tales, involving issues of control and ma-nipulation. Susan Innes writes to the author of a book that she has just finished reading and succeeds in getting an invitation to visit him. She does not know that the author, Andrew Clifton, is horribly deformed and is taken care of by a young, handsome man named Tom Parkinson. Obviously, Clifton loves Parkinson very deeply. Susan is shocked by Clifton's deformity, a fact that changes her whole attitude toward him. She stays the night but experiences a nightmare during which Tom Parkinson comes into her room to comfort her. She is very attracted to Tom and decides to "accidentally" leave a beautiful diamond pin or badge behind to ensure further contact and, perhaps, another invitation. Finally, after months of silent waiting, she reads a new story by Andrew Clifton called "The Diamond Badge" and real-izes that the story is really about her attempt to manipu-late both Andrew and Tom. Shortly after reading the story, she receives her diamond badge back without a comment. Andrew had not even sent it registered mail. Susan's attempt to control the lives of these two men merely exposed her selfish and mean-spirited attitude toward both of them.

The majority of the stories in Welch's collection *Brave and Cruel* deal with the crises of childhood and adolescence and particularly with falls from a childish innocence into the painful knowledge of emerging adulthood. The second collection, *A Last Sheaf*, con-cerns the specific difficulties that young artists experi-ence when they first attempt to practice their creative talents. In both collections, the protagonists are overly sensitive, introspective, and isolated. They feel pro-foundly separated from the normal world and suffer from that alienation. As time passes, they experience increased desperation and take dangerous and, some-times, self-destructive steps to alleviate their emptiness.

OTHER MAJOR WORKS

LONG FICTION: *Maiden Voyage*, 1943; *In Youth Is Pleasure*, 1944; *A Voice Through a Cloud*, 1950 (unfinished).

POETRY: *Dumb Instrument: Poems and Fragments*, 1976.

NONFICTION: *I Left My Grandfather's House*, 1958; *The Journals of Denton Welch*, 1984.

BIBLIOGRAPHY

Crain, Caleb. "It's Pretty, but Is It Broken?" *The New York Times*, June 20, 1999. Discusses Welch as the "champion of preciousness," fascinated with picnics and antiques. Comments on the relationship of Welch's homosexuality and physical disability to his writing.

De-la-Noy, Michael. *Denton Welch: The Making of a Writer*. New York: Viking, 1984. This standard bi-ography uses much material never before published. The biographer obtained information from many of Welch's letters, letters to Welch from his friends, and personal recollections of those who knew Welch.

Gooch, Brad. "Gossip, Lies, and Wishes." *The Nation* 240 (June 8, 1985): 711-713. Gooch praises Welch for his ability to make even the smallest objects into mementos by the precision of his writing. Though Welch seems haunted by death and time, he is never morbid and can, at times, be flippant about tombs and graveyards.

Hollinghurst, Alan. "Diminished Pictures." *The Times Literary Supplement*, no. 4264 (December 21, 1984): 1479-1480. Hollinghurst finds Welch's aes-theticism anything but precious. He argues that Welch's conceptions of beauty and art helped him focus his attention on art objects during times of great physical and mental pain; he wrote to save himself and to enrich his life.

Malcolm, Cheryl Alexander, and David Malcolm, eds. *British and Irish Short-Fiction Writers, 1945-2000*. Vol. 391 in *Dictionary of Literary Biog-raphy*. Detroit: Thomson/Gale, 2006. Includes an essay providing an overview of Welch's life and literary career and analysis of his short fiction.

Methuen-Campbell, James. *Denton Welch, Writer and Artist*. London: Tauris Parke, 2004. An updated biography that ties Welch's life to his works of literature and art. References to the individual short stories and short-story collections are listed in the index.

Phillips, Robert. *Denton Welch*. New York: Twayne, 1974. Book-length critical treatment of all Welch's work. Phillips's interpretations are thorough, though he tends to find Freudian and Jungian patterns most helpful. He also intelligently points out some of the affinities that Welch shared with D. H. Lawrence and James Joyce.

Skenazy, Paul. "The Sense and Sensuality of Denton Welch." *The Washington Post Book World*, April 6, 1986, p. 1. A review of *The Stories of Denton Welch* that comments on Welch's focus on the texture of social rituals rather than narrative structure and plot tension. Argues that one reads Welch not for character revelation but to experience his sensibility. Notes that nearly all the stories concern a confused outsider seeking security and love.

Updike, John. "A Short Life." In *Picked-Up Pieces*. New York: Alfred A. Knopf, 1975. Updike calls Welch an authentic existential writer insofar as his agony enabled him to create a world particle by particle. He sees Welch's autobiographical account of his terrible accident as "a proclamation of our terrible fragility."

Patrick Meanor

FAY WELDON

Born: Alvechurch, Worcestershire, England;
September 22, 1931
Also known as: Franklin Birkinshaw

PRINCIPAL SHORT FICTION

Watching Me, Watching You, 1981
Polaris, and Other Stories, 1985
Moon over Minneapolis: Or, Why She Couldn't Stay, 1991
Angel, All Innocence, and Other Stories, 1995
Wicked Women: A Collection of Short Stories, 1995
A Hard Time to Be a Father, 1998
Nothing to Wear and Nowhere to Hide, 2002

OTHER LITERARY FORMS

In addition to short fiction, Fay Weldon (WEHL-dehn) is a prolific author of novels and teleplays. Her best-known novel, *The Life and Loves of a She Devil* (1983), was made into a British Broadcasting Corporation (BBC) drama and a Hollywood film. Her numerous plays for television, primarily the BBC, include a 1971 award-winning episode of *Upstairs, Downstairs* and a 1980 dramatization of Jane Austen's novel *Pride and Prejudice* (1813). Weldon has also written plays for radio and the theater; nonfiction, including the memoir *Auto Da Fay* (2002); and the children's books *Wolf the Mechanical Dog* (1988), *Party Puddle* (1989), and *Nobody Likes Me* (1997).

ACHIEVEMENTS

Fay Weldon's novel *The Heart of the Country* (1987) won the 1989 *Los Angeles Times* book prize. Two other novels, *Praxis* (1978) and *Worst Fears* (1996), were finalists for the Booker McConnell Prize and the Whitbread Literary Award, respectively. The short-story collection *Wicked Women* won the PEN/Macmillan Silver Pen Award (1997). In 2001, she was made a Commander of the Order of the British Empire (CBE).

BIOGRAPHY

No doubt Fay Weldon's life has influenced her work, which often contains autobiographical elements. Her characteristic subjects--the lives of contemporary women, relations between women and men, motherhood, and distinctions of social class--reflect the extremes of her early life, spent almost exclusively among females, and her adult life, spent mostly in the company of males.

Born Franklin Birkinshaw, Weldon grew up in Britain and New Zealand, where her parents immigrated, when she was an infant, and then divorced, when she was six. When Weldon was fourteen, her mother took her and her sister back to London, where they lived in an all-female household with her grandmother. There, Weldon attended Hampstead High, a girls' school. In 1949, Weldon received a scholarship to attend Scotland's coeducational St. Andrews University, from which she received an M.A. in economics and psychology in 1952. By 1955 she had had a child (Nicholas) and was struggling to earn a living. Her assortment of jobs included writing propaganda for the British Foreign Office and later writing copy for advertising firms, a career in which she gradually advanced and prospered. She also visited a psychoanalyst, which suggested material for a number of her stories.

In 1960, she married Ronald Weldon, an antiques dealer, and became a suburban wife and mother in Primrose Hill, outside London. The Weldons had three sons, Daniel (1963), Thomas (1970), and Samuel (1977). The last pregnancy, when Weldon was forty-six, was difficult, and she thought she might die. The Weldons had moved to beautiful but distant Somerset in 1976, to an old country house where Weldon felt isolated--another familiar scene in some of her stories. Eventually the marriage broke up, and Weldon returned to London to preside as the literary lioness she had become. In 1995, Weldon married poet Nick Fox, and the couple later moved to Dorset in the south of England.

ANALYSIS

Fay Weldon could be called a contemporary Jane Austen, an entertaining, satiric chronicler of twentieth- and twenty-first-century manners centered on sex and materialism. As befits an admirer of Austen, Weldon focuses on the coupling of women and men, almost always from the women's point of view. In keeping with the contemporary world, this coupling is often shallow, insecure, and unhappy. Awful events occur in Weldon's short fiction: seductive women break up marriages, pregnant women are

Fay Weldon (Getty Images)

abandoned, babies are abused, and ghosts rattle through old houses. For the most part, however, Weldon maintains a comic tone, though again her black comedy is consistent with the times.

Weldon is able to deal with painful events and still maintain a comic tone through manipulation of narrative technique and voice. She experiments with discontinuous and fragmented narration, making sudden leaps in her characters' lives. To attain this out-of-breath pace, she sometimes sacrifices depth of characterization, especially of the male characters. What else is an author to do in an age of shallow people? The shallowness of her characters may be seen as another symptom of the times. Her narrative techniques also reflect her background in writing advertising copy--the transfer of sound bite technology to short fiction. Her stories would probably not be convincing enough to entertain if they were not also narrated in highly believable human voices, the colloquial, confused voices of single mothers, suburban housewives, daughters, and feminists.

Since the voices in Weldon's writing are almost always female, she has sometimes been claimed as a feminist writer. Her writing does not, however, express a consistent feminist ideology or agenda. There is no shortage of oppressive men in Weldon's writing, but neither is there a shortage of wicked women. In fact, some of the targets of Weldon's toughest satire are misguided women who have constructed their identity entirely around feminist ideology and who behave accordingly. Weldon's work does not so much express an ideology as, in the classic mode, hold a mirror up to nature.

"WATCHING ME, WATCHING YOU"

"Watching Me, Watching You," which gives its title to Weldon's first collection of short fiction, is ostensibly a ghost story, the first of several stories set in old houses where strange noises and happenings occur. The ghost here is rather lethargic, mostly reacting to strange happenings among the house's living inhabitants. Echoing stories by Nathaniel Hawthorne and Edgar Allan Poe, curtains rustle, wine glasses tip, walls sweat and cry, and mirrors crash to the floor only to comment on human behavior. The real story is of how Vanessa steals Anne's husband Maurice and marries him, only to have Audrey steal Maurice from her in the end, as if some crude sense of cosmic justice operates in the old house cursed by human failings. Meanwhile, two children are born to suffer, and Maurice does not make a good impression himself. The gothic conventions are used to justify the narration, which covers fifteen years because presumably the ghost can see the past, present, and future all at once. The story's comic tone is rather tentative, except in the characterization of the ghost and in a little satire at the end, in which Anne and Vanessa are communing with each other amid posters "calling on women to live, to be free, to protest, to re-claim the right, demand wages for housework, to do anything in the world but love."

MOON OVER MINNEAPOLIS

Perhaps Weldon's most popular collection of short fiction, *Moon over Minneapolis* represents the variety of her work. As in some of her other collections, the variety is indicated by groupings of stories under subheadings: "Stories of Working Life," "Four Tales from Abroad," "Tales of the New Age," "Stories for Christmas," "Three Tales of Country Life" (showing the Somerset influence), and "As Told to Miss Jacobs" (stories narrated to a silent psychoanalyst).

One of the tales from abroad is a favorite of literary anthologists, "Ind Aff or Out of Love in Sarajevo." The puzzling abbreviation in the title is one John Wesley, founder of Methodism, used for "inordinate affection," a sin "which bears the spirit away from God towards the flesh." In the story a twenty-five-year-old Cambridge graduate student feels "inordinate affection" for her professor and thesis director, to the extent of sharing a vacation with him in Sarajevo and paying for her share. The aptly named Professor Peter Piper, a forty-six-year-old married man and father of three, is a male chauvinist of the old school. While the peerless Peter imposes his opinions on his young charge, from tastes in food to theories of history, he pays little attention when she speaks. The setting finally brings her to her senses when they reflect on the local hero Gavrilo Princip, the young assassin credited with starting World War I by shooting the Archduke Francis Ferdinand, and when a handsome young waiter smiles at her:

> I smiled back, and instead of the pain in the heart I'd become accustomed to as an erotic sensation, now felt, quite violently, an associated yet different pang which got my lower stomach. The true, the real pain of Ind Aff!

"Ind Aff" can be interpreted as a prototypical feminist story, but other stories in *Moon over Minneapolis* poke fun at extreme feminist attitudes. In "Subject to Diary" a middle-aged career woman, who is close only to her diary, cancels her third abortion at the last minute on a sudden motherly impulse. In "I Do What I Can and I Am What I Am" a daughter disappoints her feminist mother by being sweet, by getting an A in her housecraft course and F's in chemistry and physics, by dressing in frilly women's clothes instead of pants, and by becoming an airline stewardess and winning the Miss Skyways Competition. Finally, in "Au Pair" a "big-busted, bovine" Danish girl gets a position with the Beaver family in England, cleans up the messy house, starts cooking good meals, takes care of the children, starts sleeping with the husband, and eventually replaces the neurotic Mrs. Beaver.

The title story, "Moon over Minneapolis," contrasts with the romantic song title "Moon over Miami." In the story, romance fails when an Englishwoman calls off her wedding to a Minneapolis man in order to return home and take care of her dependent extended family. This story, like others in the collection, makes use of some interesting techniques, such as symbolic settings, plays on names, and experiments with narration. In this particular case, the story is narrated by the English-woman to her psychoanalyst, Miss Jacobs; another story, "Au Pair," is narrated secondhand by the girl's mother back in Copenhagen (assisted by letters and phone calls) while the mother entertains sailors from around the world in bed.

"PAINS"

"Pains," subtitled "A Story of Most Contemporary Women, 1972," appears in the collection *Wicked Women*. Like some other stories in the collection, it uses engaging women's voices and narrative techniques, but the fireworks are brilliant. The story features not just one woman's voice but a whole ca-cophony, as the local Women's Liberation Group meets downstairs, while upstairs, in ironic juxtaposition, Paula undergoes labor and eventually delivers a son. At the very moment she gives birth, her husband is down-stairs trying to kiss a neighbor woman. These ironic situations are only the framework for the dazzling dis-play of voices, ranging from radical-sounding femi-nists who quote Vladimir Ilich Lenin to Audrey, the neighbor woman, who opines,

I *like* being a woman . . . I mean, what's wrong with it? I mean, it's all a bit ridiculous, isn't it, all this bra-burning and why do they make themselves so *plain*. Present company excepted, of course.

A HARD TIME TO BE A FATHER

A Hard Time to Be a Father, a collection of nineteen stories, continues with some of Weldon's familiar sub-jects and techniques. Even some of the titles are remi-niscent, but the stories are just as entertaining as earlier ones. Jealousy and revenge are still part of "Once in Love in Oslo," in which a former wife seeks retribu-tion against a present one, and in "Come on Everyone," in which the protagonist returns years later to savage her popular college roommate. The media's feeding

frenzies are satirized in "What the Papers Say" and prenatal testing in "A Libation of Blood." Other sto-ries, however, have less of a satirical edge, as if Weldon is willing to concede the possibility of happy turns of fate, if only by luck or chance. Such stories include "Spirits Fly South," "Noisy into the Night," the title story, and "GUP--Or, Falling in Love in Helsinki," in which a young woman meets her long-lost father, and GUP stands for Great Universal Paradox.

NOTHING TO WEAR AND NOWHERE TO HIDE

Like some of Weldon's previous collections of short fiction, the nineteen stories and one radio play in *Nothing to Wear and Nowhere to Hide* are divided into sections based on content and narrative devices. The stories in the section called "Things That Go Bump in the Night," for instance, all involve ghosts or an ele-ment of the supernatural, while those in "Making Do" show characters deciding to make the best of (or at least believe the best about) their unpleasant circum-stances. These section divisions, though, are somewhat arbitrary, since there is a good deal of overlap between their themes, and stories throughout the collection re-turn to conflicts and questions that the author has vis-ited before.

A common narrative move in this collection is to set up contrasts between opposites--men versus women, city versus country, career versus family--and to have the protagonist reach a crisis that invites or forces her to make an either-or choice between opposites. One question that arises for the characters in several stories is whether and/or when to have children. In the story "The Medium Is the Message," a young woman named Oriole is prompted by the presence of a teacup-throwing poltergeist in her house (likely the ghost of her grandmother) to return to her Jewish roots and to look for "a nice Jewish boy" with whom she can settle down and have a baby. Another story, "Freeze Eggs, Freeze Eggs," follows the musings of a middle-aged woman, who is afraid her daughter's high-flying career and urban lifestyle will prevent her from having chil-dren until it's too late. When the mother tells her daughter she should consider having some of her eggs frozen so that she can use them to conceive a child later in life, the daughter blithely tells her mother that that had been her plan all along, suggesting that family, in

---

Critical Survey of Short Fiction

the materialistic world, has become a thing of convenience, something to be scheduled around career advancement.

The question of materialism in modern culture arises again and again in these stories. Weldon was widely criticized in literary circles when she accepted money from the jewelry company Bulgari to feature its products in her 2001 novel *The Bulgari Connection*. Throughout *Nothing to Wear and Nowhere to Hide*, as elsewhere in Weldon's fiction, characters wear designer Italian suits and shoes, drink high-end champagne, and set up house in the glamorous and expensive parts of London, New York, or the English countryside. It's never entirely clear, though, whether Weldon is celebrating or critiquing the choices of these characters. Generally, as story titles such as "Percentage Trust" and "Trophy Wife" suggest, she makes clear at least that there is a tradeoff in human terms for such materialistic success. In the end, the human values of friendship and family are seen as important, though Weldon seems worried about the fate of these values in the modern world.

OTHER MAJOR WORKS

LONG FICTION: *The Fat Woman's Joke*, 1967 (pb. in U.S. as . . . *And the Wife Ran Away*, 1968); *Down Among the Women*, 1971; *Female Friends*, 1974; *Remember Me*, 1976; *Words of Advice*, 1977 (pb. in England as *Little Sisters*, 1978); *Praxis*, 1978; *Puffball*, 1980; *The President's Child*, 1982; *The Life and Loves of a She-Devil*, 1983; *The Shrapnel Academy*, 1986; *The Heart of the Country*, 1987; *The Hearts and Lives of Men*, 1987; *The Rules of Life*, 1987; *Leader of the Band*, 1988; *The Cloning of Joanna May*, 1989; *Darcy's Utopia*, 1990; *Growing Rich*, 1992; *Life Force*, 1992; *Affliction*, 1993 (pb. in U.S. as *Trouble*, 1993); *Splitting*, 1995; *Worst Fears*, 1996; *Big Women*, 1997 (pb. in U.S. as *Big Girls Don't Cry*, 1997); *Rhode Island Blues*, 2000; *The Bulgari Connection*, 2001; *Mantrapped*, 2004; *She May Not Leave*, 2005; *The Spa Decameron*, 2007 (pb. in U.S. as *The Spa*, 2007); *Chalcot Crescent*, 2009.

PLAYS: *Permanence*, pr. 1969, pb. 1970; *Time Hurries On*, pb. 1972; *Words of Advice*, pr., pb. 1974; *Friends*, pr. 1975; *Moving House*, pr. 1976; *Mr.*

Director, pr. 1978, pb. 1984; *Action Replay*, pr. 1979, pb. 1980 (also known as *Love Among the Women*); *After the Prize*, pr. 1981 (also known as *Woodworm*); *I Love My Love*, pr. 1981, pb. 1984; *Tess of the D'Urbervilles*, pr. 1992 (adaptation of Thomas Hardy's novel); *The Four Alice Bakers*, pr. 1999; *The Reading Group*, pb. 1999, pr. 2001.

TELEPLAYS: *The Fat Woman's Tale*, 1966; *Wife in a Blonde Wig*, 1966; *Dr. De Waldon's Therapy*, 1967; *Fall of the Goat*, 1967; *Goodnight Mrs. Dill*, 1967; *The Forty-fifth Unmarried Mother*, 1967; *What About Me*, 1967; *£13083*, 1968; *Hippy Hippy Who Cares*, 1968; *Ruined Houses*, 1968; *The Three Wives of Felix Hull*, 1968; *Venus Rising*, 1968; *Smokescreen*, 1969; *The Loophole*, 1969; *Office Party*, 1970; *Poor Mother*, 1970; *On Trial*, 1971 (in *Upstairs, Downstairs* series); *A Nice Rest*, 1972; *A Splinter of Ice*, 1972; *Hands*, 1972; *Old Man's Hat*, 1972; *The Lament of an Unmarried Father*, 1972; *Comfortable Words*, 1973; *Desirous of Change*, 1973; *In Memoriam*, 1974; *Aunt Tatty*, 1975 (adaptation of Elizabeth Bowen's story); *Poor Baby*, 1975; *The Terrible Tale of Timothy Bagshott*, 1975; *Act of Rape*, 1977; *Married Love*, 1977 (in *Six Women* series); *Honey Ann*, 1980; *Life for Christine*, 1980; *Pride and Prejudice*, 1980 (adaptation of Jane Austen's novel); *Watching Me, Watching You*, 1980 (in *Leap in the Dark* series); *Little Miss Perkins*, 1982; *Loving Women*, 1983; *Redundant! Or, The Wife's Revenge*, 1983.

RADIO PLAYS: *Spider*, 1972; *Housebreaker*, 1973; *Mr. Fox and Mr. First*, 1974; *The Doctor's Wife*, 1975; *Polaris*, 1978; *All the Bells of Paradise*, 1979; *Weekend*, 1979 (in *Just Before Midnight* series); *I Love My Love*, 1981.

NONFICTION: *Letters to Alice on First Reading Jane Austen*, 1984; *Rebecca West*, 1985; *Sacred Cows: A Portrait of Britain, Post-Rushdie, Pre-Utopia*, 1989; *Godless in Eden: A Book of Essays*, 1999; *Auto da Fay*, 2002; *What Makes Women Happy*, 2006.

CHILDREN'S LITERATURE: *Wolf the Mechanical Dog*, 1988; *Party Puddle*, 1989; *Nobody Likes Me*, 1997.

EDITED TEXT: *New Stories Four: An Arts Council Anthology*, 1979 (with Elaine Feinstein).

BIBLIOGRAPHY

Barreca, Regina, ed. *Fay Weldon's Wicked Fictions.* Hanover, N.H.: University Press of New England, 1994. A collection of eighteen critical essays, five by Weldon, dealing with leading themes and techniques in her fiction and various issues raised by it, such as her relation to feminism and her politics and moral stance. A few essays focus on specific novels, but others are relevant to both her short and long fiction. Includes "The Monologic Narrator in Fay Weldon's Short Fiction," by Lee A. Jacobus. Essays by Weldon include "The Changing Face of Fiction" and "On the Reading of Frivolous Fiction."

Dowling, Finuala. *Fay Weldon's Fiction.* Rutherford, N.J.: Fairleigh Dickinson University Press, 1998. An examination of the themes and techniques in Weldon's fiction, with emphasis on the novels but relevant to the short fiction.

Faulks, Lana. *Fay Weldon.* Boston: Twayne, 1998. An introduction to Weldon's life and work. Focusing on the novels, Faulks sees Weldon's work as "feminist comedy," contrasting with feminist writing that depicts women as oppressed. Examines Weldon's experiments with narrative techniques.

Grice, Elizabeth. "Fay Weldon: 'Dying? I Don't Want to Do That Again.'" *The Guardian,* March 12, 2009. A lively interview with Weldon, who talks about her near-death experience.

Salzmann-Brunner, Brigitte. *Amanuenses to the Present: Protagonists in the Fiction of Penelope Mortimer, Margaret Drabble, and Fay Weldon.* New York: Peter Lang, 1988. Examines the women in these authors' works, with opportunities for some comparisons and contrasts.

Saner, Emine "'I'm the Only Feminist There Is--The Others Are All Out of Step.'" *The Guardian,* August 22, 2009. The outspoken Weldon gives a frank interview about her life and her career on the occasion of the publication of her thirtieth novel.

Harold Branam
Updated by Janet E. Gardner

H. G. WELLS

Born: Bromley, Kent, England; September 21, 1866
Died: London, England; August 13, 1946

PRINCIPAL SHORT FICTION

The Stolen Bacillus, and Other Incidents, 1895
The Plattner Story, and Others, 1897
Thirty Strange Stories, 1897
Tales of Space and Time, 1899
The Vacant Country, 1899
Twelve Stories and a Dream, 1903
The Door in the Wall, and Other Stories, 1911
The Country of the Blind, and Other Stories, 1911
The Short Stories of H. G. Wells, 1927 (also known as *The Complete Stories of H. G. Wells*, 1966)
The Favorite Short Stories of H. G. Wells, 1937 (also known as *The Famous Short Stories of H. G. Wells*, 1937)
Selected Stories of H. G. Wells, 2004 (Ursula K. Le Guin, editor)

OTHER LITERARY FORMS

Beginning with *The Time Machine: An Invention* (1895) and ending with *The War in the Air, and Particularly How Mr. Bert Smallways Fared While It Lasted* (1908), H. G. Wells wrote nine fantastic, often futuristic novels, which he called scientific romances. Works like *The Invisible Man: A Grotesque Romance* (1897), *The War of the Worlds* (1898), and *The First Men in the Moon* (1901), which now fall under the rubric of science fiction, earned Wells the informal place that he shares with Jules Verne as a cofounder of that genre. Wells also wrote more than thirty realistic novels, of which the three most famous are *Kipps: The Story of a Simple Soul* (1905), *Tono-Bungay* (1908), and *The History of Mr. Polly* (1910). His fiction became increasingly speculative and utopian (or dystopian) after 1920. Wells, assisted by specialists, wrote three encyclopedic works devoted to the history of the universe, to biology, and to economics. The first, *The Outline of History: Being a Plain History of Life and Mankind* (1920), became a staple of home libraries throughout the world.

ACHIEVEMENTS

George Orwell declared that the twenty-five years between *The Time Machine* and *The Outline of History* should bear H. G. Wells's name. In fact, the reputation of Wells gave rise to a term, "Wellsian," whose mention conveys "the shape of things to come." Perhaps critic Walter Allen summed up best Wells's virtues and their defects:

I still think [Wells] had the largest natural talent of any English writer of the century. He did not always use it well, but he was a positive cornucopia of ideas. . . . Almost certainly he will look much greater in the future than he does now.

Wells anticipated the League of Nations with his World State and forecast the atom bomb thirty years before Hiroshima.

BIOGRAPHY

One of the most amply self-documented lives in the annals of English literature began on September 21, 1866, when to Sarah Neal Wells, a lady's maid, and to Joseph Wells, an unsuccessful tradesman though accomplished cricketer, was born the last of three sons, Herbert George "Bertie" Wells. The infant first "squinted and bubbled at the universe" in a shabby bedroom over a china shop in Bromley, in a residence called Atlas House. Bertie Wells's escape from the drab life of his two siblings was astonishing though brief. Her older sons safely apprenticed, Sarah Wells took thirteen-year-old Bertie with her to an estate called Uppark, where she hired on as a housekeeper in 1880. The change in outlook from shopkeeper's window to below stairs in a manor house was lifesaving. It lasted a year, during which the boy encountered great books for the first time--the satires of Voltaire, the saga of Gulliver, the liberating air of Platonic realism's *Politeia* (388-368 B.C.E.; *Republic*, 1701).

The young Wells's education was fragmentary, alternating with dismal apprenticeships one after another. He escaped anonymity through an unlikely door. He began to pass examinations and to show unusual ability in science. At eighteen he won a scholarship to the Normal School of Science in London to train to be a teacher. His zoology professor was Thomas Henry Huxley, a brilliant essayist, evolutionist, and public spokesperson for Charles Darwin and the theory of evolution. It was Huxley's example and lectures that provided Wells with vital links between the traditional religious beliefs in which he had been brought up and the scientific ideas he absorbed as a student. Huxley's fears about the pitfalls of natural selection if left unchecked by ethical and social progress took form in his student's imagination in such cosmic phenomena as colliding comets, invading Martians, and monstrous creatures seen by his time traveler.

The year 1895 was crucial for Wells on both domestic and literary fronts. He divorced his first wife, a cousin; happily married a teacher, Amy Catherine Robbins; and published *The Time Machine*, which brought him a fervent readership and contracts from England's leading editors for stories only he could write. He published more than sixty tales in magazines and in five collections, most of them written before he was thirty-five, and *The Short Stories of H. G. Wells* has remained steadily in print. These stories were products of the astonishing outburst of creative energy that turned Wells from an obscure science tutor into one of the most admired and discussed writers of his time, "the most influential writer in the English-speaking world," according to Anatole France.

The great crisis in Wells's life as a writer and a man came in his early forties when, with thirty volumes published and status as a public figure well in hand, he chose to become a force recognizable only in his own time. Wells began to write utopian blueprints disguised as novels, long tracts calling for elitist utopias, encyclopedias of knowledge which were really propaganda. He continued to publish

essays, even novels, almost into his final year. He died in 1946, one year after the dropping of the atomic bomb, an event he had predicted thirty years earlier.

ANALYSIS

By the 1890's, the golden age of the English short story had begun. Edgar Allan Poe and his theory that every story should strive for a single effect had become a pattern for imitation. Rudyard Kipling's stories of Indian life were opening a new and exotic dimension to readers worldwide. A flourishing discipleship of Guy de Maupassant, later to be led by W. Somerset Maugham, had come into existence on the English side of the channel. H. G. Wells's range is narrower than Kipling's, only rarely does Wells achieve macabre effects anywhere near Poe's, and he is incapable of the irony underlying the deceptively anecdotal stories of the French master Maupassant. However, from these three writers Wells learned the technique of the short story. "I was doing my best to write as the others wrote," Wells acknowledged, "and it was long before I realized that my exceptional origins and training gave me an almost unavoidable freshness of approach."

Often a story "starts as a joke," Wells observed in retrospect. "There is a shock of laughter in nearly every discovery." H. E. Bates, himself a master of short fiction, was one of the first to see the twinkle in the storyteller's eye. He praises Wells as

a great Kidder, a man who succeeded in telling more tall stories than any writer of his generation yet, by a genius for binding the commonplace to some astounding exploration of fancy, succeeded in getting them believed.

A close friend, the novelist and memoirist Frank Swinnerton, believes that of Wells's rich variety of writings "the short stories may well be the most characteristic."

The spellbinding tale-teller felt right at home in an end-of-century cultural anxiety--a late-Victorian sense of crisis which seemed to inhibit the large statement. The major self-contained fictions of the 1890's were mood-inducing novellas, such as Oscar Wilde's *The Picture of Dorian Gray* (1890, serial; 1891, book), Henry James's *The Turn of the Screw* (1898), and

Wells's *The Time Machine.* "Anything is possible" became the rule.

"THE MAN WHO COULD WORK MIRACLES"

A famous story, "The Man Who Could Work Miracles," is not only Wells at his playful best but also a paradigm for a vast literature about humble souls unexpectedly endowed with the power to upset their worlds. The clerk Fotheringay's supreme windfall lies in being able to conjure up miracles. Like so many who lack the proper combination of dash and restraint for the proper use of divine powers, Fotheringay lets his reach exceed his grasp. Requesting that the earth stop rotating, he precipitates a scene of comic confusion as every object about him falls off into space.

"THE LORD OF THE DYNAMOS"

From the first paragraph of this story, the reader is *shown*, never *told*, Wells's hatred of Empire. The reader is introduced to Holroyd, the uncivilized-civilized white man, the characteristically wooden product of technological society, and to Azuma-zi, the "burden" who will rise against oppression and destroy. Holroyd, the chief attendant of the dynamos that keep an electric

H. G. Wells (Library of Congress)

railway going, and his helper, who has come from the "mysterious East," are opposed at all points. Holroyd delivers a theological lecture on his big machine soon after Azuma-zi's arrival. "Where's your 'eathen idol to match 'im?" he shouts. Azuma-zi hears only a few words above the din: "Kill a hundred man. . . . That's something like a Gord!" Azuma-zi learns to worship the dynamo. Under Holroyd's sneering tutorship, the native obeys only too well. By tribal custom, he must ritualize the dynamo. One night Azuma-zi grasps the lever and sends the armature in reverse. There is a struggle; Holroyd is electrocuted. His death is taken to have been accidental, and a substitute arrives. For Azuma-zi, the newcomer is to be a second sacrifice. This time the Asian is foiled; to avoid capture, he kills himself by grabbing the naked terminals. The conclusion is phrased in mythic terms: "So ended prematurely the worship of the Dynamo Deity, perhaps the most short-lived of all religions. Yet withal it could at least boast a Martyrdom and a Human Sacrifice." The story echoes Joseph Conrad and Kipling, but it can be read simply as a good story or for wider implications beneath the parable.

"THE COUNTRY OF THE BLIND"

More effectively than anywhere except in certain of the scientific romances and in the last pages of *Tono-Bungay*, Wells's finest story, "The Country of the Blind," blends the riches of the storyteller and the mystic. To the mythmaker at the heart of Wells, no imagery proved so obsessive. From his student days under Huxley until his deathbed conviction that humankind had played itself out, Wells viewed humankind darkly: as struggling in an evolutionary whirl to fulfill its promise, but always forced back into some sealed-off country of the blind.

Essentially, the story is a pessimistic restatement of Plato's *Allegory of the Cave.* The mountaineer Nunez comes unawares on a remote place deep in the Andes, where for centuries the inhabitants have been sightless and where the idea of seeing has disappeared. At first, Nunez brazenly assumes the truth of the proverb "In the country of the blind, the one-eyed man is king," and he confidently expects to become master. However, he finds that the blind inhabitants have developed other faculties; that in a land where no one sees, the sighted are actually the disabled. Eventually Nunez is forced to submit, and his submission includes giving up his eyes, regarded by the blind as grievous and useless appendages. As Nunez rebels and endeavors to escape over the mountains, he is obliged to leave behind the woman, Medina, he has come to love.

Like the prisoners of Plato's cave, the blind have made the remote valley a symbol of self-imposed limits. They can no more conceive of a world outside their valley than the chained cave dwellers can imagine anything beyond the flickering shadows on the wall. The blind world, like the world Wells sought to reform, goes on, self-satisfied.

"THE DOOR IN THE WALL"

By the time Wells stopped writing stories, he had tired of any notion of "art for art's sake." A harassed Wells insisted to his onetime American admirer, Henry James, that he would rather be called a journalist than an artist. James broke with Wells, seeking to protect his precious territory, the novel, from the brash invasion of his younger and better-selling peer. Wells's expressed determination "to have all of life" embraced by fiction ran up against James's charges that writers like Wells "saturated" fiction.

One of Wells's least characteristic stories touches on a theme that James worked into several stories and his own favorite of his novels, *The Ambassadors* (1903), namely, the unlived life. In "The Door in the Wall," Lionel Wallace, a wealthy and famous cabinet minister, finds himself haunted by a childhood memory of a door that leads into a garden containing all the things that success has denied him--peace, delight, beauty. Three times Wallace rejects the door before yielding to its promise and stepping fatally into an excavation pit. Much of the story is told between quotation marks, but the unidentified narrator maintains a tone which suggests he has been mesmerized by Wallace's conviction into a reluctant acceptance:

And it was at school that I heard first of the 'Door in the Wall'--and that I was to hear of a second time only a month before his death. To him at least [it] was a real door, leading through a real wall to immortal realities . . .

Bernard Bergonzi, whose *The Early H. G. Wells*

(1961) is still unsurpassed in its linking of Wells's stories and scientific romances to the search for new enchantments at the turn of the century, presents a convincing case for the beautiful garden behind the closed door as a symbol of the imagination and for Wallace as a projection of Wells's split persona.

"THE BEAUTIFUL SUIT"

Three years after "The Door in the Wall," in 1909, Wells published in *Collier's* magazine another story in the same spirit. A boy is presented by his mother with a shining suit but is constrained from wearing it, except on special occasions, by the poor woman's innate caution--a reference perhaps to Wells's own mother and to her sense of Victorian propriety. The boy dreams of the fuller life he believes wearing the suit will bring him. One moonlit night he unwraps the precious gift, dons it, and in an ecstasy of fulfillment, plunges into what was by day a duck pond but which to his night sense "was a great bowl of silver moonshine . . . amidst which the stars were netted in tangled reflections of the brooding trees upon the bank." To the boy's starry eyes, his suit equips him for his journey, but next morning his body is found in the bottom of a stone pit,

with his beautiful clothes a little bloody, and foul and stained with the duckweed from the pond [but] his face . . . of such happiness . . . that you would have understood indeed . . . he had died happy.

OTHER MAJOR WORKS

LONG FICTION: *The Time Machine: An Invention*, 1895; *The Wonderful Visit*, 1895; *The Island of Dr. Moreau*, 1896; *The Wheels of Chance: A Holiday Adventure*, 1896; *The Invisible Man: A Grotesque Romance*, 1897; *The War of the Worlds*, 1898; *When the Sleeper Wakes: A Story of the Years to Come*, 1899; *Love and Mr. Lewisham*, 1900; *The First Men in the Moon*, 1901; *The Sea Lady*, 1902; *The Food of the Gods, and How It Came to Earth*, 1904; *Kipps: The Story of a Simple Soul*, 1905; *In the Days of the Comet*, 1906; *The War in the Air, and Particularly How Mr. Bert Smallways Fared While It Lasted*, 1908; *Tono-Bungay*, 1908; *Ann Veronica: A Modern Love Story*, 1909; *The History of Mr. Polly*, 1910; *The New Machiavelli*, 1910; *Marriage*, 1912; *The Passionate Friends*,

1913; *The Wife of Sir Isaac Harman*, 1914; *The World Set Free: A Story of Mankind*, 1914; *Bealby: A Holiday*, 1915; *The Research Magnificent*, 1915; *Mr. Britling Sees It Through*, 1916; *The Soul of a Bishop: A Novel---with Just a Little Love in It---About Conscience and Religion and the Real Troubles of Life*, 1917; *Joan and Peter: The Story of an Education*, 1918; *The Undying Fire: A Contemporary Novel*, 1919; *The Secret Places of the Heart*, 1922; *Men Like Gods*, 1923; *The Dream*, 1924; *Christina Alberta's Father*, 1925; *The World of William Clissold: A Novel at a New Age*, 1926 (3 volumes); *Meanwhile: The Picture of a Lady*, 1927; *Mr. Blettsworthy on Rampole Island*, 1928; *The King Who Was a King: The Book of a Film*, 1929; *The Autocracy of Mr. Parham: His Remarkable Adventure in This Changing World*, 1930; *The Buplington of Blup*, 1933; *The Shape of Things to Come: The Ultimate Resolution*, 1933; *The Croquet Player*, 1936; *Byrnhild*, 1937; *Star Begotten: A Biological Fantasia*, 1937; *The Camford Visitation*, 1937; *Apropos of Dolores*, 1938; *The Brothers*, 1938; *The Holy Terror*, 1939; *All Aboard for Ararat*, 1940; *Babes in the Darkling Wood*, 1940; *You Can't Be Too Careful: A Sample of Life, 1901-1951*, 1941.

NONFICTION: *Honours Physiography*, 1893 (with Sir Richard A. Gregory); *Text-Book of Biology*, 1893 (2 volumes); *Certain Personal Matters*, 1897; *A Text-Book of Zoology*, 1898 (with A. M. Davis); *Anticipations of the Reaction of Mechanical and Scientific Progress upon Human Life and Thought*, 1902 (also known as *Anticipations*); *The Discovery of the Future*, 1902; *Mankind in the Making*, 1903; *A Modern Utopia*, 1905; *Socialism and the Family*, 1906; *The Future in America: A Search After Realities*, 1906; *This Misery of Boots*, 1907; *First and Last Things: A Confession of Faith and Rule of Life*, 1908; *New Worlds for Old*, 1908; *The Great State: Essays in Construction*, 1912 (also known as *Socialism and the Great State*); *An Englishman Looks at the World: Being a Series of Unrestrained Remarks upon Contemporary Matters*, 1914 (also known as *Social Forces in England and America*); *The War That Will End War*, 1914; *God, the Invisible King*, 1917; *Russia in the Shadows*, 1920; *The Outline of History: Being a Plain History of Life and Mankind*, 1920; *The Salvaging of Civilization*, 1921; *A Short History of the World*, 1922; *Socialism and the Scientific Motive*, 1923; *The Open Conspiracy: Blue Prints for a World Revolution*, 1928; *Imperialism and the Open Conspiracy*, 1929; *The Science of Life: A Summary of Contemporary Knowledge About Life and Its Possibilities*, 1929-1930 (with Julian S. Huxley and G. P. Wells); *The Way to World Peace*, 1930; *The Work, Wealth, and Happiness of Mankind*, 1931 (2 volumes); *What Are We to Do with Our Lives?*, 1931 (revised edition of *The Open Conspiracy*); *After Democracy: Addresses and Papers on the Present World Situation*, 1932; *Evolution: Fact and Theory*, 1932 (with Huxley and G. P. Wells); *Experiment in Autobiography: Discoveries and Conclusions of a Very Ordinary Brain Since 1866*, 1934 (2 volumes); *The New America: The New World*, 1935; *The Anatomy of Frustration: A Modern Synthesis*, 1936; *World Brain*, 1938; *The Fate of Homo Sapiens: An Unemotional Statement of the Things That Are Happening to Him Now and of the Immediate Possibilities Confronting Him*, 1939; *The Common Sense of War and Peace: World Revolution or War Unending?*, 1940; *The New World Order: Whether It Is Obtainable, How It Can Be Attained, and What Sort of World a World at Peace Will Have to Be*, 1940; *Phoenix: A Summary of the Inescapable Conditions of World Reorganization*, 1942; *Science and the World Mind*, 1942; *The Conquest of Time*, 1942; *Crux Ansata: An Indictment of the Roman Catholic Church*, 1943; *'42 to '44: A Contemporary Memoir upon Human Behaviour During the Crisis of the World Revolution*, 1944; *Mind at the End of Its Tether*, 1945.

CHILDREN'S LITERATURE: *The Adventures of Tommy*, 1929.

BIBLIOGRAPHY

Batchelor, John. *H. G. Wells*. Cambridge, England: Cambridge University Press, 1985. Batchelor examines the wide range of Wells's writings, including some of the short stories, which are listed in the index.

Bates, H. E. *The Modern Short Story*. Boston: The Writer, 1941. Himself one of England's finest short-story writers, Bates accords high rank to Wells in the genre and rebuts charges that Wells's style lacks beauty. Calls Wells a "literary [Thomas] Edison."

Bergonzi, Bernard. *The Early H. G. Wells: A Study of the Scientific Romances*. Toronto: University of Toronto Press, 1961. Still the most knowledgeable account of the remarkable affinity of Wells's early fantasies, including his short stories, with the search for new worlds and behavior that characterized the end of the nineteenth and beginning of the twentieth century. Bergonzi, in a long third chapter, "The Short Stories," links "The Country of the Blind" and "The Door in the Wall" to Freudian-Jungian tendencies in Wells.

Coelsch-Foisner, Sabine. "H. G. Wells's Short Stories: 'The Country of the Blind' and 'The Door in the Wall.'" In *A Companion to the British and Irish Short Story*, edited by Cheryl Alexander Malcolm and David Malcolm. Malden, Mass.: Wiley-Blackwell, 2008. An explication of the two stories, which helps place them in the larger context of the British short story.

Costa, Richard Hauer. *H. G. Wells*. Boston: Twayne, 1985. A thorough study of Wells's work. Includes notes, references, and a bibliography.

_____. "Wells and the Cosmic Despair." *The Nation* (September, 12, 1966): First essay on "The Country of the Blind" to compare the original version (1904), written when Wells was in his thirties, with a revision he wrote in his seventies. Wells changes the ending to permit the hero Nunez and his blind lover Medina to escape together to the sighted--the civilized--world, only to find that Medina, her life saved by Nunez's vision, prefers the simplicity of the valley of the blind to the fearfully complicated Nunez world "that may be beautiful but terrible to *see*." Wells's cosmic pessimism may thus be symbolized.

Hammond, John. *A Preface to H. G. Wells*. New York: Longman, 2001. A concise analysis of Wells's position as a literary figure. Provides information on his life and influences, critical commentary on his science fiction and social novels, and an examination of his literary reputation.

Lynn, Andrea. *Shadow Lovers: The Last Affairs of H. G. Wells*. Westview, 2002. A lively, but rather narrowly focused, account of Wells's late-life relationships with three fascinating women.

Rainwater, Catherine. "Encounters with the 'White Sphinx': Poe's Influence on Some Early Works of H. G. Wells." *English Literature in Transition* 26, no. 1 (1983). Describes how Wells follows Edgar Allan Poe in blurring the distinction between his characters and their imaginings. Rainwater demonstrates Wells's debt to Poe with "The Red Room," a Wellsian ghost story which, like Poe's stories, depends upon a narrator's altered state of consciousness for its effects.

Rinkel, Gene K., and Margaret E. Rinkel. *The Picshuas of H. G. Wells: A Burlesque Diary*. Urbana: University of Illinois Press, 2006. "Picshuas" is the term Wells used for the sketches and cartoons he drew for his second wife, Jane. The sketches are rendered in this book, conveying the dynamics of their relationship and providing readers with insights into Wells's psyche and personal life.

Thompson, Terry. "'I Come from the Great World': Imperialism as Theme in Wells's 'The Country of the Blind.'" *English Language Notes* 42, no. 1 (September, 2004): 65-75. Argues that imperialism is the theme of Wells's story "The Country of the Blind." Analyzes the story's symbolism, examines the meaning of the protagonist's name--Nunez-- and discusses Nunez's imperialist longings. Around the same time that this article appeared, Thompson also published a shorter analysis of "The Country of the Blind" in *The Explicator* 63, no. 1 (Fall, 2004): 34-37. In this article, he discusses Nunez's rebellious character and interprets Nunez's acts of violence against the blind people.

Wagar, W. Warren. *H. G. Wells: Traversing Time*. Middletown, Conn.: Wesleyan University Press, 2004. Traces Wells's interest in the way public time unfolds by analyzing a wide range of his works, not merely the science fiction. References to the short stories are listed in the index.

Richard Hauer Costa

ANGUS WILSON

Born: Bexhill, East Sussex, England;
    August 11, 1913
Died: Bury St. Edmunds, Suffolk, England;
    May 31, 1991
Also known as: Sir Angus Wilson

PRINCIPAL SHORT FICTION

The Wrong Set, and Other Stories, 1949
Such Darling Dodos, and Other Stories, 1950
A Bit off the Map, and Other Stories, 1957
Death Dance: Twenty-five Stories, 1969
The Collected Stories of Angus Wilson, 1987

OTHER LITERARY FORMS

Although Angus Wilson enjoyed initial success with the publication of his first two short-story collections, he is better known as a novelist, particularly for *Anglo-Saxon Attitudes* (1956) and *The Old Men at the Zoo* (1961). Wilson is also an important literary critic, having published studies of Émile Zola, Charles Dickens, and Rudyard Kipling. He also wrote a play, a study of the influence of television on the arts, and a book on the relationship between his life and his fiction.

ACHIEVEMENTS

Angus Wilson was a guest lecturer, honorary fellow, and professor at a number of universities in England and America. In 1958, his third novel, *The Middle Age of Mrs. Eliot,* won the James Tait Black Memorial Prize and the French Prize for Best Foreign Novel. He was made a Fellow of the Royal Society of Literature in 1958 and was Chairman of England's National Book League between 1971 and 1974. He was made Companion of the Order of the British Empire in 1968 and Chevalier de l'Ordre des Arts et des Lettres in France in 1972. He was awarded a knighthood in 1980.

BIOGRAPHY

Angus Frank Johnstone Wilson was born on August 11, 1913, in the small resort town of Bexhill near Hastings on England's south coast. Although his father was descended from a wealthy Scottish family, the Wilsons lead a somewhat threadbare existence after World War I, moving from hotel to hotel. As a result, Wilson attended a number of different schools until he enrolled in a preparatory school run by an older brother. In 1927, he entered Westminster School as a day student, living with his parents in London in a small hotel. With the assistance of a legacy he received after his mother's death, he went to Merton College, Oxford University, in 1932 to study medieval history.

From 1936 through the early 1950's Wilson worked for the British Museum's Department of Printed Books. During World War II, he was assigned to the Foreign Office and came close to suffering a nervous breakdown. After the war, when he returned to the British Museum, he was put in charge of replacing the thousands of books destroyed in the bombings. In the late 1940's, Wilson began publishing short stories in a number of journals before putting them together in two collections published in 1949 and 1950. As a result of his increasing literary recognition, he quit the museum in 1955 to devote himself to writing, moving out of London to a cottage in a village in Suffolk. In his last years, he traveled widely and taught at several American universities, particularly in California.

ANALYSIS

Angus Wilson has most often been recognized as a satirist and an author of comedy-of-manners fiction; however, there has been some disagreement among critics as to whether he has the moral stance for satire or whether his work is more lightweight social comedy. Wilson himself said he preferred to think of himself as the author of comedy of manners.

Wilson once said he believed a short story is closer to a play or a poem than to a novel. Indeed, his stories are like one-act drawing-room comedies. Instead of probing complexities of individual psychology or establishing elaborate symbolic structures, Wilson is more interested in setting up dramatic situations in which relatively easy targets are exposed to his witty ridicule. However, even as Wilson deftly reveals the pretensions of his characters--be they upper-class snob, lower-class climber, or middle-class bureaucrat--he does not dehumanize them. Beneath the laughter, there is always a subtle groan of sympathy.

"TOTENTANZ"

"Totentanz," which means "dance of death," focuses on a Scottish couple, Brian Capper, who has been appointed to a chair of art history in London, and his wife, Isobel, who has received a legacy of half a million pounds from an uncle and aunt. In London, she cultivates four people: Professor Cadaver, Lady Maude, Guy Rice, and Tanya Mule. The will by which she has inherited her money includes a clause which insists that two seven-foot marble monuments be set in the room of her house, where she entertains friends. She and her husband devise a scheme by which they will give one party and then get rid of the monuments.

People come to the party dressed in costume: Mrs. Mule as a vampire, Lady Maude as Marie-Antoinette, Professor Cadaver as a corpse eater, and Guy Rice as the suicide of the poet Thomas Chatterton. Fulfilling these disguises, Guy kills himself because he is being blackmailed; Lady Maude dies like a queen, decapitated by a young man with an ax; Cadaver breaks his neck in a cemetery when he begins to clear away a freshly dug grave; and Mrs. Mule plays the vampire. The deaths mark the end of Isobel's social aspirations. The story is one of Wilson's most popular combinations of farce, pathos, and the grotesque. As critic Averil Gardner has suggested, it is a black comedy worthy of Evelyn Waugh.

"REALPOLITIK"

Wilson's most frequently anthologized story, "Realpolitik," is a classic example of his social satire. This comic set piece is structured like a one-act play, in which the central character, John Hobday, who has recently been made head of an art gallery, holds forth for an audience of the gallery staff. It becomes immediately apparent that Hobday is a big-mouthed bureaucrat who knows nothing about art but has vulgar and grandiose plans to boost traffic in the modest gallery. The story is primarily made up of Hobson's theatrical posturing and uncouth-salesman approach, as he sets forth plans for the gallery to compete with the cinema, football, and the fireside radio.

Throughout the story, Hobson is mildly interrupted by the staff, who plainly disapprove of his plans, but who obviously have little or no power to stop him. The final straw occurs when Hobson says he is going to bring in students from universities and experts from other museums to work at the gallery, all of which may necessitate some revisions in seniority. When one of the older staff members says that if so they will resign, Hobson, happily anticipating this, shows them out. The story ends with Hobson's secretary chiding him for lying to the staff and warning him that he is getting too fond of bullying. However, when she leaves the room, he thinks that for all her loyalty she knows him too well and that perhaps a graduate-student secretary would be more suitable for him.

Angus Wilson (Getty Images)

"WHAT DO HIPPOS EAT?"

The final story in Wilson's collection *Such Darling Dodos*, "What Do Hippos Eat?" focuses on Maurice Legge, a fifty-five-year-old former officer, who is past his prime and down on his luck, living in a boarding-house and having an affair with the landlady, Greta, who is below him in class and twenty years younger. Greta has joined forces with Legge in the hope that he will teach her some of his upper-class manners. The story centers on a trip to the zoo, which in various ways allows Wilson to expose Legge's pompous posturing and Greta's money-grubbing vulgarity.

Although Greta genuinely likes Legge and he is sentimentally fond of her, their selfish needs get in the way of any real caring; the tension between them is exacerbated by the fact that he has not paid the rent in the past two months. Greta takes great pride in Legge when he shows off by telling small children about his adventures with tigers in India, and he in turn basks in her admiration; however, the mood changes when, at the monkey cage, Legge is upstaged by a young man with more knowledge about the animals than he possesses.

When the resulting argument deteriorates to the issue of the unpaid rent, Legge loses face even more. The story ends with a final humiliation when Legge is embarrassed by a young zookeeper he tries to patronize and when Greta says in front of the young man that she is going to buy Legge a new suit, as if he were an old man in her care. In the final ironic scene, Legge puts his hands on Greta's waist and considers pushing her in the hippo pool; however, she thinks it is a gesture of affection and tries to reestablish his egoistic superiority by asking in a childlike way, "What *do* hippos eat, darling?"

The story quite deftly sets up a situation in order to satirize the efforts of the lower class to emulate their betters and rise in social esteem, while the upper class, without money to support their snobbishness, are reduced to empty posturing. As a result, the reader is not sure which is the more repellent or pathetic--Legge's boasting swagger or Greta's toadying mendacity. This story is typical of Wilson's satire, for his characters engage the reader's sympathy and judgment at once.

OTHER MAJOR WORKS

LONG FICTION: *Hemlock and After*, 1952; *Anglo-Saxon Attitudes*, 1956; *The Middle Age of Mrs. Eliot*, 1958; *The Old Men at the Zoo*, 1961; *Late Call*, 1964; *No Laughing Matter*, 1967; *As If by Magic*, 1973; *Setting the World on Fire*, 1980.

PLAY: *The Mulberry Bush*, pr., pb. 1956.

NONFICTION: *Émile Zola: An Introductory Study of His Novels*, 1952; *For Whom the Cloche Tolls: A Scrapbook of the Twenties*, 1953 (with Philippe Jullian); *The Wild Garden: Or, Speaking of Writing*, 1963; *Tempo: The Impact of Television on the Arts*, 1964; *The World of Charles Dickens*, 1970; *The Strange Ride of Rudyard Kipling: His Life and Works*, 1977; *Diversity and Depth in Fiction: Selected Critical Writings of Angus Wilson*, 1983 (Kerry McSweeney, editor); *Reflections in a Writer's Eye: Travel Pieces*, 1986.

BIBLIOGRAPHY

Binding, Paul. "No Laughing Matter." *The Times Literary Supplement*, April 27, 2007, 14-15. Examines Wilsons's works, focusing on his use of satire. Describes how he was influenced by Charles Dickens and other nineteenth-century novelists. Briefly discusses the *The Wrong Set*.

Brooke, Allen. "The Mimetic Brilliance of Angus Wilson." *New Criterion* 15 (October, 1996): 28-37. In this biographical essay, Brooke describes Wilson's childhood and youth, his early literary career, his homosexual relationship with Anthony Garrett, his disillusionment with communism, and his declining final years.

Drabble, Margaret. *Angus Wilson: A Biography*. New York: St. Martin's Press, 1995. A detailed biography of Wilson in which his friend Margaret Drabble shows the autobiographical sources of much of his fiction in his early years. Drabble describes Wilson's long-term homosexual relationship with Anthony Garrett, and she analyzes Wilson's obsession with the nature of evil in relationship to his mother's Christian faith.

Faulkner, Peter. *Angus Wilson: Mimic and Moralist*. London: Secker and Warburg, 1980. Discusses the satirist's negative judgment on the patterns of life around him in Wilson's early stories. Provides summary analyses of many of the stories in Wilson's first two collections, focusing on his developing satiric style.

Furbank, P. N. "'No Laughing Matter: A Word on Angus Wilson." In *On Modern British Fiction*, edited by Zachary Leader. New York: Oxford University Press, 2002. Furbank focuses on Wilson's use of humor and irony in his work, describing how he will "send up" his characters before he creates sympathy for them. Furbank analyzes some of the stories in *The Wrong Set*, as well as some of the novels.

Gardner, Averil. *Angus Wilson*. Boston: Twayne, 1985. In this general introduction to Wilson's life and art, Gardner devotes one chapter to *The Wrong Set* and *Such Darling Dodos*. Gardner argues that the central reality of Wilson's stories is the world of people; neither nature nor the divine nor the eternal is very important in them. Maintains that the unity of Wilson's stories lies in their milieu of personal uncertainty, social precariousness, and emotional ambivalence, which allows people to be both funny and pathetic at the same time.

Gransden, K. W. *Angus Wilson*. Essex, England: Longmans, Green, 1969. A pamphlet-length introduction to Wilson's work. Argues that the success of his early stories depends on their satirical analyses of people's vulnerability, failure, and self-deception. Suggests that many of his stories begin realistically and then are pushed to a farcical climax that involves violence or hysteria.

Halio, Jay L. *Angus Wilson*. London: Oliver and Boyd, 1964. Discusses the character types and situations in *The Wrong Set* and *Such Darling Dodos*, such as the Raffish Old Sport, the Intense Young Woman, and the Widow Who Copes. Argues that Wilson is primarily interested in the success or failure of people to understand who they are and what they are doing. Provides a detailed analysis of "Heart of Elm."

_____, ed. *Critical Essays on Angus Wilson*. Boston: G. K. Hall, 1985. A collection of reviews, interviews, and criticism covering Wilson's literary career. Includes influential reviews by Edmund Wilson, V. S. Pritchett, Kingsley Amis, and Anthony Burgess, as well as important essays by Malcolm Bradbury, A. S. Byatt, and Margaret Drabble. Halio's overview essay is a concise survey of Wilson's work and a critique of the criticism of it.

Vanatta, Dennis, ed. *The English Short Story: 1945-1980*. Boston: Twayne, 1985. In his essay on the English short story between 1945 and 1950, John Stinson describes how Wilson's characters cannot come to terms with themselves or the reality of their social situations. Stinson argues that in miniature portraits, Wilson captures psychological and social nuance through skillful irony. Dean Baldwin, in his essay on the 1950's English short story, explains that Wilson is often classed with nineteenth-century novelists, such as Charles Dickens. Baldwin discusses Wilson's themes of social cruelty and his eye for detail.

Charles E. May

TIM WINTON

Born: Karrinyup, Western Australia, Australia; August 4, 1960

PRINCIPAL SHORT FICTION

Scission, 1985
Minimum of Two, 1987
Blood and Water, 1993 (this collects the stories from *Scission* and *Minimum of Two*)
The Turning, 2004

OTHER LITERARY FORMS

In addition to his short stories, Tim Winton has written nine adult novels, including the celebrated *Cloudstreet* (1991), *The Riders* (1994), *Dirt Music* (2001), and *Breath* (2008), and a number of books for children, including *Lockie Leonard, Legend* (1997). His nonfiction work includes *Down to Earth* (1999), with photographs by Richard Woldendorp, and *Land's Edge* (1993), which both underline his love of and concern for the marine environment.

ACHIEVEMENTS

Tim Winton's oeuvre has garnered national and international recognition, beginning with the Australian Vogel Award for an unpublished manuscript for his first novel, *An Open Swimmer.* Two novels, *The Riders* and *Dirt Music,* were shortlisted for London's Booker Prize, and *Shallows* (1984), *Cloudstreet, Dirt Music,* and *Breath* (2008) won the Miles Franklin Award for the best Australian novel of the year. He also won the Commonwealth Writers' Prize for *The Riders.* His books have been translated into numerous languages.

Winton's collections of short stories and novels are studied regularly in Australian high schools. His series of Lockie Leonard novels for children were dramatized as a television series and plays, while *Cloudstreet* and *That Eye, the Sky* (1986) have been successfully adapted for the stage. Two novels, *That Eye, the Sky* and *In the Winter Dark* (1988), were adapted for the screen. Winton has been named a Living Treasure by the National Trust of Australia. He was awarded the Australian Centenary Medal for service to literature and community and is patron of the Tim Winton Award for Young Writers of short stories.

BIOGRAPHY

Timothy John Winton was born in Karrinyup, a suburb of Perth in Western Australia, in 1960. Winton's father, a motorcycle policeman, was seriously injured in a road accident when his son was five. After his father recovered from his injuries, the family, influenced by a man from a local church who helped care for the invalid, became fundamentalist Christians.

When Winton was about twelve, his family moved from the beachside city suburb of Scarborough to regional Albany, a former whaling port about 250 miles south of Perth. His father was the policeman in this country area, and the young Winton, an insomniac, eavesdropped as his father told his mother about the various road accidents, shootings, and domestic violence that punctuated a policeman's daily life. There is no doubt that these stories influenced Winton's writing, as did his sense of the relative roughness of Albany in contrast to the city and his love of fishing and surfing. The fictional town of Angelus in his stories incorporates Albany and the fishing town of Lancelin.

Winton completed a creative-writing course at the Western Australian Institute of Technology (now Curtin University) in Perth, during which time he wrote three books, including *An Open Swimmer,* first published in 1982. At that time Winton became a full-time writer. He claimed that, with a wife and young family, he needs to be a disciplined writer and often writes two or three books in tandem.

He is an active environmentalist and conservationist, and he donated the $28,000 Miles Franklin Literary Award for *Dirt Music* to the campaign to save a reef north of Perth from developers. As a patron of the Marine Conservation Society, Winton has spoken out against the overfishing of endangered shark species. Although he has lived in Australia for most of his life, he also has spent time in France, Ireland, Italy, and Greece. Winton settled in Geraldton, Western Australia.

ANALYSIS

Tim Winton is one of Australia's most prolific and popular writers. His work is admired for its minimalist yet often lyrical style, for its use of the Australian vernacular, for its representations of place with striking images of ocean, beach, and bush and the frequently fractured characters who people these sites. Common themes are those of loss, relationships in limbo, the unconscious yearning for the sacred, the nature of gender roles, and the (often unresolved) tension between characters' memories and their present situations. The misunderstandings, frustrations, possibilities, and complexities of family life are central concerns for Winton. Most stories are tied directly to a sense of place and displacement, particularly those in *Minimum of Two* and *The Turning*. In these two collections, although each story is complete, characters from one story often appear in others. This layering enables the reader to gain multiple perspectives on character motivations, themes, settings, and the relevance of events.

SCISSION

There are thirteen stories in the collection, which opens with "Secrets," a poignant third-person narrative that elides into the thoughts of Kylie, who is six. Through the child's voice, Winton evokes the sense of anguished loneliness and puzzlement Kylie feels because her mother has left Kylie's father and moved in with Philip. She does not discuss the breakup with Kylie, who spends time looking at a photo album while hidden in an old well she has been forbidden by Philip to enter. She explores photos of herself and her mother taken by her father. She does not have a photograph of her father.

She likes the photo of herself where she looks confidently at the camera as if she, like her mother, has a secret. Kylie finds a real secret when she discovers a scrawny hen and her eggs hidden in the back garden, and she guards this knowledge carefully, watching over the eggs until Philip discovers her in the well and smacks her. Kylie throws the eggs and then the hen into the disused well and later cuts out her face from the photo she likes and pushes it through the window screen. The promise of new life suggested by the fertile eggs is erased violently, as is the child's sense of self through the thoughtless betrayal of the adults in her life.

MY FATHER'S AXE

Often in this collection defining moments in childhood or adolescence haunt the adults. In "My Father's Axe," for example, Winton draws on the father and son relationships evoked in many of the stories, such as "A Blow, a Kiss," in which the compassionate child, Albie, knows his father's affection for him is God-like, and "Lantern Stalk," in which the adolescent, Egg, is kept from his father's church by his mother yet stumbles

Tim Winton (Getty Images)

upon the blessing of a baby in a farmhouse that provides him with a version of Christian masculinity far removed from the soldiering exercise he participates in at his mother's insistence.

In "My Father's Axe," memories and dream sequences suggest the unexpressed depth of feeling the protagonist has for his father. The unnamed protagonist is a married man with a son, but the disappearance of an axe that belonged to his father causes anxiety and guilt to emerge. He remembers his father as a strong, heroic woodcutter, and although he could not achieve the gracefulness of his father's swing, he was proud to keep the wood supply up when his father left for long periods in order to work. He recalls his father weeping before one departure. The boy immediately ran to cut more wood than they needed, denying his father's supposedly feminine expression of grief. Similarly, the boy at fourteen evades his father's gentle affection for him. Winton touches here on the social expectations of gender roles and tension between father and son expectations, as the protagonist notes that he and his father often looked at each other with disappointment.

It is revealed that the protagonist has placed his ailing parents in a home for the aged and he now lives with his wife and son in his father's house. He has a nightmare in which the head of the axe flies loose and decapitates his father, and his guilt about moving his parents out surfaces as he thinks someone has stolen the axe in order to murder him. After his father dies, a man and a boy come to the house to return the stolen axe, and the protagonist recognizes the positive resonances of this symbol of his father's life in all its contradictions. Other stories such as "Neighbours" and "The Oppressed" reflect the multicultural nature of the coastal town; others, such as "Wake" and "Scission," focus on marriage breakups and the consequences, the latter story ending in a graphic shooting.

MINIMUM OF TWO

More than half of the fourteen stories in this collection feature the characters of Jerra Nilsam, his wife Rachel, their son Sam, and Jerra's parents and friends. In these stories, Winton is interested in young marriage and parenthood, as the dedication to his wife Denise and their son Jesse suggests. The seven Nilsam stories are "Forest Winter," "Gravity," "Nilsam's Friend," "Bay of Angels,"

"The Strong One," "More," and, implicitly, "Death Belongs to the Dead, His Father Told Him, and Sadness to the Sad," in which an elderly man who may be Jerra's father dies, and "Blood and Water," about Sam's difficult birth.

Jerra, a musician, takes on various odd jobs to support his family as they cope with a low income, the birth of Sam, Rachel's asthma and depression, Jerra's father's cancer and death, infidelity, guilt, frustrations, and Rachel's return to study to be a social worker. Jerra's stories in the volume are not chronologically ordered. For instance, when "Winter Forest" begins, Sam is nine weeks old. In "Gravity," he is three years old, and the final story of the collection is about his birth. Much of the pleasure of reading this collection lies in the reader's involvement in reordering the stories and reading the gaps in narrative. The understanding of characters is enhanced by the different perspectives offered. The reader sees Jerra, for example, as a son, a musician, a fisherman, a friend, a worker, a husband, and a father.

In a story unrelated to the Nilsam family except for the setting, Queenie Cookson in "Laps" makes a return journey to Angelus after seven years in the city. Swimming laps at City Beach has made her think of home. Queenie and her husband Cleve were anti-whaling protesters in their hometown of Angelus, where whaling provided employment for many in the town. Their allegiance to the town was questioned, and it is clear they were forced, under threat of violence, to leave, having failed to end the whaling. Queenie is ready to return to the places she remembers as a girl. The whaling has ended, replaced by whale watching, and she wants to visit her grandfather's grave on the farm he used to own and swim in the ocean, which is her element.

The Cooksons visit the old whalers' huts and the flensing deck and later the farm. The farm caretaker, who recognizes Queenie, will not allow her on the property. Nevertheless, Queenie makes some peace with the past on the beach, as she swims freely and watches the hill on which her grandfather is buried.

THE TURNING

As one would expect, this collection shows the maturity of Winton's craft in the confidence of its structure, setting, imagery, and emotional depth. Again, although each story is self-contained, Vic Lang, the son of a country cop who moves to Angelus when he is twelve and leaves for university after completing high school, is relevant to nine of the seventeen stories in the collection.

The setting of Angelus unites all the stories in the collection in some way, with Winton evoking a real sense of the town and its history, its landscape, and its inhabitants. Angelus has beautiful beaches and rugged woods, but like any small town it can be limiting. Many stories are dark. Vic's father, Bob, for instance, becomes an alcoholic crushed by his job, the death of his baby daughter, and corrupt policemen involved in drug dealing. He leaves town and returns twenty-seven years later, when his wife Carol is dying. Bob's story is told in "Commission" and "Fog." He dies a week after Carol, and the death of both his parents devastates Vic and almost ruins his marriage to Gail.

Boredom, bullying, drinking, drugs, domestic violence, car accidents, and a shark attack pepper the Angelus stories, though there is gentle humor, too, in, for example, "Reunion," in which Vic, Gail, and Carol are invited to a party by Bob's brother and go to the wrong house. Characters strive to reconcile the buried past and communicate with each other. *The Turning* ends with a positive sense that Vic and Carol's marriage is stable, now that Vic is able to forgive and put the past behind him in "Defender."

One of the best stories in this collection is "Boner McPharlin's Moll." Boner was expelled from school and is known as the bad boy in town. Schoolgirl Jackie Martin is attracted to and repelled by him. She earns an unwarranted reputation when she goes driving with Boner, who wants to be her friend rather than her lover. He teaches her to fish and to drive. Woven into their story is the link Boner has to the corrupt cops because he, unknown to Jackie, runs drugs for them. Boner eventually has his legs smashed on a deserted beach.

Jackie goes to a city university, takes a trip overseas, and accepts a position at a Perth university. She returns to Angelus when she hears Boner has been committed to a psychiatric hospital. The police have set him up, and they make sure that Jackie is repelled by him. A royal commission into police corruption is occurring, and the police are worried that Boner will testify

against them. Later Boner dies in the hospital, supposedly from a massive heart attack. After she attends Boner's funeral, the middle-aged Jackie is furious with herself for not seeking more details from Boner and for not believing in him. Boner was a scapegoat at school and as an adult, while Jackie, rather than being Boner's "moll," is gay. This is a compassionately told story that probes beneath the surface of accepted reputations.

OTHER MAJOR WORKS

LONG FICTION: *An Open Swimmer*, 1982; *Shallows*, 1984; *That Eye, the Sky*, 1986; *In the Winter Dark*, 1988; *Cloudstreet*, 1991; *The Riders*, 1994; *Dirt Music*, 2001; *Breath*, 2008.

NONFICTION: *Land's Edge*, 1993; *Local Colour: Travels in the Other Australia*, 1994 (with Bill Bachman); *Down to Earth*, 1999.

CHILDREN'S LITERATURE: *Jesse*, 1988; *Lockie Leonard, Human Torpedo*, 1990; *The Bugalugs Bum Thief*, 1991; *Lockie Leonard, Scumbuster*, 1993; *Lockie Leonard, Legend*, 1997; *Blueback*, 1997; *The Deep*, 1998.

BIBLIOGRAPHY

Ben-Messahel, Salhia. *Mind the Country: Tim Winton's Fiction*. Crawley: University of Western Australia Press, 2006. A useful survey of the reception of Winton's writing, which also provides the geographic context for it.

Edemariam, Aida. "Waiting for the New Wave." *The Guardian*, June 28, 2008. This is a well-researched, comprehensive interview that touches on the poetry of Winton's language, the influence of the bush and the sea, and the discipline of writing.

McPhee, Hilary, ed. *Tim Winton: A Celebration*. Canberra, A.C.T.: National Library of Australia, 1999. The book features four essays: three from writers who know Winton and his work and one from McPhee, who was Winton's editor for the first ten years in which he published. The book provides biographical and literary insights into Winton's short stories.

Rossiter, Richard, and Lyn Jacobs, eds. *Reading Tim Winton*. Sydney: Angus and Robertson, 1993. Provides an accessible study guide for high school students.

Christine Ferrari

VIRGINIA WOOLF

Born: London, England; January 25, 1882
Died: The River Ouse, near Rodmell, Sussex, England; March 28, 1941
Also known as: Adeline Virginia Stephen

PRINCIPAL SHORT FICTION

Two Stories, 1917 (one by Leonard Woolf)
Kew Gardens, 1919
The Mark on the Wall, 1919
Monday or Tuesday, 1921
A Haunted House, and Other Short Stories, 1943
Mrs. Dalloway's Party, 1973 (Stella McNichol, editor)
The Complete Shorter Fiction of Virginia Woolf, 1985

OTHER LITERARY FORMS

Besides writing short stories, Virginia Woolf was an acute and detailed diarist (her diary entries occupy five volumes in the authoritative collected edition); a prolific letter writer (six volumes in the authoritative collected edition); a biographer; a perceptive, original, and argumentative essayist and reviewer (her collected essays fill six volumes in the authoritative edition); and a pioneer of the modern novel in her ten works of long prose fiction, which include the acknowledged classics *Mrs. Dalloway* (1925), *To the Lighthouse* (1927), and *The Waves* (1931).

ACHIEVEMENTS

A distinguished and distinctive prose stylist, Virginia Woolf excelled in fiction, nonfiction, and her own unique hybrid of these genres in her two whimsical books *Orlando: A Biography* (1928) and *Flush: A Biography* (1933), which are variously categorized as fiction, nonfiction, or "other" by critics of her work. In nonfiction, essays such as "The Death of the Moth,"

"How Should One Read a Book?" and "Shakespeare's Sister" have been widely anthologized, and their vividness, imagery, and keen analysis of daily life, literature, society, and women's concerns assure Woolf a place in the history of the essay.

In fiction, Woolf's classic novels, sharing much in style and theme with the nonfiction, have overshadowed the short stories. Reacting against the realistic and naturalistic fiction of her time, Woolf often emphasized lyricism, stream of consciousness, and the irresolute slice of life in both her novels and her stories, though she wrote more conventional fiction as well. Whether the conventional "well-made" or the experimental stream-of-consciousness variety, many of her approximately fifty short stories are accomplished works of art. Because of their precise and musical prose style, irony, ingenious spiral form (with narrative refrains), reversal or revelatory structure, and exploration of human nature and social life, they deserve to be better known and to be studied for themselves and not just for what they may reveal about the novels.

BIOGRAPHY

Virginia Woolf was born Adeline Virginia Stephen and grew up in the household of her father, Leslie Stephen, a Victorian and Edwardian literary lion who was visited by many prominent writers of the time. The importance of books in her life is reflected in many of the short stories, such as "Memoirs of a Novelist," "The Evening Party," and "A Haunted House"; her father's extensive personal library provided much of her education, along with some private tutoring, especially in Greek. Despite Katherine Stephen, niece of Leslie Stephen, being the principal of Newnham College at the University of Cambridge (reflected in the story "A Woman's College from Outside"), Virginia was denied a formal college education because of persistent ill health, emotional and physical, as well as her father's male bias in this matter, all of which is echoed with mild irony in "Phyllis and Rosamond" (about two sisters who resemble Virginia and Vanessa Stephen, lacking a college education) and "A Society" (in which the character Poll, lacking a college education, receives her father's inheritance on condition that she read all the books in the London Library).

The early death of Woolf's mother, Julia, in 1895; the repeated sexual molestation by her half brother George Duckworth; her father's transformation of Virginia's sisters Stella and Vanessa into surrogate mothers after Julia's death; and her own attachments to women, such as Violet Dickinson and, later, Vita Sackville-West, culminated in Virginia's cool and ambivalent sexuality, reflected by the general absence of sexual passion in many of the short stories, as well as by what Woolf herself described as the "Sapphism" of "Moments of Being: 'Slater's Pins Have No Points.'" The more regular element of her adolescence and generally happy life with Leonard Woolf, whom she married in 1912, was the social round of upper-middle-class life, including horticultural outings in London (reflected in "Kew Gardens"); parties, private concerts, and theatergoing (as in "The Evening Party," "The String Quartet," the *Mrs. Dalloway's Party* cycle of stories, "Uncle Vanya," and "The Searchlight"); and excursions to the country (as in "In the Orchard"), seashore (as in "Solid Objects" and "The Watering Place"), or foreign resorts (as in "A Dialogue upon Mount Pentelicus" and "The Symbol").

Clustering around Virginia and her sister Vanessa, when they moved to a house in the Bloomsbury district after Leslie Stephen's death in 1904, was a group of talented writers, artists, and intellectuals who came to be known as the Bloomsbury Group and were generally among the avant-garde in arts and letters. (This period is portrayed in "Phyllis and Rosamond.") Many intellectuals from the group continued to associate with Virginia and Leonard Woolf after their marriage, and some, such as T. S. Eliot, had books published by the Hogarth Press, which was set up by the Woolfs in 1917. Indeed, all Virginia Woolf's short stories in book form have been published in England by this press.

In 1919, the Woolfs, for weekend and recreational use, took a country cottage called Monks House, whose reputation for being haunted evoked "A Haunted House" and whose vicinity, Rodmell (as well as Leonard Woolf, by name), is jocularly referred to in "The Window and the Parrot: A True Story." Because of numerous family deaths, as well as the later strain and letdown of completing her novels and the anxiety from World Wars I and II (referred to in many of the stories, and responsible in 1940 for the destruction of the Woolfs' London house), Woolf had been and continued to be subject to mental breakdowns. The motifs of liquid's destructiveness and death by drowning in several of the stories ("Solid Objects," "A Woman's College from Outside," "The Widow and the Parrot," "The New Dress," "The Introduction," "A Simple Melody," and "The Fascination of the Pool") were actualized when, in early 1941, Woolf, at the onset of another breakdown, drowned herself in the Ouse River, near Rodmell and Monks House.

ANALYSIS

Perhaps related to her mental condition is Virginia Woolf's interest in perception and perspective, as well as their relationship to imagination, in many stories. In two short avant-garde pieces-- "Monday or Tuesday" (six paragraphs) and "Blue and Green" (two paragraphs, one for each color)--Woolf attempts to convey the reality of the urban and natural worlds through discrete, apparently disconnected associative impressions.

"MONDAY OR TUESDAY" AND "BLUE AND GREEN"

In "Monday or Tuesday," a series of contrasts between up and down, spatially free timelessness (a lazily flying heron) and restrictive timeliness (a clock striking), day and night, inside and outside, and present experience and later recollection of it conveys the ordinary cycle of life suggested by the title and helps capture its experiential reality, the concern expressed by the refrain question that closes the second, fourth, and fifth paragraphs: "and truth?"

Similar contrasts inform the two paragraphs describing the blue and green aspects of reality and the feelings associated with them in "Blue and Green." These two colors are dominant and symbolic throughout Woolf's short stories. Differing perspectives, which are almost cinematic or painterly, also structure "In the Orchard," as each of the story's three sections, dealing with a woman named Miranda sleeping in an orchard, focuses on, in order, the sleeping Miranda in relation to her physical surroundings, the effect of the physical surroundings on Miranda's dreaming (and thus the interconnection between imagination and external world), and finally a return to the physical environment, with a shift in focus to the orchard's apple trees and birds. The simultaneity and differing angle of the three perspectives are suggested by the narrative refrain that closes each section, a sentence referring to Miranda jumping upright and exclaiming that she will be late for tea.

The ability of the imagination, a key repeated word in Woolf's short stories, to perceive accurately the surrounding world is an issue in many of the stories. In "The Mark on the Wall," a narrator is led into associative musings from speculating about the mark, only to discover, with deflating irony, that the source of the imaginative ramblings is in reality a lowly snail (with the additional concluding ironic reversal being an unexpected reference to World War I, whose seriousness undercuts the narrator's previous whimsical free

Virginia Woolf (D.C. Public Library)

associations). Even more difficult is the imagination's perception of people (who and what individuals really are) in the surrounding world. This is the chief problem of the biographer, a task at which Woolf herself was successful, though not the self-centered and somewhat dishonest novelist's biographer who narrates "Memoirs of a Novelist." In the four stories "An Unwritten Novel," "Moments of Being: 'Slater's Pins Have No Points,'" "The Lady in the Looking Glass: A Reflection," and "The Shooting Party," a major character or the narrator is led through small details into imaginative flights about the life and personality of an individual--only, in the story's concluding reversal, to be proved incorrect or be left very doubtful about the picture or account created. Likewise showing a connection between the literary artist's problem of depicting the truth and the imagination's problem in probing reality is the story "The Three Pictures," in which the first picture, of a sailor's homecoming to a welcoming wife, leads the narrator to imagine other happy events, undercut by the second and third pictures revealing the sailor's death from a fever contracted overseas and the despair of his wife.

The problem of "and truth?" (as phrased in "Monday or Tuesday") can be comically superficial, as in the narrator's wasted sympathetic imaginings in "Sympathy" in response to a newspaper account of Humphrey Hammond's death, only to discover in the story's conclusion that the article referred to the elderly father rather than the son (with ironic undercutting of the genuineness of the narrator's sympathy because of her chagrin about the "deception" and "waste"). In contrast, in "The Fascination of the Pool," the deeply evocative imagery and symbolism of never-ending layers of stories absorbed by a pool over time, and always going inexhaustibly deeper, have a meditative and melancholic solemnity.

"KEW GARDENS"

Related to imagination and art (which may or may not bridge the gap between human beings), as well as to social criticism and feminist issues (whether roles and identities unite or divide, fulfill or thwart people), is the motif of isolation and alienation in many of the stories. In "Kew Gardens," the first paragraph's twice-repeated detail of the heart-and-tongue shape of the colorful plants symbolizes the potential of love and communication to effect communion, while the colors projected by the flowers from sunlight on various things (mentioned in the first and last paragraphs) symbolize the various couples' imaginations projected on the environs. In the social context of the park, however, the four sets of strollers are isolated from one another, as is the other major "character" described, the snail; each is solipsistically involved in its own affairs. Only in the fourth set, a romantic young couple, do love and communication seem to promise, though not guarantee, the hope of communion.

"SOLID OBJECTS"

In "Solid Objects," the first paragraph's emphasis on a changing perspective (a black dot on the horizon becomes four-legged and then two men) symbolizes how the protagonist John's perspective changes from imaginative engagements with people, politics, and ideas, to engagements with small things or concrete objects, beginning with his discovery at the beach of a smooth, irregular fragment of glass. While Charles, John's friend, at the beach casts flat slate stones into the water, aware of objects only as a means of allowing physical action and release, John becomes attached to them with the child's and artist's fascination, which lures him away from the practical and pragmatic adult world of action and politics, in which he had a bright future. John thus becomes alienated from all those around him, including Charles. Symbolically during their last encounter, both end up conversing at cross purposes, neither person understanding the other.

"A HAUNTED HOUSE" AND "LAPPIN AND LAPINOVA"

"A Haunted House" and "Lappin and Lapinova" show, respectively, success and failure in human communion. The former story uses the convention of the ghost story and gothic fiction, almost satirically or ironically, to suggest the broader theme of the mystery of the human heart. Implicitly two kinds of mystery are contrasted: the mystery of ghosts, haunted houses, secret treasures, and so on, and the real, important mystery of what is most worthwhile in the universe--the ghostly couple's lesson at the story's close that the house's hidden treasure is love, "the light in the heart." The implicitly living couple presumably have love, paralleling the ghostly couple's bond. The cyclical

repetitions in the story help convey, stylistically, the pulsation or beating of the human heart, the seat of this love. In contrast, the married couple in "Lappin and Lapinova" become alienated because the husband cannot genuinely share in the wife's imaginative fantasy of the two of them as rabbit and hare, reverting to his pragmatic and stolid family heritage and an arrogant masculine impatience.

MRS. DALLOWAY'S PARTY CYCLE

Most of the nine stories constituting the *Mrs. Dalloway's Party* cycle ("Mrs. Dalloway in Bond Street," "The New Dress," "Happiness," "Ancestors," "The Introduction," "Together and Apart," "The Man Who Loved His Kind," "A Simple Melody," and "A Summing Up") naturally deal, by their focus on a social occasion, with communion or alienation, as suggested by the title "Together and Apart." In "Mrs. Dalloway in Bond Street," the title character remains isolated or insulated from the surrounding world, symbolized by the gloves that she is going to buy (perhaps for the party), by her general disregard of traffic and other phenomena while she muses about the death of a recent acquaintance, and by her disregard of a literal explosion that ends the story (though paradoxically she communes with an acquaintance by remembering and uttering the name while ignoring the explosion). At the party itself, Mabel Waring, the protagonist of "The New Dress," is alienated because her new dress, owing to her limited means, seems a failure and source of embarrassment; Stuart Elton, protagonist of "Happiness," remains withdrawn in himself to preserve an egocentric equilibrium that is his happiness; Mrs. Vallance, protagonist of "Ancestors," is alienated by the superficial and undignified talk and values of the young around her, in contrast to her past. Woolf's feminist concerns about the unjust subordination and oppression of women (prominent in "Phyllis and Rosamond," "The Mysterious Case of Miss V.," "The Journal of Mistress Joan Martyn," "A Society," "A Woman's College from Outside," and "The Legacy") are suggested by the isolation and alienation of Lily Everit, who feels inadequate when introduced to Bob Brinsley, symbol of thoughtless male power and conceit. Despite Everit's esteemed essay writing (paralleling Woolf's), Brinsley negligently assumes that she must as a woman write poetry,

as his initial question shows. Everit feels crushed, sti-
fled, and silenced by the weight of masculine accom-
plishment in the arts and sciences.

Two impromptu pairings in the Dalloway party
cycle--Roderick Serle and Ruth Anning of "Together
and Apart," and Prickett Ellis and Miss O'Keefe of
"The Man Who Loved His Kind"--achieve temporary
communion: Serle and Anning, when they imaginatively attune to each other, sharing profound emotions about experiences in Canterbury; and Ellis and
O'Keefe, when the latter concurs with the former's
concern about the poor excluded from affairs, such as
Mrs. Dalloway's party. These couples, however, are
driven apart at story's end by the evening's experi-
ence--Serle and Anning, when the former is mock-
ingly accosted by a female acquaintance, and Ellis
and O'Keefe, when the former fails, with some self-
centered posturing, to appreciate the latter's understanding of the need for beauty and imagination in the
life lived at all social levels. Only the protagonists of
the last two stories of the cycle, George Carslake in
"A Simple Melody" and Sasha Latham in "A Summing Up," achieve a transcendence over isolation
and alienation. Carslake melds all the partygoers and
himself through a blend of imagination, art, and nature by meditating on a beautiful painting of a heath
in the Dalloways' house and imagining the various
partygoers on a walk there that reduces them all to
fundamentally decent human beings coalesced in a
common enterprise. Like Carslake, Latham achieves
wisdom by fixing on inanimate objects, the Dalloways' beautiful Queen Anne house (art) and a tree in
the garden (nature), and meditating on them; like
Carslake, Latham sees people admirably united in
motion--in her reverie, adventures and survivors
sailing on the sea.

OTHER MAJOR WORKS

LONG FICTION: *Melymbrosia*, wr. 1912, pb. 1982, revised pb. 2002 (early version of *The Voyage Out*;
Louise DeSalvo, editor); *The Voyage Out*, 1915; *Night
and Day*, 1919; *Jacob's Room*, 1922; *Mrs. Dalloway*,
1925; *To the Lighthouse*, 1927; *Orlando: A Biography*,
1928; *The Waves*, 1931; *Flush: A Biography*, 1933;
The Years, 1937; *Between the Acts*, 1941.

NONFICTION: *The Common Reader: First Series*,
1925; *A Room of One's Own*, 1929; *The Common
Reader: Second Series*, 1932; *Three Guineas*, 1938;
Roger Fry: A Biography, 1940; *The Death of the
Moth, and Other Essays*, 1942; *The Moment, and
Other Essays*, 1947; *The Captain's Death Bed, and
Other Essays*, 1950; *A Writer's Diary*, 1953; *Letters:
Virginia Woolf and Lytton Strachey*, 1956; *Granite
and Rainbow*, 1958; *Contemporary Writers*, 1965;
Collected Essays, Volumes 1-2, 1966; *Collected Es-
says, Volumes 3-4*, 1967; *The Flight of the Mind: The
Letters of Virginia Woolf, Vol. I, 1888-1912*, 1975
(pb. in U.S. as *The Letters of Virginia Woolf, Vol. I:
1888-1912*, 1975; Nigel Nicolson, editor); *The
London Scene: Five Essays*, 1975; *Moments of Being*,
1976 (Jeanne Schulkind, editor); *The Question of
Things Happening: The Letters of Virginia Woolf,
Vol. II, 1912-1922*, 1976 (pb. in U.S. as *The Letters of
Virginia Woolf, Vol. II: 1912-1922*, 1976; Nigel
Nicolson, editor); *A Change of Perspective: The Let-
ters of Virginia Woolf, Vol. III, 1923-1928*, 1977 (pb.
in U.S. as *The Letters of Virginia Woolf, Vol. III:
1923-1928*, 1978; Nigel Nicolson, editor); *Books and
Portraits*, 1977; *The Diary of Virginia Woolf*, 1977-
1984 (5 volumes; Anne Olivier Bell, editor); *A Re-
flection of the Other Person: The Letters of Virginia
Woolf, Vol. IV, 1929-1931*, 1978 (pb. in U.S. as *The
Letters of Virginia Woolf, Vol. IV: 1929-1931*, 1979;
Nigel Nicolson, editor); *The Sickle Side of the Moon:
The Letters of Virginia Woolf, Vol. V, 1932-1935*,
1979 (pb. in U.S. as *The Letters of Virginia Woolf,
Vol. V: 1932-1935*, 1979; Nigel Nicolson, editor);
*Leave the Letters Til We're Dead: The Letters of Vir-
ginia Woolf, Vol. VI, 1936-1941*, 1980 (Nigel
Nicolson, editor); *The Essays of Virginia Woolf*,
1987-1994 (4 volumes); *Carlyle's House, and Other
Sketches*, 2003 (David Bradshaw, editor).

BIBLIOGRAPHY

Banks, Joanne Trautmann. "Virginia Woolf and
    Katherine Mansfield." In *The English Short
    Story, 1880-1945: A Critical History*, edited by
    Joseph M. Flora. Boston, Mass.: Twayne, 1985.
    Briefly explores the common philosophical
    themes   of   several   stories   (imagination,

perception) and the affinities of the two writers, deriving from feminist concerns and mutual admiration of Anton Chekhov's short fiction.

Barrett, Eileen, and Patricia Cramer, eds. *Virginia Woolf: Lesbian Readings*. New York: New York University Press, 1997. This collection of conference papers features two essays on Woolf's short stories: one on Katherine Mansfield's presence in Woolf's story "Moments of Being," and another that compares lesbian modernism in Woolf's stories with lesbian modernism in the stories of Gertrude Stein.

Bleishman, Avrom. "Forms of the Woolfian Short Story." In *Virginia Woolf: Revaluation and Continuity*, edited by Ralph Freedman. Berkeley: University of California Press, 1980. Bleishman discusses abstract theoretical issues concerning genre and then divides several stories into the two categories of linear form (for example, "The New Dress" and "Kew Gardens") or circular form (for example, "The Duchess" and "Lappin and Lapinova").

Briggs, Julia. *Reading Virginia Woolf*. Edinburgh: Edinburgh University Press, 2006. Briggs, a Woolf scholar and biographer, reconsiders some of Woolf's works from her earliest fiction to her late short fiction. The chapter entitled "'Sudden Intensities': Frame and Focus in Woolf's Later Short Stories," analyzes her story "The Symbol" and other works. Some of the other chapters focus on the influence of William Shakespeare upon Woolf, the use of biography in Woolf's early fiction, and Woolf's ideas of "Englishness."

_____. *Virginia Woolf: An Inner Life*. Orlando, FL: Harcourt, Inc., 2005. A thorough biography of Woolf, shedding light on her creative process, as well as her own perceptions of her work.

Daiches, David. *Virginia Woolf*. Norfolk, Conn.: New Directions, 1942. Offers brief comments on "A Haunted House," "The Mark on the Wall," "Monday or Tuesday," "A Society," "The String Quartet," and "An Unwritten Novel."

Dick, Susan, ed. Introduction to *The Complete Shorter Fiction of Virginia Woolf*. 2d ed. San Diego: Harcourt Brace Jovanovich, 1989. Classifies the short fiction into traditional stories and fictional reveries, finding affinities in the works of nineteenth-century

writers such as Thomas De Quincey and Anton Chekhov. Provides invaluable notes on historical, literary, and cultural allusions, as well as textual problems, for every story.

Guiget, Jean. "Stories and Sketches." In *Virginia Woolf and Her Works*. Translated by Jean Stewart. London: Hogarth Press, 1965. Divides the stories into several groups by style (such as the impressionistic ones) or theme (such as the observer studying another person), with perceptive comments on specific symbols.

Head, Dominic. "Experiments in Genre." In *The Modernist Short Story: A Study in Theory and Practice*. Cambridge, England: Cambridge University Press, 1992. Head discusses Woolf's search for a narrative texture that would adequately portray her notion of life as amorphous.

Hunter, Adrian. "Virginia Woolf." In *The Cambridge Introduction to the Short Story in English*. Cambridge, England: Cambridge University Press, 2007. An incisive overview of Woolf's short fiction. Describes how Woolf used the theory and practice of the short story to build an audience response for the type of modernist fiction she wished to produce.

King, James. *Virginia Woolf*. New York: W. W. Norton, 1995. A literary biography that relates Woolf's life to her work. Shows how the chief sources of her writing were her life, her family, and her friends.

Lee, Hermione. *Virginia Woolf*. New York: Alfred A. Knopf, 1997. A detailed biography of Woolf, her complex family relationships, her lifelong battle with mental illness, and her relationship to the Bloomsbury Group.

Meyerowitz, Selma. "What Is to Console Us? The Politics of Deception in Woolf's Short Stories." In *New Feminist Essays on Virginia Woolf*, edited by Jane Marcus. Lincoln: University of Nebraska Press, 1981. Instead of emphasizing formal aspects or general philosophical themes, Meyerowitz focuses on the political and social content of several stories, discussing feminist issues of subordination and powerlessness, alienation, negative male traits, class conflict, and oppressive social institutions.

Reid, Panthea. *Art and Affection: A Life of Virginia Woolf.* New York: Oxford University Press, 1996. A biography based on new materials and facts about Woolf's life and thought. Focuses on the relationship of her letters and other writings to her relatives and circle of friends.

Reynier, Christine. *Virginia Woolf's Ethics of the Short Story.* New York: Palgrave Macmillan, 2009. An in-depth examination and appraisal of Woolf's short stories. Explains Woolf's untraditional definition and theories of short fiction. Describes how Woolf's stories create conversations between the characters and between Woolf and her readers. Discusses how the stories offer a form of resistence to social and cultural norms.

Skrbic, Nena. *Wild Outbursts of Freedom: Reading Virginia Woolf's Short Fiction.* Westport, Conn.: Praeger, 2004. An examination of Woolf's short fiction, providing close readings of many of the stories and placing these works in their literary, historical, and critical contexts. Includes discussions of the collection *Monday or Tuesday*, the *Mrs. Dalloway's Party* cycle, and ghostly motifs in Woolf's short fiction.

Norman Prinsky

Y

WILLIAM BUTLER YEATS

Born: Sandymount, near Dublin, Ireland; June 13, 1865
Died: Roquebrune-Cap-Martin, France; January 28, 1939
Also known as: W. B. Yeats

PRINCIPAL SHORT FICTION

John Sherman and Dhoya, 1891, 1969
The Celtic Twilight, 1893
The Secret Rose, 1897
The Tables of Law; The Adoration of the Magi, 1897
Stories of Red Hanrahan, 1904
Mythologies, 1959

OTHER LITERARY FORMS

William Butler Yeats (yayts), a prolific writer, composed hundreds of lyrical, narrative, and dramatic poems. It was not unusual to find characters from his short stories appearing in his poems; *Michael Robartes and the Dancer*, a collection of poems published in 1920, is one example. In addition to writing poetry, he contributed to the Irish dramatic movement, which culminated in the establishment of the Abbey Theatre in Dublin. His *Cathleen ni Houlihan* (pr., pb. 1902) and *Deirdre* (pr. 1906, pb. 1907) are typical plays of that early period. Yeats was a prolific and accomplished essayist and also produced various works of autobiography which are collected in one volume entitled *Autobiographies* (1926, 1955), as well as an ambitious philosophical treatise entitled *A Vision* (1925, 1937), which details his cosmology.

ACHIEVEMENTS

William Butler Yeats's reputation as one of the major poets of the twentieth century is unassailable, and his influence, particularly on the course of American verse, as practiced most notably by Robert Lowell, is equally well attested. His adaptation of native Irish materials for poetic ends, his mythic projection in verse of his life and times, and his conception of art as an antidote to history have exerted a powerful imaginative influence on poets succeeding him. In a more narrowly Irish context, his ideological pronouncements and cultural commitments--the latter culminating in the establishment of the Abbey Theatre--have constituted an overwhelmingly important instance of the relationship of the artist to society.

Yeats received honorary degrees from Queen's University (Belfast) and Trinity College (Dublin) in 1922. Receipt of the Nobel Prize in Literature followed in 1923, as well as honorary degrees from the University of Oxford in 1931 and the University of Cambridge in 1933.

BIOGRAPHY

Born in Dublin to the painter John Butler Yeats and Susan Pollexfen of Sligo, William Butler Yeats was of Irish Protestant background. His childhood was spent in London, Dublin, and Sligo. He was educated at the Godolphin School, Hammersmith, Dublin High School, and the Metropolitan School of Art, where he fell under the spell of George Russell and other Dublin mystics. John O'Leary, the Fenian leader, and Maud Gonne, the passionate actress and patriot, were two Irish friends, while Arthur Symons and Lionel Johnson of the Rhymers' Club were London friends. When Maud Gonne and later her daughter Iseult rejected his marriage proposals, Yeats married Georgie Hyde-Lees, an Englishwoman, in 1917. They had one son and one daughter. After the Irish Civil War, he served as a senator for the Irish Free State from 1923 to 1928. Yeats traveled extensively, including lecture tours to the United States. In 1899, Yeats with Lady Augusta Gregory, Edward Martyn, and George Moore established an Irish theater, which led to the Abbey Theatre.

With George Bernard Shaw and George Russell (Æ), Yeats founded the Irish Academy of Letters in 1932. His complex life experiences were literary source material for his works. Acutely aware of the religious and philosophical conflict facing the world, he believed that a viable literature was an alternative resolution until religion and philosophy offered another solution.

ANALYSIS

With the exception of "John Sherman," William Butler Yeats's short stories mirror his attraction to the spirit world and reflect his fascination with good and evil. Since they were written during the fin de siècle period when literary and graphic artists, epitomized by the French Symbolists, were expressing a world-weariness and pessimism that celebrated the triumph of evil, it is understandable that Yeats's tales articulate that prevailing mood. These early fictional works also identify the themes which were to occupy Yeats's poetic genius for the remainder of his life.

An integral part of the Irish literary movement, these tales have a dual purpose: to revitalize ancient Irish myths for modern Ireland and to serve as a model for artists attempting to write in Irish about Irish subjects. In the stories, Yeats celebrates the exploits of fairies and pagan Irish heroes which he discovered in the oral and written literary traditions; his tales thus become source material for other storytellers. Yeats's *The Celtic Twilight*, a collection of folklore gathered from local storytellers, became important source material for his later work. In recording the fantastic behavior of the various spirits and their relationships to the country people, Yeats stored information which he used later to dramatize his belief in communication between the material and the immaterial worlds. "Dhoya" is an excellent example of a revitalized myth, and "The Twisting of the Rope" illustrates Yeats's role as a mentor for others.

"DHOYA"

In "Dhoya," Yeats writes about a local Sligo legend. He had recently edited *Fairy and Folk Tales of the Irish Peasantry* (1888), and his imagination was stimulated by the living nature of these expressions of the conflict between the natural and preternatural worlds. "Dhoya" honors an ancient Celt who lived before the time of the

William Butler Yeats (Library of Congress)

Pharaohs, Buddha, and Thor. In predating the time of known heroes, Dhoya, the Celt, exists before recorded history. It follows then that Yeats's native Sligo has indeed an ancient history, for Dhoya is deserted at the Bay of Ballah, the fictional name of Sligo Bay. The Formorians, an ancient Irish tribe, abandon Dhoya, a giant of tremendous strength, because he cannot control the violent rages which come over him. While enraged, he kills those around him and destroys whatever he can touch. He is believed to be possessed by demons, and a plan is concocted to exile him to the Bay of Ballah.

Dhoya, living alone in the forests and along the beaches, experiences more frequent attacks, but they are directed against his shadow or the halcyon, the beautiful and peaceful legendary bird. Years pass, and a quality of timelessness adds to the mystical nature of the tale, for Dhoya is hundreds of years old. One day he kills a great bull, and the herd chases him until he eludes it by running into the deepest part of the bay, a spot called Pool Dhoya. To this day, and in Yeats's day, the deepest part of Sligo Bay is known as

Pool Dhoya, a fact which Yeats incorporates into the story to create a living legend.

Yeats also introduces legendary characters. Dhoya ranges over the mountains where Diarmuid and Grania, pagan lovers from the written Irish literature of pre-Christian Ireland, traveled. In time, Dhoya also experiences a love like Diarmuid. It comes to Dhoya as a gentle breeze upon his forehead, nothing more, but he longs for that touch, which remains only a touch for an untold number of years. Eventually, he develops a depression which he plans to shake off by building a huge bonfire at the rising of the moon. The unhappy lover prays to the moon and makes all kinds of sacrifices--strawberries, an owl, a badger, deer, swine, birds, and whatever else he can find to appease the moon. Soon thereafter, a voice calls "Dhoya, my beloved." Trembling, Dhoya looks into the forest and sees a white form which becomes a flowering plant as he touches it. Dazed, the giant returns to his cave where he finds a beautiful woman cleaning and rearranging the spears and skins.

She throws her arms about his neck, telling him that she yearns for his love. Having left her happy people from under the lake where age, sorrow, and pain are unknown, she desires love in the changing world, a mortal love which her people cannot experience. Dhoya loves her with a mad passion which is not matched by the beautiful fairy, unnamed by Yeats. Then a man from under the sea appears to reclaim the lady. Holding a spear tipped with metal, he challenges Dhoya, whose rage returns as he fights to keep his love. He wins that battle only to lose to the fairy, who reappears and challenges him to a game of chess. Before she leaves Dhoya, the fairy sings a strange love song which was part of "The Wandering of Oisin" (1889):

My love hath many evil mood
Ill words for all things soft and fair
I hold him dearer than the good
My fingers feel his amber hair.

This stanza is central to "Dhoya" and to the great poems which follow. The happy spirit is unhappy and seeks human love which is neither perfect nor perpetual--a paradox which haunts Yeats.

"JOHN SHERMAN"

"John Sherman," a realistic story which Yeats called a short romance and wanted to be judged as an Irish novel, is a variation of the Dhoya theme. Although the story lacks the cultural unity of the Irish novels of William Carleton, John Banim, and Gerald Griffin, it does demonstrate the great influence upon Yeats of William Blake, whose poetical works Yeats had recently edited.

The story takes place in Ballah and London, two contrary locations representing the virtuous countryside and the villainous city. There is also a set of contrary characters who, even if they were merged, would not represent the ideal character. John Sherman of Ballah and William Howard of London have different views on almost everything, yet they become engaged to the same woman. Mary Carton of Ballah and Margaret Leland of London are different, but both remain confused about their love for John Sherman. Sherman's mother and Margaret's mother really represent the country mother and the city mother; neither has a life beyond motherhood. Such artificial characterizations doom the plot of "John Sherman," which--although intended as a love story--with a little revision could have become a comedy or farce. Certainly, it is the lightest piece of work that Yeats produced; however, unlike other Irish writers, Yeats lacked a comic sense.

"PROUD COSTELLO, MACDERMOT'S DAUGHTER, AND THE BITTER TONGUE"

"Proud Costello, MacDermot's Daughter, and the Bitter Tongue," from *The Secret Rose*, is a love story which exhibits the intensity of Dhoya's love for the fairy, but the lovers are mortals of the sixteenth century. Costello loves Una, daughter of MacDermot, who is promised by her father to MacNamara. Una loves Costello and sends a message to him by Duallach, the wandering piper. Costello must appear at her nuptial feast, at which she will drink to the man she loves. At the betrothal drink, to the amazement of all, she drinks to Costello; he is then attacked by the members of the wedding party and barely escapes with his life. Una dies without seeing Costello again, but at her funeral procession he sees the coffin and is considered her murderer. Loving her still, Costello swims to the island where Una is buried, mourning over her grave for three days and nights. Confused, he tries to swim back to the mainland but drowns in the attempt. His body is brought to the island and buried beside his beloved; two ash trees are planted over their grave site. They grow tall and the branches, like lover's arms, entwine themselves, symbolic of the undying love between Costello and Una. This motif, common in folklore, appealed to Yeats's sensibility because of the implied relationship between the natural world and the affairs of mortals.

"THE TWISTING OF THE ROPE"

From another perspective, Yeats writes again about that relationship in "The Twisting of the Rope." This story is one of the six connected stories grouped as the *Stories of Red Hanrahan* which tell of the plight of Hanrahan, a hedge schoolmaster enchanted by a spirit on Samhain Eve, the night (the equivalent of Halloween) on which the Celts believed spirits roamed the earth searching for mortals. Since his enchantment, Hanrahan has become a traveling poet of the Gael who sings of the past heroic age when the ancient Irish kings and queens ruled Ireland. The people, although they welcome Hanrahan into their cottages, fear him because he is of the other world and is able to charm others, especially young and impressionable women.

One night Hanrahan is observed casting his spell over Oona, an attentive listener to his tales, but her mother and a neighbor woman, watching Oona drift into the spirit world, plan to thwart Hanrahan's influence. They cannot order the poet out of the house because he might cast a spell over their animals and fields, destroying cattle and corn, so they devise a scheme whereby Hanrahan is asked to twist a rope from the bundles of hay which the women bring to him. Feeding him more and more rope and praising him for the fine job of rope-making, they eventually get Hanrahan to the door and out of the cottage. Realizing that he had been tricked, he composes a song, "The Twisting of the Rope."

Douglas Hyde, who wrote the first Irish play for the new Irish dramatic movement (*Casad-an-Sugan*, 1901), selected this short tale by Yeats for production. Yeats's success in revitalizing Irish myth and encouraging the continuation of the written Irish literary tradition assures him a prominent place in Irish letters.

Another aspect of Yeats's personality was his fascination with the occult, an attraction which led him to explore Christian, Jewish, and Asian mysticism in his writings. As John O'Leary made Yeats conscious of the past political Irish culture, George Russell, to whom *The Secret Rose* was dedicated, indoctrinated Yeats into the Dublin Theosophist Circle, which was occupied with the study of Rosicrucianism. It was a subject about which Yeats could never learn enough, and in "Rosa Alchemica" he approaches the topic through the story of the life of Michael Robartes. Yeats says in an explanatory note to the collection of poems known as *Michael Robartes and the Dancer* that Robartes had returned to Dublin from Mesopotamia where he "partly found and partly thought out much philosophy."

This knowledge, which Robartes wants to share with his old friend, is revolutionary. It consists of an understanding that modern alchemy is not concerned with simply converting base metal to gold. On the contrary, the new science seeks to transform all things to the divine form; in other words, experiential life is transmuted to art. The process involves rituals through which novices are initiated gradually into the sect. Robartes brings his friend into a temple, but in order to proceed, he must first learn a series of intricate dance steps; then he is dressed in a costume of Greek and Egyptian origin for the mad dance. At this point the friend, fearing for his sanity, flees from the phantasmagoria.

"THE TABLES OF THE LAW" AND
"THE ADORATION OF THE MAGI"

"The Tables of the Law" and "The Adoration of the Magi" are two other short stories that deal with religious mysteries. In "The Tables of the Law," Owen Aherne, like Michael Robartes, returns to Dublin after studying mysticism and alchemy. He hates life and cherishes a medieval book with its secrets of the spirit. Jonathan Swift, Aherne thinks, created a soul for Dublin gentlemen by hating his neighbor as himself. A decade later, the narrator sees Aherne again at a Dublin bookstore; his face is a lifeless mask, drained of the energy to sin and repent as God planned for mortal man. God's law tablets make humankind commit sin, which is abhorrent to Aherne.

Michael Robartes, appearing again in "The Adoration of the Magi," promises the return of the Celtic heroes. Three men in the tale, perhaps demons, watch the death of the Wise Woman. Civilization has not progressed; Christianity has not fulfilled its mission. The hope of nations lies in the reestablishment of the aristocratic order of the Celtic civilization. To a greater degree, Yeats develops this theme in later verse, essays, and plays with a blurring of the character of Cuchulain, the pagan Irish hero, with Christ and Saint Patrick.

Yeats's reputation as a poet and a dramatist overshadows his renown as a storyteller. His tales have intrinsic worth nevertheless and can be read as a prelude to his later great works.

OTHER MAJOR WORKS

PLAYS: *The Countess Cathleen*, pb. 1892, pr. 1899; *The Land of Heart's Desire*, pr., pb. 1894; *Cathleen ni Houlihan*, pr., pb. 1902; *The Pot of Broth*, pr. 1902, pb. 1903 (with Lady Augusta Gregory); *The King's Threshold*, pr., pb. 1903 (with Lady Gregory); *The Hour-Glass*, pr. 1903, revised pr. 1912, pb. 1913; *On Baile's Strand*, pr. 1904, pb. 1905; *Deirdre*, pr. 1906, pb. 1907 (with Lady Gregory); *The Shadowy Waters*, pr. 1906, pb. 1907; *The Unicorn from the Stars*, pr. 1907, pb. 1908 (with Lady Gregory); *The Golden Helmet*, pr., pb. 1908; *The Green Helmet*, pr., pb. 1910; *At the Hawk's Well*, pr. 1916, pb. 1917; *The Player Queen*, pr. 1919, pb. 1922; *The Only Jealousy of Emer*, pb. 1919, pr. 1922; *The Dreaming of the Bones*, pb. 1919, pr. 1931; *Calvary*, pb. 1921; *Four Plays for Dancers*, pb. 1921 (includes *Calvary*, *At the Hawk's Well*, *The Dreaming of the Bones*, and *The Only Jealousy of Emer*); *The Cat and the Moon*, pb. 1924, pr. 1931; *The Resurrection*, pb. 1927, pr. 1934; *The Words upon the Window-Pane*, pr. 1930, pb. 1934; *The King of the Great Clock Tower*, pr., pb. 1934; *The Collected Plays of W. B. Yeats*, pb. 1934, 1952; *A Full Moon in March*, pr. 1934, pb. 1935; *The Herne's Egg*, pb. 1938; *Purgatory*, pr. 1938, pb. 1939; *The Death of Cuchulain*, pb. 1939, pr. 1949; *Variorum Edition of the Plays of W. B. Yeats*, pb. 1966 (Russell K. Alspach, editor).

POETRY: *Mosada: A Dramatic Poem*, 1886; *Crossways*, 1889; *The Wanderings of Oisin, and Other Poems*, 1889; *The Countess Kathleen and Various Legends and Lyrics*, 1892; *The Rose*, 1893; *The Wind Among the Reeds*, 1899; *In the Seven Woods*, 1903; *The Poetical Works of William B. Yeats*, 1906, 1907 (2 volumes); *The Green Helmet, and Other Poems*, 1910; *Responsibilities*, 1914; *Responsibilities, and Other Poems*, 1916; *The Wild Swans at Coole*, 1917, 1919; *Michael Robartes and the Dancer*, 1920; *The Tower*, 1928; *Words for Music Perhaps, and Other Poems*, 1932; *The Winding Stair, and Other Poems*, 1933; *The Collected Poems of W. B. Yeats*, 1933, 1950; *The King of the Great Clock Tower*, 1934; *A Full Moon in March*, 1935 (includes poems and plays); *Last Poems and Plays*, 1940; *The Poems of W. B. Yeats*, 1949 (2 volumes); *The Collected Poems of W. B. Yeats*, 1956; *The Variorum Edition of the Poems of W. B. Yeats*, 1957 (P. Allt and R. K. Alspach, editors); *The Poems*, 1983; *The Poems: A New Edition*, 1984.

NONFICTION: *Ideas of Good and Evil*, 1903; *The Cutting of an Agate*, 1912; *Per Amica Silentia Lunae*, 1918; *Essays*, 1924; *A Vision*, 1925, 1937; *Autobiographies*, 1926, 1955; *A Packet for Ezra Pound*, 1929; *Essays, 1931-1936*, 1937; *The Autobiography of William Butler Yeats*, 1938; *On the Boiler*, 1939; *If I Were Four and Twenty*, 1940; *The Letters of W. B. Yeats*, 1954; *The Senate Speeches of W. B. Yeats*, 1960 (Donald R. Pearce, editor); *Essays and Introductions*, 1961; *Explorations*, 1962; *Ah, Sweet Dancer: W. B. Yeats, Margot Ruddock--A Correspondence*, 1970 (Roger McHugh, editor); *Uncollected Prose by W. B. Yeats*, 1970, 1976 (2 volumes); *Memoirs*, 1972; *The Collected Letters of W. B. Yeats*, 1986-2005 (4 volumes); *Early Articles and Reviews: Uncollected Articles and Reviews Written Between 1886 and 1900*, 2004 (John P. Frayne and Madeleine Marchaterre, editors).

MISCELLANEOUS: *The Collected Works in Verse and Prose of William Butler Yeats*, 1908; *The Collected Works of W. B. Yeats*, 1989-2008 (13 volumes).

BIBLIOGRAPHY

Bloom, Harold. *Yeats*. New York: Oxford University Press, 1970. An influential work by a leading contemporary critic. The emphasis is on Yeats's Romanticism, and Yeats is seen as the heir to the English Romantic tradition. The prosodic, aesthetic, and imaginative implications of this inheritance are the subject of much intense and sophisticated discussion.

Brown, Terence. *The Life of W. B. Yeats: A Critical Biography*. Malden, Mass.: Blackwell, 1999. Brown's book is very much a critical biography, attending more to Yeats's art than to his life. Brown conveys the texture of Yeats's life, selecting just the right details from what is now a copious historical record.

Donoghue, Denis. *Yeats*. London: Fontana, 1971. The best brief survey of the subject. Yeats's life, works, and thoughts are clearly presented in their many complex interrelations. The study's unifying argument is the author's conception of Yeats's understanding of, and identification with, power. Contains a useful chronology and succinct bibliography.

Ellmann, Richard. *W. B. Yeats: The Man and the Masks*. New York: Macmillan, 1948. The first biography to avail itself of unrestricted access to Yeats's posthumous papers. Yeats's doctrine of the mask is adopted as a biographical trope. Life and work are perceived as being mutually reinforcing. In many ways, the most satisfactory biographical treatment of Yeats.

Fleming, Deborah. *"A Man Who Does Not Exist": The Irish Peasant in the Work of W. B. Yeats and J. M. Synge*. Ann Arbor: University of Michigan Press, 1995. Discusses how Yeats transforms Irish folklore into art, thus helping establish a new sense of cultural identity in Ireland. Examines Yeats as a postcolonial writer and his belief that peasant culture was a repository of ancient wisdom.

Foster, R. F. *W. B. Yeats: A Life*. 2 vols. New York: Oxford University Press, 1997-2003. Foster, a noted Irish historian, received the cooperation of Yeats's family to write this meticulously researched biography. His two-volume chronicle of Yeats's life defines the writer by what he did rather than what he wrote.

Holdeman, David, and Ben Levitas, eds. *W. B. Yeats in Context*. New York: Cambridge University Press, 2010. The thirty-eight essays in this collection explore the political, historical, literary, cultural, and philosophical contexts of Yeats's life and works. The first section of essays place his life within the historical events of his times, discussing the importance of church and state during his childhood in Ireland, the fin de siècle, World War I, and the Irish Free State. Other sections provide information on people, places, and philosophies associated with Yeats; the reception of his writings; and the themes of class and eugenics, nationalism and postcolonialism, gender, aesthetics, and fascism in his work. Another section looks at art movements during Yeats's lifetime, including a discussion of modern fiction. References to the short fiction are listed in the index.

Howes, Marjorie, and John Kelly, eds. *The Cambridge Companion to W. B. Yeats*. New York: Cambridge University Press, 2006. Yeats scholars from the United States, the United Kingdom, and Ireland contribute eleven essays to this work, illuminating the personal and political events in Yeats's life. The essays chronicle Yeats's early interests in theater, politics, and the occult, as well as his use of folklore and Irish legend. References to the short fiction and short-fiction collections are listed in the index.

Ingman, Heather. "W. B. Yeats and George Egerton." In *A History of the Irish Short Story*. New York: Cambridge University Press, 2009. This chapter in Ingman's examination of the development of the Irish short story provides an overview of short fiction written during the fin de siècle period, followed by detailed readings of some of Yeats and Egerton's stories.

Torchiana, Donald. *Yeats and Georgian Ireland*. Evanston, Ill.: Northwestern University Press, 1966. One of the primary ways in which Yeats derived myth from history was through his reading of the works of major Irish writers of the eighteenth century. This study analyzes Yeats's knowledge of Jonathan Swift, George Berkeley, Oliver Goldsmith, and Edmund Burke. The influence of these thinkers on Yeats's poetry and prose is then assessed. An illuminating study of the impact of the Irish context, particularly on the poet's later work.

Tratner, Michael. *Modernism and Mass Politics: Joyce, Woolf, Eliot, Yeats*. Stanford, Calif.: Stanford University Press, 1995. Discusses the political context of Yeats's modernism. Reviews Yeats's poetics of violence. Although the chapter on Yeats is primarily concerned with his poetry, it is helpful for an understanding of Yeats's literary efforts to create a national mind.

Eileen A. Sullivan
Updated by George O'Brien

RESOURCES

TERMS AND TECHNIQUES

Aestheticism: The European literary movement denied that art needed to have any utilitarian purpose and focused on the slogan "art for art's sake." The movement was predominant in the 1890's and had its roots in France. The doctrines of aestheticism were introduced to England by Walter Pater and can be found in the plays of Oscar Wilde and the short stories of Arthur Symons. In American literature, the ideas underlying the aesthetic movement can be found in the short fiction of Edgar Allan Poe.

Allegory: A literary mode in which characters in a narrative personify abstract ideas or qualities and provide a second level of meaning to the work. Two famous examples of allegory are Edmund Spenser's *The Faerie Queene* (1590, 1596) and John Bunyan's *The Pilgrim's Progress from This World to That Which Is to Come*, Part I (1678). Modern examples may be found in Nathaniel Hawthorne's story "The Artist of the Beautiful" and the stories and novels of Franz Kafka.

Allusion: A reference to a person or event, either historical or from a literary work, which gives another literary work a wider frame of reference and adds depth to its meaning. For example, Sylvia Townsend Warner's story "Winter in the Air" gains greater suggestiveness from the frequent allusions to William Shakespeare's play *The Winter's Tale* (pr. c. 1610-1611, pb. 1623), and her story "Swans on an Autumn River" is enriched by a number of allusions to the poetry of William Butler Yeats.

Ambiguity: Refers to the capacity of language to suggest two or more levels of meaning within a single expression, thus conveying a rich, concentrated effect. Ambiguity has been defined by William Empson in *Seven Types of Ambiguity* (1930) as "any verbal nuance, however, slight, which gives room for alternative reactions to the same piece of language." It has been suggested that because of the short story's highly compressed form, ambiguity may play a more important role in this genre than it does in the novel.

Anachronism: An event, person, or thing placed outside--usually earlier than--its proper historical era. William Shakespeare uses anachronism in *King John* (pr. c. 1596-1597, pb. 1623), *Antony and Cleopatra* (pr. c. 1606-1607, pb. 1723), and *Julius Caesar* (pr. c. 1599-1600, pb. 1623). Mark Twain employed anachronism to comic effect in *A Connecticut Yankee in King Arthur's Court* (1889).

Anecdote: The short narration of a single interesting incident or event. An anecdote differs from a short story in that it does not have a plot, relates a single episode, and does not range over different times and places.

Antagonist: A character in fiction who stands in opposition, or rivalry, to the protagonist. In William Shakespeare's *Hamlet, Prince of Denmark* (pr. c. 1600-1601, pb. 1603), for example, King Claudius is the antagonist of Hamlet.

Anthology: A collection of prose or poetry, usually by various writers. Often serves to introduce the work of little-known authors to a wider audience.

Aphorism: A short, concise statement that states an opinion, precept, or general truth, such as Alexander Pope's "Hope springs eternal in the human breast."

Aporia: An interpretative point in a story that basically cannot be decided, usually as the result of some gap or absence.

Apostrophe: A direct address to a person (usually absent), inanimate entity, or abstract quality. Examples are the first line of William Wordsworth's sonnet "London, 1802," "Milton! Thou should'st be living at this hour," and King Lear's speech in William Shakespeare's *King Lear* (pr. c. 1605-1606, pb. 1698), "Blow, winds, and crack your cheeks! rage! blow!"

Appropriation: The act of taking over part of a literary theory or approach for one's own ends, for example, male critics using the feminist approach.

Archetypal theme: Recurring thematic patterns in literature. Common archetypal themes include death and rebirth (Samuel Taylor Coleridge's *The Rime of the Ancient Mariner*, 1798), paradise-Hades (Coleridge's "Kubla Khan," 1816), the fatal woman (Guy de Maupassant's "Doubtful Happiness"), the earth goddess ("Yanda" by Isaac Bashevis Singer), the scapegoat (D. H. Lawrence's "The Woman Who Rode Away," 1925), and the return to the womb (Flannery O'Connor's "The River," 1953).

Archetype: This term was used by psychologist Carl Jung to describe what he called "primordial images," which exist in the "collective unconscious" of humankind and are manifested in myths, religion, literature, and dreams. Now used broadly in literary criticism to refer to character types, motifs, images, symbols, and plot patterns recurring in many different literary forms and works.

Architectonics: A term borrowed from architecture to describe the structural qualities, such as unity and balance, of a work of literature. If the architectonics are successful, the work will give the impression of organic unity and balance, like a solidly constructed building in which the total value is more than the sum of the parts.

Asides: In drama, short passages generally spoken by one dramatic character in an undertone or directed to the audience, so as not to be heard by other characters on stage.

Atmosphere: The mood or tone of a work; it is often associated with setting but can also be established by action or dialogue. The opening paragraphs of Edgar Allan Poe's "The Fall of the House of Usher" (1839) and James Joyce's "Araby" (1914) provide good examples of atmosphere created early in the works and which pervade the remainder of the story.

Ballad: Popular ballads are songs or verse that tell dramatic, usually impersonal, tales. Supernatural events, courage, and love are frequent themes, but any experience that appeals to ordinary people is acceptable material. Literary ballads--narrative poems based on popular ballads--have frequently been in vogue in English literature, particularly during the Romantic period. One of the most famous is Samuel Taylor Coleridge's *The Rime of the Ancient Mariner*.

Black humor: A general term of modern origin that refers to a form of "sick humor" that is intended to produce laughter out of the morbid and the taboo. Examples are the works of Joseph Heller, Thomas Pynchon, Günter Grass, and Kurt Vonnegut.

Broadside ballad: A ballad printed on one side of a large, single sheet of paper and sung to a popular tune. Dating from the sixteenth century in England, the subject of the broadside ballad was a topical event or issue.

Burlesque: A work that, by imitating attitudes, styles, institutions, and people, aims to amuse. Burlesque differs from satire in that it aims to ridicule simply for the sake of amusement rather than for political or social change.

Canon: The standard or authoritative list of literary works that are widely accepted as outstanding representatives of their period and genre. In recent literary criticism, however, the established canon has come under fierce assault for its alleged culture and gender bias.

Canonize: The act of adding a literary work to the list of works that form the primary tradition of a genre or literature in general. For example, a number of stories by female and African American writers previously excluded from the canon of the short story, such as Charlotte Perkins Gilman's "The Yellow Wallpaper" (1892) and Charles Waddell Chesnutt's "The Sheriff's Children (1899)," have recently been canonized.

Caricature: A form of writing that focuses on unique qualities of a person and then exaggerates and distorts those qualities in order to ridicule the person and what he or she represents. Contemporary writers, such as Flannery O'Connor, have used caricature for serious and satiric purposes in such stories as "Good Country People" (1955) and "A Good Man Is Hard to Find" (1955).

Character type: The term can refer to the convention of using stock characters, such as the *miles gloriosus* (braggart soldier) of Renaissance and Roman comedy, the figure of vice in medieval morality plays, or the clever servant in Elizabethan comedy. It can also describe "flat" characters (the term was coined by E. M. Forster) in fiction who do not grow or change during the course of the narrative and who can be easily classified.

Chronicle: The precursors of modern histories, chronicles were written accounts of national or world events. One of the best known is the *Anglo-Saxon Chronicle*, begun in the reign of King Alfred in the late ninth century. Many chronicles were written in Elizabethan times, and these were used by William Shakespeare as source documents for his history plays.

Classic/Classicism: A literary stance or value system consciously based on the example of classical Greek and Roman literature. While the term is applied to an enormous diversity of artists it generally denotes a cluster of values, including formal discipline, restrained expression, reverence of tradition, and an objective rather than subjective orientation. Often contrasted to Romanticism.

Climax: Similar to crisis, the moment in a work of fiction at which the action reaches a turning point and the plot begins to be resolved. Unlike crisis, this term is also used to refer to the moment in which the reader's emotional involvement with the work reaches its highest point of intensity.

Comic story: Encompasses a wide variety of modes and inflections, such as parody, burlesque, satire, irony, and humor. Frequently, the defining quality of comic characters is that they lack self-awareness; the reader tends not to identify with them but perceives them from a detached point of view, more as objects than persons.

Conceit: A type of metaphor that makes highly intellectualized comparisons between seemingly disparate things. It is associated with the Metaphysical poets and the Elizabethan sonneteers; examples can also be found in the poetry of Emily Dickinson and T. S. Eliot.

Conflict: The struggle that develops between the protagonist and another person, the natural world, society, or some force within the self. In short fiction, the conflict is most often between the protagonist and the self or the human condition.

Connotation/Denotation: Denotation is the explicit, formal definition of a word, exclusive of its emotional associations. When a word takes on an additional meaning, other than its denotative one, it achieves connotation. For example, the word "mercenary" denotes a soldier who is paid to fight in an army not of his own region, but connotatively a mercenary is an unprincipled scoundrel who kills for money.

Conte: French for tale, a conte was originally a short adventure tale. In the nineteenth century, the term was used to describe a tightly constructed short story. In England, the term is used to describe a work longer than a short story and shorter than a novel.

Crisis: A turning point in the plot, at which the opposing forces reach the point that a resolution must take place.

Criticism: The study and evaluation of works of literature. Theoretical criticism, as for example in Aristotle's *Peri poētikēs* (c. 334-323 b.c.e.; *Poetics*, 1705), sets out general principles for interpretation. Practical criticism (Samuel Taylor Coleridge's lectures on William Shakespeare, for example) offers interpretations of particular works or authors.

Deconstruction: A literary theory, primarily attributed to French critic Jacques Derrida, which has spawned a wide variety of practical applications, the most prominent being the critical tactic of laying bare a text's self-reflexivity, that is, showing how it continually refers to and subverts its own way of meaning.

Defamiliarization: A term coined by the Russian Formalists to indicate a process by which the writer makes the reader perceive the concrete uniqueness of an object, event, or idea that has been generalized by routine and habit.

Dénouement: Literally, "unknotting"; the conclusion of a drama or fiction, when the plot is unraveled and the mystery solved.

Detective story: The "classic" detective story (or "mystery") is a highly formalized and logically structured mode of fiction in which the focus is on a crime solved by a detective through interpretation of evidence and clever reasoning. Many modern practitioners of the genre, however, such as Raymond Chandler, Patricia Highsmith, and Ross Macdonald, have placed less emphasis on the puzzlelike qualities of the detective story and have focused instead on characterization, theme, and other elements of mainstream fiction. The form was first developed in short fiction by Edgar Allan Poe, and has been used by Jorge Luis Borges.

Deus ex machina: A Latin term meaning "god out of the machine." In the Greek theater, it referred to the use of a god lowered out of a mechanism onto the stage to untangle the plot or save the hero. The term has come to signify any artificial device for the easy resolution of dramatic difficulties.

Device: Any technique used in literature in order to gain a specific effect. The poet uses the device of figurative language, for example, while the novelist may use the devices of foreshadowing, flashback, and so on, in order to create a desired effect.

Dialogics: The theory that many different voices are held in suspension without merging into a single authoritative voice. Developed by Russian critic Mikhail Bakhtin.

Didactic literature: Literature that seeks to instruct, give guidance, or teach a lesson. Didactic literature normally has a moral, religious, or philosophical purpose, or it will expound a branch of knowledge (as in Vergil's *Georgics*, c. 37-29 b.c.e.; English translation, 1589). It is distinguished from imaginative works, in which the aesthetic product takes precedence over any moral intent.

Diegesis: Refers to the hypothetical world of a story, as if it actually existed in real space and time. It is the illusory universe of the story created by its linguistic structure.

Doggerel: Strictly speaking, doggerel refers to rough and jerky versification, but the term is more commonly applied to worthless verse that contains monotonous rhyme and rhythm and trivial subject matter.

Doppelgänger: A double or counterpart of a person, sometimes endowed with ghostly qualities. A fictional doppelgänger often reflects a suppressed side of a character's personality, as in Fyodor Dostoevski's novella *Dvoynik* (1846; *The Double*, 1917) and the short stories of E. T. A. Hoffmann. Isaac Bashevis Singer and Jorge Luis Borges, among other modern writers, have also employed the doppelgänger with striking effect.

Dream vision: An allegorical form common in the Middle Ages, in which the narrator or a character falls asleep and dreams a dream that becomes the actual framed story. Subtle variations of the form have been used by Nathaniel Hawthorne in "Young Goodman Brown" (1835) and by Edgar Allan Poe in "The Pit and the Pendulum" (1842).

Dualism: A theory that the universe is explicable in terms of two basic, conflicting entities, such as good and evil, mind and matter, or the physical and the spiritual.

Eclogue: In Greek, the term means literally "selection." It is now used to describe a formal pastoral poem. Classical eclogues are constructed around a variety of conventional themes: the singing match, the rustic dialogue, the lament, the love lay, and the eulogy. During the Renaissance, eclogues were employed as veiled satires.

Écriture Féminine: French feminist Hélène Cixous argues for a unique female kind of writing, which in its fluidity disrupts the binary oppositions of male-dominated cultural structures.

Effect: The total, unified impression, or impact, made upon the reader by a literary work. Every aspect of the work--plot, characterization, style, and so on--is seen to directly contribute to this overall impression.

Elegy: A long, rhymed, formal poem whose subject is meditation upon death or a lamentable theme; Alfred, Lord Tennyson's *In Memoriam* (1850) is a well-known example. The pastoral elegy, such as Percy Bysshe Shelley's *Adonais: An Elegy on the Death of John Keats* (1821), uses a pastoral scene to express grief at the loss of a friend or important person.

Emotive meaning: The emotion that is commonly associated with a word. In other words, the connotations of a word, not merely what it denotes. Emotive meaning is contrasted with cognitive or descriptive meaning, in which neither emotions nor connotations are involved.

Epic: Although this term usually refers to a long narrative poem that presents the exploits of a central figure of high position, the term is also used to designate a long novel that has the style or structure usually associated with an epic. In this sense, for example, Herman Melville's *Moby Dick: Or, The Whale* (1851) and James Joyce's *Ulysses* (1922) may be called epics.

Epiphany: The literary application of this religious term was popularized by James Joyce in his book *Stephen Hero* (1944): "By an epiphany he meant a sudden spiritual manifestation, whether in the vulgarity of speech or of gesture or in a memorable phase of the mind itself." Many short stories since Joyce's collection *Dubliners* (1914) have been analyzed as epiphanic stories in which a character or the reader experiences a sudden revelation of meaning.

Episode: In Greek tragedy, the segment between two choral odes. Episode now refers to an incident presented as a continuous action. In a work of literature, many discrete episodes are woven together to form a more complex work.

Epistolary fiction: A work of fiction in which the narrative is carried forward by means of letters written by the characters. Epistolary novels were a quite popular form in the eighteenth century. Examples include Samuel Richardson's *Pamela: Or, Virtue Rewarded* (1740-1741) and *Clarissa: Or, The History of a Young Lady* (1747-1748). The form has not been much used in the twentieth century.

Essay: A brief prose work, usually on a single topic, that expresses the personal point of view of the author. The essay is usually addressed to a general audience and attempts to persuade the reader to accept the author's ideas.

Essay-sketch tradition: The first sketches can be traced to the Greek philosopher Theophrastus in 300 *b.c.e.*, whose character sketches influenced seventeenth and eighteenth century writers in England, who developed the form into something close to the idea of character in fiction. The essay has an equally venerable history, and, like the sketch, had an impact on the development of the modern short story.

Euphony: Language that creates a harmonious and pleasing effect; the opposite of cacophony, which is a combination of harsh and discordant sounds.

Exemplum: A brief anecdote or tale introduced to illustrate a moral point in medieval sermons. By the fourteenth century these exempla had expanded into exemplary narratives. Geoffrey Chaucer's "The Nun's Priest's Tale" and "The Pardoner's Tale" from *The Canterbury Tales* (1387-1400) are exempla.

Existentialism: A philosophy and attitude of mind that gained wide currency in religious and artistic thought after the end of World War II. Typical concerns of existential writers are human beings' estrangement from society, their awareness that the world is meaningless, and their recognition that one must turn from external props to the self. The novels of Albert Camus and Franz Kafka provide examples of existentialist beliefs.

Exposition: The part or parts of a work of fiction that provide necessary background information. Exposition not only provides the time and place of the action but also introduces readers to the fictive world of the story, acquainting them with the ground rules of the work. In the short story, exposition is usually elliptical.

Expressionism: Beginning in German theater at the start of the twentieth century, expressionism became the dominant movement in the decade following World War I. It abandoned realism and relied on a conscious distortion of external reality in order to portray the world as it is "viewed emotionally." The movement spread to fiction and poetry. Expressionism influenced the plays of Eugene O'Neill, Tennessee Williams, and Thornton Wilder and can be found in the novels of Franz Kafka and James Joyce.

Fable: One of the oldest narrative forms. Usually takes the form of an analogy in which animals or inanimate objects speak to illustrate a moral lesson. The most famous examples are the fables of Aesop, who used the form orally in 600 *B.C.E.*

Fabliau: A short narrative poem, popular in medieval French literature and during the English Middle Ages. Fabliaux were usually realistic in subject matter, bawdy, and made a point of satirizing the weaknesses and foibles of human beings. Perhaps the most famous are Geoffrey Chaucer's "The Miller's Tale" and "The Reeve's Tale" from *The Canterbury Tales* (1387-1400).

Fabulation: A term coined by Robert Scholes and used in contemporary literary criticism to describe novels that are radically experimental in subject matter, style, and form. Like the Magical Realists, fabulators mix realism with fantasy. The works of Thomas Pynchon, John Barth, Donald Barthelme, and William H. Gass provide examples.

Fairy tale: A form of folktale in which supernatural events or characters are prominent. Fairy tales usually depict a realm of reality beyond that of the natural world and in which the laws of the natural world are suspended.

Fantastic: In his study *Introduction à la littérature fantastique* (1970; *The Fantastic: A Structural Approach to a Literary Genre*, 1973), the critic Tzvetan Todorov defines the fantastic as a genre that lies between the uncanny and the marvelous. Whereas the marvelous presents an event that cannot be explained by the laws of the natural world and the uncanny presents an event that is the result of hallucination or illusion, the fantastic exists as long as the reader cannot decide which of these two applies. Henry James's *The Turn of the Screw* (1898) is an example of the fantastic.

Figurative language: Any use of language that departs from the usual or ordinary meaning to gain a poetic or otherwise special effect. Figurative language embodies various figures of speech, such as irony, metaphor, simile, and many others.

Fin de siècle: Literally, "end of the century"; refers to the last decade of the nineteenth century, a transitional period in which artists and writers were aware that they were living at the close of a great age and deliberately cultivated a kind of languor, world weariness, and satiety. Associated with the period of aestheticism and the Decadent movement exemplified in the works of Oscar Wilde.

Flashback: A scene that depicts an earlier event; it can be presented as a reminiscence by a character in a story, or it can simply be inserted into the narrative.

Folktale: A short prose narrative, usually handed down orally, found in all cultures of the world. The term is often used interchangeably with myth, fable, and fairy tale.

Form: The organizing principle in a work of literature; the manner in which its elements are put together in relation to its total effect. The term is sometimes used interchangeably with structure and is often contrasted with content: If form is the building, content is what is in the building and what the building is specifically designed to express.

Frame story: A story that provides a framework for another story (or stories) told within it. The form is ancient and is used by Geoffrey Chaucer in *The Canterbury Tales* (1387-1400). In modern literature, the technique has been used by Henry James in *The Turn of the Screw* (1898), Joseph Conrad in *Heart of Darkness* (1899, serial; 1902, book), and John Barth in *Lost in the Funhouse* (1968).

Framework: When used in connection with a frame story, the framework is the narrative setting, within which other stories are told. The framework may also have a plot of its own. More generally, the framework is similar to structure, referring to the general outline of a work.

Gendered: When a work is approached as thematically or stylistically specific to male or female characteristics or concerns, it is said to be "gendered."

Genre study: The concept of studying literature by classification and definition of types or kinds, such as tragedy, comedy, epic, lyrical, and pastoral. First introduced by Aristotle in *Poetics*, the genre principle has been an essential concomitant of the basic proposition that literature can be studied scientifically.

Gothic genre: A form of fiction developed in the late eighteenth century which focuses on horror and the supernatural. Examples include Matthew Gregory Lewis's *The Monk: A Romance,* (1796 also published as *Ambrosio: Or, The Monk*), Mary Wollstonecraft Shelley's *Frankenstein* (1818), and the short fiction of Edgar Allan Poe. In modern literature, the gothic genre can be found in the fiction of Truman Capote.

Grotesque: Characterized by a breakup of the everyday world by mysterious forces, the form differs from fantasy in that the reader is not sure whether to react with humor or horror. Examples include the stories of E. T. A. Hoffmann and Franz Kafka.

Gynocriticism: American feminist critic Elaine C. Showalter coined this term for her theory that women read and write differently than men do because of biological and cultural differences.

Hasidic tale: Hasidism was a Jewish mystical sect formed in the eighteenth century. The term "Hasidic tale" is used to describe some American short fiction, much of it written in the 1960's, which reflected the spirit of Hasidism, particularly the belief in the immanence of God in all things. Saul Bellow, Philip Roth, and Norman Mailer have been attracted to the genre, as has the Israeli writer Shmuel Yosef Agnon, who won the Nobel Prize in Literature in 1966.

Hegemony: Italian critic Antonio Gramsci maintains that capitalists create and sustain an ideology to support their dominance or hegemony over the working class. By maintaining economic and cultural power, capitalists receive the support of the working class, who adopt their values and beliefs, and thus control the ideology or social consciousness that in turn controls individual consciousness.

Historical criticism: In contrast to formalist criticism, which treats literary works as self-contained artifacts, historical criticism emphasizes the social and historical context of literature and allows itself to take into consideration the relevant facts and circumstances of the author's life. The method emphasizes the meaning that the work had in its own time rather than interpreting it for the present.

Hyperbole: The term is Greek for "overshooting" and refers to the use of gross exaggeration for rhetorical effect, based on the assumption that the reader will not be persuaded of the literal truth of the overstatement. Can be used for serious or comic effect.

Imagery: Often defined as the verbal stimulation of sensory perception. Although the word betrays a visual bias, imagery, in fact, calls on all five senses. In its simplest form, imagery re-creates a physical sensation in a clear, literal manner; it becomes more complex when a poet employs metaphor and other figures of speech to re-create experience.

In medias res: Latin phrase used by Horace, meaning literally "into the midst of things." It refers to a literary technique of beginning the narrative when the action has already begun. The term is used particularly in connection with the epic, which traditionally begins *in medias res*.

Initiation story: A story in which protagonists, usually children or young persons, go through an experience, sometimes painful or disconcerting, that carries them from innocence to some new form of knowledge and maturity. William Faulkner's "The Bear" (1942), Nathaniel Hawthorne's "Young Goodman Brown" (1835), Alice Walker's "To Hell with Dying" (1967), and Robert Penn Warren's "Blackberry Winter" (1946) are examples of the form.

Interior monologue: Defined as the speech of a character designed to introduce the reader directly to the character's internal life, the form differs from other monologues in that it attempts to reproduce thought before any logical organization is imposed upon it. An example is Molly Bloom's long interior monologue at the conclusion of James Joyce's *Ulysses* (1922).

Interpretation: An analysis of the meaning of a literary work. Interpretation will attempt to explicate the theme, structure, and other components of the work, often focusing on obscure or ambiguous passages.

Irrealism: A term often used to refer to modern or postmodern fiction that is presented self-consciously as a fiction or fabulation rather than a mimesis of external reality. The best-known practitioners of irrealism are John Barth, Robert Coover, and Donald Barthelme.

Lai/Lay: A song or short narrative poem. The term was first applied to twelfth and thirteenth centuries French poems and to English poems in the fourteenth century that were based on them, including Geoffrey Chaucer's "The Franklin's Tale" (1387-1400). In the nineteenth century, the term was applied to historical ballads, such as Sir Walter Scott's *The Lay of the Last Minstrel* (1805).

Legend: A narrative that is handed down from generation to generation, usually associated with a particular place and a specific event. A legend may often have more historical truth than a myth, and the protagonist is usually a person rather than a supernatural being.

Leitmotif: From the German, meaning "leading motif." Any repetition--of a word, phrase, situation, or idea--that occurs within a single work or group of related works.

Literary short story: A term that was current in American criticism in the 1940's to distinguish the short fiction of Ernest Hemingway, Eudora Welty, Sherwood Anderson, and others from the popular pulp and slick fiction of the day.

Local color: Usually refers to a movement in literature, especially in the United States, in the latter part of the nineteenth century. The focus was on the environment, atmosphere, and milieu of a particular region. For example, Mark Twain wrote about the Mississippi region; Sarah Orne Jewett wrote about New England. The term can also be used to refer to any work that represents the characteristics of a particular region.

Logocentrism: Jacques Derrida argues that all Western thought is based on the quest for a nonexistent "transcendental signifier," a sort of primal origin that makes ultimate meaning possible. The Western assumption of some ultimate center, that it calls God, reason, truth, or essence, is what Derrida calls Logocentrism.

Lyric short story: A form in which the emphasis is on internal changes, moods, and feelings. The lyric story is usually open-ended and depends on the figurative language usually associated with poetry. Examples of lyric stories are the works of Ivan Turgenev, Anton Chekhov, Katherine Mansfield, Sherwood Anderson, Conrad Aiken, and John Updike.

Lyrical ballad: The term is preeminently associated with William Wordsworth and Samuel Taylor Coleridge, whose *Lyrical Ballads* (1798), which drew on the ballad tradition, was one of the seminal books of the Romantic age. *Lyrical Ballads* was a revolt against eighteenth century poetic diction; it was an attempt to create a new kind of poetry by using simple language and taking as subject the everyday lives of common folk and the strong emotions they experience.

Malaprop/Malapropism: A malapropism occurs when one word is confused with another because the two words have a similar sound. The term is derived from the character Mrs. Malaprop in Richard Brinsley Sheridan's *The Rivals* (1775), who, for example, uses the word "illiterate" when she really means "obliterate" and mistakes "progeny" for "prodigy."

Märchen: German fairy tales, as collected in the works of Wilhelm and Jacob Grimm or in the works of nineteenth century writers, such as Novalis and E. T. A. Hoffmann.

Marginalization: The process by which an individual or a group is deemed secondary to a dominant group in power and thus denied access to the benefits enjoyed by the dominant group; for example, in the past women were marginalized by men and nonwhites were marginalized by whites.

Medieval romance: Medieval romances, which originated in twelfth century France, were tales of adventure in which a knight would embark on a perilous quest to win the hand of a lady, perform a service for his king, or seek the Holy Grail. He had to overcome many obstacles, including dragons and other monsters; magic spells and enchantments were prominent, and the romance embodied the chivalric ideals of courage, honor, refined manners, and courtly love. English romances include the anonymous *Sir Gawain and the Green Knight* (fourteenth century) and Sir Thomas Malory's *Le Morte d'Arthur* (1485).

Memoir: Usually written by a person prominent in public life, a memoir is the authors' recollections of famous people they have known and great events they have witnessed. Memoir differs from autobiography in that the emphasis in the latter is on the life of the authors.

Metafiction: Refers to fiction that manifests a reflexive tendency, such as Vladimir Nabokov's *Pale Fire* (1962), and John Fowles's *The French Lieutenant's Woman* (1969). The emphasis is on the loosening of the work's illusion of reality to expose the reality of its illusion. Such terms as "irrealism," "postmodernist fiction," and "antifiction" are also used to refer to this type of fiction.

Metaphor: A figure of speech in which two dissimilar objects are imaginatively identified (rather than merely compared) on the assumption that they share one or more qualities: "She is the rose, the glory of the day" (Edmund Spenser). The term is often used in modern criticism in a wider sense to identify analogies of all kinds in literature, painting, and film.

Metonymy: A figure of speech in which an object that is closely related to a word comes to stand for the word itself, such as when one says "the White House" when meaning the "president."

Minimalist movement: A school of fiction writing that developed in the late 1970's and early 1980's and that Roland Barthes has characterized as the "less is more school." Minimalism attempts to convey much by saying little, to render contemporary reality in precise, pared-down prose that suggests more than it directly states. Leading minimalist writers are Raymond Carver and Ann Beattie. A character in Beattie's short story "Snow" (in *Where You'll Find Me*, 1986) seems to sum up minimalism: "Any life will seem dramatic if you omit mention of most of it."

Mise en abîme: A small story inside a larger narrative that echoes or mirrors the larger narrative, thus containing the larger within the smaller.

Modern short story: The modern short story dates from the nineteenth century and is associated with the names of Edgar Allan Poe (who is often credited with inventing the form) and Nathaniel Hawthorne in the United States, Honoré de Balzac in France, and E. T. A. Hoffmann in Germany. In his influential critical writings, Poe defined the short story as being limited to "a certain unique or single effect," to which every detail in the story should contribute.

Monologue: Any speech or narrative presented by one person. It can sometimes be used to refer to any lengthy speech, in which one person monopolizes the conversation.

Moral tract: A propaganda pamphlet on a political or religious topic, usually distributed free. The term is often associated with the Oxford Movement in nineteenth century England, which was a movement to reform the Church of England.

Motif: An incident or situation in a story that serves as the basis of its structure, creating by repetition and variation a patterned recurrence and consequently a general theme. Russian Formalist critics distinguish between bound motifs, which cannot be omitted without disturbing the thematic structure of the story, and unbound motifs, which serve merely to create the illusion of external reality. In this sense, motif is the same as leitmotif.

Myth: An anonymous traditional story, often involving supernatural beings or the interaction between gods and human beings and dealing with the basic questions of how the world and human society came to be as they are. Myth is an important term in contemporary literary criticism. Northrop Frye, for example, has said that "the typical forms of myth become the conventions and genres of literature." By this, he means that the genres of comedy, romance, tragedy, and irony (satire) correspond to seasonal myths of spring, summer, autumn, and winter.

Narrative: An account in prose or verse of an event or series of events, whether real or imagined.

Narrative persona: Persona means literally "mask": It is the self created by the author and through whom the narrative is told. The persona is not to be identified with the author, even when the two may seem to resemble each other. The narrative persona in Lord Byron's *Don Juan* (1819-1824), for example, may express many sentiments of which Byron would have approved, but he is nevertheless a fictional creation who is distinct from the author.

Narratology: The theoretical study of narrative structures and ways of meaning. Most all major literary theories have a branch of study known as narratology.

Narrator: The character who recounts the narrative. There are many different types of narrators: The first-person narrator is a character in the story and can be recognized by his or her use of "I"; third-person narrators may be limited or omniscient. In the former, the narrator is confined to knowledge of the minds and emotions of one or, at most, a few characters. In the latter, the narrator knows everything, seeing into the minds of all the characters. Rarely, second-person narration may be used. (An example can be found in Edna O'Brien's *A Pagan Place*, 1973.)

Novel: A fictional prose form, longer than a short story or novelette. The term embraces a wide range of types, but the novel usually includes a more complicated plot and a wider cast of characters than the short story. The focus is often on the development of individual characterization and the presentation of a social world and a detailed environment.

Novella, novelette, Novelle, nouvelle: These terms all refer to the form of fiction that is longer than a short story and shorter than a novel. Novella, the Italian term, is the term usually used to refer to American works in this genre, such as Joseph Conrad's *Heart of Darkness* (1899, serial; 1902, book) and Henry James's *The Turn of the Screw* (1898). *Novelle* is the German term; *nouvelle* the French; "novelette" the British. The term "novel" derived from these terms.

Objective correlative: A key concept in modern formalist criticism, coined by T. S. Eliot in *The Sacred Wood* (1920). An objective correlative is a situation, an event, or an object that, when presented or described in a literary work, expresses a particular emotion and serves as a precise formula by which the same emotion can be evoked in the reader.

Oral tale: A wide-ranging term that can include everything from gossip to myths, legends, folktale, and jokes. Among the terms used by Saith Thompson to classify oral tales (*The Folktale*, 1951) are märchen, fairy tale, household tale, *conte populaire*, novella, hero tale, local tradition, migratory legend, explanatory tale, humorous anecdote, and merry tale.

Oral tradition: Material that is transmitted by word of mouth, often through chants or songs, from generation to generation. Homer's epics, for example, were originally passed down orally and employ formulas to make memorization easier. Often, ballads, folklore, and proverbs are also passed down in this way.

Oriental tale: An eighteenth century form made popular by the translations of *Alf layla wa-layla* (fifteenth century; *The Arabian Nights' Entertainments*, 1706-1708) collected during the period. Oriental tales were usually solemn in tone, contained little characterization, and focused on improbable events and supernatural places.

Other: By a process of psychological or cultural projection, an individual or a dominant group accuses those of a different race or gender of all the negative qualities they themselves possess and then respond to them as if they were "other" than themselves.

Oxymoron: Closely related to paradox, an oxymoron occurs when two words of opposite meaning are placed in juxtaposition, such as "wise fool," "devilish angel," or "loving hate."

Parable: A short, simple, and usually allegorical story that teaches a moral lesson. In the West, the most famous parables are those told in the Gospels by Jesus Christ.

Paradox: A statement that initially seems to be illogical or self-contradictory yet eventually proves to embody a complex truth. In New Criticism, the term is used to embrace any complexity of language that sustains multiple meanings and deviates from the norms of ordinary language use.

Parataxis: The placing of clauses or phrases in a series without the use of coordinating or subordinating terms.

Parody: A literary work that imitates or burlesques another work or author for the purpose of ridicule. Twentieth century parodists include E. B. White and James Thurber.

Periodical essay/sketch: Informal in tone and style and applied to a wide range of topics, the periodical essay originated in the early eighteenth century. It is associated in particular with Joseph Addison and Sir Richard Steele and their informal periodical, *The Spectator.*

Personification: A figure of speech which ascribes human qualities to abstractions or inanimate objects, as in these lines by W. H. Auden: "There's Wrath who has learnt every trick of guerrilla warfare,/ The shamming dead, the night-raid, the feinted retreat." Richard Crashaw's "Hope, thou bold taster of delight" is another example.

Plot: The sequence of events in a play or story and how those events are connected in a cause-and-effect relationship. There are a great variety of plot patterns, each of which is designed to create a particular effect.

Point of view: The perspective from which a story is presented to the reader. In simplest terms, it refers to whether narration is first person (directly addressed to the reader as if told by one involved in the narrative) or third person (usually a more objective, distanced perspective.)

Portmanteau words: The term was coined by Lewis Carroll to describe the creation of a new word by telescoping two existing words. In this way, "furious" and "fuming" can be combined to create "frumious." The works of James Joyce, as well as Carroll's *Through the Looking Glass and What Alice Found There* (1871), provide many examples of portmanteau words.

Postcolonial: A literary approach that focuses on English-language texts from countries and cultures formerly colonized or dominated by America, the British Empire, and other European countries. Postcolonialists focus on the literature of such countries as Australia, New Zealand, Africa, and South America, and such cultural groups as African Americans and Native Americans.

Postmodern: Although this term is so broad it is interpreted differently by many different critics, it basically refers to a trend by which the literary work calls attention to itself as an artifice rather than a mirror held up to external reality.

Prosody: The study of the principles of verse structure. Includes meter, rhyme, and other patterns of sound, such as alliteration, assonance, euphony and onomatopoeia, and stanzaic patterns.

Protagonist: Originally, in the Greek drama, the "first actor," who played the leading role. The term has come to signify the most important character in a drama or story. It is not unusual for a work to contain more than one protagonist.

Pun: A pun occurs when words that have similar pronunciations have entirely different meanings. The result may be a surprise recognition of an unusual or striking connection, or, more often, a humorously accidental connection.

Realism: A literary technique in which the primary convention is to render an illusion of fidelity to external reality. Realism is often identified as the primary method of the novel form; the realist movement in the late nineteenth century coincided with the full development of the novel form.

Reception theory: Theorist Hans Robert Jauss argues that since readers from any historical milieu create their own criteria for judging a text, one should examine how a text was received by readers contemporary with it. Since every period creates its own "horizon of expectation," the meaning of a text changes from one period to another.

Reminiscence: An account, written or spoken, of remembered events.

Rhetorical device: Rhetoric is the art of using words clearly and effectively, in speech or writing, in order to influence or persuade. A rhetorical device is a figure of speech, or a way of using language, employed to this end. It can include such elements as choice of words, rhythms, repetition, apostrophe, invocation, chiasmus, zeugma, antithesis, and the rhetorical question (a question to which no answer is expected).

Rogue literature: From Odysseus to William Shake-speare's Autolocus to Huckleberry Finn, the rogue is a common literary type. He is usually a robust and energetic comic or satirical figure whose roguery can be seen as a necessary undermining of the rigid complacency of conventional society. The pica-resque novel (*picaro* is Spanish for "rogue"), in which the picaro lives by his wits, is perhaps the most common form of rogue literature.

Romance: Originally, any work written in Old French. In the Middle Ages, romances were about knights and their adventures. In modern times, the term has also been used to describe a type of prose fiction in which, unlike the novel, realism plays little part. Prose romances often give expression to the quest for transcendent truths. Examples of the form include Nathaniel Hawthorne's *The Scarlet Letter* (1850) and Herman Melville's *Moby Dick* (1851).

Romanticism: A movement of the late eighteenth and nineteenth centuries which exalted individualism over collectivism, revolution over conservatism, in-novation over tradition, imagination over reason, and spontaneity over restraint. Romanticism re-garded art as self-expression; it strove to heal the cleavage between object and subject and expressed a longing for the infinite in all things. It stressed the innate goodness of human beings and the evils of the institutions that would stultify human creativity.

Saga: Originally applied to medieval Icelandic and other Scandinavian stories of heroic exploits and handed down by oral tradition. The term has come to signify any tale of heroic achievement or great adventure.

Satire: A form of literature that employs the comedic devices of wit, irony, and exaggeration to expose, ridicule, and condemn human folly, vice, and stu-pidity. Justifying satire, Alexander Pope wrote that "nothing moves strongly but satire, and those who are ashamed of nothing else are so of being ridiculous."

Setting: The circumstances and environment, both tem-poral and spatial, of a narrative. The term also ap-plies to the physical elements of a theatrical produc-tion, such as scenery and properties. Setting is an important element in the creation of atmosphere.

Shishōsetsu: Literally translated as "I novel," *shishōsetsu* is a Japanese genre, a form of autobio-graphical or confessional writing used in novels and short stories. The protagonist and writer are closely identified. The genre originated in the early part of the twentieth century; a good example is *An'ya Koro* (1921-1928; *A Dark Night's Passing*, 1958) by Shiga Naoya.

Short story: A concise work of fiction, shorter than a novella, that is usually more concerned with mood, effect, or a single event than with plot or extensive characterization.

Signifier/Signified: Linguist Ferdinand de Saussure proposed that all words are signs made up of a "sig-nifier," which is the written mark or the spoken sound of the word, and a "signified," which is the concept for which the mark or sounds stands.

Simile: A type of metaphor in which two things are compared. It can usually be recognized by the use of the words "like," "as," "appears," or "seems": "Float like a butterfly, sting like a bee" (Muhammad Ali); "The holy time is quiet as a nun" (William Wordsworth).

Skaz: A term used in Russian criticism to describe a narrative technique that presents an oral narrative of a lowbrow speaker.

Sketch: A brief narrative form originating in the eigh-teenth century, derived from the artist's sketch. The focus of a sketch is on a single person, place, or inci-dent; it lacks a developed plot, theme, or characterization.

Story line: The story line of a work of fiction differs from the plot. Story line is merely the events that happen; plot is how those events are arranged by the author to suggest a cause-and-effect relationship.

Stream of consciousness: A narrative technique used in modern fiction by which an author tries to embody the total range of consciousness of a character, without any authorial comment or explanation. Sen-sations, thoughts, memories, and associations pour out in an uninterrupted, prerational and prelogical flow. Examples are James Joyce's *Ulysses* (1922), Virginia Woolf's *To the Lighthouse* (1927), and Wil-liam Faulkner's *The Sound and the Fury* (1929).

Structuralism: Structuralism is based on the idea of intrinsic, self-sufficient structures that do not require reference to external elements. A structure is a system of transformations that involves the interplay of laws inherent in the system itself. The structuralist literary critic attempts, by using models derived from modern linguistic theory, to define the structural principles that operate intertextually throughout the whole of literature, as well as principles that operate in genres and in individual works.

Style: Style is the manner of expression, or how the writer tells the story. The most appropriate style is that which is perfectly suited to conveying whatever idea, emotion, or other effect that the author wishes to convey. Elements of style include diction, sentence structure, imagery, rhythm, and coherence.

Subjective/Objective: Terms used in critical theory. Subjective refers to works that express the ideas and emotions, the values and judgments of the authors, such as William Wordsworth's *The Prelude* (1850). Objective works are those that appear to be free of the personal sentiments of authors, who take a detached view of the events they record.

Supplement: A term used by Jacques Derrida to refer to the unstable relationship between the two elements in a set of binary opposites. For example, in the opposition between truth and lies, although Western thought assumes that truth is superior to lies, closer study reveals that so-called lies frequently reveal profound truths.

Symbolism: A literary movement encompassing the work of a group of French writers in the latter half of the nineteenth century, a group that included Charles Baudelaire, Stéphane Mallarmé, and Paul Verlaine. According to Symbolism, a mystical correspondence exists between the natural and spiritual worlds.

Synesthesia: Synesthesia occurs when one kind of sense experience is described in terms of another. Sounds may be described in terms of colors, and so on. For example, these lines from John Keats's poem "Isabella," "O turn thee to the very tale,/ And taste the music of that vision pale," combine the senses of taste, hearing, and

sight. Synesthesia was used especially by the nineteenth century French Symbolists.

Tale: A general term for a simple prose or verse narrative. In the context of the short story, a tale is a story in which the emphasis is on the course of the action rather than on the minds of the characters.

Tall tale: A humorous tale popular in the American West; the story usually makes use of realistic detail and common speech, but it tells a tale of impossible events that most often focus on a single legendary, superhuman figure, such as Paul Bunyan or David Crockett.

Technique: Refers both to the method of procedure in creating an artistic work and to the degree of expertise shown in following the procedure.

Thematics: According to Northrop Frye, when a work of fiction is written or interpreted thematically, it becomes an illustrative fable. Murray Krieger defines thematics in *The Tragic Vision* (1960) as "the study of the experiential tensions which, dramatically entangled in the literary work, become an existential reflection of that work's aesthetic complexity."

Theme: Loosely defined as what a literary work means, theme is the underlying idea, the abstract concept, that the author is trying to convey: "the search for love," "the growth of wisdom," or some such formulation. The theme of William Butler Yeats's poem "Sailing to Byzantium" (1928), for example, might be interpreted as the failure of the attempt to isolate oneself within the world of art.

Tone: Strictly defined, tone is the authors' attitude toward their subject, their persona, themselves, their audience, or their society. The tone of a work may be serious, playful, formal, informal, morose, loving, ironic, and so on; it can be thought of as the dominant mood of a work, and it plays a large part in the total effect.

Trope: Literally "turn" or "conversion"; a figure of speech in which a word or phrase is used in a way that deviates from the normal or literal sense.

Vehicle: Used with the term "tenor" to understand the two elements of a metaphor. The tenor is the subject of the metaphor, and the vehicle is the image by which the subject is presented. The terms were coined by I. A. Richards. As an example, in T. S. Eliot's line, "The whole earth is our hospital," the tenor is "whole earth" and the vehicle is the "hospital."

Verisimilitude: When used in literary criticism, verisimilitude refers to the degree to which a literary work gives the appearance of being true or real, even though the events depicted may in fact be far removed from the actual.

Vignette: A sketch, essay, or brief narrative characterized by precision, economy, and grace. The term can also be applied to brief short stories, less than five hundred words long.

Yarn: An oral tale or a written transcription of what purports to be an oral tale. The yarn is usually a broadly comic tale, the classic example of which is Mark Twain's "Jim Baker's Bluejay Yarn" (1879). The yarn achieves its comic effect by juxtaposing realistic detail and incredible events; tellers of the tale protest that they are telling the truth; listeners know differently.

Bryan Aubrey
Updated by Charles E. May

BIBLIOGRAPHY

THEORETICAL AND CRITICAL DISCUSSIONS OF SHORT FICTION

Aycock, Wendell M., ed. *The Teller and the Tale: Aspects of the Short Story*. Lubbock: Texas Tech Press, 1982. A collection of papers presented at a scholarly conference focusing on various aspects of short fiction, including its oral roots, the use of silences in the text, and realism versus antirealism.

Bader, A. L. "The Structure of the Modern Short Story." *College English* 7 (1945): 86-92. Counters the charge that the short story lacks narrative structure by contrasting the traditional "plotted" story with the "modern story," which is more suggestive, indirect, and technically patterned.

Baker, Falcon O. "Short Stories for the Millions." *Saturday Review*, December 19, 1953, 7-9, 48-49. Argues that as a result of formalist New Criticism, the short story has begun to ignore entertainment value and the ordinary reader.

Baldeshwiler, Eileen. "The Lyric Short Story: The Sketch of a History." *Studies in Short Fiction* 6 (1969): 443-453. A brief survey of the lyrical (as opposed to the epical) story from Ivan Turgenev to John Updike. The lyric story focuses on internal changes, moods, and feelings, using a variety of structural patterns depending on the "shape of the emotion itself."

Bates, H. E. *The Modern Short Story: A Critical Survey*. Boston: The Writer, 1941, 1972. A history of the major short-story writers and their work since Edgar Allan Poe and Nikolai Gogol. More focus on English and European short-story writers than most histories.

Bayley, John. *The Short Story: Henry James to Elizabeth Bowen*. New York: St. Martin's Press, 1988. A discussion of some of what Bayley calls the "special effects" of the short-story form, particularly its relationship to poetic techniques and devices. Much of the book consists of analyses of significant stories by Henry James, Ernest Hemingway, Rudyard Kipling, Anton Chekhov, D. H. Lawrence, James Joyce, and Elizabeth Bowen.

Benjamin, Walter. "The Storyteller: Reflections on the Words of Nikolai Leskov." Reprinted in *Modern Literary Criticism: 1900-1970*, *edited by* Lawrence Lipking and A. Walton Litz. New York: Atheneum, 1972. Benjamin claims that the art of storytelling is coming to an end because of the widespread dissemination of information and explanation. The compactness of a story precludes analysis and appeals to readers through the rhythm of the work itself. For the storyteller, the old religious chronicle is secularized into an ambiguous network in which the worldly and the eschatological are interwoven.

Bonheim, Helmut. *The Narrative Modes: Techniques of the Short Story*. Cambridge, England: D. S. Brewer, 1982. A systematic and statistical study of the short-story form, focusing on basic short-story techniques, especially short-story beginnings and endings. Argues that a limited set of techniques is used repeatedly in story endings. Discusses open and closed endings and argues that dynamic modes are more apt to be open, while static ones are more apt to be closed.

Boulanger, Daniel. "On the Short Story." *Michigan Quarterly Review* 26 (Summer, 1987): 510-514. A highly metaphoric and impressionistic study of the form, focusing primarily on the detached nature of the short story. Claims that there is a bit of Pontius Pilate in the short-story writer, for he or she is always removed from the tragic outcome. Points out how there are no class distinctions in the short story and no hierarchy.

Bowen, Elizabeth, ed. *The Faber Book of Modern Short Stories*. London: Faber & Faber, 1936. Bowen suggests that the short story, because it is exempt from the novel's often forced conclusiveness, more often approaches aesthetic and moral truth. She also suggests that the short story, more than the novel, is able to place the individual alone on that "stage which, inwardly, every man is conscious of occupying alone."

Brickell, Herschel. "What Happened to the Short Story?" *The Atlantic Monthly* 188 (September, 1951): 74-76. Argues that many contemporary writers have succeeded in breaking the short story away from its formal frame by drawing it nearer to poetry.

Brown, Suzanne Hunter. "The Chronotope of the Short Story: Time, Character, and Brevity." In *Creative and Critical Approaches to the Short Story*, *edited by* Noel Harold Kaylor, Jr. Lewiston, N.Y.: Edwin Mellen Press, 1997. A survey and analysis of the frequent critical assumption that short stories deal with characters as eternal essence and that novels deal with characters who change over time. Argues that Mikhail Bakhtin's concept of "chronotrope," a literary work's projection of time and space, will help develop a generic theory of the short story that considers both historical and technical factors.

_____. "Discourse Analysis and the Short Story." In *Short Story Theory at a Crossroads*, *edited by* Susan Lohafer and Jo Ellyn Clarey. Baton Rouge: Louisiana State University Press, 1989. A helpful analytical survey of the research being conducted by psychologists into the nature of discourse, storyness, and cognitive response to narrative.

Cortázar, Julio. "Some Aspects of the Short Story." *Arizona Quarterly*, Spring, 1982, 5-17. Cortázar, an Argentine writer and notable practitioner of the short story, discusses the invariable elements that give a good short story its particular atmosphere. He compares the novel and the short story to film and the photograph; the short story's most significant element is its subject, the act of choosing a real or imaginary happening that has the mysterious property of illuminating something beyond itself.

Cox, Alisa, ed. *The Short Story*. Newcastle, England: Cambridge Scholars, 2008. A collection of essays that provides a critical international overview of short fiction. Includes A. L. Kennedy's reflections on writing short stories, a discussion of the contemporary short story sequence, an essay pondering a definition of the short story, and analyses of stories by Italo Calvino, Jorge Luis Borges, Anita Desai, Martin Amis, Ray Bradbury, and others.

Dawson, W. J. "The Modern Short Story." *North American Review* 190 (December, 1909): 799-810. Argues that a short story must be complete in itself and consist of a single incident. The finest writing in a short story, Dawson maintains, is that which takes the reader most quickly to the very heart of the matter at hand.

Eichenbaum, Boris. *O. Henry and the Theory of the Short Story*. Translated by I. R. Titunik. Ann Arbor: University of Michigan, 1968. Originally published in 1925, this essay is a good example of the early Russian Formalist approach to fiction through a consideration of genre. Eichenbaum poses a generic distinction between the novel and the short story. Short stories are constructed on the basis of a contradiction, incongruity, error, or contrast and, like the anecdote, build their weight toward the ending.

Eldred, Janet Carey. "Narratives of Socialization: Literacy in the Short Story." *College English* 53 (October, 1991): 686-700. Based on the critical assumption that all fiction historicizes problems of socialization. Argues that the short story is a narrative of arrested socialization that ends with characters between two cultures who find their own speech inadequate but their new language problematic.

Elliott, George P. "A Defense of Fiction." *Hudson Review* 16 (1963): 9-48. Elliott, himself a short-story writer, discusses the four basic impulses that mingle with the storytelling impulse: to dream, to tell what happened, to explain the sense of things, and to make a likeness.

Ermida, Isabel. *The Language of Comic Narratives: Humor Construction in Short Stories*. New York: Mouton de Gruyter, 2008. Analyzes how humor works in short fiction, examining short stories by Dorothy Parker, Graham Greene, Woody Allen, David Lodge, Evelyn Waugh, and other English and American writers.

Farrell, James T. *The League of Frightened Philistines and Other Papers*. New York: Vanguard Press, 1945. Ridicules the short-story handbooks published in the 1920's and 1930's and claims that in many contemporary short stories, the revolutionary point of view appears more tacked on than integral to the story.

Ferguson, Suzanne C. "Defining the Short Story: Impressionism and Form." *Modern Fiction Studies* 28 (Spring, 1982): 13-24. Argues that there is no single characteristic or cluster of characteristics that distinguishes the short story from the novel. Suggests that what is called the modern short story is a manifestation of impressionism rather than a discrete genre.

_____. "The Rise of the Short Story in the Hierarchy of Genres." In *Short Story Theory at a Crossroads*, *edited by* Susan Lohafer and Jo Ellyn Clarey. Baton Rouge: Louisiana State University Press, 1989. A historical and critical survey of the development of the English short story, showing how social factors influenced the rise and fall of the form's prestige.

FitzGerald, Gregory. "The Satiric Short Story: A Definition." *Studies in Short Fiction* 5 (1968): 349-354. Defines the satiric short story as a subgenre that sustains a reductive attack upon its objects and conveys to its readers a significance different from its apparent surface meaning.

Fonlon, Bernard, "The Philosophy, the Science, and the Art of the Short Story, Part II." *Abbia* 34 (1979): 429-438. A discussion of the basic elements of a story, including character and conflict. Lists elements of intensity, detachment, skill, and unity of effect. Primarily presents a set of rules aimed at inexperienced writers.

Friedman, Norman. "Recent Short Story Theories: Problems in Definition." In *Short Story Theory at a Crossroads*, *edited by* Susan Lohafer and Jo Ellyn Clarey. Baton Rouge: Louisiana State University Press, 1989. A critical review of major short-story critics, including Mary Rohrberger, Charles May, Susan Lohafer, and John Gerlach. Argues against those critics who support a deductive, single-term, mixed category approach to definition of the form. Urges that what is needed is a more inductive approach that follows the principle of suiting the definition to the facts rather than trying to suit the facts to the definition.

_____. "What Makes a Short Story Short?" *Modern Fiction Studies* 4 (1958): 103-117. Makes use of neo-Aristotelian literary theory to determine the issue of the short story's shortness. To deal with the problem, Friedman argues, one must ask the following questions: What is the size of the action? Is the action composed of a speech, a scene, an episode, or a plot? Does the action involve a change? If so, is the change a major one or a minor one?

Gerlach, John. "The Margins of Narrative: The Very Short Story, the Prose Poem, and the Lyric." In *Short Story Theory at a Crossroads*, *edited by* Susan Lohafer and Jo Ellyn Clarey. Baton Rouge: Louisiana State University Press, 1989. Explores the basic requirements of a story, focusing particularly on two minimalist stories by Enrique Anderson Imbert and Scott Sanders, as well as a short prose poem by W. S. Merwin. Argues that point, not mere length nor fictionality, is the principal constituent of story.

Gordimer, Nadine. "South Africa." *The Kenyon Review* 30 (1968): 457-461. Gordimer, a Nobel Prize-winning writer, argues that the strongest convention of the novel, its prolonged coherence of tone, is false to the nature of what can be grasped as reality in the modern world. Short-story writers deal with the only thing one can be sure of--the present moment.

Görtschacher, Wolfgang, and Holger Klein, eds. *Tale, Novella, Short Story: Currents in Short Fiction*. Tübingen, Germany: Stauffenburg, 2004. Reprints the papers delivered at the Tenth International Salzburg Conference, which focused on the short fictional forms of the tale, novella, and short story. Among the topics discussed are the influence of English short fiction on historical texts, such as *The Arabian Nights' Entertainments*; theoretical issues, including the aesthetic principles of compactness and brevity; and analyses of contemporary short fiction from Australia, Africa, the United States, Great Britain, and Ireland.

Gullason, Thomas A. "Revelation and Evolution: A Neglected Dimension of the Short Story." *Studies in Short Fiction* 10 (1973): 347-356. Challenges Mark Schorer's distinction between the short story as an "art of moral revelation" and the novel as an "art of moral evolution." Analyzes D. H. Lawrence's "The Horse Dealer's Daughter" and John Steinbeck's "The Chrysanthemums" to show that the short story embodies both revelation and evolution.

_____. "The Short Story: An Underrated Art." *Studies in Short Fiction* 2 (1964): 13-31. Points out the lack of serious criticism of the short story, suggests some of the reasons for this neglect, and concludes with an analysis of Anton Chekhov's "Gooseberries" and Nadine Gordimer's "The Train from Rhodesia" to disprove the charges that the short story is formulaic and lacks life.

Hanson, Clare, ed. Introduction to *Re-Reading the Short Story*. New York: St. Martin's Press, 1989. Claims that the short story is a vehicle for different kinds of knowledge, knowledge that may be in some way at odds with the "story" of dominant culture. The formal properties of the short story--disjunction, inconclusiveness, and obliquity--connect with its ideological marginality and with the fact that the form may be used to express something suppressed or repressed in mainstream literature.

_____. *Short Stories and Short Fictions, 1880-1980*. New York: St. Martin's Press, 1985. Argues that during this period, the authority of the teller, usually a first-person "framing" narrator who guaranteed the authenticity of the tale, was questioned by many modernist writers. Argues that the movements from "teller" to indirect free narration, and from "tale" to "text," were part of a more general movement from "discourse" to "image" in the art and literature of the period. Includes chapters on Rudyard Kipling, Saki, W. Somerset Maugham, James Joyce, Virginia Woolf, Katherine Mansfield, Samuel Beckett.

_____. "Things out of Words: Towards a Poetics of Short Fiction." In *Re-Reading the Short Story*, *edited by* Clare Hanson. New York: St. Martin's Press, 1989. Argues that the short story is a more literary form than the novel. Maintains that short stories are framed, an aesthetic device that gives a sense of completeness that allows gaps and absences to remain in the story; thus readers accept a degree of mystery or elision in the short story that they would not accept in the novel.

Hardy, Sarah. "A Poetics of Immediacy: Oral Narrative and the Short Story." *Style* 27 (Fall, 1993): 352-368. Argues that the oral-epic episode clarifies basic characteristics of the short story: It gives the reader a way to understand the density of meaning in the short story and provides a paradigm of the short-story audience as that of a participating community.

Hedberg, Johannes. "What Is a 'Short Story?' and What Is an 'Essay'?" *Moderna Sprak* 74 (1980): 113-120. Reminds readers of the distinction between the Chekhovian story (lack of plot) and the Maupassantian story (anecdotal and therefore commercial). Discusses basic characteristics of the essay and the story; maintains they are similar in that they are both a whole picture in miniature, not merely a detail of a larger picture--a complete work, not an extract.

Hendricks, William O. "Methodology of Narrative Structural Analysis." In *Essays in Semiolinguistics and Verbal Art*. The Hague, Netherlands: Mouton, 1973. Structuralists, in the tradition of Vladimir Propp and Claude Levi-Strauss, usually bypass the actual sentences of a narrative and analyze a synopsis. This essay is a fairly detailed discussion of the methodology of synopsizing (using William Faulkner's "A Rose for Emily" as an example), followed by a brief discussion of the methodology of structural analysis of the resultant synopsis.

Hesse, Douglas. "A Boundary Zone: First-Person Short Stories and Narrative Essays." In *Short Story Theory at a Crossroads*, *edited by* Susan Lohafer and Jo Ellyn Clarey. Baton Rouge: Louisiana State University Press, 1989. Argues that the precise boundary point between essays and short stories does not exist. Analyzes George Orwell's essay "A Hanging" as a short story and William Carlos Williams's short story "Use of Force" as an essay. Discusses essays and stories that fall in a boundary zone between essay and story.

Hicks, Granville. "The Art of the Short Story." *Saturday Review* 41 (December 20, 1958): 16. Maintains that the focus of the contemporary short story is an emotional experience for the reader rather than character or plot.

Holloway, John. "Identity, Inversion, and Density Elements in Narrative: Three Tales by Chekhov, James, and Lawrence." In *Narrative and Structure: Exploratory Essays*. Cambridge, England. Cambridge University Press, 1979. Holloway looks at stories in which almost nothing happens. He says there is a distinctive kind of narrative episode introduced by an item that is then followed by another item in inverse relationship to the first, which cancels it out and brings the reader back to where he or she started.

Howe, Irving. "Tone in the Short Story." *Sewanee Review* 57 (Winter, 1949): 141-152. Maintains that because the short story lacks prolonged characterization and a structured plot, it depends mostly on tone to hold it together.

Ibáñez, José R., José Francisco Fernández, and Carmen M. Bretones, eds. *Contemporary Debates on the Short Story*. New York: Peter Lang, 2007. Collection of critical essays about short fiction, some of which are written from the perspectives of globalization and deconstructionism. Includes a discussion of dissent in the modern Irish short story; an overview of short fiction, including a historical overview of the mystery story; and analyses of short fiction by Wyndham Lewis, Henry James, Salman Rushdie, and Judith Ortiz Cofer.

"International Symposium on the Short Story" in *Kenyon Review*. Contributions from short-story writers from all over the world on the nature of the form, its current economic status, its history, and its significance. Part 1, vol. 30, no. 4 (1969): 443-490 features contributions by Christina Stead (England), Herbert Gold (United States), Erih Koš (Yugoslavia), Nadine Gordimer (South Africa), Benedict Kiely (Ireland), Hugh Hood (Canada), and Henrietta Drake-Brockman (Australia); part 2, vol. 31, no. 1 (1969): 58-94 contains comments by William Saroyan (United States), Jun Eto (Japan), Maurice Shadbolt (New Zealand), Chanakya Sen (India), John Wain (England), and Hans Bender (Germany) and "An Agent's View" by James Oliver Brown; part 3, vol. 31, no. 4 (1969): 450-502 features Ana María Matute (Spain), Torborg Nedreaas (Norway), George Garrett (United States), Elizabeth Taylor (England), Ezekiel Mphahlele (South Africa), Elizabeth Harrower (Australia), Mario Picchi (Italy), Junzo Shono (Japan), and Khushwant Singh (India); part 4, vol. 32, no. 1 (1969): 78-108 includes Jack Cope (South Africa), James T. Farrell (United States), Edward Hyams (England), Luigi Barzini (Italy), David Ballantyne (New Zealand), and H. E. Bates (England).

Jarrell, Randall. "Stories." In *The Anchor Book of Stories*. New York: Doubleday, 1958. Jarrell's introduction to this collection focuses on stories as being closer to dream reality than the waking world of everyday life. He argues that there are basically two kinds of stories: stories in which everything is a happening (in which each event is so charged that the narrative threatens to disintegrate into energy), and stories in which nothing happens (in which even the climax may lose its charge and become one more portion of a lyric continuum).

Jouve, Nicole Ward. "Too Short for a Book." In *Re-Reading the Short Story*, edited by Clare Hanson. New York: St. Martin's Press, 1989. An impressionistic, noncritical essay about story length. Discusses *The Arabian Nights' Entertainments* as an archetypal model standing behind all stories, collections of stories, and storytelling. Makes a case for collections of stories that stand together as organic wholes rather than single individual stories that stand alone.

Lewis, C. S. "On Stories." In *Essays Presented to Charles Williams*. Grand Rapids, Mich.: Wm. B. Eerdmans, 1966. Although stories are series of events, this series, or what is called plot, is only a necessary means to capture something that has no sequence, something more like a state or quality. Thus, the "means" of a story is always at war with its "end"; this very tension, however, constitutes the story's chief resemblance to life: "We grasp at a state and find only a succession of events in which the state is never quite embodied."

Lohafer, Susan. "A Cognitive Approach to Story-Ness." *Short Story* (Spring, 1990), 60-71. A study of what Lohafer calls "preclosure," those points in a story where it could end but does not. Studies the characters of such preclosure sentences--where they appear and what they signal--as part of a more general effort to clarify what constitutes story-ness.

_____. *Coming to Terms with the Short Story*. Baton Rouge: Louisiana State University Press, 1983. A highly suggestive theoretical study of the short story that focuses on the sentence unit of the form as a way of showing how it differs from the novel.

_____. "Interdisciplinary Thoughts on Cognitive Science and Short Fiction Studies." In *The Tales We Tell: Perspectives on the Short Story*, edited by Barbara Lounsberry et al. Westport, Conn.: Greenwood Press, 1998. A brief summary of psychological approaches to cognitive strategies for reading short fiction. Makes a number of suggestions about the future of short-story criticism based on the cooperation between narrative theorists and cognitive scientists.

_____. "Preclosure and Story Processing." In *Short Story Theory at a Crossroads*, edited by Susan Lohafer and Jo Ellyn Clarey. Baton Rouge: Louisiana State University Press, 1989. Analyzes responses to a story by Kate Chopin in terms of identifying those sentences that could end the story but do not. This essay is a continuation of Lohafer's study of what she has defined as preclosure in short fiction.

_____. "Preclosure in an 'Open' Story." In *Creative and Critical Approaches to the Short Story*, edited by Noel Harold Kaylor, Jr. Lewiston, N.Y.: Edwin Mellen Press, 1997. Presents the results of an experiment in preclosure studies in which 114 students were asked to read Julio Cortázar's story "Orientation of Cats" and report on their understanding of it. Lohafer asks the students to identify points at which the story might have ended, a preclosure procedure that makes them more aware of reading tactics and their inherent sense of story-ness.

_____. *Reading for Storyness: Preclosure Theory, Empirical Poetics, and Culture in the Short Story*. Baltimore: Johns Hopkins University Press, 2003. Lohafer discusses many of the literary theories presented in her previous articles, arguing that "imminent closure" is the defining trait of the short story. She demonstrates her theories by analyzing stories by Kate Chopin, Katherine Mansfield, Julio Cortázar, Raymond Carver, Bobbie Ann Mason, Ann Beattie, and other writers.

_____. "Why the 'Life of Ma Parker' Is Not So Simple: Preclosure in Issue-Bound Stories." *Studies in Short Fiction* 33 (Fall, 1996): 475-486. In this particular experiment with student reaction to preclosure markers in a story by Katherine Mansfield, Lohafer is interested in showing how attention to preclosure encourages readers to temporarily suppress their ready-made concepts and engage their story competence.

March-Russell, Paul. *The Short Story: An Introduction*. Edinburgh: Edinburgh University Press, 2009. Historical overview of short fiction, defining its origins, the concept of the well-made story, the short story cycle, and specific types of stories, such as ghost stories and modernist, postmodernist, minimalist, and postcolonial short fiction.

Marcus, Mordecai. "What Is an Initiation Story?" *The Journal of Aesthetics and Art Criticism* 14 (1960): 221-227. Distinguishes three types of initiation stories: those that lead protagonists only to the threshold of maturity, those that take the protagonists across the threshold of maturity but leave them in a struggle for certainty, and decisive initiation stories that carry protagonists firmly into maturity.

Matthews, Brander. *The Philosophy of the Short-Story*. New York: Longmans, Green, 1901. An expansion of an 1882 article in which Matthews sets himself forth as the first critic since Edgar Allan Poe to discuss the "short-story" (Matthews contributed the hyphen) as a genre. By asserting that the short story must have a vigorous compression, must be original, must be ingenious, must have a touch of fantasy, and so on, Matthews set the stage for the subsequent host of textbook writers on the short story.

Maugham, W. Somerset. "The Short Story." In *Points of View: Five Essays*. Garden City, N.Y.: Doubleday, 1958. As might be expected, Maugham's preference is for the well-made story exemplified by Guy de Maupassant's "The Necklace." Most of the essay, however, deals with biographical material about Anton Chekhov and Katherine Mansfield.

May, Charles E. "Artifice and Artificiality in the Short Story." *Story* 1 (Spring, 1990): 72-82. Discusses the artificial and formalized nature of the endings of short stories, arguing that the short story is the most aesthetic narrative form. Discusses the ending of several representative stories.

_____. "Metaphoric Motivation in Short Fiction: 'In the Beginning Was the Story.'" In *Short Theory at a Crossroads*, edited by Susan Lohafer and Jo Ellyn Clarey. Baton Rouge: Louisiana State University Press, 1989. A discussion of how short fiction moves from the "tale" form to the "short story" form through motivation by metaphor in "The Fall of the House of Usher," "Bartleby the Scrivener," "The Legend of Sleepy Hollow," and "Young Goodman Brown."

_____. "The Nature of Knowledge in Short Fiction." *Studies in Short Fiction* 21 (Fall, 1984): 227-238. A theoretical study of the epistemological bases of short fiction. Argues that the short story originates as a primal mythic mode that develops into a metaphoric mode.

_____. "Obsession and the Short Story." In *Creative and Critical Approaches to the Short Story*, edited by Noel Harold Kaylor, Jr. Lewiston, N.Y.: Edwin Mellen Press, 1997. An examination of the common charge that the short story is unhealthily limited and obsessed. Discusses the origins of the relationship between psychological obsession and aesthetic unity in the stories of Edgar Allan Poe, Nathaniel Hawthorne, and Herman Melville. Attempts to account for this relationship as a generic characteristic of the short story.

_____. "Prolegomenon to a Generic Study of the Short Story." *Studies in Short Fiction* 33 (Fall, 1996): 461-474. Tries to lay the groundwork for a generic theory of the short story in terms of new theories of this genre. Discusses the short story's historical focus on the strange and unexpected and the formal demands made by this thematic focus. Argues for a mixed genre theory of the short story that can account for the form's essential, as well as historically changing, characteristics.

_____. "Reality in the Modern Short Story. *Style* 27 (Fall, 1993): 369-379. Argues that realism in the modern short story from Anton Chekhov to Raymond Carver is not the simple mimesis of the realistic novel but rather the use of highly compressed selective detail configured to metaphorically

objectify that which cannot be described directly. The result is a "hyperrealism" in which story is unified by tone and meaning is created by aesthetic pattern.

_____. *The Short Story: The Reality of Artifice*. New York: Routledge, 2002. A historical survey of the short story, tracing its origins in the tales of Geoffrey Chaucer and Giovanni Boccaccio through the nineteenth-century and its contemporary renaissance.

_____. *Short Story Theories*. Athens: Ohio University Press, 1976. A collection of twenty previously published essays on the short story as a genre in its own right.

_____. "A Survey of Short Story Criticism in America." *The Minnesota Review*, Spring, 1973, 163-169. An analytical survey of criticism beginning with Edgar Allan Poe and focusing on the short story's underlying vision and characteristic mode of understanding and confronting reality.

_____. "The Unique Effect of the Short Story: A Reconsideration and an Example." *Studies in Short Fiction* 13 (1976): 289-297. An attempt to redefine Edgar Allan Poe's "unique effect" in the short story in terms of mythic perception. Maintains that the short story demands intense compression and focusing because its essential subject is a manifestation of what philosopher Ernst Cassirer calls the "momentary deity." A detailed discussion of Stephen Crane's story "An Episode of War" illustrates the concept.

McSweeney, Kerry. *The Realist Short Story of the Powerful Glimpse: Chekhov to Carver*. Columbia: University of South Carolina Press, 2007. Focuses on the short fiction of five writers--Anton Chekhov, James Joyce, Ernest Hemingway, Flannery O'Connor, and Raymond Carver--to argue that the realist realist short story is a "glimpse--powerful and tightly focused, into a world that the writer must precisely craft and in which the reader must fully invest."

Menikoff, Barry. "The Problematics of Form: History and the Short Story." *Journal of the Short Story in English*, no. 2 (1984): 129-146. After a brief introduction discussing how the short story has been neglected, Menikoff comments briefly on the importance of Charles E. May's *Short Story Theories*

(1976) and then discusses essays on the short story that appeared in *Critical Survey of Short Fiction* (1981) and a special issue of *Modern Fiction Studies* (1982).

Miall, David. "Text and Affect: A Model for Story Understanding." In *Re-Reading the Short Story*, edited by Clare Hanson. New York: St. Martin's Press, 1989. A discussion of what readers are doing in emotional terms when they read, using the defamiliarization model of the Russian Formalists. Focuses on three aspects of emotion: self-reference, domain crossing, and anticipation. Basically determines that whereas literary texts constrain response by means of their shared frames and conventions, their affective responses are highly divergent.

Millhauser, Steven. "The Ambition of the Short Story." *The New York Times Book Review*, October 5, 2008, p. 31. Discussion of the short story's essential characteristics and how the form differs from the novel.

Moffett, James. "Telling Stories: Methods of Abstraction in Fiction." *ETC* 21 (1964): 425-450. Charts a sequence covering an "entire range" of ways in which stories can be told, from the most subjective and personal (interior monologue and dramatic monologue) to the most objective and impersonal (anonymous narration). Includes examples of each type.

Moravia, Alberto. "The Short Story and the Novel." In *Man as End: A Defense of Humanism*. Translated by Bernard Wall. New York: Farrar, Straus & Giroux, 1969. Moravia, who wrote many novels and short stories, maintains that the basic difference between the two is that the novel has a bone structure of ideological themes whereas the short story is made up of intuitions of feelings.

Munson, Gorham. "The Recapture of the Storyable." *University Review* 10 (Autumn, 1943): 37-44. Maintains that the best short-story writers are concerned with only three questions: whether they have found a "storyable" incident, how they should cast their characters, and who would best tell their story.

Oates, Joyce Carol. "Beginnings: The Origin and Art of the Short Story." In *The Tales We Tell: Perspectives on the Short Story*, edited by Barbara Lounsberry et al. Westport, Conn.: Greenwood Press, 1998.

Defines the short story as a form that represents an intensification of meaning rather than an expansion of the imagination. Briefly discusses the importance of Edgar Allan Poe's aesthetic and Mark Twain's oral tale to the development of the American short story.

_____. "The Short Story." *Southern Humanities Review* 5 (1971): 213-214. Maintains that the short story is a "dream verbalized," a manifestation of desire; its most interesting aspect is its "mystery."

O'Connor, Frank. *The Lonely Voice: A Study of the Short Story*. 1963. Reprint. Hoboken, N.J.: Melville House, 2004. O'Connor, an accomplished master of the short-story form, presented his observations of the genre in this study. The introductory chapter contains extremely valuable "intuitive" criticism. O'Connor maintains that the basic difference between the novel and the short story is that in the latter readers always find an intense awareness of human loneliness. He believes that the protagonist of the short story is less an individual with whom readers can identify than a "submerged population group," that is, someone outside the social mainstream. The remaining chapters of the book treat this theme in the works of Ivan Turgenev, Anton Chekhov, Guy de Maupassant, Rudyard Kipling, James Joyce, Katherine Mansfield, D. H. Lawrence, A. E. Coppard, Isaac Babel, and Mary Lavin.

O'Faoláin, Seán. *The Short Story*. New York: Devin-Adair, 1951. This book on the technique of the short story claims that technique is the "least part of the business." O'Faoláin illustrates his thesis that personality is the most important element in short fiction by describing the personal struggles of Alphonse Daudet, Anton Chekhov, and Guy de Maupassant. He does his duty to the assigned subject of the book by also discussing the technical problems of convention, subject, construction, and language.

O'Rourke, William. "Morphological Metaphors for the Short Story: Matters of Production, Reproduction, and Consumption." In *Short Story Theory at a Crossroads*, edited by Susan Lohafer and Jo Ellyn Clarey. Baton Rouge: Louisiana State University Press, 1989. Explores a number of analogies drawn from the social and natural sciences to suggest ways of seeing how the short story is different from the novel: The novel has a structure like a vertebrate, whereas the short story is like an animal with an exoskeleton; the novel is a macro form, whereas the short story is a micro form.

Overstreet, Bonaro. "Little Story, What Now?" *Saturday Review of Literature*, 24 (November 22, 1941): 3-5, 25-26. Overstreet argues that as a result of a loss of faith in the old verities of the nineteenth century, the twentieth-century short story is concerned with psychological materials, not with the events in the objective world.

Pain, Barry. *The Short Story*. London: Martin Secker, 1916. Pain claims that the primary difference between the short story and the novel is that the short story, because of its dependence on suggestive devices, demands more of the reader's participation.

Palakeel, Thomas. "Third World Short Story as National Allegory?" *Journal of Modern Literature* 20 (Summer, 1996): 97-102. Argues against Frederic Jameson's claim that Third World fictions are always national allegories. Points out that this claim is even more damaging to the short story than to the novel because the short story is the most energetic literary activity in the Third World. He argues that Jameson's theory cripples any non-Western literature that tries to deal with the psychological or spiritual reality of the individual.

Pasco, Allan H. "The Short Story: The Short of It." *Style* 27 (Fall, 1993): 442-451. Suggests a list of qualities of the short story generated by its brevity, such as the assumptions of considerable background on the part of the readers and that readers will absorb and remember all elements of the work. Claims that the short story shuns amplification in favor of inference, that it is usually single rather than multivalent, that it tends toward the general, and that it remains foreign to loosely motivated detail.

Patrick, Walton R. "Poetic Style in the Contemporary Short Story." *College Composition and Communication* (1957): 77-84. Argues that the poetic style appears more consistently in the short story than in the novel because metaphorical dilations are

essential to the writer who "strives to pack the utmost meaning into his restricted space."

Penn, W. S. "The Tale as Genre in Short Fiction." *Southern Humanities Review* 15 (Summer, 1981): 231-241. Discusses the genre from the perspective of structure. Primarily uses suggestions made by Jonathan Culler in *Structuralist Poetics* for constructing a poetic persona in the lyric poem, what Culler calls an "enunciative posture," that is, the detectable or intuited moral relation of the implied author to both the world at large and the world he or she creates. Develops two kinds of tales: the radical oral and the exponential oral.

Perry, Bliss. *A Study of Prose Fiction*. Boston: Houghton Mifflin, 1920. Perry claims that the short story differs from the novel by presenting unique and original characters, by focusing on fragments of reality, and by making use of the poetic devices of impressionism and symbolism.

Pickering, Jean. "Time and the Short Story." In *Re-Reading the Short Story*, edited by Clare Hanson. New York: St. Martin's Press, 1989. Discusses the distinction between the short story as an art of revelation and the novel as an art of evolution. General implications that derive from this distinction are that short-story writers do not need to know all the details of their characters' lives and that the short story is doubly symbolic. Structure, theme, characterization, and language are influenced by the short story's particular relation to time as a moment of revelation.

Poe, Edgar Allan. Review of *Twice-Told Tales*. *Graham's Magazine*, May, 1842. The first critical discussion of the short story, or the "tale" as Poe terms it, to establish the genre as distinct from the novel. Because of its sense of totality, its single effect, and its patterned design, the short story is second only to the lyric in its demands on high genius and in its aesthetic beauty.

Pratt, Mary Louise. "The Short Story: The Long and the Short of It." *Poetics* 10 (1981): 175-194. A theoretical discussion of the form. Presents eight ways that the short story is better understood if its dependence on the novel is understood.

Prince, Gerald. *A Grammar of Stories: An Introduction.* The Hague, Netherlands: Mouton, 1973. An attempt to establish rules to account for the structure of all the syntactical sets that readers intuitively recognize as stories. The model used is Noam Chomsky's theories of generative grammar.

_____. "The Long and the Short of It." *Style* 27 (Fall, 1993): 327-331. Provides a definition of the short story as "an autonomous, short, fictional story written in prose and offered for display." Admits that such a definition has limited usefulness but argues that this is characteristic of generic definitions; maintains that texts belong not to one but to an indefinitely large number of textual families and use an indefinitely large number of clusters of features.

Pritchett, V. S. "Short Stories." *Harper's Bazaar* 87 (July, 1953): 31, 113. In Pritchett's opinion the short story is a hybrid, owing much to the quickness and objectivity of the cinema, much to the poet and the newspaper reporter, and everything to the "restlessness, the alert nerve, the scientific eye and the short breath of contemporary life." He makes an interesting point about the collapse of standards, conventions, and values which has so bewildered the impersonal novelist but has been the making of the story writer.

Reid, Ian. *The Short Story.* London: Methuen, 1977. A brief study that deals with problems of definition, historical development, and related generic forms. Offers a good introduction to the short story as a genre.

Rohrberger, Mary. "Between Shadow and Act: Where Do We Go from Here?" In *Short Story Theory at a Crossroads,* edited by Susan Lohafer and Jo Ellyn Clarey. Baton Rouge: Louisiana State University Press, 1989. A thought-provoking review of a number of modern short-story critics and theorists, largely by way of responding to, and disagreeing with, the strictly scientific and logical approach to definition of the form suggested by Norman Friedman. Also includes a restatement of the view that Rohrberger enunciated in her earlier book on Nathaniel Hawthorne, in which she argued for the essentially romantic nature of the short-story form.

_____. *Hawthorne and the Modern Short Story: A Study in Genre.* The Hague, Netherlands: Mouton, 1966. Attempts a generic definition of the short story as a form that derives from the Romantic metaphysical view that there is more to the world than can be apprehended through the senses. Nathaniel Hawthorne is the touchstone for Rohrberger's definition, which she then applies to twentieth-century stories by Eudora Welty, Ernest Hemingway, Sherwood Anderson, William Faulkner, and others.

Ruthrof, Horst. "Bracketed World and Reader Construction in the Modern Short Story." In *The Reader's Construction of Narrative.* London: Routledge & Kegan Paul, 1981. Discusses the "boundary situation" as the basis for the modern short story. In the pure boundary situation, the reader's act of bracketing transforms the presented crisis into the existential experience of the reading act.

Scott, A. O. "A Good Tale Isn't Hard to Find." *The New York Times,* April 5, 2009, p. WK1. Discussion of the remarkable durability of the short story, suggesting that it may be poised for a resurgence at the end of the first decade of the twenty-first century.

Shaw, Valerie. *The Short Story: A Critical Introduction.* London: Longman, 1983. A discussion of the form that primarily focuses on British writers, with one chapter on the transitional figure Robert Louis Stevenson. The rest of book deals with the patterned form to the artless tale form, with chapters on character, setting, and subject matter. Shaw argues that the short story cannot be defined by unity of effect or by a history of its "favorite devices and eminent practitioners."

Siebert, Hilary. "'Outside History': Lyrical Knowledge in the Discourse of the Short Story." In *Creative and Critical Approaches to the Short Story,* edited by Noel Harold Kaylor, Jr. Lewiston, N.Y.: Edwin Mellen Press, 1997. A discussion of how readers of short stories must often shift from expectations of a revealed, discursive meaning typical of prose to a gradually apprehended suggestive meaning typical of lyric poetry.

Stanzel, Franz K. "Textual Power in (Short) Short Story and Poem." In *Modes of Narrative: Approaches to American, Canadian, and British Fiction,* edited by

Reingard M. Vischik and Barbara Korte. Wursburg, Germany: Konigshausen and Neumann, 1990. Argues that the short story and poetry, which at the beginning of the twentieth-century were far apart, have come closer together in both form and content. Suggests some of the similarities between the two forms, such as their focusing the reader's attention on beginnings and endings and their insistence on close readings of the structure of each line and sentence.

Stevick, Philip, ed. *Anti-Story: An Anthology of Experimental Fiction*. New York: Free Press, 1971. An influential collection of contemporary short fiction with a helpful introduction that characterizes anti-story as against mimesis, reality, event, subject, the middle range of experience, analysis, and meaning.

Stroud, Theodore A. "A Critical Approach to the Short Story." *Journal of General Education* 9 (1956): 91-100. Makes use of American New Criticism to determine the pattern of the short story, that is, why apparently irrelevant episodes are included and why some events are expanded and others excluded.

Suckow, Ruth. "The Short Story." *Saturday Review of Literature* 4 (November 19, 1927): 317-318. Suckow strongly argues that no one can define the short story, for it is an aesthetic method for dealing with diversity and multiplicity.

Sullivan, Walter. "Revelation in the Short Story: A Note of Methodology." In *Vanderbilt Studies in Humanities*, edited by Richard C. Beatty, John Philip Hyatt, and Monroe K. Spears. Vol. 1. Nashville, Tenn.: Vanderbilt University Press, 1951. The fundamental methodological concept of the short story is a change of view from innocence to knowledge. This change can be either "logical" (coming at the end of the story) or "anticipated" (coming near the beginning); it can be either "intraconcatinate" (occurring within the main character) or "extra-concatinate" (occurring within a peripheral character). Thus defined, the short story did not begin until the final years of the nineteenth century.

Summers, Hollis, ed. *Discussions of the Short Story*. Boston: D. C. Heath, 1963. The nine general pieces on the short story include essays by Edgar Allan Poe and A. L. Bader; excerpts of books by Ray B. West,

Seán O'Faoláin, and Brander Matthews; a chapter each from Percy Lubbock's *Craft of Fiction* (1954) and Kenneth Payson Kempton's *The Short Story* (1947); and Bret Harte's "The Rise of the Short Story." Also includes seven additional essays on specific short-story writers.

Szávai, János. "Towards a Theory of the Short Story." *Acta Litteraria Academiae Scientiarum Hungariae, Tomus* 24 (1982): 203-224. Discusses the Giovanni Boccaccio model as a genre is a complex, structured entity that both retains and enriches the basic structure of the story. The enrichment resides, both in the careful preparation of the point and its attachment to a key motif and in the introduction of a new dimension in addition to the anecdote.

Todorov, Tzvetan. "The Structural Analysis of Literature." In *Structuralism: An Introduction, edited by* David Robey. London: Clarendon Press, 1973. The "figure in the carpet" in Henry James's stories is the quest for an absolute and absent cause. This cause is either a character, an event, or an object; its effect is the story readers are told. Everything in the story owes its existence to this cause, but because it is absent, the reader sets off in quest of it.

Trask, Georgianne, and Charles Burkhart, ed. *Storytellers and Their Art*. New York: Doubleday Anchor, 1963. A valuable collection of comments on the short-story form by practitioners from Anton Chekhov to Truman Capote. Noteworthy in part 1 are "Definitions of the Short Story" and "Short Story vs. Novel."

Trussler, Michael. "The Short Story: Interview with Charles May and Susan Lohafer." *Wascana Review* 33 (Spring, 1998): 14-24. Interview with two well-known theorists of the short story who discuss reasons for past critical neglect of the form, conditions of the recent renaissance of interest in the form by both critics and general readers, unique generic characteristics of the short story, and current and future trends in the short story and theoretical approaches to it.

_____. "Suspended Narratives: The Short Story and Temporality." *Studies in Short Fiction* 33 (Fall, 1996): 557-577. An analysis of the critical view that the short-story form focuses on atemporality.

Synthesizes a number of theories that emphasize short fiction's focus on existential confrontations while refusing to mitigate such experiences with abstraction, context, or continuity.

Wain, John. "Remarks on the Short Story." *Journal of the Short Story in English* 2 (1984): 49-66. Wain, himself a short-story writer, argues that the short story is a form of its own, with its own laws and logic, and that it is a modern form, beginning with Edgar Allan Poe. He observes that the novel is like a painting, whereas the short story is like a drawing, which catches a moment and is satisfying on its own grounds. He says there are perfectly successful short stories and totally unsuccessful ones, and nothing in between.

Welty, Eudora. "The Reading and Writing of Short Stories." *The Atlantic Monthly*, February, 1949, 54-58; March, 1949, 46-49. An impressionistic but suggestive essay in two installments that focuses on the mystery of the story and the fact that one cannot always see the solid outlines of the story because of the atmosphere that it generates.

West, Ray B. "The Modern Short Story and the Highest Forms of Art." *English Journal* 46 (1957): 531-539. Describes how the rise of the short story in the nineteenth-century was a result of the shift in narrative view from the "telescopic" (viewing nature and society from the outside) to the "microscopic" (viewing the unseen world of inner motives and impulses).

Wharton, Edith. "Telling a Short Story." In *The Writing of Fiction*. New York: Charles Scribner's Sons, 1925. Wharton maintains that the chief technical difference between the novel and the short story is that the novel focuses on character while the short story focuses on situation, "and it follows that the effect produced by the short story depends almost entirely on its form."

Williams, William Carlos. *A Beginning on the Short Story: Notes*. Yonkers, N.Y.: The Alicat Bookshop Press, 1950. In these notes from a writers' workshop session, Williams makes several interesting, if fragmentary and impressionistic, remarks about the short-story form: The short story, as contrasted with the novel, is a brushstroke instead of a picture.

Stressing virtuosity instead of story structure, it is "one single flight of the imagination, complete: up and down." It is best suited to depicting the life of "briefness, brokenness, and heterogeneity."

Winther, Per, Jacob Lothe, and Hans H. Skei, eds. *The Art of Brevity: Excursions in Short Fiction Theory and Analysis*. Columbia: University of South Carolina Press, 2004. Collection of essays that examine reasons for readers' neglect of short stories. Other essays analyze short fiction by Robert Olen Butler, Chris Offutt, James Joyce, Sarah Orne Jewett, Linda Hogan, Flannery O'Connor, Eudora Welty, William Faulkner, and Herman Melville; Danish short stories from the 1990's; and works by Australian writers.

Wright, Austin. "On Defining the Short Story: The Genre Question." In *Short Story Theory at a Crossroads*, *edited by* Susan Lohafer and Jo Ellyn Clarey. Baton Rouge: Louisiana State University Press, 1989. Discusses some of the theoretical problems involved in defining the short story as a genre. Argues for the formalist view of a genre definition as a cluster of conventions.

_____. "Recalcitrance in the Short Story." In *Short Story Theory at a Crossroads*, *edited by* Susan Lohafer and Jo Ellyn Clarey. Baton Rouge: Louisiana State University Press, 1989. A discussion of stories with endings that resist the reader's efforts to assimilate them and to make sense of them as a whole. Such final recalcitrance, Wright claims, is the extreme kind of resistance that the short story has developed to thwart final closure and reduce the complexity of the story to a conceptual understanding.

BRITISH SHORT FICTION

Allen, Walter. *The Short Story in English*. Oxford, England: Clarendon Press, 1981. A historical study of the development of the form in England and the United States. Primarily a series of biographical discussions of authors and summary discussions of stories. Good for providing a framework for the development of the form.

Baldwin, Dean. "The English Short Story in the Fifties." In *The English Short Story, 1945-1980*, *edited by* Dennis Vanatta. Boston: Twayne, 1985. Argues that after World War II, Great Britain experienced a bureaucratization of everyday life. Focuses on stories of social protest, especially those of Alan Sillitoe; the supernatural stories of Sylvia Townsend Warner and Muriel Spark; the mainstream writers H. E. Bates, V. S. Pritchett, Spark, and Rhys Davies; and the major writers Doris Lessing, Sillitoe, Roald Dahl, Angus Wilson, William Sansom, and Elizabeth Taylor.

_____. "The Tardy Evolution of the English Short Story." *Studies in Short Fiction* 30 (Winter, 1993): 23-34. Discusses how the business of literary production, as well as various aesthetic issues, retarded the evolution of the short story in England until late in the nineteenth century.

Beachcroft, T. O. *The Modest Art: A Survey of the Short Story in English*. London: Oxford University Press, 1968. A historical survey of the major figures of the English short story from Geoffrey Chaucer to Doris Lessing. The result of the basic difference between antique stories (listening) and modern stories (reading) is that modern short-story writers attempt to portray rather than expound; they remove their own personalities from the stories and present the flashes of insight through poetic needs.

Boyce, Benjamin. "English Short Fiction in the Eighteenth-century: A Preliminary View." *Studies in Short Fiction* 5 (1968): 95-112. Discusses the types of short fiction found in periodicals and inserted in novels: character sketches, Oriental tales, and stories of passion. Usually the purpose of these works was didactic and the mode was either "hovering pathos" or "hovering irony." The most distinctive characteristic is the formal, even elegant language.

Broich, Ulrich. "Muted Postmodernism: The Contemporary British Short Story." *Zeitschrift für Anglistik und Amerikanistik* 41 (1993): 31-39. Analyzes the market conditions of contemporary British short fiction. Argues that in spite of a remarkable number of excellent British short stories, the form is neglected by readers and critics. Surveys three major types of British short stories: the feminist story, the cultural conflict story, and the experimental postmodernist story.

Canby, Henry S. *The Short Story in English*. New York: Holt, Rinehart, and Winston, 1909. A classic historical survey of English-language short fiction from the Middle Ages through the nineteenth century, with discussion of both British and American writers. Canby argues that the Romantic movement gave birth to the modern short story and that Edgar Allan Poe is its first important figure; the rest of the nineteenth-century writers applied Poe's theory of single effect to new subjects, primarily the contrasts of civilization in flux.

Carruthers, Gerard. *Scottish Literature*. Edinburgh: Edinburgh University Press, 2009. A comprehensive history of Scottish literature. Includes debate about Scotland's languages and analyses of writers, such as Sir Walter Scott, Margaret Oliphant, and Alasdair Gray, among many others.

Chan, Winnie. *The Economy of the Short Story in British Periodicals of the 1890's*. New York: Routledge, 2007. Focuses on the commercial pressures of the publishing industry and how they contributed to the types of short stories that were published in three periodicals of the period: *Strand*, *Yellow Book*, and *Black and White*.

Crawford, Robert. *Scotland's Books: A History of Scottish Literature*. Oxford, England: Oxford University Press, 2009. An excellent introduction to Scottish literature, written in accessible and engaging language. Crawford argues that the development of the short-story genre owes much to the literary reviews and journals of eighteenth-century Edinburgh.

Duncan, Edgar Hill. "Short Fiction in Medieval English: A Survey." *Studies in Short Fiction* 9 (1972): 1-28. A survey of short pieces in the Old English period, primarily in verse, that have in common the characteristic of "artfully telling a story in a relatively brief compass" and that focus on "singleness of character, of action, and/or impression." The fall of the angels and the fall of man in the *Genesis B*, the St. Guthlac poems, and *The Dream of the Rood* are analyzed.

_____. "Short Fiction in Medieval English: 2. The Middle English Period." *Studies in Short Fiction* 11 (1974): 227-241. A brief sampling of short fiction elements in the "shorter romance" form, the exemplary narrative, the beast tale, and the fabliau introduced to Middle English by the French. Also noted are paraphrases of biblical stories, saints' lives, the dream visions of *The Pearl*, and Geoffrey Chaucer's "The Book of the Duchess" and the "Prologue to the Legend of Good Women."

Dunn, Douglas. *The Oxford Book of Scottish Stories*. Oxford, England: Oxford University Press, 1995. A collection of stories, including traditional and oral examples, dating from the eighteenth-century through the twentieth-century. Dunn notes in his introduction that Scottish short stories largely relate to and are written in the language of common people.

Evans, Walter. "The English Short Story in the Seventies." In *The English Short Story, 1945-1980, edited by* Dennis Vanatta. Boston: Twayne, 1985. Focuses on new writers of the period, such as Susan Hill, Angela Carter, Gabriel Josipovici, and Christine Brooke-Rose. The emphasis here is on different themes in these works, such as personal crises and the individual in conflict with society. Briefly discusses the avant-garde, especially Josipovici and Brooke-Rose. Claims the decade's finest collection of stories is *The Ebony Tower* by John Fowles.

Fallon, Erin, et al., eds. *A Reader's Companion to the Short Story in English*. Westport, Conn.: Greenwood Press, 2001. Produced under the auspices of the Society for the Study of the Short Story, this collection of essays, aimed at the general reader, provides brief biographies of numerous writers and analyses of their short fiction. Some of the writers examined are Chinua Achebe, Margaret Atwood, Alice Munro, Jean Rhys, Salman Rushdie, and Olive Senior.

Ferguson, Suzanne. "Local Color and the Function of Setting in the English Short Story." In *Creative and Critical Approaches to the Short Story*, *edited by* Noel Harold Kaylor, Jr. Lewiston, N.Y.: Edwin Mellen Press, 1997. Ferguson argues that whereas the function of setting in early stories was to establish a degree of verisimilitude, greater emphasis on setting in later stories served to establish the emotional interaction of the characters with elements of the physical environment.

Flora, Joseph M., ed. *The English Short Story, 1880-1945*. Boston: Twayne, 1985. A collection of essays on a number of British short-story writers during the period, including Rudyard Kipling, D. H. Lawrence, Virginia Woolf, Saki, A. E. Coppard, P. G. Wodehouse, and V. S. Pritchett.

Harris, Wendell V. "Beginnings of and for the True Short Story in England." *English Literature in Transition* 15 (1972): 296-276. Argues that the true short story did not begin in England until Rudyard Kipling discovered the means to control the reader's angle of vision and establish a self-contained world within the story that keeps the reader at a distance. Maintains that the externality of the reader to the story's participants is a basic characteristic of the short story.

_____. "English Short Fiction in the Nineteenth Century." *Studies in Short Fiction* 6 (1968): 1-93. After distinguishing between "short fiction" appearing before 1880 and the "short story" after 1880, Harris surveys examples from both periods. The turning point was the definition posed by Brander Matthews, which first appeared in the *Saturday Review* in 1884.

_____. "Vision and Form: The English Novel and the Emergence of the Short Story." *Victorian Newsletter*, no. 47 (1975): 8-12. The short story did not begin in England until the 1880's because the presentation of isolated individuals, moments, or scenes was not considered a serious intellectual task for fiction to undertake. Only at the end of the century was reality perceived as congeries of fragments; the primary vehicle of this perception is the short story.

Hunter, Adrian. *The Cambridge Introduction to the Short Story in English*. Cambridge, England: Cambridge University Press, 2007. Hunter begins his literary history in the nineteenth century, describing the form and cultural context of short fiction from that time until the late twentieth-century. He discusses the works of Charles Dickens, Thomas Hardy, Rudyard Kipling, Joseph Conrad, James Joyce, Virginia Woolf, Katherine Mansfield, Samuel Beckett, Frank O'Connor, Seán O'Faoláin, Elizabeth Bowen, V. S. Pritchett, Angela Carter, Ian McEwan, Chinua Achebe, James Kelman, Alice Munro, and others.

Killick, Tim. *British Short Fiction in the Early Nineteenth Century: The Rise of the Tale*. Burlington, Vt.: Ashgate, 2008. Describes how nineteenth-century British writers and publishers sought to publish short fiction in book-length volumes in order to compete with the more prestigious novels. Discusses the publishing conditions of the period that promoted the creation of short fiction, explaining how the popular collections of American writer Washington Irving influenced the British periodical market for short fiction. Analyzes the stories and sketches of Mary Russell Mitford, James Hogg, Hannah More, Maria Edgeworth, and other writers.

Malcolm, Cheryl Alexander, and David Malcolm, eds. *A Companion to the British and Irish Short Story*. Malden, Mass.: Wiley-Blackwell, 2008. Collection of essays focusing on British and Irish short fiction from 1880 to the present day. Includes discussions of detective and crime stories, ghost stories, science-fiction tales, and gay and lesbian short stories, as well as women's writing. Analyzes the work of Rudyard Kipling, Robert Louis Stevenson, Thomas Hardy, Joseph Conrad, Saki, James Joyce, D. H. Lawrence, Virginia Woolf, Katherine Mansfield, Frank O'Connor, Liam O'Flaherty, Elizabeth Bowen, Ben Okri, Salman Rushdie, Hanif Kureishi, Alan Sillitoe, and John McGahern, among others.

Maunder, Andrew, ed. *The Facts On File Companion to the British Short Story*. New York: Facts On File, 2007. Provides more than 450 alphabetically arranged encyclopedia entries about short stories, novellas, short-fiction collections, writers, concepts, terms, themes, and literary movements in literature written from 1790 until the early twenty-first century. Although the entries focus on Great Britain, Ireland, and the Commonwealth, they also include some writers, such as Henry James and Salman Rushdie, who have strong ties to the British short-story tradition.

Mish, Charles C. "English Short Fiction in the Seventeenth Century." *Studies in Short Fiction* 6 (1969): 223-330. Mish divides the period into two parts: 1600-1660, in which short fiction declined into sterile imitation and preciousness, and 1660-1700, in which it was revitalized by the French influence

of such works as Madame de la Fayette's *La Princesse de Clèves* (1678; *The Princess of Clèves*, 1679). The French direction toward interiorization, psychological analysis, and verisimilitude in action and setting, combined with the English style of the self-conscious narrator, moves fiction toward the novel of the eighteenth-century.

Orel, Harold. *The Victorian Short Story: Development and Triumph of a Literary Genre*. Cambridge, England: Cambridge University Press, 1986. Contains chapters on Joseph Sheridan Le Fanu, Charles Dickens, Anthony Trollope, Thomas Hardy, Robert Louis Stevenson, Rudyard Kipling, H. G. Wells, and Joseph Conrad. Focuses on the relevant biographical and sociocultural factors and discusses writers' relationships with editors and periodicals. Does not attempt a formal history of the evolution of the genre.

Pache, Walter. "Towards the Modern English Short Story." In *Modes of Narrative: Approaches to American, Canadian, and British Fiction*, edited by Reingard M. Vischik and Barbara Korte. Wurzburg, Germany: Konigshausen and Neumann, 1990. A study of the relationship between the short fiction of the 1890's and the modern short story. Surveys changes in periodical publishing during the period, analyzes new directions in short-story theory at the turn of the twentieth-century, and suggests some of the basic structural patterns of the end-of-the-nineteenth-century short story.

Pickering, Jean. "The English Short Story in the Sixties." In *The English Short Story, 1945-1980*, edited by Dennis Vanatta. Boston: Twayne, 1985. Pickering says that few of the cultural developments in England in the 1960's were reflected in the short story and claims that the short story was in decline during this period. Focuses on short-story collections by Roald Dahl, William Sansom, Doris Lessing, V. S. Pritchett, and H. E. Bates.

Schlauch, Margaret. "English Short Fiction in the Fifteenth and Sixteenth Centuries." *Studies in Short Fiction* 3 (1966): 393-434. A survey of types of short fiction from the romantic *lai* to the exemplum, and from the bawdy fabliau to the novella. Schlauch's conclusions are that modern short-story writers are heirs both in subject matter (for example internal psychological conflict) and in technique (such as the importance of dialogue) to a long tradition that antedates the seventeenth century, a tradition that is still worth studying.

Schoene-Harwood, Berthold, ed. *The Edinburgh Companion to Contemporary Scottish Literature*, Edinburgh: Edinburgh University Press, 2007. International critics discuss Scottish writing in the context of devolution and self-rule, voted by referendum in 1997, in nearly four-dozen essays.

Stevenson, Lionel. "The Short Story in Embryo." *English Literature in Transition* 15 (1972): 261-268. A discussion of the "agglomerative urge" in the English fiction of the eighteenth and nineteenth centuries that contributed to the undervaluing of the short story. Not until 1880, when the fragmentation of the well-integrated view of society began in England, did the short story come into its own in that country.

Stinson, John J. "The English Short Story, 1945-1950." In *The English Short Story, 1945-1980, edited by* Dennis Vanatta. Boston: Twayne, 1985. Discusses some of the reasons why the short story was in decline in England during this period and claims there was no new direction in the form at the time. Discusses W. Somerset Maugham, A. E. Coppard, Graham Greene, Sylvia Townsend Warner, V. S. Pritchett, and Angus Wilson.

Sullivan, C.W. *Welsh Celtic Myth in Modern Fantasy*, Greenwood, 1989. A fascinating study that shows the constant interplay of fantasy elements in otherwise realistic Welsh fiction. Makes the essential connection between the earliest writings in Welsh having a modern-day influence on short fiction and poetry writing by Welsh authors.

Vanatta, Denis, ed. *The English Short Story, 1945-1980*. Boston: Twayne, 1985. Includes survey essays by various critics on the short story in England in the 1950's, 1960's, and 1970's.

Windholz, Anne M. "The American Short Story and Its British Critics: *Athenaeum* Reviews, 1880-1900." *Victorian Periodicals Review* 23 (Winter, 1990): 156-166. Argues that between 1880 and 1900, reviews of British and American short stories in the British journal *Athenaeum* helped establish an aesthetic that dominated critical analysis of the Anglo-American short story. Surveys reviewers' comments on American humor, dialect, and local color, as well as the importance of conciseness and unity of effect in both British and American short stories between 1880 and 1900.

IRISH SHORT FICTION

Averill, Deborah. *The Irish Short Story from George Moore to Frank O'Connor*. Washington, D.C.: University Press of America, 1982. An introductory study of the Irish short story intended primarily for teachers and students. Surveys historical conditions in the nineteenth and early twentieth centuries that contributed to the development of the Irish short story and discusses the major stories of George Moore, James Joyce, Seumas O'Kelly, Daniel Corkery, Liam O'Flaherty, Seán O'Faoláin, and Frank O'Connor. Discusses each writer's basic style or concept of form and recurrent themes.

Carens, James F. "In Quest of a New Impulse: George Moore's *The Untilled Field* and James Joyce's *Dubliners*." In *The Irish Short Story: A Critical History*, *edited by* James F. Kilroy. Boston: Twayne, 1984. Carens provides analyses of the major stories in these two most influential collections of Irish short fiction. Discusses the major contributions of the stories of Moore and Joyce that were responsible for creating the modern Anglo-Irish short story. Explains Moore's influence on Joyce, analyzing Joyce's "Counterparts" as a reworking of Moore's "The Clerk's Quest."

Chatman, Seymour. "New Ways of Analyzing Narrative Structure, with an Example from Joyce's *Dubliners*." *Language and Style* 2 (1969): 3-36. A "test" of the narrative theories of Ronald Barthes and Tzvetan Todorov, with a detailed analysis of James Joyce's "Eveline." The story is considered both in terms of the internal relations of the narrative and the external relations between narrator and reader.

Delargy, J. H. "The Gaelic Story-Teller." *Proceedings of the British Academy* 31 (1945). An important study of the early Irish oral tradition of storytelling.

Dunleavy, Janet Egleson. "Mary Lavin, Elizabeth Bowen, and a New Generation: The Irish Short Story at Mid-Century." In *The Irish Short Story: A Critical History, edited by* James F. Kilroy. Boston: Twayne, 1984. Discusses Lavin's art as economic, disciplined, and compressed; argues that she neither romanticizes nor trivializes Irish experience. Examines the basic characteristics of the fiction of Bowen, Benedict Kiely, Michael McLaverty, and Bryan MacMahon.

Hogan, Robert. "Old Boys, Young Bucks, and New Women: The Contemporary Irish Short Story." In *The Irish Short Story: A Critical History, edited by* James F. Kilroy. Boston: Twayne, 1984. A general survey of contemporary Irish short-story writers, such as old guards Anthony C. West, James Plunkett, William Trevor, and Patrick Boyle; young-buck writers Eugene McCabe, John Morrow, Bernard Mac Laverty, Desmond Hogan, and Gillman Noonan; and women writers, such as Edna O'Brien, Maeve Kelly, Emma Cooke, Kate Cruise O'Brien, and Juanita Casey.

Ingman, Heather. *A History of the Irish Short Story.* New York: Cambridge University Press, 2009. A historical survey of Irish short fiction from its beginnings in the nineteenth-century to the present day. Each chapter concludes with an analysis of major stories from the period discussed, including works by William Carleton, Emily Lawless, William Butler Yeats, George Egerton, James Joyce, Frank O'Connor, Norah Hoult, Mary Lavin, Seán O'Faoláin, William Trevor, Edno O'Brien, John McGahern, and Eilis Ni Dhuibhne.

Kiberd, Declan. *Inventing Ireland: The Literature of the Modern Nation.* Cambridge, Mass.: Harvard University Press, 1996. An important study of the development of Irish literature from Oscar Wilde to the late twentieth-century.

Kilroy, James F. Introduction to *The Irish Short Story: A Critical History.* Boston: Twayne, 1984. Collection of five essays surveying the development of the Irish short story in the nineteenth and twentieth centuries. Kilroy's focus is on the relationship between historical and social events in Ireland and the development of fiction in this country, including political conflicts and upheavals and the rise of periodical publication.

_____. "Setting the Standards: Writers of the 1920's and 1930's." In *The Irish Short Story: A Critical History, edited by* Kilroy. Boston: Twayne, 1984. Argues that the major Irish writers who set the standards for short fiction in the 1920's and 1930's were Liam O'Flaherty, Frank O'Connor, and Seán O'Faoláin. Kilroy compares and contrasts the three writers by analyzing some of their best-known stories. The essay also includes brief discussions of writers Daniel Corkery and Seamus O'Kelley.

Malcolm, Cheryl Alexander, and David Malcolm, eds. *A Companion to the British and Irish Short Story.* Malden, Mass.: Wiley-Blackwell, 2008. Collection of essays focusing on British and Irish short fiction from 1880 to the present day. Includes discussions of detective and crime stories, ghost stories, science-fiction tales, and gay and lesbian short stories, as well as women's writing. Analyzes the work of Rudyard Kipling, Robert Louis Stevenson, Thomas Hardy, Joseph Conrad, Saki, James Joyce, D. H. Lawrence, Virginia Woolf, Katherine Mansfield, Frank O'Connor, Liam O'Flaherty, Elizabeth Bowen, Ben Okri, Salman Rushdie, Hanif Kureishi, Alan Sillitoe, and John McGahern, among others.

Martin, Augustine, ed. *The Genius of Irish Prose.* Dublin: Mercier Press, 1985. Includes two relevant essays: "The Short Story: 1900-1945" and "The Short Story After the Second World War."

Mercier, Vivian. "The Irish Short Story and Oral Tradition." In *The Celtic Cross: Studies in Irish Culture and Literature, edited by* Ray B. Browne, William John Roselli, and Richard Loftus. West Lafayette, Ind.: Purdue University Studies, 1964. An influential essay that examines the relationship between the Irish folktale and the contemporary Irish short story.

Orel, Harold. *The Victorian Short Story.* Cambridge, England: Cambridge University Press, 1986. A helpful historical study with important chapters on William Carleton and Joseph Sheridan Le Fanu.

Rafroidi, Patrick, ed. *The Irish Short Story.* Atlantic Highlands, N.J.: Humanities Press, 1979. Collection of essays on general historical-critical issues concerning the Irish short story and on a number of important Irish short-story writers from William Carleton and Joseph Sheridan Le Fanu to Patrick Boyle and John McGahern.

Schirmer, Gregory A. "Tales from Big House and Cabin: The Nineteenth Century." In *The Irish Short Story: A Critical History*, edited by James F. Kilroy. Boston: Twayne, 1984. Surveys the short fiction of Maria Edgeworth, William Carleton, and Joseph Sheridan Le Fanu, among others. Schirmer emphasizes the ironic voice of Edgeworth's *Castle Rackrent*, the comic realism and the sophisticated use of narrative voice by William Carleton, and the use of the gothic tradition and psychological complexity by Joseph Sheridan Le Fanu.

Storey, Michael L. *Representing the Troubles in Irish Short Fiction*. Washington, D.C.: Catholic University of America Press, 2004. Examines short stories about Ireland's longstanding conflict with England during the period beginning with the 1916 Easter Rising to the 1990's sectarian violence in Northern Ireland, placing these stories in their political and historical contexts. Chronicles how depictions of the "troubles" evolved from expressions of Romantic Irish nationalism to realistic depictions of violence and sectarian strife. Some of the writers whose works are analyzed include Daniel Corkery, Frank O'Connor, Liam O'Flaherty, Seán O'Faoláin, Mary Lavin, Benedict Kiely, William Trevor, Bernard MacLaverty, and Colum McCann.

Thompson, Richard J. *Everlasting Voices: Aspects of the Modern Irish Short Story*. Troy, N.Y.: Whitston, 1989. A study of George Moore's *The Untilled Field*, James Joyce's *Dubliners*, and the stories of Frank O'Connor, Seán O'Faoláin, Liam O'Flaherty, and Mary Lavin.

CANADIAN SHORT FICTION

Bennett, Bruce. "Short Fiction and the Canon: Australia and Canada." *Antipodes* 7, no. 2 (1993): 109-114. A useful introductory essay, concentrating particularly on the "new" writing of the 1960's and 1970's.

Dvořák, Marta, and W. H. New, eds. *Tropes and Territories: Short Fiction, Postcolonial Readings, Canadian Writing in Context*. Montreal: McGill-Queen's

University Press, 2007. Examines contemporary short fiction written in Canada and the Commonwealth, including works by Native Canadians, Maoris, and writers Katherine Mansfield, Janet Frame, Alice Munro, Mavis Gallant, R. K. Narayan, and David Malouf, among others. Two of the essays provide general analyses of short fiction from South Asia and Australia, while another discusses Caribbean diasporic writing.

Huang, Guiyou, ed. *Asian American Short Story Writers: An A-to-Z Guide*. Westport, Conn.: Greenwood Press, 2003. An encyclopedia containing alphabetically arranged entries about forty-nine Asian American authors living in the United States and Canada, including Frank Chin, Bharti Mukherjee, and Toshio Mori. Each entry provides a biography, a discussion of the writer's major works and themes, and a bibliography. Also contains an introductory overview of Asian American short fiction.

Kruk, Laurie. *The Voice Is the Story: Conversations with Canadian Writers of Short Fiction*. Oakville, Ont.: Mosaic Press, 2003. Sandra Birdsell, Timothy Findley, Alistair MacLeod, Carol Sheilds, and Guy Vanderhaeghe are among the short-fiction writers who discuss their work.

Lynch, Gerald. *The One and the Many: English-Canadian Short Story Cycles*. Toronto: University of Toronto Press, 2001. A literary-historical survey of the Canadian short-story cycle. Lynch examines Stephen Leacock's *Sunshine Sketches of a Little Town* in order to describe how a short-story cycle conveys meaning and the significant function of its concluding story. He then examines six other cycles, including works by Duncan Campbell Scott, Frederick Philip Grove, and Alice Munro.

New, W. H. *Dreams of Speech and Violence: The Art of the Short Story in Canada and New Zealand*. Toronto: University of Toronto Press, 1987. An excellent analysis of the development of the short story and its relationship to the development of a Canadian national literary identity. The comparison between the short story in New Zealand and in Canada is interesting.

_____, ed. *Encyclopedia of Literature in Canada*. Toronto, Ont.: University of Toronto Press, 2002. A thousand-page reference covering the full panoply of Canada's literary heritage. Includes discussions of literature in English and French, as well as other languages, First Nation writers, and historical and cultural events that have influenced Canadian literature.

Nischik, Reingard M., ed. *The Canadian Short Story: Interpretations*. Rochester, N.Y.: Camden House, 2007. Collection of essays providing a comprehensive overview of Canadian short fiction. Includes a historical survey of the nation's short fiction and discussions of animal stories, the Canadian writer as an expatriate, Canadian modernism, prairie fiction, and the work of numerous writers, including Stephen Leacock, Frederick Philip Grove, Morley Callaghan, Ethel Wilson, Hugh Garner, Mordecai Richler, Mavis Gallant, Alice Munro, Margaret Laurence, Leon Rooke, and Carol Shields.

AUSTRALIA AND NEW ZEALAND SHORT FICTION

Bennett, Bruce. *Australian Short Fiction: A History*. St. Lucia, Qld..: University of Queensland Press, 2002. Examines short fiction of the nineteenth and twentieth centuries, including works by Henry Lawson and Steele Rudd.

_____. "Short Fiction and the Canon: Australia and Canada." *Antipodes* 7, no. 2 (1993): 109-114. A useful introductory essay, concentrating particularly on the "new" writing of the 1960's and 1970's.

Goldsworthy, Kerryn. "Short Fiction." In *The Penguin New Literary History of Australia*, edited by Laurie Hergenhan. Ringwood, Vic.: Penguin Australia, 1988. One of the few essays that covers the development of the Australian short story from the 1890's to the 1980's in detail, with attention paid to the form and its relationship to the development of a national literary identity.

Goodwin, Ken. *A History of Australian Literature*. Basingstoke, England: Macmillan, 1986. A useful general text that covers the development of the short story from the 1890's to the 1980's, with particular attention paid to the Social Realist writers of the 1940's and 1950's and the "new" writing of the 1960's and 1970's.

Hadgraft, Cecil, ed. *The Australian Short Story Before Lawson*. Melbourne, Vic.: Oxford University Press, 1986. A collection of early short stories with a comprehensive and entertaining introduction not only covering the early writing but also touching on the short story of the 1890's.

New, W. H. *Dreams of Speech and Violence: The Art of the Short Story in Canada and New Zealand*. Toronto: University of Toronto Press, 1987. An excellent analysis of the development of the short story and its relationship to the development of a New Zealand national literary identity. New provides an interesting general discussion of particular writers and close readings of stories by Katherine Mansfield and others. The comparison between the short story in New Zealand and in Canada is interesting.

Pierce, Peter, ed. *The Cambridge History of Australian Literature*. New York: Cambridge University Press, 2009. This overview of Australian literature contains two essays focusing on short fiction: "Short Story, 1890's to 1950," by Bruce Bennett, and "Short Story Since 1950," by Stephen Torre.

Wevers, Lydia. "The Short Story." In *The Oxford History of New Zealand Literature, edited by* Terry Sturm. Auckland, New Zealand: Oxford University Press, 1991. An excellent account of the development of the short story in New Zealand. Contains detailed discussions not only of the development of the form but also of individual writers and particular literary movements.

TYPES OF SHORT FICTION

MODERNIST SHORT FICTION

Childs, Peter. *Modernism*. 2d ed. New York: Routledge, 2008. Chronicles the origins of the modernist movement and describes its impact on late nineteenth- and early twentieth-century literature. Devotes a chapter to the short story.

Goldberg, Michael E. "The Synchronic Series as the Origin of the Modernist Short Story." *Studies in Short Fiction* 33 (Fall, 1996): 515-527. Goldberg suggests that the cumulative power of modernist collections of stories, such as James Joyce's *Dubliners* (1914) and Ernest Hemingway's *In Our Time*

(1924, 1925), is modeled after a synchronic series of stories innovated by Sir Arthur Conan Doyle.

Head, Dominic. *The Modernist Short Story*. Cambridge: Cambridge University Press, 1992. An examination of the short story's formal characteristics from a theoretical framework derived from Louis Althusser and Mikhail Bakhtin. Argues that the short story's emphasis on literary artifice lends itself to modernist experimentalism. Illustrates this thesis with chapters on James Joyce, Tobias Woolf, Katherine Mansfield, and Wyndham Lewis.

POSTMODERN SHORT FICTION

Clark, Miriam Marty. "After Epiphany: American Stories in the Postmodern Age." *Style* 27 (Fall, 1993): 387-394. Argues that contemporary short stories can no longer be read in terms of epiphany. Claims that critics must develop a new reading strategy, shifting from metaphoric ways of meaning to metonymic ones to redefine the short story in its postmodern context.

Ifterkharrudin, Farhat, et al., eds. *Postmodern Approaches to the Short Story*. Westport, Conn.: Praeger, 2003. This volume, created under the auspices of the Society for the Study of the Short Story, analyzes elements of postmodernism in the works of Jorge Luis Borges, Italo Calvino, Katherine Mansfield, Henry James, Janette Turner Hospital, Jean Toomer, Homi K. Bhabba, and other writers.

_____. *The Postmodern Short Story: Forms and Issues*. Westport, Conn.: Praeger, 2003. Created under the auspices of the Society for the Study of the Short Story, this collection of essays demonstrates how postmodernism has altered the styles and themes of short fiction. Includes analyses of the personal essay, the nonfiction short story, Canadian and American postmodern stories, and works of short fiction by Sandra Cisneros, Lelie Marmon Silko, Joyce Carol Oates, Lorrie Moore, Thom Jones, Tom Paine, Denis Johnson, Edmund White, Ernest Hemingway, Richard Ford, Richard Brautigam, and R. R. R. Dhlomo.

THE HYPERSTORY

Coover, Robert. "Storying in Hyperspace: 'Linkages.'" In *The Tales We Tell: Perspectives on the Short Story*, *edited by* Barbara Lounsberry et al. Westport, Conn.: Greenwood Press, 1998. A discussion of the future of the short story in computerized hyperspace as a form that is nonsequential, multidirectional, and interactive. Discusses linked short fictional pieces in the past in the Bible, in medieval romances, and by Giovanni Boccaccio, Miguel de Cervantes, and Geoffrey Chaucer.

May, Charles E. "HyperStory: Teaching Short Fiction with Computers." In *The Tales We Tell: Perspectives on the Short Story*, *edited by* Barbara Lounsberry et al. Westport, Conn.: Greenwood Press, 1998. Describes HyperStory, a computer program developed by the author, which teaches students how to read short fiction more carefully and thoughtfully. Uses Edgar Allan Poe's "The Cask of Amontillado" as an example; attempts to explain, with the help of student comments, the success of the program.

MAGICAL REALISM

Benito, Jesús, Ana Ma Manzanas, and Begoña Simal. *Uncertain Mirrors: Magical Realisms in U.S. Ethnic Literatures*. New York: Rodopi, 2009. Examines Magical Realism in comparison to other literary movements, such as postmodernism and postcolonialism, Studies the use of Magical Realism in works by various authors, discussing how these writers represent themselves and their characters.

Bowers, Maggie Ann. *Magic(al) Realism*. London: Routledge, 2004. Serves as a helpful introduction to the Magical Realism movement. Bowers provides an overview of the genre and a close examination of the genre's connections with postcolonialism.

Faris, Wendy B. *Ordinary Enchantments: Magical Realism and the Remystification of Narrative*. Nashville, Tenn.: Vanderbilt University Press, 2004. Faris discusses key components of Magic Realist fiction and explores the work of authors from around the world. Each chapter focuses on a different aspect of Magical Realism, ranging from studies of narrative structure to the representation of women. Examines the importance of the Magical Realism tradition and its greater cultural implications.

Gaylard, Gerald. *After Colonialism: African Postmodernism and Magical Realism*. Johannesburg: Wits University, 2006. Gaylard describes how two genres of fiction--postmodernism and Magical Realism--provide reflections on and responses to colonialism in Africa. He argues that genres such as Magical Realism, which allow writers freedom and release, provide African writers a sense of liberty in an era of colonization and assimilation.

Hart, Stephen, and Wen-chin Ouyang, eds. *A Companion to Magical Realism*. Rochester, N.Y.: Tamesis, 2006. Collection of essays providing a close examination of the Magical Realism genre. Essayists trace the genre's history, its common symbols, and the politics of representation in close readings of texts, including works by Gabriel García Márquez, Jorge Luis Borges, and Isabel Allende.

Hegerfeldt, Anne C. *Lies That Tell the Truth: Magic Realism Seen Through Contemporary Fiction in Britain*. New York: Rodopi, 2005. Hegerfeldt discusses the debate over the definition of the genre and gives in-depth analyses of literary techniques employed often in Magical Realism.

Schroeder, Shannin. *Rediscovering Magical Realism in the Americas*. Westport, Conn.: Praeger, 2004. Examines works of Magical Realism in North and South America, paying special attention to North American Magical Realists. Schroeder acknowledges that the genre is often associated primarily or only with Latin and Central American writers and confronts this assumption with discussion of often neglected Magical Realist writers.

Takolander, Maria. *Catching Butterflies: Bringing Magical Realism to Ground*. Bern, Switzerland: Peter Lang, 2007. Takolander, like other scholars of Magical Realism, discusses the debate over how the genre should be defined, as well as its inception and its influence around the world. By examining historical context, Takolander attempts to provide answers to questions about the genre's presence, dominance, and influence in the literary world.

Zamora, Lois Parkinson, and Wendy B. Faris, eds. *Magical Realism: Theory, History, Community*. London: Duke University Press, 1995. Collection of essays about developments in the Magical Realism movement in art, literature, and other media.

FOLK TALES AND FAIRY TALES

Ashliman, D. L. *Folk and Fairy Tales: A Handbook*. Westport, Conn.: Greenwood Press, 2004. Ashliman provides readers with a history of fairy tales and folktales, examines the definitions of these genres, and explores some examples of each type of tale.

Bettelheim, Bruno. *The Uses of Enchantment: The Meaning and Importance of Fairy Tales*. New York: Alfred A. Knopf, 1977. This book discusses the tradition of and patterns present in fairy tales, then gives extensive analyses of well-known fairy tales, including "Hansel and Gretel," "Little Red Riding Hood," "Snow White," "Goldilocks and the Three Bears," "The Sleeping Beauty," and "Cinderella."

Bottigheimer, Ruth B. *Grimms' Bad Girls and Bold Boys: The Moral and Social Vision of the Tales*. New Haven, Conn.: Yale University Press, 1987. Bottigheimer discusses the fairy-tale tradition, including specific patterns of the characters' speech, how they endure punishment, their struggle for power, and the value systems implicit in these tales.

Georges, Robert A., and Michael Owen Jones. *Folkloristics: An Introduction*. Bloomington: Indiana University Press, 1995. Defines folklore as a historical tradition, focusing on its role in various cultures, in human psychology, and as a historical science.

Jones, Steven Swann. *The Fairy Tale: The Magic Mirror of the Imagination*. New York: Routledge, 2002. Provides a history of the fairy-tale genre, awarding special attention to the roles of men and women in fairy tales of the past and describing how those figures influenced more contemporary stories.

Leeming, David Adams, ed. *Storytelling Encyclopedia*. Phoenix, Ariz.: Oryx Press, 1997. Provides a general discussion of the storytelling tradition and a look at a number of countries and their specific cultural contributions to the tradition. In addition, there are brief entries regarding the most popular people and theories related to the oral and written traditions.

Propp, Vladimir. *Morphology of the Folktale. Edited by* Svatava Pirkova-Jakovson, translated by Laurence Scott. Bloomington: Indiana University Research Center, 1958. All formalist and structuralist studies of narrative owe a debt to this pioneering early twentieth-century study. Using one hundred fairy tales, Propp defines the genre itself by analyzing the stories according to characteristic actions or functions.

_____. *Theory and History of Folklore*. Minneapolis: University of Minnesota Press, 1984. This collection of Propp's essays expands on his theory of the narrative that he presented in *Morphology of the Folktale*.

Tatar, Maria. *Off With Their Heads: Fairy Tales and the Culture of Childhood*. Princeton, N.J.: Princeton University Press, 1992. Tatar examines how important writers in the fairy-tale tradition revised these stories in order to be more didactic for children. She argues that the typical portrayal of children in fairy tales is problematic, especially since the contemporary target audience of fairy tales is children.

Thompson, Stith. *The Folktale*. New York: Dryden Press, 1946. Discusses the nature, theories, and form of the folktale and presents a varied collection of international tales. Selected are tales from many categories, such as the complex and the simple tale.

Warner, Marina. *From the Beast to the Blonde: On Fairy Tales and Their Tellers*. New York: Farrar, Straus and Giroux, 1994. Warner studies the characters whose role is the telling of fairy tales and analyzes gender roles, specifically those of women, including the typical portrayals of daughters, mothers, stepmothers, brides, and runaway girls.

Zipes, Jack. *Fairy Tales and the Art of Subversion: The Classical Genre for Children and the Process of Civilization*. New York: Routledge, 1991. Zipes focuses on the didactic function of fairy tales, ranging from the work of the Grimm brothers to later fairy tales. He argues that the primary function of fairy tales is to instill morals and lessons in their child readers.

_____. *Fairy Tale as Myth, Myth as Fairy Tale*. Lexington: University Press of Kentucky, 1994. Examines the history of the fairy tale and its rise as the genre preceding the folktale. Discusses many well-known fairy tales and their role in society.

SCIENCE-FICTION SHORT STORIES

Amis, Kingsley. *New Maps of Hell: A Survey of Science Fiction*. London: Gollancz, 1960. A slightly superficial study by a critic whose relative ignorance of the genre's history is amply compensated by his insights into the distinctive forms and merits of short science fiction.

Ashley, Michael. *The Time Machines: The Story of the Science-Fiction Pulp Magazines from the Beginning to 1950*. Liverpool, England: Liverpool University Press, 2000. *Transformations: The Story of the Science-Fiction Magazines from 1950 to 1970, the History of the Science-Fiction Magazine*. Liverpool, England: Liverpool University Press, 2005. *Gateways to Forever: The Story of the Sience-Fction Magazines from 1970 to 1980, the History of the Science-Fiction Magazine*. Liverpool, England: Liverpool University Press, 2007. A three-volume history of the American and English pulp science-fiction magazines and the types of short stories they published.

Carter, Paul A. *The Creation of Tomorrow: Fifty Years of Magazine Science Fiction*. New York: Columbia University Press, 1977. An intelligent and well-informed history of the genre, which pays more careful attention to short fiction than most other books on the subject.

Clute, John, and Peter Nicholls. *The Encyclopedia of Science Fiction*. London: Orbit, 1993. By far the most comprehensive guide to the genre's history, practitioners, and themes.

Monk, Patricia. *Alien Theory: The Alien as Archetype in the Science Fiction Short Story*. Lanham, Md.: Scarecrow Press, 2006. Examines the use of alien characters in science-fiction short stories, including stories published in pulp magazines and contemporary works of the genre. Argues that the creation of the alien contributes to readers' understanding of their present-day lives and the future potential of their universe.

Scholes, Robert. *Structural Fabulation: An Essay on Fiction of the Future*. Notre Dame, Ind.: University of Notre Dame Press, 1975. Scholes argues that fabular futuristic fictions are more pertinent to present concerns in a fast-changing world than any fiction set in the present-day can be.

MYSTERY AND DETECTIVE SHORT FICTION

Haining, Peter. *The Classic Era of American Pulp Magazines*. Chicago: Chicago Review Press, 2001. This American edition of a book originally published in England provides historical, biographical, and literary analyses of pulp stories published in a number of genres. Chapter 3, "The Coming of the Hardboiled Dicks," focuses on the "crime" pulps which published detective stories.

Herbert, Rosemary, ed. *The Oxford Companion to Crime and Mystery Writing*. New York: Oxford University Press, 1999. Essays and brief entries by hundreds of authorities span every conceivable aspect of the genre, making this an invaluable reference work for the student, casual reader, and scholar.

Kayman, Martin A. "The Short Story from Poe to Chesterton." In *The Cambridge Companion to Crime Fiction*, *edited by* Martin Priestman. Cambridge, England; Cambridge University Press, 2003. This section will be of particular interest to those looking for information about the development of the genre. The work as a whole is a useful reference tool for all genres, eras, styles, and writers of crime fiction in eighteenth-, nineteenth-, and twentieth-century England and America.

Moore, Lewis D. *Cracking the Hard-Boiled Detective: A Critical History from the 1920's to the Present*. Jefferson, N.C.: McFarland, 2006. Traces the development of the private investigator subgenre from the early days of Raymond Chandler and Dashiell Hammett to current practitioners.

Rzepka, Charles J. *Detective Fiction*. Cambridge, England: Polity, 2005. Rzepka's well-written survey of the genre pays particular attention to the development of scientific investigative methods and cultural issues that shaped the genre. Includes specific essays on Edgar Allan Poe, Sir Arthur Conan Doyle, Dorothy Sayers, and Raymond Chandler.

Symons, Julian. *Bloody Murder*. New York: Mysterious Press, 1993. Written by a leading critic and mystery-fiction writer, this is one of the most thorough, balanced, and readable histories and critical analyses of the genre. Although a bit dated now, it remains indispensable both for the fan and for the student of crime fiction.

THE SHORT-STORY CYCLE

Davis, Rocío G. *Transcultural Reinventions: Asian American and Asian Canadian Short-Story Cycles*. Toronto: TSAR, 2001. Examines how Asian American and Asian Canadian writers have adopted the short-story cycle as a means of both self-representation and empowerment. Some of the writers whose works are analyzed include Amy Tan, Rohinton Mistry, Sara Suleri, Garrett Hongo, Terry Watada, Sylvia Watanabe, M. G. Vassanji, and Wayson Choy.

Harde, Roxanne, ed. *Narratives of Community: Women's Short Story Sequences*. Newcastle, England: Cambridge Scholars, 2007. Collection of essays analyzing women's roles in domestic, social, and literary communities and how they attain their identities in these communities. Some of the writers whose works are examined include Sandra Cisneros, Margaret Laurence, Salwa Bakr, Mary Caponegro, Gloria Naylor, Elizabeth Gaskell, Virginia Woolf, Alice Munro, and Maxine Hong Kingston.

Ingram, Forrest L. "The Dynamics of Short Story Cycles." *New Orleans Review* 2 (1979): 7-12. A historical and critical survey and analysis of short stories that form a single unit, such as James Joyce's *Dubliners* (1914), Ernest Hemingway's *In Our Time* (1924, 1925), and Sherwood Anderson's *Winesburg, Ohio* (1919). Attempts to define some of the basic devices used in such cycles.

Kennedy, J. Gerald, ed. *Modern American Short Story Sequences: Composite Fictions and Fictive Communities*. Cambridge, England: Cambridge University Press, 1995. An anthology of essays by various critics on short-story sequence collections, such as Jean Toomer's *Cane* (1923), Ernest Hemingway's *In Our Time* (1924, 1925), William Faulkner's *Go Down, Moses* (1942), John Updike's *Olinger Stories: A Selection* (1964), Sherwood Anderson's *Winesburg, Ohio* (1919), and several others. Kennedy's introduction provides a brief survey of the short-story cycle, a definition of the cycle, and a discussion of the implications of the short-story sequence.

Kuttainen, Victoria. *Unsettling Stories: Settler Postcolonialism and the Short Story Composite*. Newcastle upon Tyne, England: Cambridge Scholars, 2010.

Examines how the interconnected short-story collection has been used to express issues of postcolonialism in American, Canadian, and Australian literature. Analyzes works by Tim Winton, Margaret Laurence, William Faulkner, Stephen Leacock, Sherwood Anderson, Tim O'Brien, and others to describe how they describe the nature of the colonial settlement experience.

Lundén, Rolf. *The United Stories of America: Studies in the Short Story Composite.* Amsterdam: Rodopi, 1999. Analyzes short-story cycles, focusing on the authors' strategies for closing these texts and attaining a sense of unity. Some of the authors who are examined include Eudora Welty, William Faulkner, Ernest Hemingway, and Sherwood Anderson.

Luscher, Robert M. "The Short Story Sequence: An Open Book." In *Short Story Theory at a Crossroads*, *edited by* Susan Lohafer and Jo Ellyn Clarey. Baton Rouge: Louisiana State University Press, 1989. Discusses the need for readers of story cycles, such as *Winesburg, Ohio*, to extend their drive to find a pattern to cover a number of individual sequences. Compares story cycles with mere aggregates of stories, as well as with novelistic sequences.

Lynch, Gerald. *The One and the Many: English-Canadian Short Story Cycles.* Toronto: University of Toronto Press, 2001. A literary-historical survey of the Canadian short-story cycle. Lynch examines Stephen Leacock's *Sunshine Sketches of a Little Town* in order to describe how a short-story cycle conveys meaning and the significant function of its concluding story. He then examines six other cycles, including works by Duncan Campbell Scott, Frederick Philip Grove, and Alice Munro.

Nagel, James. *The Contemporary American Short-Story Cycle: The Ethnic Resonance of Genre.* Baton Rouge: Louisiana State University Press, 2001. Argues that the concentric plot of the short-story cycle lends itself particularly well to issues of ethnic assimilation. Demonstrates this argument by analyzing short-story cycles by eight authors: Louise Erdrich, Jamaica Kincaid, Susan Minot, Sandra Cisneros, Tim O'Brien, Julia Alvarez, Amy Tan, and Robert Olen Butler.

Pacht, Michelle. *The Subversive Storyteller: The Short Story Cycle and the Politics of Identity in America.* Newcastle upon Tyne, England: Cambridge Scholars, 2009. Analyzes the works of nineteenth - and twentieth-century American authors to demonstrate how they adapted the short-story cycle in order to convey controversial ideas without alienating readers and publishers. Focuses on short stories by Washington Irving, Nathaniel Hawthorne, Sarah Orne Jewett, Charles Waddell Chesnutt, Willa Cather, Henry James, Ernest Hemingway, William Faulkner, Flannery O'Connor, Raymond Carver, Maxine Hong Kingston, and Louise Erdrich.

SHORT FICTION AND WOMEN

Bande, Usha, and Atma Ram. *Woman in Indian Short Stories: Feminist Perspective.* Jaipur, India: Rawat, 2003. Examines women writers' depiction of the "new woman" in Marathi, Hindi, Punjab, and Indian-English short stories published from the mid-1940's through the late 1990's.

Bloom, Harold, ed. *Caribbean Women Writers.* Philadelphia: Chelsea House, 1997. A thorough examination of contemporary, female Caribbean authors who write in English, including Jean Rhys, Jamaica Kincaid, Beryl Gilroy, and Edwidge Danticat. Includes bibliographical references and an index.

Brown, Julie, ed. *American Women Short Story Writers: A Collection of Critical Essays.* New York: Garland, 2000. Collection of essays that analyze short fiction by nineteenth- and twentieth-century women writers, ranging from serious works of literature to popular tales about "sob sisters." Some of the writers whose works are examined are Lydia Maria Child, Elizabeth Stoddard, Louisa May Alcott, Ellen Glasgow, Edith Wharton, Eudora Welty, Dorothy Parker, Joyce Carol Oates, and Denise Chávez.

Burgin, Mary. "The 'Feminine' Short Story: Recuperating the Moment." *Style* 27 (Fall, 1993): 380-386. Argues that there is a connection between so-called feminine writing that focuses on isolated moments and the concerns of women who have chosen the short story as a form. Claims that the twentieth-century epiphanic short story is a manifestation of women's tradition of temporal writing as opposed to the spatial writing of men.

Daiya, Krishna. *Post-Independence Women Short Story Writers in Indian English*. New Delhi, India: Sarup and Sons, 2006. Provides an overview of the works of women short-story writers, analyzing the themes, characterization, and styles of their stories. Assesses the status of the short-fiction genre and describes the contributions of women's short fiction to the genre and to Indian literature. Some of the writers whose works are analyzed are Shashi Deshpande, Anita Desai, Jhumpa Lahiri, Githa Hariharan, and Ruth Prawer Jhabvala.

Erro-Peralta, Nora, and Caridad Silva-Núñez, eds. *Beyond the Border: A New Age in Latin American Women's Fiction*. Pittsburgh, Pa.: Cleis Press, 1991. Covers works by Latin American female writers. Includes bibliographical references.

Hanson, Clare. "The Lifted Veil: Women and Short Fiction in the 1880's and 1890's." *The Yearbook of English Studies* 26 (1996): 135-142. Argues that British women writers in the early modernist period chose the short story to challenge the existing dominant order. Shows how this challenge is embodied in such stories as Charlotte Mew's "Mark Stafford's Wife" as an encounter, presented in iconic, painterly terms, between a male protagonist and a woman, who is then unveiled.

Harde, Roxanne, ed. *Narratives of Community: Women's Short Story Sequences*. Newcastle, England: Cambridge Scholars, 2007. Collection of essays analyzing women's roles in domestic, social, and literary communities and how they attain their identities in these communities. Some of the writers whose works are examined are Sandra Cisneros, Margaret Laurence, Salwa Bakr, Mary Caponegro, Gloria Naylor, Elizabeth Gaskell, Virginia Woolf, Alice Munro, and Maxine Hong Kingston.

Harrington, Ellen Burton, ed. *Scribbling Women and the Short Story Form: Approaches by American and British Women Writers*. New York: Peter Lang, 2008. Collection of essays providing feminist analyses of short fiction by British and American women, focusing on how this genre "liberated" women writers in the period from 1850 through the

late twentieth-century. Some of the women writers whose works are analyzed are Rebecca Harding Davis, Louise May Alcott, Kate Chopin, Katherine Anne Porter, Flannery O'Connor, Cynthia Ozick, and Lydia Davis.

Palumbo-DeSimone, Christine. *Sharing Secrets: Nineteenth-Century Women's Relations in the Short Story*. Madison, N.J.: Fairleigh Dickinson University Press, 2000. Palumbo-DeSimone contradicts the criticism that many short stories by nineteenth-century women writers are framed around a "seemingly meaningless incident," arguing that these stories are detailed, meaningful, and intricately designed works of serious fiction.

Partnoy, Alicia, ed. *You Can't Drown the Fire: Latin American Women Writing in Exile*. Pittsburgh, Pa.: Cleis Press, 1988. Covers twentieth-century female writers whose works have been translated into English. Includes bibliographical references.

PERSONAL ACCOUNTS BY SHORT-FICTION WRITERS

Allende, Isabel. "The Short Story." *Journal of Modern Literature* 20 (Summer, 1996): 21-28. This personal account of storytelling makes suggestions about the differences between the novel and the short story, the story's demand for believability, the story's focus on change, the story's relationship to dream, and the story as events transformed by poetic truth.

Bailey, Tom, ed. *On Writing Short Stories*. 2d ed. New York: Oxford University Press, 2011. In addition to containing a sampling of some classic short stories, this book also features a section in which short-story writers discuss some basic issues regarding the definition and form of these works. These writers include Francine Prose, who explains what makes a short story, and Andre Dubus, who explores the "habit of writing." Bailey also contributes an essay about character, plot, setting, time, metaphor, and voice in short fiction.

Barth, John. "It's a Short Story." In *Further Fridays: Essays, Lectures, and Other Nonfiction, 1984-1994*. New York: Little, Brown, 1995. A personal account by a "congenital novelist" of his brief love affair with the short story during the writing of *Chimera* (1972) and the stories in *Lost in the Funhouse* (1968).

Blythe, Will, ed. *Why I Write: Thoughts on the Craft of Fiction*. Boston: Little, Brown, 1998. A collection of essays by various authors about writing fiction. The essays most relevant to the short story are those by Joy Williams, who says that writers must cherish the mystery of discovery in the process of writing; Thom Jones, who discusses his passionate engagement in the writing of short stories; and Mary Gaitskill, who calls stories the "rich, unseen underlayer of the most ordinary moments."

Burgess, Anthony. "Anthony Burgess on the Short Story." *Journal of the Short Story in English*, no. 2 (1984): 31-47. Burgess admits that he disdains the short story because he cannot write it. He says that the novel presents an epoch, while the short story presents a revelation. Discusses different types of stories, distinguishing between the literary short story, which is patterned, and the commercial form, which is anecdotal.

Charters, Ann, ed. *The Story and Its Writer: An Introduction to Short Fiction*. 6th ed. Boston: Bedford/St. Martin's, 2003. A collection of classic short stories, with commentaries by their authors and other writers that analyze the works and describe how the stories were written. Includes appendixes chronicling storytelling before the emergence of the short story and the history of the short story.

Gioia, Dana, and R. S. Gwynn, eds. *The Art of the Short Story*. New York: Pearson Longman, 2006. This anthology includes an "author's perspective" from each of its fifty-two authors, in which the writers comment on the aims, context, and workings of their short stories. For example, Sherwood Anderson and Raymond Carver provide advice on the craft of writing; Margaret Atwood discusses Canadian identity; Alice Walker writes about race and gender; and Flannery O'Connor explains the importance of religious grace in her work. Some of the other authors included in the anthology are John Cheever, Albert Camus, F. Scott Fitzgerald, Ernest Hemingway, Anton Chekhov, James Joyce, Jorge Luis Borges, William Faulkner, Chinua Achebe, Ha Jin, Sandra Cisneros, and Gabriel García Márquez.

Iftekharuddin, Farhat, Mary Rohrberger, and Maurice Lee, eds. *Speaking of the Short Story: Interviews with Contemporary Writers*. Jackson: University Press of Mississippi, 1997. Collection of twenty-one interviews with short-story writers, such as Isabel Allende, Rudolfo A. Anaya, Ellen Douglas, Richard Ford, Bharati Mukherjee, and Leslie Marmon Silko, and short story critics, such as Susan Lohafer, Charles E. May, and Mary Rohrberger.

Lee, Maurice A., ed. *Writers on Writing: The Art of the Short Story*. Westport, Conn.: Praeger, 2005. A collection of essays in which short-story writers from around the world discuss their craft and analyze stories and types of short fiction. Some of the contributors include Amiri Baraka, Olive Senior, Jayne Anne Philips, Janette Turner Hospital, Kirpal Singh, and Ivan Wolfers.

Mandelbaum, Paul, ed. *Twelve Short Stories and Their Making*. New York: Persea Books, 2005. These twelve stories by contemporary writers have been selected to illustrate six elements of the short story: character, plot, point of view, theme, setting, and structure. The book also includes individual interviews with the twelve authors in which they describe their writing processes and the challenges they faced in composing their selected stories. The featured writers include Elizabeth Tallent, Charles Johnson, Allan Gurganus, Ursula K. Le Guin, Jhumpa Lahiri, Sandra Cisneros, and Tobias Wolff.

O'Connor, Flannery. "Writing Short Stories." In *Mystery and Manners*, edited by Sally and Robert Fitzgerald. New York: Farrar, Straus & Giroux, 1969. In this lecture at a southern writers' conference, O'Connor discusses the two qualities necessary for the short story: "sense of manners," which writers get from the texture of their immediate surroundings, and "sense of mystery," which is always the mystery of personality-- "showing how some specific folks *will* do, in spite of everything."

Senior, Olive. "Lessons from the Fruit Stand: Or, Writing for the Listener." *Journal of Modern Literature* 20 (Summer, 1996): 40-44. An account of one writer's development of the short story as a personal engagement between teller and listener. Discusses the relationship between the oral tradition of gossip and folklore and the development of short-story conventions. Claims that the short story is a form based on bits and pieces of human lives for which there is no total picture.

Turchi, Peter, and Andrea Barrett, eds. *The Story Behind the Story: Twenty-six Writers and How They Work*. New York: W. W. Norton, 2004. The stories in this collection were written by faculty members in the writing program at Warren Wilson College, including Antonya Nelson, Margot Livesey, David Shields, C. J. Hribal, Andrea Barrett, Steven Schwartz, and Jim Shepard. Accompanying each story is a brief essay in which the writer describes how his or her story was created.

Wright, Austin. "The Writer Meets the Critic on the Great Novel/Short Story Divide." *Journal of Modern Literature* 20 (Summer, 1996): 13-19. A personal account by a short-story critic and novelist of some of the basic differences between the critical enterprise and the writing of fiction, as well as some of the generic differences between the short story and the novel.

Charles E. May
Updated by Rebecca Kuzins

GUIDE TO ONLINE RESOURCES

WEB SITES

The following sites were visited by the editors of Salem Press in 2011. Because URLs frequently change, the accuracy of these addresses cannot be guaranteed; however, long-standing sites, such as those of colleges and universities, national organizations, and government agencies, generally maintain links when sites are moved or updated.

Australian Literature
http://www.middlemiss.org/lit/lit.html

Perry Middlemiss, a Melbourne-based blogger, created this useful resource about Australian writers and their works. It features an alphabetical list of authors which links to biographies and lists of their works; some of the listed works link to a synopsis and an excerpt. Peter Carey, David Malouf, and Frank Moorhouse are among the writers listed. The site also contains information about Australian literary awards.

Bibliomania: Short Stories
http://www.bibliomania.com/0/5/frameset.html

Among Bibliomania's more than two thousand texts are short stories written by American and foreign writers, including Mark Twain, O. Henry, Stephen Crane, and Anton Chekhov, as well as James Joyce's story collection *Dubliners*. The stories can be retrieved via lists of titles and authors.

Books and Writers
http://www.kirjasto.sci.fi/indeksi.htm

A broad, comprehensive, and easy-to-use resource about hundreds of authors throughout the world, extending from 70 B.C.E to the twenty-first century. Books and Writers contains an alphabetical list of authors with links to pages featuring a biography, a list of works, and recommendations for further reading about each author; each writer's page also includes links to related pages in the site. Although brief, the biographical essays provide a solid overview of the authors'

careers, their contributions to literature, and their literary influence.

A Celebration of Women Writers
http://digital.library.upenn.edu/women

An extensive compendium of information about the contributions of women writers throughout history. The "Local Editions by Authors" and "Local Editions by Category" pages enable users to retrieve electronic texts of the works of numerous writers, including Katherine Mansfield and Virginia Woolf. Users can also access biographical and bibliographical information about women writers by browsing writers' names, countries of origin, ethnicities, and centuries in which they lived.

Classic Short Stories
http://www.classicshorts.com

Features the texts of British and American short stories, as well as some stories by Guy de Maupassant, Anton Chekhov, and other European writers. Stories can be accessed via title or author's name.

Contemporary Writers
http://www.contemporarywriters.com

Created by the British Council, this site offers, in its own words, "up-to-date profiles of some of the U.K. [United Kingdom] and Commonwealth, and Republic of Ireland's most important living writers." The available information includes biographies, bibliographies, critical reviews, news about literary prizes, and photographs. Users can search the site by author, genre, nationality, gender, publisher, book title, and prize name and date.

The Literary Gothic
http://www.litgothic.com/index_html.html

The Literary Gothic describes itself as a guide to "all things concerned with literary Gothicism," including ghost stories, with the majority of its resources related to literary works written and published from 1764 through 1820. The site defines gothic literature in broad terms, including some authors usually not associated with the genre, such as Joseph Addison and Willa Cather. An alphabetical list of authors and of titles provides links to biographies and other Web-based resources, including electronic texts of many works of gothic literature.

LiteraryHistory.com
http://www.literaryhistory.com

An excellent source of Web-based academic, scholarly, and critical literature about eighteenth-, nineteenth-, and twentieth-century American and English writers. The site provides numerous pages about specific eras and literary genres, including individual pages for eighteenth-, nineteenth-, and twentieth-century literature and for African American and postcolonial literature. These pages contain alphabetical lists of authors which link to articles, reviews, overviews, excerpts of works, teaching guides, podcast interviews, and other materials.

Literary Resources on the Net
http://andromeda.rutgers.edu/~jlynch/Lit

Jack Lynch of Rutgers University maintains this extensive collection of links to Internet sites that are useful to academics, including Web sites about a broad range of literary topics. The site is organized chronically, with separate pages for information about classical Greece and Rome, the Middle Ages, the Renaissance, the eighteenth-century, Romantic and Victorian eras, and twentieth-century British and Irish literature. There are also separate pages providing links to Web sites

about American literature and to women's literature and feminism.

Literature: What Makes a Good Short Story
http://www.learner.org/interactives/literature

Annenberg Learner.org, a site providing interactive resources for teachers, contains this section describing the elements of short fiction, including plot construction, point of view, character development, setting, and theme. The section also features the text of "A Jury of Her Peers," a short story by Susan Glaspell, in order to illustrate the components of short fiction.

LitWeb
http://litweb.net

LitWeb provides biographies of more than five hundred world authors throughout history which can be accessed via an alphabetical listing. The pages about each writer contain a list of his or her works, suggestions for further reading, and illustrations. LitWeb also offers information about past and present winners of major literary prizes

Luminarium: Anthology of English Literature
http://www.luminarium.org/lumina.htm

Luminarium has been a reliable source for more than a decade, providing information about English literature from the Middle Ages through the eighteenth-century. Some of the authors it covers are Geoffrey Chaucer, Robert Greene, Sir Thomas Malory, Sir Richard Steele, and Samuel Johnson. Users can assess a biography, list of quotable remarks, and bibliographies of books about each author, as well as links to electronic texts of the writers' works, essays about the writers, and related Web sites.

The Modern Word: The Libyrinth
http://www.themodernword.com/authors.html

The Modern Word provides a great deal of critical information about postmodern writers and contemporary experimental fiction. The core of the site is "The Libyrinth," which lists authors for which there are links to essays and other resources. There are also sections devoted to Samuel Beckett, Jorge Luis Borges, Gabriel García Márquez, James Joyce, Franz Kafka, and Thomas Pynchon.

The Short Story Library at American Literature

http://www.americanliterature.com/sstitleindex.html

A compilation of more than two thousand short stories which can be accessed via alphabetical lists of story titles and authors. Although the majority of the authors are American, the site also features English translations of stories by Anton Chekhov, Guy de Maupassant, and other writers, as well as works by British authors, such as Charles Dickens, Saki, and Rudyard Kipling.

The Victorian Web

http://www.victorianweb.org

One of the finest Web sites about the nineteenth century, providing a wealth of material about Great Britain during the reign of Queen Victoria, including information about the era's literature. The home page links to a section called "Authors," offering an alphabetical listing of more than one hundred nineteenth-century writers; the list links to additional pages of information about the individual authors, including biographies, bibliographies, analyses of their work, and, in some cases, excerpts of their writings. "Authors" also links to lists of pre- and post-Victorian writers and to British and other European authors associated with the Aesthetic and Decadent movements. The information about some of the writers, such as Charles Dickens, Thomas Hardy, George Eliot, and William Makepeace Thackeray, is quite extensive, with discussions of the themes, characterization, imagery, narration, and other aspects of their work and essays and other resources placing their writings in social, political, and economic context.

Voice of the Shuttle

http://vos.ucsb.edu

The most complete and authoritative place for online information about literature. Created and maintained by professors and students in the English department at the University of California, Santa Barbara, Voice of the Shuttle is a database with thousands of links to electronic books, academic journals, association Web sites, sites created by university professors, and many other resources about the humanities. Its "Literature in English" page provides links to separate pages about the literature of the Anglo-Saxon era, Middle Ages, Renaissance and seventeenth century, Restoration and eighteenth-century, Romantic age, Victorian age, and modern and contemporary periods in Great Britain and the United States, as well as a page about minority literature. Another page in the site, "Literatures Other than English," offers a gateway to information about the literature of numerous countries and world regions, including Africa, Eastern Europe, Arabic-speaking nations, China, France, and Germany.

Voices from the Gaps

http://voices.cla.umn.edu

This site from the English department at the University of Minnesota is "dedicated to bringing together marginalized resources and knowledge about women artists of color," including women writers. Users can retrieve information by artists' names or by a selection of keywords, including Chinese Canadians, Indian Canadians, Indo-Caribbean Canadians, and Japanese Canadians.

Western European Studies Section: British Studies Web

http://wess.lib.byu.edu/index.php/Great_Britain_%28British_Studies%29

The Western European Studies Section of the Association of College and Research Libraries maintains a collection of resources useful to students of Western European history and culture. The site includes the British Studies Web, with links to a separate page of information about the language and literature of England, the Republic of Ireland, Northern Ireland, Scotland, and Wales.

Electronic databases usually do not have their own URLs. Instead, public, college, and university libraries subscribe to these databases, provide links to them on their Web sites, and make them available to library card holders or specified patrons. Readers can check library Web sites or ask reference librarians to check availability.

Bloom's Literary Reference Online

Facts On File publishes this database of thousands of articles by renowned scholar Harold Bloom and other literary critics, examining the lives and works of great writers worldwide. The database also includes information on more than forty-six thousand literary characters, literary topics, themes, movements, and genres, plus video segments about literature. Users can retrieve information by browsing writers' names, titles of works, time periods, genres, or writers' nationalities.

Canadian Literary Centre

Produced by EBSCO, the Canadian Literary Centre database contains full-text content from ECW Press, a Toronto-based publisher, including *Canadian Writers and Their Work*, *George Woodcock's Introduction to Canadian Fiction*, and *Essays on Canadian Writing*. Author biographies, essays and literary criticism, and book reviews are among the database's offerings.

Literary Reference Center

EBSCO's Literary Reference Center (LRC) is a comprehensive full-text database containing information from reference works, books, literary journals, and other materials. Its contents include more than 34,000 plot summaries, synopses, and overviews of literary works; almost 100,000 essays and articles of literary criticism; about 180,000 author biographies; more than 683,000 book reviews; and more than 6,200 author interviews. It also contains the entire contents of Salem Press's MagillOnLiterature Plus. Users can retrieve information by browsing a list of authors' names or titles of literary works; they can also use an advanced search engine to access information by numerous categories, including authors' names, genders, cultural identities, national identities, and the years in which they lived, or by literary title, character, locale, genre, and publication date.

Literary Resource Center

Published by Gale, this comprehensive literary database contains information on the lives and works of more than 135,000 authors from Gale reference sources in all genres, all time periods, and throughout the world. In addition, the database offers more than 75,000 full-text critical essays and reviews from some of Gale's reference publications, including *Short Story Criticism*; more than 11,000 overviews of frequently studied works; and more than 300,000 full-text short stories, poems, and plays. Literary Resource Center also features a literary-historical time line and an encyclopedia of literature.

MagillOnLiterature Plus

MagillOnLiterature Plus is a comprehensive, integrated literature database produced by Salem Press and available on the EBSCO host platform. The database contains the full-text of Salem's many literature-related reference works, including *Masterplots* (series I and II), *Cyclopedia of World Authors*, *Cyclopedia of Literary Characters*, *Cyclopedia of Literary Places*, and *Critical Surveys of Literature*. Among its contents are critical essays, brief plot summaries, extended character profiles, and detailed setting discussions about works of literature by more than eighty-five hundred short- and long-fiction writers, poets, dramatists, essayists, and philosophers. It also features biographical essays on more than twenty-five hundred authors, with lists of each author's principal works and current secondary bibliographies.

NoveList

NoveList is a readers' advisory service produced by EBSCO Publishing. The database provides access to 155,000 titles of both adult and juvenile fiction, including collections of short fiction. Users can type the words "short story" into the search engine and retrieve more than fourteen thousand short-story collections;

users can also search by author's name to access titles of books, information about the author, and book reviews.

Short Story Index

This index, created by the H. W. Wilson Company, features information on more than 76,500 stories from more than 4,000 collections. Users can retrieve information by author, title, keyword, subject, date, source, literary technique, or a combination of these categories. The subject searches provide information about the stories' themes, locales, narrative techniques, and genres.

Rebecca Kuzins

TIMELINE

10th century	*The Maginogion*, a collection of Welsh prose tales, both oral and written, begins to take shape. These tales will be collated from medieval manuscripts and published in book form beginning in 1838.
1387-1400	Geoffrey Chaucer creates *The Canterbury Tales*, a collection of stories about a group of pilgrims en route to Canterbury. The collection is unprecedented in its use of a wide variety of short-story types, including the Breton lai, fabliau, beast-fable, exemplum, and allegory.
1485	*Le Morte d'Arthur* is written by Sir Thomas Mallory and is the first text to bring unity and coherence to the mass of material regarding the Arthurian legend.
1592	English Renaissance writer Robert Greene publishes *A Disputation Between a Hee Conny-Catcher and a Shee Conny-Catcher*.
1692	Playwright William Congreve publishes his only work of short fiction, *Incognita: Or, Love and Duty Reconcil'd*.
1697	Aphra Behn, better known as a dramatist and novelist, creates one of the most important works of Restoration short fiction, *The Nun: Or, The Perjur'd Beauty*.
1706	Daniel Defoe's publishes "A True Relation of the Apparition of One Mrs. Veal," the earliest short narrative in English literature to contribute to the development of the short story.
1711-1712, 1714	Joseph Addison and Sir Richard Steele write their semifictional essays for *The Spectator* newspaper, in which they create the characters of Sir Roger de Coverley and Mr. Spectator.
1759	Samuel Johnson publishes *Rasselas, Prince of Abyssinia*.
1760-1761	*The Public Ledger* publishes *The Citizen of the World*, Oliver Goldsmith's version of the "Asian tale," a popular genre of the time.
1827	Sir Walter Scott publishes "The Two Drovers." In his book *The Short Story in English* (1981), Walter Allen begins his survey of the genre with Scott's story, which Allen describes as "the first modern short story in English."
1830-1833	William Carleton publishes his most popular short-story collection, the five-volume *Traits and Stories of the Irish Peasantry*. Carleton was the first Irish writer to provide a realistic depiction of his nation's peasants.

1843	*A Christmas Carol*, Charles Dickens's best-known holiday story, is published.
1882	Robert Louis Stevenson publishes his first short-fiction collection, *The New Arabian Nights*. He will follow this up three years later with a sequel, *More New Arabian Nights*.
1888	Thomas Hardy publishes *Wessex Tales*, a volume of short stories that will prove a popular success.
1890	Welsh writer Arthur Machen publishes *The Great God Pan*, which some critics consider the best horror story ever written.
1892	The detective story gains sophistication and popularity with the publication of *The Adventures of Sherlock Holmes* by Sir Arthur Conan Doyle.
1894	At the height of his career, popular Australian writer Henry Lawson publishes a short-fiction collection *While the Billy Boils*.
1897	H. G. Wells, whose "scientific romances" gave shape to the science-fiction genre, publishes *Thirty Strange Stories*.
1899	Joseph Conrad's *Heart of Darkness* is serialized and will be published in book form three years later.
1901	Brander Matthews, a Columbia University professor, publishes *The Philosophy of Short Fiction*, the first full-length study of the short story.
1904	M. R. James, an academic and scholar who wrote ghost stories for his friends, publishes his first collection of these tales, *Ghost Stories of an Antiquary*.
1907	Rudyard Kipling, an accomplished short-story writer, wins the Nobel Prize in Literature.
1911	Katherine Mansfield publishes her first short-story collection, *In a German Pension*. This New Zealand-born writer will attain a reputation as one of the greatest practitioners of short-fiction writing.
1914	D. H. Lawrence publishes his first short-fiction collection, *The Prussian Officer, and Other Stories*.
1914	James Joyce publishes *Dubliners*, which shapes the modernist conception of short fiction.
1915	*The Best American Short Stories* debuts and will continue to be published annually. The anthology features the best short stories published that year in American and Canadian magazines.

1924	Agatha Christie publishes her first collection of stories, *Poirot Investigates*, featuring one of her best-known sleuths, Belgian detective Hercule Poirot.
1928	H. E. Bates publishes his second collection of short fiction, *Day's End, and Other Stories*.
1932	British writer John Galsworthy receives the Nobel Prize in Literature.
1943	Mary Lavin wins the James Tait Black Memorial Prize for *Tales from Bective Bridge*. As of 2011, her collection was the only work of short fiction to receive this prestigious award.
1951	Canadian writer Mavis Gallant publishes her first short story, "Madeline's Birthday," in *The New Yorker*. Gallant will earn a reputation as one of the premiere short-fiction writers of her time, and in 2002 she will receive the Rea Award for the Short Story.
1963	Irish writer Frank O'Connor publishes *The Lonely Voice*, a study of short fiction focusing on nine writers, including Ernest Hemingway, Guy de Maupassant, and Anton Chekhov.
1964	J. G. Ballard publishes *The Terminal Beach*, an innovative work of short fiction he describes as a "condensed novel."
1974	Angela Carter publishes *The Bloody Chamber, and Other Stories*. Carter's stories combine eroticism with feminist criticism of patriarchal legends and folk tales.
1991	Janis Galloway publishes her first short-fiction collection, *Blood*, in which she depicts postindustrial Scotland as a bleak and often violent place.
1995	*The Collected Stories of Peter Carey* is published. Carey, the world's most famous Australian writer, is one of only two authors to twice win the prestigious Man Booker Prize.
1999	John Updike edits *The Best American Short Stories of the Century*, featuring one of the stories that appeared in each edition of *The Best American Short Stories* from 1915 through 1999.
2000	Australian writer David Malouf wins the Neustadt International Prize for Literature for his body of work. *The Complete Stories*, a compendium of his short fiction, will appear seven years later.
2003	The four-volume collection *The Complete Stories* of Canadian writer Morley Callaghan is posthumously published.

2005	*Natasha, and Other Stories* by David Bezmozgis receives the Danuta Gleed Literary Awarded, presented annually by the Writers' Union of Canada to a Canadian writer who has written the best first collection of short fiction in English.
2007	Nam Le wins the Pushcart Prize for his story "Cartagena."
2007	*Walk the Blue Fields*, the second short-fiction collection by Claire Keegan, establishes the Irish writer's reputation as one the most significant practitioners of the short-story genre.
2007	Doris Lessing receives the Nobel Prize in Literature.
2009	Alice Munro, often called the "Canadian Chekhov," receives the Man Booker International Prize.
2010	The Bank of New Zealand (BNZ) Katherine Mansfield Short Story Awards inaugurated in New Zealand in 1958, is renamed the BNZ Literary Awards, with the Premier Award becoming the BNZ Katherine Mansfield Award. Recipients in the twenty-first century have included Tracey Slaughter for "Wheat" (2004), Susan Wylie for "Lolly" (2005), Charlotte Grimshaw for "Plain Sailing" (2006), and Carl Nixon for "My Beautiful Balloon" (2007).

Rebecca Kuzins

MAJOR AWARDS

AMERICAN AND CANADIAN AWARDS

THE BEST AMERICAN SHORT STORIES
Published annually since 1915, *The Best American Short Stories* includes the best stories that were published in American or Canadian magazines during the year. Selection for the volume is considered a high honor.

The Best Short Stories of 1915, and the Yearbook of the American Short Story, *edited by* Edward J. O'Brien

Burt, Maxwell Struthers-- "The Water-Hole"
Byrne, Donn-- "The Wake"
Comfort, Will Levington-- "Chautonville"
Dwiggins, W. A.-- "La Derniere Mobilisation"
Dwyer, James Francis-- "The Citizen"
Gregg, Frances-- "Whose Dog?"
Hecht, Ben-- "Life"
Hurst, Fannie-- "T. B."
Johnson, Arthur-- "Mr. Eberdeen's House"
Jordan, Virgil-- "Vengeance Is Mine"

Lyon, Harris Merton-- "The Weaver Who Clad the Summer"
Muilenburg, Walter J.-- "Heart of Youth"
Noyes, Newbold-- "The End of the Path"
O'Brien, Seumas-- "The Whale and the Grasshopper"
O'Reilly, Mary Boyle-- "In Berlin"
Roof, Katharine Metcalf-- "The Waiting Years"
Rosenblatt, Benjamin-- "Zelig"
Singmaster, Elsie-- "The Survivors"
Steele, Wilbur Daniel-- "The Yellow Cat"
Synon, Mary-- "The Bounty-Jumper"

The Best Short Stories of 1916, and the Yearbook of the American Short Story, *edited by* Edward J. O'Brien

Atherton, Gertrude-- "The Sacrificial Altar"
Benefield, Barry-- "Miss Willett"
Booth, Frederick-- "Supers"
Burnet, Dana-- "Fog"
Buzzell, Francis-- "Ma's Pretties"
Cobb, Irvin S.-- "The Great Auk"

Dreiser, Theodore-- "The Lost Phoebe"
Gordon, Armistead C.-- "The Silent Infare"
Greene, Frederick Stuart-- "The Cat of the Cane-Brake"
Hallet, Richard Matthews-- "Making Port"
Hurst, Fannie-- "'Ice water, Pl--!'"

The Best Short Stories of 1917, and the Yearbook of the American Short Story, *edited by* Edward J. O'Brien

Babcock, Edwina Stanton-- "Excursion"
Beer, Thomas-- "Onnie"
Burt, Maxwell Struthers-- "Cup of Tea"
Buzzell, Francis-- "Lonely Places"
Cobb, Irvin S.-- "Boys Will Be Boys"

Dobie, Charles Caldwell-- "Laughter"
Dwight, H. G.-- "Emperor of Elam"
Ferber, Edna-- "Gay Old Dog"
Gerould, Katharine Fullerton-- "Knight's Move"
Glaspell, Susan-- "Jury of Her Peers"

Greene, Frederick Stuart-- "Bunker Mouse"
Hallet, Richard Matthews-- "Rainbow Pete"
Hurst, Fannie-- "Get Ready the Wreaths"
Johnson, Fanny Kemble-- "Strange Looking Man"
Kline, Burton-- "Caller in the Night"

O'Sullivan, Vincent-- "Interval"
Perry, Lawrence-- "Certain Rich Man"
Pulver, Mary Brecht-- "Path of Glory"
Steele, Wilbur Daniel-- "Ching, Ching, Chinaman"
Synon, Mary-- "None So Blind"

The Best Short Stories of 1918, and the Yearbook of the American Short Story, *edited by* **Edward J. O'Brien**

Abdullah, Achmed-- "A Simple Act of Piety"
Babcock, Edwina Stanton-- "Cruelties"
Brown, Katharine Holland-- "Buster"
Dobie, Charles Caldwell-- "The Open Window"
Dudly, William-- "The Toast to Forty-five"
Freedley, Mary Mitchell-- "Blind Vision"
Gerould, Gordon Hall-- "Imagination"
Gilbert, George-- "In Maulmain Fever-Ward"
Humphrey, G.-- "The Father's Hand"
Johnson, Arthur-- "The Visit of the Master"
Kline, Burton-- "In the Open Code"

Lewis, Sinclair-- "The Willow Walk"
Moseley, Katharine Prescott-- "The Story Vinton Heard at Mallorie"
Rhodes, Harrison-- "Extra Men"
Springer, Fleta Campbell-- "Solitaire"
Steele, Wilbur Daniel-- "The Dark Hour"
Street, Julian-- "The Bird of Serbia"
Venable, Edward C.-- "At Isham's"
Vorse, Mary Heaton-- "De Vilmarte's Luck"
Wood, Frances Gilchrist-- "The White Battalion"

The Best Short Stories of 1919, and the Yearbook of the American Short Story, *edited by* **Edward J. O'Brien**

Alsop, G. F.-- "The Kitchen Gods"
Anderson, Sherwood-- "An Awakening"
Babcock, Edwina Stanton-- "Willum's Vanilla"
Barnes, Djuna-- "A Night Among the Horses"
Bartlett, Frederick Orin-- "Long, Long Ago"
Brownell, Agnes Mary-- "Dishes"
Burt, Maxwell Struthers-- "The Blood-Red One"
Cabell, James Branch-- "The Wedding-Jest"
Fish, Horace-- "The Wrists on the Door"
Glaspell, Susan-- "'Government Goat'"

Goodman, Henry-- "The Stone"
Hallet, Richard Matthews-- "To the Bitter End"
Hergesheimer, Joseph-- "The Meeker Ritual"
Ingersoll, Will E.-- "The Centenarian"
Johnston, Calvin-- "Messengers"
Jones, Howard Mumford-- "Mrs. Drainger's Veil"
La Motte, Ellen N.-- "Under a Wine-Glass"
Lieberman, Elias-- "A Thing of Beauty"
Vorse, Mary Heaton-- "The Other Room"
Yezierska, Anzia-- "'The Fat of the Land'"

The Best Short Stories of 1920, and the Yearbook of the American Short Story, *edited by* **Edward J. O'Brien**

Anderson, Sherwood-- "The Other Woman"
Babcock, Edwina Stanton-- "Gargoyle"
Bercovici, Konrad-- "Ghitza"
Bryner, Edna Clare-- "The Life of Five Points"
Camp, Wadsroth-- "The Signal Tower"
Crew, Helen Oale-- "The Parting Genius"
Gerould, Katharine Fullerton-- "Habakkuk"
Hartman, Lee Foster-- "The Judgment of Vulcan"
Hughes, Rupert-- "The Stick-in-the-Muds"
Mason, Grace Sartwell-- "His Job"

Oppenheim, James-- "The Rending"
Roche, Arthur Somers-- "The Dummy-Chucker"
Sidney, Rose-- "Butterflies"
Springer, Fleta Campbel-- "The Rotter"
Steele, Wilbur Daniel-- "Out of Exile"
Storm, Ethel-- "The Three Telegrams"
Wheelwright, John T.-- "The Roman Bath"
Whitman, Stephen French-- "Amazement"
Williams, Ben Ames-- "Sheener"
Wood, Frances Gilchrist-- "Turkey Red"

The Best Short Stories of 1921, and the Yearbook of the American Short Story, *edited by* Edward J. O'Brien

Anderson, Sherwood-- "Brothers"

Bercovici, Konrad-- "Fanutza"

Burt, Maxwell Struthers-- "Experiment"

Cobb, Irvin S.-- "Darkness"

Colcord, Lincoln-- "An Instrument of the Gods"

Finger, Charles J.-- "The Lizard God"

Frank, Waldo-- "Under the Dome"

Gerould, Katherine Fullerton-- "French Eva"

Glasgow, Ellen-- "The Past"

Glaspell, Susan-- "His Smile"

Hallet, Richard Matthews-- "The Harbor Master"

Hart, Frances Noyes-- "Green Gardens"

Hurst, Fannie-- "She Walks in Beauty"

Komroff, Manuel-- "The Little Master of the Sky"

Mott, Frank Luther-- "The Man with the Good Face"

O'Sullivan, Vincent-- "Master of Fallen Years"

Steele, Wilbur Daniel-- "The Shame Dance"

Thayer, Harriet Maxon-- "Kindred"

Towne, Charles Hanson-- "Shelby"

Vorse, Mary Heaton-- "The Wallow of the Sea"

The Best Short Stories of 1922, and the Yearbook of the American Short Story, *edited by* Edward J. O'Brien

Aiken, Conrad-- "The Dark City"

Anderson, Sherwood-- "I'm a Fool"

Bercovici, Konrad-- "The Death of Murdo"

Boogher, Susan M.-- "An Unknown Warrior"

Booth, Frederick-- "The Helpless Ones"

Bryner, Edna-- "Forest Cover"

Cohen, Rose Gollup-- "Natalka's Portion"

Finger, Charles J.-- "The Shame of Gold"

Fitzgerald, F. Scott-- "Two for a Cent"

Frank, Waldo-- "John the Baptist"

Freedman, David-- "Mendel Marantz: Housewife"

Gerould, Katharine Fullerton-- "Belshazzar's Letter"

Hecht, Ben-- "Winkelburg"

Hergesheimer, Joseph-- "The Token"

Jitro, William-- "The Resurrection and the Life"

Lardner, Ring-- "The Golden Honeymoon"

Oppenheim, James-- "He Laughed at the Gods"

Rosenblatt, Benjamin-- "In the Metropolis"

Steele, Wilbur Daniel-- "From the Other Side of the South"

Wood, Clement-- "The Coffin"

The Best Short Stories of 1923, and the Yearbook of the American Short Story, *edited by* Edward J. O'Brien

Adams, Bill-- "Way for a Sailor"

Anderson, Sherwood-- "The Man's Story"

Babcock, Edwina Stanton-- "Mr. Cardeezer"

Bercovici, Konrad-- "Seed"

Burnet, Dana-- "Beyond the Cross"

Clark, Valma-- "Ignition"

Cobb, Irvin S.-- "The Chocolate Hyena"

Cournos, John-- "The Samovar"

Dreiser, Theodore-- "Reina"

Ferber, Edna-- "Home Girl"

Goodman, Henry-- "The Button"

Hemingway, Ernest-- "My Old Man"

Hurst, Fannie-- "Seven Candle"

Montague, Margaret Prescott-- "The Today Tomorrow"

Stewart, Solon K.-- "The Contract of Corporal Twing"

Stimson, F. J.-- "By Due Process of Law"

Sukow, Ruth-- "Renters"

Toomer, Jean-- "Blood-Burning Moon"

Vorse, Mary Heaton-- "The Promise"

Wilson, Harry Leon-- "Flora and Fauna"

The Best Short Stories of 1924, and the Yearbook of the American Short Story, *edited by* Edward J. O'Brien

Burke, Morgan-- "Champlin"

Cram, Mildred-- "Billy"

Dell, Floyd-- "Phantom Adventure"

Dobie, Charles Caldwell-- "The Cracked Teapot"

Drake, Carlos-- "The Last Dive"

Finger, Charles J.-- "Adventures of Andrew Lang"

Gale, Zona-- "The Biography of Blade"

Greenwald, Tupper-- "Corputt"

Hervey, Harry-- "The Young Men Go Down"

Hess, Leonard L.-- "The Lesser Gift"

Hughes, Rupert-- "Grudges"

Morris, Gouverneur-- "A Postscript to Divorce"

Reese, Lizette Woodworth-- "Forgiveness"

Sergel, Roger-- "Nocturne: A Red Shawl"

Shiffrin, A. B.-- "The Black Laugh"

Suckow, Ruth-- "Four Generations"

Van den Bark, Melvin-- "Two Women and Hog-Back Ridge"

Van Dine, Warren L.-- "The Poet"

Wescott, Glenway-- "In a Thicket"

Wood, Frances Gilchrist-- "Shoes"

The Best Short Stories of 1925, and the Yearbook of the American Short Story, *edited by* **Edward J. O'Brien**

Alexander, Sandra-- "The Gift"

Anderson, Sherwood-- "The Return"

Asch, Nathan-- "Gertude Donovan"

Benefield, Barry-- "Guard of Honor"

Bercovici, Konrad-- "The Beggar of Alcazar"

Cohen, Bella-- "The Laugh"

Dobie, Charles Caldwell-- "The Hands of the Enemy"

Fisher, Rudolph-- "The City of Refuge"

Gerould, Katherine Fullerton-- "An Army with Banners"

Gilkyson, Walter-- "Coward's Castle"

Komroff, Manuel-- "How Does It Feel to Be Free?"

Lardner, Ring-- "Haircut"

Robinson, Robert-- "The Ill Wind"

Scott, Evelyn-- "The Old Lady"

Stanley, May-- "Old Man Ledge"

Steele, Wilber Daniel-- "Six Dollars"

Waldman, Milton-- "The Home Town"

Wescott, Glenway-- "Fire and Water"

Willoughby, Barrett-- "The Devil Drum"

Wylie, Elinor-- "Gideon's Revenge"

The Best Short Stories of 1926, and the Yearbook of the American Short Story, *edited by* **Edward J. O'Brien**

Benefield, Barry-- "Carrie Snyder"

Carver, Ada Jack-- "Maudie"

Corley, Donald-- "The Glass Eye of Throgmorton"

Crowell, Chester T.-- "Take the Stand, Please"

Dingle, A. E.-- "Bound for Rio Grande"

Dudley, Henry Walbridge-- "Query"

Fauset, Arthur Huff-- "Symphonesque"

Gale, Zona-- "Evening"

Greenwald, Tupper-- "Wheels"

Hemingway, Ernest-- "The Undefeated"

Komroff, Manuel-- "The Christian Bite"

Krunich, Milutin-- "Then Christs Fought Hard"

Lardner, Ring-- "Travelogue"

Mason, Grace Sartwell-- "The First Stone"

Meriwether, Susan-- "Grimaldi"

Morris, Ira V.-- "A Tale from the Grave"

Sherwood, Robert E.-- "'Extra! Extra!'"

Steele, Wilbur Daniel-- "Out of the Wind"

Strater, Edward L.-- "The Other Road"

Tracy, Virginia-- "The Giant's Thunder"

The Best Short Stories of 1927, and the Yearbook of the American Short Story, *edited by* **Edward J. O'Brien**

Anderson, Sherwood-- "Another Wife"

Bradford, Roark-- "Child of God"

Brecht, Harold W.-- "Vienna Roast"

Burman, Ben Lucien-- "Minstrels of the Mist"

Finley-Thomas, Elisabeth-- "Mademoiselle"

Hare, Amory-- "Three Lumps of Sugar"

Hemingway, Ernest-- "The Killers"

Hergesheimer, Joseph-- "Trial by Armes"

Heyward, DuBose-- "The Half Pint Flask"

Hopper, James-- "When it Happens"

La Farge, Oliver-- "North Is Black"

Lane, Rose Wilder-- "Yarbwoman"

Le Sueur, Meridel-- "Persephone"

Marquand, J. P.-- "Good Morning, Major"

Saxon, Lyle-- "Cane River"

Sexton, John S.-- "The Pawnshop"

Shay, Frank-- "Little Dombey"

Sullivan, Alan-- "In Portofino"

Weeks, Raymond-- "The Hound-Tuner of Callaway"

Wister, Owen-- "The Right Honorable the Strawberries"

The Best Short Stories of 1928, and the Yearbook of the American Short Story,
edited by Edward J. O'Brien

Brennan, Frederick Hazlitt-- "The Guardeen Angel"

Bromfield, Louis-- "The Cat That Lived at the Ritz"

Brush, Katharine-- "Seven Blocks Apart"

Callaghan, Morley-- "A Country Passion"

Canfield, Dorothy-- "At the Sign of the Three Daughters"

Chambers, Maria Cristina-- "John of God, the Water Carrier"

Cobb, Irvin S.-- "No Dam' Yankee"

Connolly, Myles-- "The First of Mr. Blue"

Edmonds, Walter D.-- "The Swamper"

Harris, Eleanor E.-- "Home to Mother's"

Hughes, Llewellyn-- "Lady Wipers--of Ypres"

Hurst, Fannie-- "Give This Little Girl a Hand"

McKenna, Edward L.-- "Battered Armor"

Parker, Dorothy-- "A Telephone Call"

Paul, L.-- "Fences"

Roberts, Elizabeth Madox-- "On the Mountain-Side"

Seaver, Edwin-- "The Jew"

Stevens, James-- "The Romantic Sailor"

Suckow, Ruth-- "Midwestern Primitive"

Ware, Edmund-- "So-Long, Oldtimer"

The Best Short Stories of 1929, and the Yearbook of the American Short Story,
edited by Edward J. O'Brien

Addington, Sarah-- "'Hound of Heaven'"

Anderson, Sherwood-- "The Lost Novel"

Beede, Ivan-- "The Country Doctor"

Bercovici, Konrad-- "'There's Money in Poetry'"

Callaghan, Morley-- "Soldier Harmon"

Cather, Willa-- "Double Birthday"

Coates, Grace Stone-- "Wild Plums"

Edmonds, Walter D.-- "Death of Red Peril"

Glover, James Webber-- "First Oboe"

Hall, James Norman-- "Fame for Mr. Beatty"

Herald, Leon Srabian-- "Power of Horizon"

Jenkins, MacGregor-- "Alcantara"

Leech, Margaret-- "Manicure"

McAlmon, Robert-- "Potato Picking"

McCarty, Wilson-- "His Friend the Pig"

McKenna, Edward L.-- "I Have Letters for Marjorie"

Mullen, Robert-- "Light Without Heat"

Patterson, Pernet-- "'Cunjur'"

Wescott, Glenway-- "A Guilty Woman"

Williams, William Carlos-- "The Venus"

The Best Short Stories of 1930, and the Yearbook of the American Short Story,
edited by Edward J. O'Brien

Bishop, Ellen-- "Along a Sandy Road"

Bragdon, Clifford-- "Suffer Little Children"

Burnett, Whit-- "Two Men Free"

Callaghan, Morley-- "The Faithful Wife"

Coates, Grace Stone-- "The Way of the Transgressor"

Draper, Edythe Squier-- "The Voice of the Turtle"

Furniss, Ruth Pine-- "Answer"

Gilkyson, Walter-- "Blue Sky"

Gordon, Caroline-- "Summer Dust"

Hahn, Emily-- "Adventure"

Hartwick, Harry-- "Happiness up the River"

Kittredge, Eleanor Hayden-- "September Sailing"

Komroff, Manuel-- "A Red Coat for Night"

Lewis, Janet-- "At the Swamp"

March, William-- "The Little Wife"

Parker, Dorothy-- "The Cradle of Civilization"

Paulding, Gouverneur-- "The White Pidgeon"

Polk, William-- "The Patriot"

Porter, Katherine Anne-- "Theft"

Upson, William Hazlett-- "The Vineyard at Schloss Ramsburg"

The Best Short Stories of 1931, and the Yearbook of the American Short Story,
edited by **Edward J. O'Brien**

Adamic, Louis-- "The Enigma"

Barber, Solon R.-- "The Sound That Frost Makes"

Bessie, Alvah C.-- "Only We Are Barren"

Boyle, Kay-- "Rest Cure"

Bromfield, Louis-- "Tabloid News"

Burnett, Whit-- "A Day in the Country"

Caldwell, Erskine-- "Dorothy"

Callaghan, Morley-- "The Yound Priest"

Edmonds, Walter D.-- "Water Never Hurt a Man"

Faulkner, William-- "That Evening Sun Go Down"

Fitzgerald, F. Scott-- "Babylon Revisited"

Foley, Martha-- "One with Shakespeare"

Gilpatric, Guy-- "The Flaming Chariot"

Gowen, Emmett-- "Fiddlers of Moon Mountain"

Herbst, Josephine-- "I Hear You, Mr. and Mrs. Brown"

Horgan, Paul-- "The Other Side of the Street"

March, William-- "Fifteen from Company K"

Marquis, Don-- "The Other Room"

Milburn, George-- "A Pretty Cute Little Stunt"

Parker, Dorothy-- "Here We Are"

Read, Allen-- "Rhodes Scholar"

Stevens, James-- "The Great Hunter of the Woods"

Upson, William Hazlett-- "The Model House"

Ward, Leo L.-- "The Threshing Ring"

Wilson, Anne Elizabeth-- "The Miracle"

Wimberly, Lowry Charles-- "White Man's Town"

The Best Short Stories of 1932, and the Yearbook of the American Short Story,
edited by **Edward J. O'Brien**

Adams, Bill-- "The Foreigner"

Bessie, Alvah C.-- "Horizon"

Bragdon, Clifford-- "Love's So Many Things"

Brennan, Louis-- "Poisoner in Motley"

Burnett, Wanda-- "Sand"

Burnett, Whit-- "Sherrel"

Caldwell, Erskine-- "Warm River"

Callaghan, Morley-- "The Red Hat"

Caperton, Helena Lefroy-- "The Honest Wine Merchant"

Cournos, John-- "The Story of the Stranger"

DeJong, David Cornel-- "So Tall the Corn"

Diefenthaler, Andra-- "Hansel"

Faulkner, William-- "Smoke"

Komroff, Manuel-- "Napoleon's Hat under Glass"

Le Sueur, Meridel-- "Spring Story"

Lockwood, Scammon-- "An Arrival at Carthage"

March, William-- "Mist on the Meadow"

Milburn, George-- "Heel, Toe, and a 1, 2, 3, 4"

Morris, Ira V.-- "The Kimono"

Neagoe, Peter-- "Shepherd of the Lord"

Schnabel, Dudley-- "Load"

Stallings, Laurence-- "Gentlemen in Blue"

Tuting, Bernhard Johann-- "The Family Chronicle"

Villa, José García-- "Untitled Story"

Ward, Leo L.-- "The Quarrel"

The Best Short Stories of 1933, and the Yearbook of the American Short Story,
edited by **Edward J. O'Brien**

Albee, George-- "Fame Takes the J Car"

Bessie, Alvah C.-- "A Little Walk"

Bishop, John Peale-- "Toadstools Are Poison"

Boyd, Albert Truman-- "Elmer"

Burnett, Whit-- "Serenade"

Caldwell, Erskine-- "The First Autumn"

Callaghan, Morley-- "A Sick Call"

Cantwell, Robert-- "The Land of Plenty"

Dobie, Charles Caldwell-- "The Honey Pot"

Edmonds, Walter D.-- "Black Wolf"

Farrell, James T.-- "Helen, I Love You!"

Fitzgerald, F. Scott-- "Crazy Sunday"

Flandrau, Grace-- "What Was Truly Mine"

Foley, Martha-- "Martyr"

Gowen, Emmett-- "Fisherman's Luck"

Hale, Nancy-- "Simple Aveu"

Halper, Albert-- "Going to Market"

Joffe, Eugene-- "In the Park"

Lambertson, Louise-- "Sleet Storm"

Leenhouts, Grant-- "The Facts in the Case"

Milburn, George-- "The Apostate"

Morris, Ira V.-- "The Sampler"

Morris, Lloyd-- "Footnote to a Life"

Porter, Katherine Anne-- "The Cracked Looking-Glass"

Reed, Louis-- "Episode at the Pawpaws"

Shumway, Naomi-- "Ike and Us Moons"

Steele, Wilbur Daniel-- "How Beautiful with Shoes"

Thomas, Dorothy-- "The Joybell"

Villa, José García-- "The Fence"

The Best Short Stories of 1934, and the Yearbook of the American Short Story, *edited by* **Edward J. O'Brien**

Appel, Benjamin-- "Winter Meeting"

Bessie, Alvah C.-- "No Final Word"

Burnett, Whit-- "The Cats Which Cried"

Caldwell, Erskine-- "Horse Thief"

Callaghan, Morley-- "Mr. and Mrs. Fairbanks"

Childs, Marquis W.-- "The Woman on the Shore"

Corle, Edwin-- "Amethyst"

Corning, Howard McKinley-- "Crossroads Woman"

Faulkner, William-- "Beyond"

Fisher, Rudolph-- "Miss Cynthie"

Foley, Martha-- "She Walks in Beauty"

Godin, Alexander-- "My Dead Brother Comes to America"

Gordon, Caroline-- "Tom Rivers"

Goryan, Sirak-- "The Broken Wheel"

Hall, James Norman-- "Lord of Marutea"

Hughes, Langston-- "Cora Unashamed"

Joffe, Eugene-- "Siege of Love"

Komroff, Manuel-- "Hamlet's Daughter"

Lineaweaver, John-- "Mother Tanner"

Mamet, Louis-- "The Pension"

March, William-- "This Heavy Load"

Marshall, Alan-- "Death and Transfiguration"

McCleary, Dorothy-- "Winter"

Ryan, Paul-- "The Sacred Thing"

Sabsay, Nahum-- "In a Park"

Sheean, Vincent-- "The Hemlock Tree"

Sherman, Richard-- "Now There Is Peace"

Tate, Allen-- "The Immortal Woman"

Terrell, Upton-- "Money at Home"

Zugsmith, Leane-- "Home Is Where You Hang Your Childhood"

The Best Short Stories of 1935, and the Yearbook of the American Short Story, *edited by* **Edward J. O'Brien**

Appel, Benjamin-- "Outside Yuma"

Benson, Sally-- "The Overcoat"

Brace, Ernest-- "The Party Next Door"

Brown, Carlton-- "Suns That Our Hearts Harden"

Burnett, Whit-- "Division"

Caldwell, Erskine-- "The Cold Winter"

Callaghan, Morley-- "Father and Son"

Cole, Madelene-- "Bus to Biarritz"

Cooke, Charles-- "Triple Jumps"

DeJong, David Cornel-- "Home-Coming"

Faulkner, William-- "Lo!"

Godchaux, Elma-- "Wild Nigger"

Haardt, Sara-- "Little White Girl"

Haines, William Wister-- "Remarks: None"

Hale, Nancy-- "The Double House"

Horgan, Paul-- "A Distant Harbour"

Mamet, Louis-- "Episode from Life"

McCleary, Dorothy-- "Sunday Morning"

McHugh, Vincent-- "Parish of Cockroaches"

Morang, Alfred-- "Frozen Stillness"

Morris, Edita-- "Mrs. Lancaster-Jones"

Saroyan, William-- "Resurrection of a Life"

Seager, Allan-- "This Town and Salamanca"

Sylvester, Harry-- "A Boxer: Old"

Thielen, Benedict-- "Souvenir of Arizona"

White, Max-- "A Pair of Shoes"

Wolfe, Thomas-- "The Sun and the Rain"

The Best Short Stories of 1936, and the Yearbook of the American Short Story,
edited by Edward J. O'Brien

Burlingame, Roger-- "In the Cage"

Callaghan, Morley-- "The Blue Kimono"

Canfield, Dorothy-- "The Murder on Jefferson Street"

Carr, A. H. Z.-- "The Hunch"

Cooke, Charles-- "Catafalque"

Coombes, Evan-- "The North Wind Doth Blow"

Faulkner, William-- "That Will Be Fine"

Fessier, Michael-- "That's What Happened to Me"

Field, S. S.-- "Torrent of Darkness"

Flannagan, Roy-- "The Doorstop"

Foley, Martha-- "Her Own Sweet Simplicity"

Gilkyson, Walter-- "Enemy Country"

Hall, Elizabeth-- "Two Words Are a Story"

Kelly, Frank K.-- "With Some Gaiety and Laughter"

Kelm, Karlton-- "Tinkle and Family Take a Ride"

Komroff, Manuel-- "That Blowzy Goddess Fame"

Larsen, Erling-- "A Kind of a Sunset"

Le Sueur, Meridel-- "Annuciation"

Maltz, Albert-- "Man on a Road"

McCleary, Dorothy-- "The Shroud"

Porter, Katherine Anne-- "The Grave"

Richmond, Roaldus-- "Thanks for Nothing"

Seager, Allan-- "Fugue for Harmonica"

Slesinger, Tess-- "A Life in the Day of a Writer"

Thomas, Elisabeth Wilkins-- "Traveling Salesman"

Vines, Howell-- "The Mustydines Was Ripe"

Whitehand, Robert-- "American Nocturne"

Williams, Calvin-- "On the Sidewalk"

Wilson, William E.-- "The Lone Pioneer"

Wolfe, Thomas-- "Only the Dead Know Brooklyn"

The Best Short Stories of 1937, and the Yearbook of the American Short Story,
edited by Edward J. O'Brien

Buckner, Robert-- "The Man Who Won the War"

Burlingame, Roger-- "The Last Equation"

Callaghan, Morley-- "The Voyage Out"

Cooke, Charles-- "Enter Daisy; to Her, Alexandra"

Faulkner, William-- "Fool About a Horse"

Field, S. S.-- "Goodbye to Cap'm John"

Foley, Martha-- "Glory, Glory, Hallelujah!"

Godchaux, Elma-- "Chains"

Halper, Albert-- "The Poet"

Hemingway, Ernest-- "The Snows of Kilimanjaro"

Heth, Edward Harris-- "Homecoming"

Horgan, Paul-- "The Surgeon and the Nun"

Komroff, Manuel-- "The Girl with the Flaxen Hair"

Krantz, David E.-- "Awakening and the Destination"

Kroll, Harry Harrison-- "Second Wife"

Linn, R. H.-- "The Intrigue of Mr. S. Yamamoto"

MacDougall, Ursula-- "Titty's Dead and Tatty Weeps"

March, William-- "Maybe the Sun Will Shine"

McGinnis, Allen-- "Let Nothing You Dismay"

Morris, Edita-- "A Blade of Grass"

Morris, Ira V.-- "Marching Orders"

Porter, Katharine Anne-- "The Old Order"

St. Joseph, Ellis-- "A Passenger to Bali"

Saroyan, William-- "The Crusader"

Stuart, Jesse-- "Hair"

Thielen, Benedict-- "Lieutenant Pearson"

Thompson, Lovell-- "The Iron City"

Wright, Wilson-- "Arrival on a Holiday"

Zugsmith, Leane-- "Room in the World"

The Best Short Stories of 1938, and the Yearbook of the American Short Story,
edited by Edward J. O'Brien

Ayre, Robert-- "Mr. Sycamore"

Benedict, Libby-- "Blind Man's Buff"

Benét, Stephen Vincent-- "A Tooth for Paul Revere"

Bond, Nelson S.-- "Mr. Mergenthwirker's Lobblies"

Callaghan, Morley-- "The Cheat's Remorse"

Cheever, John-- "The Brothers"

Cherkasski, Vladimir-- "What Hurts Is That I Was in a Hurry"

Cook, Whitfield-- "Dear Mr. Flessheimer"

Creyke, Richard Paulett-- "Niggers Are Such Liars"

Di Donato, Pietro-- "Christ in Concrete"
Fessier, Michael-- "Black Wind and Lightning"
Hannum, Alberta Pierson-- "Turkey Hunt"
Komroff, Manuel-- "The Whole World Is Outside"
Le Sueur, Meridel-- "The Girl"
Ludlow, Don-- "She Always Wanted Shoes"
March, William-- "The Last Meeting"
McCleary, Dorothy-- "Little Bride"
Moll, Elick-- "To Those Who Wait"
Pereda, Prudencio de-- "The Spaniard"
Prokosch, Frederic-- "A Russian Idyll"

Rayner, George Thorp-- "A Real American Fellow"
Roberts, Elizabeth Madox-- "The Haunted Palace"
Schorer, Mark-- "Boy in the Summer Sun"
Seager, Allan-- "Pro Arte"
Steinbeck, John-- "The Chrysanthemums"
Stuart, Jesse-- "Huey, the Engineer"
Swados, Harvey-- "The Amateurs"
Warren, Robert Penn-- "Christmas Gift"
Welty, Eudora-- "Lily Daw and the Three Ladies"
Wolfert, Ira-- "Off the Highway"

The Best Short Stories of 1939, and the Yearbook of the American Short Story, *edited by* **Edward J. O'Brien**

Beck, Warren-- "The Blue Sash"
Caldwell, Ronald-- "Vision in the Sea"
Callaghan, Morley-- "It Had to Be Done"
Cheever, John-- "Frère Jacques"
Clark, Gean-- "Indian on the Road"
Coates, Robert M.-- "Passing Through"
Cohn, David L.-- "Black Troubadour"
Danielson, Richard Ely-- "Corporal Hardy"
Ellson, Hal-- "The Rat Is a Mouse"
Halper, Albert-- "Prelude"
Horgan, Paul-- "To the Mountains"
Jenison, Madge-- "True Believer"
Komroff, Manuel-- "What Is a Miracle?"
Le Sueur, Meridel-- "Salutation to Spring"
MacDonald, Alan-- "An Arm Upraised"
Maltz, Albert-- "The Happiest Man on Earth"

St. Joseph, Ellis-- "Leviathan"
Saroyan, William-- "Piano"
Schoenstedt, Walter-- "The Girl from the River Barge"
Seager, Allan-- "Berkshire Comedy"
Seide, Michael-- "Bad Boy from Brooklyn"
Stuart, Jesse-- "Eustacia"
Sylvester, Harry-- "The Crazy Guy"
Thielen, Benedict-- "The Thunderstorm"
Warren, Robert Penn-- "How Willie Proudfit Came Home"
Welty, Eudora-- "A Curtain of Green"
Werner, Heinz-- "Black Tobias and the Empire"
Wolfert, Ira-- "The Way the Luck Runs"
Wright, Eugene-- "The White Camel"
Wright, Richard-- "Bright and Morning Star"

The Best Short Stories of 1940, and the Yearbook of the American Short Story, *edited by* **Edward J. O'Brien**

Boyle, Kay-- "Anschluss"
Caldwell, Erskine-- "The People vs. Abe Lathan, Colored"
Callaghan, Morley-- "Getting on in the World"
Eisenberg, Frances-- "Roof Sitter"
Farrell, James T.-- "The Fall of Machine Gun McGurk"
Faulkner, William-- "Hand upon the Waters"
Fitzgerald, F. Scott-- "Design in Plaster"
Gordon, Caroline-- "Frankie and Thomas and Bud Asbury"

Hemingway, Ernest-- "Under the Ridge"
King, Mary-- "The Honey House"
Komroff, Manuel-- "Death of an Outcast"
Lull, Roderick-- "That Fine Place We Had Last Year"
Lussu, Emilio-- "Your General Does Not Sleep"
McCleary, Dorothy-- "Something Jolly"
Morris, Edita-- "Kullan"
Morris, Ira V.-- "The Beautiful Fire"
Pasinetti, P. M.-- "Family History"
Pereda, Prudencio de-- "The Way Death Comes"
Pooler, James-- "Herself"

Porter, Katherine Anne-- "The Downward Path to Wisdom"
Saroyan, William-- "The Presbyterian Choir Singers"
Seide, Michael-- "Words Without Music"
Shaw, Irwin-- "Main Currents of American Thought"
Slocombe, George-- "The Seven Men of Rouen"
Stern, Morton-- "Four Worms Turning"

Storm, Hans Otto-- "The Two Deaths of Kaspar Rausch"
Stuart, Jesse-- "Rich Men"
Sylvester, Harry-- "Beautifully and Bravely"
Thielen, Benedict-- "Night and the Lost Armies"
Welty, Eudora-- "The Hitch-Hikers"
Zara, Louis-- "Resurgam"

The Best Short Stories of 1941, and the Yearbook of the American Short Story, *edited by* **Martha Foley**

Ashton, E. B.-- "Shadow of a Girl"
Benét, Stephen Vincent-- "All Around the Town"
Caldwell, Erskine-- "Handy"
Callaghan, Morley-- "Big Jules"
Coates, Robert M.-- "The Net"
DeJong, David Cornel-- "Mamma Is a Lady"
Exall, Henry-- "To the Least . . ."
Fante, John-- "A Nun No More"
Faulkner, William-- "Gold Is Not Always"
Garfinkel, Harold-- "'Color Trouble'"
Gizycka, Felicia-- "The Magic Wire"
Herman, Justin-- "Smile for the Man, Dear"
Kees, Weldon-- "The Life of the Mind"
King, Mary-- "The White Bull"
Kober, Arthur-- "Some People Are Just Plumb Crazy"

La Farge, Christopher-- "Scorn and Comfort"
Levin, Meyer-- "The System Was Doomed"
Lull, Roderick-- "Don't Get Me Wrong"
Maltz, Albert-- "Sunday Morning on Twentieth Street"
Neagoe, Peter-- "Ill-Winds from the Wide World"
Saroyan, William-- "The Three Swimmers and the Educated Grocer"
Shaw, Irwin-- "Triumph of Justice"
Shore, Wilma-- "The Butcher"
Stegner, Wallace-- "Goin' to Town"
Stuart, Jesse-- "Love"
Thielen, Benedict-- "The Psychologist"
Weidman, Jerome-- "Houdini"
Weller, George-- "Strip-Tease"
Wright, Richard-- "Almos' a Man"

The Best American Short Stories, 1942, and the Yearbook of the American Short Story, *edited by* **Martha Foley**

Algren, Nelson-- "Biceps"
Bemelmans, Ludwig-- "The Valet of the Splendide"
Benson, Sally-- "Fifty-one Thirty-five Kensington: August, 1903"
Boyle, Kay-- "Nothing Ever Breaks Except the Heart"
Bryan, Jack Y.-- "For Each of Us"
Clark, Walter Van Tilburg-- "The Portable Phonograph"
DeJong, David Cornel-- "That Frozen Hour"
Eakin, Boyce-- "Prairies"
Fineman, Morton-- "Tell Him I Waited"
Gibbons, Robert-- "A Loaf of Bread"
Hale, Nancy-- "Those Are as Brothers"
Kantor, MacKinlay-- "That Greek Dog"
Knight, Eric-- "Sam Small's Better Half"
Lavin, Mary-- "At Sallygap"
Medearis, Mary-- "Death of a Country Doctor"
Morris, Edita-- "Caput Mortuum"

O'Hara, Mary-- "My Friend Flicka"
Peattie, Margaret Rhodes-- "The Green Village"
Saroyan, William-- "The Hummingbird That Lived Through Winter"
Schulberg, Budd Wilson-- "The Real Viennese Schmalz"
Seide, Michael-- "Sacrifice of Isaac"
Shaw, Irwin-- "Search Through the Streets of the City"
Stegner, Wallace-- "In the Twilight"
Steinbeck, John-- "How Edith McGillcuddy Met R. L. Stevenson"
Stuart, Jesse-- "The Storm"
Taylor, Peter-- "The Fancy Woman"
Thomas, Dorothy-- "My Pigeon Pair"
Thurber, James-- "You Could Look It Up"
Vatsek, Joan-- "The Bees"
Worthington, Marjorie-- "Hunger"

The Best American Short Stories, 1943, and the Yearbook of the American Short Story,
edited by **Martha Foley**

Baum, Vicki-- "The Healthy Life"
Beck, Warren-- "Boundary Line"
Boyle, Kay-- "Frenchman's Ship"
Cheever, John-- "The Pleasures of Solitude"
D'Agostino, Guido-- "The Dream of Angelo Zara"
Dyer, Murray-- "Samuel Blane"
Faulkner, William-- "The Bear"
Field, Rachel-- "Beginning of Wisdom"
Fisher, Vardis-- "A Partnership with Death"
Flandrau, Grace-- "What Do You See, Dear Enid?"
Gibbons, Robert-- "Time's End"
Gray, Peter-- "Threnody for Stelios"
Hale, Nancy-- "Who Lived and Died Believing"
Horgan, Paul-- "The Peach Stone"
Knight, Laurette MacDuffie-- "The Enchanted"
Laidlaw, Clara-- "The Little Black Boys"

Lavin, Mary-- "Love Is for Lovers"
Morris, Edita-- "Young Man in an Astrakhan Cap"
Saroyan, William-- "Knife-like, Flower-like, Like Nothing at All in the World"
Schwartz, Delmore-- "An Argument in 1934"
Shaw, Irwin-- "Preach on the Dusty Roads"
Shedd, Margaret-- "My Public"
Stegner, Wallace-- "Chip off the Old Block"
Stuart, Alison-- "Death and My Uncle Felix"
Stuart, Jesse-- "Dawn of Remembered Spring"
Sullivan, Richard-- "The Women"
Thurber, James-- "The Catbird Seat"
Treichler, Jessie-- "Homecoming"
Weidman, Jerome-- "Philadelphia Express"
Welty, Eudora-- "Asphodel"

The Best American Short Stories, 1944, and the Yearbook of the American Short Story,
edited by **Martha Foley**

Alexander, Sidney-- "The White Boat"
Barrett, William E.-- "Señor Payroll"
Bellow, Saul-- "Notes of a Dangling Man"
Canfield, Dorothy-- "The Knot Hole"
De Lanux, Eyre-- "The S.S. Libertad"
Eastman, Elizabeth-- "Like a Field Mouse over the Heart"
Eustis, Helen-- "The Good Days and the Bad"
Fifield, William-- "The Fishermen of Patzcuaro"
Fleming, Berry-- "Strike up a Stirring Music"
Hawthorne, Hazel-- "More Like a Coffin"
Houston, Noel-- "A Local Skirmish"
Jackson, Shirley-- "Come Dance with Me in Ireland"
Johnson, Josephine W.-- "The Rented Room"
Kaplan, H. J.-- "The Mohammedans"
McCullers, Carson-- "The Ballad of the Sad Café"

March, William-- "The Female of the Fruit Fly"
Meighan, Astrid-- "Shoe the Horse and Shoe the Mare"
Mian, Mary-- "Exiles from the Creuse"
Morris, Edita-- "Heart of Marzipan"
Nabokov, Vladimir-- "'That in Aleppo Once . . . '"
Portugal, Ruth-- "Neither Here nor There"
Powers, J. F.-- "Lions, Harts, Leaping Does"
Schmitt, Gladys-- "All Souls'"
Shaw, Irwin-- "The Veterans Reflect"
Stiles, George-- "A Return"
Surmelian, Leon Z.-- "My Russian Cap"
Trilling, Lionel-- "Of This Time, of That Place"
Warner, Elizabeth-- "An Afternoon"
West, Jessamyn-- "The Illumination"
Winters, Emmanuel-- "God's Agents Have Beards"

The Best American Short Stories, 1945, and the Yearbook of the American Short Story,
edited by **Martha Foley**

Algren, Nelson-- "How the Devil Came Down Division Street"
Beck, Warren-- "The First Fish"

Bromfield, Louis-- "Crime Passionnel"
Bulosan, Carlos-- "My Brother Osong's Career in Politics"

Deasy, Mary-- "Harvest"

Fenton, Edward-- "Burial in the Desert"

Fineman, Morton-- "The Light of Morning"

Gerry, Bill-- "Understand What I Mean?"

Gill, Brendan-- "The Test"

Hagopian, Richard-- "'Be Heavy'"

Hahn, Emily-- "It Never Happened"

Hardy, W. G.-- "The Czech Dog"

Johnson, Josephine W.-- "Fever Flower"

McLaughlin, Robert-- "Poor Everybody"

McNulty, John-- "Don't Scrub off These Names"

Miller, Warren-- "The Animal's Fair"

Panetta, George-- "Papa, Mama, and Economics"

Pennell, Joseph Stanley-- "On the Way to Somewhere Else"

Portugal, Ruth-- "Call a Solemn Assembly"

Pratt, Theodore-- "The Owl That Kept Winking"

Rosenfeld, Isaac-- "The Hand That Fed Me"

Rowell, Donna-- "A War Marriage"

Schmitt, Gladys-- "The Mourners"

Shaw, Irwin-- "Gunners' Passage"

Stafford, Jean-- "The Wedding: Beacon Hill"

Tartt, Ruby Pickens-- "Alabama Sketches"

Taylor, Peter-- "Rain in the Heart"

Warren, Robert Penn-- "Cass Mastern's Wedding Ring"

West, Jessamyn-- "First Day Finish"

Zugsmith, Leane-- "This Is a Love Story"

Zukerman, William-- "A Ship to Tarshish"

The Best American Short Stories, 1946, and the Yearbook of the American Short Story, *edited by* **Martha Foley**

Angoff, Charles-- "Jerry"

Beck, Warren-- "Out of Line"

Berryman, John-- "The Lovers"

Bradbury, Ray-- "The Big Black and White Game"

Breuer, Bessie-- "Bury Your Own Dead"

Brown, T. K., III-- "The Valley of the Shadow"

Burnett, W. R.-- "The Ivory Tower"

Clark, Walter Van Tilburg-- "The Wind and the Snow of Winter"

Critchell, Laurence-- "Flesh and Blood"

Deasy, Mary-- "A Sense of Danger"

Elkin, Samuel-- "In a Military Manner"

Gottlieb, Elaine-- "The Norm"

Hardwick, Elizabeth-- "The Mysteries of Eleusis"

Johnson, Josephine W.-- "Story Without End"

Lampman, Ben Hur-- "Old Bill Bent to Drink"

Liben, Meyer-- "The Caller"

Liebling, A. J.-- "Run, Run, Run, Run"

Mitchell, W. O.-- "The Owl and the Bens"

Nabokov, Vladimir-- "Time and Ebb"

Petry, Ann-- "Like a Winding Sheet"

Ruml, Wentzle, III-- "For a Beautiful Relationship"

Schmitt, Gladys-- "The King's Daughter"

Stark, Irwin-- "The Bridge"

Stern, James-- "The Woman Who Was Loved"

Still, James-- "Mrs. Razor"

Taylor, Peter-- "The Scout Master"

Trilling, Lionel-- "The Other Margaret"

Weigel, Henrietta-- "Love Affair"

West, Jessamyn-- "The Singing Lesson"

Woods, Glennyth-- "Death in a Cathedral"

The Best American Short Stories, 1947, and the Yearbook of the American Short Story, *edited by* **Martha Foley**

Broderick, Francis L.-- "Return by Faith"

Canfield, Dorothy-- "Sex Education"

Capote, Truman-- "The Headless Hawk"

Fontaine, Robert-- "Day of Gold and Darkness"

Gerstley, Adelaide-- "The Man in the Mirror"

Goodwin, John B. L.-- "The Cocoon"

Goss, John Mayo-- "Bird Song"

Griffith, Paul-- "The Horse like September"

Guérard, Albert J.-- "Turista"

Hardwick, Elizabeth-- "The Golden Stallion"

Harris, Ruth McCoy-- "Up the Road a Piece"

Heggen, Thomas-- "Night Watch"

Heth, Edward Harris-- "Under the Ginkgo Trees"

Humphreys, John Richard-- "Michael Finney and the Little Men"

Lincoln, Victoria-- "Down in the Reeds by the River"
Lowry, Robert-- "Little Baseball World"
Martenet, May Davies-- "Father Delacroix"
Mayhall, Jane-- "The Darkness"
Powers, J. F.-- "Prince of Darkness"
Raphaelson, Samson-- "The Greatest Idea in the World"
Schorer, Mark-- "What We Don't Know Hurts Us"
Seager, Allan-- "Game Chickens"

Shaw, Irwin-- "Act of Faith"
Shirley, Sylvia-- "The Red Dress"
Stafford, Jean-- "The Interior Castle"
Stark, Irwin-- "Shock Treatment"
Stegner, Wallace-- "The Women on the Wall"
Tucci, Niccolò-- "The Seige"
Weaver, John D.-- "Bread and Games"
Williams, Lawrence-- "The Hidden Room"

The Best American Short Stories, 1948, and the Yearbook of the American Short Story,
edited by **Martha Foley**

Alexander, Sidney-- "Part of the Act"
Bowles, Paul-- "A Distant Episode"
Bradbury, Ray-- "I See You Never"
Canfield, Dorothy-- "The Apprentice"
Cheever, John-- "The Enormous Radio"
Clay, George R.-- "That's My Johnny-Boy"
Clayton, John Bell-- "Visitor from Philadelphia"
Cousins, Margaret-- "A Letter to Mr. Priest"
Fisher, M. F. K.-- "The Hollow Heart"
Garrigan, Philip-- "'Fly, Fly, Little Dove'"
Gellhorn, Martha-- "Miami-New York"
Grennard, Elliott-- "Sparrow's Last Jump"
Gustafson, Ralph-- "The Human Fly"
Hersey, John-- "Why Were You Sent out Here?"
Jeffers, Lance-- "The Dawn Swings In"

Lincoln, Victoria-- "Morning, a Week Before the Crime"
Lowry, Robert-- "The Terror in the Streets"
Lynch, John A.-- "The Burden"
McHugh, Vincent-- "The Search"
Morse, Robert-- "The Professor and the Puli"
Portugal, Ruth-- "The Stupendous Fortune"
Post, Mary Brinker-- "That's the Man"
Root, Waverley-- "Carmencita"
Sharp, Dolph-- "The Tragedy in Jancie Brierman's Life"
Stegner, Wallace-- "Beyond the Glass Mountain"
Sulkin, Sidney-- "The Plan"
Welty, Eudora-- "The Whole World Knows"
White, E. B.-- "The Second Tree from the Corner"

The Best American Short Stories, 1949, and the Yearbook of the American Short Story,
edited by **Martha Foley**

Albee, George-- "Mighty, Mighty Pretty"
Biddle, Livingston, Jr.-- "The Vacation"
Bishop, Elizabeth-- "The Farmer's Children"
Bowles, Paul-- "Under the Sky"
Brookhouser, Frank-- "My Father and the Circus"
Deal, Borden-- "Exodus"
Dolokhov, Adele-- "Small Miracle"
Dorrance, Ward-- "The White Hound"
Felsen, Henry Gregor-- "Li Chang's Million"
Gibbons, Robert-- "Departure of Hubbard"
Griffith, Beatrice-- "In the Flow of Time"
Hardwick, Elizabeth-- "Evenings at Home"
Heller, Joseph-- "Castle of Snow"
Herschberger, Ruth-- "A Sound in the Night"

Hunter, Laura-- "Jerry"
Kjelgaard, Jim-- "Of the River and Uncle Pidcock"
Lull, Roderick-- "Footnote to American History"
Mabry, Thomas-- "The Vault"
Macdonald, Agnes-- "Vacia"
Mayhall, Jane-- "The Men"
Morgan, Patrick-- "The Heifer"
Pfeffer, Irving-- "All Prisoners Here"
Rogers, John-- "Episode of a House Remembered"
Salinger, J. D.-- "A Girl I Knew"
Segre, Alfredo-- "Justice Has No Number"
Shapiro, Madelon-- "An Island for My Friends"
Stafford, Jean-- "Children Are Bored on Sunday"
West, Jessamyn-- "Road to the Isles"

The Best American Short Stories, 1950, and the Yearbook of the American Short Story, *edited by* Martha Foley

Angoff, Charles-- "Where Did Yesterday Go?"
Aswell, James-- "Shadow of Evil"
Babb, Sanora-- "The Wild Flower"
Beck, Warren-- "Edge of Doom"
Bellow, Saul-- "A Sermon by Doctor Pep"
Bennett, Peggy-- "Death Under the Hawthornes"
Bowles, Paul-- "Pastor Dowe at Tacaté"
Christopher, Robert-- "Jishin"
Elliott, George P.-- "The NRACP"
Fiedler, Leslie A.-- "The Fear of Innocence"
Gustafson, Ralph-- "The Pigeon"
Hauser, Marianne-- "The Mouse"
Johnson, Josephine W.-- "The Author"
Kaplan, Ralph-- "The Artist"

Karchmer, Sylvan-- "'Hail Brother and Farewell'"
Lamkin, Speed-- "Comes a Day"
Lincoln, Victoria-- "The Glass Wall"
Maier, Howard-- "The World Outside"
McCoy, Esther-- "The Cape"
Newhouse, Edward-- "My Brother's Second Funeral"
Norris, Hoke-- "Take Her Up Tenderly"
Parker, Glidden-- "Bright and Morning"
Putman, Clay-- "The Old Acrobat and the Ruined City"
Rothberg, Abraham-- "Not with Our Fathers"
Stewart, Ramona-- "The Promise"
Still, James-- "A Master Time"
Strong, Joan-- "The Hired Man"
Taylor, Peter-- "A Wife of Nashville"

The Best American Short Stories, 1951, and the Yearbook of the American Short Story, *edited by* Martha Foley, *assisted by* Joyce F. Hartman

Angell, Roger-- "Flight Through the Dark"
Asch, Nathan-- "Inland, Western Sea"
Bennett, Peggy-- "A Fugitive from the Mind"
Bolté, Mary-- "The End of the Depression"
Calisher, Hortense-- "In Greenwich There Are Many Gravelled Walks"
Casper, Leonard-- "Sense of Direction"
Cassill, R. V.-- "Larchmoor Is Not the World"
Cheever, John-- "The Season of Divorce"
Downey, Harris-- "The Hunters"
Enright, Elizabeth-- "The Temperate Zone"
Gardon, Ethel Edison-- "The Value of the Dollar"
Goodman, J. Carol-- "The Kingdom of Gordon"
Goyen, William-- "Her Breath upon the Windowpane"
Jackson, Shirley-- "The Summer People"

Johnson, Josephine W.-- "The Mother's Story"
Karmel, Ilona-- "Fru Holm"
La Farge, Oliver-- "Old Century's River"
Lanning, George-- "Old Turkey Neck"
Lewis, Ethel G.-- "Portrait"
Livesay, Dorothy-- "The Glass House"
Macauley, Robie-- "The Wishbone"
Malamud, Bernard-- "The Prison"
Patt, Esther-- "The Butcherbirds"
Powers, J. F.-- "Death of a Favorite"
Rader, Paul-- "The Tabby Cat"
Stafford, Jean-- "The Nemesis"
West, Ray B., Jr.-- "The Last of the Grizzly Bears"
Williams, Tennessee-- "The Resemblance Between a Violin Case and a Coffin"

The Best American Short Stories, 1952, and the Yearbook of the American Short Story, *edited by* Martha Foley, *assisted by* Joyce F. Hartman

Berge, Bill-- "That Lovely Green Boat"
Bethel, Laurence-- "The Call"
Bowen, Robert O.-- "The Other River"
Boyle, Kay-- "The Lost"
Bradbury, Ray-- "The Other Foot"
Calisher, Hortense-- "A Wreath for Miss Totten"

Cardozo, Nancy-- "The Unborn Ghosts"
Chaikin, Nancy G.-- "The Climate of the Family"
Chidester, Ann-- "Wood Smoke"
Eaton, Charles Edward-- "The Motion of Forgetfulness Is Slow"
Elliott, George P.-- "Children of Ruth"

Enright, Elizabeth-- "The First Face"

Garner, Hugh-- "The Conversion of Willie Heaps"

Gellhorn, Martha-- "Weekend at Grimsby"

Glen, Emilie-- "Always Good for a Belly Laugh"

Hale, Nancy-- "Brahmin Beachhead"

Horton, Philip-- "What's in a Corner?"

Kuehn, Susan-- "The Searchers"

Rooney, Frank-- "Cyclists' Raid"

Saroyan, William-- "Palo"

Schulberg, Stuart-- "I'm Really Fine"

Stafford, Jean-- "The Healthiest Girl in Town"

Stegner, Wallace-- "The Traveler"

Still, James-- "A Ride on the Short Dog"

Swados, Harvey-- "The Letters"

Van Doren, Mark-- "Nobody Say a Word"

Waldron, Daniel-- "Evensong"

Weston, Christine-- "Loud Sing Cuckoo"

Yamamoto, Hisaye-- "Yoneko's Earthquake"

The Best American Short Stories, 1953, and the Yearbook of the American Short Story, *edited by* **Martha Foley,** *assisted by* **Joyce F. Hartman**

Agee, James-- "A Mother's Tale"

Ballard, James-- "A Mountain Summer"

Becker, Stephen-- "The Town Mouse"

Carroll, Joseph-- "At Mrs. Farrelly's"

Cassill, R. V.-- "The Life of the Sleeping Beauty"

Coates, Robert M.-- "The Need"

Deasy, Mary-- "Morning Sun"

Downey, Harris-- "Crispin's Way"

Duke, Osborn-- "Struttin' with Some Barbecue"

Elliott, George P.-- "Faq'"

Froscher, Wingate-- "A Death in the Family"

Gregory, Vahan Krikorian-- "Athens, Greece, 1942"

Hall, James B.-- "A Spot in History"

Jackson, Charles Tenney-- "The Bullalo Wallow"

Jackson, Roberts-- "Fly away Home"

Jones, Madison P., Jr.-- "Dog Days"

Marsh, Willard-- "Beachhead in Bohemia"

Marshall, Elizabeth-- "The Hill People"

Noland, Felix-- "The Whipping"

Pendergast, Constance-- "The Picnic"

Purdy, Ken-- "Change of Plan"

Putman, Clay-- "Our Vegetable Love"

Shattuck, Roger-- "Workout on the River"

Shultz, Henry-- "Oreste"

Sultan, Stanley-- "The Fugue of the Fig Tree"

Van Doren, Mark-- "Still, Still So"

Wesely, Donald-- "A Week of Roses"

Weston, Christine-- "The Forest of the Night"

Williams, Tennessee-- "Three Players of a Summer Game"

Wincelberg, Simon-- "The Conqueror"

The Best American Short Stories, 1954, and the Yearbook of the American Short Story, *edited by* **Martha Foley**

Bush, Geoffrey-- "A Great Reckoning in a Little Room"

Clay, Richard-- "A Beautiful Night for Orion"

DeMott, Benjamin-- "The Sense That in the Scene Delights"

Dorrance, Ward-- "A Stop on the Way to Texas"

Doughty, LeGarde S.-- "The Firebird"

Enright, Elizabeth-- "Apple Seed and Apple Thorn"

Frazee, Steve-- "My Brother Down There"

Gold, Ivan-- "A Change of Air"

Heath, Priscilla-- "Farewell, Sweet Love"

Hebert, Anne-- "The House on the Esplanade"

Holwerda, Frank-- "Char on Raven's Bench"

Jarrell, Randall-- "Gertrude and Sidney"

Jenks, Almet-- "No Way Down"

Loveridge, George-- "The Latter End"

Patton, Frances Gray-- "The Game"

Payne, Robert-- "The Red Mountain"

Robinson, Rosanne Smith-- "The Mango Tree"

Shaw, Irwin-- "In the French Style"

Stafford, Jean-- "The Shorn Lamb"

Taylor, Kressmann-- "The Pale Green Fishes"

Traven, B.-- "The Third Guest"

Weston, Christine-- "The Man in Gray"

Wolfert, Ira-- "The Indomitable Blue"

Yentzen, Vurell-- "The Rock"

The Best American Short Stories, 1955, and the Yearbook of the American Short Story,
edited by **Martha Foley**

Bowen, Robert O.-- "A Matter of Price"
Cardozo, Nancy-- "The Excursionists"
Chaikin, Nancy G.-- "Bachelor of Arts"
Cheever, John-- "The Country Husband"
Connell, Evan S., Jr.-- "The Fisherman from Chihuahua"
Coogan, Joe-- "The Decline and Fall of Augie Sheean"
Curley, Daniel-- "The Day of the Equinox"
Eastlake, William-- "Little Joe"
Elliott, George P.-- "Brother Quintillian and Dick the Chemist"
Hyman, Mac-- "The Hundredth Centennial"
La Farge, Oliver-- "The Resting Place"
Malumud, Bernard-- "The Magic Barrel"

Merril, Judith-- "Dead Center"
Middleton, Elizabeth H.-- "Portrait of My Son as a Young Man"
Mudrick, Marvin-- "The Professor and the Poet"
Nemerov, Howard-- "Yore"
O'Connor, Flannery-- "A Circle in the Fire"
Shaw, Irwin-- "Tip on a Dead Jockey"
Stegner, Wallace-- "Maiden in a Tower"
Stuart, David-- "Bird Man"
Swados, Harvey-- "Herman's Day"
Van Doren, Mark-- "I Got a Friend"
Vukelich, George-- "The Scale Room"
Welty, Eudora-- "Going to Naples"

The Best American Short Stories, 1956, and the Yearbook of the American Short Story,
edited by **Martha Foley**

Angell, Roger-- "In an Early Winter"
Brown, Morris-- "The Snow Owl"
Clay, George R.-- "We're All Guests"
Coates, Robert M.-- "In a Foreign City"
Davis, Wesley Ford-- "The Undertow"
Dorrance, Ward-- "The Devil on a Hot Afternoon"
Downey, Harris-- "The Hobo"
Eastlake, William-- "The Quiet Chimneys"
Elliott, George P.-- "Is He Dead?"
Granit, Arthur-- "Free the Canaries from Their Cages!"
Housepian, Marjorie-- "How Levon Dai Was Surrendered to the Edemuses"

Jackson, Shirley-- "One Ordinary Day, with Peanuts"
Kerouac, Jack-- "The Mexican Girl"
LaMar, Nathaniel-- "Creole Love Song"
Lyons, Augusta Wallace-- "The First Flower"
Molloy, Ruth Branning-- "Twenty Below, at the End of a Lane"
O'Connor, Flannery-- "The Artificial Nigger"
Roth, Philip-- "The Contest for Aaron Gold"
Shepley, John-- "The Machine"
Weston, Christine-- "Four Annas"
Yellen, Samuel-- "Reginald Pomfret Skelton"

The Best American Short Stories, 1957, and the Yearbook of the American Short Story,
edited by **Martha Foley**

Algren, Nelson-- "Beasts of the Wild"
Berriault, Gina-- "Around the Dear Ruin"
Betts, Doris-- "The Proud and Virtuous"
Blassingame, Wyatt-- "Man's Courage"
Butler, Frank-- "To the Wilderness I Wander"
Clemons, Walter-- "The Dark Roots of the Rose"
Connell, Evan S., Jr.-- "Arcturus"
Downey, Harris-- "The Song"
Eastlake, William-- "The Unhappy Hunting Grounds"
Hale, Nancy-- "A Summer's Long Dream"

Langdon, John-- "The Blue Serge Suit"
Mabry, Thomas-- "Lula Borrow"
McClintic, Winona-- "A Heart of Furious Fancies"
O'Connor, Flannery-- "Greenleaf"
Olsen, Tillie-- "I Stand Here Ironing"
Robinson, Anthony-- "The Farlow Express"
Robinson, Rosanne Smith-- "The Impossible He"
Smith, John Campbell-- "Run, Run away, Brother"
Weigel, Henrietta-- "Saturday Is a Poor Man's Port"
Woodward, Gordon-- "Escape to the City"

The Best American Short Stories, 1958, and the Yearbook of the American Short Story, *edited by* **Martha Foley** *and* **David Burnett**

Agee, James-- "The Waiting"

Baldwin, James-- "Sonny's Blues"

Bowles, Paul-- "The Frozen Fields"

Bradbury, Ray-- "The Day It Rained Forever"

Bradshaw, George-- "'The Picture Wouldn't Fit in the Stove'"

Chester, Alfred-- "As I Was Going up the Stair"

Grau, Shirley Ann-- "Hunter's Home"

Hill, Pati-- "Ben"

Macauley, Robie-- "Legend of Two Swimmers"

McCord, Jean-- "Somewhere out of Nowhere"

Nemerov, Howard-- "A Delayed Hearing"

O'Connor, Flannery-- "A View of the Woods"

Ostroff, Anthony-- "La Bataille des Fleurs"

Parker, Dorothy-- "The Banquet of Crow"

Robin, Ralph-- "Mr. Pruitt"

Scoyk, Bob Ban-- "Home from Camp"

Stafford, Jean-- "A Reasonable Facsimile"

Swados, Harvey-- "Joe, the Vanishing American"

Thurman, Richard-- "Not Another Word"

White, Robin-- "House of Many Rooms"

Wright, Richard-- "Big, Black, Good Man"

The Best American Short Stories, 1959, and the Yearbook of the American Short Story, *edited by* **Martha Foley** *and* **David Burnett**

Berry, John-- "Jawaharlal and the Three Cadavers"

Bingham, Sallie-- "Winter Term"

Butler, Frank-- "Amid a Place of Stone"

Cheever, John-- "The Bella Lingua"

Coates, Robert M.-- "Getaway"

Finney, Charles G.-- "The Iowan's Curse"

Gass, William H.-- "Mrs. Mean"

Geeslin, Hugh, Jr.-- "A Day in the Life of the Boss"

Gold, Herbert-- "Love and Like"

Holwerda, Frank-- "In a Tropical Minor Key"

Malamud, Bernard-- "The Last Mohican"

Nemerov, Howard-- "A Secret Society"

Rosten, Leo-- "The Guy in Ward Four"

Roth, Philip-- "The Conversion of the Jews"

Sayre, Anne-- "A Birthday Present"

Swados, Harvey-- "The Man in the Toolhouse"

Taylor, Peter-- "Venus, Cupid, Folly, and Time"

Updike, John-- "A Gift from the City"

Williams, Thomas-- "The Buck in Trotevale's"

Wilson, Ethel-- "The Window"

The Best American Short Stories, 1960, and the Yearbook of the American Short Story, *edited by* **Martha Foley** *and* **David Burnett**

Babb, Sanora-- "The Santa Ana"

Ellin, Stanley-- "The Day of the Bullet"

Elliott, George P.-- "Words Words Words"

Fast, Howard-- "The Man Who Looked Like Jesus"

Gallant, Mavis-- "August"

Garrett, George-- "An Evening Performance"

Graves, John-- "The Last Running"

Hall, Lawrence Sargent-- "The Ledge"

Hardwick, Elizabeth-- "The Purchase"

MacDonald, Lachlan-- "The Hunter"

Malamud, Bernard-- "The Maid's Shoes"

Miller, Arthur-- "I Don't Need You Any More"

Nemerov, Howard-- "Unbelievable Characters"

Roberts, Phyllis-- "Hero"

Roth, Philip-- "Defender of the Faith"

Sturgeon, Theodore-- "The Man Who Lost the Sea"

Swados, Harvey-- "A Glance in the Mirror"

Taylor, Peter-- "Who Was Jesse's Friend and Protector?"

Young, Elisabeth Larsh-- "Counterclockwise"

The Best American Short Stories, 1961, and the Yearbook of the American Short Story,
edited by **Martha Foley** *and* **David Burnett**

Baldwin, James-- "This Morning, This Evening, So Soon"

Berry, John-- "The Listener"

Chester, Alfred-- "Berceuse"

Gass, William H.-- "The Love and Sorrow of Henry Pimber"

Gold, Ivan-- "The Nickel Misery of George Washington Carver Brown"

Goyen, William-- "A Tale of Inheritance"

Harris, Mark-- "The Self-Made Brain Surgeon"

Hurlbut, Kaatje-- "The Vestibule"

Jacobs, Theodore-- "A Girl for Walter"

Lavin, Mary-- "The Yellow Beret"

Ludwig, Jack-- "Confusions"

Marsh, Willard-- "Mexican Hayride"

McKelway, St. Clair-- "First Marriage"

Olive, Jeannie-- "Society"

Olsen, Tillie-- "Tell Me a Riddle"

Peden, William-- "Night in Funland"

Pynchon, Thomas-- "Entropy"

Sandmel, Samuel-- "The Colleagues of Mr. Chips"

Taylor, Peter-- "Miss Leonora When Last Seen"

White, Ellington-- "The Perils of Flight"

The Best American Short Stories, 1962, and the Yearbook of the American Short Story,
edited by **Martha Foley** *and* **David Burnett**

Arkin, Frieda-- "The Light of the Sea"

Choy, Wayson S.-- "The Sound of Waves"

Dahlberg, Edward-- "Because I Was Flesh"

Deal, Borden-- "Antaeus"

Elkin, Stanley-- "Criers and Kibbitzers, Kibbitzers and Criers"

Epstein, Seymour-- "Wheat Closed Higher, Cotton Was Mixed"

Garrett, George-- "The Old Army Game"

Gass, William H.-- "The Pedersen Kid"

Gilbert, Sister Mary-- "The Model Chapel"

Hall, Donald-- "A Day on Ragged"

Karmel-Wolfe, Henia-- "The Last Day"

Lavin, Mary-- "In the Middle of the Fields"

Leahy, Jack Thomas-- "Hanging Hair"

Maddow, Ben-- "'To Hell the Rabbis'"

McKenzie, Miriam-- "Déjà vu"

Miller, Arthur-- "The Prophecy"

Myers, E. Lucas-- "The Vindication of Dr. Nestor"

O'Connor, Flannery-- "Everything That Rises Must Converge"

Selz, Thalia-- "The Education of a Queen"

Shaw, Irwin-- "Love on a Dark Street"

Updike, John-- "Pigeon Feathers"

The Best American Short Stories, 1963, and the Yearbook of the American Short Story,
edited by **Martha Foley** *and* **David Burnett**

Andersen, U. S.-- "Turn Ever So Quickly"

Blattner, H. W.-- "Sound of a Drunken Drummer"

Carter, John Stewart-- "The Keyhole Eye"

Cheever, John-- "A Vision of the World"

Dawkins, Cecil-- "A Simple Case"

Dickerson, George-- "Chico"

Dikeman, May-- "The Sound of Young Laughter"

Elkin, Stanley-- "I Look out for Ed Wolfe"

Godfrey, Dave-- "Newfoundland Night"

Gordon, William J. J.-- "The Pures"

Hermann, John-- "Aunt Mary"

Loeser, Katinka-- "Beggarman, Rich Man, or Thief"

McKelway, St. Clair-- "The Fireflies"

Molinaro, Ursule-- "The Insufficient Rope"

Oates, Joyce Carol-- "The Fine White Mist of Winter"

Phelan, R. C.-- "Birds, Clouds, Frogs"

Richler, Mordecai-- "Some Grist for Mervyn's Mill"

Saroyan, William-- "What a World, Said the Bicycle Rider"

Sassoon, Babette-- "The Betrayal"

Shaw, Irwin-- "Noises in the City"

Taylor, Peter-- "At the Drugstore"

Tucci, Niccolò-- "The Desert in the Oasis"

West, Jessamyn-- "The Picnickers"

The Best American Short Stories, 1964, and the Yearbook of the American Short Story, *edited by* **Martha Foley** *and* **David Burnett**

Arkin, Frieda-- "The Broomstick on the Porch"
Brown, Richard G.-- "Mr. Iscariot"
Carter, John Stewart-- "To a Tenor Dying Old"
Curley, Daniel-- "A Story of Love, Etc."
Dikeman, May-- "The Woman Across the Street"
Eastlake, William-- "A Long Day's Dying"
Goyen, William-- "Figure over the Town"
Horgan, Paul-- "Black Snowflakes"
Humphrey, William-- "The Pump"
Jackson, Shirley-- "Birthday Party"

Konecky, Edith-- "The Power"
Lolos, Kimon-- "Mule No. 095"
Malamud, Bernard-- "The German Refugee"
McCullers, Carson-- "Sucker"
Moriconi, Virginia-- "Simple Arithmetic"
Oates, Joyce Carol-- "Upon the Sweeping Flood"
Price, Reynolds-- "The Names and Faces of Heroes"
Randal, Vera-- "Waiting for Jim"
Swados, Harvey-- "A Story for Teddy"
Warren, Robert Penn-- "Have You Seen Sukie?"

The Best American Short Stories, 1965, and the Yearbook of the American Short Story, *edited by* **Martha Foley**

Amster, L. J.-- "Center of Gravity"
De Paola, Daniel-- "The Returning"
Elkin, Stanley-- "The Transient"
Gilchrist, Jack-- "Opening Day"
Groshong, James W.-- "The Gesture"
Hamer, Martin J.-- "Sarah"
Howard, Maureen-- "Sherry"
Hutter, Donald-- "A Family Man"
Karmel-Wolfe, Henia-- "The Month of His Birthday"
Lavin, Mary-- "Heart of Gold"
Lynds, Dennis-- "A Blue Blonde in the Sky over Pennsylvania"

Morton, Frederic-- "The Guest"
Neugeboren, Jay-- "The Application"
Oates, Joyce Carol-- "First Views of the Enemy"
Robinson, Leonard Wallace-- "The Practice of an Art"
Singer, Isaac Bashevis-- "A Sacrifice"
Somerlott, Robert-- "Eskimo Pies"
Spencer, Elizabeth-- "The Visit"
Stafford, Jean-- "The Tea Time of Stouthearted Ladies"
Stein, Gerald-- "For I Have Wept"
Taylor, Peter-- "There"
Yu-Hwa, Lee-- "The Last Rite"

The Best American Short Stories, 1966, and the Yearbook of the American Short Story, *edited by* **Martha Foley** *and* **David Burnett**

Cady, Jack-- "The Burning"
Dickerson, George-- "A Mussel Named Ecclesiastes"
Downey, Harris-- "The Vicar-General and the Wide Night"
Ely, David-- "The Academy"
Faulkner, William-- "Mr. Acarius"
Grau, Shirley Ann-- "The Beach Party"
Hedin, Mary-- "Places We Lost"
Hood, Hugh-- "Getting to Williamstown"
Jackson, Shirley-- "The Bus"
Jacobsen, Josephine-- "On the Island"

Kreisel, Henry-- "The Broken Globe"
Lavin, Mary-- "One Summer"
Leviant, Curt-- "Mourning Call"
Maxwell, William-- "Further Tales About Men and Women"
O'Connor, Flannery-- "Parker's Back"
Rothberg, Abraham-- "Pluto Is the Furthest Planet"
Terry, Walter S.-- "The Bottomless Well"
Wakefield, Dan-- "Autumn Full of Apples"
Whitehill, Joseph-- "One Night for Several Samurai"
Wilner, Herbert-- "Dovisch in the Wilderness"

The Best American Short Stories, 1967, and the Yearbook of the American Short Story,
edited by **Martha Foley** *and* **David Burnett**

Ayer, Ethan-- "The Promise of Heat"

Blake, George-- "A Place Not on the Map"

Boyle, Kay-- "The Wild Horses"

Carver, Raymond-- "Will You Please Be Quiet, Please?"

Francis, H. E.-- "One of the Boys"

Harris, MacDonald-- "Trepleff"

Hazel, Robert-- "White Anglo-Saxon Protestant"

Hunt, Hugh Allyn-- "Acme Rooms and Sweet Marjorie Russell"

Lee, Lawrence-- "The Heroic Journey"

Miller, Arthur-- "Search for a Future"

Moore, Brian-- "The Apartment Hunter"

Morgan, Berry-- "Andrew"

Oates, Joyce Carol-- "Where Are You Going, Where Have You Been?"

Radcliffe, Donald-- "Song of the Simidor"

Roth, Henry-- "The Surveyor"

Rubin, David-- "Longing for America"

Stuart, Jesse-- "The Accident"

Sturm, Carol-- "The Kid Who Fractioned"

Travers, Robert-- "The Big Brown Trout"

Wiser, William-- "House of the Blues"

The Best American Short Stories, 1968, and the Yearbook of the American Short Story,
edited by **Martha Foley** *and* **David Burnett**

Baldwin, James-- "Tell Me How Long the Train's Been Gone"

Bruce, Janet-- "Dried Rose Petals in a Silver Bowl"

Deck, John-- "Greased Samba"

Farrell, James T.-- "An American Student in Paris"

Freitag, George H.-- "An Old Man and His Hat"

Gardner, Herb-- "Who Is Harry Kellerman and Why Is He Saying Those Terrible Things About Me?"

Gass, William H.-- "In the Heart of the Heart of the Country"

Gavell, Mary Ladd-- "The Rotifer"

Gropman, Donald-- "The Heart of This or That Man"

Harrison, William-- "The Snooker Shark"

Higgins, Judith-- "The Only People"

Hudson, Helen-- "The Tenant"

Litwak, Leo E.-- "In Shock"

McKenna, Richard-- "The Sons of Martha"

Moseley, William-- "The Preacher and Margery Scott"

Ostrow, Joanna-- "Celtic Twilight"

Parker, Nancy Huddleston-- "Early Morning, Lonely Ride"

Phillips, John-- "Bleat Blodgette"

Spingarn, Lawrence P.-- "The Ambassador"

Weathers, Winston-- "The Games That We Played"

The Best American Short Stories, 1969, and the Yearbook of the American Short Story,
edited by **Martha Foley** *and* **David Burnett**

Brennan, Maeve-- "The Eldest Child"

Cady, Jack-- "Play Like I'm Sherrif"

Costello, Mark-- "Murphy's Xmas"

Gerald, John Bart-- "Walking Wounded"

Hughes, Mary Gray-- "The Foreigner in the Blood"

Klein, Norma-- "The Boy in the Green Hat"

Lavin, Mary-- "Happiness"

MacLeod, Alistair-- "The Boat"

Madden, David-- "The Day the Flowers Came"

Malamud, Bernard-- "Pictures of Fidelman"

McGregor, Matthew W.-- "Porkchops with Whiskey and Ice Cream"

McPherson, James Alan-- "Gold Coast"

Milton, John R.-- "The Inheritance of Emmy One Horse"

Oates, Joyce Carol-- "By the River"

Pansing, Nancy Pelletier-- "The Visitation"

Plath, Sylvia-- "Johnny Panic and the Bible of Dreams"

Rugel, Miriam-- "Paper Poppy"

Shipley, Margaret-- "The Tea Bowl of Ninsei Nomura"

Singer, Isaac Bashevis-- "The Colony"

Winslow, Joyce Madelon-- "Benjamen Burning"

The Best American Short Stories, 1970, and the Yearbook of the American Short Story,
edited by **Martha Foley** *and* **David Burnett**

Cady, Jack-- "With No Breeze"

Cleaver, Eldridge-- "The Flashlight"

Coover, Robert-- "The Magic Poker"

Davis, Olivia-- "The Other Child"

Dubus, Andre-- "If They Knew Yvonne"

Gerald, John Bart-- "Blood Letting"

Gillespie, Alfred-- "Tonight at Nine Thirty-six"

Leffland, Ella-- "The Forest"

Matthews, Jack-- "Another Story"

Maxwell, William-- "The Gardens of Mont-Saint-Michel"

Morris, Wright-- "Green Grass, Blue Sky, White House"

Oates, Joyce Carol-- "How I Contemplated the World from the Detroit House of Correction and Began My Life over Again"

Olsen, Paul-- "The Flag Is Down"

Ozick, Cynthia-- "Yiddish in America"

Siegel, Jules-- "In the Land of the Morning Calm, Deja Vu"

Singer, Isaac Bashevis-- "The Key"

Stone, Robert-- "Porque no tiene, porque le falta"

Taylor, Peter-- "Daphne's Lover"

Weisbrod, Rosine-- "The Ninth Cold Day"

The Best American Short Stories, 1971, and the Yearbook of the American Short Story,
edited by **Martha Foley** *and* **David Burnett**

Banks, Russell-- "With Che in New Hampshire"

Bennett, Hal-- "Dotson Gerber Resurrected"

Blake, James-- "The Widow, Bereft"

Cady, Jack-- "I Take Care of Things"

Canzoneri, Robert-- "Barbed Wire"

Drake, Albert-- "The Chicken Which Became a Rat"

Eastlake, William-- "The Dancing Boy"

Harvor, Beth-- "Pain Was My Portion"

Madden, David-- "No Trace"

Mitchell, Don-- "Diesel"

Montgomery, Marion-- "The Decline and Fall of Officer Fergerson"

Morris, Wright-- "Magic"

O'Connor, Philip F.-- "The Gift Bearer"

Olsen, Tillie-- "Requa I"

Prashker, Ivan-- "Shirt Talk"

Rush, Norman-- "In Late Youth"

Santiago, Danny-- "The Somebody"

Strong, Jonathan-- "Xavier Fereira's Unfinished Book: Chapter One"

Tushnet, Leonard-- "The Klausners"

Valgardson, W. D.-- "Bloodflowers"

Woiwode, Larry-- "The Suitor"

The Best American Short Stories, 1972, and the Yearbook of the American Short Story,
edited by **Martha Foley**

Beal, M. F.-- "Gold"

Brautigan, Richard-- "The World War I Los Angeles Airplane"

Cherry, Kelly-- "Convenant"

Gold, Herbert-- "A Death on the East Side"

Greenberg, Joanne-- "The Supremacy of the Hunza"

Heath, Mary-- "The Breadman"

Holmes, Edward M.-- "Drums Again"

Hughes, Mary Gray-- "The Judge"

Jones, Ann-- "In Black and White"

Just, Ward-- "Three Washington Stories"

Kalechofsky, Roberta-- "His Day Out"

Kavaler, Rebecca-- "The Further Adventures of Brunhild"

L'Heureux, John-- "Fox and Swan"

Malony, Ralph-- "Intimacy"

Mandell, Marvin-- "The Aesculapians"

Ozick, Cynthia-- "The Dock-Witch"

Porter, Joe Ashby-- "The Vacation"

Street, Penelope-- "The Magic Apple"

Warren, Robert Penn-- "Meet Me in the Green Glen"

Weesner, Theodore-- "Stealing Cars"

Yglesias, José-- "The Guns in the Closet"

The Best American Short Stories, 1973, the Yearbook of the American Short Story,
edited by **Martha Foley**

Barthelme, Donald-- "A City of Churches"

Bromell, Henry-- "The Slightest Distance"

Cheever, John-- "The Jewels of the Cabots"

Clayton, John J.-- "Cambridge Is Sinking!"

Corrington, John William-- "Old Men Dream Dreams, Young Men See Visions"

Davenport, Guy-- "Robot"

Eastlake, William-- "The Death of Sun"

Greenberg, Alvin-- "The Real Meaning of the Faust Legend"

Hayden, Julie-- "In the Words Of"

Higgins, George V.-- "The Habits of Animals: The Progress of the Seasons"

Just, Ward-- "Burns"

Kenary, James S.-- "Going Home"

Knight, Wallace E.-- "The Way We Went"

Lardas, Konstantinos-- "The Broken Wings"

Malamud, Bernard-- "God's Wrath"

McPherson, James Alan-- "The Silver Bullet"

Oates, Joyce Carol-- "Silkie"

Plath, Sylvia-- "Mothers"

Sandberg-Diment, Erik-- "Come away, Oh Human Child"

Shetzline, David-- "Country of the Painted Freaks"

Williams, Tennessee-- "Happy August the Tenth"

The Best American Short Stories, 1974, and the Yearbook of the American Short Story,
edited by **Martha Foley**

Boyer, Agnes-- "The Deserter"

Bumpus, Jerry-- "Beginnings"

Clark, Eleanor-- "A Summer in Puerto Rico"

Esslinger-Carr, Pat M.-- "The Party"

Horne, Lewis B.-- "Mansion, Magic, and Miracle"

Ignatow, Rose Graubart-- "Down the American River"

Kumin, Maxine-- "Opening the Door on Sixty-second Street"

Lavin, Mary-- "Tom"

L'Heureux, John-- "A Family Affair"

Lopate, Phillip-- "The Chamber Music Evening"

Minot, Stephen-- "The Tide and Isaac Bates"

Mitchell, Beverly-- "Letter from Sakaye"

Rothschild, Michael-- "Dog in the Manger"

Sandberg, Peter L.-- "Calloway's Climb"

Saroyan, William-- "Isn't Today the Day?"

Schneider, Philip H.-- "The Gray"

Targan, Barry-- "Old Vemish"

Updike, John-- "Son"

Vivante, Arturo-- "Honeymoon"

Walker, Alice-- "The Revenge of Hannah Kemhuff"

The Best American Short Stories, 1975, and the Yearbook of the American Short Story,
edited by **Martha Foley**

Banks, Russell-- "The Lie"

Barthelme, Donald-- "The School"

Brown, Rosellen-- "How to Win"

Bumpus, Jerry-- "Desert Matinee"

Busch, Frederick-- "Bambi Meets the Furies"

Chaikin, Nancy G.-- "Waiting for Astronauts"

Clearman, Mary-- "Paths unto the Dead"

De Jenkins, Lyll Becerra-- "Tyranny"

Dubus, Andre-- "Cadence"

Ford, Jesse Hill-- "Big Boy"

Hoffman, William-- "The Spirit in Me"

Hunter, Evan-- "The Analyst"

Kaser, Paul-- "How Jerem Came Home"

MacLeod, Alistair-- "The Lost Salt Gift of Blood"

McNamara, Eugene-- "The Howard Parker Montcrief Hoax"

Matthews, Jack-- "The Burial"

Price, Reynolds-- "Night and Day at Panacea"

Rothberg, Abraham-- "Polonaise"

Silko, Leslie Marmon-- "Lullaby"

Targan, Barry-- "The Who Lived"

Yglesias, José-- "The American Sickness"

The Best American Short Stories, 1976, and the Yearbook of the American Short Story, *edited by* **Martha Foley**

Adams, Alice-- "Roses, Rhododendron"

Battin, M. Pabst-- "Terminal Procedure"

Briskin, Mae Seidman-- "The Boy Who Was Astrid's Mother"

Chaikin, Nancy G.-- "Beautiful, Helpless Animals"

Corrington, John William-- "The Actes and Documents"

Francis, H. E.-- "A Chronicle of Love"

Hagge, John-- "Pontius Pilate"

Just, Ward-- "Dietz at War"

McCluskey, John-- "John Henry's Home"

Minot, Steven-- "Grubbing for Roots"

Nelson, Kent-- "Looking into Nothing"

Ozick, Cynthia-- "A Mercenary"

Price, Reynolds-- "Broad Day"

Rothschild, Michael-- "Wondermonger"

Targan, Barry-- "Surviving Adverse Seasons"

Taylor, Peter-- "The Hand of Emmagene"

Updike, John-- "The Man Who Loved Extinct Mammals"

The Best American Short Stories, 1977, and the Yearbook of the American Short Story, *edited by* **Martha Foley**

Busch, Frederick-- "The Trouble with Being Food"

Caldwell, Price-- "Tarzan Meets the Department Head"

Cheever, John-- "Falconer"

Copeland, Ann-- "At Peace"

Corrington, John William-- "Pleadings"

Damon, Philip-- "Growing up in No Time"

Epstein, Leslie-- "The Steinway Quintet"

Garber, Eugene K.-- "The Lover"

Hampl, Patricia-- "Look at a Teacup"

Kerr, Baine-- "Rider"

Matthews, Jack-- "A Questionnaire for Rudolph Gordon"

Minot, Stephen-- "A Passion for History"

Newman, Charles-- "The Woman Who Thought like a Man"

Oates, Joyce Carol-- "Gay"

O'Brien, Tim-- "Going After Cacciato"

Robbins, Tom-- "The Chink and the Clock People"

Saroyan, William-- "A Fresno Fable"

Sayles, John-- "Breed"

Tyler, Anne-- "Your Place Is Empty"

Wilson, William S.-- "Anthropology: What Is Lost in Rotation"

The Best American Short Stories, 1978: Selected from U.S. and Canadian Magazines, including the Yearbook of the American Short Story, *edited by* **Ted Solotaroff,** *with* **Shannon Ravenel**

Baumbach, Jonathan-- "The Return of Service"

Bowles, Jane-- "Two Scenes"

Brodkey, Harold-- "Verona: A Young Woman Speaks"

Cullinan, Elizabeth-- "A Good Loser"

Elkin, Stanley-- "The Conventional Wisdom"

Epstein, Leslie-- "Skaters on Wood"

Gardner, John-- "Redemption"

Helprin, Mark-- "The Schreuderspitze"

Kaplan, James-- "In Miami, Last Winter"

Marsh, Peter-- "By the Yellow Lake"

McCarthy, Tim-- "The Windmill Man"

McEwan, Ian-- "Psychopolis"

Oates, Joyce Carol-- "The Translation"

Petesch, Natalie L. M.-- "Main Street Morning"

Rishel, Mary Ann Malinchak-- "Staus"

Schott, Max-- "Murphy Jones: Pearblossom, California"

Schwartz, Lynne Sharon-- "Rough Strife"

Sintetos, L. Hluchan-- "Telling the Bees"

Sorrells, Robert T.-- "The Blacktop Champion of Ickey Honey"

Sorrentino, Gilbert-- "Decades"

Taylor, Peter-- "In the Miro District"

Williams, Joy-- "Bromeliads"

The Best American Short Stories, 1979: Selected from U.S. and Canadian Magazines,
edited by **Joyce Carol Oates,** *with* **Shannon Ravenel**

Barthelme, Donald-- "The New Music"
Bellow, Saul-- "A Silver Dish"
Bowles, Paul-- "The Eye"
Brown, Rosellen-- "The Wedding Week"
Coffin, Lyn-- "Falling off the Scaffold"
Hedin, Mary-- "The Middle Place"
Hurlbut, Kaatje-- "A Short Walk into Afternoon"
Kumin, Maxine-- "The Missing Person"
LaSalle, Peter-- "Some Manhattan in New England"
Malamud, Bernard-- "Home Is the Hero"
McLaughlin, Ruth-- "Seasons"
Munro, Alice-- "Spelling"
O'Connor, Flannery-- "An Exile in the East"

Phillips, Jayne Anne-- "Something That Happened"
Rubin, Louis D., Jr.-- "Finisterre"
Sanford, Annette-- "Trip in a Summer Dress"
Schwartz, Lynne Sharon-- "Plaisir D'amour"
Singer, Isaac Bashevis-- "A Party in Miami Beach"
Styron, William-- "Shadrach"
Tennenbaum, Silvia-- "A Lingering Death"
Thompson, Jean-- "Paper Covers Rock"
Virgo, Sean-- "Home and Native Land"
Wilner, Herbert-- "The Quarterback Speaks to His God"
Wilson, Robley, Jr.-- "Living Alone"
Yngve, Rolf-- "The Quail"

The Best American Short Stories, 1980: Selected from U.S. and Canadian Magazines,
edited by **Stanley Elkin,** *with* **Shannon Ravenel**

Barthelme, Donald-- "The Emerald"
Busch, Frederick-- "Long Calls"
Evanier, David-- "The One-Star Jew"
Gallant, Mavis-- "The Remission; Speck's Idea"
Gass, William H.-- "The Old Folks"
Gertler, T.-- "In Case of Survival"
Hardwick, Elizabeth-- "The Faithful"
Heinemann, Larry-- "The First Clean Fact"
Henderson, Robert-- "Into the Wind"
Johnson, Curt-- "Lemon Tree"
Paley, Grace-- "Friends"

Robison, James-- "Home"
Rooke, Leon-- "Mama Tuddi Done Over"
Sayles, John-- "At the Anarchist's Convention"
Singer, Isaasc Bashevis-- "The Safe Deposit"
Stern, Richard-- "Dr. Cahn's Visit"
Targan, Barry-- "The Rags of Time"
Taylor, Peter-- "The Old Forest"
Updike, John-- "Gesturing"
Waksler, Norman-- "Markowitz and the Gypsies"
Weaver, Gordon-- "Hog's Heart"

The Best American Short Stories, 1981: Selected from U.S. and Canadian Magazines,
edited by **Hortense Calisher,** *with* **Shannon Ravenel**

Abish, Walter-- "The Idea of Switzerland"
Apple, Max-- "Small Island Republics"
Beattie, Ann-- "Winter: 1978"
Coover, Robert-- "A Working Day"
Dethier, Vincent G.-- "The Moth and the Primrose"
Dubus, Andre-- "The Winter Father"
Gallant, Mavis-- "The Assembly"
Hardwick, Elizabeth-- "The Bookseller"
Mason, Bobbie Ann-- "Shiloh"
McElroy, Joseph-- "The Future"
McGrath, Elizabeth-- "Fogbound in Avalon"

Moseley, Amelia-- "The Mountains Where Cithaeron Is"
Munro, Alice-- "Wood"
Oates, Joyce Carol-- "Presque Isle"
Ozick, Cynthia-- "The Shawl"
Rubin, Louis D., Jr.-- "The St. Anthony Chorale"
Stern, Richard-- "Wissler Remembers"
Tallent, Elizabeth-- "Ice"
Updike, John-- "Still of Some Use"
Woiwode, Larry-- "Change"

The Best American Short Stories, 1982: Selected from U.S. and Canadian Magazines,
edited by **John Gardner,** *with* **Shannon Ravenel**

Baker, Nicholson-- "K. 590"

Baxter, Charles-- "Harmony of the World"

Carver, Raymond-- "Cathedral"

Coggeshall, Rosanne-- "Lamb Says"

Ferry, James-- "Dancing Ducks and Talking Anus"

Freeman, Anne Hobson-- "The Girl Who Was No Kin to the Marshalls"

Greenberg, Alvin-- "The Power of Language Is Such That Even a Single Word Taken Truly to Heart Can Change Everything"

Gupta, Roberta-- "The Cafe de Paris"

Hauptmann, William-- "Good Rockin' Tonight"

Higgins, Joanna-- "The Courtship of Widow Sobcek"

Johnson, Charles-- "Exchange Value"

Licht, Fred-- "Shelter the Pilgrim"

MacMillan, Ian-- "Proud Monster: Sketches"

McLaughlin, Lissa-- "The Continental Heart"

Milton, Edith-- "Coming Over"

Oates, Joyce Carol-- "Theft"

Renwick, Joyce-- "The Dolphin Story"

Robison, Mary-- "Coach"

Rosner, Anne F.-- "Prize Tomatoes"

Smith, R. E.-- "The Gift Horse's Mouth"

The Best American Short Stories, 1983: Selected from U.S. and Canadian Magazines,
edited by **Anne Tyler,** *with* **Shannon Ravenel**

Barich, Bill-- "Hard to Be Good"

Bly, Carol-- "The Dignity of Life"

Bond, James-- "A Change of Season"

Carver, Raymond-- "Where I'm Calling From"

Chute, Carolyn-- "'Ollie, Oh . . .'"

Colwin, Laurie-- "My Mistress"

Epstein, Joseph-- "The Count and the Princess"

Erdrich, Louise-- "Scales"

Le Guin, Ursula K.-- "The Professor's Houses; Sur"

Mason, Bobbie Ann-- "Graveyard Day"

Morris, Wright-- "Victrola"

Schumacher, Julie-- "Reunion"

Stark, Sharon Sheehe-- "Best Quality Glass Company, New York"

Taylor, Robert-- "Colorado"

Thurm, Marian-- "Starlight"

Updike, John-- "Deaths of Distant Friends"

Vanderhaeghe, Guy-- "Reunion"

Vreuls, Diane-- "Beebee"

Woiwode, Larry-- "Firstborn"

The Best American Short Stories, 1984: Selected from U.S. and Canadian Magazines,
edited by **John Updike,** *with* **Shannon Ravenel**

Abbott, Lee K.-- "The Final Proof of Fate and Circumstance"

Bell, Madison Smartt-- "The Naked Lady"

Benedict, Dianne-- "Unknown Feathers"

Bowles, Paul-- "In the Red Room"

Brown, Mary Ward-- "The Cure"

DeMarinis, Rick-- "Gent"

Dubus, Andre-- "A Father's Story"

Gallant, Mavis-- "Lena"

Hood, Mary-- "Inexorable Progress"

Justice, Donald-- "The Artificial Moonlight"

Kirk, Stephen-- "Morrison's Reaction"

Minot, Susan-- "Thorofare"

Morris, Wright-- "Glimpse into Another Country"

Oates, Joyce Carol-- "Nairobi"

Ozick, Cynthia-- "Rosa"

Pei, Lowry-- "The Cold Room"

Penner, Jonathan-- "Things to Be Thrown Away"

Rush, Norman-- "Bruns"

Salter, James-- "Foreign Shores"

Schinto, Jeanne-- "Caddie's Day"

The Best American Short Stories, 1985: Selected from U.S. and Canadian Magazines,
edited by **Gail Godwin,** *with* **Shannon Ravenel**

Banks, Russell-- "Sarah Cole: A Type of Love Story"

Bishop, Michael-- "Dogs' Lives"

Canin, Ethan-- "Emperor of the Air"

Doctorow, E. L. -- "The Leather Man"

Edwards, Margaret-- "Roses"

Flythe, Starkey-- "Walking, Walking"

Francis, H. E.-- "The Sudden Trees"

Jafek, Bev-- "You've Come a Long Way, Mickey Mouse"

L'Heureux, John-- "Clothing"

Meinke, Peter-- "The Piano Tuner"

Morris, Wright-- "Fellow-Creatures"

Mukherjee, Bharati-- "Angela"

Nugent, Beth-- "City of Boys"

Oates, Joyce Carol-- "Raven's Wing"

Rush, Norman-- "Instruments of Seduction"

Sandor, Marjorie-- "The Gittel"

Seabrooke, Deborah-- "Secrets"

Smiley, Jane-- "Lily"

Stark, Sharon Sheehe-- "The Johnstown Polka"

Williams, Joy-- "The Skater"

The Best American Short Stories, 1986: Selected from U.S. and Canadian Magazines,
edited by **Raymond Carver,** *with* **Shannon Ravenel**

Barthelme, Donald-- "Basil from Her Garden"

Baxter, Charles-- "Gryphon"

Beattie, Ann-- "Janus"

Burke, James Lee-- "The Convict"

Canin, Ethan-- "Star Food"

Conroy, Frank-- "Gossip"

Ford, Richard-- "Communist"

Gallagher, Tess-- "Bad Company"

Hempel, Amy-- "Today Will Be a Quiet Day"

Kaplan, David Michael-- "Doe Season"

Lipsky, David-- "Three Thousand Dollars"

McGuane, Thomas-- "Sportsmen"

McIlroy, Christopher-- "All My Relations"

Munro, Alice-- "Monsieur Les Deux Chapeaux"

Neely, Jessica-- "Skin Angels"

Nelson, Kent-- "Invisible Life"

Paley, Grace-- "Telling"

Simpson, Mona-- "Lawns"

Williams, Joy-- "Health"

Wolff, Tobias-- "The Rich Brother"

The Best American Short Stories, 1987: Selected from U.S. and Canadian Magazines,
edited by **Ann Beattie,** *with* **Shannon Ravenel**

Abbott, Lee K.-- "Dreams of Distant Lives"

Baxter, Charles-- "How I Found My Brother"

Bell, Madison Smartt-- "Lie Detector"

Carlson, Ron-- "Milk"

Carver, Raymond-- "Boxes"

Gallant, Mavis-- "Kingdom Come"

Haruf, Kent-- "Private Debts/Public Holdings"

Lombreglia, Ralph-- "Men Under Water"

Miller, Sue-- "Lover of Women"

Mukherjee, Bharati-- "Tenant"

Munro, Alice-- "Circle of Prayer"

Nova, Craig-- "Prince"

O'Brien, Tim-- "Things They Carried"

Sontag, Susan-- "Way We Live Now"

Stern, Daniel-- "Interpretation of Dreams by Sigmund Freud: A Story"

Tallent, Elizabeth-- "Favor"

Taylor, Robert-- "Lady of Spain"

Updike, John-- "Afterlife"

Williams, Joy-- "Blue Men"

Wolff, Tobias-- "Other Miller"

The Best American Short Stories, 1988: Selected from U.S. and Canadian Magazines,
edited by **Mark Helprin,** *with* **Shannon Ravenel**

Bass, Rick-- "Cats and Students, Bubbles and Abysses"
Bausch, Richard-- "Police Dreams"
Blythe, Will-- "Taming Power of the Small"
Carver, Raymond-- "Errand"
Currey, Richard-- "Waiting for Trains"
Erdrich, Louise-- "Snares"
Gallant, Mavis-- "Dede"
Godshalk, C. S.-- "Wonderland"
Goldman, E. S.-- "Way to the Dump"
Honig, Lucy-- "No Friends, All Strangers"
Jen, Gish-- "Water-Faucet Vision"
Johnson, Hilding-- "Victoria"
Kiteley, Brian-- "Still Life with Insects"
Lacy, Robert-- "Natural Father"
Lombreglia, Ralph-- "Inn Essence"
Milton, Edith-- "Entrechat"
Sandor, Marjorie-- "Still Life"
Stone, Robert-- "Helping"
Taylor-Hall, Mary Ann-- "Banana Boats"
Wolff, Tobias-- "Smorgasbord"

The Best American Short Stories, 1989: Selected from U.S. and Canadian Magazines,
edited by **Margaret Atwood,** *with* **Shannon Ravenel**

Baxter, Charles-- "Fenstad's Mother"
Bell, Madison Smartt-- "Customs of the Country"
Boswell, Robert-- "Living to Be a Hundred"
Boyd, Blanche McCrary-- "The Black Hand Girl"
Brown, Larry-- "Kubuku Riders (This Is It)"
Busch, Frederick-- "Ralph the Duck"
Cunningham, Michael-- "White Angel"
DeMarinis, Rick-- "The Flowers of Boredom"
Doerr, Harriet-- "Edie: A Life"
Gallant, Mavis-- "The Concert Party"
Glover, Douglas-- "Why I Decided to Kill Myself and Other Jokes"
Gowdy, Barbara-- "Disneyland"
Hogan, Linda-- "Aunt Moon's Young Man"
Louie, David Wong-- "Displacement"
Mukherjee, Bharati-- "The Management of Grief"
Munro, Alice-- "Meneseteung"
Phillips, Dale Ray-- "What Men Love For
Richard, Mark-- "Strays"
Robinson, Arthur-- "The Boy on the Train"
Sharif, M. T.-- "The Letter Writer"

The Best American Short Stories, 1990: Selected from U.S. and Canadian Magazines,
edited by **Richard Ford,** *with* **Shannon Ravenel**

Allen, Edward-- "River of Toys"
Bausch, Richard-- "The Fireman's Wife"
Bausch, Richard-- "A Kind of Simple, Happy Grace"
Bell, Madison Smartt-- "Finding Natasha"
Godshalk, C. S.-- "The Wizard"
Henley, Patricia-- "The Secret of Cartwheels"
Houston, Pam-- "How to Talk to a Hunter"
Hustvedt, Siri-- "Mr. Morning"
Johnson, Denis-- "Car-Crash While Hitchhiking"
McFarland, Dennis-- "Nothing to Ask For"
Millhauser, Steven-- "Eisenheim the Illusionist"
Moore, Lorrie-- "You're Ugly, Too"
Munro, Alice-- "Differently"
Munro, Alice-- "Wigtime"
Powell, Padgett-- "Typical"
Segal, Lore--The Reverse Bug"
Tallent, Elizabeth-- "Prowler"
Tilghman, Christopher-- "In a Father's Place"
Wickersham, Joan-- "Commuter Marriage"
Williams, Joy-- "The Little Winter"

The Best American Short Stories, 1991: Selected from U.S. and Canadian Magazines, edited by **Alice Adams,** *with* **Katrina Kenison**

Bass, Rick-- "Legend of Pig-Eye"
Baxter, Charles-- "The Disappeared"
Bloom, Amy-- "Love Is Not a Pie"
Braverman, Kate-- "Tall Tales from the Mekong Delta"
Butler, Robert Olen-- "The Trip Back"
D'Ambrosio, Charles, Jr.-- "The Point"
Dillon, Millicent-- "Oil and Water"
Doerr, Harriet-- "Another Short Day in La Luz"
Eisenberg, Deborah-- "The Custodian"
Gordon, Mary-- "Separation"

Graver, Elizabeth-- "The Body Shop"
Hustvedt, Siri-- "Houdini"
Iossel, Mikhail-- "Bologoye"
Jauss, David-- "Glossolalia"
Michaels, Leonard-- "Viva la Tropicana"
Moore, Lorrie-- "Willing"
Munro, Alice-- "Friend of My Youth"
Oates, Joyce Carol-- "American, Abroad"
Prose, Francine-- "Dog Stories"
Updike, John-- "A Sandstone Farmhouse"

The Best American Short Stories, 1992: Selected from U.S. and Canadian Magazines, edited by **Alice Adams,** *with* **Katrina Kenison**

Adams, Alice-- "The Last Lovely City"
Bass, Rick-- "Days of Heaven"
Beller, Thomas-- "A Different Kind of Imperfection"
Bloom, Amy-- "Silver Water"
Butler, Robert Olen-- "A Good Scent from a Strange Mountain"
Gallant, Mavis-- "Across the Bridge"
Gautreaux, Tim-- "Same Place, Same Things"
Johnson, Denis-- "Emergency"
Jones, Thom-- "The Pugilist at Rest"
Klimasewiski, Marshall N.-- "JunHee"

Moore, Lorrie-- "Community Life"
Munro, Alice-- "Carried Away"
Oates, Joyce Carol-- "Is Laughter Contagious?"
Price, Reynolds-- "The Fare to the Moon"
Smith, Annick-- "It's Come to This"
Tilghman, Christopher-- "The Way People Run"
Wallace, David Foster-- "Forever Overhead"
Wheeler, Kate-- "Under the Roof"
Winthrop, Elizabeth-- "The Golden Darters"
Wolff, Tobias-- "Firelight"

The Best American Short Stories, 1993: Selected from U.S. and Canadian Magazines, edited by **Louise Erdrich,** *with* **Katrina Kenison**

Berry, Wendell-- "Pray Without Ceasing"
Dixon, Stephen-- "Man, Woman, and Boy"
Earley, Tony-- "Charlotte"
Edwards, Kim-- "Gold"
Ellison, Harlan-- "The Man Who Rowed Christopher Columbus Ashore"
Fulton, Alice-- "Queen Wintergreen"
Gaitskill, Mary-- "The Girl on the Plane"
Gordon, Mary-- "The Important Houses"
Johnson, Diane-- "Great Barrier Reef"
Jones, Thom-- "I Want to Live!"

Lee, Andrea-- "Winter Barley"
Moore, Lorrie-- "Terrific Mother"
Munro, Alice-- "A Real Life"
Nelson, Antonya-- "Naked Ladies"
Peery, Janet-- "What the Thunder Said"
Power, Susan-- "Red Moccasins"
Scott, Joanna-- "Concerning Mold upon the Skin, Etc."
Shapiro, Jane-- "Poltergeists"
Updike, John-- "Playing with Dynamite"
Woiwode, Larry-- "Silent Passengers"

The Best American Short Stories, 1994: Selected from U.S. and Canadian Magazines, *edited by* **Tobias Wolff,** *with* **Katrina Kenison**

Alexie, Sherman-- "This Is What It Means to Say Phoenix, Arizona"

Anshaw, Carol-- "Hammam"

Butler, Robert Olen-- "Salem"

Chang, Lan Samantha-- "Pipa's Story"

Cummins, Ann-- "Where I Work"

Dark, Alice Elliott-- "In the Gloaming"

Dybek, Stuart-- "We Didn't"

Earley, Tony-- "The Prophet from Jupiter"

Ferrell, Carolyn-- "Proper Library"

Gardiner, John Rolfe-- "The Voyage Out"

Gates, David-- "The Mail Lady"

Hannah, Barry-- "Nicodemus Bluff"

Jones, Thom-- "Cold Snap"

Keeble, John-- "The Chasm"

Krusoe, Nancy-- "Landscape and Dream"

Louis, Laura Glen-- "Fur"

Offutt, Chris-- "Melungeons"

Robinson, Roxana-- "Mr. Sumarsono"

Shepard, Jim-- "Batting Against Castro"

Tilghman, Christopher-- "Things Left Undone"

Wilson, Jonathan-- "From Shanghai"

The Best American Short Stories, 1995: Selected from U.S. and Canadian Magazines, *edited by* **Jane Smiley,** *with* **Katrina Kenison**

Barrett, Andrea-- "The Behavior of the Hawkweeds"

Braverman, Kate-- "Pagan Night"

Cornell, Jennifer C.-- "Undertow"

Cozine, Andrew-- "Hand Jive"

Davies, Peter Ho-- "The Ugliest House in the World"

Delaney, Edward J.-- "The Drownings"

DeLillo, Don-- "The Angel Esmeralda"

Doybyns, Stephen-- "So I Guess You Know What I Told Him"

Falco, Edward-- "The Artist"

Garland, Max-- "Chiromancy "

Gilchrist, Ellen-- "The Stucco House"

Gordon, Jaimy-- "A Night's Work"

Jen, Gish-- "Birthmates"

Jones, Thom-- "Way down Deep in the Jungle"

Kincaid, Jamaica-- "Xuela"

Mandelman, Avner-- "Pity"

Orozco, Daniel-- "Orientation"

Polansky, Steven-- "Leg"

Thon, Melanie Rae-- "First, Body"

Williams, Joy-- "Honored Guest"

The Best American Short Stories, 1996: Selected from U.S. and Canadian Magazines, *edited by* **John Edgar Wideman,** *with* **Katrina Kenison**

Adams, Alice-- "Complicities"

Bass, Rick-- "Fires"

Brown, Jason-- "Driving the Heart"

Butler, Robert Olen-- "Jealous Husband Returns in Form of Parrot"

Chang, Lan Samantha-- "The Eve of the Spirit Festival"

Chaon, Dan-- "Fitting Ends"

Davies, Peter Ho-- "The Silver Screen"

Díaz, Junot-- "Ysrael"

Dixon, Stephen-- "Sleep"

Dybek, Stuart-- "Paper Lantern"

Galyan, Deborah-- "The Incredible Appearing Man"

Gordon, Mary-- "Intertextuality"

Huddle, David-- "Past My Future"

Keesey, Anna-- "Bright Winter"

Kincaid, Jamaica-- "In Roseau"

Lewis, William Henry-- "Shades"

Lychack, William--A Stand of Fables"

Oates, Joyce Carol-- "Ghost Girls"

Patrinos, Angela-- "Sculpture I"

Perabo, Susan-- "Some Say the World"

Schwartz, Lynne Sharon-- "The Trip to Halawa Valley"

Sharma, Akhil-- "If You Sing Like That for Me"

Thompson, Jean-- "All Shall Love Me and Despair"

Thon, Melanie Rae-- "Xmas, Jamaica Plain"

The Best American Short Stories, 1997: Selected from U.S. and Canadian Magazines,
edited by **E. Annie Proulx,** *with* **Katrina Kenison**

Bausch, Richard-- "Nobody in Hollywood"

Bender, Karen E.-- "Eternal Love"

Boyle, T. Coraghessan-- "Killing Babies"

Byers, Michael-- "Rites of Passage: Shipmates down Under"

Cliff, Michelle-- "Identifying the Stranger: Transactions"

Cooke, Carolyn-- "Bob Darling"

Davis, Lydia-- "St. Martin"

Díaz, Junot-- "Perceived Social Values: Fiesta, 1980"

Durban, Pam-- "Soon"

Edgerton, Clyde-- "Send Me to the Electric Chair"

Eugenides, Jeffrey-- "Air Mail"

Franzen, Jonathan-- "Chez Lambert"

Gautreaux, Tim-- "Little Frogs in a Ditch"

Hagy, Alyson-- "Search Bay"

Hall, Donald-- "From Willow Temple"

Jin, Ha-- "Manners and Right Behavior: Saboteur"

Michaels, Leonard-- "A Girl with a Monkey"

Ozick, Cynthia-- "Save My Child!"

Spence, June-- "Missing Women"

Stone, Robert-- "Under the Pitons"

Wolff, Tobias-- "Powder"

The Best American Short Stories, 1998: Selected from U.S. and Canadian Magazines,
edited by **Garrison Keillor,** *with* **Katrina Kenison**

Adrian, Chris-- "Every Night for a Thousand Years"

Anshaw, Carol-- "Elvis Has Left the Building"

Ballantine, Poe-- "The Blue Devils of Blue River Avenue"

Broyard, Bliss-- "Mr. Sweetly Indecent"

Carter, Emily-- "Glory Goes and Gets Some"

Chetkovich, Kathryn-- "Appetites"

Crain, Matthew-- "Penance"

Gautreaux, Tim-- "Welding with Children"

Kaplan, Hester-- "Would You Know It Wasn't Love"

Larson, Doran-- "Morphine"

Moore, Lorrie-- "People Like That Are the Only People Here"

Nelson, Antonya-- "Unified Front"

Pearlman, Edith-- "Chance"

Powell, Padgett-- "Wayne in Love"

Proulx, Annie-- "The Half-Skinned Steer"

Schoemperlen, Diane-- "Body Language"

Sharma, Akhil-- "Cosmopolitain"

Swann, Maxine-- "Flower Children"

Updike, John-- "My Father on the Verge"

Wolitzer, Meg-- "Tea at the House"

The Best American Short Stories, 1999: Selected from U.S. and Canadian Magazines,
edited by **Amy Tan,** *with* **Katrina Kenison**

Bass, Rick-- "The Hermit's Story"

Díaz, Junot-- "The Sun, the Moon, the Stars"

Divakaruni, Chitra-- "Mrs. Dutta Writes a Letter"

Dobyns, Stephen-- "Kansas"

Englander, Nathan-- "The Tumblers"

Gautreaux, Tim-- "The Piano Tuner"

Hardy, Melissa-- "The Uncharted Heart"

Harrar, George-- "The Five Twenty-two"

Hemon, A.-- "Islands"

Houston, Pam-- "The Best Girlfriend You Never Had"

Jin, Ha-- "In the Kindergarten"

Julavits, Heidi-- "Marry the One Who Gets There First"

Kaplan, Hester-- "Live Life King-Sized"

Kohler, Sheilia-- "Africans"

Lahiri, Jhumpa-- "Interpreter of Maladies"

Moore, Lorrie-- "Real Estate"

Munro, Alice-- "Save the Reaper"

Proulx, Annie-- "The Bunchgrass Edge of the World"

Spencer, James-- "The Robbers of Karnataka"

Upadhyay, Samrat-- "The Good Shopkeeper"

Yarbrough, Steve-- "The Rest of Her Life"

The Best American Short Stories of the Century, *edited by* John Updike

To compile this volume, Updike selected the best stories that appeared in *The Best American Short Stories* series from 1915 through 1999; the stories are listed in chronological order of their publication in the series.

Rosenblatt, Benjamin-- "Zelig" (1915)

Lerner, Mary-- "Little Selves" (1916)

Glaspell, Susan-- "A Jury of Her Peers" (1917)

Anderson, Sherwood-- "The Other Woman" (1920)

Lardner, Ring-- "The Golden Honeymoon" (1922)

Toomer, Jean-- "Blood-Burning Moon" (1923)

Hemingway, Ernest-- "The Killers" (1927)

Cather, Willa-- "Double Birthday" (1929)

Coates, Grace Stone-- "Wild Plums" (1929)

Porter, Katherine Anne-- "Theft" (1930)

Faulkner, William-- "That Evening Sun Go Down" (1931)

Parker, Dorothy-- "Here We Are" (1931)

Fitzgerald, F. Scott-- " Crazy Sunday" (1933)

Godin, Alexander-- "My Dead Brother Comes to America" (1934)

Saroyan, William-- "Resurrection of a Life" (1935)

Warren, Robert Penn-- "Christmas Gift" (1938)

Wright, Richard-- "Bright and Morning Star" (1939)

Welty, Eudora-- "The Hitch-Hikers" (1940)

Horgan, Paul-- "The Peach Stone" (1943)

Nabokov, Vladimir-- "'That in Aleppo Once . . .'" (1944)

Stafford, Jean-- "The Interior Castle" (1947)

Gellhorn, Martha-- "Miami-New York" (1948)

White, E. B.-- "The Second Tree from the Corner" (1948)

Bishop, Elizabeth-- "The Farmer's Children" (1949)

Powers, J. F.-- "Death of a Favorite" (1951)

Williams, Tennessee-- "The Resemblance Between a Violin Case and a Coffin" (1951)

Cheever, John-- "The Country Husband" (1955)

O'Connor, Flannery-- "Greenleaf" (1957)

Hall, Lawrence Sargent-- "The Ledge" (1960)

Roth, Philip-- "Defender of the Faith" (1960)

Elkin, Stanley-- "Criers and Kibitzers, Kibitzers and Criers" (1962)

Malamud, Bernard-- "The German Refugee" (1964)

Oates, Joyce Carol-- "Where Are You Going, Where Have You Been?" (1967)

Gavell, Mary Ladd -- "The Rotifer" (1968)

McPherson, James Alan-- "Gold Coast" (1969)

Singer, Isaac Bashevis-- "The Key" (1970)

Barthelme, Donald-- "A City of Churches" (1973)

Brown, Rosellen-- "How to Win" (1975)

Adams, Alice-- "Roses, Rhododendron" (1976)

Brodkey, Harold-- "Verona: A Young Woman Speaks" (1978)

Bellow, Saul-- "A Silver Dish" (1979)

Updike, John-- "Gesturing" (1980)

Ozick, Cynthia-- "The Shawl" (1981)

Carver, Raymond-- "Where I'm Calling From" (1983)

Beattie, Ann-- "Janus" (1986)

Sontag, Susan-- "The Way We Live Now" (1987)

O'Brien, Tim-- "The Things They Carried" (1987)

Munro, Alice-- "Meneseteung" (1989)

Moore, Lorrie-- "You're Ugly, Too" (1990)

Jones, Thom-- "I Want to Live!" (1993)

Dark, Alice Elliott-- "In the Gloaming" (1994)

Ferrell, Carolyn-- "Proper Library" (1994)

Jen, Gish-- "Birthmates" (1995)

Durban, Pam-- "Soon" (1997)

Proulx, Annie-- "The Half-Skinned Steer" (1998)

Houston, Pam-- "The Best Girlfriend You Never Had" (1999)

The Best American Short Stories, 2000: Selected from U.S. and Canadian Magazines, *edited by* E.L. Doctorow, *with* Katrina Kenison.

Becker, Geoffrey-- "Black Elvis"

Bloom, Amy-- "The Story"

Byers, Michael-- "The Beautiful Days"

Carlson, Ron-- "The Ordinary Son"

Carver, Raymond-- "Call if You Need Me"

Davenport, Kiana-- "Bones of the Inner Ear"

Díaz, Junot-- "Nilda"

Englander, Nathan-- "The Gilgul of Park Avenue"

Everett, Percival-- "The Fix"

Gautreaux, Tim-- "Good for the Soul"

Gurganus, Allan-- "He's at the Office"

Hemon, Aleksandar-- "Blind Jozef Pronek"

Hill, Kathleen-- "The Anointed"

Jin, Ha-- "The Bridegroom"

Krysl, Marilyn-- "The Thing Around Them"

Lahiri, Jhumpa-- "The Third and Final Continent"

Mosley, Walter-- "Pet Fly"

Packer, ZZ-- "Brownies"

Pearlman, Edith-- "Allog"

Proulx, Annie-- "People in Hell Just Want a Drink of Water"

Sherwood, Frances-- "Basil the Dog"

The Best American Short Stories, 2001: Selected from U.S. and Canadian Magazines, *edited by* Barbara Kingsolver, *with* Katrina Kenison

Barrett, Andrea-- "Servants of the Map"

Bass, Rick-- "The Fireman"

Davies, Peter Ho-- "Think of England"

Davis, Claire-- "Labors of the Heart"

Graver, Elizabeth-- "The Mourning Door

Jin, Ha-- "After Cowboy Chicken Came to Town"

Lee, Andrea-- "Brothers and Sisters Around the World"

Moody, Rick-- "Boys"

Moss, Barbara Klein-- "Rug Weaver"

Munro, Alice-- "Post and Beam"

Orner, Peter-- "The Raft"

Parvin, Roy-- "Betty Hutton"

Reisman, Nancy-- "Illumination"

Row, Jess--The Secrets of Bats"

Sanford, Annette-- "Nobody Listens When I Talk"

Shonk, Katherine-- "My Mother's Garden"

Silver, Marisa-- "What I Saw from Where I Stood"

Trevanian-- "The Apple Tree"

Updike, John-- "Personal Archeology"

West, Dorothy-- "My Baby . . ."

The Best American Short Stories, 2002: Selected from U.S. and Canadian Magazines, *edited by* Sue Miller, *with* Katrina Kenison

Chabon, Michael-- "Along the Frontage Road"

Cooke, Carolyn-- "The Sugar-Tit"

Cummins, Ann-- "The Red Ant House"

Danticat, Edwidge-- "Seven"

Doctorow, E. L.-- "A House on the Plains"

Ford, Richard-- "Puppy"

Hardy, Melissa-- "The Heifer"

Iagnemma, Karl-- "Zilkowski's Theorem"

Lahiri, Jhumpa-- "Nobody's Business"

Lordan, Beth-- "Digging"

Mattison, Alice-- "In Case We're Separated"

McCorkle, Jill-- "Billy Goats"

McNeal, Tom-- "Watermelon Days"

Michaels, Leonard-- "Nachman from Los Angeles"

Miller, Arthur-- "Bulldog"

Mullins, Meg-- "The Rug"

Munro, Alice-- "Family Furnishings"

Sharma, Akhil-- "Surrounded by Sleep"

Shepard, Jim-- "Love and Hydrogen"

Waters, Mary Yukari-- "Aftermath"

The Best American Short Stories, 2003: Selected from U.S. and Canadian Magazines, *edited by* Walter Mosley, *with* Katrina Kenison

Allison, Dorothy-- "Compassion"

Brockmeier, Kevin-- "Space"

Chaon, Dan-- "The Bees"

Cooper, Rand Richards-- "Johnny Hamburger"

Danticat, Edwidge-- "Night Talkers"

Doctorow, E. L.-- "Baby Wilson"

Doerr, Anthony-- "The Shell Collector"

Erdich, Louise-- "Shamengwa"

Harty, Ryan-- "Why the Sky Turns Red When the Sun Goes Down"

Haslett, Adam-- "Devotion"

Krauss, Nicole-- "Future Emergencies"

Packer, ZZ-- "Every Tongue Shall Confess"

Paschal, Dean-- "Moriya"

Phipps, Marilene-- "Marie-Ange's Ginen"

Pomerantz, Sharon-- "Ghost Knife"

Raboteau, Emily Ishem-- "Kavita Through Glass"
Row, Jess-- "Heaven Lake"
Simpson, Mona-- "Coins"

Straight, Susan-- "Mines"
Waters, Mary Yukari-- "Rationing"

The Best American Short Stories, 2004: Selected from U.S. and Canadian Magazines, *edited by* **Lorrie Moore,** *with* **Katrina Kenison**

Alexie, Sherman-- "What You Pawn I Will Redeem"
Boyle, T. Coraghessan-- "Tooth and Claw"
Brady, Catherine-- "Written in Stone"
Bynum, Sarah Shun-lien-- "Accomplice"
D'Ambrosio, Charles-- "Screenwriter"
Dybek, Stuart-- "Breasts"
Eisenberg, Deborah-- "Some Other, Better Otto"
Fox, Paula-- "Grace"
Freudenberger, Nell-- "The Tutor"
Jones, Edward P.-- "A Rich Man"
Lewis, Trudy-- "Limestone Diner"

McCorkle, Jill-- "Intervention"
McGuane, Thomas-- "Gallatin Canyon"
Munro, Alice-- "Runaway"
Pneuman, Angela-- "All Saints Day"
Proulx, Annie-- "What Kind of Furniture Would Jesus Pick"
Smith, R. T.-- "Docent"
Updike, John-- "The Walk with Elizanne"
Waters, Mary Yukari-- "Mirror Studies"
Wideman, John Edgar-- "What We Cannot Speak About We Must Pass over in Silence"

The Best American Short Stories, 2005: Selected from U.S. and Canadian Magazines, *edited by* **Michael Chabon,** *with* **Katrina Kenison**

Bellows, Nathaniel-- "First Four Measures"
Bezmozgis, David-- "Natasha"
Bissell, Tom-- "Death Defier"
D'Ambrosio, Charles-- "The Scheme of Things"
Doctorow, Cory-- "Anda's Game"
Jones, Edward P.-- "Old Boys, Old Girls"
Lehane, Dennis-- "Until Gwen"
Lennon, J. Robert-- "Eight Pieces for the Left Hand"
Link, Kelly-- "Stone Animals"
McGuane, Thomas-- "Old Friends"
Means, David-- "The Secret Goldfish"

Munro, Alice-- "Silence"
Oates, Joyce Carol-- "The Cousins"
Ohlin, Alix-- "Simple Exercises for the Beginning Student"
Perotta, Tom-- "The Smile on Happy Chang's Face"
Pratt, Tom-- "Heart and Boot"
Reddi, Rishi-- "Justice Shiva Ram Murthy"
Saunders, George-- "Bohemians"
Schwartz, Lynn Sharon -- "A Taste of Dust"
Williams, Joy-- "The Girls"

The Best American Short Stories, 2006: Selected from U.S. and Canadian Magazines, *edited by* **Ann Patchett,** *with* **Katrina Kenison**

Beattie, Ann, with Harry Matthews-- "Mr. Nobody at All"
Bell, Katherine-- "The Casual Car Pool"
Bezmozgis, David-- "A New Gravestone for an Old Grave"
Coover, Robert-- "Grandmother's Nose"
Englander, Nathan-- "How We Avenged the Bums"
Gaitskill, Mary-- "Today I'm Yours"
Hemon, Aleksandar-- "The Conductor"
Li, Yiyun-- "After a Life"
Livings, Jack-- "The Dog"

McGuane, Thomas-- "Cowboy"
Moffett, Kevin-- "Tattooizm"
Munro, Alice-- "The View from Castle Rock"
Pearlman, Edith-- "Self-Reliance"
Percy, Benjamin-- "Refresh, Refresh"
Ryan, Patrick-- "So Much for Artemis"
Slouka, Mark-- "Dominion"
Swann, Maxine-- "Secret"
Tartt, Donna-- "The Ambush"
Woolf, Tobias-- "Awaiting Orders"
Yoon, Paul-- "Once the Shore"

The Best American Short Stories, 2007: Selected from U.S. and Canadian Magazines,
edited by **Stephen King,** *with* **Heidi Pitlor**

Auchincloss, Louis-- "Pa's Darling"
Barth, John-- "Toga Party"
Beattie, Ann-- "Solid Wood"
Boyle, T. Coraghessan-- "Balto"
DeVita, Randy-- "Riding the Doghouse"
Epstein, Joseph-- "My Brother Eli"
Gay, William-- "Where Will You Go When Your Skin Cannot Contain You?"
Gordon, Mary-- "Eleanor's Music"
Groff, Lauren-- "L. DeBard and Aliette, a Love Story"
Jensen, Beverly-- "Wake"
Kesey, Roy-- "Wait"
Kim, Stellar-- "Findings and Impressions"
Kyle, Aryn-- "Allegiance"
McAllister, Bruce-- "Boy in Zaquitos"
Munro, Alice-- "Dimension"
Pollack, Eileen-- "Bris"
Russell, Karen-- "St. Lucy's Home for Girls Raised by Wolves"
Russo, Richard-- "Horseman"
Shepard, Jim-- "Sans Farine"
Walbert, Kate-- "Do Something"

The Best American Short Stories, 2008: Selected from U.S. and Canadian Magazines,
edited by **Salman Rushdie,** *with* **Heidi Pitlor**

Boyle, T. Coraghessan-- "Admiral"
Brockmeier, Kevin-- "The Year of Silence"
Brown, Karen-- "Galatea"
Chase, Katie-- "Man and Wife"
Evans, Danielle-- "Virgins"
Goodman, Allegra-- "Closely Held"
Homes, A. M.-- "May We Be Forgotten"
Krauss, Nicole-- "From the Desk of Daniel Varsky"
Lethem, Jonathan-- "The King of Sentences"
Makkai, Rebecca-- "The Worst You Ever Feel"
Millhauser, Steven-- "The Wizard of West Orange"
Mueenuddin, Daniyal-- "Nawabdin Electrician"
Munro, Alice-- "Child's Play"
Penkov, Miroslav-- "Buying Lenin"
Russell, Karen-- "Vampires in the Lemon Grove"
Saunders, George-- "Puppy"
Sneed, Christine-- "Quality of Life"
Tice, Bradford-- "Missionaries"
Wisniewski, Mark-- "Straightaway"
Wolff, Tobias-- "Bible"

The Best American Short Stories, 2009: Selected from U.S. and Canadian Magazines,
edited by **Alice Sebold,** *with* **Heidi Pitlor**

Alarcón, Daniel-- "The Idiot President"
Bynum, Sarah Shun-lien-- "Yurt"
De Jarnatt, Steve-- "Rubiaux Rising"
Epstein, Joseph-- "Beyond the Pale"
Fulton, Alice-- "A Shadow Table"
Greenfeld, Karl Taro-- "NowTrends"
Henderson, Eleanor-- "The Farms"
Hrbek, Greg-- "Sagittarius"
Johnson, Adam-- "Hurricanes Anonymous"
Lancelotta, Victoria-- "The Anniversary Trip"
Li, Yiyun-- "A Man Like Him"
Makkai, Rebecca-- "The Briefcase"
McCorkle, Jill-- "Magic Words"
Moffett, Kevin-- "One Dog Year"
Powers, Richard-- "Modulation"
Proulx, Annie-- "Them Old Cowboy Songs"
Rash, Ron-- "Into the Gorge"
Rose, Alex-- "Ostracon"
Rutherford, Ethan-- "The Peripatetic Coffin"
Serpell, Namwali-- "Muzungu"

The Best American Short Stories, 2010: Selected from U.S. and Canadian Magazines,
edited by **Richard Russo,** *with* **Heidi Pitlor**

Almond, Steve-- "Donkey Greedy, Donkey Gets Punched"
Barton, Marlin-- "Into Silence"
Baxter, Charles-- "The Cousins"
Egan, Jennifer-- "Safari"
Evans, Danielle-- "Someone Ought to Tell Her There's No Place to Go"
Ferris, Joshua-- "The Valetudinarian"
Groff, Lauren-- "Delicate Edible Birds"
Harrison, Wayne-- "Least Resistance"
Lasdun, James-- "The Hollow"
Makkai, Rebecca-- "Painted Ship, Painted Ocean"
Matthews, Brendan-- "My Last Attempt to Explain What Happened to the Lion Tamer"

McCorkle, Jill-- "P. S."
Moffett, Kevin-- "Further Interpretations of Real Life Events"
Obreht, Téa-- "The Laugh"
Ostlund, Lori-- "All Boy"
Rash, Ron-- "The Ascent"
Russell, Karen-- "The Seagull Army Descends on Strong Beach"
Shepard, Jim-- "The Netherlands Lives with Water"
Shipstead, Maggie-- "Cowboy Tango"
Tower, Wells-- "Raw Water"

Danuta Gleed Literary Award

The Writers' Union of Canada presents this $10,000 prize annually to a Canadian author who has written the best first collection of short fiction in the English language.

1998: Curtis Gillespie--*The Progress of an Object in Motion*
1999: Mike Barnes--*Aquarium*
2000: Ivan E. Coyote--*Close to Spiderman*
2001: Barbara Lamber--*The Allegra Series*
2002: Gloria Sawai--*A Song for Nettie Johnson*
2003: Lee Henderson--*The Broken Record Technique*
2004: Jacqueline Baker--*A Hard Witching, and Other Stories*

2005: David Bezmozgis--*Natasha, and Other Stories*
2006: Charlotte Gill--*Ladykiller*
2007: Nathan Sellyn--*Indigenous Beasts*
2008: Andrew Hood--*Pardon Our Monsters*
2009: Pasha Malla--*The Withdrawal Method*
2010: Sarah Roberts--*Wax Boats*

PEN/Malamud Award

The PEN/Malamud Award and Memorial Reading, awarded annually by the PEN/Faulkner Foundation, recognizes excellence in "the art of the short story." This list includes only Commonwealth writers who have received the award.

2009: Alistair MacLeod

2010: Nam Le

PEN/O. Henry Award

The O. Henry Awards, published each year in a volume entitled *Prize Stories*, were established in 1919; in 2009, prize officials partnered with the PEN American Center and the prize was renamed the PEN/O. Henry Award. The annual volume of prize-winners features stories written in English that were published in American and Canadian magazines.

1919

First Prize

Montague, Margaret Prescott-- "England to America"

Second Prize

Steele, Wilbur Daniel-- "For They Know Not What They Do"

Other Selected Stories

Alsop, Guglielma-- "The Kitchen Gods"

Cabell, James Branch-- "Porcelain Cups"

Derieux, Samuel A.-- "The Trial in Tom Belcher's Store"

Ferber, Edna-- "April Twenty-fifth as Usual"

Hurst, Fannie-- "Humoresque"

Marshall, Edison-- "The Elephant Remembers"

Post, Melville D.-- "Five Thousand Dollars Reward"

Ravenel, Beatrice-- "The High Cost of Conscience"

Rice, Louise-- "The Lubbeny Kiss"

Springer, Thomas Grant-- "The Blood of the Dragon"

Terhune, Albert Payson-- "On Strike"

Williams, Ben Ames-- "They Grind Exceedingly Small"

Wood, Frances Gilchrist-- "Turkey Red"

1920

First Prize

Burt, Maxwell Struthers-- "Each in His Generation"

Second Prize

Hart, Frances Noyes-- "Contact!"

Other Selected Stories

Fitzgerald, F. Scott-- "The Camel's Back"

Forbes, Esther-- "Break-Neck Hill"

Gilpatric, Guy-- "Black Art and Ambrose"

Hartman, Lee Foster-- "The Judgement of Vulcan"

Hull, Alexander-- "The Argosies"

Lewis, O. F.-- "Alma Mater"

Miller, Alice Duer-- "Slow Poison"

Pelley, William Dudley-- "The Face in the Window"

Perry, Lawrence-- "A Matter of Loyalty"

Robbins, L. H.-- "Professor Todd's Used Car"

Rutledge, Maurice-- "The Thing They Loved"

Sidney, Rose-- "Butterflies"

Smith, Gordon Arthur-- "No Flowers"

Steele, Wilbur Daniel-- "Footfalls"

Whitman, Stephen French-- "The Last Room of All"

1921

First Prize

Marshall, Edison-- "The Heart of Little Shikara"

Second Prize

Jackson, Charles Tenney-- "The Man Who Cursed the Lillies"

Other Selected Stories

Allen, Maryland-- "The Urge"

Beer, Thomas-- "Mummery"

Chittenden, Gerald-- "The Victim of His Vision"

Cooper, Courtney Ryley, and Lee F. Creagan-- "Martin Gerrity Gets Even"

Cram, Mildred-- "Stranger Things"

Derieux, Samuel A.-- "Comet"

Heerman, Elizabeth Alexander-- "Fifty-two Weeks for Florette"

Kerr, Sophie-- "Wild Earth"

Kniffin, Harry Anable-- "The Tribute"

Lewis, O. F.-- "The Get-Away"

Mumford, Ethel Watts-- "Aurore"

Robbins, L. H.-- "Mr. Downey Sits Down"

Steele, Wilbur Daniel-- "The Marriage in Kairwan"

Tupper, Tristram-- "Grit"

1922

First Prize

Cobb, Irvin S.-- "Snake Doctor"

Second Prize

Lane, Rose Wilder-- "Innocence"

Best Short Short

Buckley, F. R.-- "Gold-Mounted Guns"

Other Selected Stories

Alexander, Charles-- "As a Dog Should"

Barrett, Richmond Brooks-- "Art for Art's Sake"

Beer, Thomas-- "Tact"

Bennett, James W.-- "The Kiss of the Accolade"

Derieux, Samuel A.-- "The Sixth Shot"

Horn, R. de S.-- "The Jinx of the Shandon Belle"

Hull, Helen R.-- "His Sacred Family"

Jackson, Charles Tenney-- "The Horse of Hurricane Reef"

Lewis, O. F.-- "Old Peter Takes an Afternoon Off"

Morris, Gouverneur-- "Ig's Amock"

Steele, Wilbur Daniel-- "The Anglo-Saxon"

Terhune, Albert Payson-- "The Writer-Upward"

Vorse, Mary Heaton-- "Twilight of the God"

1923

First Prize

Smith, Edgar Valentine-- "Prelude"

Second Prize

Connell, Richard-- "A Friend of Napoleon"

Best Short Short

Folsom, Elizabeth Irons-- "Towers of Fame"

Other Selected Stories

Dell, Floyd-- "Phantom Adventure"

Farogoh, Francis Edwards-- "The Distant Street"

Glenn, Isa Urquhart-- "The Wager"

Hopper, James-- "Célestine"

Larsson, Genevieve-- "Witch Mary"

Lemmon, Robert S.-- "The Bamboo Trap"

Mahoney, James-- "The Hat of Eight Reflections"

Mason, Grace Sartwell-- "Home Brew"

Morris, Gouverneur-- "Derrick's Return"

Synon, Mary-- "Shadowed"

Tarkington, Booth-- "The One Hundred Dollar Bill"

Watts, Mary S.-- "Nice Neighbors"

Williams, Jesse Lynch-- "Not Wanted"

1924

First Place

Irwin, Inez Haynes-- "The Spring Flight"

Second Place

Crowell, Chester T.-- "Margaret Blake"

Best Short Short

Newman, Frances-- "Rachel and Her Children"

Other Selected Stories

Benét, Stephen Vincent-- "Uriah's Son"

Connell, Richard-- "The Most Dangerous Game"

Dobie, Charles Caldwell-- "Horse and Horse"

Mirrielees, Edith R.-- "Professor Boynton Rereads History"

Mosley, Jefferson-- "The Secret at the Crossroads"

Pattullo, George-- "The Tie That Binds"

Singmaster, Elsie-- "The Courier of the Czar"

Smith, Edgar Valentine-- "'Lijah"

Spears, Raymond S.-- "A River Combine-Professional"

Steele, Wilbur Daniel-- "What Do You Mean--Americans?"

Stone, Elinore Cowan-- "One Uses the Handkerchief"

Welles, Harriet-- "Progress"

1925

First Prize

Street, Julian-- "Mr. Bisbee's Princess"

Second Prize

Williams, Wythe-- "Splendid with Swords"

Best Short Short

Austin, Mary-- "Papago Wedding"

Other Selected Stories

Anderson, Sherwood-- "The Return"

Babcock, Edwina Stanton-- "Dunelight"

Brady, Mariel-- "Peter Projects"

Brecht, Harold W.-- "Two Heroes"

Carver, Ada Jack-- "Redbone"

Eliot, Ethel Cook-- "Maternal"

Hackett, Francis-- "Unshapely Things"

Heyward, DuBose-- "Crown's Bess"

Peterkin, Julia-- "Maum Lou"

Steele, Wilbur Daniel-- "The Man Who Saw Through Heaven"-- "Cornelia's Mountain"

Whitlock, Brand-- "The Sofa"

1926

First Prize

Steele, Wilbur Daniel-- "Bubbles"

Second Prize

Anderson, Sherwood-- "Death in the Woods"

Best Short Short

Wetjen, Albert Richard-- "Command"

Other Selected Stories

Carver, Ada Jack-- "Threeshy"

Detzer, Karl W.-- "The Wreck Job"

Dobie, Charles Caldwell-- "The Thrice Bereft Widow of Hung Gow"

Fauset, Arthur Huff-- "Symphonesque"

Goodloe, Abbie Carter-- "Claustrophobia"

Graeve, Oscar-- "A Death on Eighth Avenue"

Jacobs, Marguerite-- "Singing Eagles"

Kelly, Eleanor Mercein-- "Basquerie"

Saxon, Lyle-- "Cane River"

Skinner, Constance Lindsay-- "The Dew on the Fleece"

Tarkington, Booth-- "Stella Crozier"

Vorse, Mary Heaton-- "The Madelaine"

Williams, Ben Ames-- "The Nurse"

1927

First Prize

Bradford, Roark-- "Child of God"

Second Prize

Hemingway, Ernest-- "The Killers"

Best Short Short

Bromfield, Louis-- "The Scarlet"

Other Selected Stories

Adams, Bill-- "Jukes"

Bellah, James Warner-- "Fear"

Brush, Katherine-- "Night Club"

Carver, Ada Jack-- "Singing Woman"

Chapman, Elizabeth Cobb-- "With Glory and Honor"

Daniels, Roger-- "Bulldog"

Douglas, Marjory Stoneman-- "He Man"

Ellerbe, Alma, and Paul Ellerbe-- "Don Got Over"

Kelly, Eleanor Mercein-- "Monkey Motions"

Sawyer, Ruth-- "Four Dreams of Gram Perkins"

Suckow, Ruth-- "The Little Girl from Town"

Taylor, Ellen Dupois-- "Shades of George Sand"

1928

First Prize

Duranty, Walter-- "The Parrot"

Second Prize

Douglas, Marjory Stoneman-- "The Peculiar Treasure of Kings"

Best Short Short

Gale, Zona-- "Bridal Pond"

Other Selected Stories

Adams, Bill-- "Home Is the Sailor"

Aldrich, Bess Streeter-- "The Man Who Caught the Weather"

Avery, Stephen Morehouse-- "Never in This World"

Blackman, M. C.-- "Hot Copy"

Bradford, Roark-- "River Witch"

Brown, Cambray-- "Episode in a Machine Age"

Cobb, Irvin S.-- "An Episode at Pintail Lake"

Connell, Richard-- "The Law Beaters"

Hartman, Lee Foster-- "Mr. Smith" (or "Two Minutes to Live")

Johnson, Nunnally-- "The Actor"

Marquis, Don-- "O'Meara, the Mayflower--and Mrs. MacLirr"

Steele, Wilbur Daniel-- "Lightning"

Tarleton, Fiswoode-- "Curtains" (or "Bloody Ground")

Steele, Wilbur Daniel -- "Lightning"

Wescott, Glenway-- "Prohibition"

1929

First Prize

Parker, Dorothy-- "Big Blonde"

Second Prize

Howard, Sidney-- "The Homesick Ladies"

Best Short Short

Brush, Katherine-- "Him and Her"

Other Selected Stories

Anderson, Sherwood-- "Alice"

Benét, Stephen Vincent-- "The King of the Cats"

Bromfield, Louis-- "The Skeleton at the Feast"

Brush, Katherine-- "Speakeasy"

Chapman, Maristan-- "Treat You Clever"

Johnston, Mary-- "Elephants Through the Country"

Leech, Margaret-- "Manicure"

Marquis, Don-- "The Red-Haired Woman"

Norris, Kathleen-- "Sinners"

Patterson, Pernet-- "Buttin' Blood"

Rushfeldt, Elise-- "A Coffin for Anna"

Sanborn, Ruth Burr-- "Professional Pride"

Slade, Caroline-- "Mrs. Sabin"

Steele, Wilbur Daniel-- "The Silver Sword"

1930

First Prize

Burnett, W. R.-- "Dressing-Up"

John, William H.-- "Neither Jew Nor Greek"

Second Prize

Roberts, Elizabeth Madox-- "The Sacrifice of the
    Maidens"

Best Short Short

Connelly, Marc-- "Coroner's Inquest"

Other Selected Stories

Bradford, Roark-- "Careless Love"

Burt, Katherine Newlin-- "Herself"

Clements, Colin-- "Lobster John's Annie"

Cobb, Irvin S.-- "Faith, Hope and Charity"

Cooper, Courtney Ryley-- "The Elephant Forgets"

DeFord, Miriam Allen-- "The Silver Knight"

Hallet, Richard Matthews-- "Misfortune's Isle"

Held, John, Jr.-- "A Man of the World"

Johnson, Nunnally-- "Mlle. Irene the Great"

March, William-- "The Little Wife"

Overbeck, Alicia O'Reardon-- "Encarnatión"

Pelley, William Dudley-- "The Continental Angle"

Peterkin, Julia-- "The Diamond Ring"

Ryerson, Florence-- "Lobster John's Annie"

Steele, Wilbur Daniel-- "Conjuh"

Street, Julian-- "A Matter of Standards"

Thomason, Capt. John W., Jr.-- "Born on an Iceberg"

1931

First Prize

Steele, Wilbur Daniel-- "Can't Cross Jordan by Myself"

Second Prize

Swain, John D.-- "One Head Well Done"

Third Prize

Bradley, Mary Hastings-- "The Five-Minute Girl"

Best Short Short

La Farge, Oliver-- "Haunted Ground"

Other Selected Stories

Beems, Griffith-- "Leaf Unfolding"

Brush, Katharine-- "Good Wednesday"

Chase, Mary Ellen-- "Salesmanship"

Ryerson, Florence, and Colin Clements-- "Useless"

Dobie, Charles Caldwell-- "The False Talisman"

Faulkner, William-- "Thrift"

Hume, Cyril-- "Forrester"

Loomis, Alfred F.-- "Professional Aid"

Luhrs, Marie-- "Mrs. Schwellenbach's Receptions"

March, William-- "Fifteen from Company K"

Rice, Laverne-- "Wings for Janie"

Smith, Edgar Valentine-- "Cock-a-Doodle-Done!"

Tarkington, Booth-- "Cider of Normandy"

Thorne, Crichton Alston-- "Chimney City"

1932

First Prize

Benét, Stephen Vincent-- "An End to Dreams"

Second Prize

Cozzens, James Gould-- "Farewell to Cuba"

Best Short Short

Granberry, Edwin-- "A Trip to Czardis"

Other Selected Stories

Boone, Jack H.-- "Big Singing"

Boyle, Kay-- "The First Lover"

Brush, Katherine-- "Football Girl"

Canfield, Dorothy-- "Ancestral Home"

Cobb, Irvin S.-- "A Colonel of Kentucky"

Constiner, Merle-- "Big Singing"

Coombes, Evan-- "Kittens Have Fathers"

Edmonds, Walter D.-- "The Cruise of the Cashalot"

Faulkner, William-- "Turn About"

Marquand, J. P.-- "Deep Water"

Tarkington, Booth-- "She Was Right Once"

1933

First Prize

Rawlings, Marjorie Kinnan-- "Gal Young Un"

Second Prize

Buck, Pearl S.-- "The Frill"

Best Short Short

Hale, Nancy-- "To the Invader"

Other Selected Stories

Adams, Bill-- "The Lubber"

Aiken, Conrad-- "The Impulse"

Arnold, Len-- "Portrait of a Woman"

Caldwell, Erskine-- "Country Full of Swedes"

Fitzgerald, F. Scott-- "Family in the Wind"

Frost, Francis M.-- "The Heart Being Perished"

Haardt, Sarah-- "Absolutely Perfect"

Lane, Rose Wilder-- "Old Maid"

Robinson, Selma-- "The Departure"

Smith, Robert-- "Love Story"

Thomas, Dorothy-- "The Consecrated Coal Scuttle"

Wilde, Hagar-- "Little Brat"

1934
First Prize
Paul, Louis-- "No More Trouble for Jedwick"
Second Prize
Gordon, Caroline-- "Old Red"
Third Prize
Saroyan, William-- "The Daring Young Man on the Flying Trapeze"
Other Selected Stories
Appel, Benjamin-- "Pigeon Flight"
Buck, Pearl S.-- "Shanghai Scene"
Caldwell, Erskine-- "Maud Island"
Cole, Madelene-- "Bus to Biarritz"
DeFord, Miriam Allen-- "Pride"
Edmonds, Walter D.-- "Honor of the County"
Faulkner, William-- "Wash"
Fisher, Vardis-- "The Scarecrow"
Johnson, Josephine W.-- "Dark"
Sherman, Richard-- "First Flight"
Steinbeck, John-- "The Murder"
Stribling, T. S.-- "Guileford"
Sylvester, Harry-- "A Boxer: Old"
Wexley, John-- "Southern Highway Fifty-one"
Wolfe, Thomas-- "Boom Town"
Zugsmith, Leane-- "King Lear in Evansville"

1935
First Prize
Boyle, Kay-- "The White Horses of Vienna"
Second Prize
Thomas, Dorothy-- "The Home Place"
Third Prize
Johnson, Josephine W.-- "John the Six"
Other Selected Stories
Algren, Nelson-- "The Brother's House"
Benét, Stephen Vincent-- "The Professor's Punch"
Hamill, Katherine-- "Leora's Father"
Kantor, MacKinlay-- "Silent Grow the Guns"
Mamet, Louis-- "A Writer Interviews a Banker"
Marquis, Don-- "Country Doctor"
McCleary, Dorothy-- "Little Elise"
O'Donnell, E. P.-- "Jesus Knew"
Paul, Louis-- "Lay Me Low!"
Santee, Ross-- "Water"
Saroyan, William-- "Five Ripe Pears"

Shenton, Edward-- "When Spring Brings Back. . ."
Sherman, Richard-- "First Day"
Terrell, Upton-- "Long Distance"
Weidman, Jerome-- "My Father Sits in the Dark"
Wolfe, Thomas-- "Only the Dead Know Brooklyn"

1936
First Prize
Cozzens, James Gould-- "Total Stranger"
Second Prize
Benson, Sally-- "Suite Twenty Forty-nine"
Best Short Short
March, William-- "A Sum in Addition"
Other Selected Stories
Bessie, Alvah C.-- "A Personal Issue"
Bird, Virginia-- "Havoc Is Circle"
Brace, Ernest-- "Silent Whistle"
Cain, James M.-- "Dead Man"
Coatsworth, Elizabeth-- "The Visit"
Colby, Nathalie-- "Glass Houses"
Driftmier, Lucille-- "For My Sister"
Edmonds, Walter D.-- "Escape from the Mine"
Faulkner, William-- "Lion"
Gale, Zona-- "Crisis"
Godchaux, Elma-- "Chains"
Heth, Edward Harris-- "Big Days Beginning"
Horgan, Paul-- "The Trunk"
Katterjohn, Elsie-- "Teachers"
Knight, Eric-- "The Marne"
Owen, Janet Curren-- "Afternoon of a Young Girl"

1937
First Prize
Benét, Stephen Vincent-- "The Devil and Daniel Webster"
Second Prize
Moll, Elick-- "To Those Who Wait"
Third Prize
Coates, Robert M.-- "The Fury"
Other Selected Stories
Appel, Benjamin-- "Awroopdedoop!"
Bird, Virginia-- "For Nancy's Sake"
DeJong, David Cornel-- "The Chicory Neighbors"
Hale, Nancy-- "To the North"
Hilton, Charles-- "Gods of Darkness"
Hunt, Hamlen-- "The Saluting Doll"

March, William-- "The Last Meeting"

Martin, Charles-- "Hobogenesis"

McKeon, J. M.-- "The Gladiator"

O'Hara, John-- "My Girls"

Patten, Katherine-- "Man Among Men"

Pereda, Prudencio de-- "The Spaniard"

Seager, Allan-- "Pro Arte"

Still, James-- "Job's Tears"

Stuart, Jesse-- "Whip-Poor-Willie"

Thibault, David-- "A Woman Like Dilsie"

Warren, Robert Penn-- "Christmas Gift"

Weidman, Jerome-- "Thomas Hardy's Meat"

1938
First Prize

Maltz, Albert-- "The Happiest Man on Earth"

Second Prize

Wright, Richard-- "Fire and Cloud"

Third Prize

Steinbeck, John-- "The Promise"

Other Selected Stories

Benét, Stephen Vincent-- "Johnny Pye and the Fool-Killer"

Caldwell, Erskine-- "Man and Woman"

Daly, Maureen-- "Sixteen"

Fuchs, Daniel-- "The Amazing Mystery at Storick, Dorschi, Pflaumer, Inc."

Hale, Nancy-- "Always Afternoon"

Bradley, Mary Hastings-- "The Life of the Party"

Hunt, Hamlen-- "Only by Chance Are Pioneers Made"

Moll, Elick-- "Memoir of Spring"

Saroyan, William-- "The Summer of the Beautiful White Horse"

Still, James-- "So Large a Thing as Seven"

Whitehand, Robert-- "The Fragile Bud"

1939
First Prize

Faulkner, William-- "Barn Burning"

Second Prize

Still, James-- "Bat Flight"

Third Prize

DeJong, David Cornel-- "Calves"

Other Selected Stories

Baker, Dorothy-- "Keeley Street Blues"

Boyle, Kay-- "Anschluss"

Brand, Millen-- "The Pump"

Burt, Maxwell Struthers-- "The Fawn"

Caldwell, Erskine-- "The People V. Abe Lathan, Colored"

Cooke, Charles-- "Nothing Can Change It"

Foster, Joseph O'Kane-- "Gideon"

Gordon, Caroline-- "Frankie and Thomas and Bud Asbury"

Shaw, Irwin-- "God on a Friday Night"

St. Joseph, Ellis-- "A Knocking at the Gate"

Thielen, Benedict-- "Silver Virgin"

Welty, Eudora-- "Petrified Man"

1940
First Prize

Benét, Stephen Vincent-- "Freedom's a Hard-Bought Thing"

Second Prize

Lull, Roderick-- "Don't Get Me Wrong"

Third Prize

Havill, Edward-- "The Kill"

Other Selected Stories

Boyle, Kay-- "Poor Monsieur Panalitus"

Brooks, Roy Patchen-- "Without Hal"

Coates, Robert M.-- "Let's Not Talk About It Now"

Faulkner, William-- "Hand upon the Waters"

Hale, Nancy-- "That Woman"

King, Mary-- "Chicken on the Wind"

Lumpkin, Grace-- "The Treasure"

McCleary, Dorothy-- "Mother's Helper"

Porter, Katherine Anne-- "The Downward Path to Wisdom"

Rawlings, Marjorie Kinnan-- "The Pelican's Shadow"

Robinson, Mabel L.-- "Called For"

Saroyan, William-- "The Three Swimmers and the Educated Grocer"

Tracy, Tom-- "Homecoming"

Wright, Richard-- "Almos' a Man"

1941
First Prize

Boyle, Kay-- "Defeat"

Second Prize

Welty, Eudora-- "A Worn Path"

Third Prize

Abbett, Hallie Southgate-- "Eighteenth Summer"

Best First-Published Story
Logan, Andy-- "The Visit"
Other Selected Stories
Aiken, Conrad-- "Hello, Tib"
Algren, Nelson-- "A Bottle of Milk for Mother (Biceps)"
Benson, Sally-- "Retreat"
Cheever, John-- "I'm Going to Asia"
Clark, Walter Van Tilburg-- "Hook"
DeJong, David Cornel-- "Seven Boys Take a Hill"
Faulkner, William-- "The Old People"
Gallico, Paul-- "The Snow Goose"
Hale, Nancy-- "Those Are as Brothers"
Kunasz, Paul-- "I'd Give It All up for Tahiti"
Maltz, Albert-- "Afternoon in the Jungle"
Morris, Edita-- "Caput Mortum"
O'Hara, Mary-- "My Friend Flicka"
Sheean, Vincent-- "The Conqueror"
Still, James-- "The Proud Walkers"
Thomas, Dorothy-- "My Pigeon Pair"

1942
First Prize
Welty, Eudora-- "The Wide Net"
Second Prize
Stegner, Wallace-- "Two Rivers"
Third Prize
Schramm, Wilbur L.-- "Windwagon Smith"
Best First-Published Story
Wylie, Jeanne E.-- "A Long Way to Go"
Other Selected Stories
Boyle, Kay-- "Their Name Is Macaroni"
Clark, Walter Van Tilburg-- "The Portable Phonograph"
Davis, Robert Gorham-- "An Interval Like This"
DeJong, David Cornel-- "Snow-on-the-Mountain"
Faulkner, William-- "Two Soldiers"
Green, Eleanor-- "The Dear Little Doves"
Hale, Nancy-- "Sunday-1913"
Jaynes, Clare-- "The Coming of Age"
Johnson, Josephine W.-- "Alexander to the Park"
Laing, Alexander-- "The Workmanship Has to be Wasted"
McCullers, Carson-- "The Jockey"
Shuman, John Rogers-- "Yankee Odyssey"
Steinbeck, John-- "How Edith McGillcuddy Met R. L. Stevenson"

Stuart, Alison-- "The Yodeler"
Sullivan, Richard-- "Feathers"
Weidman, Jerome-- "Basket Carry"
Worthington, Marjorie-- "Hunger"

1943
First Prize
Welty, Eudora-- "Livvie Is Back"
Second Prize
Canfield, Dorothy-- "The Knot Hole"
Third Prize
Fifield, William-- "The Fisherman of Patzcuaro"
Best First-Published Story
Laidlaw, Clara-- "The Little Black Boys"
Other Selected Stories
Boyle, Kay-- "The Canals of Mars"
Breuer, Bessie-- "Pigeons en Casserole"
Buck, Pearl S.-- "The Enemy"
Clark, Walter Van Tilburg-- "The Ascent of Ariel Goodbody"
Cook, Whitfield-- "The Unfaithful"
Grinnell, Sarah-- "Standby"
Grossberg, Elmer-- "Black Boy's Good Time"
Hale, Nancy-- "Who Lived and Died Believing"
Johnson, Josephine W.-- "The Glass Pigeon"
Lampman, Ben Hur-- "Blinker was a Good Dog"
McCullers, Carson-- "A Tree. A Rock. A Cloud"
Saroyan, William-- "Knife-like, Flower-like, Like Nothing at All in the World"
Smith, Margarita G.-- "White for the Living"
Strong, Austin-- "She Shall Have Music"
Stuart, Alison-- "Death and My Uncle Felix"
Thurber, James-- "The Cane in the Corridor"
Von der Goltz, Peggy-- "The Old She 'Gator"
White, William C.-- "Pecos Bill and the Willful Coyote"

1944
First Prize
Shaw, Irwin-- "Walking Wounded"
Second Prize
Breuer, Bessie-- "Home Is a Place"
Third Prize
Beems, Griffith-- "The Stagecoach"
Best First-Published Story
Yerby, Frank G.-- "Health Card"

Other Selected Stories

Clark, Walter Van Tilburg-- "The Buck in the Hills"

Eastman, Elizabeth-- "Like a Field Mouse over the Heart"

Fineman, Morton-- "Soldier of the Republic"

Fleming, Berry-- "Strike up a Stirring Music"

Hope, Marjorie-- "That's My Brother"

Johnson, Josephine W.-- "Night Flight"

Knight, Ruth Adams-- "What a Darling Little Boy"

Loveridge, George-- "The Fur Coat"

Osborne, Margaret-- "Maine"

Powers, J. F.-- "Lions, Harts, Leaping Does"

Roane, Marianne-- "Quitter"

Schmitt, Gladys-- "All Souls'"

Schorer, Mark-- "Blockbuster"

Stuart, Alison-- "Sunday Liberty"

Weston, Christine-- "Raziya"

Wilcox, Wendall-- "The Pleasures of Travel"

Young, Marguerite-- "Old James"

1945

First Prize

Clark, Walter Van Tilburg-- "The Wind and the Snow of Winter"

Second Prize

Shaw, Irwin-- "Gunner's Passage"

Third Prize

Lampman, Ben Hur-- "Old Bill Bent to Drink"

Other Selected Stories

Breuer, Bessie-- "Bury Your Own Dead"

Critchell, Laurence-- "Flesh and Blood"

Deasy, Mary-- "Long Shadow on the Lawn"

Fenton, Edward-- "Burial in the Desert"

Gerry, Bill-- "Understand What I Mean"

Gordon, Ethel Edison-- "War Front: Louisiana"

Hardwick, Elizabeth-- "The People on the Roller Coaster"

Heyert, Murray-- "The New Kid"

Hubbell, Catherine-- "Monday at Six"

Lavin, Mary-- "The Sand Castle"

Martin, Hansford-- "The Thousand-Yard Stare"

Patton, Frances Gray-- "A Piece of Bread"

Portugal, Ruth-- "Call a Solemn Assembly"

Powers, J. F.-- "The Trouble"

Seager, Allan-- "The Conqueror"

Shattuck, Katharine-- "Subway System"

Smith, Louise Reinhardt-- "The Hour of Knowing"

West, Jessamyn-- "Lead Her Like a Pigeon"

Wilson, Michael-- "Come Away Home"

1946

First Prize

Goss, John Mayo-- "Bird Song"

Second Prize

Shedd, Margaret-- "The Innocent Bystander"

Third Prize

Ullman, Victor-- "Sometimes You Break Even"

Best First-Published Story

Meyer, Cord, Jr.-- "Waves of Darkness"

Other Selected Stories

Berryman, John-- "The Imaginary Jew"

Boyle, Kay-- "Winter Night"

Brookhouser, Frank-- "Request for Sherwood Anderson"

Canfield, Dorothy-- "Sex Education"

Capote, Truman-- "Miriam"

Enright, Elizabeth-- "I Forgot Where I Was"

Hardwick, Elizabeth-- "What We Have Missed"

Highsmith, Patricia-- "The Heroine"

Hutchins, M. P.-- "Innocents"

Le Sueur, Meridel-- "Breathe Upon These Slain"

Lytle, Andrew-- "The Guide"

McCleary, Dorothy-- "Not Very Close"

Rawlings, Marjorie Kinnan-- "Black Secret"

Savler, David S.-- "The Beggar"

Shaw, Irwin-- "Act of Faith"

Thielen, Benedict-- "The Empty Sky"

Welty, Eudora-- "A Sketching Trip"

West, Jessamyn-- "The Blackboard"

1947

First Prize

Clayton, John Bell-- "The White Circle"

Second Prize

Burdick, Eugene L.-- "Rest Camp on Maui"

Third Prize

Parsons, Elizabeth-- "The Nightingales Sing"

Best First-Published Story

Lewis, Robert-- "Little Victor"

Other Selected Stories

Bowles, Paul-- "The Echo"

Bradbury, Ray-- "Homecoming"
Breuer, Bessie-- "The Skeleton and the Easter Lily"
Cobb, Jane-- "The Hot Day"
Deasy, Mary-- "The Holiday"
DeJong, David Cornel-- "The Record"
Elder, Walter-- "You Can Wreck It"
Eustis, Helen-- "An American Home"
Govan, Christine Noble-- "Miss Winters and the Wind"
Kuehn, Susan-- "The Rosebush"
Lynch, John A.-- "The Burden"
Powers, J. F.-- "The Valiant Woman"
Shedd, Margaret-- "The Great Fire of 1945"
Shorer, Mark-- "What We Don't Know Hurts Us"
Smith, John Caswell, Jr.-- "Fighter"
Stafford, Jean-- "The Hope Chest"
Thielen, Benedict-- "Old Boy--New Boy"
Welty, Eudora-- "The Whole World Knows"
West, Jessamyn-- "Horace Chooney, M.D."

1948
First Prize
Capote, Truman-- "Shut a Final Door"
Second Prize
Stegner, Wallace-- "Beyond the Glass Mountain"
Third Prize
Bradbury, Ray-- "Powerhouse"
Best First-Published Story
Grennard, Elliot-- "Sparrow's Last Jump"
Other Selected Stories
Brookhouser, Frank-- "She Did Not Cry at All"
Gidney, James B.-- "The Muse and Mr. Parkinson"
Gordon, Caroline-- "The Petrified Woman"
Greene, Mary Frances-- "The Silent Day"
Hartley, Lodwick-- "Mr. Henig's Wall"
Hauser, Marianne-- "The Other Side of the River"
Ingles, James Wesley-- "The Wind Is Blind"
Janeway, Elizabeth-- "Child of God"
La Farge, Christopher-- "The Three Aspects"
Malkin, Richard-- "Pico Never Forgets"
Morse, Robert-- "The Professor and the Puli"
Parsons, Elizabeth-- "Welcome Home"
Shattuck, Katharine-- "The Answer"
Shelton, William R.-- "The Snow Girl"
Sorenson, Virginia-- "The Talking Stick"
Sulkin, Sidney-- "The Plan"

Terrett, Courtenay-- "The Saddle"
Watson, John-- "The Gun on the Table"
West, Ray B., Jr.-- "The Ascent"

1949
First Prize
Faulkner, William-- "A Courtship"
Second Prize
Van Doren, Mark-- "The Watchman"
Third Prize
Dorrance, Ward-- "The White Hound"
Other Selected Stories
Ashworth, John-- "High Diver"
Bowles, Paul-- "Pastor Dowe at Tacate"
Calisher, Hortense-- "The Middle Drawer"
Coatsworth, Elizabeth-- "Bremen's"
Connell, Evan S., Jr.-- "I'll Take You to Tennessee"
Conrad, Barnaby-- "Cayetano the Perfect"
Cramer, Alice Carver-- "The Boy Next Door"
Downey, Harris-- "The Mulhausen Girls"
Enright, Elizabeth-- "The Trumpeter Swan"
Goss, John Mayo-- "Evening and Morning Prayer"
Jackson, Shirley-- "The Lottery"
Lavin, Mary-- "Single Lady"
Pierce, Phoebe-- "The Season of Miss Maggie Reginald"
Plagemann, Bentz-- "The Best Bread"
Rice, John Andrew-- "You Can Get Just So Much Justice"
Salinger, J. D.-- "Just Before the War with the Eskimos"
Stafford, Jean-- "A Summer Day"
Weaver, John D.-- "Meeting Time"
West, Jessamyn-- "Public Address System"
Wilson, Leon-- "Six Months Is No Long Time"

1950
First Prize
Stegner, Wallace-- "The Blue-Winged Teal"
Second Prize
Leiper, Gudger Bart-- "The Magnolias"
Third Prize
Lowry, Robert-- "Be Nice to Mr. Campbell"
Other Selected Stories
Algren, Nelson-- "The Captain Is Impaled"
Bennett, Peggy-- "Death Under the Hawthorns"

Berry, John-- "New Shoes"
Boyle, Kay-- "Summer Evening"
Cheever, John-- "Vega"
Chidester, Ann-- "Mrs. Ketting and Clark Gable"
Enright, Elizabeth-- "The Sardillion"
Humphrey, William-- "The Hardy's"
Justice, Donald-- "The Lady"
Kuehn, Susan-- "The Hunt"
Lamkin, Speed-- "Comes a Day"
Newhouse, Edward-- "Seventy Thousand Dollars"
Parsons, Elizabeth-- "Not a Soul Will Come Along"
Putman, Clay-- "The Wounded"
Robinson, Leonard Wallace-- "The Ruin of Soul"
Salinger, J. D.-- "For Esmé--With Love and Squalor"
Switzer, Robert-- "Death of a Prize Fighter"
Taylor, Peter-- "Their Losses"
Van Ness, Lilian-- "Give My Love to Maggie"
Winslow, Anne Goodwin-- "Seasmiles"

1951
First Prize
Downey, Harris-- "The Hunters"
Second Prize
Welty, Eudora-- "The Burning"
Third Prize
Capote, Truman-- "The House of Flowers"
Other Selected Stories
Casper, Leonard-- "Sense of Direction"
Cheever, John-- "The Pot of Gold"
Connell, Evan S., Jr.-- "I Came from Yonder Mountain"
Culver, Monty-- "Black Water Blues"
Faulkner, William-- "A Name for the City"
Hall, James B.-- "In the Time of Demonstrations"
Hersey, John-- "Peggety's Parcel of Shortcomings"
Kensinger, Faye Riter-- "A Sense of Destination"
La Farge, Oliver-- "Old Century's River"
Love, Peggy Harding-- "The Jersey Heifer"
Macauley, Robie-- "The Invaders"
McCullers, Carson-- "The Sojourner"
Miller, Arthur-- "Monte Saint Angelo"
Patt, Esther-- "The Butcherbirds"
Patterson, Elizabeth Gregg-- "Homecoming"
Phillips, Thomas Hal-- "The Shadow of an Arm"
Rooney, Frank-- "Cyclists' Raid"
Shirley, Sylvia-- "Slow Journey"

Smith, John Campbell-- "Who Too Was a Soldier"
Stafford, Jean-- "A Country Love Story"
Thompson, R. E.-- "It's a Nice Day--Sunday"

1954
First Prize
Mabry, Thomas-- "The Indian Feather"
Second Prize
Putman, Clay-- "The News from Troy"
Third Prize
Wilbur, Richard-- "A Game of Catch"
Other Selected Stories
Cassill, R. V.-- "The War in the Air"
Clay, Richard-- "Very Sharp for Jagging"
Elliott, George P.-- "A Family Matter"
Gold, Herbert-- "The Witch"
Hall, James B.-- "Estate and Trespass: A Gothic Story"
Harnden, Ruth-- "Rebellion"
Justice, Donald-- "Vineland's Burning"
Lowrey, P. H.-- "Too Young to Have a Gun"
Maxwell, James A.-- "Fighter"
O'Connor, Flannery-- "The Life You Save May Be Your Own"
Rugel, Miriam-- "The Flower"
Stafford, Jean-- "The Shorn Lamb"
Stern, Richard G.-- "The Sorrows of Captain Schreiber"
Walker, Augusta-- "The Day of the Cipher"
Wallace, Robert-- "The Secret Weapon of Joe Smith"
West, Jessamyn-- "Breach of Promise"
Whitmore, Stanford-- "Lost Soldier"
Whittemore, Reed-- "The Stutz and the Tub"
Wilner, Herbert-- "Whistle and the Heroes"
Worthington, Rex-- "A Kind of Scandal"

1955
First Prize
Stafford, Jean-- "In the Zoo"
Second Prize
O'Connor, Flannery-- "A Circle in the Fire"
Third Prize
Buechner, Frederick-- "The Tiger"
Other Selected Stories
Bingham, Robert-- "The Unpopular Passenger"
Calisher, Hortense-- "A Christmas Carillon"
Cassill, R. V.-- "The Inland Years"

Cheever, John-- "The Five-forty-eight"

Elliott, George P.-- "Miss Cudahy of Stowes Landing"

Enright, Elizabeth-- "The Operator"

Fowler, Mary Dewees-- "Man of Distinction"

Fuchs, Daniel-- "Twilight in Southern California"

Grau, Shirley Ann-- "Joshua"

Graves, John-- "The Green Fly"

Powers, J. F.-- "The Presence of Grace"

Shultz, William Henry-- "The Shirts off Their Backs"

Steele, Max-- "The Wanton Troopers"

Stegner, Wallace-- "The City of the Living"

Wolfert, Ira-- "The Indomitable Blue"

1956
First Prize

Cheever, John-- "The Country Husband"

Second Prize

Buechler, James-- "Pepicelli"

Third Prize

Cassill, R. V.-- "The Prize"

Other Selected Stories

Bellow, Saul-- "The Gonzaga Manuscripts"

Calisher, Hortense-- "The Night Club in the Woods"

Carr, Archie-- "The Black Beach"

Coates, Robert M.-- "In a Foreign City"

Faulkner, William-- "Race at Morning"

Gold, Herbert-- "A Celebration for Joe"

Macauley, Robie-- "The Chevigny Man"

Nemerov, Howard-- "Tradition"

Stafford, Jean-- "Beatrice Trueblood's Story"

Steinbeck, John-- "The Affair at Seven, Rue de M--- "

Whitehill, Joseph-- "Able Baker"

Yates, Richard-- "The Best of Everything"

1957
First Prize

O'Connor, Flannery-- "Greenleaf"

Second Prize

Gold, Herbert-- "Encounter in Haiti"

Third Prize

Elliott, George P.-- "Miracle Play"

Other Selected Stories

Blassingame, Wyatt-- "Man's Courage"

Cassill, R. V.-- "When Old Age Shall This Generation Waste"

Cheever, John-- "The Journal of an Old Gent"

Faulkner, William-- "By the People"

Granit, Arthur-- "Free the Canaries from Their Cages!"

Langdon, John-- "The Blue Serge Suit"

Liberman, M. M.-- "Big Buick to the Pyramids"

Marsh, Willard-- "Last Tag"

McCarthy, Mary-- "Yellowstone Park"

Miller, Nolan-- "A New Life"

Rich, Cynthia Marshall-- "My Sister's Marriage"

Settle, Mary Lee-- "The Old Wives' Tale"

Shaw, Irwin-- "Then We Were Three"

Stafford, Jean-- "The Warlock"

Sunwall, Betty-- "Things Changed"

Thurman, Richard Young-- "The Credit Line"

Walter, Eugene-- "I Love You Batty Sisters"

1958
First Prize

Gellhorn, Martha-- "In Sickness as in Health"

Second Prize

Calisher, Hortense-- "What a Thing, to Keep a Wolf in a Cage!"

Third Prize

Steiner, George-- "The Deeps of the Sea"

Other Selected Stories

Berriault, Gina-- "The Stone Boy"

Blanton, Lowell D.-- "The Long Night"

Brown, T. K., III-- "A Drink of Water"

Clemons, Walter-- "A Summer Shower"

Enright, Elizabeth-- "The Eclipse"

Granat, Robert-- "My Apples"

Hale, Nancy-- "A Slow Boat to China"

Litwak, Leo-- "The Making of a Clock"

Matthiessen, Peter-- "Travelin Man"

Newhouse, Edward-- "The Ambassador"

Shore, Wilma-- "A Cow on the Roof"

Stafford, Jean-- "My Blithe, Sad Bird"

White, Robin-- "First Voice"

Wilner, Herbert-- "The Passion for Silver's Arm"

1959
First Prize

Taylor, Peter-- "Venus, Cupid, Folly, and Time"

Second Prize

Elliott, George P.-- "Among the Dangs"

Third Prize

Turner, Thomas C.-- "Something to Explain"

Other Selected Stories

Baldwin, James-- "Come Out of the Wilderness"

Buchwald, Emilie Bix-- "The Present"

Cheever, John-- "The Trouble of Marcie Flint"

Currie, Ellen-- "Tib's Eve"

Eastlake, William-- "Flight of the Circle Heart"

Filer, Tom-- "The Last Voyage"

Harris, MacDonald-- "Second Circle"

O'Connor, Flannery-- "A View of the Woods"

Sandburg, Helga-- "Witch Chicken"

Stafford, Jean-- "A Reasonable Facsimile"

Stone, Alma-- "The Bible Salesman"

Williams, Thomas-- "Goose Pond"

1960

First Prize

Hall, Lawrence Sargent-- "The Ledge"

Second Prize

Roth, Philip-- "Defender of the Faith"

Third Prize

White, Robin-- "Shower of Ashes"

Other Selected Stories

Berkman, Sylvia-- "Ellen Craig"

Berriault, Gina-- "Sublime Child"

Enright, Elizabeth-- "A Gift of Light"

Fowler, Janet-- "A Day for Fishing"

Gold, Herbert-- "Love and Like"

Granat, Robert-- "To Endure"

Henderson, Robert-- "Immortality"

Kentfield, Calvin-- "In the Cauldron"

Ogden, Maurice-- "Freeway to Wherever"

Purdy, James-- "Encore"

Spencer, Elizabeth-- "First Dark"

Swarthout, Glendon-- "A Glass of Blessings"

Ziller, Eugene-- "Sparrows"

1961

First Prize

Olson, Tillie-- "Tell Me a Riddle"

Second Prize

Gold, Ivan-- "The Nickel Misery of George Washington Carver Brown"

Third Prize

Price, Reynolds-- "One Sunday in Late July"

Other Selected Stories

Burgess, Jackson-- "The Magician"

Currie, Ellen-- "O Lovely Appearance of Death"

Ford, Jesse Hill-- "How the Mountains Are Made"

Krause, Ervin D.-- "The Quick and the Dead"

Ludwig, Jack-- "Thoreau in California"

Miller, Arthur-- "I Don't Need You Any More"

Shaber, David-- "A Nous La Liberté"

Taylor, Peter-- "Heads of Houses"

Updike, John-- "Wife-Wooing"

1962

First Prize

Porter, Katherine Anne-- "Holiday"

Second Prize

Pynchon, Thomas-- "Under the Rose"

Third Prize

Cole, Tom-- "Familiar Usage in Leningrad"

Other Selected Stories

Adams, Thomas E.-- "Sled"

Deasy, Mary-- "The People with the Charm"

Grau, Shirley Ann-- "Eight O'Clock One Morning"

Graves, John-- "The Aztec Dog"

Howard, Maureen-- "Bridgeport Bus"

Jackson, David-- "The English Gardens"

McKenzie, Miriam-- "Deja Vu"

Price, Reynolds-- "The Warrior Princess Ozimba"

Schoonover, Shirley W.-- "The Star Blanket"

Shaber, David-- "Professorio Collegio"

Updike, John-- "The Doctor's Wife"

Whitbread, Thomas-- "The Rememberer"

1963

First Prize

O'Connor, Flannery-- "Everything That Rises Must Converge"

Second Prize

Krause, Ervin D.-- "The Snake"

Third Prize

Selz, Thalia-- "The Education of a Queen"

Other Selected Stories

Ansell, Helen Essary-- "The Threesome"

Berkman, Sylvia-- "Pontifex"

Cox, James Trammell-- "That Golden Crane"

Douglas, Ellen-- "On the Lake"

Klein, Norma-- "The Burglar"

Maddow, Ben-- "In a Cold Hotel"
McClure, J. G.-- "The Rise of the Proletariat"
Oates, Joyce Carol-- "The Fine White Mist of Winter"
Saroyan, William-- "Gaston"
Southern, Terry-- "The Road Out of Axotle"
West, Jessamyn-- "The Picknickers"

1964
First Prize
Cheever, John-- "The Embarkment for Cythera"
Second Prize
Oates, Joyce Carol-- "Stigmata"
Third Prize
Shedd, Margaret-- "The Everlasting Witness"
Other Selected Stories
Bingham, Sallie-- "The Banks of the Ohio"
Calisher, Hortense-- "The Scream on Fifty-seventh
    Street"
Lanning, George-- "Something Just for Me"
Malamud, Bernard-- "The Jewbird"
Ross, Lillian-- "Night and Day, Day and Night"
Roth, Philip-- "Novotnoy's Pain"
Sara-- "So I'm Not Lady Chatterly, So Better I Should
    Know It Now"
Schoonover, Shirley W.-- "Old and Country Tale"
Shaw, Irwin-- "The Inhabitants of Venus"
Stacton, David-- "The Metamorphosis of Kenko"
Stegner, Wallace-- "Carrion Spring"
Zorn, George A.-- "Thompson"

1965
First Prize
O'Connor, Flannery-- "Revelation"
Second Prize
Friedman, Sanford-- "Ocean"
Third Prize
Humphrey, William-- "The Ballad of Jesse
    Neighbours"
Other Selected Stories
Barthelme, Donald-- "Margins"
Beagle, Peter S.-- "Come Lady Death"
Cavanaugh, Arthur-- "What I Wish (Oh, I Wish) I Had
    Said"
Curley, Daniel-- "Love in the Winter"
Ludwig, Jack-- "A Woman of Her Age"
Manoff, Eva-- "Mama and the Spy"

Mayer, Tom-- "Homecoming"
McCarthy, Mary-- "The Hounds of Summer"
McCullers, Carson-- "Sucker"
Miller, Warren-- "Chaos, Disorder, and the Late Show"
Oates, Joyce Carol-- "First Views of the Enemy"
Potter, Nancy A. J.-- "Sunday's Children"
Rooke, Leon-- "If Lost Return to the Swiss Arms"
Taylor, Peter-- "There"
Wolf, Leonard-- "Fifty-Fifty"

1966
First Prize
Updike, John-- "The Bulgarian Poetess"
Second Prize
Howard, Maureen-- "Sherry"
Third Prize
Cole, Tom-- "On the Edge of Arcadia"
Other Selected Stories
Berriault, Gina-- "The Birthday Party"
Bingham, Sallie-- "Bare Bones"
Davis, Christopher-- "A Man of Affairs"
Ford, Jesse Hill-- "To the Open Water"
Greene, Philip L.-- "One of You Must Be Wendell
    Corey"
Hale, Nancy-- "Sunday Lunch"
McKinley, Georgia-- "The Mighty Distance"
Michaels, Leonard-- "Sticks and Stones"
Petrakis, Harry Mark-- "The Prison"
Randall, Vera-- "Alice Blaine"
Spencer, Elizabeth-- "Ship Island"
Williams, Joy-- "The Roomer"
Zorn, George A.-- "Mr. and Mrs. McGill"

1967
First Prize
Oates, Joyce Carol-- "In the Region of Ice"
Second Prize
Barthelme, Donald-- "See the Moon?"
Third Prize
Strong, Jonathan-- "Supperburger"
Other Selected Stories
Buechler, James-- "The Second Best Girl"
Finney, Ernest J.-- "The Investigator"
Ford, Jesse Hill-- "The Bitter Bread"
Jacobsen, Josephine-- "On the Island"
Knickerbocker, Conrad-- "Diseases of the Heart"

Kurtz, M. R.-- "Waxing Wroth"

Macauley, Robie-- "Dressed in Shade"

Mudrick, Marvin-- "Cleopatra"

Oliver, Diane-- "Neighbors"

Updike, John-- "Marching Through Boston"

Wheelis, Allen-- "Sea-Girls"

Yates, Richard-- "A Good and Gallant Woman"

1968

First Prize

Welty, Eudora-- "The Demonstrators"

Second Prize

Broner, E. M.-- "The New Nobility"

Third Prize

Katz, Shlomo-- "My Redeemer Cometh . . ."

Other Selected Stories

Branda, Eldon-- "The Dark Days of Christmas"

Brower, Brock-- "Storm Still"

Franklin, F. K.-- "Nigger Horse"

Gration, Gwen-- "Teacher"

Hale, Nancy-- "The Most Elegant Drawing Room in Europe"

Hall, James B.-- "A Kind of Savage"

Harris, Marilyn-- "Icarus Again"

Kentfield, Calvin-- "Near the Line"

Klein, Norma-- "Magic"

Neugeboren, Jay-- "Ebbets Field"

Oates, Joyce Carol-- "Where Are You Going, Where Have You Been?"

Stacton, David-- "Little Brother Nun"

Tyner, Paul-- "How You Play the Game"

Updike, John-- "Your Lover Just Called"

1969

First Prize

Malamud, Bernard-- "Man in the Drawer"

Second Prize

Oates, Joyce Carol-- "Accomplished Desires"

Third Prize

Barth, John-- "Lost in the Funhouse"

Other Selected Stories

Corfman, Eunice Luccock-- "To Be an Athlete"

Engberg, Susan-- "Lambs of God"

Litwak, Leo-- "In Shock"

Maddow, Ben-- "You, Johann Sebastian Bach"

Michaels, Leonard-- "Manikin"

Mountzoures, H. L.-- "The Empire of Things"

Packer, Nancy Huddleston-- "Early Morning, Lonely Ride"

Paley, Grace-- "Distance"

Rubin, Michael-- "Service"

Shefner, Evelyn-- "The Invitations"

Steele, Max-- "Color the Daydream Yellow"

Sterling, Thomas-- "Bedlam's Rent"

Taylor, Peter-- "First Heat"

Tyler, Anne-- "The Common Courtesies"

1970

First Prize

Hemenway, Robert-- "The Girl Who Sang with the Beatles"

Second Prize

Eastlake, William-- "The Biggest Thing Since Custer"

Third Prize

Rindfleisch, Norval-- "A Cliff of Fall"

Special Award for Continuing Achievement

Oates, Joyce Carol-- "How I Contemplated the World from the Detroit House of Correction and Began My Life Over Again"

Other Selected Stories

Blake, George-- "A Modern Development"

Buchan, Perdita-- "It's Cold out There"

Cole, Tom-- "Saint John of the Hershey Kisses: 1964"

Donahue, H. E. F.-- "Joe College"

Griffith, Patricia Browning-- "Nights at O'Rear's"

Grinstead, David-- "A Day in Operations"

Malamud, Bernard-- "My Son the Murderer"

McPherson, James Alan-- "Of Cabbages and Kings"

Oates, Joyce Carol-- "Unmailed, Unwritten Letters"

Salter, James-- "Am Strande Von Tanger"

Strong, Jonathan-- "Patients"

Updike, John-- "Bech Takes Pot Luck"

Willard, Nancy-- "Theo's Girl"

1971

First Prize

Hecht, Florence M.-- "Twin Bed Bridge"

Second Prize

Cardwell, Guy A.-- "Did You Once See Shelley?"

Third Prize

Adams, Alice-- "Gift of Grass"

Other Selected Stories

Cleaver, Eldridge-- "The Flashlight"

Greene, Philip L.-- "The Dichotomy"

Harter, Evelyn-- "The Stone Lovers"

Hoagland, Edward-- "The Final Fate of the Alligators"

Inman, Robert-- "I'll Call You"

Jacobsen, Josephine-- "The Jungle of Lord Lion"

Larson, Charles R.-- "Up From Slavery"

Mazor, Julian-- "The Skylark"

Michaels, Leonard-- "Robinson Crusoe Liebowitz"

Minot, Stephen-- "Mars Revisited"

Oates, Joyce Carol-- "The Children"

Parker, Thomas-- "Troop Withdrawal--The Initial Step"

Price, Reynolds-- "Waiting at Dachau"

Taylor, Eleanor Ross-- "Jujitsu"

1972

First Prize

Batki, John-- "Strange-Dreaming Charlie, Cow-Eyed Charlie"

Second Prize

Oates, Joyce Carol-- "Saul Bird Says: Relate! Communicate! Liberate!"

Third Prize

Rascoe, Judith-- "Small Sounds and Tilting Shadows"

Other Selected Stories

Adams, Alice-- "Ripped Off"

Barthelme, Donald-- "Subpoena"

Brown, Rosellen-- "A Letter to Ismael in the Grave"

Brown, Margery Finn-- "In the Forests of the Riga the Beasts Are Very Wild Indeed"

Eaton, Charles Edward-- "The Case of the Missing Photographs"

Flythe, Starkey, Jr.-- "Point of Conversion"

Gill, Brendan-- "Fat Girl"

Gold, Herbert-- "A Death on the East Side"

Gottlieb, Elaine-- "The Lizard"

Matthews, Jack-- "On the Shore of Chad Creek"

McClatchy, J. D.-- "Allonym"

Salter, James-- "The Destruction of the Goetheanum"

Tyler, Anne-- "With All Flags Flying"

Zelver, Patricia-- "On the Desert"

1973

First Prize

Oates, Joyce Carol-- "The Dead"

Second Prize

Malamud, Bernard-- "Talking Horse"

Third Prize

Brown, Rosellen-- "Mainlanders"

Other Selected Stories

Adams, Alice-- "The Swastika on Our Door"

Bromell, Henry-- "Photographs"

Carver, Raymond-- "What Is It?"

Cheever, John-- "The Jewels of the Cabots"

Jacobsen, Josephine-- "A Walk with Raschid"

Johnson, Diane-- "An Apple, An Orange"

Johnson, Curt-- "Trespasser"

Malone, John-- "The Fugitives"

Mayhall, Jane-- "The Enemy"

McPherson, James Alan-- "The Silver Bullet"

Rascoe, Judith-- "A Line of Order"

Reid, Randall-- "Detritus"

Shaber, David-- "Scotch Sour"

Sikes, Shirley-- "The Death of Cousin Stanley"

Zelver, Patricia-- "The Flood"

1974

First Prize

Adler, Renata-- "Brownstone"

Second Prize

Henson, Robert-- "Lizzie Borden in the P.M."

Third Prize

Adams, Alice-- "Alternatives"

Other Selected Stories

Busch, Frederick-- "Is Anyone Left This Time of Year?"

Carver, Raymond-- "Put Yourself in My Shoes"

Clayton, John J.-- "Cambridge Is Sinking!"

Davenport, Guy-- "Robot"

Eastlake, William-- "The Death of Sun"

Fuller, Blair-- "Bakti's Hand"

Gardner, John-- "The Things"

Hemenway, Robert-- "Troy Street"

Hill, Richard-- "Out in the Garage"

Hochstein, Rolaine-- "What Kind of a Man Cuts His Finger Off"

Klein, Norma-- "The Wrong Man"

Leach, Peter-- "The Fish Trap"

McPherson, James Alan-- "The Faithful"

Salter, James-- "Via Negativa"

1975

First Prize

Brodkey, Harold-- "A Story in an Almost Classical Mode"

Ozick, Cynthia-- "Usurpation (Other People's Stories)"

Other Selected Stories

Arensberg, Ann-- "Art History"

Arking, Linda-- "Certain Hard Places"

Banks, Russell-- "With Che at Kitty Hawk"

Bayer, Ann-- "Department Store"

Carver, Raymond-- "Are You a Doctor?"

Disch, Thomas M.-- "Getting into Death"

Doctorow, E. L.-- "Ragtime"

Kotzwinkle, William-- "Swimmer in the Secret Sea"

Maxwell, William-- "Over by the River"

McCorkle, Susannah-- "Ramona by the Sea"

McPherson, James Alan-- "The Story of a Scar"

Schell, Jessie-- "Alvira, Lettie, and Pip"

Shelnutt, Eve-- "Angel"

Updike, John-- "Nakedness"

Zelver, Patricia-- "Norwegians"

1976

First Prize

Brodkey, Harold-- "His Son in His Arms, in Light, Aloft"

Second Prize

Sayles, John-- "I-80 Nebraska, M. 490-M. 205"

Third Prize

Adams, Alice-- "Roses, Rhododendrons"

Special Award for Continuing Achievement

Updike, John-- "Separating"

Other Selected Stories

Berryman, John-- "Wash Far Away"

Brown, Rosellen-- "Why I Quit the Gowanus Liberation Front"

Bumpus, Jerry-- "The Idols of Afternoon"

Corrington, John William-- "The Actes and Monuments"

Davenport, Guy-- "The Richard Nixon Freischutz Rag"

Francis, H. E.-- "A Chronicle of Love"

Goyen, William-- "Bridge of Music, River of Sand"

Griffith, Patricia Browning-- "Dust"

Halley, Anne-- "The Sisterhood"

Helprin, Mark-- "Leaving the Church"

Hudson, Helen-- "The Theft"

Jacobsen, Josephine-- "Nel Bagno"

O'Brien, Tim-- "Night March"

Oates, Joyce Carol-- "Blood-Swollen Landscape"

Sadoff, Ira-- "An Enemy of the People"

Shreve, Anita-- "Past the Island, Drifting"

1977

First Prize

Hazzard, Shirley-- "A Long Story Short"

Leffland, Ella-- "Last Courtesies"

Other Selected Stories

Adams, Alice-- "Flights"

Ballantyne, Sheila-- "Perpetual Care"

Cheever, John-- "The President of the Argentine"

Colwin, Laurie-- "The Lone Pilgrim"

Dixon, Stephen-- "Mac in Love"

Engberg, Susan-- "A Stay by the River"

Fetler, Andrew-- "Shadows on the Water"

Hedin, Mary-- "Ladybug, Fly Away Home"

McCully, Emily Arnold-- "How's Your Vacuum Cleaner Working?"

Minot, Stephen-- "A Passion for History"

Russ, Joanna-- "Autobiography of My Mother"

Sayles, John-- "Breed"

Simmons, Charles-- "Certain Changes"

Summers, Hollis-- "A Hundred Paths"

Theroux, Paul-- "The Autumn Dog"

Zelver, Patricia-- "The Little Pub"

1978

First Prize

Allen, Woody-- "The Kugelmass Episode"

Second Prize

Schorer, Mark-- "A Lamp"

Third Prize

Henson, Robert-- "The Upper and the Lower Millstone"

Other Selected Stories

Adams, Alice-- "Beautiful Girl"

Apple, Max-- "Paddycake, Paddycake . . . A Memoir"

Brodkey, Harold-- "Verona: A Young Woman Speaks"

Clayton, John J.-- "Bodies Like Mouths"
Engberg, Susan-- "Pastorale"
Fuller, Blair-- "All Right"
Helprin, Mark-- "The Schreuerspitze"
Jacobsen, Josephine-- "Jack Frost"
Leviant, Curt-- "Ladies and Gentlemen, The Original Music of the Hebrew Alphabet"
O'Brien, Tim-- "Speaking of Courage"
Oates, Joyce Carol-- "The Tattoo"
Pearlman, Edith-- "Hanging Fire"
Schaeffer, Susan Fromberg-- "The Exact Nature of Plot"
Schell, Jessie-- "Undeveloped Photographs"
Schevill, James-- "A Hero in the Highway"

1979
First Prize
Weaver, Gordon-- "Getting Serious"
Second Prize
Bromell, Henry-- "Travel Stories"
Third Prize
Hecht, Julie-- "I Want You, I Need You, I Love You"
Other Selected Stories
Adams, Alice-- "The Girl Across the Room"
Baumbach, Jonathan-- "Passion?"
Caputi, Anthony-- "The Derby Hopeful"
Disch, Thomas M.-- "Xmas"
Gold, Herbert-- "The Smallest Part"
Goldberg, Lester-- "Shy Bearers"
Heller, Steve-- "The Summer Game"
Leaton, Anne-- "The Passion of Marco Z--- "
Molyneux, Thomas W.-- "Visiting the Point"
Oates, Joyce Carol-- "In the Autumn of the Year"
Peterson, Mary-- "Travelling"
Pfeil, Fred-- "The Quality of Light in Maine"
Schwartz, Lynne Sharon-- "Rough Strife"
Smith, Lee-- "Mrs. Darcy Meets the Blue-eyed Stranger at the Beach"
Thomas, Annabel-- "Coon Hunt"
Van Dyke, Henry-- "Du Cote de Chez Britz"
Yates, Richard-- "Oh, Joseph, I'm So Tired"
Zelver, Patricia-- "My Father's Jokes"

1980
First Prize
Bellow, Saul-- "A Silver Dish"

Second Prize
Hallinan, Nancy-- "Woman in a Roman Courtyard"
Third Prize
Michaels, Leonard-- "The Men's Club"
Other Selected Stories
Adams, Alice-- "Truth or Consequences"
Arensberg, Ann-- "Group Sex"
Beattie, Ann-- "The Cinderella Waltz"
Chasin, Helen-- "Fatal"
Dillon, Millicent-- "All the Pelageyas"
Dubus, Andre-- "The Pitcher"
Dunn, Robert-- "Hopeless Acts Performed Properly, with Grace"
Gertler, T.-- "In Case of Survival"
Godwin, Gail-- "Amanuensis: A Tale of the Creative Life"
Krysl, Marilyn-- "Looking for Mother"
L'Heureux, John-- "The Priest's Wife"
Phillips, Jayne Anne-- "Snow"
Rose, Daniel Asa-- "The Goodbye Present"
Stafford, Jean-- "An Influx of Poets"
Sullivan, Walter-- "Elizabeth"
Taggart, Shirley Ann-- "Ghosts Like Them"
Targan, Barry-- "Old Light"
Taylor, Peter-- "The Old Forest"
Vaughn, Stephanie-- "Sweet Talk"

1981
First Prize
Ozick, Cynthia-- "The Shawl"
Other Selected Stories
Adams, Alice-- "Snow"
Boyle, Kay-- "St. Stephen's Green"
Flowers, Sandra Hollin-- "Hope of Zion"
Goodman, Ivy-- "Baby"
Irving, John-- "Interior Space"
L'Heureux, John-- "Brief Lives in California"
Matthews, Jack-- "The Last Abandonment"
Novick, Marian-- "Advent"
Oates, Joyce Carol-- "Mutilated Woman"
Packer, Nancy Huddleston-- "The Women Who Walk"
Reid, Barbara-- "The Waltz Dream"
Rottenberg, Annette T.-- "The Separation"
Smith, Lee-- "Between the Lines"
Stern, Steve-- "Isaac and the Undertaker's Daughter"

Tabor, James-- "The Runner"

Theroux, Paul-- "World's Fair"

Thomas, Annabel-- "The Photographic Woman"

Walker, Alice-- "The Abortion"

Wetherell, W. D.-- "The Man Who Loved Levittown"

Wolff, Tobias-- "In the Garden of North American Martyrs"

1982
First Prize

Kenney, Susan-- "Facing Front"

Second Prize

McElroy, Joseph-- "The Future"

Third Prize

Brooks, Ben-- "A Postal Creed"

Special Award for Continuing Achievement

Adams, Alice-- "Greyhound People"-- "To See You Again"

Other Selected Stories

Carkeet, David-- "The Greatest Slump of All Time"

Dixon, Stephen-- "Layaways"

Gewertz, Kenneth-- "I Thought of Chatterton, The Marvelous Boy"

Goodman, Ivy-- "White Boy"

Holt, T. E.-- "Charybdis"

Johnson, Nora-- "The Jungle of Injustice"

Malone, Michael-- "Fast Love"

O'Brien, Tim-- "The Ghost Soldiers"

Oates, Joyce Carol-- "The Man Whom Women Adored"

Smiley, Jane-- "The Pleasure of Her Company"

Taylor, Peter-- "The Gift of the Prodigal"

Trefethen, Florence-- "Infidelities"

Wheeler, Kate-- "La Victoire"

Wolff, Tobias-- "Next Door"

1983
First Prize

Carver, Raymond-- "A Small, Good Thing"

Second Prize

Oates, Joyce Carol-- "My Warsawa"

Third Prize

Morris, Wright-- "Victrola"

Other Selected Stories

Benedict, Elizabeth-- "Feasting"

Bienen, Leigh Buchanan-- "My Life as a West African Gray Parrot"

Faust, Irvin-- "Melanie and the Purple People Eaters"

Gordon, Mary-- "The Only Son of a Doctor"

Jauss, David-- "Shards"

Klass, Perri-- "The Secret Lives of Dieters"

Lloyd, Lynda-- "Poor Boy"

Meinke, Peter-- "The Ponoes"

Norris, Gloria-- "When the Lord Calls"

Plante, David-- "Work"

Schwartz, Steven-- "Slow-Motion"

Spencer, Elizabeth-- "Jeanne-Pierre"

Svendsen, Linda-- "Heartbeat'

Updike, John-- "The City"

Van Wert, William F.-- "Putting & Gardening"

Wetherell, W. D.-- "If a Woodchuck Could Chuck Wood"

Whelan, Gloria-- "The Dogs in Renoir's Garden"

1984
First Prize

Ozick, Cynthia-- "Rosa"

Other Selected Stories

Abbott, Lee K.-- "Living Alone in Iota"

Adams, Alice-- "Alaska"

Baumbach, Jonathan-- "The Life and Times of Major Fiction"

Dickinson, Charles-- "Risk"

Fetler, Andrew-- "The Third Count"

Johnson, Willis-- "Prayer for the Dying"

Justice, Donald-- "The Artificial Moonlight"

Klass, Perri-- "Not a Good Girl"

Leavitt, David-- "Counting Months"

Lish, Gordon-- "For Jerome--with Love and Kisses"

Malamud, Bernard-- "The Model"

Menaker, Daniel-- "The Old Left"

Norris, Gloria-- "Revive Us Again"

Norris, Helen-- "The Love Child"

Paley, Grace-- "The Story Hearer"

Pearlman, Edith-- "Conveniences"

Pritchard, Melissa Brown-- "A Private Landscape"

Salter, James-- "Lost Sons"

Tallent, Elizabeth-- "The Evolution of Birds of Paradise"

1985
First Prize

Dybek, Stuart-- "Hot Ice"

Smiley, Jane-- "Lily"
Other Selected Stories
Beattie, Ann-- "In the White Night"
Cameron, Peter-- "Homework"
Erdrich, Louise-- "Saint Marie"
Hamilton, R. C.-- "Da Vinci Is Dead"
Heller, Steve-- "The Crow Woman"
Hochstein, Rolaine-- "She Should Have Died Hereafter"
Jacobsen, Josephine-- "The Mango Community"
Just, Ward-- "About Boston"
Koch, Claude-- "Bread and Butter Questions"
McElroy, Joseph-- "Daughter of the Revolution"
Minot, Susan-- "Lust"
Morris, Wright-- "Glimpse into Another Country"
Norris, Helen-- "The Quarry"
Oates, Joyce Carol-- "The Seasons"
Raymond, Ilene-- "Taking a Chance on Jack"
Updike, John-- "The Other"
Wilson, Eric-- "The Axe, the Axe, the Axe"
Wolff, Tobias-- "Sister"

1986
First Prize
Walker, Alice-- "Kindred Spirits"
Special Award for Continuing Achievement
Oates, Joyce Carol-- "Master Race"
Other Selected Stories
Adams, Alice-- "Molly's Dog"
Cameron, Peter-- "Excerpts from Swan Lake"
DiFranco, Anthony-- "The Garden of Redemption"
Dybek, Stuart-- "Pet Milk"
Eisenberg, Deborah-- "Transactions in a Foreign Currency"
Faust, Irvin-- "The Year of the Hot Jock"
Gerber, Merrill Joan-- "I Don't Believe This"
Johnson, Greg-- "Crazy Ladies"
Just, Ward-- "The Costa Brava, 1959"
Kornblatt, Joyce R.-- "Offerings"
L'Heureux, John-- "The Comedian"
Lish, Gordon-- "Resurrection"
Mason, Bobbie Ann-- "Big Bertha Stories"
Meinke, Peter-- "Uncle George and Uncle Stefan"
Norris, Gloria-- "Holding On"
Spencer, Elizabeth-- "The Cousins"

Vaughn, Stephanie-- "Kid MacArthur"
Wilmot, Jeanne-- "Dirt Angel"

1987
First Prize
Erdrich, Louise-- "Fleur"
Johnson, Joyce-- "The Children's Wing"
Other Selected Stories
Adams, Alice-- "Tide Pools"
Barthelme, Donald-- "Basil from Her Garden"
Bausch, Richard-- "What Feels Like the World"
Berriault, Gina-- "The Island of Ven"
Boswell, Robert-- "The Darkness of Love"
Dillon, Millicent-- "Monitor"
Dybek, Stuart-- "Blight"
Home, Lewis-- "Taking Care"
Lavers, Norman-- "Big Dog"
Lott, James-- "The Janeites"
Norris, Helen-- "The Singing Well"
Oates, Joyce Carol-- "Ancient Airs, Voices"
Paley, Grace-- "Midrash on Happiness"
Pitzen, Jim-- "The Village"
Robison, Mary-- "I Get By"
Stern, Daniel-- "The Interpretation of Dreams by Sigmund Freud: A Story"
Taylor, Robert, Jr.-- "Lady of Spain"
Wallace, Warren-- "Up Home"

1988
First Prize
Carver, Raymond-- "Errand"
Other Selected Stories
Adams, Alice-- "Ocrakoke Island"
Baumbach, Jonathan-- "The Dinner Party"
Beattie, Ann-- "Honey"
Currey, Richard-- "The Wars of Heaven"
Deaver, Philip F.-- "Arcola Girls"
Dubus, Andre-- "Blessings"
Hazzard, Shirley-- "The Place to Be"
Kohler, Sheila-- "The Mountain"
La Puma, Salvatore-- "The Gangster's Ghost"
LaSalle, Peter-- "Dolphin Dreaming"
Mason, Bobbie Ann-- "Bumblebees"
Neugeboren, Jay-- "Don't Worry About the Kids"
Oates, Joyce Carol-- "Yarrow"
Plant, Richard-- "Cecil Grounded"

Sayles, John-- "The Halfway Diner"
Smiley, Jane-- "Long Distance"
Spencer, Elizabeth-- "The Business Venture"
Updike, John-- "Leaf Season"
Williams, Joy-- "Rot"

1989
First Prize
Finney, Ernest J.-- "Peacocks"
Second Prize
Oates, Joyce Carol-- "House Hunting"
Third Prize
Doerr, Harriet-- "Edie: A Life"
Other Selected Stories
Adams, Alice-- "After You're Gone"
Bass, Rick-- "The Watch"
Boyle, T. Coraghessan-- "Sinking House"
Casey, John-- "Avid"
Dickinson, Charles-- "Child in the Leaves"
Dillon, Millicent-- "Wrong Stories"
Harrison, Barbara Grizzuti-- "To Be"
Herman, Ellen-- "Unstable Ground"
Lary, Banning K.-- "Death of a Duke"
Minot, Susan-- "Île Séche"
Petroski, Catherine-- "The Hit"
Ross, Jean-- "The Sky Fading Upward to Yellow: A Footnote to Literary History"
Salter, James-- "American Express"
Sherwook, Frances-- "History"
Simmons, Charles-- "Clandestine Acts"
Starkey, Flythe, Jr.-- "CV Ten"
Wallace, David Foster-- "Here and There"

1990
First Prize
Litwak, Leo-- "The Eleventh Edition"
Second Prize
Matthiessen, Peter-- "Lumumba Lives"
Third Prize
Segal, Lore-- "The Reverse Bug"
Other Selected Stories
Ackerman, Felicia-- "The Forecasting Game: A Story"
Adams, Alice-- "1940: Fall"
Blaylock, James P.-- "Unidentified Objects"
Boyle, T. Coraghessan-- "The Ape Lady in Retirement"

Brinson, Claudia Smith-- "Einstein's Daughter"
Eidus, Janice-- "Vito Loves Geraldine"
Fleming, Bruce-- "The Autobiography of Gertrude Stein"
Gillette, Jane Brown-- "Sins Against Animals"
Greenberg, Joanne-- "Elizabeth Baird"
Jersild, Devon-- "In Which John Imagines His Mind as a Pond"
Kaplan, David Michael-- "Stand"
McKnight, Reginald-- "The Kind of Light That Shines on Texas"
Oates, Joyce Carol-- "Heat"
Osborn, Carolyn-- "The Grands"
Schumacher, Julie-- "The Private Life of Robert Shumann"
Sides, Marilyn-- "The Island of the Mapmaker's Wife"
Steinbach, Meredith-- "In Recent History"

1991
First Prize
Updike, John-- "A Sandstone Farmhouse"
Selected Stories
Adams, Alice-- "Earthquake Damage"
Averill, Thomas Fox-- "During the Twelfth Summer of Elmer D. Peterson"
Baxter, Charles-- "Saul and Patsy Are Pregnant"
Broughton, T. Alan-- "Ashes"
Dillon, Millicent-- "Oil and Water"
Hall, Martha Lacy-- "The Apple-Green Triumph"
Johnson, Wayne-- "Hippies, Indians, Buffalo"
Klass, Perri-- "For Women Everywhere"
Le Guin, Ursula K.-- "Hand, Cup, Shell"
Lear, Patricia-- "Powwow"
Levenberg, Diane-- "The Ilui"
McFarland, Dennis-- "Nothing to Ask For"
Norris, Helen-- "Raisin Faces"
Oates, Joyce Carol-- "The Swimmers"
Stark, Sharon Sheehe-- "Overland"
Sukenick, Ronald-- "Ecco"
Swick, Marly-- "Moscow Nights"
Walker, Charlotte Zoe-- "The Very Pineapple"
Watanabe, Sylvia A.-- "Talking to the Dead"

1992
First Prize
Ozick, Cynthia-- "Puttermesser Paired"

Other Selected Stories

Adams, Alice-- "The Last Lovely City"

Barnes, Yolanda-- "Red Lipstick"

Braverman, Kate-- "Tall Tales from the Mekong Delta"

Chowder, Ken-- "With Seth in Tana Toraja"

Dillon, Millicent-- "Lost in L.A."

Doerr, Harriet-- "Way Stations"

Herrick, Amy-- "Pinocchio's Nose"

Honig, Lucy-- "English as a Second Language"

Klass, Perri-- "Dedication"

Long, David-- "Blue Spruce"

McNeal, Tom-- "What Happened to Tully"

Meltzer, Daniel-- "People"

Myers, Les-- "The Kite"

Nelson, Kent-- "The Mine from Nicaragua"

Nelson, Antonya-- "The Control Group"

Oates, Joyce Carol-- "Why Don't You Come Live with Me It's Time"

Packer, Ann-- "Babies"

Pomerance, Murray-- "Decor"

Sherwood, Frances-- "Demiurges"

Wagner, Mary Michael-- "Acts of Kindness"

1993

First Prize

Jones, Thom-- "The Pugilist at Rest"

Second Prize

Lee, Andrea-- "Winter Barley"

Third Prize

Van Wert, William F.-- "Shaking"

Other Selected Stories

Adams, Alice-- "The Islands"

Askew, Rilla-- "The Killing Blanket"

Dixon, Stephen-- "The Rare Muscovite"

Eastman, Charles-- "Yellow Flags"

Egan, Jennifer-- "Puerto Vallerta"

Jacobsen, Josephine-- "The Pier-Glass"

Johnson, Charles-- "Kwoon"

Levenberg, Diane-- "A Modern Love Story"

Moore, Lorrie-- "Charades"

Nelson, Antonya-- "Dirty Words"

Nixon, Cornelia-- "Risk"

Oates, Joyce Carol-- "Goose-Girl"

Poverman, C. E.-- "The Man Who Died"

Richardson, John H.-- "The Pink House"

Schwartz, Steven-- "Madagascar"

Stern, Daniel-- "A Hunger Artist by Franz Kafka: A Story"

Svendsen, Linda-- "The Edger Man"

Van Kirk, John-- "Newark Job"

Weltner, Peter-- "The Greek Head"

Wheeler, Kate-- "Improving My Average"

1994

First Prize

Baker, Alison-- "Better Be Ready 'Bout Half Past Eight"

Second Prize

Gardiner, John Rolfe-- "The Voyage Out"

Third Place

Moore, Lorrie-- "Terrific Mother"

Other Selected Stories

Bain, Terry-- "Games"

Barton, Marlin-- "Jeremiah's Road"

Bloom, Amy-- "Semper Fidelis"

Cherry, Kelly-- "Not the Phil Donahue Show"

Cox, Elizabeth-- "The Third of July"

Dybek, Stuart-- "We Didn't"

Eidus, Janice-- "Pandora's Box"

Fox, Michael-- "Rise and Shine"

Fremont, Helen-- "Where She Was"

Graver, Elizabeth-- "The Boy Who Fell Forty Feet"

Hester, Katherine L.-- "Labor"

Kennedy, Thomas E.-- "Landing Zone X-Ray"

McLean, David-- "Marine Corps Issue"

Oness, Elizabeth-- "The Oracle"

Ortiz Cofer, Judith-- "Nada"

Richards, Susan Starr-- "The Hanging in the Foaling Barn"

Tannen, Mary-- "Elaine's House"

Trudell, Dennis-- "Gook"

1995

First Prize

Nixon, Cornelia-- "The Women Come and Go"

Second Prize

Clayton, John J.-- "Talking to Charlie"

Other Selected Stories

Adams, Alice-- "The Haunted Beach"

Baker, Alison-- "Loving Wanda Beaver"

Baxter, Charles-- "Kiss Away"

Bradford, Robin-- "If This Letter Were a Beaded Object"

Byers, Michael-- "Settled on the Cranberry Coast"

Cameron, Peter-- "Departing"

Cooper, Bernard-- "Truth Serum"

Delaney, Edward J.-- "The Drowning"

Eisenberg, Deborah-- "Across the Lake"

Gates, David-- "The Intruder"

Gilchrist, Ellen-- "The Stucco House"

Goodman, Allegra-- "Sarah"

Hardwick, Elizabeth-- "Shot: A New York Story"

Klass, Perri-- "City Sidewalks"

Krieger, Elliot-- "Cantor Pepper"

Oates, Joyce Carol-- "You Petted Me and I Followed You Home"

Pierce, Anne Whitney-- "Star Box"

Powell, Padgett-- "Trick or Treat"

Updike, John-- "The Black Room"

1996

First Prize

King, Stephen-- "The Man in the Black Suit"

Second Prize

Sharma, Akhil-- "If You Sing Like That for Me"

Other Selected Stories

Adams, Alice-- "His Women"

Baker, Alison-- "Convocation"

Dillen, Frederick G.-- "Alice"

Douglas, Ellen-- "Grant"

Graver, Elizabeth-- "Between"

Hagenston, Becky-- "'Til Death Do Us Part"

Hoffman, William-- "Stones"

Honig, Lucy-- "Citizens Review"

Kriegel, Leonard-- "Players"

Lombreglia, Ralph-- "Somebody Up There Likes Me"

McNally, T. M.-- "Skin Deep"

Menaker, Daniel-- "Influenza"

Mosley, Walter-- "The Thief"

Oates, Joyce Carol-- "Mark of Satan"

Paine, Tom-- "Will You Say Something Monsieur Eliot"

Schumacher, Julie-- "Dummies"

Smiley, Jane-- "The Life of the Body"

Wiegand, David-- "Buffalo Safety"

1997

First Prize

Gordon, Mary-- "City Life"

Second Prize

Saunders, George-- "The Falls"

Third Prize

Abbott, Lee K.-- "The Talk Talked Between Worms"

Other Selected Stories

Barth, John-- "On with the Story"

Bradford, Arthur-- "Catface"

Cooke, Carolyn-- "The TWA Corbies"

Davenport, Kiana-- "The Lipstick Tree"

Dubus, Andre-- "Dancing After Hours"

Eisenberg, Deborah-- "Mermaids"

Gaitskill, Mary-- "Comfort"

Glave, Thomas-- "The Final Inning"

Klam, Matthew-- "The Royal Palms"

MacMillan, Ian-- "The Red House"

Moody, Rick-- "Demonology"

Morgan, Robert-- "The Balm of Gilead Tree"

Munro, Alice-- "The Love of a Good Woman"

Ruff, Patricia Elam-- "The Taxi Ride"

Schaeffer, Susan Fromberg-- "The Old Farmhouse and the Dog-Wife"

Schutt, Christine-- "His Chorus"

Shields, Carol-- "Mirrors"

1998

First Prize

Moore, Lorrie-- "People Like That Are the Only People Here"

Second Prize

Millhauser, Steven-- "The Knife Thrower"

Third Prize

Munro, Alice-- "The Children Stay"

Other Selected Stories

Bass, Rick-- "The Myths of Bears"

Cooke, Carolyn-- "Eating Dirt"

Davies, Peter Ho-- "Relief"

Erdrich, Louise-- "Satan: Hijacker of a Planet"

Evenson, Brian-- "Two Brothers"

Heuler, Karen-- "Me and My Enemy"

Jones, Thom-- "Tarantula"

MacDonald, D. R.-- "Ashes"

McKnight, Reginald-- "Boot"

Mehta, Suketu-- "Gare du Nord"

Novakovich, Josip-- "Crimson"

Proulx, Annie-- "Brokeback Mountain"

Saunders, George-- "Winky"
Sharma, Akhil-- "Cosmopolitan"
Swann, Maxine-- "Flower Children"
Weltner, Peter-- "Movietone: Detour"
Zancanella, Don-- "The Chimpanzees of Wyoming Territory"

1999
First Prize
Baida, Peter-- "A Nurse's Story"
Second Prize
Holladay, Cary-- "Merry-Go-Sorry"
Third Prize
Munro, Alice-- "Save the Reaper"
Other Selected Stories
Benedict, Pinckney-- "Miracle Boy"
Boyle, T. Coraghessan-- "The Underground Gardens"
Chabon, Michael-- "Son of the Wolfman"
Cunningham, Michael-- "Mister Brother"
Davenport, Kiana-- "Fork Used in Eating Reverend Baker"
Forbes, Charlotte-- "Sign"
Houston, Pam-- "Cataract"
Lahiri, Jhumpa-- "Interpreter of Maladies"
Potok, Chaim-- "Moon"
Proulx, Annie-- "The Mud Below"
Reilly, Gerald-- "Nixon Under the Bodhi Tree"
Saunders, George-- "Sea Oak"
Schirmer, Robert-- "Burning"
Schwartz, Sheila-- "Afterbirth"
Wallace, David Foster-- "The Depressed Person"
Wetherell, W. D.-- "Watching Girls Play"
Whitty, Julia-- "A Tortoise for the Queen of Tonga"

2000
First Prize
Wideman, John Edgar-- "Weight"
Second Prize
Lordan, Beth-- "The Man with the Lapdog"
Third Prize
Gordon, Mary-- "The Deacon"
Other Selected Stories
Banks, Russell-- "Plains of Abraham"
Banner, Keith-- "The Smallest People Alive"
Barrett, Andrea-- "Theories of Rain"
Bertles, Jeannette-- "Whileaway"

Biguenet, John-- "Rose"
Budnitz, Judy-- "Flush"
Brockmeier, Kevin-- "These Hands"
Byers, Michael-- "The Beautiful Days"
Carver, Raymond-- "Kindling"
Dark, Alice Elliott-- "Watch the Animals"
Davenport, Kiana-- "Bones of the Inner Ear"
Englander, Nathan-- "The Gilgul of Park Avenue"
Gautreux, Tim-- "Easy Pickings"
Gurganus, Allan-- "He's at the Office"
Lennon, J. Robert-- "The Fool's Proxy"
Pritchard, Melissa-- "Salve Regina"
Walbert, Kate-- "The Gardens of Kyoto"

2001
First Prize
Swan, Mary-- "The Deep"
Second Prize
Chaon, Dan-- "Big Me"
Third Prize
Munro, Alice-- "Floating Bridge"
Other Selected Stories
Barrett, Andrea-- "Servants of Map"
Benedict, Pinckney-- "Zog 19: A Scientific Romance"
Boyle, T. Coraghessan-- "The Love of My Life"
Carlson, Ron-- "At the Jim Bridger"
Erdrich, Louise-- "Revival Road"
Gay, William-- "The Paperhanger"
Graver, Elizabeth-- "The Mourning Door"
Kalam, Murad-- "Bow Down"
Leebron, Fred G.-- "That Winter"
Nelson, Antonya-- "Female Trouble"
Oates, Joyce Carol-- "The Girl with the Blackened Eye"
Peck, Dale-- "Bliss"
Saunders, George-- "Pastoralia"
Schickler, David-- "The Smoker"

2002
First Prize
Brockmeier, Kevin-- "The Ceiling"
Second Prize
Lewis, Mark Ray-- "Scordatura"
Third Prize
Erdrich, Louise-- "The Butcher's Wife"
Other Selected Stories
Beattie, Ann-- "The Last Odd Day in L.A."

Danticat, Edwidge-- "Seven"
Divakaruni, Chitra Banerjee-- "The Lives of Strangers"
Doerr, Anthony-- "The Hunter's Wife"
Eisenberg, Deborah-- "Like It or Not"
Ford, Richard-- "Charity"
Gates, David-- "George Lassos Moon"
Homes, A. M.-- "Do Not Disturb"
Leavitt, David-- "Speonk"
Lee, Andrea-- "Anthropology"
Lee, Don-- "The Possible Husband"
Munro, Alice-- "Family Furnishings"
Nolan, Jonathan-- "Memento Mori"
Roorbach, Bill-- "Big Bend"
Schmidt, Heidi Jon-- "Blood Poison"
Wallace, David Foster-- "Good Old Neon"
Waters, Mary Yukari-- "Egg-Face"

2003
Juror Favorites
Byatt, A. S-- "The Thing in the Forest"
Johnson, Denis-- "Train Dreams"
Other Selected Stories
Adichie, Chimamanda Ngozi-- "The American
   Embassy"
Boyle, T. Coraghessan-- "Swept Away"
Connell, Evan S., Jr.-- "Election Eve"
Desnoyers, Adam-- "Bleed Blue in Indonesia"
Doerr, Anthony-- "The Shell Collector"
Giles, Molly-- "Two Words"
Harleman, Ann-- "Meanwhile"
Johnston, Tim-- "Irish Girl"
Kemper, Marjorie-- "God's Goodness"
Kittredge, William-- "Kissing"
Leff, Robyn Jay-- "Burn Your Maps"
Light, Douglas-- "Three Days. A Month. More"
Morrow, Bradford-- "Lush"
Munro, Alice-- "Fathers"
O'Brien, Tim-- "What Went Wrong"
Pearlman, Edith-- "The Story"
Silber, Joan-- "The High Road"
Trevor, William--Sacred Statues"

2004 (No prizes awarded)

2005
Juror Favorites
Alexie, Sherman-- "What You Pawn I Will Redeem"

Jhabvala, Ruth Prawer-- "Refuge in London"
Stuckey-French, Elizabeth-- "Mudlavia"
Other Selected Stories
Berry, Wendell-- "The Hurt Man"
Brockmeier, Kevin-- "The Brief History of the Dead"
Crouse, Timothy-- "Sphinxes"
D'Ambrosio, Charles-- "The High Divide"
Fountain, Ben-- "Fantasy for Eleven Fingers:
Fox, Paula-- "Grace"
Freudenberg, Nell-- "The Tutor"
Hadley, Tessa-- "The Card Trick"
Jones, Edward P.-- "A Rich Man"
Jones, Gail-- "Desolation"
Macy, Caitlin-- "Christie"
Parker, Michael-- "The Golden Era of Heartbreak"
Peck, Dale-- "Dues"
Peebles, Frances de Pontes-- "The Drowned Woman"
Rash, Ron-- "Speckle Trout"
Reisman, Nancy-- "Tea"
Ward, Liza-- "Snowbound"

2006
Juror Favorites
Eisenberg, Deborah-- "Window"
Jones, Edward P.-- "Old Boys, Old Girls"
Munro, Alice-- "Passion"
Other Selected Stories
Brown, Karen-- "Unction"
Clark, George Makana-- "The Center of the World"
Erdrich, Louise-- "The Plague of Doves"
Fox, Paula-- "The Broad Estates of Death"
Kay, Jackie-- "You Go When You Can No Longer
   Stay"
Means, David-- "Saulte Ste. Marie
Morse, David Lawrence-- "Conceived"
Peelle, Lydia-- "Mule Killers"
Reents, Stepahnie-- "Disquisition on Tears"
Schaeffer, Susan Fromberg-- "Wolves"
Svoboda, Terese-- "'80's Lilies"
Thon, Melanie Rae-- "Letters in the Snow . . . "
Trevor, Douglas-- "Girls I Know"
Trevor, William--The Dressmaker's Child"
Vapnyar, Lara-- "Puffed Rice and Meatballs"
Vaswani, Neela-- "The Pelvis Series"
Xu Xi-- "Famine"

2007
Juror Favorites
Chuculate, Eddie-- "Galveston Bay, 1826"
Trevor, William--The Room"
Other Selected Stories
Altschul, Andrew Foster-- "A New Kind of Gravity"
Anapol, Bay-- "A Stone House"
Curtis, Rebecca-- "Summer, with Twins"
Dorfman, Ariel-- "Gringos"
D'Souza, Tony-- "Djamilla"
Dymond, Justine-- "Cherubs"
Ellison, Jan-- "The Company of Men"
Evenson, Brian-- "Mudder Tongue"
Haslett, Adam-- "City Visit"
Kraskikov, Sana-- "Companion"
Lambert, Charles-- "The Scent of Cinnamon"
McCann, Richard-- "The Diarist"
Munro, Alice-- "The View from Castle Rock"
Murphy, Yannick-- "In a Bear's Eye"
Schutt, Christine-- "The Duchess of Albany"
Silbert, Joan-- "War Buddies
Straight, Susan-- "El Ojo de Agua"
Tran, Vu-- "The Gift of Years"

2008
Juror Favorites
Munro, Alice-- "What Do You Want to Know For?"
Trevor, William--Folie à Deux"
Zentner, Alexi-- "Touch"
Other Selected Stories
Cain, Shannon-- "The Necessity of Certain Behaviors"
Doerr, Anthony-- "Village 113"
Faber, Michel-- "Bye-Bye Natalia"
Gaitskill, Mary-- "The Little Boy"
Gass, William H.-- "A Little History of Modern Music"
Jin, Ha-- "A Composer and His Parakeets"
Jones, Edward P.-- "Bad Neighbors"
Kohler, Sheila-- "The Transitional Object"
Li, Yiyun-- "Prison"
Malouf, David-- "Every Move You Make"
McDonald, Roger-- "The Bullock Run"
Millhauser, Steven-- "A Change in Fashion"
Olafsson, Olaf-- "On the Lake"
Segal, Lore-- "Other People's Deaths"

Sonnenberg, Brittani-- "Taiping"
Tremain, Rose-- "A Game of Cards"
Tulathimutte, Tony-- "Scenes from the Life of the Only Girl in Water Shield, Alaska"

2009
Juror Favorites
Díaz, Junot-- "Wildwood"
Graham, Joyce-- "An Ordinary Soldier of the Queen"
Other Selected Stories
Brown, Karen-- "Isabel's Daughter"
Burnside, John-- "The Bell Ringer"
Dien, Viet-- "Substitutes"
Godimer, Nadine-- "A Beneficiary"
Greer, Andrew Sean-- "Darkness"
Horrocks, Caitlin-- "This Is Not Your City"
Jin, Ha-- "The House Behind a Weeping Cherry"
Lunstrum, Kristen Sundberg-- "The Nursery"
Miller, L. E.-- "Kind"
Morgan, Alistair-- "Icebergs"
Muñoz, Manuel-- "Tell Him About Brother John"
Nash, Roger-- "The Camera and the Cobra"
Sikka, Mohan-- "Uncle Musto Takes a Mistress"
Silver, Marisa-- "The Visitor"
Slate, E. V.-- "Purple Bamboo Park"
Theroux, Paul-- "Twenty-Two Stories"
Troy, Judy-- "The Order of Things"
Yoon, Paul-- "And We Will Be Here"

2010
Juror Awards
Lasdun, John-- "On Death"
Mueenuddi, Daniyal-- "A Spoiled Man"
Trevor, William--The Woman of the House
Other Selected Stories
Adichie, Chimamanda Ngozi-- "Stand by Me"
Alarcón, Daniel-- "The Bridge"
Allio, Kirstin-- "Clothed, Female Figure
Bakopoulos, Natalie-- "Fresco, Byzantine"
Berry, Wendell-- "Sheep May Safely Graze"
Bradley, George-- "An East Egg Update"
Cameron, Peter-- "The End of My Life in New York"
Galgut, Damon-- "The Lover"
Munro, Alice-- "Some Women"
Proulx, Annie-- "Them Old Cowboy Songs"
Rash, Ron-- "Into the Gorge"

Row, Jess-- "Sheep May Safely Graze"
Samarasan, Pretta-- "Birth Memorial"
Sanders, Ted-- "Obit"

Segal, Lore-- "Making Good"
Watson, Brad-- "Visitation"
Wideman, John Edgar-- "Microstories"

WRITERS' TRUST OF CANADA/MCCLELLAND AND STEWART *JOURNEY* PRIZE

The Journey Prize is awarded annually to an emerging writer for the best short story published in a Canadian literary publication. The award is endowed with the Canadian royalties that James A. Michener earned from his novel *Journey*, which was published in 1988 by McClelland and Stewart. This company also publishes an annual anthology of the year's nominated short stories.

1989: Holley Rubinsky-- "Rapid Transits"
1990: Cynthia Flood--My Father Took a Cake to France"
1991: Yann Martel--The Facts Behind the Helsinki Roccamatios"
1992: Rozena Maart-- "No Rosa No District Six"
1993: Gayla Reid--Sister Doyle's Men"
1994: Melissa Hardy-- "Long Man the River"
1995: Kathryn Woodward-- "Of Marranos and Gilded Angels"
1996: Elyse Gasco-- "Can You Wave Bye Bye Baby?"
1997: Gabriella Goliger-- "Maladies of the Inner Ear" and Anne Simpson-- "Dreaming Snow" (tie)

1998: John Brooke-- "The Finer Points of Apples"
1999: Alissa York-- "The Back of the Bear's Mouth"
2000: Timothy Taylor-- "Doves of Townsend"
2001: Kevin Armstrong-- "The Cane Field"
2002: Jocelyn Brown-- "Miss Canada"
2003: Jessica Grant-- "My Husband's Jump"
2004: Devin Krukoff-- "The Last Spark"
2005: Matt Shaw-- "Matchbook for a Mother's Hair"
2006: Heather Birrell-- "BriannaSusannaAlana"
2007: Craig Boyko-- "Ozy"
2008: Saleema Nawaz-- "My Three Girls"
2009: Yasuko Thanh-- "Floating like the Dead"
2010: Devon Code-- "Uncle Oscar

INTERNATIONAL AWARDS FRANK O'CONNOR INTERNATIONAL SHORT STORY AWARD

Named in honor of Irish writer Frank O'Connor, this award is presented annually for a collection of short stories. The award was inaugurated in 2005.

2005: Yiyun Li--*A Thousand Years of Good Prayers*--China/United States
2006: Haruki Murakami--*Blind Willow, Sleeping Woman*--Japan
2007: Miranda July--*No One Belongs Here More than You*--United States

2008: Jhumpa Lahiri--*Unaccustomed Earth*--United States
2009: Simon Van Booy--*Love Begins in Winter*--England
2010: Ron Rash--*Burning Bright*--United States

JERUSALEM PRIZE FOR THE FREEDOM OF THE INDIVIDUAL IN SOCIETY

The Jerusalem Prize is a biennial literary award presented to writers whose works have dealt with themes of human freedom in society. This listing cites only the prize-winning authors whose works include short fiction.

1965: Max Frisch--Switzerland
1969: Ignazio Silone--Italy
1971: Jorge Luis Borges--Argentina
1973: Eugene Ionesco--Romania/France

1975: Simone de Beauvoir--France
1981: Graham Green--England
1983: V. S. Naipaul--Trinidad and Tobago/England
1985: Milan Kundera--Czech Republic/France

1993: Stefan Heym--Germany
1995: Mario Vargas Llosa--Peru
1999: Don DeLillo--United States

2001: Susan Sontag--United States
2003: Arthur Miller--United States
2009: Haruki Murakami--Japan

MAN BOOKER INTERNATIONAL PRIZE

Established in 2005, this award is presented biennially to a living author of any nationality for fiction published in English or generally available in English translation. The first four winners have all written short fiction.

2005: Ismail Kadaré--Albania
2007: Chinua Achebe--Nigeria

2009: Alice Munro--Canada
2011: Philip Roth--United States

NEUSTADT INTERNATIONAL PRIZE FOR LITERATURE

Awarded biennially since 1970, this award, sponsored by the University of Oklahoma, honors writers for a body of work. This listing cites only the prize-winning authors whose works include short fiction.

1970: Giuseppe Ungaretti--Italy
1972: Gabriel García Márquez--Colombia
1976: Elizabeth Bishop--United States
1980: Josef Škvorecký--Czechoslovakia/Canada
1984: Paavo Haavikko--Finland
1986: Max Frisch--Switzerland

1988: Raja Rao--India/United States
1998: Nuruddin Farah--Somalia
2000: David Malouf--Australia
2002: Álvaro Mutis--Colombia
2006: Claribel Alegría--Nicaragua/El Salvador
2008: Patricia Grace--New Zealand

NOBEL PRIZE IN LITERATURE

Awarded annually since 1901, this award is generally regarded as the highest honor that can be bestowed upon an author for his or her total body of literary work. This listing of winners includes only authors whose works include short fiction.

1904: José Echegaray y Eizaguirre--Spain
1905: Henryk Sienkiewicz--Poland
1907: Rudyard Kipling--England
1909: Selma Lagerlöf--Sweden
1910: Paul Heyse--Germany
1912: Gerhart Hauptmann--Germany
1913: Rabindranath Tagore--India
1916: Verner von Heidenstam--Sweden
1917: Henrik Pontoppidan--Denmark
1920: Knut Hamsun--Norway
1921: Anatole France--France
1922: Jacinto Benavente--Spain
1923: William B. Yeats--Ireland
1924: Władyslaw Reymont--Poland
1925: George Bernard Shaw--Ireland
1926: Grazia Deledda--Italy

1928: Sigrid Undset--Norway
1929: Thomas Mann--Germany
1930: Sinclair Lewis--United States
1932: John Galsworthy--England
1933: Ivan Bunin--Russia
1934: Luigi Pirandello--Italy
1938: Pearl S. Buck--United States
1939: Frans Eemil Sillanpää--Finland
1944: Johannes V. Jensen--Denmark
1946: Hermann Hesse--Switzerland
1947: André Gide--France
1949: William Faulkner--United States
1951: Pär Lagerkvist--Sweden
1954: Ernest Hemingway--United States
1955: Halldór Laxness--Iceland
1957: Albert Camus--France

1958: Boris Pasternak (declined)--Russia

1961: Ivo Andrić--Yugoslavia

1962: John Steinbeck--United States

1964: Jean-Paul Sartre (declined)--France

1965: Mikhail Sholokhov--Russia

1966: Shmuel Yosef Agnon--Israel; Nelly
   Sachs--Sweden

1967: Miguel Angel Asturias--Guatemala

1968: Yasunari Kawabata--Japan

1969: Samuel Beckett--Ireland

1970: Aleksandr Solzhenitsyn--Russia

1972: Heinrich Böll--Germany

1973: Patrick White--Australia

1974: Eyvind Johnson--Sweden

1976: Saul Bellow--United States

1978: Isaac Bashevis Singer--United States

1982: Gabriel García Márquez--Colombia

1983: William Golding--England

1988: Naguib Mahfouz--Egypt

1989: Camilo José Cela--Spain

1991: Nadine Gordimer--South Africa

1994: Kenzaburō Ōe--Japan

1998: José Saramago--Portugal

2000: Gao Xingjian--China

2001: V. S. Naipaul--Trinidad and Tobago/England

2007: Doris Lessing--England

2008: J. M. G. Le Clézio--France/Mauritias

2009: Herta Müller--Germany

2010: Mario Vargas Llosa--Peru

UNITED KINGDOM AND THE COMMONWEALTH AWARDS COMMONWEALTH SHORT STORY COMPETITION

The Commonwealth Short Story Competition aims to promote new writing for radio. The prize has been awarded since 2008 and is funded and administered by the Commonwealth Foundation and the Commonwealth Broadcasting Association. Competition for the prize is open to all citizens of the Commonwealth countries.

2008

Overall Winner: Julie Curwin-- "World
   Backwards"--Canada

Regional Winner, Africa: Taddeo Bwambale Nyonda--
   "Die, Dear Tofa"--Uganda

Regional Winner, Asia: Salil Chaturvedi-- "The
   Bombay Run"--India

Regional Winner, Europe: Tania Hershman-- "Straight
   Up"--England

Regional Winner, Pacific: Jennifer Mills-- "Jack's Red
   Hat"--Australia

2009

Overall Winner: Jennifer Moore-- "Table
   Talk"--England

Regional Winner, Africa: Kachi A. Ozumba-- "The
   One-Armed Thief"--Nigeria

Regional Winner, Asia: Manasi Subramaniam-- "Deb-
   bie's Call"--India

Regional Winner Caribbean Alake Pilgrim--
   "Shades"--Trinidad and Tobago

Regional Winner, Pacific: Terri-Anne Green-- "The
   Colour of Rain"--Australia

2010

Overall Winner: Shachi Kaul-- "Retirement"--India

Regional Winner, Africa: Karen Jennings-- "From
   Dark"--South Africa

Regional Winner,Canada and Europe: Melissa
   Madore-- "Swallow Dive"--Canada

Regional Winner, Caribbean: Barbara Jenkins--
   "Something from Nothing"--Trinidad and Tobago

Regional Winner, Pacific: Jena Woodhouse-- "Praise
   Be"--Australia

Special Prize, Science, Technology and Society:
   Anuradha Kumar-- "The First Hello"--India

Special Prize, Story for Children: Iona Massey--
   "Grandma Makes Meatballs"--Australia

Anietie Isong Special Prize for a Story from Nigeria:
   Shola Olowu-Asante-- "Dinner for
   Three"--Nigeria

COMMONWEALTH WRITERS' PRIZE

Established in 1987, this prize recognizes the best works of fiction written by an established writer from the Commonwealth countries. Only one work of short fiction has received the prize:

1987: Olive Senior--*Summer Lightning, and Other Stories*--Jamaica

JAMES TAIT BLACK MEMORIAL PRIZE

One of the oldest and most prestigious literary awards in the United Kingdom, the James Tait Black Memorial Prize has been presented annually since 1919 for a work of fiction written in the English language. Only one work of short fiction has received the prize.

1943: Mary Lavin--*Tales from Bective Bridge*

CHRONOLOGICAL LIST OF WRITERS

This chronology lists authors covered in this subset in order of their dates of birth. This arrangement serves as a supplemental time line for those interested in the development of short fiction over time.

BORN UP TO 1800
Chaucer, Geoffrey (c. 1343)
Malory, Sir Thomas (early fifteenth century)
Greene, Robert (c. July, 1558)
Congreve, William (January 24, 1670)
Steele, Sir Richard (March 12, 1672 baptized)
Addison, Joseph (May 1, 1672)
Johnson, Samuel (September 18, 1709)
Hawkesworth, John (1715?)
Goldsmith, Oliver (November 10, 1728 or 1730)
Edgeworth, Maria (January 1, 1768)
Scott, Sir Walter (August 15, 1771)
Austen, Jane (December 16, 1775)
Carleton, William (March 4, 1794)

BORN 1801-1850
Thackeray, William Makepeace (July 18, 1811)
Dickens, Charles (February 7, 1812)
Le Fanu, Joseph Sheridan (August 28, 1814)
Eliot, George (November 22, 1819)
O'Brien, Fitz-James (c. 1828)
Hardy, Thomas (June 2, 1840)
Stevenson, Robert Louis (November 13, 1850)

BORN 1851-1875
Moore, George (February 24, 1852)
Conrad, Joseph (December 3, 1857)
Doyle, Sir Arthur Conan (May 22, 1859)
James, M. R. (August 1, 1862)
Machen, Arthur (March 3, 1863)
Jacobs, W. W. (September 8, 1863)
Yeats, William Butler (June 13, 1865)
Kipling, Rudyard (December 30, 1865

Wells, H. G. (September 21, 1866)
Lawson, Henry (June 17, 1867)
Galsworthy, John (August 14, 1867)
Blackwood, Algernon (March 14, 1869)
Saki (December 18, 1870)
Beerbohm, Max (August 24, 1872)
de la Mare, Walter (April 25, 1873)
Maugham, W. Somerset (January 25, 1874)
Chesterton, G. K. (May 29, 1874)

BORN 1876-1900
Coppard, A. E. (January 4, 1878)
Dunsany, Lord (July 24, 1878)
Forster, E. M. (January 1, 1879)
Woolf, Virginia (January 25, 1882)
Joyce, James (February 2, 1882)
Lewis, Wyndham (November 18, 1882)
Lawrence, D. H. (September 11, 1885)
Mansfield, Katherine (October 14, 1888)
Christie, Agatha (September 15, 1890)
Warner, Sylvia Townsend (December 6, 1893)
Huxley, Aldous (July 26, 1894)
Rhys, Jean (August 24, 1894)
O'Flaherty, Liam (August 28, 1896)
Bowen, Elizabeth (June 7, 1899)
O'Faoláin, Seán (February 22, 1900)
Pritchett, V. S. (December 16, 1900)

BORN 1901-1910
Kavan, Anna (April 10, 1901)
Collier, John (May 3, 1901)
Davies, Rhys (November 9, 1901 or 1903)
O'Connor, Frank (1903)

BORN 1901-1910 (*continued*)
Callaghan, Morley (February 22, 1903)
Plomer, William (December 10, 1903)
Greene, Graham (October 2, 1904)
Boyle, Patrick (1905)
Bates, H. E. (May 16, 1905)

BORN 1911-1920
Sansom, William (January 18, 1912)
Lavin, Mary (June 11, 1912)
Taylor, Elizabeth (July 3, 1912)
Wilson, Angus (August 11, 1913)
Thomas, Dylan (October 27, 1914)
Welch, Denton (March 29, 1915)
Dahl, Roald (September 13, 1916)
Fitzgerald, Penelope (December 17, 1916)
Clarke, Arthur C. (December 16, 1917)
Spark, Muriel (February 1, 1918)
Kiely, Benedict (August 15, 1919)
Lessing, Doris (October 22, 1919)

BORN 1921-1930
Gallant, Mavis (August 11, 1922)
Wain, John (March 14, 1925)
Tuohy, Frank (May 2, 1925)
Fowles, John (March 31, 1926)
Laurence, Margaret (July 18, 1926)
Higgins, Aidan (March 3, 1927)
Jhabvala, Ruth Prawer (May 7, 1927)
Sillitoe, Alan (March 4, 1928)
Trevor, William (May 24, 1928)
Friel, Brian (January 9, 1929)
Ballard, J. G. (November 15, 1930)
O'Brien, Edna (December 15, 1930)

BORN 1931-1940
Richler, Mordecai (January 27, 1931)
Munro, Alice (July 10, 1931)
Weldon, Fay (September 22, 1931)
Gilliatt, Penelope (March 25, 1932)
Malouf, David (March 20, 1934)
Rooke, Leon (September 11, 1934)
McGahern, John (November 12, 1934)
Kinsella, W. P. (May 25, 1935)
Shields, Carol (June 2, 1935)

MacLeod, Alistair (July 20, 1936)
Byatt, A. S. (August 24, 1936)
Callaghan, Barry (July 5, 1937)
Atwood, Margaret (November 18, 1939)
Carter, Angela (May 7, 1940)

BORN 1941-1950
Marshall, Owen (August 17, 1941)
MacLaverty, Bernard (September 14, 1942)
Hospital, Janette Turner (November 12, 1942)
Carey, Peter (May 7, 1943)
Tremain, Rose (August 2, 1943)
Barnes, Julian (January 19, 1946)
Boylan, Clare (April 21, 1948)
McEwan, Ian (June 21, 1948)
Swift, Graham (May 4, 1949)
Amis, Martin (August 25, 1949)
Jordan, Neil (February 25, 1950)
Hogan, Desmond (December 10, 1950)

BORN 1951-1960
Vanderhaeghe, Guy (April 5, 1951)
Mistry, Rohinton (July 3, 1952)
Mars-Jones, Adam (October 26, 1954)
Ishiguro, Kazuo (November 8, 1954)
Kureishi, Hanif (December 5, 1954)
Bissoondath, Neil (April 19, 1955)
Tóibín, Colm (May 30, 1955)
Galloway, Janice (December 2, 1956)
Lasdun, James (June 8, 1958)
Donovan, Gerard (1959)
Winton, Tim (August 4, 1960)

BORN 1961 AND LATER
Enright, Anne (October 11, 1962)
McCann, Colum (February 28, 1965)
Kennedy, A. L. (October 22, 1965)
Barker, Nicola (March 30, 1966)
Kelman, James (June 9, 1966)
Keegan, Claire (September 2, 1968)
Seiffert, Rachel (January, 1971)
Bezmogis, David (June 2, 1973)
Le, Nam (October 15, 1978)

INDEX

CATEGORICAL INDEX

ADVENTURE

Bates, H. E., 41
Conrad, Joseph, 152
Doyle, Sir Arthur Conan, 194
Greene, Robert, 282
Johnson, Samuel, 336
Stevenson, Robert Louis, 636
Wells, H. G., 711
Winton, Tim, 721

AFRICAN CULTURE

Laurence, Margaret, 403
Plomer, William, 565

ALLEGORY

Addison, Joseph, 1
Amis, Martin, 6
Carleton, William, 98
Carter, Angela, 104
Coppard, A. E., 162
Forster, E. M., 231
Hardy, Thomas, 288
Hawkesworth, John, 294
Johnson, Samuel, 336
Steele, Sir Richard, 631
Stevenson, Robert Louis, 636

ANTISTORY

Fowles, John, 237

ASIAN CULTURE

Hawkesworth, John, 294

AUSTRALIAN CULTURE

Carey, Peter, 94
Hospital, Janette Turner, 308
Lawson, Henry, 424
Malouf, David, 473
Winton, Tim, 721

AUTOBIOGRAPHICAL STORIES

Bowen, Elizabeth, 64
Higgins, Aidan, 298
Hogan, Desmond, 303
Jhabvala, Ruth Prawer, 332
Jordan, Neil, 342
Laurence, Margaret, 403
Lavin, Mary, 408
Lawrence, D. H., 415
O'Faoláin, Seán, 552
Plomer, William, 565
Richler, Mordecai, 583

BLACK HUMOR

Atwood, Margaret, 11
Collier, John, 143
Richler, Mordecai, 583
Weldon, Fay, 705
Wilson, Angus, 717

BRITISH CULTURE

Amis, Martin, 6
Bowen, Elizabeth, 64
Carter, Angela, 104
Coppard, A. E., 162
Dahl, Roald, 168
Davies, Rhys, 174
Delamare, Walter, 179
Dickens, Charles, 184
Doyle, Sir Arthur Conan, 194
Eliot, George, 218
Fitzgerald, Penelope, 227
Forster, E. M., 231
Fowles, John, 237
Galsworthy, John, 258
Greene, Graham, 275
Greene, Robert, 282
Hardy, Thomas, 288
Kelman, James, 364
Kipling, Rudyard, 385

BRITISH CULTURE *(continued)*

Kureishi, Hanif, 394
Lawrence, D. H., 415
MacEwan, Ian, 505
Malory, Sir Thomas, 469
Pritchett, V.S., 569
Saki, 595
Sillitoe, Alan, 620
Spark, Muriel, 625
Taylor, Elizabeth, 646
Thackeray, William Makepeace, 650
Tremain, Rose, 666
Wain, John, 688
Warner, Sylvia Townsend, 692
Wilson, Angus, 717

CANADIAN CULTURE

Atwood, Margaret, 11
Bezmogis, David, 52
Bissoondath, Neil, 56
Callaghan, Barry, 83
Callaghan, Morley, 87
Kinsella, W. P., 379
Laurence, Margaret, 403
MacLeod, Alistair, 465
Munro, Alice, 523
Richler, Mordecai, 583
Vanderhaeghe, Guy, 684

CHARACTER STUDIES

Addison, Joseph, 1
Barker, Nicola, 32
Bezmogis, David, 52
Bissoondath, Neil, 56
Boyle, Patrick, 74
Callaghan, Barry, 83
Donovan, Gerard, 190
Enright, Anne, 222
Fitzgerald, Penelope, 227
Galloway, Janice, 254
Goldsmith, Oliver, 269
Higgins, Aidan, 298
Hogan, Desmond, 303
Ishiguro, Kazuo, 318
Jordan, Neil, 342
Keegan, Claire, 360
Kelman, James, 364
Kennedy, A. L., 368

Kureishi, Hanif, 394
Lasdun, James, 399
Le, Nam, 429
Maccann, Colum, 501
MacLaverty, Bernard, 461
MacLeod, Alistair, 465
Malouf, David, 473
Marshall, Owen, 490
Mistry, Rohinton, 514
Rooke, Leon, 589
Steele, Sir Richard, 631

COLONIALISM

Conrad, Joseph, 152
Kipling, Rudyard, 385
Laurence, Margaret, 403
Maugham, W. Somerset, 494
Plomer, William, 565

DETECTIVE AND MYSTERY

Barnes, Julian, 36
Chesterton, G. K., 122
Christie, Agatha, 129
Conrad, Joseph, 152
Delamare, Walter, 179
Dickens, Charles, 184
Doyle, Sir Arthur Conan, 194
LeFanu, Joseph Sheridan, 432

DIDACTIC STORIES

Addison, Joseph, 1
Chaucer, Geoffrey, 108
Dickens, Charles, 184
Edgeworth, Maria, 209
Goldsmith, Oliver, 269
Greene, Robert, 282
Hawkesworth, John, 294
Johnson, Samuel, 336
Lawrence, D. H., 415
Sillitoe, Alan, 620
Steele, Sir Richard, 631

DOMESTIC REALISM

Bates, H. E., 41
Bezmogis, David, 52
Bowen, Elizabeth, 64
Boyle, Patrick, 74

Callaghan, Morley, 87
Enright, Anne, 222
Gallant, Mavis, 248
Jhabvala, Ruth Prawer, 332
Jordan, Neil, 342
Keegan, Claire, 360
Kureishi, Hanif, 394
Maccann, Colum, 501
MacLaverty, Bernard, 461
Malouf, David, 473
Mansfield, Katherine, 477
Marshall, Owen, 490
Munro, Alice, 523
O'Brien, Edna, 534
O'Connor, Frank, 545
Shields, Carol, 615
Tóibín, Colm, 662
Tremain, Rose, 666

EPIC

Joyce, James, 346

EPIPHANY

Boyle, Patrick, 74
Joyce, James, 346
Pritchett, V.S., 569

EROTIC STORIES

Carter, Angela, 104

ESSAY-SKETCH TRADITION

Addison, Joseph, 1
Goldsmith, Oliver, 269
Steele, Sir Richard, 631

EXEMPLUM

Chaucer, Geoffrey, 108

EXISTENTIALISM

Lessing, Doris, 439

EXPERIMENTAL STORIES

Ballard, J. G., 25
Byatt, A. S., 78
Carey, Peter, 94
Fowles, John, 237
Galloway, Janice, 254

Gilliatt, Penelope, 263
Higgins, Aidan, 298
Lewis, Wyndham, 447
Marshall, Owen, 490
Swift, Graham, 642
Weldon, Fay, 705
Woolf, Virginia, 725

EXPRESSIONISM

Joyce, James, 346

FABLE

Callaghan, Barry, 83
Chaucer, Geoffrey, 108
Delamare, Walter, 179
Hawkesworth, John, 294
Kinsella, W. P., 379
Kipling, Rudyard, 385

FAIRY TALE

Byatt, A. S., 78
Carter, Angela, 104
Delamare, Walter, 179
Dunsany, Lord, 203
Rooke, Leon, 589
Warner, Sylvia Townsend, 692
Yeats, William Butler, 732

FANTASY

Amis, Martin, 6
Beerbohm, Max, 47
Byatt, A. S., 78
Carey, Peter, 94
Carter, Angela, 104
Clarke, Arthur C., 136
Coppard, A. E., 162
Delamare, Walter, 179
Dunsany, Lord, 203
Enright, Anne, 222
Forster, E. M., 231
Kinsella, W. P., 379
Kipling, Rudyard, 385
Machen, Arthur, 457
Sansom, William, 599
Warner, Sylvia Townsend, 692

FOLKTALES

Barnes, Julian, 36
Carleton, William, 98
Carter, Angela, 104
Friel, Brian, 243
Hardy, Thomas, 288
Moore, George, 518
Scott, Sir Walter, 606
Yeats, William Butler, 732

GAY AND LESBIAN ISSUES

Forster, E. M., 231
Hogan, Desmond, 303
Mars-Jones, Adam, 486
O'Brien, Fitz James, 541
Welch, Denton, 699
Woolf, Virginia, 725

GERMAN CULTURE

Seiffert, Rachel, 611

GHOST

Blackwood, Algernon, 60
Clarke, Arthur C., 136
Delamare, Walter, 179
Dickens, Charles, 184
James, M. R., 327
LeFanu, Joseph Sheridan, 432
Scott, Sir Walter, 606

GOTHIC

Carter, Angela, 104
Dahl, Roald, 168
Delamare, Walter, 179
O'Brien, Edna, 534
O'Brien, Fitz James, 541

GROTESQUE STORIES

Sansom, William, 599

HISTORICAL STORIES

Atwood, Margaret, 11
Barnes, Julian, 36
Le, Nam, 429
MacLaverty, Bernard, 461
Scott, Sir Walter, 606

Swift, Graham, 642
Tóibín, Colm, 662
Tremain, Rose, 666

HORROR

Blackwood, Algernon, 60
Bowen, Elizabeth, 64
Collier, John, 143
Delamare, Walter, 179
Doyle, Sir Arthur Conan, 194
Dunsany, Lord, 203
Jacobs, W. W., 323
James, M. R., 327
Kipling, Rudyard, 385
LeFanu, Joseph Sheridan, 432
Machen, Arthur, 457
O'Brien, Fitz James, 541
Sansom, William, 599
Stevenson, Robert Louis, 636

HUMANISM

Callaghan, Morley, 87
Forster, E. M., 231
Johnson, Samuel, 336
Shields, Carol, 615

IMPRESSIONISM

Mansfield, Katherine, 477

INDIAN CULTURE

Bissoondath, Neil, 56
Jhabvala, Ruth Prawer, 332
Kipling, Rudyard, 385
Kureishi, Hanif, 394
Mistry, Rohinton, 514

IRISH CULTURE

Bowen, Elizabeth, 64
Boylan, Clare, 70
Boyle, Patrick, 74
Carleton, William, 98
Donovan, Gerard, 190
Dunsany, Lord, 203
Edgeworth, Maria, 209
Enright, Anne, 222
Friel, Brian, 243
Hogan, Desmond, 303

Jordan, Neil, 342
Joyce, James, 346
Keegan, Claire, 360
Kiely, Benedict, 373
Lavin, Mary, 408
LeFanu, Joseph Sheridan, 432
Maccann, Colum, 501
MacGahern, John, 510
MacLaverty, Bernard, 461
Moore, George, 518
O'Brien, Edna, 534
O'Connor, Frank, '45
O'Faoláin, Seán, 552
O'Flaherty, Liam, 558
Tóibín, Colm, 662
Yeats, William Butler, 732

IRONIC STORIES

Boylan, Clare, 70
Chaucer, Geoffrey, 108
Collier, John, 143
Gallant, Mavis, 248
Goldsmith, Oliver, 269
Hardy, Thomas, 288
Lavin, Mary, 408
Pritchett, V.S., 569
Saki, 595
Spark, Muriel, 625
Wain, John, 688
Warner, Sylvia Townsend, 692
Woolf, Virginia, 725

IRREALISM

Fowles, John, 237

JAPANESE CULTURE

Ishiguro, Kazuo, 318

JEWISH CULTURE

Bezmogis, David, 52
Jhabvala, Ruth Prawer, 332
Richler, Mordecai, 583

LOCAL COLOR

Tóibín, Colm, 662
Winton, Tim, 721

LYRICAL SHORT STORIES

Bates, H. E., 41
Hogan, Desmond, 303
Lawrence, D. H., 415
MacGahern, John, 510
Mansfield, Katherine, 477
Thomas, Dylan, 656
Woolf, Virginia, 725

METAFICTION

Atwood, Margaret, 11
Fowles, John, 237
Kinsella, W. P., 379

MINIMALISM

MacGahern, John, 510

MODERNISM

Bates, H. E., 41
Callaghan, Morley, 87
Joyce, James, 346
Lewis, Wyndham, 447
Mansfield, Katherine, 477

MODERN SHORT STORY

Carleton, William, 98
Coppard, A. E., 162
Joyce, James, 346
Mansfield, Katherine, 477
Moore, George, 518
Pritchett, V.S., 569
Sansom, William, 599
Scott, Sir Walter, 606
Stevenson, Robert Louis, 636

MORAL STORIES

Austen, Jane, 20
Dickens, Charles, 184
Edgeworth, Maria, 209
Eliot, George, 218
Hawkesworth, John, 294
Joyce, James, 346
Stevenson, Robert Louis, 636
Wain, John, 688

MYTHIC STORIES

Lawrence, D. H., 415
Lawson, Henry, 424
Maccann, Colum, 501
Rooke, Leon, 589
Yeats, William Butler, 732

NATURALISM

Barker, Nicola, 32
Bowen, Elizabeth, 64
Callaghan, Morley, 87
Davies, Rhys, 174
Lawrence, D. H., 415
O'Flaherty, Liam, 558

NEW ZEALAND CULTURE

Marshall, Owen, 490

OCCULT

Blackwood, Algernon, 60
Carter, Angela, 104
Christie, Agatha, 129

PAKISTANI CULTURE

Kureishi, Hanif, 394

PARABLE

Callaghan, Barry, 83

PARODY

Austen, Jane, 20
Beerbohm, Max, 47
Dunsany, Lord, 203
Rooke, Leon, 589
Saki, 595

PHILOSOPHICAL STORIES

Amis, Martin, 6
Callaghan, Morley, 87
Goldsmith, Oliver, 269
Hospital, Janette Turner, 308
Johnson, Samuel, 336
Vanderhaeghe, Guy, 684

POETIC SHORT STORIES

Chaucer, Geoffrey, 108
Yeats, William Butler, 732

POSTMODERNISM

Amis, Martin, 6
Atwood, Margaret, 11
Barnes, Julian, 36
Fowles, John, 237
Galloway, Janice, 254
Higgins, Aidan, 298
Hospital, Janette Turner, 308
Jordan, Neil, 342
MacEwan, Ian, 505
Swift, Graham, 642

PSYCHOLOGICAL REALISM

Atwood, Margaret, 11
Bowen, Elizabeth, 64
Callaghan, Morley, 87
Conrad, Joseph, 152
Coppard, A. E., 162
Forster, E. M., 231
Gallant, Mavis, 248
Greene, Graham, 275
Hospital, Janette Turner, 308
Ishiguro, Kazuo, 318
Lawson, Henry, 424
Lessing, Doris, 439
Munro, Alice, 523
O'Brien, Edna, 534
Seiffert, Rachel, 611
Shields, Carol, 615
Tóibín, Colm, 662
Winton, Tim, 721

PSYCHOLOGICAL STORIES

Chaucer, Geoffrey, 108
Conrad, Joseph, 152
Galloway, Janice, 254
Hardy, Thomas, 288
Higgins, Aidan, 298
Kavan, Anna, 355
LeFanu, Joseph Sheridan, 432
Seiffert, Rachel, 611
Spark, Muriel, 625

REALISM

Barnes, Julian, 36
Bates, H. E., 41
Bissoondath, Neil, 56
Byatt, A. S., 78
Carleton, William, 98
Coppard, A. E., 162
Forster, E. M., 231
Gallant, Mavis, 248
Hospital, Janette Turner, 308
Joyce, James, 346
Kinsella, W. P., 379
Lasdun, James, 399
Laurence, Margaret, 403
Lavin, Mary, 408
Lawrence, D. H., 415
Lawson, Henry, 424
Lewis, Wyndham, 447
MacEwan, Ian, 505
MacGahern, John, 510
Maugham, W. Somerset, 494
Moore, George, 518
Munro, Alice, 523
O'Brien, Fitz James, 541
O'Connor, Frank, 545
O'Faoláin, Seán, 552
Richler, Mordecai, 583
Sansom, William, 599
Trevor, William, 671
Tuohy, Frank, 679
Vanderhaeghe, Guy, 684
Warner, Sylvia Townsend, 692

REGIONAL STORIES

Hospital, Janette Turner, 308
Laurence, Margaret, 403
Lawson, Henry, 424
O'Flaherty, Liam, 558
Vanderhaeghe, Guy, 684

RELIGIOUS STORIES

Boyle, Patrick, 74
Chesterton, G. K., 122
Greene, Graham, 275
Hawkesworth, John, 294

ROMANCE

Malory, Sir Thomas, 469

ROMANTICISM

Goldsmith, Oliver, 269
O'Brien, Fitz James, 541
Scott, Sir Walter, 606
Stevenson, Robert Louis, 636

SATIRE

Addison, Joseph, 1
Beerbohm, Max, 47
Boylan, Clare, 70
Higgins, Aidan, 298
Jacobs, W. W., 323
Jhabvala, Ruth Prawer, 332
Kinsella, W. P., 379
Lewis, Wyndham, 447
Saki, 595
Spark, Muriel, 625
Steele, Sir Richard, 631
Taylor, Elizabeth, 646
Thackeray, William Makepeace, 650
Thomas, Dylan, 656
Wain, John, 688
Weldon, Fay, 705
Wilson, Angus, 717

SCIENCE FICTION

Atwood, Margaret, 11
Ballard, J. G., 25
Carey, Peter, 94
Clarke, Arthur C., 136
Doyle, Sir Arthur Conan, 194
Forster, E. M., 231
Huxley, Aldous, 312
Kavan, Anna, 355
O'Brien, Fitz James, 541
Wells, H. G., 711

SKETCHES

Addison, Joseph, 1
Callaghan, Morley, 87
Dickens, Charles, 184
Gilliatt, Penelope, 263
Goldsmith, Oliver, 269
Huxley, Aldous, 312

SKETCHES *(continued)*
Jhabvala, Ruth Prawer, 332
Lessing, Doris, 439
Mansfield, Katherine, 477
Steele, Sir Richard, 631
Thackeray, William Makepeace, 650

SOCIAL CRITICISM

Galsworthy, John, 258
Kureishi, Hanif, 394
Taylor, Elizabeth, 646
Wain, John, 688

SOCIAL REALISM

Atwood, Margaret, 11
Bowen, Elizabeth, 64
Carleton, William, 98
Gallant, Mavis, 248
Huxley, Aldous, 312
Kelman, James, 364
Lavin, Mary, 408
MacLaverty, Bernard, 461
Moore, George, 518
Richler, Mordecai, 583
Shields, Carol, 615
Tóibín, Colm, 662
Vanderhaeghe, Guy, 684

SOCIAL SATIRE

Boylan, Clare, 70

SOUTH AFRICAN CULTURE

Lessing, Doris, 439
Plomer, William, 565

SPANISH CULTURE

Tóibín, Colm, 662

SUPERNATURAL STORIES

Ballard, J. G., 25
Barnes, Julian, 36
Blackwood, Algernon, 60
Bowen, Elizabeth, 64
Collier, John, 143
Dickens, Charles, 184
Doyle, Sir Arthur Conan, 194
Fowles, John, 237

Greene, Graham, 275
Hardy, Thomas, 288
James, M. R., 327
Kipling, Rudyard, 385
LeFanu, Joseph Sheridan, 432
Machen, Arthur, 457
Moore, George, 518
O'Brien, Firz James, 541
Saki, 595
Spark, Muriel, 625
Yeats, William Butler, 732

SURREALISM

Carey, Peter, 94
Carter, Angela, 104
Enright, Anne, 222
Kavan, Anna, 355
Kinsella, W. P., 379
Sansom, William, 599
Thomas, Dylan, 656

SUSPENSE

Dahl, Roald, 168

SYMBOLIC REALISM

Conrad, Joseph, 152

SYMBOLISM

Carter, Angela, 104
Conrad, Joseph, 152
Delamare, Walter, 179
Joyce, James, 346
Lawrence, D. H., 415
Mansfield, Katherine, 477
Welch, Denton, 699

TALES

Clarke, Arthur C., 136
Thackeray, William Makepeace, 650
Wells, H. G., 711
Yeats, William Butler, 732

UTOPIAN STORIES

Wells, H. G., 711

WAR

Bates, H. E., 41
Dahl, Roald, 168
O'Faoláin, Seán, 552
Seiffert, Rachel, 611
Wells, H. G., 711

WEST INDIAN CULTURE

Bissoondath, Neil, 56

WIT AND HUMOR

Addison, Joseph, 1
Beerbohm, Max, 47
Chesterton, G. K., 122
Collier, John, 143
Congreve, William, 149
Dickens, Charles, 184
Gilliatt, Penelope, 263
Goldsmith, Oliver, 269
Greene, Graham, 275
Higgins, Aidan, 298
Kennedy, A. L., 368
Kinsella, W. P., 379
Lawson, Henry, 424
Lewis, Wyndham, 447
Mars-Jones, Adam, 486
Maugham, W. Somerset, 494
O'Connor, Frank, 545
O'Faoláin, Seán, 552
Pritchett, V.S., 569
Rooke, Leon, 589
Saki, 595
Sansom, William, 599
Steele, Sir Richard, 631

Taylor, Elizabeth, 646
Thackeray, William Makepeace, 650
Vanderhaeghe, Guy, 684
Warner, Sylvia Townsend, 692
Weldon, Fay, 705
Wells, H. G., 711
Wilson, Angus, 717

WOMEN/S ISSUES

Atwood, Margaret, 11
Austen, Jane, 20
Bowen, Elizabeth, 64
Boylan, Clare, 70
Byatt, A. S., 78
Carter, Angela, 104
Edgeworth, Maria, 209
Eliot, George, 218
Enright, Anne, 222
Gallant, Mavis, 248
Galloway, Janice, 254
Gilliatt, Penelope, 263
Hospital, Janette Turner, 308
Kavan, Anna, 355
Kennedy, A. L., 368
Laurence, Margaret, 403
Lavin, Mary, 408
Mansfield, Katherine, 477
Munro, Alice, 523
O'Brien, Edna, 534
Rhys, Jean, 578
Shields, Carol, 615
Spark, Muriel, 625
Taylor, Elizabeth, 646
Tremain, Rose, 666
Weldon, Fay, 705

SUBJECT INDEX

All personages whose names appear in **boldface** *type in this index are the subjects of articles in* Critical Survey of Short Fiction, Fourth Revised Edition.

A

"Accompanist, The" (Pritchett), 575
"Across the Bridge" (Gallant), 252
Addison, Joseph, 1-6
"Admiral and the Nuns, The" (Tuohy), 680
"Adoration of the Magi, The" (Yeats), 735
"Adventure of the Dancing Men, The" (Doyle), 199
"Adventure of the Empty House, The" (Doyle), 199
Aesthetic movement, 48
"After Long Absence" (Hospital), 309
After Rain (Trevor), 676
All Looks Yellow to the Jaundiced Eye (Boyle), 76
"All Sorts of Impossible Things" (McGahern), 512
All the Stories (Spark), 629
Almoran and Hamet (Hawkesworth), 297
"Almost 1948" (Galloway), 256
"American Dreams" (Carey), 97
American Ghosts and Old World Wonders (Carter), 106
Amis, Martin, 6-10
"Among the Dahlias" (Sansom), 603
"Among the Ruins" (Friel), 244
"Amos Barton" (Eliot), 219
"Amuck in the Bush" (Callaghan, M.), 89
"Amurath the Sultan" (Hawkesworth), 296
"Angelina: Or, L'Amie Inconnue" (Edgeworth), 213
"Animal to the Memory, An" (Bezmozgis), 54
"Another Time" (O'Brien, E.), 538
Antarctica (Keegan), 361
Antic Jezebel, The (Malouf), 475
"Anxious Man, The" (Lasdun), 401
"Apple Tree, The" (Galsworthy), 259
"Arabesque: The Mouse" (Coppard), 165
"Archaeologists" (Donovan), 193
Asian tale, 270
"Asylum Piece" (Kavan), 357
At Night All Cats Are Grey (Boyle), 75
Atrocity Exhibition, The (Ballard), 28

"At Sallygap" (Lavin), 410
"At Sea" (Welch), 700
"At the Bay" (Mansfield), 483
Atwood, Margaret, 11-19
"Auspicious Occasion" (Mistry), 515
Austen, Jane, 20-24
"Autumn Day" (Gallant), 250

B

Ballard, J. G., 25-31
"Ball of Malt and Madame Butterfly, A" (Kiely), 374
"Bang-Bang You're Dead" (Spark), 628
"Barbara of the House of Grebe" (Hardy), 291
"Bardon Bus" (Munro), 526
Barker, Nicola, 32-35
Barnes, Julian, 36-40
"Basement Room, The" (Greene, G.), 278
Bates, H. E., 41-47
"Beach of Falesá, The" (Stevenson), 639
"Bears in Mourning" (Mars-Jones), 488
Beast-fable, 117
"Beautiful Suit, The" (Wells), 714
Beerbohm, Max, 47-52
"Beggars, The" (O'Flaherty), 562
"Beginning of an Idea, The" (McGahern), 512
Beginning of Spring, The (Fitzgerald, P.), 229
Between Trains (Callaghan, B.), 85
"Beyond the Pale" (Kipling), 387
Bezmozgis, David, 52-55
Bird in the House, A (Laurence), 405
"Birthmark, The" (Kavan), 356
Bissoondath, Neil, 56-60
Bit on the Side, A (Trevor), 676
Black Boxer, The (Bates), 43
"Black Peril" (Plomer), 567
"Black Queen, The" (Callaghan, B.), 84
Black Venus (Carter), 106
Blackwood, Algernon, 60-63

"Blind Love" (Pritchett), 573
"Blind Man, The" (Lawrence), 417
"Bliss" (Mansfield), 480
"Blood" (Galloway), 256
Blood (Galloway), 256
"Blue and Green" (Woolf), 726
"Bluebeard's Egg" (Atwood), 14
"Bluebell Meadow" (Kiely), 376
"Blue Cross, The" (Chesterton), 124
"Blue Kimono, The" (Callaghan, M.), 91
"Blundell's Improvement" (Jacobs), 325
"Blush, The" (Taylor, E.), 648
Body, The (Kureishi), 396
"Bolt of White Cloth, A" (Rooke), 591
"Book Buyers, The" (Kinsella), 380
Book of the Duchess (Chaucer), 109
Bookshop, The (Fitzgerald, P.), 228
Bowen, Elizabeth, 64-70
"Bowmen, The" (Machen), 459
Boylan, Clare, 70-73
Boyle, Patrick, 74-77
"Brave and Cruel" (Welch), 703
"Breakfast for Enrique" (McCann), 502
Breton lais, 119
"Broken Homes" (Trevor), 675
"Brother Frank's Gospel Hour" (Kinsella), 383
"Brothers" (Sillitoe), 624
"Brushwood Boy, The" (Kipling), 388
"Bujak and the Strong Force" (Amis), 8
"Bull" (Kinsella), 383
"But at the Stroke of Midnight" (Warner), 696
Byatt, A. S., 78-82

C

"Cage, The" (Bissoondath), 58
"Cage of Sand, The" (Ballard), 27
Callaghan, Barry, 83-86
Callaghan, Morley, 87-94
"Camberwell Beauty, The" (Pritchett), 575
Canterbury Tales, The (Chaucer), 114
"Cap for Steve, A" (Callaghan, M.), 92
Carey, Peter, 94-98
Carleton, William, 98-104
"Carmilla" (Le Fanu), 435
"Cartagena" (Le), 431
Carter, Angela, 104-108
"Casualty" (Lessing), 443
"Celestial Omnibus, The" (Forster), 234

"Cellists" (Ishiguro), 321
"Chaser, The" (Collier), 145
Chaucer, Geoffrey, 108-121
Cheating at Canasta (Trevor), 677
"Cheat's Remorse, The" (Callaghan, M.), 92
Chesterton, G. K., 122, 128
"Child of God, The" (O'Flaherty), 560
"Child of Queen Victoria, The" (Plomer), 566
Children of Lir (Hogan), 305
"Childybawn" (O'Faoláin), 554
Christie, Agatha, 129-136
Christmas Carol, A (Dickens), 188
Christmas Garland, Woven by Max Beerbohm, A
       (Beerbohm), 50
Citizen of the World, The (Goldsmith), 270
Clarke, Arthur C., 136-142
"Clerk's Tale, The" (Chaucer), 118
"Cloud, The" (Fowles), 241
"Coffin on the Hill, The" (Welch), 700
"Coincidence of the Arts, The" (Amis), 9
Collected Stories of Mavis Gallant, The
       (Gallant), 251
Collectors, The (Mistry), 516
Collier, John, 143-149
Colonel Julian, and Other Stories (Bates), 44
Colonel's Daughter, and Other Stories, The
       (Tremain), 667
"Company of Wolves, The" (Carter), 105
Complaint, 109
"Concentration City" (Ballard), 27
"Concerning Virgins" (Boylan), 72
"Confessions of Fitz-Boodle" (Thackeray), 653
Congreve, William, 149-152
Conrad, Joseph, 152-161
Consolatio, 109
"Contest of Ladies, A" (Sansom), 603
"Contraband" (Jacobs), 324
"Conversion of an English Courtizan, The"
       (Greene, R.), 285
Coppard, A. E., 162-167
"Cords" (O'Brien, E.), 536
"Country Funeral, The" (McGahern), 511
"Country of the Blind, The" (Wells), 713
"Country of the Grand" (Donovan), 192
"Country Passion, A" (Callaghan, M.), 89
"Course of English Studies, A" (Jhabvala), 333
"Cousin Theresa" (Saki), 596
"Cow in the House, A" (Kiely), 374

"Credit Repair" (Hospital), 310
"Crooner" (Ishiguro), 320
"Crown, The" (Lawrence), 419
"Curtain Blown by the Breeze, The"
        (Spark), 627
"Cynthia" (Huxley), 314

D

Daffodil Sky, The (Bates), 45
Dahl, Roald, 168-174
"Damned, The" (Blackwood), 62
"Dance of the Happy Shades" (Munro), 524
"Dancing" (Bissoondath), 58
"Dancing Girls" (Atwood), 13
Darkness of Wallis Simpson, and Other Stories, The
        (Tremain), 669
Dark Room, The (Seiffert), 613
"Daughters of the Late Colonel, The"
        (Mansfield), 481
Davies, Rhys, 174-178
Day Hemingway Died, The (Marshall), 492
Day's End, and Other Stories (Bates), 43
"Dayspring Mishandled" (Kipling), 391
"Dead, The" (Joyce), 352
"Dead as They Come" (McEwan), 507
"Dead Astronaut, The" (Ballard), 28
"Death of King Arthur, The" (Malory), 471
Death of the Hind Legs, and Other Stories
        (Wain), 690
"Dedicated Man, A" (Taylor,), 647
De la Mare, Walter, 179-184
"Demon Lover, The" (Bowen), 67
"De Mortuis" (Collier), 145
"Destructors, The" (Greene, G.), 279
Devil and All, The (Collier), 144
"Dhoya" (Yeats), 733
"Diamond Badge, The" (Welch), 703
"Diamond Lens, The" (O'Brien, F. J.), 542
Diamonds at the Bottom of the Sea, The (Hogan), 305
Dickens, Charles, 184-190
"Difficulty with a Bouquet" (Sansom), 602
"Digging Up the Mountains" (Bissoondath), 57
"Dilemma of Catherine Fuchsias, The"
        (Davies, R.), 177
"Dimond Cut Dimond" (Thackeray), 652
Disputation Between a Hee Conny-Catcher and a
        Shee Conny-Catcher, A (Greene, R.), 285
"Distracted Preacher, The" (Hardy), 290

"Diver, The" (Pritchett), 574
"Dividends" (O'Faoláin), 555
"Diviner, The" (Friel), 245
"Doctor, The" (Gallant), 252
"Doll's House, The" (Mansfield), 483
Donovan, Gerard, 190-193
"Door in the Wall, The" (Wells), 714
"Down Then by Derry" (Kiely), 377
Doyle, Sir Arthur Conan, 194-202
"Do You Love Me?" (Carey), 96
"Dragons" (Barnes), 37
"Dream of a Beast, The" (Jordan), 345
"Dressing Up for the Carnival" (Shields), 618
"Drover's Wife, The" (Lawson), 426
"Drummer Boy, The" (Trevor), 674
"Drunkard, The" (O'Connor), 548
Dubliners (Joyce), 347
"Duel, The" (Conrad), 157
"Duke Humphrey's Dinner" (O'Brien, F. J.), 543
"Dun, The" (Edgeworth), 215
Dunsany, Lord, 203-208

E

"Ebony Tower, The" (Fowles), 238
Edgeworth, Maria, 209-218
Einstein's Monsters (Amis), 8
"Eliduc" (Fowles), 240
Eliot, George, 218-222
Empty Family, The (Tóibín), 664
"Empty House, The" (Blackwood), 61
"Enigma, The" (Fowles), 240
"Enormous Space, The" (Ballard), 29
Enright, Anne, 222-226
"Epilogue II" (Mansfield), 479
"Eterna" (Lavin), 412
"Eternal Moment, The" (Forster), 233
"Eustace" (Malouf), 474
"Evangeline's Mother" (Kinsella), 380
Evangelista's Fan, and Other Stories (Tremain), 668
"Evening Primrose" (Collier), 146
"Evening with John Joe Dempsey, An" (Trevor), 673
"Evermore" (Barnes), 37
Everything in This Country Must (McCann), 504
"Executor, An" (Mars-Jones), 487
Exemplum, 118
"Expatriates' Party, The" (Vanderhaeghe), 686
"Eye of Apollo, The" (Chesterton), 124

F

Fabliaux, 116, 117
"Fairy Goose, The" (O'Flaherty), 560
Fanatic Heart, A (O'Brien, E.), 538
Fancies and Goodnights (Collier), 146
"Fard" (Huxley), 315
"Fat Man in History, The" (Carey), 96
Felo de Se (Higgins), 300
"Few Crusted Characters, A" (Hardy), 291
"Fiddler of the Reels, The" (Hardy), 290
"Fidelity" (Jhabvala), 334
"Field of Mustard, The" (Coppard), 163
Field Study (Seiffert), 614
"Fight, The" (Thomas), 659
"Final Problem, The" (Doyle), 198
"Fingers in the Door" (Tuohy), 681
"Fire in the Wood, The" (Welch), 703
"First Confession" (O'Connor), 548
"First Death of Her Life, The" (Taylor), 646
First Love, Last Rites (McEwan), 507
"First Year of My Life, The" (Spark), 628
"Fishing the Sloe-Black River" (McCann), 502
Fitzgerald, Penelope, 227-230
"Flights of Fancy" (Trevor), 674
"Flitting Behavior" (Shields), 617
"Fly, The" (Mansfield), 481
"Foring Parts" (Thackeray), 653
Forster, E. M., 231-236
"Foster" (Keegan), 363
"Foundry House" (Friel), 245
Fowles, John, 237-243
Frank, I-IV (Edgeworth), 212
"Franklin's Tale, The" (Chaucer), 119
Friel, Brian, 243-247
"Frostbite" (Galloway), 256
"Fur Coat, The" (O'Faoláin), 554

G

Gallant, Mavis, 248-254
Galloway, Janice, 254-258
Galsworthy, John, 258-263
Garden of the Villa Mollini, and Other Stories, The (Tremain), 668
"Garden-Party, The" (Mansfield), 483
"Gaspar Ruiz" (Conrad), 158
Gate of Angels, The (Fitzgerald), 229
"Gavin O'Leary" (Collier), 146
"General's Day, The" (Trevor), 672

George Silverman's Explanation (Dickens), 186
Gilliatt, Penelope, 263-269
"Girl on the Bus, The" (Sansom), 602
"Giving Birth" (Atwood), 14
"Glass Coffin, The" (Byatt), 80
"Go-Away Bird, The" (Spark), 628
"Going up in the World" (Kavan), 356
"Golden Girl" (Hospital), 309
Goldsmith, Oliver, 269-275
Good Bones and Simple Murders (Atwood), 16
"Good Women, The" (Sillitoe), 623
"Grandmothers, The" (Lessing), 444
Great God Pan, The (Machen), 458
Greene, Graham, 275-282
Greene, Robert, 282-287
"Green Tunnels" (Huxley), 315
"Grosse Fifi, La" (Rhys), 579
Guardian, The (Steele), 634
"Guests of the Nation" (O'Connor), 546

H

"Hammer of God, The" (Chesterton), 125
"Hammer of God, The" (Clarke), 140
"Handsome Is as Handsome Does" (Pritchett), 571
"Happily Ever After" (Huxley), 314
"Happiness" (Lavin), 412
"Happy Death, A" (Lavin), 410
Hard Time to Be a Father, A (Weldon), 708
Hardy, Thomas, 288-294
"Hateful Word, The" (Welch), 703
Hateship, Friendship, Courtship, Loveship, Marriage (Munro), 529
"Haunted House, A" (Woolf), 728
Hawkesworth, John, 294-298
Heading Inland (Barker), 34
Heart of Darkness (Conrad), 155
"Hee-Haw!" (Warner), 693
"Hermitage" (Barnes), 38
"Her Table Spread" (Bowen), 66
Higgins, Aidan, 298-302
"Higgler, The" (Coppard), 164
"Highland Widow, The" (Scott), 608
"Hint of an Explanation, The" (Greene, G.), 276
"Hiroshima" (Le), 431
"Hoffmeier's Antelope" (Swift), 643
Hogan, Desmond, 303-307
"Hollow, The" (Lasdun), 402
"Horse Dealer's Daughter, The" (Lawrence), 418

Hospital, Janette Turner, 308-311
House of Fame (Chaucer), 111
House of Sleep, The (Kavan), 357
"How I Became a Holy Mother" (Jhabvala), 334
"How I Finally Lost My Heart" (Lessing), 441
"Human Element, The" (Maugham), 498
Huxley, Aldous, 312-317
"Hymeneal" (O'Faoláin), 555

I

I Am Lazarus (Kavan), 357
"Ideal Craftsman, An" (De la Mare), 182
"Idle Days on the Yann" (Dunsany), 206
In a Café (Lavin), 413
"In a Café" (Mansfield), 479
"In a Glass Darkly" (Christie), 132
In a Glass Darkly (Le Fanu), 434
"In Between the Sheets" (McEwan), 507
Incognita (Congreve), 150
"Indian Summer of a Forsyte, The"
        (Galsworthy), 260
In His Own Country (Callaghan, M.), 90
Innocent and the Guilty, The (Warner), 696
"Interference" (Barnes), 37
"In the Fall" (MacLeod), 467
"In the Forest" (De la Mare), 181
"In the Train" (O'Connor), 547
Ishiguro, Kazuo, 318-322
"It's Beginning to Hurt" (Lasdun), 400
"I Used to Live Here Once" (Rhys), 581

J

Jacobs, W. W., 323-326
James, M. R., 327-331
"Janet's Repentance" (Eliot), 220
"Je Ne Parle Pas Français" (Mansfield), 480
Jhabvala, Ruth Prawer, 332-335
"John Sherman" (Yeats), 734
John Silence (Blackwood), 62
Johnson, Samuel, 336-342
Jordan, Neil, 342-345
"Journey to the Seven Streams, A" (Kiely), 374
Joyce, James, 346-354
"Judas Tree, The" (Welch), 702
"Julia and the Bazooka" (Kavan), 358
Julia and the Bazooka, and Other Stories,
        (Kavan), 358
Just So Stories (Kipling), 389

K

Kavan, Anna, 355-360
Keegan, Claire, 360-364
Kelman, James, 364-368
Kennedy, A. L., 368-372
"Kew Gardens" (Woolf), 727
Kiely, Benedict, 373-379
"Killachter Meadow" (Higgins), 301
"King Caliban" (Wain), 689
Kingdoms of Elfin (Warner), 697
"King's Ankus, The" (Kipling), 389
Kinsella, W. P., 379-384
Kipling, Rudyard, 385-394
Kiss Is Still a Kiss, A (Callaghan, B.), 85
"Knight's Tale, The" (Chaucer), 115
"Korea" (McGahern), 511
"Kristu-Du" (Carey), 96
Kureishi, Hanif, 394-398

L

"Labor Day Dinner" (Munro), 527
"Lady on the Grey, The" (Collier), 146
Lady Susan (Austen), 22
"Lagoon, The" (Conrad), 155
"Lamb to the Slaughter" (Dahl), 169
"Lamia in the Cévennes, A" (Byatt), 80
"Lappin and Lapinova" (Woolf), 728
Lasdun, James, 399-402
"Last Pennant Before Armageddon, The"
        (Kinsella), 381
"Last Rites" (Jordan), 344
Laurence, Margaret, 403-408
Lavin, Mary, 408-414
Lawrence, D. H., 415-423
Lawson, Henry, 424-428
"Learning to Swim" (Swift), 642
Lebanon Lodge (Hogan), 306
Le Fanu, Joseph Sheridan, 432-438
Left Bank, and Other Stories, The (Rhys), 579
Legend of Good Women, The (Chaucer), 112
Lemon Table, The (Barnes), 36
Le, Nam, 429-432
Lessing, Doris, 439-446
"Letter 13" (Goldsmith), 272
"Letter 48" (Goldsmith), 271
"Letter 49" (Goldsmith), 271
Lewis, Wyndham, 447-455
"Life, Death" (Sansom), 603

"Lifted Veil, The" (Eliot), 220
Lingo (Gilliatt), 267
"Litany for the Homeland" (Hospital), 309
Little Black Book of Stories (Byatt), 81
"Little Madonna, The" (Boylan), 72
"Little Momento" (Collier), 145
"Little Puppy That Could, The" (Amis), 8
Live Bait, and Other Stories (Tuohy), 681
Living as a Moon (Marshall), 493
"Lodging for the Night, A" (Stevenson), 637
"Loneliness of the Long-Distance Runner, The"
        (Sillitoe), 621
Lonely Voice, The (O'Connor), 549
"Long Road to Ummera, The"
        (O'Connor), 548
"Lord of the Dynamos, The" (Wells), 713
"Lost Battle, The" (Mansfield), 480
"Lost Hearts" (James), 328
"Lottery, The" (Edgeworth), 214
"Lotus, The" (Rhys), 579
"Lough Derg Pilgrim, The" (Carleton), 100
"Love, A" (Jordan), 344
Love and Freindship (Austen), 21
"Love and Honor and Pity and Pride and Compassion
        and Sacrifice" (Le), 430
"Love Child, A" (Lessing), 444
Love in a Blue Time (Kureishi), 396
"Love Match, A" (Warner), 694
Love of a Good Woman, The (Munro), 528
"Love-o'-Women" (Kipling), 387
"Lovers of Their Time" (Trevor), 674
"Love's Lesson" (O'Brien, E.), 538
Love Your Enemies (Barker), 33

M

Machen, Arthur, 457-460
MacLaverty, Bernard, 461-465
MacLeod, Alistair, 465-468
"Mademoiselle Panache" (Edgeworth), 213
"Maiden's Leap" (Kiely), 375
Malory, Sir Thomas, 469, 473
Malouf, David, 473-477
"Mama Tuddi Done Over" (Rooke), 591
"Man and Two Women, A" (Lessing), 442
"Man Descending" (Vanderhaeghe), 685
"Man from Mars, The" (Atwood), 12
"Man from the South" (Dahl), 170
"Manhole Sixty-nine" (Ballard), 27

Mansfield, Katherine, 477-485
"Man Who Could Work Miracles, The" (Wells), 713
Man Who Died, The (Lawrence), 421
"Man Whom the Trees Loved, The" (Blackwood), 61
"Man Without a Temperament, The" (Mansfield), 481
"Maritain, Jacques", 91
"Markheim" (Stevenson), 638
"Marmalade Bird, The" (Sansom), 604
Marshall, Owen, 490-494
Mars-Jones, Adam, 486-489
"Mary Postgate" (Kipling), 391
Master of Big Jingles, The (Marshall), 492
"Master Richard" (Wain), 689
"Matter of Taste, A" (Collier), 145
Matters of Life and Death (MacLaverty), 463
Maugham, W. Somerset, 494-501
McCann, Colum, 501-505
McEwan, Ian, 505-509
McGahern, John, 510-513
Means of Escape, The (Fitzgerald, P.), 230
"Medusa's Ankles" (Byatt), 79
"Meeting with Medusa, A" (Clarke), 139
"Memories of the Space Age" (Ballard), 28
Menaphon (Greene, R.), 284
"Merchant's Tale, The" (Chaucer), 119
"Message from the Pig-Man, A" (Wain), 689
Midnight All Day (Kureishi), 396
"Miller's Tale, The" (Chaucer), 115
Minimum of Two (Winton), 723
"Miss Brill" (Mansfield), 480
"Miss Holland" (Lavin), 409
"Miss Shum's Husband" (Thackeray), 651
Mistry, Rohinton, 514-517
Modern Griselda, The (Edgeworth), 215
"Monday or Tuesday" (Woolf), 726
"Monkey's Paw, The" (Jacobs), 325
Moon over Minneapolis (Weldon), 707
Moore, George, 518-522
Moral Disorder (Atwood), 17
Moral Tales for Young People (Edgeworth), 212
Morley Callaghan's Stories (Callaghan, M.), 92
"Morning Swimmers" (Donovan), 192
"Moslem Wife, The" (Gallant), 251
Mothers and Sons (Tóibín), 663
"Mountain Tavern, The" (O'Flaherty), 562
"Mr. and Mrs. Frank Berry" (Thackeray), 653
"Mr. Gilfil's Love Story" (Eliot), 219
"Mrs. Bathurst" (Kipling), 389

Mrs. Dalloway's Party (Woolf), 728
"Mr. Solomon Wept" (Jordan), 344
Mr. Spectator, 4
Mrs. Reinhardt, and Other Stories (O'Brien, E.), 537
"Mrs. Turner Cutting the Grass" (Shields), 617
Munro, Alice, 523-533
"My Father and the Sergeant" (Friel), 245
"My Oedipus Complex" (O'Connor), 548
"My Son the Fanatic" (Kureishi), 397
My Soul in China: A Novella and Stories (Kavan), 358
"Mystery of the Blue Jar, The" (Christie), 131
My Uncle Silas (Bates), 44

N

"Nail on the Head, A" (Boylan), 71
"Natasha" (Bezmozgis), 54
"Nativity" (Hospital), 310
"Neck" (Dahl), 171
"New Café, The" (Lessing), 443
"Nice Day at School" (Trevor), 673
Night Geometry and the Garscadden Trains (Kennedy), 370
"Nightgown, The" (Davies, R.), 176
"Night in Tunisia" (Jordan), 343
"Nine Billion Names of God, The" (Clarke), 139
"N" (Machen), 459
Nobody's Business (Gilliatt), 265
"Nocturne" (Ishiguro), 320
Nocturnes (Ishiguro), 320
Notable Discovery of Cozenage, A (Greene, R.), 284
Nothing to Wear and Nowhere to Hide (Weldon), 708
Not Not While the Giro (Kelman), 366
Novel of sensibility, 21
Now That April's Here, and Other Stories (Callaghan, M.), 91
"Nun's Priest's Tale, The" (Chaucer), 117

O

O'Brien, Edna, 534-540
O'Brien, Fitz-James, 541-545
O'Connor, Frank, 545-552
"Odour of Chrysanthemums" (Lawrence), 417
O'Faoláin, Seán, 552-557
"Office Romances" (Trevor), 674
Offshore (Fitzgerald), 229
O'Flaherty, Liam, 558-564
"Oh, Whistle, and I'll Come to You, My Lad"

(James), 329
"Old Address, The" (Kavan), 358
"Old Lady, The" (Jhabvala), 333
"Old Master, The" (O'Faoláin), 553
On Forsyte 'Change (Galsworthy), 260
"On Saturday Afternoon" (Sillitoe), 621
"On the Edge of the Cliff" (Pritchett), 575
Open to the Public: New and Collected Stories (Spark), 628
"Open Window, The" (Saki), 597
"Orange Fish, The" (Shields), 618
"Orchards, The" (Thomas), 660
"Orgy, The" (De la Mare), 181
"Other Kingdom" (Forster), 234
"Other Paris, The" (Gallant), 249
"Outpost of Progress, An" (Conrad), 155
"Overloaded Man, The" (Ballard), 29
"Oxenhope" (Warner), 696

P

"Pains" (Weldon), 708
"Palace of Sleep, The" (Kavan), 357
"Paradise Lounge, The" (Trevor), 675
Parlement of Foules (Chaucer), 111
"Patricia, Edith and Arnold" (Thomas), 658
"Patriot, The" (O'Faoláin), 556
"Pawnbroker's Wife, The" (Spark), 627
"Peace of Utrecht, The" (Munro), 525
"Peaches" (McGahern), 511
"Peaches, The" (Thomas), 657
"Phantom 'Rickshaw, The" (Kipling), 388
"Phelim O'Toole's Courtship" (Carleton), 101
"Phonefun Limited" (MacLaverty), 463
Pictures in the Fire (Collier), 145
"Pit Strike" (Sillitoe), 623
"Playing Ball on Hampstead Heath" (Richler), 586
Plomer, William, 565-568
"Polarities" (Atwood), 13
"Poor Franzi" (Gallant), 251
"Poor Koko" (Fowles), 240
Popular Tales (Edgeworth), 213
Portable Virgin, The (Enright), 223
"Portobello Road, The" (Spark), 628
"Portrait, The" (Huxley), 315
"Post Office, The" (O'Flaherty), 562
"Predicament, A" (Callaghan, M.), 90
"Prelude" (Mansfield), 482
"Princess, The" (Lawrence), 420

Pritchett, V. S., 569-577
"Prospect of the Sea, A" (Thomas), 659
"Proud Costello, MacDermot's Daughter, and the
         Bitter Tongue" (Yeats), 734
"Prowlers" (Callaghan, B.), 84
"Prussian Officer, The" (Lawrence), 418
"Prussian Vase, The" (Edgeworth), 212
"Psychology" (Mansfield), 480
"Psychopolis" (McEwan), 508
Puck of Pook's Hill (Kipling), 389
"Purple Jar, The" (Edgeworth), 211

Q

"Queer Client" (Dickens), 185
"Quest of the Holy Grail, The" (Malory), 470
Quotations from Other Lives (Gilliatt), 266

R

"Rain" (Maugham), 497
Rasselas (Johnson), 338
"Realpolitik" (Wilson), 718
"Red Barbara" (O'Flaherty), 561
"Red-Headed League, The" (Doyle), 197
"Red-Letter Day, A" (Taylor), 647
"Red" (Maugham), 496
"Red Petticoat, The" (O'Flaherty), 561
"Reeve's Tale, The" (Chaucer), 116
"Reflections" (Carter), 105
"Remember Young Cecil" (Kelman), 366
"Remission" (Mars-Jones), 488
"Rescue Party" (Clarke), 137
Returning (O'Brien, E.), 537
"Revelation" (Davies), 177
Rhys, Jean, 578-582
Richler, Mordecai, 583-588
"Riddle, The" (De la Mare), 180
"Road from Colonus, The" (Forster), 234
Rooke, Leon, 589-593
Rotting Hill (Lewis), 451
"Royal Jelly" (Dahl), 170
Runaway (Munro), 529

S

Saints' lives, 117
Saki, 595-598
"Sally's Story" (Malouf), 475
Sansom, William, 599-605
"Sarah Gwynn" (Moore, G.), 519

"Saucer of Larks, The" (Friel), 245
"Say Could That Lad Be I" (Lavin), 411
"Scandal in Bohemia, A" (Doyle), 196
"Scandalous Woman, A" (O'Brien, E.), 536
Scenes of Childhood (Warner), 697
"Schalken the Painter" (Le Fanu), 433
Scission (Winton), 722
Scott, Sir Walter, 606-611
"Scream, The" (Mistry), 517
"Secret Garden, The" (Chesterton), 125
"Secret of Father Brown, The" (Chesterton), 124
"Secret Sharer, The" (Conrad), 158
"Secrets" (MacLaverty), 462
Seiffert, Rachel, 611-615
"Senility" (Lavin), 411
"Sense of Humour" (Pritchett), 572
Sentimental fiction, 21, 273
"Sentinel, The" (Clarke), 138
"Seraph and the Zambesi, The" (Spark), 627
Seven Men (Beerbohm), 48
Shields, Carol, 616-619
"Shoplifting in the USA" (Donovan), 192
"Shut-In Number, The" (Rooke), 591
"Sick Call, A" (Callaghan, M.), 91
"Siege, The" (Lasdun), 400
"Significant Moments in the Life of My Mother"
         (Atwood), 15
"Silence, The" (Barnes), 39
Sillitoe, Alan, 620-625
"Simple Susan" (Edgeworth), 211
"Sisters" (McCann), 502
Six Stories Written in the First Person Singular
         (Maugham), 498
"Skeleton, The" (Pritchett), 573
"Sleep It Off, Lady" (Rhys), 580
Sleep It Off, Lady (Rhys), 580
"Slim" (Mars-Jones), 487
"Small Spade, A" (Mars-Jones), 488
"Solid Objects" (Woolf), 728
"Some Grist for Mervyn's Mill" (Richler), 585
Something Short and Sweet (Bates), 44
"Something Terrible, Something Lovely"
         (Sansom), 601
"So on He Fares" (Moore), 520
Spark, Muriel, 625-631
"Sparrows" (Lessing), 443
Spectator, The (Steele, R.), 633
Spectator Club, 4

Splendid Lives (Gilliatt), 266
"Squatter" (Mistry), 516
"Sredni Vashtar" (Saki), 597
"Star, The" (Clarke), 139
"State of England" (Amis), 9
Steele, Sir Richard, 631-635
Stevenson, Robert Louis, 636-641
St. Mawr (Lawrence), 421
"Storms" (Lessing), 443
"Story by Maupassant, A" (O'Connor), 549
"Story of Mats Israelson, The" (Barnes), 38
Story-Teller's Holiday, A (Moore), 520
"Sugar" (Byatt), 79
"Sugawn Chair, The" (O'Faoláin), 554
"Summer Lightning" (Mars-Jones), 488
"Summer My Grandmother Was Supposed to Die,
       The" (Richler), 584
"Summer Night" (Bowen), 65
"Survivor in Salvador, A" (Tuohy), 680
"Swans on an Autumn River" (Warner), 695
Swift, Graham, 642-645
"Swimming Lessons" (Mistry), 517
"Sword of Welleran, The" (Dunsany), 204

T

"Tables of the Law, The" (Yeats), 735
Taking Pictures (Enright), 224
"Tale of Balin, The" (Malory), 470
"Tale of King Arthur, The" (Malory), 469
"Talking About My Wife" (Kelman), 367
"Tapka" (Bezmozgis), 53
Tatler, The (Steele, R.), 632
Tatler 163, The (Addison), 3
Taylor, Elizabeth, 646-649
"Tea and Biscuits" (Kennedy), 370
"Tell Me Yes or No" (Munro), 527
Tent, The (Atwood), 17
Terminal Beach, The (Ballard), 28
Thackeray, William Makepeace, 650-655
"That Bad Woman" (Boylan), 73
"There Is No End" (Kavan), 357
"They" (Kipling), 391
They Sleep Without Dreaming (Gilliatt), 266
Thomas, Dylan, 656-662
"Three Dogs of Siena" (Sansom), 602
Three Impostors, The (Machen), 458
"Three Tasks, The" (Carleton), 100
"Thrill of the Grass, The" (Kinsella), 381

"Through the Field" (McCann), 503
"Till September Petronella" (Rhys), 580
Tóibín, Colm, 662-666
"Tom" (Lavin), 411
Tomorrow-Tamer, The (Laurence), 404
Too Much Happiness (Munro), 531
"Totentanz" (Wilson), 718
"Tree, The" (Thomas), 660
Tremain, Rose, 666-670
Trembling of a Leaf, The (Maugham), 495
Trevor, William, 671-679
"Trip to London, The" (Davies, R.), 176
Troilus and Criseyde (Chaucer), 112
"Tubber Derg" (Carleton), 101
"Tuning of Perfection, The" (MacLeod), 467
"Tunnel" (Barnes), 38
"Tunnel, The" (Swift), 643
Tuohy, Frank, 679-683
Turning, The (Winton), 723
"Tutti-Frutti" (Sansom), 602
"Twisting of the Rope, The" (Yeats), 735
"Two Drovers, The" (Scott), 608
"Two Lovely Beasts" (O'Flaherty), 561
"Two Old Women and a Young One" (Lessing), 444
"Typhoon" (Conrad), 156
Typical Day in a Desirable Woman's Life"
       (Rooke), 592

U

"Ula Masonda" (Plomer), 566
"Umberto Verdi, Chimney-Sweep"
       (MacLaverty), 462
"Uncle Ernest" (Sillitoe), 621
"Uncle Spencer" (Huxley), 315
"Unearthing Suite" (Atwood), 15
"Union Buries Its Dead, The" (Lawson), 426
"Unperformed Experiments Have No Results"
       (Hospital), 309

V

"Valley of Lagoons, The" (Malouf), 476
Vanderhaeghe, Guy, 684-687
"Vertical Ladder, The" (Sansom), 601
View from Calvary, A (Boyle), 77
View from Castle Rock, The (Munro), 530
"Vision of Mizrah, The" (Addison), 3
"Visitor, The" (Thomas), 660

W

Wain, John, 688-692
"Walking the Dog" (MacLaverty), 463
Walking the Dog (MacLaverty), 463
"Walk in the Park, A" (Kelman), 367
Walk the Blue Fields (Keegan), 362
"Wall, The" (Sansom), 600
"Wandering Willie's Tale" (Scott), 607
"War Fever" (Ballard), 29
Warner, Sylvia Townsend, 692-699
"Watch, The" (Swift), 644
"Watcher, The" (Vanderhaeghe), 686
"Watching Me, Watching You" (Weldon), 707
"Wedding Dress, A" (Callaghan, M.), 90
"Weddings and Beheadings" (Kureishi), 397
Welch, Denton, 699-705
Weldon, Fay, 705-710
Wells, H. G., 711-716
"What Becomes" (Kennedy), 371
What Becomes (Kennedy), 371
"What Do Hippos Eat?" (Wilson), 719
"What Jorkens Has to Put Up with" (Dunsany), 206
What's It Like Out? (Gilliatt), 265
"What Was It?" (O'Brien, F. J.), 543
"When I Was Thirteen" (Welch), 701
"When My Girl Comes Home" (Pritchett), 572
"When the Sardines Came" (Plomer), 567
"While the Sun Shines" (Wain), 690
"White People, The" (Machen), 459

"Who Do You Love?" (Rooke), 591
"Wife of Bath's Tale, The" (Chaucer), 118
Wild Body, The (Lewis), 449
Wilderness Tips (Atwood), 15
"Wilfrid Holmes" (Moore), 519
"Willows, The" (Blackwood), 62
Wilson, Angus, 717-720
"Winter Dog" (MacLeod), 467
"Winter in the Air" (Warner), 694
"Winter Swimmers" (Hogan), 306
Winton, Tim, 721-724
"Wish House, The" (Kipling), 388
"Withdrawal" (Carey), 97
"Withered Arm, The" (Hardy), 289
"With Your Tongue Down My Throat" (Kureishi), 397
"Witness, The" (Sansom), 601
"Woman Who Rode Awa', The" (Lawrence), 420
"Wondersmith, The" (O'Brien, F. J.), 542
Woolf, Virginia, 725-731
"World of Heroes, The" (Kavan), 358
"Wronged Wife, The" (Boylan), 72

Y

Yeats, William Butler, 732-737
"You Gave Me Hyacinths" (Hospital), 309
"Young Archimedes" (Huxley), 316
"Youth" (Conrad), 155
"You Touched Me" (Lawrence), 418